Encyclopaedia OF DATES & EVENTS

L. C. Pascoe
A. J. Lee
E. S. Jenkins, B.A.
H. V. Ralph, A.L.A.

Edited by
L. C. Pascoe

This edition revised by
Brian Phythian

Headway • Hodder & Stoughton

First published 1968
Second edition 1974
Fifth impression 1981
Third edition 1991

British Library Cataloguing in Publication Data
Encyclopaedia of dates and events. – 3rd ed.
1. World, history
I. Pascoe, L. C. (Lionel Craman) II. Phythian, B. A.
(Brian Arthur)
909

ISBN 0 340 539909

Phototypeset by Input Typesetting Ltd, London

Printed in Great Britain for the education division of Hodder and Stoughton Limited, Mill Road, Dunton Green, Sevenoaks, Kent, by St Edmundsbury Press Ltd

Preface to the Second Edition

Since the publication of the first edition of this book in 1968, a substantial number of corrections and modifications have been made. A few additional entries have been added where subsequent investigation has indicated that their inclusion is desirable.

It has, furthermore, been decided to extend the final chronological date from 1950 to 1970. This has the advantage of including matters that are almost contemporary. It should, however, be borne in mind that it is not easy to assess the true impact of these events on tomorrow's history. Will, for example, a current work of art adjudged as of outstanding merit today be so valued twenty-five years or more hence? Is an international confrontation, of concern to us now, going to be of more than fleeting interest in the future? This we do not know, but such entries can always be amended in the light of experience gained later. In the interim, they give a greater measure of completeness to the book.

I should like to express my deep appreciation to the many readers who have written to me offering helpful suggestions for improving the book. Quite a number of the additions that appear do so as a direct consequence of their interest, and so do some of the amendments!

In conclusion, my sincere thanks go to Mr. H. V. Ralph, who prepared the entries of the years 1951–70 for editing, and to Mr. Nicholas Chapman, Managing Editor of Teach Yourself Books, for his interest and help.

L. C. Pascoe
Manchester, 1974

Preface to the Third Edition

New material has been added to bring the chronology up to 1988, and the earlier edition has also been updated by the incorporation of some 200 amendments. The pre-history section has been revised by Dr G. Bailey of the University of Cambridge.

Brian Phythian
London, 1990

How to Use this Book

In ancient history many events, and in later times some events, are shown with *c.* (standing for *circa*, "about"). The margin of error is variable; in very early dates the approximation is naturally less reliable than is the case with more recent entries. Nevertheless, the great majority of the records are well authenticated, and the following points should help the reader.

With the exception of entries in the history column, dates of the birth and death of prominent people are indicated by * and † respectively, e.g. (*1823, †1894) means *born* 1823, *died* 1894. Such dates are, in general, given only in the earliest entry for the person concerned, which is at the time of his first important achievement. Thus the reader might find:

1821	James Fenimore Cooper (*1789, †1851), American writer: *The Spy*, popular novel.

and then later:

1826	Cooper: *The Last of the Mohicans*, American Story.

However, where the date of the death of a V.I.P. terminates an important era, an entry may be found thus:

1509	†Henry VII and accession of Henry VIII.

Death by violence is usually indicated in words, e.g.:

1645	Execution of Laud.

In cases where the date of an achievement is unknown, the entry has generally been made at the date of birth of the person concerned, e.g.:

1316*c.*	*John Barbour (†1395), Scottish Poet who wrote *The Brus*.

Where a major historical undertaking was of several years' duration, an indication has been given as to whether the date shown is at the start or the completion of the project. In such cases, where known, the second relevant date is shown in brackets in the entry.

The names of books, paintings, musical compositions and so on are given in italics.

There is a short introduction of pre-history with dates given in the number of years before the present. This is not comprehensive but is merely a lead-in to the main body of the work, which is dated using the B.C./A.D. system and runs from 5000 B.C. to A.D. 1988. Pre-Christian dates are indicated with a minus, e.g. –275 means 275 B.C..

The main part of the book is divided into four columns. The first gives events in Political, Constitutional and Religious History; the second in Language, Literature and Drama; the third in Art, Architecture, Sculpture, Music, Ballet, Education, Sports and Pastimes; and the fourth in Economics, Exploration, Science and Technology. Some events do not fall more naturally into one column rather than another, and in such cases space has been the main consideration. The column headings are represented pictorially as follows:

Political, Constitutional and Religious History

Language, Literature and Drama

Art, Architecture, Music, Ballet, Sports and Pastimes

Economics, Exploration, Science and Technology

Although, for reasons of space, full details cannot be given in entries, they are whenever possible logically explained and developed. Each is placed in the framework of surrounding events, and it is possible to see the state of civilization and of knowledge at any time.

The comprehensive index lists both people (or places) and events, and thus most entries have a cross-reference. This enables the reader to look up any topic quickly and easily.

Pre–history

3,500,000 *Australopithecus afarensis*, a bipedal ape-like human ancestor was present in East Africa, probably lived off plant foods.

2,000,000 Pleistocene Age: a period of recurrent ice-ages which had profound effect on plant and animal life. *Homo habilis* made simple chipped stone artefacts (beginning of the Lower Palaeolithic) in Africa and may have scavenged for meat.

1,500,000 *Homo erectus* made bifacially flaked hand-axes and used fire, scavenged meat in Africa. Hunting of large mammals not certain.

800,000 Europe and Asia colonised by *Homo erectus*.

250,000 Archaic *Homo sapiens* in Africa and Europe. Variety of stone tools including scrapers (Middle Palaeolithic), use of caves for shelter, hunting probable.

100,000 Onset of Last Ice Age. Neanderthals (archaic *Homo sapiens*) appear in Europe and parts of south-west Asia and North Africa. Burial of dead. Early varieties of anatomically modern *Homo sapiens sapiens* in Africa and south-west Asia.

60,000 Sea-borne colonisation of Melanesia and Australia by *Homo sapiens sapiens*.

30,000 *Homo sapiens sapiens* entirely replaced archaic humans. Stone tools made on blades (Upper Palaeolithic) widespread. Use of bone, antler and ivory for making tools. Use of clothing and artificial huts or tents. Musical instruments made of bone. Large-scale hunting of herd mammals.

25,000 Cave painting and rock engraving in Europe, Africa and Australia. Ornaments of bone, stone, shell, antler, ivory and fired clay. Ground-stone axes in Australia. Colonisation of the Americas probable by this time across the Bering land bridge from Siberia.

18,000 Height of Last Ice Age. Most of Britain and Scandinavia covered by ice sheets. Sea-levels 100 metres lower than present.

15,000 Immense and impressive wall paintings in the Lascaux caves (see 1940). Ice sheets begin to retreat and sea-levels rise. Dog domesticated and use of bow and arrow by 12,000.

10,000 Ice finally retreated, beginnings of Holocene (or Postglacial period). Spread of forests in Europe and Mesolithic period to about 5,500. Hunters, fishers and gatherers with use of flaked axes, boats, fishing tackle. Sedentary villages. Harvesting and storage of wild seed grains in south-west Asia. Pottery in Japan.

8,000 Beginnings of so-called Neolithic revolution in south-west Asia, with cultivation of domesticated wheats and barleys, domestic sheep and goat, combined with permanent villages of sun-dried brick houses, use of pottery and polished stone. Cultivation of maize in MesoAmerica. Domestication of pig and drainage of swamps for cultivation in New Guinea. Agricultural origins probably occurred independently in multiple centres of origin, with successive introduction and diffusion of different domesticates over several millennia. Onset of postglacial climatic optimum, with temperatures in Europe c. 3° C higher than present.

History
Literature
Arts
Science
5000BC to AD1988

LITERATURE

	History	Literature
−5000	*c.* Sumerians from Central Asia settled in southern part of plain of Shinar called Sumer (renamed Babylonia after −2000).	*c.* Sumerian language in use.
−4700		
−4300	*c.* Egyptians advanced beyond Neolithic stage.	
−4241		
−4000	*c.* The end of the Mesolithic period along the Mediterranean coastline, with spread of Neolithic culture.	*c.* Sumerian pictographic writing: about 2,000 signs in use; writing done on clay tablets.
−3700		*c.* Earliest Omen tablets of Babylon.
−3760		
−3750		
−3500	*c.* Great period of prosperity of Sumerian Civilization. *c.* Neolithic period in Western Europe to *c.* −1700. *c.* Beginnings of true Bronze Age, in Bohemia.	*c.* Sumerian temple of Ianna at Eridu built; clay tablets of cuneiform writing of Sumerian language were found here in 1952.
−3400	*c.* Upper, or White Egypt, joined to Lower, or Red Egypt, by Menes the Fighter, King of Upper Egypt.	*c.* Cuneiform (wedge-shaped) writing of Sumerian civilization; earliest writing known.
−3200	*c.* Archaic period, first and second dynasties, of Egypt to *c.* −2800 (possibly −3188 to −2815).	*c.* Early stages of Egyptian hieroglyphics.
−3000	*c.* Semitic tribes occupied Assyria in northern part of the plain of Shinar and Akkad; wars with Sumerians already settled there. *c.* Other Semitic tribes settled on Syrian coast; these were Phoenicians with centres at Tyre, Sidon and, later, Carthage. *c.* Neolithic settlements known to have existed in Crete by this date (possibly as early as −5000).	

c. Bee-hive houses of Khirokitia, Cyprus.
c. Neolithic (?) cave temples of Malta.

c. Ropes believed to have been used
c. Australo-Melanesoid race of people settled in Malay Peninsula.

c. Ornamental pottery existed.

c. White painted pottery in Egypt.

Egyptians had year of 365 days; Calendar regulated by Sun and Moon, 12 months of 30 days each; with 5 feast days at the end; first exactly dated year in history.

c. Painted pottery in S.E. Europe.
c. Harps and flutes played in Egypt.

c. Egyptians glazed soap-stone beads.
c. Sumerians settled on site of City of Babylon.
c. Cretan shipping gained eminence.

c. Painted fabric, found in tomb at El Gebelein, Egypt.

First year of Jewish Calendar.

c. Multi-coloured ceramic ware, originating from region of Ukraine; influence spread to China.

c. Earliest known bronze alloy; used by Egyptians and Sumerians.

c. Temple at Tell-el-Obeid and tomb of Mes-Kalam-Dug (see 1927), near Ur, Chaldea, built.
c. Carved alabaster vases of Thinite dynasty of Egypt (for unguents).

c. Craftsmen such as masons and smiths active.
c. Egyptian ships probably traded in Mediterranean.
c. Wheeled vehicles believed to have been in use in Sumeria.

c. Pots in the shape of animals made in Egypt.
c. Period of the mastaba, rectangular structure of sun-baked mud bricks covering a buried pit.

c. Flax used for textiles in Middle East; Egyptians did not use wool.
c. Earliest known *numerals* (Egyptian), hieroglyphic and hieratic.

c. The White Temple, Uruk, erected.
c. Temple of Tepe Gawra (Al'Ubaid period) built.

c. Record of ploughing, raking and manuring by Egyptians.

c. Religious art of Sumeria: brick temples with coloured pillars.
c. Earliest date of Trojan culture.
c. Sumerians played lyres and drums.
c. Earliest extant glass bead in Egypt (imported).
c. Murals at Beni Hassan, Egypt, and records at Kyafaje, Iraq, indicate existence of wrestling.
c. Cities of Indus valley; flourished until about –1500.

c. Oil-burning lamps used by Sumerians.
c. Earliest reference to use of animals (asses) as beasts of burden, in Egypt.
c. Utensils made in precious metals e.g. gold; metals tools also in use.
c. Practice of trepanning took place.
c. Horizontal ground loom used in Middle East; possibly of much earlier origin.
c. Domesticated dogs in Egypt.
c. Woven cloth at Mohenjo-daro, India.

LITERATURE

	History	Literature
–2900	*c.* Peak of great Danubian culture, possibly evolved from Vardas-Morava farmers who lived in houses (wattle and daub or mud-brick).	*c.* Sumerian signs condensed to about 550; Sumerians had no alphabet.
–2850	*c.* Legendary Golden Age of China; beginning of the period of the Sage Kings (so-named).	
–2800	*c.* Old Kingdom of Egypt; third To Sixth Dynasties (possibly –2815 to –2294; *or* –2778 to –2263). *c.* Beginnings of Early Dynastic Period of Mesopotamia (to *c.* –2350).	
–2750		*Code of Urukagina*, Babylon.
–2700	*c.* Fourth Dynasty of Egypt, comprising Sneferu, Khufu, Chephren and Men-kau-re.	
–2650		
–2640		
–2600	Egyptian punitive expedition to Palestine by land and sea, as reprisal for attacks on Egyptian trade caravans.	
–2500	*c.* Settlement of Semitic tribes in Syria and North Africa complete. *c.* Aramean nomads from area of Euphrates settled in Palestine. *c.* Beginnings of Indus civilization of India (to *c.* –1500). *c.* Canaanite tribes of Semitic stock settled in Palestine. *c.* Early Minoan I period in Crete.	*c.* Recorded evidence of libraries: stories, poetry, prayers and religious plays as well as books on medicine, mathematics and census lists and tax registers from Egypt. *c.* On clay tablets are earliest known maps; these are of estates of Babylonian merchants.
–2350	*c.* Under Sargon of Akkad, the Semites occupied the whole plain of Shinar; greatest Mesopotamia empire established.	*c. Code of Gudea*, Babylon, set out.
–2300		*c. Pyramid Texts*, religious documents of Egyptian 6th dynasty.
–2250		

c. Egyptians used standard measure calibrated in cubit, hand and palm.

c. Rock carving of Pharaoh Semempses at Sinai.

c. Egyptian metal mirrors in use.
c. Agriculture and medicine were reaching high standards in the period after this date (to –2200).

c. Third Dynasty: Zoser pyramid and complex, Sakkara, erected.

c. Pewter, alloy of tin and lead, may have been used by Egyptians and Chinese (date very doubtful).
c. Plaster used by Egyptians.

First known picture of a ship, an Egyptian trading vessel.

c. Erection of pyramid at Meidum by Sneferu.

c. Khufu (Cheops) erected Great Pyramid at Gizeh.
c. Chephren erected second Great Pyramid, the Great Sphinx and diorite statue.
c. Men-kau-re built the third Pyramid at Gizeh.

Huang-Ti ordered Ling-lun to cut a bamboo pole to give musical note Huang-chung.

Reputed date of start of Chinese silk industry with discovery of use of silkworms.

c. Statue of acacia wood, tomb of Sakkara; Fifth Dynasty of Egypt.
c. Huge palace platform of Lagash, Chaldea.

c. Probable date of earliest iron objects being manufactured; iron not seriously used until much later (see –1400).
c. Mesopotamian lime-kilns in use.

c. Beginnings of barrow-building in Britain.
c. By this date, fine neolithic pottery was produced in Honan, Shantung and Kansu, in China (colours—black, grey or red).
c. Monument of King Naram-sin, Susa, erected.
c. Pottery extant indicates establishment of Indus civilization at Mohen-jo-daro.

c. Egyptians discovered uses of papyrus.
c. Glass objects made in Mesopotamia; glass vessels 1,000 years later. N. Indian system of measurements; later passed into Europe.
c. Oldest houses at Kahun, Egypt.
c. Dolmen Period of Scandinavian neolithic age (to –2200).

c. Egyptian tombs at Beni Hasan.
c. Basalt statue of Gudea, priest-king of Lagash.

c. Sumerian talent; weighed about one hundredweight.
c. Probable period of erection of first observatory; perhaps Temple of Belus in Babylon.
c. Wine appears to have been known in Eygpt.

c. The great Stele of Naram-Sin (grandson of Sargon); monolith 6 ft high.

c. Equinoxes and solstices determined in China.

c. (doubtful) Oldest surviving ski, Swedish hoting ski.

c. Oldest existing irrigation dam.

Year		
–2230		
–2200	*c.* Traditional date for foundation of first of the three Chinese dynasties, the Hsia, reputed to have lasted until –1760; their history is obscure.	
–2188		
–2183	Beginning of the Seventh Dynasty of Pharaohs in Egypt; lasted until about – 525.	
–2124	*c.* Ur-Nammu founded Third Dynasty of Ur; kings of Ur ruled all Mesopotamia until –2016.	*c.* Athotes: *History of Egypt*.
–2100	(to –1790) Middle Kingdom of Egypt, eleventh and twelfth dynasties. *c.* Abraham migrated from Ur.	
–2065		
–2000	*c.* Middle Minoan period in Crete; true Bronze Age (to –1700). *c.* Indo-European tribes, the Hittites, of Asia Minor, began to join together to form a single kingdom. *c.* Bronze Age in Britain and Northern Europe. *c.* Egyptians in control of Crete and Aegean islands. *c.* Beginning of Greek movement into the eastern Mediterranean from original home on shores of Caspian Sea; movement completed by –1000.	*c.* Egyptians mastered the use of an alphabet of 24 signs, each representing one letter or sound; the earliest known alphabet.
–1950	Sesostris I of Egypt led a military expedition into Canaan.	
–1925	*c.* The Hittites attacked and plundered Babylon.	*c.* *The Story of Sinuhe*, Egyptian historical novel (12th dynasty); earliest form of novel known. *c.* Ugaritic cuneiform writing.
–1860	Sesostris III of Egypt invaded Canaan, conquered Nubia as far as the Second Cataract of the Nile.	*c.* Beginnings of Semitic alphabet. *c.* *Coffin Texts*, religious documents of Egyptian 12th dynasty.

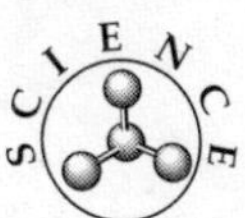

c. Possible date for compilation of first volumes of astronomy: *Chaldean Registers of Celestial Observation*.

c. Painted pottery in N.W. China.
c. Minyan ware appeared in Greece.

c. Indonesian people replaced much earlier Melanesoid type in Malaya; development of agriculture in this region.
c. Passage-grave Period of Scandinavian neolithic age (to –1650).

Memphis built by Mizraim.

c. End of Akkadian civilization in Mesopotamia (see –2350); city of Akkad disappeared.

c. Erection of Ziggurat (holy pyramidal mountain) at Ur; rebuilt much later by Nebuchadnezzar; kiln-baked brick set in asphalt.

Temple of Mentuhotep, Der-el-Bahari, Thebes.

c. City of Babylon, capital of the empire.
c. Palaces of this date have been excavated recently at Ugarit, in Syria.
c. Earliest extant dyed cloth (mummy linen).
c. Treasure of Priam, fine collection of jewels and plate; found on site of Troy.
c. Unique silver cup of Gournia; Middle Minoan period.
c. Stones of Callanish (17 ft. tall) on Lewis, Outer Hebrides, erected; earlier than Stonehenge.
c. Camp with causeway established at Maiden Castle (see –1500).

c. Settlement of Jomon people in Japan.
c. First Chinese maps believed to have been produced.
c. Cretans exported copper, olives, grapes, timber and pottery and imported gold, silver and marble.
c. Method of joinery understood; furniture no longed needed to be lashed together.
c. Three-legged utensils used in Hwang-Ho plain (China).
c. Period of greatest obliquity of ecliptic.
c. Earliest record of use of locks and latches.
c. Signs of the Zodiac (Babylonian); some signs, e.g. Virgo, seem to be 1,000 years older.
c. Introduction, by accident, of house mouse into Britain.

c. Erection of great temple of Dagon and palace, at Mari.

c. Tomb of Chnemhotep near Beni Hassan; beautifully painted.

c. Earliest references to medical contraceptive methods; Egyptian.

LITERATURE

Date	History	Literature
–1800	*c.* Hammurabi of Babylon set laws of kingdom in order and provided first known legal system.	*c. Code of Hammurabi*—famous for information on customs of the times; 282 laws inscribed on a black basalt stele.
–1760	Foundation of the Shang Dynasty in China; lasted until –1122.	
–1750	Beginnings of Persian Empire (to *c.* –550).	
1700	*c.* Bronze Age in Western Europe, to *c.* –750. *c.* Late Minoan period in Crete (to –1400). *c.* Disturbances in Asia Minor began to threaten the prosperity of Egypt. *c.* Hittite attacks on Syria caused Asiatic peoples to move into the Nile Valley.	Reputed date for the foundation of libraries in Chaldea. *c.* Chinese writing known to have been well established by this date; first period (of seven) of Chinese literature (to *c.* –600, *q.v.*).
–1650	Egyptians driven south by Asiatic refugees known as the Hyksos, who formed a kingdom in the Nile Delta.	
–1575	Ahmosis, first king of new Egyptian dynasty, defeated and expelled the Hyksos, who were forced back into Syria and Canaan.	
–1550	The settlement of Cecrops in Attica, *c.* (to –1150) New Kingdom of Egypt, Eighteenth to Twentieth Dynasties.	*c. Book of the Dead*, religious documents of Egyptian 18th dynasty.
–1540	Thutmosis I began a period of Egyptian conquest lasting until *c.* –1479	
–1500	*c.* Ganges civilization in India (to *c.* –400). *c.* Immigration into Asia Minor of race (to become Phrygians) from Thrace; led to establishment of Phrygia. *c.* Middle Mycenaean period of culture (to *c.* –1400). *c.* Peak of Canaanitish civilization in Palestine.	By this time Sumerian ceased to be spoken, but was used as erudite written language, as later occurred with Latin. *c.* Hymns of the *Rig Veda* composed: Upanishad tradition of Hindus (to –1000).
–1475		

c. Vast temple of Ischali erected.
c. Early period of development of Stonehenge, megalithic temple; main construction –1600 to –1400.
c. Construction of Woodhenge, being 6 circles of wooden posts.

c. Ancient trumpet of Denmark is known to have existed.

c. Horses used to draw vehicles.

c. Palace of Minos, Knossos, built (to *c*. –1450); destroyed *c*. –1400: excavated 1899 *et seq*. by Sir Arthur Evans (*1851, †1941).
c. European bronze statuettes, gold objects and painted pottery made.

c. Earliest record of lubrication: Ra-Em-Ka tomb, Egypt.
c. Possible period of Teutonic settlement in S. Norway.

c. Six small sphinxes of gold, of this period; found in a tomb of the acropolis of Mycenae; beginnings of Early Mycenaean period (to *c*. –1500).

c. Rhind mathematical papyrus; contains primitive algebraic equations.
c. Long Stone Cist Period of Scandinavian neolithic age (to –1500).

c. Percussion instruments added to Egyptian orchestras.
c. Famous faience statuette of the Earth Goddess; Middle Minoan III period; found at Knossos.

c. Animal glue used by Egyptians for furniture making.
c. Bronze used in Egypt; much earlier, copper had been in use.

c. Temple of Ammon, Karnak.
c. Beautiful Cretan terracotta vases made.
c. Development of the Avebury megalithic temple circles (two phases), in Wiltshire.

c. Four "elements" accepted in India; based on Brahma; earth, air, fire and water.
c. Earliest botanical record; on the walls of Karnak temple.

c. Temple of Queen Hatsephut, Der-el-Bahari.
c. Mycenaeans begun to use tholos tombs for royal burials; e.g. Treasury of Atreus.

c. Egyptian royal cubit (approx. 21 in.).

c. City of Mohenjo-daro, Indus valley, destroyed by barbarians; details found in recent excavations indicated brick houses laid out on rectangular plan.
c. Beautiful bronze vessels made in Shang period of China.
c. Maiden Castle over-built by a long barrow; abandoned in Bronze Age (but see Iron Age, –350).

c. Shaduf used for irrigation in Egypt.
c. Egyptians made glass vessels.
c. Mercury discovered in Egyptian tomb of this period.
c. Beginnings of Bronze Age in Scandinavia.
c. Shadow clock in use; sand-glass dates from about the same period.

c. Earliest extant tapestry; Egyptian.
c. Cleopatra's Needle, so-called; actually an obelisk of the region of Thutmosis III.

−1449		
−1411	The Egyptian Empire reached its highest point of development under Amenhotep III.	
−1400	*c*. The Hittite Empire centred at Hatti had become the strongest kingdom in western Asia. Burning of Knossos. *c*. Pheonicians colonized Malta. *c*. Late Mycenaean period of culture (to *c*. −1150).	*c*. Primitive Greek alphabet at Knossos (see −675).
−1360	Amenhotep IV destroyed old gods of Egypt and set up worship of one god only, the Sun God, Aton.	
−1350		
−1313	Hittite invasions of Egypt resumed; Sethos I and Rameses II failed to defeat invaders in struggle which lasted until −1292.	
−1300	*c*. Regulations concerning beer-shops in Egypt.	*c*. Introduction of alphabetical letters into Boeotia by Cadmus.
−1225	*c*. Cretan sea-raiders joined Libyan desert tribes in attacks on Nile Delta; others, having broken Hittite kingdom, raided Egypt by −1175. *c*. Exodus, under Moses, of Israelites from Egypt.	
−1200	*c*. The Hebrews occupied Canaan.	
−1196	*c*. The crossing of Jordan.	
−1193	Destruction of Troy.	
−1175	Egypt attacked and invaded; divided into two kingdoms, Upper and Lower Egypt, centred on the Delta and at Thebes.	

Thutmosis III erected Lateran obelisk, now in Rome.

c. Ruins of fine temple of Amenhotep III at Amara in Sudan.

c. Tomb of Tut-ankh-Amen commenced; possibly originally intended for the high priest, Ay, and his family; on excavation, this tomb proved to contain some of the finest known golden relics of ancient Egypt.
c. Temple of Luxor built.
c. Colossus of Thebes, erected by Amenhotep III.
c. *Painting of a Pond* (from Thebes).

c. Iron tools, including plough-shares, in use in India.
c. Iron began to be extensively used in Asia Minor, the most important mines in Southern Syria being owned by the Hittites.
c. Leprosy in India.

c. Treasury of Atreus, Mycenae; bee-hive tomb.
c. Painted sculpture of Queen Nefertiti, Egypt.

c. Egyptian beam balances in use for weighing.
c. Record of existence of a Suez Canal; reconstructed from time to time.

c. Tut-ankh-Amen's mummy embalmed; placed in magnificent wood and gold sarcophagus.

c. Alleged foundation of Corinth.
c. Reference to leprosy in Egypt.

c. Aqueducts and reservoirs in use for irrigation in Egypt.

c. Great Temple of Abu-Simbel, Nubia; created for Rameses II.
c. Paintings of harps at Thebes; the instrument is, however, much older—remains found in Egypt.
c. Terracotta group of dancers (one of the earliest records of dancing) at Knossos.

c. First official survey under Rameses II (Egypt—Nile Valley).
Papyrus plan of Nubian gold-fields; still extant (at Turin).

c. Tchoga Zambil Ziggurat, Susa, constructed.
c. The Lion Gate, Palace of Minos, Micenae; earliest European monumental sculpture (possibly older, 14th cen. B.C.).

c. Revival of ancient Nemean Games; lasted until 396.

c. Temple of Rameses III, at Medinet Habu, having bud-type columns.

c. Rise of Phoenician power in sea trading in Mediterranean.

The Trojan horse constructed.

c. Development of Tyre and establishment of Phoenician (trading) settlements beyond Pillars of Hercules; foundation of Lixus and Utica.

LITERATURE

	History	Literature
–1122	Shang supremacy in China ended and replaced by Chou Dynasty, which lasted until –480	
–1104	Conqest of Peloponnesus by the Dorians.	
–1100	*c.* Assyrian Empire set up in Mesopotamia (to –612).	By this date some 2000 Chinese characters had developed (from the Shang period).
–1045	Abolition of monarchy at Athens; Medon made First Archon for life.	
–1012		
–1000	*c.* Israelitish kingdoms set up by David and Solomon: extended from Euphrates to Egypt by –900. *c.* Zoroaster developed form of religious belief based on struggle between good and evil; views accepted by Medes and Persians by about –700.	*c.* Hebrew alphabet developed; differing from earlier Semitic alphabet (see –1860).
–935	*c.* Division of Hebrew kingdom into Israel and Judah.	
–900	*c.* Damascus, strongest kingdom along the western coast of Asia; remained so until *c.* –850.	
–854	War between Damascus and Assyria began.	
–850	*c.* Indo-European tribes set up kingdom in Chaldea, north-west of Assyria, in region now known as Armenia.	*c. Iliad* and *Odyssey*, Greek epics; traditional author is Homer; the *Iliad* related siege of Troy; the *Odyssey* the adventures of Odysseus (Ulysses). *c.* Moabitic and Aramaic alphabets.
–813		
–800		*c.* Oldest Chinese poems are to be found in the *Book of Songs* (to –600).
–781		
–776	Victory of Coraebus at Olympia.	

Ten drums of Chou dynasty have survived; date unknown (–1122 to –221).

c. The *Chou-pi*, first text of the *Suan-ching* (see 619).
c. Chinese completed map of entire country.

c. Chinese first calculated obliquity of ecliptic.
c. Tin, mined in England, imported by Phoenicians.

Solomon commenced building of the temple at Jerusalem.

Minstrels known to have been present in Greece.
c. Temple of Hera, Olympia; the oldest surviving Greek temple.
c. Period of Geometrical Style (dots, lines and key patterns) in Greek pottery (to –700).
c. Jomon *doki*, rope-design ware, earliest Japanese objects of art.
c. Combs made in Syria.

c. Chinese knowledge of astronomy recorded; they also possessed silk-weaving looms superior to those of earlier civilizations; also probably used coal.
c. Austrian iron industry developing.
c. Use of the water-wheel with vertical axis began (see –100).
c. Charaka, Indian physician, gave details for nursing the sick.
c. Foundation of Cadiz and of Ephesus and Smyrna.

c. Bronze Age barrow at Kivik, Sweden, with remarkable carved stones.

c. Introduction of weights and measures into Greece; attributed to Phaedon of Argos.
c. Samaria first settled by Omri.

c. The Moabite Stone, monument inscribed with oldest known Phoenician characters, erected.

c. Horse-riding introduced from the steppes of Asia; hitherto horses used for drawing vehicles (see –1800).
c. First reference, in the *Odyssey*, to use of drugs for dulling consciousness, and in the *Iliad* to diving for oysters.

Carthage founded as trading centre for Tyre.

c. Earliest recorded music; a hymn on a Sumerian tablet.

c. Use of positive integers and zero by Hindus.

Eclipse recorded by Chinese.

First recorded Olympic Games, possibly dating from *c*. –1350; lasted intermittently for 1,000 years; recently revived.

c. Two-decked ship built by the Tyrians.

–753	Foundation of City of Rome, probably as an outpost of Latin tribes against Etruscans who could have forded the Tiber at this point.	*c.* Hesiod, Greek poet, author of *Works and Days* and *Theogony*; didactic poetry dealing with maxims and origin of world.
–750	*c.* Greeks began settling in S. Italy.	
–743	First Messenian War; Messenian power overthrown –723.	
–738		
–735		
–732	Damascus overthrown by Assyria.	
–722	Sargon II of Assyria captured Samaria; kingdom of Israel ended.	
–721	Chou citadel in Shensi taken by Barbarian army; Chou capital removed to Loyang.	
–713		
–710	Destruction of kingdom of Chaldea by the Assyrians.	
–701	Sennacherib, successor of Sargon II, invaded Judah; invasion failed.	
–700	*c.* Stone of Scone, reputedly Jacob's pillar, reached Ireland through Egypt.	*c.* Etruscan inscriptions known to exist, but language not fully understood.
–689	Assyrians destroyed Babylon and turned the Euphrates to flow over place where city had stood.	
–685	Second Messenian war broke out and lasted for seventeen years.	*c.* Age of Aristomenes and Tyrtaeus, military elegiac poet of Sparta.
–684	Institution of Annual Archonship in Athens.	
–682	Submission of Hebrew kingdom of Judah to Assyria.	
–675		*c.* Classical Greek alphabet believed to have originated from Miletus.
–670	Assyrians destroyed Memphis and Thebes, but failed to hold Egypt.	
–650	Cimmarian and Scythian raiders ravaged Syria and Palestine.	*c.* Earliest extant Latin inscriptions.

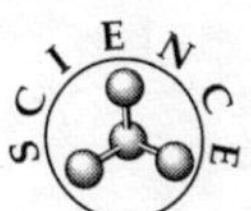

Romulus, founder of Rome, divided the year into ten months.

Phoenicians founded trading colony in Sicily.

c. Hezekiah's aqueduct at Jerusalem.

Sargon II, king of Assyria, set up his capital at Assur.

c. Fine wall-painting of throne-room of Sargon II at Khorsabad (to –705).

c. Electrum staters of Lydia coined; possibly world's earliest money.

Numa Pompilius added January and February to year of ten months set up by Romulus.

c. Appearance of Etruscan art forms (in Tuscany).

c. Spartans founded Taras (Taranto).

Sennacherib settled Assyrian capital at Ninevah.

c. Fortified city of Khorsabad, Assyria; noted for its symmetry.
c. Orientalized style of Greek pottery, largely Corinthian (Archaic Period, to –480).

c. Silver mined at Laurion.
c. Phoenicians believed to have circumnavigated Africa.

c. Aqueduct of Sennacherib constructed.

Remains of a palace of this date exist at Ninevah.

Assyrians rebuilt city of Babylon in effort to placate Babylonians.

c. Superb Etruscan gold clasp from Regolini-Galassi tomb at Cerveteri.

c. Iron came into general use in Egypt.

–647	Assyrians destroyed Susa.	
–626	Chaldean general Nabopolassar (†–605) seized Babylonian throne; declared independence from Assyria.	
–621		The Laws of Dracon; first written laws of Athens; noted for harshness.
–612	Medes, allied with Babylonians and Scythians, destroyed Nineveh; end of Assyrian Empire.	
–606	Nebuchadnezzar made Judah tributary; beginning of the captivity.	
–604	Nebuchadnezzar, with Chaldean army, defeated Egyptian force under Necha.	
–600	Assyrian empire divided among its conquerors; Chaldeans took Babylon and western provinces; Medes took Assyria and most of northern Asia; Persians became Lord of Elam.	*c.* Beginning of second period of Chinese literature (to *c.* –200); classical age of highest Chinese civilization.
–594		Promulgation of Laws of Solon in Athens.
–588		
–586	Nebuchadnezzar burned Jerusalem.	
–585		
–581	Nebuchadnezzar deposed Arries.	
–580		
–573		
–564	Corsica colonized by Phoenicians.	

SCIENCE

Bas-relief Palace of Assurbanipal at Kuyunjik, Ninevah.

c. Attic marble statue of a youth; now in New York.

Commencement of another canal joining the Red Sea and the Nile; completed 100 years later.

Erection of New Palace of Babylon.

c. Black-figured pottery in Greece.
c. Nebuchadnezzar began building temples, developed fine irrigation canals and rebuilt Babylon.
c. *The Green Head*, Egyptian portrait sculpture.
c. Temple of the Sun, near Pyramids of Meroë, Sudan.

c. First attempt to establish bases for matter, other than supernatural, made by Thales of Miletus; later ideas suggested (1) air, (2) fire, were bases of life. Static electricity in amber, observed by Thales, in form of attracting light objects.
c. Foundation of: (i) Paestum; (ii) Massalia (Marseilles).
c. Earliest known period for windmills (used in Persian corn grinding).

Cloaca Maxima, great sewer of Rome, constructed; still in existence.

The Pythian Games first held; ceased −394

Shwe Dagon Pagoda, Burma, built; reconstructed in 16th cent.

Thales first predicted eclipse of the sun.

Erection of the Olympieum on hill of Polichne, Syracuse, Sicily; one of two earliest stone peripteral temples; ruins extant.

*Pythagoras (†−497), to whom is attributed theroem concerning right-angled triangles; great philosopher and mathematician, but scientific approach was prejudiced by mysticism.

c. Nebuchadnezzar built walls of the Hanging Gardens of Babylon (one of the Seven Wonders).
c. Polymedes of Argos; *Statue of a Youth*; found at Delphi.

Anaximander (*−611, †−547): first Greek map of world, which he diagnosed as hanging in space but to which he gave wrong shape.

Papyrus introduced into Greece.

c. Evolution of Doric column, earliest order of Greek architecture.

Year	History	Literature
–560	*Sakya Muni, founder of Buddhist religion (†–480) as Buddha, the "Enlightened One"). Peisistratus usurped government of Athens.	*c.* Lao-tsze, founder of Taoism: *Tao Teh King*, Chinese philosophical work advocating unselfishness.
–553	Cyrus II of Persia deposed Median king and became king of Medes and Persians.	
–550	*c.* Period called La Têne culture; name is that of Celtic settlement at Neuchâtel, Switzerland, occupied in –250 to –100.	*c.* Aesop's *Fables*, written in Greek prose; by tradition Aesop was a Phrygian slave. *c.* *K'ung-tse (†–478), known to posterity as Confucius; Chinese philosopher and teacher of Ethics.
–546	Cyrus II conquered Asia Minor; captured Croesus; end of Lydian monarchy.	
–543	Sakya Muni, later Buddha, left home to devote himself to philosophy and asceticism.	
–538	Cyrus II conquered Babylonia; Judah a Persian province until –333.	*c.* Public libraries in use in Athens.
–536	Edict of Cyrus; the Return—some Jewish exiles returned to Judah.	
–530	Having received enlightenment, Sakya Muni, now Buddha, preached first sermon in deer park of holy city of Benares.	*c.* Anacreon (*–560, †–475): *Odes*, Greek poetry in praise of love and wine.
–529	Egypt conquered by Cambyses of Persia, who had himself crowned as king of Egypt.	
–527	†Peisistratus of Athens; succeeded by his sons Hippias and Hipparchus.	
–525	Psammenitus of Egypt murdered; dynasty of Pharaohs ended.	*c.* *Aeschylus (†–456) Greek tragic dramatist; seven of seventy-two plays survive.
–522	Darius, successor to Cambyses of Persia, divided Persian empire into twenty provinces or satrapies.	
–518		

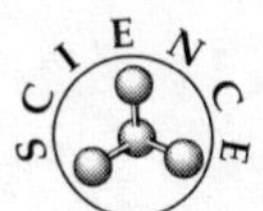

c. Archaic temple of Diana, Ephesus erected; displays Ionic pillars, second order of Greek architecture.

The twelve signs of the Zodiac named by Anaximander; he also determined solstices and equinoxes.

Pythagoras considered planetary movement.
Prediction of eclipses by Babylonians.

c. Attempts made in Egypt to revive ancient ritualistic music.
c. Fine Greek *Blackfigured* vase, made by Exekias.
c. Treasure of Oxus; collection of Persian goldsmiths' work.

c. Earliest type of Chinese abacus; bamboo rods used for computation.
c. Medical schools at Cos and Cnidus flourished.
c. Anaximenes (*–590, †–525), theory of condensation (into earth or water) and rarefaction (into fire) of air (primary matter).

Pythagoras attributed with introduction of the octave in music.

c. Erection of Temple of Ceres, Paestum.

Jews began rebuilding of the Temple at Jerusalem.
c. Temple of Apollo, Corinth, possessing Doric columns.

c. Modes used in music.
Erection of Syphnian Treasure at Delphi; finely sculptured.

c. Development of Greek deductive mathematics, through Thales and Pythagoras, as distinct from Babylonian empirical work.

Tomb of Cyrus, Pasargadae, erected; possessing rusticated masonry.

Phythian Games chronologically recorded, although earlier in origin; devoted to musical competitions.

c. Introduction of red-figure ornamented pottery in Greece.
c. Erection of Basilica at Paestum, S, Italy, fine Greek temple.

c. Eusebius reported introduction of the Isthmian Games.

c. Porsenna, king of Etruria, built labyrinth at Clusium.

(to –465) Persepolis, Persia: seat of Achaemenian kings.

Year	History	Literature
–517		
–514	Conspiracy of Harmonius and Aristogeiton.	
–510	Rome declared a Republic: last king, Tarquin the Proud, expelled. Expulsion of the Peisistratidae from Athens. Reforms of Cleisthenes.	
–506	Settlement of 5,000 Attic colonists in Chalcis of Eubae; first Greek colony in Greece.	
–500	Sardinia captured by Phoenicians, Greeks and Carthaginians. Aristagorus solicited aid from Sparta and Athens against Darius.	*c*. Use of letter A by Greeks, based on earlier form, *c*. –850. *c*. Heraclitus: *Concerning Nature*, philosophic concept of fire as centre of creation and dissolution. *c*. The *Ramayana*, ancient Hindu poem originally composed; known version *c*. –300.
–499	Start of Ionian War. Sardis burned by Athenians.	
–498	Tarquin defeated and slain at battle of Lake Regulus.	
–494	Thirty cities of Latium formed the Latin League under leadership of Rome; alliance mainly against the Etruscans. Capture of Miletus. End of the Ionian war.	
–493	Plebeians of Rome to have two magistrates of their own who could not be interfered with by patricians.	
–492	Darius demanded tribute of Earth and Water from Greece. Invasion of Mardonius.	
–490	Persian armies defeated by Greeks at Marathon.	*c*. Aeschylus: *The Supplicant Women*, earliest of his extant plays.
–485	†Darius of Persia; accession of Xerxes (to –464); decline of Persia began.	
–484		

Ancient map of the world, by Hecataeus, showing it as a disc.

c. Theatre at Delphi constructed.

c. Completion of Temple of Jupiter Optimus Maximus, Rome; called the Capitol.

Harpy Tomb, Xanthos; now in British Museum.
c. The Treasury of the Athenians, Delphi; first entirely marble Doric edifice.
c. Capitoline Wolf, bronze casting, of Etruria; later removed to Rome.
c. Statue of Jupiter on the Capitol constructed by Volca of Veii, Etruscan artist.

c. Lathe widely used in woodwork.
c. Hindus familiar with plastic surgery, especially production of artificial noses.
c. Astronomer Naburiannu (Babylonian) determined length of lunar month.
c. Dams constructed in India.

Erection of Temple of Saturn, Rome, by Titus Larcius; badly rebuilt −42 and again A.D..

Doxandros erected Vouni Palace, Cyprus; oriental style.

Temple of Ceres, Cosmedin, ornamented with terracotta figures by Gorgasus and Damophilus of Himera.

c. Temple of Aphaia, Aegina, built.

Hypostyle Hall of Xerxes, Persepolis; architectural word hypostyle implies having a roof supported by pillars.

Erection of Temple of Castor and Pollux, Rome; restored −117 and again in A.D. 6

*Herodotus (†−425), Greek historian, who was one of the first men to refer to insects.

Year		
–480	Battle of Thermopylae: †Leonidas and 400 Spartans in vain attempt to stem Persian invasions of Greece. Period of Warring States in China (to –221).	*c.* *Euripides (†–406), Greek tragic dramatist, whose plays are noted for their humanity.
–479	Battle of Platea; end of Persian invasion of Greece.	
–477	Commencement of Athenian ascendancy.	
–471	Plebians in Rome to choose own Tribunes.	*c.* Aeschylus: *The Persians*, Greek play.
–470	†Confucius (see –550).	
–466	Victories of Cimon over Persians at Eurymedon.	*c.* Aeschylus: *Seven Against Thebes*, Greek play.
–460	Athens controlled by Pericles the Athenian; Age of Pericles lasted until –429.	*c.* Aeschylus: *Prometheus Bound*, Greek play.
–458	Cincinnatus rescued a Roman army, surrounded by the Aequi, in a campaign lasting 16 days.	Aeschylus: *Oresteia* trilogy awarded first prize at the festival of Dionysius.
–451	Three Senators sent from Rome to Athens to study Laws of Solon.	*c.* Pindar (*–522, †–438), Greek lyric poet; completed *Epinicia*, Odes of Victory; begun –502.
–450	Romans agreed laws of city be written down so that plebeians should know with which offence they were charged if brought before a magistrate.	Written laws of Rome, called the Twelve Tables. *c.* Samaritan text of the Pentateuch.
–449	Assembly of the Plebeians given right to share in making laws.	
–447		
–445	The conflict between Athens and Sparta ended with thirty years truce.	
–444	Nehemiah's first visit to Jerusalem.	*c.* Age of Sophocles and Euripides.

c. Tomb of the Leopards, Tarquinii (Etruscan city).
c. Classical Period of Greek pottery (to −323).

Greek navy destroyed Persian fleet of Xerxes at the battle of Salamis.

c. *Birth of Aphrodite*, part of an altar.
c. Fine Grecian bronze horse; possibly by Calamis.

c. Hanno of Carthage explored by sea as far as Sierra Leone.
c. Rapid development in technology and agriculture in China.

c. Temple of Zeus, Olympia, erected.
c. Marble statue of Apollo from West Gate of the above-named temple.
c. *The Charioteer of Delphi*, fine Greek life-size bronze figure.

*Hippocrates, Greek physician (†−357), considered to be Father of Medicine; after him is named Hippocratic oath taken by medical practitioners (see −260).

c. Myron: *Discobolus*, in praise of discus throwing.

c. Empedocles's philosophical enunciation of conservation of matter (scientifically stated 1789).

c. *The Ephebus of Subiaco*, fine Greek statue (headless), formerly at Nero's Villa.

Zeno of Elea (*c*. *−490, †−420) formulated eight famous paradoxes, which remained unanswered for some 2,000 years; they required mathematical concept of limit.

Foundations of the Parthenon laid at Athens; designed by Ictinus and Callicrates; completed −433.

c. Nehemiah rebuilt the walls of Jerusalem; opposed by Samaritans.

*c*Anaxagoras (†−428) believed that there were many forms of primal matter and that *reason* established them in order.

Temple of Poseidon, Sunium, built (completed −440); Doric columns.

−440	Plebeians given the right to marry patricians.	
−433	Nehemiah's second visit to Jerusalem.	
−431	Peloponnesian War between Athens and Sparta began; lasted to −404.	Pericles' "Funeral Oration"; as recorded by Thucydides.
−430		
−429	†Pericles of Athens, during plague. Siege and destruction of Plataea.	*Plato (†−347), widely travelled Athenian philosopher, disciple of Socrates and would-be aristocratic politician; about 30 dialogues survive.
−423	Revival, under Nicias, of festival of Delos.	Aristophanes (*−448, †−380); *The Clouds,* Greek satirical comedy.
−421	Fifty years' truce, *Peace of Nicias,* concluded between Athens and Sparta.	Aristophanes: *Peace,* opposing conflict between Athens and Sparta.
−420		
−415	War renewed between Athens and Sparta.	
−414	Destruction of Athenian forces in Sicily.	Aristophanes: *The Birds,* satirical Greek comedy.
−411	Revolution broke out in Athens; power transferred to assembly of the people.	*c.* *Diogenes the Cynic; Greek philosopher who in later years lived in a barrel.
−408		
−407	Alcibiades restored authority of Athens in the revolted cities.	
−406	Victory of Athenian fleet off the Arginuae; eight of ten generals condemned to death for failing to save ship-wrecked sailors; six executed but two escaped.	†Euripides, author of *Medea, Andromache, Iphigenia* and *Alcestis* and numerous other Greek tragedies. †Sophocles (*−495), author of *Antigone, Oedipus Rex, Electra.*
−405	Lysander of Sparta destroyed the Athenian fleet at Aegos-Potami.	Aristophanes: *The Frogs,* Greek satirical comedy.

Erection of Concordia Temple, Agrigento, Sicily; became Christian cathedral 597.
c. Pheidias: The Elgin Marbles (from the Parthenon).

c. Melissus, Greek philosopher, reasoned reality to be infinite; existence was unity, not an aggregate of discrete ideas (or things); interesting parallel with modern mathematical concept of unbounded set.

Temple of Appollo in Rome erected; reconstructed –179.

c. *Nike untying her sandal*; Greek marble sculpture.

The Plague at Athens.
Democritus (*–460, †–370) believed matter to be made up of very small indestructible particles; Greek atomic theory.

Completion of the Acropolis (began –437).

Spartans used chemical smoke in warfare; charcoal, sulphur and pitch.
Hippochrates of Chios reduced problem of "duplication of the cube".

End of the Plague at Athens.

c. Completion of the Theseum, Greek temple at Athens.

c. Temple of Apollo Epicurius, Bassae, having columns of all three orders of Greek Architecture.

c. Hippias of Elis discovered quadratrix, a mathematical curve.

Mutilation of the *Hermes* statue.

*Eudoxus (†–355), who investigated ideas of proportion, basis of 5th book of Euclid.
Foundation of Rhodes.

c. The Erechtheion, Athens Ionic temple of excellent design.

Year	History	Literature
−404	Athens surrendered to Spartans. Assassination of Alcibiades.	
−403	Overthrow of the Thirty Tyrants; council set up by Lysander to rule Athens.	
−400	Greek Army successfully withdrawn after defeat at Cunaxa by Xenophon; "Retreat of the Ten Thousand".	*c.* Hebrew traditions collected in the Priestly Code (or Code of Holiness).
−399		Socrates, accused of teachings contrary to established beliefs, condemned to death.
−396	Etruscan city of Veii captured by Romans after ten years' siege.	*c.* Plato: *Euthyphro, Apology* and *Crito,* appreciation of Socrates.
−395	Coalition among Athens, Thebes, Corinth and Argos against the Spartans; Lysander killed at Hailiartus.	
−394	Spartan general, Agisilaus, defeated Allies at Coronae.	
−391	All Etruria brought under Roman rule by dictator Camillus.	
−390	Gauls from northern Italy took Rome, except for Capital; unable to capture this, they withdrew after sacking the city. Camillus subdued risings in Latin League and reconquered Etruria by −367.	
−387	Conon's plans to use Persian aid to restore Athens failed. Peace of Antalcidas: Greek cities in Asia Minor surrendered to Artaxerxes II.	*c.* Plato: *Symposium* and *Phaedrus,* dialogues dealing with ideal love.
−384		*c.* Plato: *Logic.*
−379	Massacre of Spartan tyrants at Thebes restored Theban liberty.	*c.* Plato: *Phaedo,* supporting faith in immortality.
−371	Sparta defeated by Thebans under Epaminondas at battle of Leuctra.	Xenophon (*c.* *−430): *Anabasis* completed; a record of his travels on campaign.
−369	Epaminondas restored Messenians.	
−367	Camillus returned to Rome; recognized that plebeians needed share in government.	Plato: *Theaetetus*, Greek dialogue. *c.* Aristotle began his *dialogues,* of which only fragments remain.
−366	First plebeian elected to office of Consul; henceforward at least one Consul had to be a plebeian.	

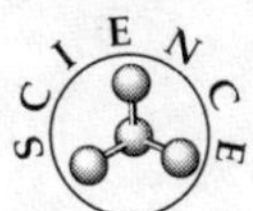

Trumpet competitions held by Greeks.

c. Use of Catapult as weapon of war.
c. Metallic mirrors, Etruscan and Greek, in use.

c. The marble Tholos, Delphi; Doric and Corinthian orders of Greek architecture.
c. *Praxiteles, prominent Greek sculptor.

c. Plato developed logical reasoning in mathematical proofs.

Camillus rebuilt Rome after the Gallic fire; grotto oscura stone used for walls instead of poorer capellaccio.

Plato opened Academy in Athens, inscribed: "Let no one who knows no geometry come under my roof."

†Theaetetus, who founded solid geometry.

Aristotle (*−384, † −322), Greek philosopher, joined Plato at Athens and remained at Academy for 20 years.

Original erection of Temple of Concordia, Rome (rebuilt −120).

	History	Literature
−362	Athens and Sparta allied against Thebes; defeated and killed Epaminondas at battle of Mantinaea, Arcadia.	
−359	Philip of Macedon became King of Macedonia; defeated Athenian force under Pretender Argaeus.	*c*. Xenophon: *Hellenica*, an account of period −411 to −362 of Greek history.
−358	Philip of Macedon reduced the trading city of Amphipolis.	
−357	"Social War"; Athens fought islands of Rhodes, Cos and Chios when they refused to continue to pay protection money; Athens defeated −355.	
−356	Phocis and Thebes quarrelled over guardianship of temple at Delphi; Phocians, supported by Athenians, seized Delphi and so started the Sacred War.	
−351		Demosthenes (*c*. *−384, † −322), Athenian orator, delivered his first *Philippic* attacking Philip of Macedon.
−350	*c*. Etruscan power began to decline when Celts over-ran northern Italy and Romans advanced from south; last city fell −264. *c*. Revolt of the Jews against Artaxerxes III of Persia; suppressed.	*c*. *The Parian Chronicle*, an account of Greek history engraved on marble.
−347	Philip of Macedon destroyed Republic of Olynthus.	Aristotle began his travels at Assos, Lesbos and Pella (to −335).
−346	Peace between Philip of Macedon and Athens. Philip joined with Thebans against Phocians and ended Sacred War.	
−340		*Epicurus (†−270), Greek philosopher, founder of Epicurean School.
−338	Philip of Macedon invaded Greece; Athens, Thebes, Corinth, Achaea and Euboea against him; Allies defeated at Chaeronea; end of Greek independence. Cities of Latium revolted and were defeated; Latin League dissolved.	

Theatrical productions in Rome.

c. Indication that the aristocracy of Plato's republic studied the *quadrivium* (arithmetic, astronomy, geometry, music).

Philip of Macedon founded Philippi in gold-fields area.

c. Menaechmus studied parabola and hyperbola (particular plane sections of a cone) in connection with mean proportional.

Temple of Diana at Ephesus destroyed by fire; rebuilt soon afterwards; again largely destroyed in 262, by Goths.

c. Tomb of Mausolus (one of the Seven Wonders) completed; whence is word *mausoleum*.

c. Aristotle: *Historia Animalium*, classfied animals; he believed some animals mated and had progeny, while others developed spontaneously from mud and water.

c. Bronze head of Brutus; now in Rome.
c. Arezzo Chimera, bronze casting; Etruscan work discovered at Arezzo in 16th cent.
c. Beautiful theatre at Epidaurus built; best preserved of Greek theatres, typical of this deisgn; 387 ft. diameter.

c. Greeks understood Earth to be spherical in shape.
c. First Greek herbal appeared.
c. Theophrastus recorded use of coal in Italy and Greece (by metalworkers).
c. Creation of the *Shan-hai-ching*, a Chinese cosmography.
c. Hill fort constructed at Maiden Castle (see –149).

c. Aristotle seems to have been first man to study musical theory.

c. Romans began to use coins.

–336	Assassination of Philip of Macedon at Aegae.	
–335	Thebans revolted on reported death of Alexander, Philip's successor; Alexander completely destroyed Thebes. Samaritan Schism.	Aristotle returned to Athens and became head of Peripatetic school; extant work mainly dates from this period (to –322).
–334	Alexander defeated Persians at Granicus.	
–333	Darius III of Persia defeated by Alexander at Issus.	
–332	Alexander destroyed Tyre. Egypt accepted Alexander as ruler. Jerusalem submitted to Alexander; Palestine under Greek influence to –63.	
–331	Alexander defeated Darius III at Gaugamela and destroyed Persian empire. Babylon surrendered to Alexander.	
–330	Assassination of Darius III by Bessus, Satrap of Bactria; Alexander attacked the Bactrians, executed Bessus. Alexander burned Persepolis.	*c.* Aristotle: *Organon, Poetics, Politics*.
–327	Renewal of war between Rome and neighbouring Samnites.	
–326	Alexander's campaign in Punjab extended his empire to River Indus.	
–325		*c.* Earliest extant papyrus written in Greek: the *Persae* of Timotheus.
–323	Beginning of the Final Egyptian Dynasty, under Ptolemy Soter, lasting until †Cleopatra (–31).	
–321	†Alexander in Babylon. Roman army entrapped and defeated by Samnites at Claudine Pass.	
–320	Ptolemy Soter of Egypt invaded Syria; captured Jerusalem.	*Theocritus (†–250), Greek bucolic poet who wrote *Epigrams, Idylls*.
–319	Antipater (†–318) marched against Ptolemy Soter, governor of Egypt; won Regency of Asia.	
–316	Olympias, mother of Alexander the Great, put to death by Cassander, son of Antipater.	

Erection of Choragic Monument of Lysicrates, at Athens; white marble cylinder with earliest extant external Corinthian columns.

c. Aristotle; various scientific and quasi-scientific works, e.g. *Physica; De Anima; Meterologica.*

Alexander recognized Samaritan High Priesthood.

Port of Alexandria founded by Alexander.

Erection, at Sidon, of Alexander's Cenotaph; sarcophagus now at Constantinople.

Pytheas, Greek seaman who found how to determine latitude, sailed round Britain.

*c.*Important surveys of land and other geographical records carefully made during Alexander's travels.

c. Praxiteles: *Hermes with young Dionysus,* Greek statue; the only original statue definitely by the master.

Alexander ordered exploration of Indian Ocean, Persian Gulf and Euphrates; opened trade route to India and Egypt via Red Sea.

Alexandria became centre of Greek learning.
Hellenistic Period of Greek arts (to –30).

c. *Euclid (†–283), famous for *Elements,* great work on geometry in standard use until about A.D. 1900 (dates doubtful).

c. Rise of Mauryan culture in India some 1,500 years after last known period (Mohenjo-daro).

*c.*Aristoxenus defined rhythm as tripartite: (*a*) speech; (*b*) melody; (*c*) movement.

Colonies of Jews settled in Egypt and Cyrene for commercial purposes.

Cassander founded Salonika (Thessaloniki).

LITERATURE

	History	Literature
–314	Palestine subject to Seleucid rule of Syria.	
–313	Tibet founded by union of pastoral tribes; ruled by king, Nya-Thri Tempo.	
–312	Commencement of the Seleucidae in Syria; continued 240 years, until last king deposed by Roman general Pompey (see –65).	
–311	Civil wars in Alexander's empire ended; Treaty of Partition allocated Macedonia to Cassander as Regent, Thrace to Lysimachus, Egypt to Ptolemy Soter and Asia to Antigonus.	
–310	Samnites and Etrurian allies totally defeated by Rome at Vadimonian Lake.	*c.* Epicureans developed philosophy that knowledge was useful only for practical purposes.
–307	Demetrius released Athens from Cassander and restored popular government.	
–306	Demetrius defeated Ptolemy Soter at sea; Alexander's successors assumed title of "King" in various parts of his empire.	
–305	Bovianum, last Samnite fortress, fell to Rome. Campania and southern Italian provinces under Roman rule.	*c. Jus Flavianum* issued.
–301	Battle of the Kings at Ipsus; †Antigonus. Palestine reverted to Egyptian rule.	
–300		*c.* Zeno of Crete (*c.* *–336, †–264), philosopher, flourished; associated with Stoics, who attached no value to knowledge as such; believed the universe to possess body and soul. *c.* First six books of the Bible collected together.
–299	Demetrius captured Athens; usurped Macedonian throne.	
–298	Samnites revolted a third time; planned to unite with Gauls and Etruscans against Rome.	

c. Ptolemy Soter founded academy at Alexandria.

Construction of Aqua Appia, oldest Roman aqueduct; subterranean.

Appius Claudius began work on the Appian Way; most celebrated and one of the earliest Roman roads.

Rome created commissioners: first *permanent* navy in the world.

c. Herophilus of Chalcedon, of Alexandria school of medicine, flourished.

c. Chares, Rhodian sculptor, began Colossus of Rhodes, gigantic statue of Apollo which stood, not astride the harbour but on one side of it; one of the Seven Wonders (see –280, –224).
c. Pylon of great temple to Amen, associated with Ethiopian Queen Candace, Sudan.

c. Theophrastus (*–372, †–287) wrote earliest surviving work on fossils and minerals; used word *anatomy*.
c. Clepsydra (water-clock) used in Greece.
c. Erasistratus, Greek anatomist, observed function of motor and sensory nerves; the *trachea* was named by him; he also invented the catheter.
c. Erection of great observatory at Alexandria by Ptolemy Soter.
Seleucus Nicator founded Antioch, in Syria.

Tomb of Scipius Berbatus, Rome.

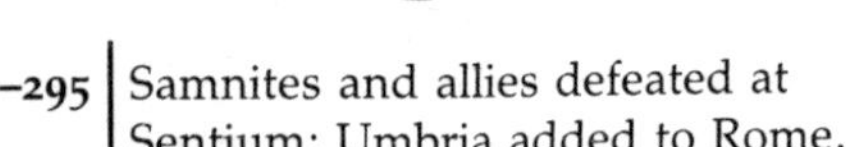

Date	History	Literature
–295	Samnites and allies defeated at Sentium; Umbria added to Rome.	
–293	Lucius Papirius led Romans to victory over Samnites at Aquiloneia.	
–290	War between Rome and Samnites ended with surrender of Samnites.	
–289	Romans defeated by Senones at Arretium.	*c.* †Mencius (Meng-Tzu), great Sung philosopher, (**c.* –372).
–287	Demetrius of Macedon deposed by army revolt; replaced by Pyrrhus, king of Epirus; in turn replaced by Lysimachus, former general of Alexander the Great.	
–284	Senones exterminated by Romans under Dolabella; Lucanians also crushed; Roman garrisons placed in all Greek towns in Italy, except Tarentum.	*c.* Foundation of great Library of Alexandria by Ptolemy Soter.
–283	Corsica captured by Romans.	
–282	War between Tarentum and Rome over presence of Roman ships in Tarentum harbour.	
–280	Pyrrhus defeated Romans at Pandosia; Greek cities supported Pyrrhus, who was joined by Samnites. Formation of Achaean League.	
–279	Romans defeated by Pyrrhus at Asculum. Gauls invaded Greece by way of Macedonia, their object being loot.	
–275	Pyrrhus finally defeated by Romans at Beneventum.	
–274	Pyrrhus invaded Macedonia, and again crowned king.	
–270		
–268		

c. Euclid: *Optica* and *Catoptica*.

c. Herophilus dissected human body and distinguished veins and arteries.

c. Strato appears to have expounded hydrodynamical principle that the smaller the cross-section of liquid flow with a given head the greater the speed of flow.

*Archimedes (†–212), early applied mathematician; to him are attributed the screw, screw pump, laws of levers and "Principle of Archimedes" (law of flotation); he also designed war engines—powerful catapults; pure mathematics included his "spiral".

(to –247) Ptolomaic Isis Temple, Philae.

c. Completion of the Colossus of Rhodes; destroyed by earthquake –224.

Elephants used in battle at Pandosia were the first seen in Europe.

Completion of lighthouse at Pharos, Alexandria; one of the Seven Wonders (begun –283).

Babylonians re-established in new city of Seleucia; end of history of Babylon.

c. Aristarchus of Samos believed the Sun to be larger than the Earth and was first to evolve the theory that the latter rotated around the former.

c. The quadratic equation, stated in words, was probably solved more or less by drawing geometrical diagrams; symbols followed much later.

Aratus recorded 45 constellations.

First appearance of the denarius; hence symbol (*d*) for one old penny arose U.K.

Year	History	Literature
–266	Calabria conquered by Romans.	
–264		
–260	Outbreak of First Punic War between Rome and Carthage; main cause was conflict of imperial interests; Carthaginian fleet defeated by Romans at Mylae.	
–256	Roman fleet defeated Carthaginians at Ecnomus.	
–255	Regulus, attacking Carthage, captured by Carthaginians under Xanthippus the Spartan.	*c.* Writing of the *Septuagint*, Greek version of Old Testament.
–254	New Roman fleet, under Cornelius Scipio, captured Panormus, best harbour in Sicily.	*Plautus (†–184), Latin comic playwright.
–251	Rome occupied all Sicily except Lilybaeum and Drepana.	
–250	Unsuccessful siege of Lilybaeum by Romans. *c.* Invasion of Britain by *La Têne* Iron Age people.	Parchment produced at Pergamium. *c.* Arcesilaus founded second Academy in Athens.
–243	Aratus of Achaean League captured Corinth from Macedonian garrison.	
–242	Roman naval victory over Carthage led to Roman capture of Drepana.	
–241	Hamilcar, Carthaginian general, made peace with Rome and surrendered Sicily to Rome.	
–239		*Ennius (†–170) father of Latin literature, epic poet, who wrote *Annals*.
–238	Carthage, under Hamilcar, began conquest of Spain. Sardinia became part of Roman Republic.	
–236	Outbreak of war between Sparta and Achaean League.	
–229	Hamilcar's conqeust of southern Spain complete.	
–225	Gauls defeated by the Romans at Telaman; Gauls south of River Po exterminated.	

First public combats of gladiators (see 325).

c. The *Hippocratic Corpus*, earliest collected works of Greek medicine, assembled in Alexandria.

c. Portico of Temple of Horus, Edfu; still in fine preservation.

c. Erection of the Tullianum, first Roman prison.
c. Asoka, emperor of N. and C. India erected great columns (40 ft. high) inscribed with his laws.

Ctesibius constructed water-clocks at Alexandria.
c. Eratosthenes (c. *–276, †–194) mapped the course of the Nile.
c. Herophilus, Greek anatomist, realized that human beings belong to animal kingdom.

c. Ctesibius developed *hydraulus*, water-controlled organ.

c. Eratosthenes suggested that the Earth moves round the Sun.

Hasdrubal founded Cartagena, Spain.

c. Eratosthenes made good estimate of Earth's circumference.

Introduction of leap year into calendar by Egyptians.

Port of New Carthage constructed.

c. Spurius Carvilius opened first grammar school (stated by Plutarch; see 47).

c. Apollonius (*–260, †–190), mathematician, concerned with geometry of conics; calculated π; a standard theorem is named after him.

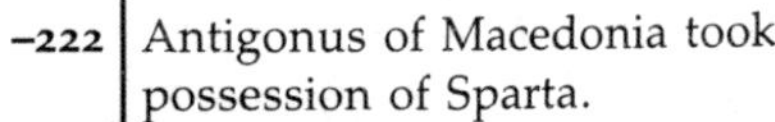

	History	Literature
−222	Antigonus of Macedonia took possession of Sparta.	
−221	The Ch'ins, a borderland tribe, seized Imperial power in China; Ch'in dynasty (to −206).	
−220	Hannibal of Carthage besieged Sarguntum, Greek town in eastern Spain allied to Rome.	
−219	Renewal of war between Carthage and Rome: Second Punic War.	
−218	Hannibal invaded Italy from north, crossing the Little St Bernard Pass; captured Turin; defeated Scipio at River Ticinus and Sempronius at River Trebia.	
−217	Romans, under Gaius Flaminius, defeated by Hannibal at Lake Trasimene.	
−216	Romans defeated at Cannae. Philip V of Macedon made alliance with Hannibal.	
−215	Roman armies in Spain under Publius and Cornelius Scipio defeated; both generals killed.	
−213	†Aratus by slow poison, for having criticized tyrannies of Philip V of Macedon.	*c.* Shih Huang Ti, Chinese Emperor, responsible for great Burning of the Books.
−210	Revolution in Sparta; tyranny under Machanidas.	
−209	Insurrection in China; Ch'in dynasty exterminated; Liu Pang, former bandit leader, gained control; became Han prince −206.	
−207	Carthaginian relief force defeated by Romans on the Metaurus. Machanidas, Tyrant of Sparta, killed by Achaean League.	
−205	Scipio completed conquest of Spain begun by his father in −215.	*c.* Plautus: *Miles Gloriosus*, Roman comedy.
−204	Scipio landed at Utica to attack Carthage but was repulsed.	*c.* †Naevius, first major Latin poet.
−203	Romans, under Scipio, defeated a Carthaginian army; Hannibal recalled from Italy to lead against Scipio.	

Construction of the Flaminian Way from Rome to Rimini.

c. Chinese prepared *Arithmetic in Nine Sections,* a work on mensuration.

Oldest extant Roman bridge built at Martorell, Spain.

c. Great Wall of China; built to keep out invaders; 1,400 miles long.

c. Period of Chinese Bronze Age.

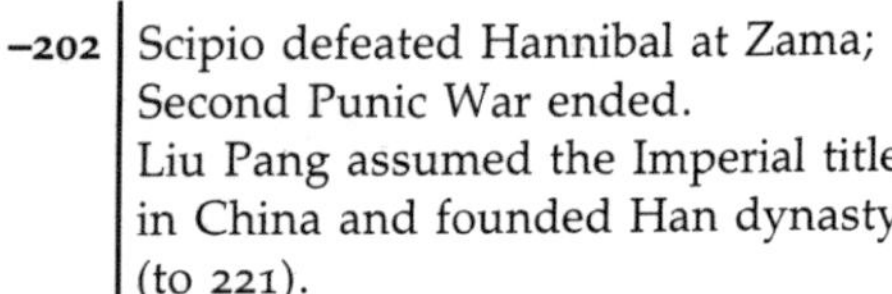

Date	History	Literature
–202	Scipio defeated Hannibal at Zama; Second Punic War ended. Liu Pang assumed the Imperial title in China and founded Han dynasty (to 221).	
–200	Abydus destroyed by Philip V of Macedon; Attica ravaged. *c.* Yayoi people ousted Jomon people from Japan.	*c.* Inscription engraved on Rosetta Stone. *c.* The *Mahābhārata*, ancient Hindu poem; survives in form from this date.
–198	Antiochus III of Syria took Palestine from Egypt.	*c.* Third period of Chinese literature; deteriorated because of state examinations, (lasted to *c.* +200).
–197	Philip of Macedon, defeated by Flaminius in Thessaly, fled.	
–196	Peace made at Corinth among Rome, Achaean League and states which had taken part in war against Philip.	
–195	The Aetolians invited Antiochus III of Syria to conquer Greece.	*c.* *Terence (†–159), Roman dramatist, who wrote *Andria, Hecyra, Adelphi* and three other plays.
–192	Antiochus III, aided by Hannibal in exile at his court, landed in Greece. War between Sparta and Rome; Sparta defeated and joined Achaean League.	
–191	Romans, under Glabrio, defeated Antiochus III at Thermoplyae	*c.* Plautus: *Pseudolus* Latin comedy, produced.
–189	Hannibal defeated at River Eurymedon by Rhodian fleet.	
–188	Antiochus III defeated by Romans at Magnesia.	
–185	Shunga dynasty (to –30) replaced Mauryan in India.	
–182	Hannibal committed suicide. †Scipio Africanus.	
–179	†Philip of Macedon succeeded by son Perseus, who continued hostility to Rome.	
–175	†Antiochus III: succeeded by Antiochus IV (Epiphanes).	
–174		
–172	War again broke out between Rome and Macedonia; Perseus defeated badly-led Roman army.	

SCIENCE

c. Confucianism and Taoism adopted as Chinese way of life during Han dynasty.

c. With rise of (Western) Han dynasty, Chinese discovered secret of manufacturing porcelain; considerable doubt as to precise date.

c. Silver cauldron of Gundestrup, Denmark, Celtic votive offering.
c. Oldest paintings on walls of caves of Ajanta (see +50).

c. Use of gears led to invention of ox-driven water-wheel for irrigation.

Independence of Greece proclaimed at Isthmian Games.

c. Salerno became a Roman colony.

c. Foundation of Roman town of Florentia (later Florence; see 313).

Foundation of Aquileia, Italy, great city; destroyed by Attila the Hun 452.

Original foundation of Basilica Aemilia, Rome.

First Roman stone bridge: Aemilian Bridge.

Construction of earliest known Roman pavement; no paved streets earlier.

Temple of Zeus, Athens; later completed by Hadrian (*76, †138).

	History	Literature
–168	Perseus routed by Roman army at Pydna; Macedonia placed under Roman governor. Persecution of the Jews by Antiochus IV.	
–167	Maccabean revolt against Antiochus IV to defend Jewish religion. 1,000 Achaeans exiled to Italy for 17 years.	*c.* First performance of *Andrea*, a comedy by Terence, in Rome; remaining five plays produced by –160.
–165		
–160	†Judas Maccabaeus; succeeded by Jonathan Maccabaeus; Asmonaean line of priestly rulers established.	*c.* Public libraries in existence in Rome.
–153	Independence of Jews (to –63).	
–149	Roman war with Carthage resumed: Third Punic War.	
–147	War between Sparta and Achaea; Roman force besieged Corinth and completely destroyed it; Greece now directly under Roman control.	
–146	Romans utterly destroyed Carthage.	
–144	Jonathan Maccabaeus murdered; succeeded by Simon.	
–140		
–133	Asia Minor made into province of Rome, now ruler of whole civilized world round Mediterranean, except Egypt. Tiberius Gracchus, Roman reformer, assassinated at instigation of Senate.	Polybius (*c.* *–204, †–122) concluded his forty books of history; written in Greek.
–125		
–123	Caius Gracchus, brother of Tiberius, elected Tribune; started wide plan of reform and assistance to poorer subjects of Rome.	
–121	†Caius Gracchus in a riot.	

Desecration of Temple at Jerusalem by Antiochus IV.

Temple at Jerusalem rededicated by Maccabaeus.

c. Stupas; (mound graves) at Sanchi, India; Shunga dynasty.

*Hipparchus (†–125), who invented trigonometry.

First month of Roman year changed from March to January.

c. Massive reconstruction of Maiden Castle (by the Veneti?); soon under hegemony of Belgic chiefs (see 45).

c. *Heron of Alexandria (*c.* †–100), Greek mathematician and mechanist; it is far from certain exactly when he lived.

c. Marcius constructed first high-level aqueduct.

c. Hipparchus responsible for establishment of observatory at Rhodes.

c. *Venus de Milo*, famous statue of Parian marble, sculpted (see 1820).

c. Crates of Mallos made great globe of world.

c. Hipparchus discovered new star in constellation of Scorpio; gave rise to idea of producing a star catalogue.
c. *Posidonius, who observed relationship between tides and moon.

Completion of the Pylons of the Temple of Horus, Edfu.

Star catalogue by Hipparchus.

c. Grand College in China for Civil Service training.

c. Early use of concrete in Temple of Concord, Rome.

	History	Literature
−115	Under Han Emperor Wu Ti, Chinese army crossed Lop Nor Desert and occupied Tarim basin and imposed Chinese authority on local rulers there.	
−112	Outbreak of slave war in Sicily. War began in Africa between Rome and Jugurtha, king of Numidia. *c.* Rise of Pharisees and Sadducees.	
−106	Gaius Marius elected Consul and sent to Africa to replace Caecilius Metellus.	*Cicero (†−43), Roman politician and orator; 57 speeches survive, including *In Verrem, Pro Cluentio, Pro Milone*.
−105	Marius, assisted by Sulla, defeated Jugurtha of Numidia and ally, Bocchus of Mauretania. Gauls slaughtered 80,000 Roman soldiers at battle of Arausio.	
−102	Chinese army crossed Pamir mountains and imposed rule on area which brought them into contact with the West. Marius defeated Teutonic tribes attacking Roman province of Southern Gaul; wiped out Teutones and Ambrones.	
−101	Romans, under Marius, exterminated Cimbri at battle of Vercellae.	
−100	Marius again elected Consul; year of incessant riot and murders of prominent men.	*c. The Book of Enoch*, collection of writings of Pharisees; supposed to have been written by Enoch. *c.* Dionysius Thrax, author of first Greek grammar, flourished.
−91	Livius Drusus, reformer of Roman Law and proposer of votes for all Italians, murdered.	
−90	Central Italy formed separate state; war with Rome. Civil war in Rome between Marius and Sulla: Marius driven out.	
−89	Led by Sulla, Roman army regained control of Italy, but had to grant to all Italians right of Roman citizenship.	
−88	Mithradates VI, king of Pontus, invaded Asia; Athens rose against Roman rule.	

c. Early form of fire-engine known.

c. Hermagos of Temnos, Aeolis, founded school of "scholastic" rhetoric.

c. Development of commerce around the Indian Ocean.

c. Heron developed a School of Mechanics and Surveying at Alexandria; very early form of College of Technology.

Silk trade developed between China and the West.
c. Heron invented *Sphere of Aeolus*, early form of steam turbine (not developed); described in his book *Pneumatica*.

c. Erection of the Great Stupa, Sanchi, India (Shunga Period).
By now Yayoi pottery vessels had largely replaced Jomon type; frequently dark red colour.

c. †Heron, who enunciated Laws of Reflection; also invented the syphon.
c. Cissoid of Diocles, mathematical curve.

c. Vitruvius: *De Architectura Libri Decem*, on architecture and machines; known in 12th cent.; rediscovered 1486, *q.v.*
Asclepiades, Greek physician, practised nature curing in Rome.

–87	Sulla sent to East to crush Mithradates, took Athens.	
–86	Marius returned to Rome and seized power; Sulla outlawed; †Marius. †Wu Ti, Han Emperor; civil war in China.	*Sallust (†–34), Roman historian, who wrote *De coniuratione Catilinae* and *Bellum Jugurthinum*.
–85	Mithradates again defeated by Sulla at Orchomenus.	
–84	Roman army, sent to arrest Sulla, joined him.	
–83	Sulla made peace with Mithradates.	
–82	Sulla returned to Italy from Asia, and made himself Dictator of Rome.	
–79	Sulla voluntarily laid down Dictatorship because of old age, after a period of reform.	
–78	†Sulla.	
–73	Mithradates renewed war against Rome; defeated by Roman army under Lucullus.	
–72	Lucullus overthrew Armenian allies of Mithradates. Sertorius murdered by his officers; end of war in Spain.	
–71	Revolt of slaves and gladiators under Spartacus crushed by consuls Pompey and Crassus.	
–70	Lucullus recalled from Asia following a revolt among his troops inspired by men in Pompey's pay.	*Virgil (†–19), great Roman poet.
–69	Dynastic war in Palestine; Hyrcanus II deposed; rise of House of Antipater.	
–68	Crete captured by the Romans.	
–67	Mediterranean pirates crushed by Pompey.	Publication of *Lex Cornelia*. Sallust: *Historiarum libri V*; contemporary history, a fragment only surviving.
–66	Pompey defeated Mithradates, who committed suicide.	*c.* Gaius Valerius Catullus (*c.* *–84, †–54) great Roman lyric poet at work on his 116 odes.
–65	Pompey entered Syria; conquest of Palestine complete by –63; Palestine now part of Roman province of Syria.	*Horace (†–8), Roman poet, who wrote *Odes, Satires, Epistles*.

c. Crateuas, Asiatic herbalist, first drew plants scientifically.

c. Oldest extant amphitheatre erected: at Pompeii.

c. Erection of Temple of Hercules, Cori; Doric order.

Posidonius of Apamea attempted to find basis for theory of tides (see –133, 1683).

Catulus erected Tabularium, Rome, holding tablets of laws.

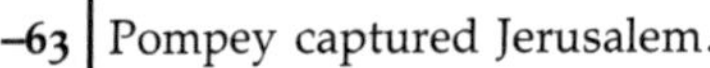

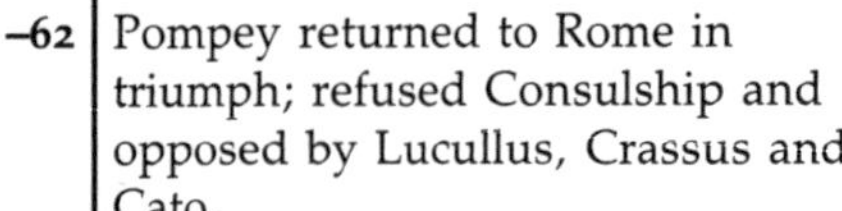

Year	History	Literature
−63	Pompey captured Jerusalem.	
−62	Pompey returned to Rome in triumph; refused Consulship and opposed by Lucullus, Crassus and Cato.	
−61	Gaius, Julius Caesar, nephew of Marius, victorious in Spain.	
−60	Caesar returned to Rome from Spain and was elected Consul. Pompey, Crassus and Caesar formed the First Triumvirate.	Caesar created *Acta Diurna*, daily bulletin, forerunner of newsletter.
−58	Caesar departed for Gaul and secured Upper and Middle Rhine frontier.	
−55	North Gaul conquered by Caesar. Punitive expeditions sent to Britain.	Cicero: *De oratore*. Gauls began to use Latin instead of their native Celtic.
−54	Caesar invaded Britain a second time; Cassivelanus, king of south Britain, agreed to pay tribute to Rome:	*Albius Tibullus (†−18), Roman poet who wrote *Elegies*. Cicero: *De Re Publica*.
−53	Roman army under Crassus defeated by Parthians; Crassus killed. Nervii completely defeated by Caesar.	
−52	Pompey became sole consul after rioting in Rome. Caesar crushed revolt of Vercingetorix in Central Gaul.	
−51	Caesar set about Romanization of Gaul; work complete by −50.	*c*. Caesar: *De Bello Gallico* account of Gallic wars.
−50	Pompey and Caesar, both with armies under their command, rivals for control of Rome; Republic nearing its end.	*c*. Possible date of collection of psalms into present form (Nos. 1–150).
−49	Pompey, supported by Senate, against Caesar; Mark Antony, supporter of Caesar, expelled from Senate; Caesar crossed the Rubicon to invade Italy and start civil war.	
−48	Pompey defeated by Caesar at Pharsalia; Hyrcanus II restored.	

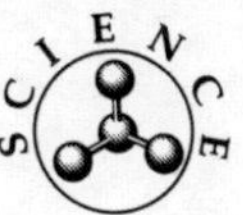

Marcus Tullius Tiro of Rome invented system of shorthand (in use for over 600 years).

The Ponte Fabricio erected over the Tiber, Rome.

c. Lucretius (*–98, †–55): *De natura rerum,* Epicurean doctrine of universe, including many scientific ideas; he described magnets, known earlier in China.

Roman colonies established in Switzerland.

Pompey built first permanent theatre at Rome.

Erection of new (Julian) forum, Rome, commenced.
Crassus plundered Temple at Jerusalem.

Fortified town of Lutetia (later, Paris) burned during Gallic War of Independence.

Early form of oboe known.
c. Erection of House of Livia, Rome.
c. *Father Nile and his Children,* Graeco-Egyptian marble.
c. Buddhist golden reliquary from Bimaran.

c. Landscape gardening in Rome.

	History	Literature
−47	Pompey murdered in Egypt by order of Cleopatra; Caesar settled affairs in Egypt; reduced Asia Minor at Zela. Antipater became Procurator of Judaea; Herod, governor of Galilee.	*c.* Caesar: *De Bello Civili*, account of civil wars.
−46	Pompey's supporters in Africa defeated by Caesar at Thapsus; Africa made Roman Province; Caesar returned to Rome and set about reconstruction.	
−45	Final Pompeian revolt in Spain defeated by Caesar at Mundi; Caesar virtually Dictator of Rome; adopted nephew, Gaius Octavius, as heir.	
−44	Caesar murdered by conspirators led by Brutus and Cassius.	Cicero issued his first *Philippic*, in reply to Mark Antony.
−43	Second Triumvirate formed: Mark Antony, Lepidus and Octavius Caesar. Cleopatra became Queen of Egypt. †Antipater.	*Ovid (†17), Roman poet, in exile from 8 onwards.
−42	Triumvirs defeated Brutus and Cassius at Philippi.	Virgil: *Eclogues*, pastoral poems (to −37).
−40	Open quarrels between Mark Antony and Octavius. Hyracanus II banished; Antigonus succeeded; last of Asmonaean priestly line. Herod, at Rome, appointed king of Judaea.	
−38	Mark Antony returned to Egypt and Octavius declared war on him.	
−37	Herod captured Jerusalem.	
−34	Dalmatia made into Roman Province.	
−31	Combined fleets of Antony and Cleopatra defeated by Roman fleet of Octavius at Actium; Mark Antony and Cleopatra committed suicide; Egypt became Roman province.	*c.* Virgil completed the *Georgics* (Art of Husbandry).
−27	Octavius, now Augustus Caesar, laid down pattern of government of Empire.	

Extensive damage by fire of Great Library of Ptolemy I (Egypt); disaster in scientific history; library again burned in 391 (see also 641).

Erection of Basilica Julia, Rome, begun. Caesar rebuilt Corinth.

Adoption of Julian Calendar of 365+105 days; leap year introduced (see –4241).

The Romans built a fort near the confluence of Saône and Rhône rivers which was to become the city of Lyons.

Temple of Julius Caesar, Rome, begun.

c. Chinese octave had 60 notes.

Erection of Tower of the Winds, Athens; octagonal clock-tower with sundial on each face and clepsydra below.
†Asclepiades of Bithynia, first scientific physician in Rome.

c. Famous marble sculpture, *Laocoon Group*, created; discovered 1506.

c. Sallust laid out Horti Sallustiani, magnificent gardens of Quirinal.

c. Oldest known computer constructed; made of bronze; recovered 1953 from wreck of Greek ship.

Erection of Temple of Portunus, Rome; of circular form.

c. (date doubtful) Discovery in Sidon of blowpipe method of constructing glassware from glass bubbles.
Galleys in general use in Mediterranean.

Agrippa commenced building the Pantheon at Rome (see 120).
Erection of Arch of Augustus at Rimini.

c. Agrippa built Pont du Gard, Nîmes, great Roman aqueduct bridge 900 ft. long.

LITERATURE

	History	Literature
–20	Parthia induced to return captured standards of Crassus and Antony.	*c.* Sextus Propertius, Roman elegiac poet: four books of poetry, including *Cynthia*, written from –25 to –16. *c.* Virgil completed the *Aeneid*, epic poem.
–18	Adultery made an offence against State of Rome.	
–16	Augustus planned establishment of Danube-Elbe frontier.	
–9	Roman forces under Drusus penetrated Germania as far as the Elbe.	Livy (*–59, †17) ceased his history of Rome, which covered period from its foundation.
–6	Judaea annexed by Rome.	
–4	†Herod; Judaea divided among his sons. *Jesus Christ (probably correct year after adjustment of calendar), at Bethlehem.	*Seneca (†65), Roman philosopher, who wrote *Dialogues, Moral Letters*.
–2	Julia, daughter of Augustus, banished for immorality.	*c.* Ovid: *Ars Amatoria*, which aroused anger of Augustus.
1		
3		
5	Cunobelinus (Cymbeline), king of the Catuvellauni, recognized by Romans as king of Britain.	*c.* Ovid: *Metamorphoses*, Roman narrative fables.
6	Revolts in Danubian provinces crushed by Tiberius. Judaea became Roman province.	
9	Roman army, under Varus, destroyed by Cherusci, under Arminius; Roman provinces between Rhine and Elbe lost.	*c.* Ovid began *Tristia*, five books of poetic complaints.
14	†Augustus; succeeded by weak Tiberius.	
16	Arminius defeated by Germanicus at Idistaviso.	*c.* Ovid: *Epistolae ex Ponto*, Roman poetic epistles.
19	Germanicus poisoned by Piso, Roman governor of Syria.	
22	Han dynasty set up by Liu Hsin; "Eastern" or "Later" Han.	

c. The *Aldobrandine Wedding*, Roman mural, discovered in 1605.
Herod began rebuilding Temple at Jerusalem.

The *Miliarium Aureum*, or Golden Milestone, bearing the names and distances from Rome of the chief towns in the Empire set up in the Via Sacra.

c. Erection of Maison Carrée, Nîmes, finest extant small Roman shrine.

Dedication of Temple of Mars Ultor, Rome.

c. Work begun on theatre at Leptis Magna, Tripolitania, by Annobal Tapiapus Rufus.

During Han dynasty (China) astronomy at its peak; calculations made on phases of moon, planetary motion and calendar.
Voice pipes in use for communication in Roman palaces.

Erection of Palaces of Emperors of Rome (to 212).

Reconstruction of Temple of Castor and Pollux (commenced –7).

Examinations for Civil Service in China.

Erection of Porte d'Auguste, Roman gates at Nîmes; still extant.

First definite reference to diamonds.

Chinese capital removed to Loyang.

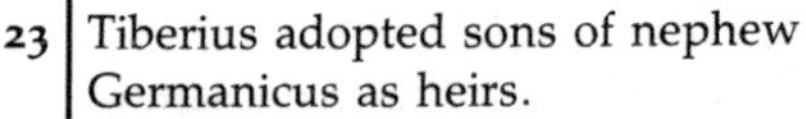

	History	Literature
23	Tiberius adopted sons of nephew Germanicus as heirs.	*Pliny the Elder (†79), Roman author.
25	*c.* Roman colony at S. Indian port of Muziris, modern Cranganore.	
26	Tiberius settled in Capri, leaving Rome in charge of Sejanus, Prefect of Praetorian Guard. Pontius Pilate, Procurator of Judaea (to 36).	
27	Baptism of Jesus Christ; Ministry (to 30).	
28	Execution of John the Baptist.	Records of John the Baptist's teaching.
30	Crucifixion of Jesus Christ (possibly 29). Sejanus murdered widow and two sons of Germanicus; Gaius survived.	I.N.R.I.; Iesus Nazarenus Rex Iudaeorum, the letters on the Cross of Christ.
32	Conversion of Saul of Tarsus; baptized as Paul.	
37	†Tiberius; succeeded by Gaius, nicknamed *Caligula*.	
40	Arminius, son of Cunobelinus, forced to take refuge with Caligula. Emperor announced conquest of Britain.	*c.* (Date very doubtful) I.H.S. (IHΣ) interpreted (falsely) as Iesus Hominum Salvator.
41	Mauretania annexed by Romans.	Seneca began series of philosophical essays (to 64).
42	Caligula assassinated by Praetorian Guard to check misrule; succeeded by Claudius.	
43	Roman invasion of Britain under Aulus Plautius; British of South-east, under Caractacus, defeated at Medway.	*Martial (†104) Roman poet, who wrote *Epigrams*.
47	Ostorius Scapula appointed Governor of Britain; pursued conquest vigorously.	*Plutarch (†120), Greek historian who wrote *Parallel Lives of Greeks and Romans*.
50	Alexandria now within few weeks' sailing of India. Gothic Kingdom set up on Lower Vistula.	

c. Volto Santo, famous wood-carving of Christ; possibly work of S. Nicodemus.

c. During unrest in China (to 600), fine painted grey clay human figures made.

c. Celsus's important work on medicine translated into Latin; original Greek text appears to have been lost; Latin name *De Re Medica*.

c. Foundation of a church at Corinth; one of earliest Christian houses.

c. Seneca: *Questiones Naturalis*.

c. Erection of Temple of Augustus, Vienne, France; rusticated stone.

c. Maiden Castle, Dorset, fell to Vespasian, because of superiority of Roman iron ballistae over sling-stones.

London believed to have been founded by this date.

Early period of caves at Karle and Ajanta, India, early Buddhist rock-cut temples (see 525).

c. Two silver cups (Roman); found near Copenhagen (1922).

c. Roman fortresses erected at Glevum and Lindum (later Gloucester and Lincoln respectively).

c. Dioscorides: *De Materia Medica*, describing some 600 medicinal plants; little further progress in Europe for some 1,500 years.

Hippalus, Alexandrian merchant, discovered monsoon wind; made passage to India possible.

c. Romans took control of Mendip lead mines.

LITERATURE

	History	Literature
51	Caractacus defeated and captured.	
53		
57	First records of direct communication between China and Japan.	*c*. St Paul believed to have written Epistle to the Galatians.
58	Ming-Ti became Emperor of China; introduced Buddhism. St Paul imprisoned in Rome (to 60).	
60	Campaign of Suetonius Paulinus in Wales; massacre of Druids in Anglesey. St Paul released at Rome.	*Juvenal (†130) Roman poet and satirist of Roman vices.
61	Nero became Emperor of Rome on murder of Claudius. Boudicca led British revolt; sacked Camulodonum, London and Verulamium; defeated; suicide of Boudicca.	*Pliny the Younger (†113) Roman author.
64	Great Fire of Rome blamed on the Christians; persecution renewed; intermittent to 314. SS. Peter and Paul martyred at Rome.	
65		*c*. Gospel according to St. Mark.
68	Suicide of Nero.	*c*. Flavius Josephus (*37, †98); *A History of the Jewish War*.
70	Revolt of Jews against Rome; Jerusalem captured and destroyed by Romans under Titus.	
72		
74	Petilius Cerealis conquered the Brigantes.	*c*. Gospel according to St. Matthew.
78	Julius Frontinus subdued Silures of South Wales. Julius Agricola Governor of Britain; conquered the Ordovices of mid-Wales and Anglesey.	*c*. Cornelius Tacitus (*c*. *55, †120), Roman historian: *Dialogue on Orators*.
79	Agricola commenced conquest of North Britain; complete by 84.	†Pliny the Elder at Stabiae.
80		*c*. Wang Ch'ung, Chinese philosopher, published *Lun Heng*, exposing apocryphal teaching of Confucius. *c*. Gospel according to St. Luke.

Pompeii possessed a central hot-water supply.

c. Foundation of Glastonbury Abbey originally made by Joseph of Arimathea (traditional).

c. Paintings believed to have been produced on canvas at Rome.

Early book on agriculture, land-drainage and veterinary surgery.

Romans destroyed Herod's temple at Jerusalem.
c. Bust of Vespasian carved.

c. Glass-blowing in France and Spain.

Vespasian began building Colosseum.
Erection of temple of Vespasian, Brescia.

c. Pliny the Edler: *Historia Naturalis* (*Natural History*) (Books I to X), on mathematics of heavens, geography and ethnography (unscientific but informative) and zoology.

c. Roman fort of Mamucium, later Manchester.

Destruction of Pompeii, Stabiae and Herculaneum by eruption of Vesuvius.

Domitian completed the Colosseum, Rome; designed to hold 50,000 people.
Baths of Titus, Rome, built.

c. Probably, remaining books of Pliny the Elder's *Natural History* were published Books XI to XXXVII); great influence until 12th cent.

81		
84	Agricola won battle of Mons Granpius in Scotland, but failed to subdue Caledonia.	
85		
94		*c.* Gospel according to St. John.
96	Domitian persecuted the Christians. Conquest of western and southern Germany by Rome complete.	*c.* †Quintilian, Roman orator, who wrote *Instituio Oratoria*.
98	Trajan became Emperor; Empire at its greatest geographical extent.	*c.* Pliny the Younger: *Letters*, Books I and II. *c.* Tacitus: *Life of Agricola* and *Germania*.
100		*c. Targums*, Aramaic versions of sections of Old Testament, written down.
105		*c.* Development of written literature as the result of Chinese paper manufacture.
110		Pliny the Younger: *Letters*, Books III to IX completed by this date.
114		*c.* *Apuleius, who wrote *The Golden Ass*, satirical romance of young man transformed into an ass.
115		*c.* Tacitus: *Historiae*.
120	Accession of Kanishka, a Kushan, as King of Northern India. Brigantes revolted against Roman rule and defeated IX Legion at York.	*c.* Tacitus (†) completed *Annales*. Oldest known Chinese Dictionary published, by Hsu Shen; contained about 10,000 characters. Dictionary produced by Hsu Shen (*c.* *–86) Shuo Wen Chieh Tzu; finally published posthumously *c.* 120.
122	Hadrian visited Britain.	
123	Roman conquests beyond Euphrates renounced.	
130		*Perpetual Edict* drawn up by Julius Salvianus.

Arch of Titus, Rome, erected.

Construction of Rome baths at Bath, Somerset, begun.

c. Agricola built line of forts from the Forth to the Clyde.

c. Nicomachus: *Introductio arithmetica*, first work on arithmetic; using ordinary *numbers*.

Domitian erected Temple of Vespasian, Rome; Corinthian style.

c. Foundation of Colonia at Lindum (later Lincoln).

Roman fortified frontier road called the Limes.

c. Chinese of Han dynasty developed technique of fine metal and lacquer work to high degree in art forms.

c. Foundation of Colonia Nervia Glevensis (later Gloucester).

c. Nicomachus: *Enchiridion Harmonices*, work concerning Pythagorean musical theory.
c. Legionary fortress at Isca and many Welsh forts rebuilt in stone.

c. Menelaus of Alexandria propounded his theorem concerning triangles, in treatise on lines and chords in a circle (six volumes).
Lighthouse at La Corunna erected; used until recently.
c. Methods of extracting rare metals (gold, silver, etc.) from minerals known.

Fine Roman bridge built at Alcantara.

c. Paper manufacture in China; many years before process used in Europe.

c. Great aqueduct, El Puente del Diablo, erected at Segovia; Roman.

Archigenes performed operation for cancer of the chest.

Trajan's Column erected in Rome; inscribed on base in fine Roman majuscules (capitals).

Celsian library, Ephesus (Roman).

The Pantheon, Rome, (completed 124): great circular building, erected on site of earlier temple (see –27).

c. Ptolemy (**c*. 100, †*c*. 178) mathematician, astronomer and geographer, experimented with refraction of light (Law enunciated by Snell about 1,500 years later), described in *Optics*.

Hadrian commenced wall (73 miles long) from the Tyne to Solway Firth; completed *c*. 127.

First reference to lodestone in Chinese literature.

c. Roman fort erected at Lancaster.

c. Ptolemy organized musical scale.

c. Ptolemy observed persistence of vision (used 1895 for first cinema).

135		
140		
142		
150	*c.* Gothic settlements appeared in Black Sea area.	Earliest known Sanskrit inscription; in general use (in India) by 4th cent. *c.* Greek Bible translated into old Latin for use in Africa.
157		
160		
161		*c.* Gaius, Roman jurist: *Institutiones*.
164		
166		
170		*c.* Aulus Gellius (*c.* *123, †180), Latin grammarian: *Noctes Atticae*, a miscellany.
176		*c.* Pausanias, Greek traveller, completed *Description of Greece*; 10 volumes.
180	Romans defeated in Caledonia and retired to Hadrian's Wall. †Marcus Aurelius ended century of peace and good government after Nero; began period of 90 years in which there were 80 Emperors.	*c.* Longus, *Daphnis and Chloe*, Greek pastoral romance; date uncertain.
190		
195		
196	Albinus proclaimed himself Emperor in Britain; first recognized by Severus, but later defeated and killed at battle of Lyons, 197	
200	*c.* Afghanistan invaded by White Huns, who retained control until 540.	*c.* Period of neo-Platonism, last of Greek philosophies, combining Eastern theosophy with Platonic thought. *c.* Fourth period of Chinese literature (to 600).
203		

c. Completion of Temple of Zeus Olympus, Athens.

Roman theatre built at Verulamium; Herts.

Lollius Urbicus completed Antonine Wall, from the Forth to the Clyde (begun 139).

c. Erection of 400–ft-high tower at Peshawar, covering remains of Buddha.

c. Herodes Atticus built Odeum, Athens.

Erection of the Acropolis, Athens.

c. Calpurnius Agricola rebuilt forts in Roman Britain.

Firt church at Glastonbury erected.

c. Completion of Roman theatre (begun 166) at Thugga (now Dougga) in Tunisia.

Martyrdom of St Cecilia, patron saint of music, in Sicily.

c. Mosaic of Oceanus (Neptune) at Roman baths in Sabratha, Tripolitania.
c. Wall painting in Roman room under church of SS. John and Paul, Rome; very fine.
c. Antonine wall breached.

c. Erection of Column of Marcus Aurelius, Rome.

Hadrian's Wall overrun and extensively damaged by the Maecatae.

c. Period of carvings on Amaravati stupa, Madras; 160 pieces in British Museum; end of Bharhat-Sanchi period.

Construction of Arch of Septimus Severus, Rome.

SCIENCE

Operations on pharynx and arteries by Antyllus.

c. Ptolemy; *Almagest* great work on astronomy; but placed Earth at centre of universe; theory accepted until time of Copernicus.

Claudius Galen (c. *130, †200), surgeon to gladiators; famous for 500 medical treatises.

Galen read pulse-rate as a guide to illness.
c. Ptolemy: *Syntaxis*, his second great work.

Outbreak of Great Plague which lasted until 180

26 maps of various countries made by Ptolemy; inaccurate, but possessing useful scientific ideas.

c. System of counting numbers in tens (i.e. the scale of ten) known in India (see 815).

c. Practice grew up in China of carving Confucian texts in stone and then taking rubbings; prelude to printing (see 400 and 650).
c. Earliest known Christian tomb-stone; at Kutahya in Turkey.

Medicinal extraction of plant juices by Galen.

Sextus Julius Africanus, historian (*c. 150), suggested idea of semaphore signalling.

208	Severus divided Britain into two Provinces.	
210		
211	Severus visited Britain; †at York.	
212	Roman citizenship given to every free-born subject in Empire; *Constitutio Antoniniana*.	
220	End of Han Dynasty in China; start of four centuries of division. Gothic invasions of Asia Minor and Balkan Peninsula.	*c.* Kalidasa: *Sakuntala*, important Sanskrit drama; date speculative.
221	Three Kingdoms in China (to 265).	
225	Demise of Andgra kings, who had ruled Deccan Provinces in India since −230; Southern India broke up into various kingdoms.	*c.* Origen (*c.* *185, †254) began *Hexapla*; record of Biblical translations.
226	Sassanid dynasty established in Persia.	
240		
242	Mani, founder of Manichaean sect, began preaching in Persia.	
247	Great Goth raid over the Danube.	
250	Persecution of Christians under Decius. St Paul of Thebes took refuge in Egyptian desert to escape Decian persecution; first recorded hermit.	*c.* In S.W. Denmark, oldest extant runic writings which can be translated; they have been recovered from bogland.
251	Emperor Decius defeated at Beroea; killed by Goths at Abrittus.	*c.* Termination of Nubian literacy; last known demotic inscription in Nubia.
257	Goths occupied Dacia (Roumania). Goths divded into Visigoths and Ostrogoths.	
258	Goths invaded Black Sea area.	St Cyprian (*200), author of *De Unitate Catholicae Ecclesiae*, beheaded.
260	Emperor Valerian captured by Shapur I of Persia.	
263	Yuan Chi, eccentric Chinese recluse, founded a cult of nudism.	

Severus rebuilt Hadrian's Wall.

c. Catacombs of St. Callixtus; first Christian cemetery.

c. Roman temple of Minerva in Tebessa, North Africa.

c. Thermae of Caracalla, Rome; huge public bath, centre of social activity (to 217).

c. *The Twelve Apostles*, wall-painting in the Aurelium Hypogeum; early Christian catacomb paintings date from about this time.

Portrait medallion (Roman) of Serverus and mother and grandmother; now at Brescia.

c. Erection of Mars Gate, Rheims, a triumphal arch (date conjectural).

c. Establishment of school of technology in Rome.

c. Amphitheatre of El Djem, Tripolitania.

Chinese travellers visiting Japan recorded high standard of organization in tribal life.
c. (to 6th cent.) Period of great gravemounds in Japan, surrounded by moats, and having numerous *haniwa*, clay statues.

c. Diophantus of Alexandria; *Arithmetica*, first book of algebra; he is remembered by indeterminate equations of type known as *diophantine*.
c. Development of modern form of hand-saw.
c. 75-ft. clinker-built boat of this period recovered from peat-bog at Nydam.

c. Wall-painting; *Moses Striking Water from the Rock*; from synagogue at Dura-Europos.

c. Erection of Sun temple of Baal in Palmyra, Syrian desert oasis.

	History	Literature
265	Period of Six Dynasties in China (to 581).	
268	Goths sacked Athens, Corinth and Sparta.	
270		
283		
284	Diocletian became Emperor of Rome, and for 21 years checked its decline.	
285	*c.* Carausius, Roman commander of British Fleet, proclaimed himself independent Emperor of Britain. Diocletian partitioned Empire into Western and Eastern Empires.	
290		
293	Carausius defeated and killed by Alectus, who succeeded him as "Emperor in Britain".	Diocletian introduced stringent system of laws.
296	Revolt of Alectus crushed by Constantius.	
297	Romans took Armenia from Persians.	
300	Buddhism increased in influence in China. Christianity introduced into Armenia.	(to 630) Byzantine period of the "biblical" handwriting. *c.* Tune Stone, S.E. Norway; possesses longest runic inscription. *c.* Records of early religious plays.
303	Beginning of Diocletian persecution of Christians; martyrdom of St Alban.	
305	Diocletian abdicated on grounds of age; succeeded in the West by Constantius. Persecution under Galerius continued in the East. St Anthony the Hermit controlled N. Egyptian Desert; advocated celibate priesthood (see 325).	*c.* Pamphilus (†309) founded large library at Caesarea.

Aurelian rebuilt the Walls of Rome.

c. Compass may have been used in China (very speculative).

Forum destroyed in great fire of Carinus.

c. Pappus of Alexandria described 5 simple machines used in mechanics—cogwheel, lever, pulley, screw, wedge.

Amphitheatre at Verona constructed; all stone seats still intact.

c. Pappus evolved important mathematical theorems concerning areas and volumes, re-enunciated by Guldin in 1641.
Lactantius recorded use of window-glass on Continent.

Hadrian's Wall and fortress of Eboracum and Deva rebuilt.

Diocletian ordered total destruction of scientific books.

c. Mosaics largely replaced paintings as Roman art by this time.

Sushruta, who knew many diseases, used observation in clinical medicine.
Reference to Chinese "millionaires" such as Shih Ch'ung reputed to own 30 silk "mills".
c. Scientific progress in Europe greatly restricted for 1,000 years.

c. Thermae of Diocletian (larger than Caracalla).

c. First church built at St Albans, after martyrdom of St Alban.

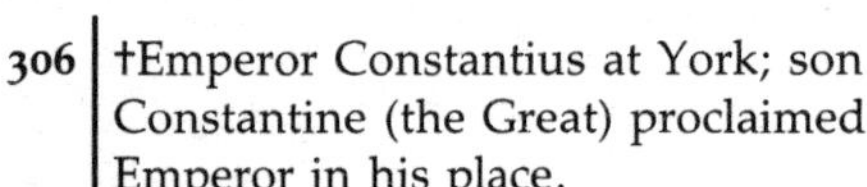

Year	History	Literature
306	†Emperor Constantius at York; son Constantine (the Great) proclaimed Emperor in his place.	
311	Galerius abandoned persecution of Christians.	
312	Constantine became sole Emperor, re-uniting the two Empires under Rome.	
313	Ch'in Dynasty in China ended. Edict of Milan; Constantine established toleration of Christianity.	
314	Synod of Arles included bishops from the Church in Britain. Start of Arian controversy in early Christian Church.	
315	*c.* Religious sect called Donatists founded by Donatus.	
316	Severe persecution of Donatists.	
320	Chandragupta, having made himself master of Ganges-Jumna plain, crowned first Gupta emperor of Northern India.	
325	Council of Nicaea considered Arian question; decided in favour of Athanasius and against Arians. *c.* St Pachomius, disciple of St Anthony the Hermit, attributed with introduction of monastic life (in Egypt).	*c.* Eusebius (*265, †340): *History of the Christian Church.* Council of Nicaea produced *Nicene Creed.*
330	New capital founded on site of old Greek colony of Byzantium; called, after the emperor "Constantinople" and dedicated to the Virgin Mary.	*c.* Uncial manuscript of *Codex Sinaiticus* written; New Testament.
331	Seat of Roman Empire moved to Constantinople.	Constantine founded Library of Constantinople.
337	Constantine the Great baptized on his death-bed.	
342	Goths destroyed Roman protectorate of Bosporus.	
343	Emperor Constans visited Britain.	
350	*c.* Ruling class in Abyssinia accepted Christianity from Syrian missionaries. Evidences of close contacts between Japan and Korea.	*c.* Bishop Wulfila (*311, †383); *Codex Argentaeus,* earliest extant text of Gothic Bible. *c.* Sanskrit inscriptions of this period discovered in Kedah.

c. The Multangular Tower, York, built by Constantine.

Circus Maxentius, Rome; a racetrack.

Jerome mentioned manufacture of plate glass by casting.

Erection of Constantine Arch in Rome, celebrating his victory over Maxentius.

Erection of Basilica of Maxentius (begun 310).

Earliest mention of existence of Florence.

c. Beginnings of Gupta art in India (to 600).

c. Rise of Gupta power led to great advances in mathematics, astronomy and medicine, reaching peak in 5th cent.

Erection of first Church of the Nativity, Bethlehem, destroyed 527; rebuilt *c.* 540.
Council of Nicea decreed that paintings must be in accordance with Church tradition, not invention of artists.

c. (to *c.* 900) Teotihuacán, ancient city of Mexico, developed.
Constantine stopped gladiators' public combats (see –264).

c. Basilican Church of St. Peter's, Rome, erected; pulled down in 1506 to make room for present cathedral.

c. Vuolfvinus created gem-studded reliefs of St Ambroglio altar (see 386).

c. *Ku K'ai-Chuh (*c.* †406), great Chinese silk-roll painter.

c. Palace of Feruz-abad (Sassanian dynasty) erected.
c. Foundation of Schola Cantorum, for Church Song, in Rome.

Pelagonius wrote on veterinary surgery.
c. The *Sūrya,* Indian work on astronomy using sexagesimal fractions; tables of trigonometrical sines exist.
c. Record of existence of goldfish.

	History	Literature
350	Persians regained Armenia from Romans.	*Erh Ya*, Chinese dictionary; contains earliest authentic record of tea-drinking.
360	Picts and Scots attacked Britain and crossed Hadrian's Wall. *c*. Start of Hun invasions of Europe.	
361	Emperor Julian attempted to revive paganism in empire.	
364	Roman Empire divided; Valeus became the first Greek, or Eastern, Emperor.	
365	Union of Persia and Armenia.	
367	Theodosius began victorious campaign against Picts and Scots.	
369	Picts and Scots driven out of Britain by Theodosius.	
376	Huns invaded Russia.	
378	Valeus defeated and killed by Visigoths at Adrianople in Thrace.	
380	*c*. Goths expelled from Hungary.	*c*. St Jerome (*331, †420) applied name *Apocrypha* to sections dropped from Bible.
382	Institution of death penalty for heresy.	
383	Magnus Maximus set himself up as Emperor in Britain; crossed Channel; conquered Spain and Gaul.	
384		*c*. St. Jerome translated the Bible into the Latin *Vulgate* (completed 405).
386	Persia and Armenia became separate countries again. Barbarian Tartars from eastern Mongolia set up Wei dynasty in North China; lasted until 534.	
387	Romans and Persians partitioned Armenia.	
388	Magnus Maximus defeated and killed at Aquileia.	
392	Accession of Theodosius the Great as Emperor of East and West.	

c. Fortification of London.

Lo-tsun, Chinese monk, founded Caves of the Thousand Buddhas, Kansu; elaborated some centuries later.

c. Scrolls began to be replaced by books.

Law against magicians enacted by Rome.

Roman road maps of this date were copied by Peutinger (*1465, †1547), German antiquary.

Agorus Pretestatus erected Portico of the Twelve Gods, Rome.

St. Basil of Cappadocia founded hospital at Caesarea.

c. Probable date of manufacture of true soap.

c. Saint Ursus built Ravenna cathedral; destroyed *c*. 1734; except campanile and crypt; rebuilt.

Basilican Church of St Paolo fuori le Mura, Rome, begun; destroyed 1823; rebuilt.

c. Water-driven marble-cutting saw recorded in use by Ausonius (Moselle area).

Final over-running of Hadrian's Wall, which was not reconstructed.

Magnus Maximus opened up long disused mint at London.

Bishop Ambrose of Milan (*340, †397), set plainsong in order and introduced four modes.

Ambrose built church of St Ambroglio, Milan (to 389); now 11th cent. Romanesque basilica.

	History	Literature
395	†Theodosius; successors, Honorius and Arcadius, re-divided the Empire with Stilicho and Alaric as their masters and protectors. Alaric became King of the Visigoths.	
396	Alaric invaded Greece; Athens plundered. Augustine (*354, †430) became Bishop of Hippo.	
398	Balkans plundered by Alaric.	
400	*c.* Recorded history of Japan commenced at about this date.	*c.* Beginnings of writing in Japan, using Chinese ideographs.
405	Japanese kingdom of Yamato, having gained supremacy over the rest, adopted use of Chinese characters.	*c.* Pope Innocent I first listed prohibited books for R.C.s (see 1559).
406	Celibacy among clergy condemned by Vigilantius of Barcelona.	
408	*c.* Visigoth invasions of Italy. Fa-Hien, a Chinese pilgrim, crossed Pamir mountains to study Buddhism in India.	Jerusalem Talmud developed modern form.
410	Italy invaded by Alaric; Rome captured and sacked; Roman legions withdrawn from Britain to protect Rome. Christianity tolerated in Persia.	
411	Start of Pelagian struggle in Early Church by British theologian, Pelagius, who affirmed doctrine of Freedom of Will. Council of Carthage condemned Donatist movement, which died out.	*c.* Augustine wrote *City of God* after sack of Rome by Visigoths.
418	Roman troops probably returned to Britain for a short period.	
420	Nanking again capital of Northern China.	

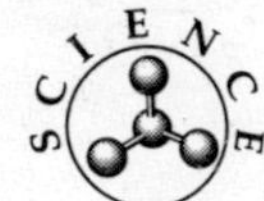

c. Fine mosaic in apse of S. Pudenziana, Rome.

Olympic Games held for last time in old Greece; terminated by Theodosius I.

c. Sarcophagus of St. Ambrose, Milan, fabricated.

c. The Iron Pillar, in Delhi (24 ft. high), erected in honour of Chandragupta Vikramaditya.
c. Villa of Piazza Armerina, Sicily, containing some 40 fine mosaics in the form of paving, showing 10 girls in bikinis round a swimming pool.

c. Peak period for Indian mathematics, to last for some 700 years.
c. Chinese discovered lamp-black, using it to take rubbings (see 650).

c. Macrobius: *In Somnium Scorpionis.*

Roman ivory diptych of Honorius; now in Aosta.

c. Chinese pilgrim, Fa-Hien, visited Mathura, on R. Jumna, recorded high cultural standard in this part of India; many monasteries.

c. Beginnings of alchemy, chief objects of which were to search for Philosopher's Stone and Elixir of Life.

Franks settled in parts of Gaul.

c. Gupta temple, Sanchi, India; early Hindu single-cell temple; date doubtful.

Year	History	Literature
425	Barbarians settled in Roman provinces—Vandals in South Spain, Huns in Pannonia, Goths in Dalmatia, Visigoths and Suevi in Portugal and Northern Spain.	
428	Re-union of Persia and Armenia. Foundation of Merovingian kings of France; line lasted to 752.	
429	Germanus of Auxerre and Lupus of Troyes visited Britain to counteract influence of Pelagianism. Jutes and Angles expelled Picts and Scots from S. England.	
430	Persecution of Christians in Persia.	Prosper of Aquitaine (*c.* *390, *c.* †465): *Adversus ingratos* against Pelagians.
432	Commencement of St Patrick's mission to Ireland.	Prosper of Aquitaine: *De Gratia Dei ut Libero Arbitrio*, against Cassian.
433	Attila (†453) became ruler of Huns.	
436	Roman troops probably left Britain.	
439	Vandals captured Carthage.	*c.* Theodosian Code summarized Roman law.
441		
446	Romano-British people made vain appeal for military aid from Aetius, chief minister of Emperor Valentinian III (†455).	
449	Kent invaded by Jutes; West Britain invaded by Angles and Saxons.	
450	*c.* Contact between Britain and Rome appeared severed.	*c.* Popularity of *Bestiaries*, allegorical odes depicting humans as animals, developed; continued into 14th cent.
451	Attila invaded Gaul; defeated by alliance of Franks, Alemanni and Romans under Aetius at Chalons.	
452	Northern Italy invaded by Huns under Attila; turned back by Pope Leo I.	
455	Rome sacked by Vandals.	
457	Britons defeated by Hengest, at Crayford; abandoned Kent to Jutes.	

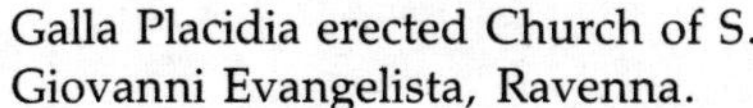

Galla Placidia erected Church of S. Giovanni Evangelista, Ravenna.

c. Chinese musical octave had 360 notes; reduced to 18 (by 1180) and to 12 (by 1593, *q.v.*).

c. Mosaic in baptistry of Orthodox Church, Ravenna.

c. Work begun on basilica of S. Maria Maggiore, Rome.

(to 449) Erection of Chapel of S. Pier Crisologo, Ravenna; contains original mosaics.

Ancient town of Ys, Brittany, probably submerged in great flood.

c. Galla Placidia erected so-called Mausoleum, containing fine Christian mosaics.

c. Yun Kang caves, Shansi; rock-cut Buddhist shrines.

c. First ideas of negative numbers in the Orient.

c. San Lorenzo, Milan, erected; fine early church (see 1574).

c. Valentinian III constructed walls of Naples.

Foundation of Venice, in impregnable swamp, by refugees from Hun invaders; united under first Doge in 697.

Year	History	Literature
460	Cologne captured by Franks.	
468	Hun invaders withdrew from Europe.	
476	Gothic leader, Odoacer, forced Romulus Augustus to lay down power; end of Western Roman Empire; Gothic kingdom set up in Italy.	
478		
481	Accession of Clovis the Great as King of France.	
484	Gupta Empire in N. India overthrown by Epthalite or White Hun invaders from beyond River Oxus.	
486	Last Roman governor of Gaul defeated by Clovis at Soissons.	
489	Ostrogoths invaded Italy.	
491	Saxons captured Pevensey, Sussex.	
493	Theodoric, the Ostrogoth, conquered Italy; became king, but subject to Constantinople.	
496	Clovis defeated the Alemanni.	Final compilation of the Missal, R.C. book of Mass.
500	*c.* British victory over the English at Mount Badon. *c.* Clovis accepted Christianity. Saxon kingdom of Wessex founded. *c.* Period known as the Middle Ages, lasting until the Renaissance (*c.* 1500) began. *c.* Mayan city of Chichen Itza flourished in the Yucatan.	*c.* *Codex Bezae*, New Testament in Greek on left-hand page and Latin on right, written.
507	Franks under Clovis conquered Visigothic kingdom of Toulouse.	
511	†Clovis; Frankish kingdom divided among his four sons.	
523		Boëthius: *Consolation of Philosophy*, best-known work of the Roman Christian philosopher; written in prison.

c. Beginnings of Buddhist carvings in Yun-kang caves, China; Wei dynasty.

c. Martianus Capella: *Satyricon, sive De Nuptiis Mercurii et Philologiae et de Septem Artibus Liberalibus*.

*Aryabhata, Indian mathematician, who wrote on powers and roots of numbers and other important algebraic concepts.

Earliest Shinto shrines, Japan.

Tomb of Childeric (see 1653).

c. St Stephen Rotunda, Rome, built.

c. Emperor Seno built Church of St Simeon Stylites around the saint's 50 ft pillar.

c. The "cloud maidens" of caves of Sigiriya, Ceylon, were painted.

c. Transition from Basket Maker-period (commenced *c*. 0 A.D.) to Modified Basket Maker in S.W.North America.
c. Evolution of Hopewellian phase of Mississippi valley culture; mound-builders, N. America.
Anicius M.S. Boethius (*480, †524): *De Institutione Musica* groundwork of music.

c. Indo-Chinese technically developed weaving with looms; ideas known by cave-dwellers much earlier.
c. Indians understood use of zero in mathematics.

c. Head of Death God, Mayan altar, Copan, Honduras.

Pagoda of Sung Yueh Temple, Honan, China.
c. Boethius introduced Greek musical letter notation to the west.

Boëthius: *Categories* and *De Interpretatione*, Latin works on mathematics and logic.

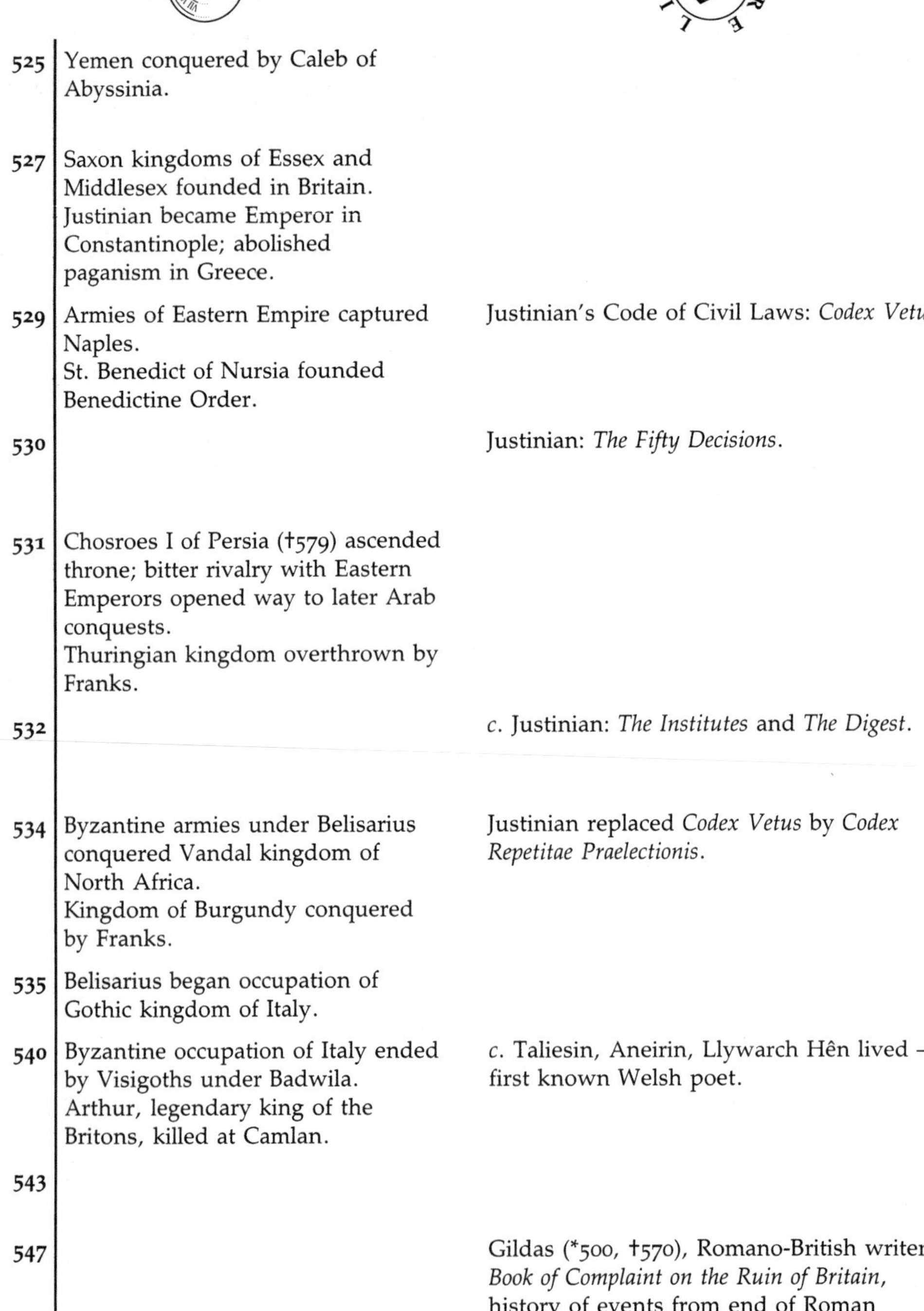

Year	History	Literature
525	Yemen conquered by Caleb of Abyssinia.	
527	Saxon kingdoms of Essex and Middlesex founded in Britain. Justinian became Emperor in Constantinople; abolished paganism in Greece.	
529	Armies of Eastern Empire captured Naples. St. Benedict of Nursia founded Benedictine Order.	Justinian's Code of Civil Laws: *Codex Vetus*.
530		Justinian: *The Fifty Decisions*.
531	Chosroes I of Persia (†579) ascended throne; bitter rivalry with Eastern Emperors opened way to later Arab conquests. Thuringian kingdom overthrown by Franks.	
532		*c.* Justinian: *The Institutes* and *The Digest*.
534	Byzantine armies under Belisarius conquered Vandal kingdom of North Africa. Kingdom of Burgundy conquered by Franks.	Justinian replaced *Codex Vetus* by *Codex Repetitae Praelectionis*.
535	Belisarius began occupation of Gothic kingdom of Italy.	
540	Byzantine occupation of Italy ended by Visigoths under Badwila. Arthur, legendary king of the Britons, killed at Camlan.	*c.* Taliesin, Aneirin, Llywarch Hên lived – first known Welsh poet.
543		
547		Gildas (*500, †570), Romano-British writer; *Book of Complaint on the Ruin of Britain*, history of events from end of Roman occupation.
549		

SCIENCE

c. Medieval Buddhist caves at Ajanta; carvings now suited to stone; earlier work (see 50) wood-replica type.

(to 565) Church of the Nativity, Bethlehem, first Constantine church, rebuilt.

Justinian closed the thousand-year-old Schools at Athens.
St. Benedict founded Monte Cassino monastery.

Migration to Persia and Syria of numerous philosophers from Athens School.

c. Theodoric's mausoleum, Ravenna, constructed; two-storied ugly building still intact.

Ἁγία Σοφία (St. Sophia), great Christian church of Constantinople, built by Justinian (to 537).

c. Earliest extant Chinese roll paintings to include landscapes.

Tomb of Galla Placidia, Ravenna, oldest cruciform tomb to survive.

Great earthquake shook entire world.
Terrible pandemic of the plague 542–3.

Church of San Vitale, Ravenna, of double octagonal shape, consecrated; begun before 534.
Ida built Bamburgh Castle, Northumberland; frequently destroyed and rebuilt.

c. Gildas described plague of boils, first known genuine plague in Britain.

Church of S. Apollinaire in Classe, near Ravenna, completed; on site of the saint's grave.

	History	Literature
550	Migration of Turkish tribes began. *c.* Anglian kingdoms of East Anglia, Mercia and Northumbria founded. *c.* Conversion of Wales to Christianity by St David.	*c.* Dionysius Exiguus assembled papal decrees; *decretals*. *c.* Procopius: *The Vandal War*.
552	Narses and Byzantine armies expelled Goths from Italy. Buddhism introduced into Japan from Korea; end of Japanese pre-history and beginning of Asuka period (to 645).	No exactly dateable Japanese documents exist before this date.
553	Rome annexed to Eastern Empire by Narses, general of Justinian.	
558	Clothaire I, son of Clovis, reunited Frankish kingdom.	
560		
561	†Clothaire I; Frankish kingdom divided among his four sons.	
563	St Columba (†597) went to Iona and began conversion of Picts.	
565	†Emperor Justinian. Ravenna in Byzantine hands.	
567	Partition of Frankish kingdom into: (1) Austrasia (Eastern kingdom): Lorraine, Belgium and right bank of Rhine, later Germany; (2) Neustria (Western kingdom): later France; (3) Burgundy.	
568	Lombards conquered N. Italy.	
570	Persians overthrew Abyssinian rule in Yemen.	
575	*c.* Buddhism firmly established in Japan.	
577	West Saxons defeated British at Deorham in Gloucestershire.	
579	Lombards dominated Italy.	
581	Accession of Yan Ch'ien and foundation of Sui Dynasty (to 619) in China.	

Bells believed to have been used in France.

c. Draw looms in use in Egypt for patterned silk weaving.
c. Cosmas of Alexandria: *Topographia Christiana;* flat rectangular Earth theory.

Throne of Archbishop Maximium; in Ravenna cathedral (still extant).

Justinian sent missionaries to China to smuggle out a supply of silk-worms.

Foundation of first English abbey, at Bangor, N. Ireland.

c. Foundation of Abbey of St. Médard, Soissons.

St Columba founded monastery on Iona.

c. Mosaic of Justinian, in S. Vitale Church, Ravenna.

c. St Deniol founded Bangor Cathedral, Wales; destroyed 1071; see 1496.

c. St Gregory the Great (*c.* *540, †604), standardized Plainsong in Church Music; added 4 (Gregorian) modes to existing musical scales.

Pelagius II rebuilt St. Lorenzo fuori le Mura, Rome.

Year	History	Literature
589	Visigoths converted to Roman Catholicism.	
590	Accession of Chosroes II and renewal of struggle with Byzantium.	
593	Northumbria supreme among English kingdoms.	
594		Gregory of Tours: *Historia Francorum.*
595		
597	St Augustine (†604) landed in Thanet and introduced Benedictine Order into England; baptism of Ethelbert of Kent.	
598		
600	*c.* Korean and Chinese monks, scholars, artists and craftsmen settled in Japan.	*c.* Standard Chinese language developed; fifth period of Chinese literature (to 900).
602	Foundation of Archiepiscopal See of Canterbury by St Augustine.	
603	Lombards converted to Roman Catholicism.	
604		Code of Shōtoku Taishi (Sage Virtue), Japan: people should venerate Buddha, the Law and the Priesthood.
605		
607	Accession of Harsha, of Thanesar, kingdom on the Ganges.	
609		
610	Accession of Heraclius at Constantinople; long period of Byzantine-Persian wars. Vision of Mohammed (*570, †632).	
612	Harsha of Thanesar took title of Emperor of the Five Indies (Punjab, Kanauj, Bengal, Darbhanga and Orissa).	

Sarcophagus of Empress Helena; late Rome work; in Vatican.

c. Gregory of Tours (*538, †594) referred to church window-glass.

Rome devastated by plague.

Work begun on Temple of Four Heavenly Kings (Shitennō-ji), Osaka; entirely rebuilt later.

End of terrible plague (begun 542) in Roman Empire; half the population died.

Erection of Hokō-ji, near Nara, Japan; none of original building survives.

First authenticated record of decimal notation (Hindu).

St Augustine founded a Benedictine monastery at Canterbury.

Probable date of earliest English school (at Canterbury).

c. Castellain brooch, cloisonné enamelled.

c. Development of Coptic art in Egypt.

c. St Augustine founded Christ Church Cathedral, Canterbury, on site of an old Christian Roman church.

First St Paul's Church built in London (finally rebuilt by Wren).

St Augustine founded cathedral church of St Andrew, Rochester.

An-chi bridge, Chou-hsien, Hopei, China, constructed.

Construction of the Grand Canal of China.

Completion of Hōryū-jitemple, Japan, by Shōtoku Taishi; oldest surviving wooden building in the world (possibly burned down in 670 and immediately rebuilt).

Hōryū Gakumon-ji developed as hospital centre as well as shrine for Buddhist study.

The Pantheon dedicated to S. Maria and Martyres: now called St. Maria Rotunda.

First record of use of episcopal rings.

LITERATURE

	History	Literature
615	*c.* Battle of Chester; Britons defeated by Ethelfrith of Bernicia. Anglian penetration to Irish Sea; massacre of monks of Bangor.	Evidence of early written records of some of Mohammed's teachings.
616	Egypt overrun by Persians. Kingdom of Kent declined and passed to Wessex.	
619	Chosroes II extended Persian rule to include Egypt, Jerusalem and Damascus and had armies at the Hellespont. Beginning of T'ang Dynasty in China (to 906).	
620	Isle of Man subdued by king of Northumbria.	
622	The Hegira: the flight of Mohammed from Mecca to Medina.	
623		
624	Buddhism made established religion in Japan.	
625	Paulinus, Roman Church Missionary, sent by Justus to Northumbria.	*c.* Mohammed began dictation of the *Koran*, sacred book of his followers.
626	Egypt regained from Byzantium by Heraclius, who expelled Persians.	
627	Persians defeated at Nineveh by Heraclius. Tsai-tsung became Emperor of China.	
628	Mohammed and followers captured Mecca. Chosroes II murdered by his son, who succeeded him as Kavadh II.	Mohammed wrote letters of all rulers of world setting out principles of Moslem faith.
629	Mohammed returned to Mecca. Heraclius regained Jerusalem from Persians.	
630	Olaf Tratelia, expelled from Sweden, set up colony in Vermeland, later known as Norway.	

SCIENCE

c. Revival of Indian architecture and sculpture, through Harsavardhana and Mahendravarman I; stone replaced earlier brick and timber.

Use of "burning water" (petroleum) in Japan.

c. Benedictine nunnery and church built at Folkestone; present church Early English.

c. Huge Chinese orchestras with hundreds of players performed during T'ang and Sung dynasties (to 1279).

c. (to 907) The *Suan-Ching* (Ten Classics); mathematical and astronomical texts used for Chinese state examinations.

First authenticated Chinese porcelain produced.

Isidore of Seville (*c.* *570, †636), Spanish encyclopaedist: *Originum sive etymologiarum libri XX*, on architecture, sciences, etc.

Year One of the Moslem Calendar.

Tori Bushi created famous *Shaka Trinity*, altarpiece of the Kōndō, Japan.
Mamalhapuram temple, Shore dynasty, erected.

Erection of Wild Goose pagoda Ch'ang-an, China (to 705); rebuilt 8th cent.
c. Gourdon gold paten and chalice, France.
c. Original Ise Shrine, Japan; demolished and rebuilt every 20 years at Ujiyamada.

c. Period of Brahmagupta, Indian mathematician at Ujjain; he found general solution of indeterminate linear equations.

Edwin of Northumbria founded Edinburgh.

Edwin, after his baptism, replaced wooden first York Minster (founded 601) by one of stone.

Lincoln Church founded; present cathedral mainly 12th and 13th cent. (see 1185).

Brahmagupta wrote an important mathematical work, *Brahma Siddhanta*.

A set of Byzantine silver plates depicting life of David; made 610–629; found 1902 near Kyrenia.

c. Cotton supposedly introduced into Arabia.

	History	Literature
634	Moslems conquered Syria, defeating armies of Heraclius.	
635	Moslems captured Damascus and overthrew Persian empire. Emperor Tsai-tsung received missionaries from west. Chalukyas, a people of the Deccan, repulsed invasion by Harsha.	
637	Battle of Kadessia, between Moslems and Persians; latter routed.	
638	Persia appealed to China for aid against Moslems. Jerusalem surrendered to Caliph Omar.	
639	Armenia attacked by Arabs (and in 642, 645, 646); Arab governor 654–658).	
640	St Aidan began missionary work in Northumbria.	
641	Moslem conquest of Egypt completed.	Last traces of book-copying industry at Alexandria Library destroyed by Arabs.
642	Byzantines left Alexandria. †Emperor Heraclius.	
643	Moslem conquest of Persia and of Tripoli completed.	
645	The Taikwa, great reform edict, issued in Japan; centralized government; beginning of Nara period (to 784).	
646	Byzantine fleet recaptured Alexandria.	
647	†Harsha; Empire of Five Indies disintegrated.	
649	Cyprus overcome by Moslems.	
650		
652		
655	Moslem fleet based on Alexandria destroyed Byzantine fleet at Lycia.	

St. Aidan (†651) founded Lindisfarne Priory; destroyed 793.

Persian fire worshippers, evicted by Moslems, settled in Gujarat in Central India.

Persian refugees settled in China.

Erection of Syracuse Cathedral; integrated into Doric temple of *c.* –470.

Amr founded Fustat, later renamed Cairo. End of the Alexandrian School, centre of western culture.

Dome of the Rock, Jerusalem, earliest extant Mohammedan architecture, begun.

c. Yen Li-pen (†673), greatest of T'ang period Chinese artists, at work.

Early Nara period of Japanese art (to 710).

c. Neumes, notation for groups of notes, used in music in 7th cent. and up to 11th cent.

c. Chinese practice of using lamp-black ink for taking rubbings led to introduction of wood blocks for printing (see 400).

Southern limit of Moslem expansion agreed as Aswan with Nubians.

c. Benedictine monastery at Peterborough (Medehamstede) founded (see 870).

LITERATURE

	History	Literature
657	Accession of Clothaire III, king of the Franks. United kingdom lasted until 663, when Clothaire became king of Neustria.	*c.* Caedmon (†680?), first English poet of known name, dreamed of divine call to poetry.
660		
661		
664	Synod of Whitby; Oswy of Northumbria decided in favour of Roman date for Easter; England became attached to R.C. Church.	
669	Bishopric of Lichfield founded by St Chad, who carried on missionary work in Mercia. Theodore of Tarsus became Archbishop of Canterbury.	
670	Successful Moslem campaigns in North Africa.	
673	Moslems commenced siege of Constantinople (lasted until 678). First Council of English Church held at Hertford.	
675	*c.* Bulgars settled in districts south of Danube.	
680		
681		
685	Battle of Nechtansmere; Picts prevented Northumbria gaining control of Scotland; resulted in independence of Scotland for centuries.	
687	†St Cuthbert at Lindisfarne. Pepin II subdued Neustria and united whole Frankish kingdom.	
695		Law Code of Wihtred.
700		Psalms translated into Anglo-Saxon. *c.* The Lindisfarne Gospels (or Gospel of St Cuthbert), illuminated Manuscript in insular half-uncials by Eadfrith; Aldred added Anglo-Saxon translation in 10th cent.

Foundation of Streanaeshalch (now Whitby) monastery by St Hild.

c. Sutton Hoo burial (see 1939).

Ripon Monastery founded; destroyed *c.* 950; rebuilt 12th, 14th, 15th cents.

St Peter's York, boys' public school, founded by this date.
St Cuthbert came to Lindisfarne.

Plague attacked Saxon England; again in 672, 679 and 683.

Foundation of Lichfield cathedral; present building mainly 13th cent. (see 1193).

Quairawan tower, Tunis, built.
c. Cross of St Osyth (Saxon relic at Ely).

Ethelreda founded Ely Abbey; refounded 970 by Ethelwold; see 1083.

"Greek Fire" used in sea battle by Constantine Pogonatus.

Foundation of monastery at Wearmouth.
Glass windows in church in England.

Foundation of Hereford cathedral; burned 1055 by Welsh; rebuilt.

Gloucester Abbey founded (see 1089).
Biscop founded Jarrow monastery, home of Bede.

c. Foundation of (Saxon) Winchester cathedral; see 1079.

c. The Ravenna Cosmography, index of all known countries, towns and rivers.

First Arab coinage used.

c. The Franks Casket, a whalebone box carved with Christian and pagan scenes; possibly Northumbrian work.
Basket-maker culture of S.W. North America replaced by Pueblo period, with its enlarged underground houses.
c. Pagoda of Tzu-en temple, Sian, China.

c. Tapestry weaving believed to have been well established in Peru.

Year	History	Literature
705		
710	Moslem pressure led Kashgarian principalities to ask help from China; aid refused. Japanese capital transferred from Fujiwara to Nara.	
712	Moslem state established in Sindh in India. Moslems conquered Seville (invaded 711)	Compilation of *Kojiki,* first history of Japan and first written book in Japanese language.
714		
715	Moslem Empire extended from Pyrenees to China; capital at Damascus.	*c. Beowulf,* Old English epic, oldest heroic poem in any Germanic language (*c.* 3200 lines).
716	Church at Iona accepted Roman Easter.	
717	Accession of Leo III to Byzantine throne; first of Iconoclast Emperors (see 720).	
718	Suleiman the Caliph failed to capture Constantinople; Moslem fleet destroyed.	
720	Moslem armies crossed Pyrenees into France. First Moslem settlement in Sardinia.	Period of *Tchhouen-Khi,* Chinese heroic drama (to 907).
725		Venerable Bede (*672, †735), monk from Jarrow: *De Temporum Ratione.*
727		
731		Bede: *Historia Ecclesiastica Gentis Anglorum,* Latin history of the English.
732	Leo III withdrew Byzantine provinces of southern Italy from jurisdiction of Rome. Moslem armies defeated by Charles Martel at Poitiers; Europe outside the sphere of Mohammedanism.	

Wells Cathedral founded; present building mainly 14th cent.
Great Mosque, Damascus built; Omayad dynasty.

Main period of Nara art (to 784).
c. Creation of triad of figures in Tōindō of Yakushiji monastery.
c. Taunton castle first built (see 1100).

New capital of Japan built at Nara on lines of Chinese capital at Hsian.

Foundation of Liège Cathedral, Belgium.

Foundation of Reichenau Abbey by Pirminius.

Great Byzantine mosaic at Damascus erected (begun 707).
Earliest extant Islamic paintings are of this date.

Opposition to use of images in churches led to the term *iconoclast*.

c. In India great period of building under Rajput rule; e.g. Palace of Winds at Udaipur.

Foundation of Oxford Cathedral; present building mainly 12th to 15th cent.

	History	Literature
734	Image worship condemned by Greek Christian Church.	
735	Archbishopric of York established.	*Alcuin (†804), learned scholar who maintained English reputation after Bede's death.
740	Pope Gregory III appealed to Charles Martel for help against Lombards, Arabs and Greeks.	*Ecloga*, legal code, issued by Leo III; greatly influenced developments in Byzantium and Slavonic countries.
744		School of singing established at Fulda.
748	Moslem fleet destroyed during attack on Cyprus; not re-formed until *c.* 850.	
750	*c.* St Boniface, missionary from England, took Christianity into central Germany.	*c.* Earliest records of existence of the Tamil language.
751	Pepin, son of Charles Martel, liquidated last of descendants of Clovis; crowned king of the French. Ravenna taken from Byzantium by Aistulf, king of the Lombards.	
756	Caliph of Baghdad sent military aid to Hsuan Tsung in China, to crush rebellion. Pepin III reduced Lombardy to vassal state of France; donated land to Papacy, so creating a Papal state.	*Manyoshu*, anthology of Japanese poetry; some 4,000 pieces, mainly in *tanka* (5 lines of 5, 7, 5, 7, 7, syllables).
759		
760	Foundation of Turkish Empire by a Tartar tribe who seized part of Armenia.	*c.* The *Book of Kells*, Latin gospels now in library of Trinity College, Dublin; written in Irish half-uncials of the finest penmanship.
763		
765	*c.* Tibetan forces invaded China; later retired.	
771	Accession of Charlemagne (*742, †814) as king of the French.	
773	Pope Hadrian I appealed to Charlemagne for help against Lombards; Charlemagne annexed Lombardy.	

Hachibushu, Eight Guardian Divas, earliest extant dry-lacquer statues, now in Nara, Japan.

Penny piece introduced by Offa, king of Mercia; made of silver.

c. Church of York burned down; rebuilt and again destroyed 1069 (see 1070).

Earthquake in Asia Minor.

Foundation of Abbey of Fulda.

c. Work on the Great Buddha (53 ft high), Nara, Japan; no longer extant.

c. Shore temple, Mamallapuram, India, erected.
c. Hôriu-ji Pagoda, oldest existing pagoda in Japan, constructed.
c. Developmental Pueblo period in S.W. North America (to *c*. 900).

Kiev reported as fortress and trading station.
c. Continuation of cultural knowledge of Alexandria by Arabs settled in Spain.

c. *Gigaku* masks, early wood carving of Japan, made for inaugural ceremony of Great Buddha (752); 164 survive.

Chinese paper-makers captured at Samarkand enabled its manufacture to spread throughout Arab dominions.

†St. John of Damascus (*676), who organized the arrangement of Plainsong.

Earliest extant examples of cloisonné enamel; mirrors in *Shōsō in*, Nara, Japan.

Foundation of temple of Tōshōdai-ji, near Nara, Japan.

c. Kailasanatha, Ellora, begun by Krishna I: rock-cut temple in India.

c. Arabic numerals, of Indian origin, reached Baghdad region.

Al-Mansur founded Baghdad; to be capital of Moslem world.

c. Foundation of Kasuga shrine, Nara, Japan.

c. Pictorial block printing known in Japan.

c. Translation of Euclid's *Elements* into Arabic.

	History	Literature
778	Charlemagne defeated at Roncesvalles.	
779	Offa of Mercia subdued West Saxons at battle of Benson; regarded as king of all England.	*c. Ch'a Ching,* first (Chinese) handbook of tea.
781	Christianity widespread at Chinese Court.	*c. Wessobrunner Gebet,* earliest German ecclesiastical verse.
782	Alcuin left monastery at York to become minister of public instruction to Charlemagne at Aachen.	*c.* Godescalc: *Evangelistary* illustrated with figures of Christ and the Evangelists; oldest *Ada*-school MS. of Aachen.
786	Accession of Haroun-al-Rashchid as Caliph in Baghdad.	
787	Offa created Archbishop of Lichfield as metropolitan see in addition to Canterbury. Danish attacks on England begin.	
788	Bavaria annexed by Charlemagne.	
793	East Anglia annexed to Mercia by Offa.	
794	Heian period of Japan (to 1185, so-named on removal of capital to Heian (Kyoto); Japanese culture developed independently of China.	
795	Egypt in state of factional turmoil.	*c.* Cynewulf, Anglo-Saxon poet, author of *Elena; Juliana; Christ; Fates of the Apostles.*
796	†Offa.	
799	Port of Fiume destroyed by Charlemagne.	
800	Charlemagne crowned in Rome as Emperor of the West by Pope Leo III. *c.* Sale of Indulgences begun in Rome by Leo III. *c.* Rajputs occupied Kana uj, cultural centre of Northern India; set up kingdom extending from Bihar to Sutlej. *c.* First Norse attacks on England. Charlemagne invaded Bohemia and imposed tributes.	*c. Hildebrandslied,* the lay of Hildebrand, old High German poem. *c.* Development of miniscule handwriting. *c.* Earliest records of Persian literature (poetry), possibly by Abbās of Mārv (recorded *c.* 846).

c. The Fejo Bowl, nielloed bowl in Copenhagen – believed British.

c. Japanese pictorial prints exist, the earliest extant printing in the world.

Christian monasteries built in China.

Construction of Offa's Dyke, earthwork from River Dee to River Wye against Welsh attacks on Mercia; completed 783.

c. Jabir (*722), great Arab chemist developed knowledge of chemical reactions and compounds substantially; beginnings of chemistry as distinct from alchemy.

c. Work begun on Great Mosque at Cordoba; completed 990.

Offa founded St Alban's abbey.
Danish raid destroyed Lindisfarne Priory.

c. Hereford Cathedral first dedicated; to St Ethelbert (murdered 793).

Foundation of Heian (later called Kyoto), Japan.

State-owned paper-mill established in Baghdad.

Palatine Chapel, Aachen, built by Charlemagne (to 805) as Royal Tomb; many modifications since; primarily a 16-sided polygon.

Commercial treaty between Charlemagne and Offa of Mercia.

c. Poems sung to music at Charlemagne's court.
c. Li Chen painted five portraits of saints, T'ang period of China; pictures damaged.
c. Chou Fang, Chinese artist: *Tuning the lute and drinking tea*.
c. Possible date of Charioteer silk, found in Charlemagne's tomb.

Paper Manufacture in Turkey.
The Gokstad Ship, Norwegian state vessel, believed to have been built at about this time; discovered recently in excellent preservation.
c. City of Machu Pichu, Peru, developed; discovered 1911.
c. Charlemagne abandoned gold standard; ordered 240 denarii (silver pennies) to be made from one pound weight of silver; hence 240*d*. = £1

		LITERATURE
802	Egbert, formerly English refugee at court of Charlemagne, established himself as king of Wessex.	Charlemagne codified German tribal laws.
803		
805	Archbishopric of Lichfield ended; Canterbury restored to Metropolitan See.	
806		
810	Krum, king of Bulgaria, defeated and killed Emperor Nicephorus.	*c.* Nennius: *Historia Britonum*, early British history by Welsh monk, Nynniaw.
811		
813		Ecclesiastical Council of Tours noted that subjects of Charlemagne no longer understood Latin of clergy: "Birth certificate" of French language.
814	†Charlemagne. From 814 to 888 Bulgaria extended to include much of Balkans; nomadic Bulgars assimilated by Slavs.	
825	Mercia overthrown by Egbert at battle of Ellandun.	
826	Crete captured by Arabs. Danish king baptized at Mainz; returned to Denmark with missionary monk Anskar.	
828	Egbert of Wessex recognized as Overlord of England by other English kingdoms.	
829		Conclusion of *Annales Regni Francorum*, official chronical of French history.
830		*c. Heliand Epic* (The Saviour); author unknown, Saxon.
831	Bishopric of Hamburg set up; raised to Archbishopric in 832.	
832	Sicily captured by Saracens (conquest begun 827). Caliph Al Ma'mun invaded Egypt and broke Arab military power.	*c.* Einhard (*c.* *775, †840), medieval scholar, wrote during retirement *Life of Charles the Great* (on Charlemagne).

SCIENCE

Charlemagne founded Münster Abbey.

c. Mosaic work in Church of St. Germigny-les-Près.

Monastery of Iona sacked by Norsemen.

Lex Frisionum indicated Frisian occupation of 350 miles of marshy coastland; over 2,000 artificial village-hillocks.

Erection of Mosque of Mulai Idris, Fez, three years after foundation of the Moroccan city.

Foundation of Hamburg, usually attributed to Charlemagne.

School of astronomy in Baghdad.

c. Arabs developed scale of ten (see 176), including use of zero to multiply by 10.

Pavia became centre of learning; early university (see 1361).

c. Mohammed ibn Mûsâ al-Kho-wârizmî: *Al-jebr w'al-muqâbalah* (Baghdad); gave rise to name "algebra".

Original foundation of St. Mark's, Venice, rebuilt 976; altered 1063 *et seq.* (see 1094).

c. Ptolemy's *Almagest* translated into Arabic (see 150).

Milfrid rebuilt Hereford Cathedral in stone; destroyed 1056; rebuilt 1107.

Foundation of Venetian Order of St. Marc, oldest order of chivalry (probably).

c. *Utrecht Psalter* written at Rheims; profusely illustrated with interesting line-drawings.

	History	Literature
835	Egbert defeated Danes and Britons in Cornwall.	
840	Mojmir, Slav chief, formed confederation of Slav tribes in Bohemia, Moravia, Slovakia, Hungary and Transylvannia.	
842	Danish attack on London bought off by a ransom.	*Strassburg Oaths*: Louis the German and Charles the Bald swore allegiance at Strasbourg (Strassburg); Charles used Romance language of Western Franks, Louis the German tongue; dialects used were ancestors of modern English and German.
843	Pictish and Scottish kingdoms coalesced into Scotland to resist Danish attacks. †Louis the Pious; collapse of Carlovingian empire; no regular succession of Holy Roman Emperors until 962. Treaty of Verdun: Empire of Charlemagne divided; Charles had France; Louis the German kept Germany; Lothair took Lotharingia and Italy. Great persecution in China; all alien faiths except Islam to be obliterated.	
845		*c. Vivian Bible*, one of earliest illustrated Old and New Testaments, written at Tours.
846	Rome pillaged by Arabs.	†Po Ch'ui (*772), great T'ang poet.
848	Archiepiscopal See of Hamburg transferred to Bremen after attack by Norsemen; Bremen became centre for German and Scandinavian missionary work.	
849	Pope Leo IV organized fleet which defeated Saracens at Ostia.	*Glossa ordinaria*, commentary on Bible, appeared.
850	*c.* Buddhism disappeared in Northern India; replaced by Jainism and Hinduism. Rurik, a Norseman, became ruler of Kiev; Rus settled in trading towns and served local traders as mercenaries. Tibetan power collapsed.	*c.* The *Edda*, mythological poems dating from 9th cent.; discovered in 1643 by an Icelandic bishop. *c.* Photius (*820, †893): patriarch of Constantinople; *Bibliotheca*, extracts of ancient lost books. *c.* The Alcuin Bible, illuminated manuscript.

SCIENCE

c. Gold ring of Ethelwulf, decorated with niello work, made; now in British Museum.

Danish settlers founded Dublin and Limerick.

Johannes Scotus (Erigena) (*801, †886) appointed head of palace school to Charles the Bald.

Basilica of Vatican extensively damaged by Saracens.

c. Pope Leo IV built Leonine Wall round Vatican hill to protect it from attack.

c. Chinese used paper money.

c. The acropolis of Zimbabwe, Rhodesia, constructed.
c. Kaneoka, Japanese painter, produced secular and religious pictures which, while retaining Chinese influences, showed marked native characteristics.
c. Anskar, Archbishop of Hamburg, built first Christian church in Denmark.
c. Foundation of Salerno University, earliest known university.

c. Astrolabe perfected by Arabs.
Rus or Varangians, Swedish Northmen began trade with Constantinople and Khazans along waterways of Russia.
(to 1200) Great period of Islamic science, developed by translation of old Greek scientists into Syriac and hence into Arabic.
c. Kaldi, Arabian goatherd, accredited with discovery of coffee.

851	Main Danish forces entered Thames, landed and marched on Canterbury.	Erigena: *De divina praedestinatione*, against predestination.
855	Ethelwulf of Wessex and son, Alfred, went on pilgrimage to Rome.	
857		
860	†Kenneth MacAlpine, first king of united realm of Scotland.	Erigena: translation into Latin of Dionysius the Areopagite.
862	Rus seized power in Russian settlement area.	
865	Fleet of Russian Northmen attacked Constantinople.	
866	York seized by Danes; Danish kingdom established.	
868	Tulunid dynasty set up in Egypt and Syria; lasted until 905. Fen country ravaged by Danes.	First printed book: Buddhist sutra. *c.* Earliest printed newspaper, Chinese, dates from about the same period.
869	Malta captured by Arabs.	†Jahiz, Arab scholar, famed for literary discourses on varied subjects.
870	Danes conquered East Anglia, killing St Edmund, its last English king. Treaty of Mersen: Lotharingia divided between Germany and France.	*c.* Otfrid, first German poet whose name is known. *Codex Aureus* (the Gold Book), having fine gold cover, produced at Regensburg.
871	Accession of Alfred the Great (*849, †900) as king of Wessex.	
873		
876		
877	Mercia partitioned between English and Danes.	
878	Danes under Guthrum attacked Wessex; Alfred driven out; Guthrum defeated by Alfred at Edington. Treaty of Wedmore set up Danelaw.	

Canterbury Cathedral sacked by Danes; rebuilt *c.* 950 by Odo.

Terrible earthquake in Rome.

c. Earliest attempts at polyphonic music. Fresco *Ascension of Christ* in lower church of St Clement, Rome.

Ko Fuang temple, Shansi; oldest Chinese wooden building.

c. Work begun on Angkor Thom, city of Khmer civilization, Cambodia; ruins survive.

Accepted date of foundation of Novgorod by the Rus under Rurik.

c. Musica Enchiriadis, 9th cent. MS. using Latin letters A to P for musical notation. Danes destroyed first Medehampstead Monastery.

Erigena wrote Latin encyclopaedia on Nature.
c. Calibrated candles used in England to measure the time.

First church built on site of present Cologne Cathedral; later destroyed by Normans.

c. †Alkindi, who wrote original Arabic of *De Aspectibus; De Umbris et de Diversitate Aspectuum*.

c. Trewhiddle hoard, Cornwall; contains decorated metal objects.

Southern Northumbria colonized by Danes.

c. The Alfred Jewel, brooch believed to have belonged to King Alfred.

Start of observations by Arab astronomer Al-Battānī (Albategnius); by 918, determined inclination of ecliptic and precession of equinoxes with greater accuracy; used cotangents.

LITERATURE

Year	History	Literature
879	France partitioned: Louis III, king of Northern France; Carloman, king of Southern France. Nepal gained independence from Tibet.	
880	*c.* Eastern Emperor, Basil I, recovered Italy from Arabs. *c.* Igor, Rurik's son, and his cousin, Oleg, moved south from Novgorod to Kiev.	
881	Constantine II of Scotland defeated and killed by Danes. Norsemen defeated Louis III at Saucourt.	*c. Ludwsigslied*, first German historical ballad, written.
883	Sighelm, envoy of Alfred the Great, reputed to have visited S. India on pilgrimage to tomb of St. Thomas at Mylapore.	*c.* Notker Balbulus (*c.* *840, †912): *Gesta Karoli*, epic on deeds of Charlemagne.
885	*c.* Harold Fairhair of Eastern Norway conquered whole country and united it under his rule. Norsemen besieged Paris; defended by Odo, later Count of Paris.	Alfred translated Gregory's *Cura Pastoralis* into English. *c. Vie de Sainte Eulalie*, life of a saint; first French poem (29 lines).
886	Alfred captured London and gave it, with English Mercia, to his son-in-law, Ethelred.	
890		*c. Taketori Monogatari*, earliest Japanese narrative work.
891		*Anglo-Saxon Chronicle*, source of much early English history, begun in Alfred's reign; continued until 1154.
893	Renewal of Danish attacks on England; Danish leader Hasting defeated by Alfred.	
894	Gradual ending of close connection between Japan and the political and cultural life of Ch'ang-an capital of China.	*c.* Alfred translated Orosius' *Historia Adversus Paganos* into English.
895	Alfred defeated and captured Danish fleet on the River Lea.	Earliest Hebrew manuscript of Old Testament.
900	Schleswig captured by Swedish sea raiders. *c.* Great Moravian confederate state destroyed by advent of Magyars from Asia to Middle Danube. *c.* The Czechs, Bohemian tribe,	*c.* Asser, Welsh cleric who became bishop of Sherborne, wrote Latin *Life of Alfred the Great*, earliest biography of an English layman. *c.* Sixth period of Chinese literature (to 1900).

c. Ibn Tulun mosque, Cairo, oldest in the city, containing early examples of pointed arch.

Foundation of the Monserrat monastery, Benedictine order, in Catalonia.

c. Norway founded colony in Iceland.

Rebuilding of London begun by Alfred.

Ratpert (†895): Latin hymns.
c. Reliquary of the Tooth of St John, Carolingian jewel.

c. Probable date of foundation of Hastings.

Alfred's fleet to oppose Danes; beginnings of Royal Navy.

c. Introduction of Part Song, sung in fourths, fifths and octaves (*organum*, not to be confused with *polyphony*; see 855).
c. Second Pueblo period in S.W. states of N. America produced houses built entirely above ground (to 1250).

c. Thabit ibn Qurra, who wrote original Arabic of *Liber Charastonis*, concerning "Roman" steelyard, fl.
c. Rhazes, Islamic alchemist, described how to equip chemical laboratory; was first to distinguish between measles and smallpox.

LITERATURE

Year	History	Literature
900	asserted authority over all other Bohemian tribes. *c.* Bulgaria Christianized as part of Orthodox Church. Fujiwara family supreme in Japan; power behind rulers; aspect of Japanese history repeated in all ages. Succession of Edward the Elder to Alfred. *c.* Arab conquest of Sicily completed.	*c.* Japanese language replaced Chinese as language of culture and art in Japan. *c.* Jewish *Sepher Yetzirah* (Book of Creation) compiled. *c.* Japanese developed cursive signs, Kana, from single Chinese logographs; these become phonetic syllabary accurately recording Japanese sounds (*hiragana*).
902		*c. Genesis, Exodus, Daniel*: Biblical stories in crude Old English verse (once attributed to Caedmon).
904	Salonika sacked by Moslem pirates. Further attacks against Constantinople by Russian Northmen.	
905	Tulunid dynasty in Egypt suppressed; Egypt returned to misrule of caliphal governors.	*c. Kokinshu*, anthology of Japanese poetry of preceding 150 years; contents exceeded 1,100 pieces, mainly in *tanka*.
906	Start of Magyar invasions of Germany; continued until mid-tenth century.	
907	End of T'ang dynasty in China; civil strife: 907–960 "The Epoch of the Five Dynasties".	
910	Edward the Elder took possession of Oxford and London on death of brother-in-law, Ethelred of Mercia.	
911	Treaty of St. Claire-sur-Epte set up Dukedom of Normandy with Rollo as first Duke.	
912	Northmen under Rolf and Ranger settled in Normandy.	†Notker Balbulus, Monk of St Gallen (see 883).
913	Essex taken from Danes by Edward the Elder. Symeon of Bulgaria, after invading Thrace and Macedonia, threatened Constantinople but failed to reduce city.	
914		
915	Egypt invaded from Tunisia by Fatimid armies.	

c. Earliest Gothic wood-carvings; some Scandinavian objects have survived, more or less in fragmentary form.

c. Foundation of School of Medicine of Salerno.

Work begun on campanile of St Mark's, Venice; collapsed 1902.

Commencement of era of pornocracy in Rome; lasted until 963.

In St Cuthbert's tomb of this year was found the earliest extant Anglo-Saxon embroidery – a stole and maniple.

Epoch of Five Dynasties in China (to 960), remarkable for stimulating painting.

Commercial treaty between Kiev and Constantinople.

William, Duke of Aquitaine, founded Cluny Abbey.

c. Foundation of Witney; later to become famous for its blankets.
Earliest mention of Oxford as town.

Spendour of Omayyid Caliphate of Cordova (to 961).

c. Ethelfleda, daughter of Alfred the Great, erected great earthen mound of Warwick Castle.

Rouen became capital of Normandy.

Consecration of first Cluny Abbey Church.

	History	Literature
916	Renewal of Danish attacks on Ireland; Danes established themselves in Munster. Arabs expelled from central Italy.	*Codex Babylonicus Petropolitanus*, Masoretic text of Old Testament.
917	Edward the Elder annexed English Mercia to Wessex on †sister Ethelfleda, Lady of Mercia.	
919	Henry the Fowler became king of Germany. Fatimid armies again invaded Egypt.	
924	Symeon of Bulgaria devastated Greece and again threatened Constantinople without success.	
925	†Edward the Elder of Wessex; accession of Athelstan.	
926	Athelstan drove out Guthfrith of Northumbria and annexed his realm. Kings of Strathclyde, Wales, and of Picts and Scots submitted to Athelstan.	*c. Yengishiki*: Part I—Shinto liturgies; Part II—organization of Japanese government.
929	Wenceslas of Bohemia murdered by the Pagan Party led by his brother Boleslav I.	
930	*c.* Cluniac reform in Benedictine Order extended over France and Lorraine by Odo, Abbot of Cluny.	*c.* Ekkehart (†973), monk of St Gall, Switzerland: *Waltharius* (Walter of Aquitaine), Latin poem.
934	Swedish sea-kings driven out of Schleswig by German king, Henry I (the Fowler).	
935	*c.* Khitans, reindeer-using inhabitants of Siberia, invaded China from north. Fatimid armies defeated in Egypt; control of Alexandria, Faiyum and southern Syria regained by Mohammed ibn Tughj.	*c.* Tsurayuki (†946): *Tosa Nikki*, oldest extant diary; describes journey to Kyoto at end of his term of office in another province.
936	Otto I, king of Germany, succeeded his father, Henry I.	
937	Battle of Brunnanburh: Athelstan defeated alliance of Danes, Scots and Strathclyde Britons.	*Brunanburh*, Old English poem of victory included in *Anglo-Saxon Chronicle*.

(to 1130) Period of Pueblo Bonito ruins in N.W. New Mexico.

c. *Concert at the Palace,* Chinese picture depicting costumes and musical instruments of the time.

c. †Rhazes, who wrote original Arabic version of *De Aluminibus et Salibus,* on chemistry.

c. Odo of Cluny (*879, †942), abbot in 927, used letters A to G only in music as in modern times.

†Al-Battānī, Arab astronomer(*c.* *858).

c. Athelstan formulated rules for controlling the Mint.

Year	History	Literature
938	Khitans deserted old Chinese capital on Liaotung peninsula and set up new capital at Yenching, later called Peking.	
940	Revolt of a Taira chieftain against imperial rule set off period of civil war in Japan lasting to 1185.	
943	Caliph of Baghdad confirmed Egypt to Mohammed ibn Tughj and his heirs for 30 years.	*c.* Hywel Dda's Code of Welsh Laws.
944		
945	Cumberland and Westmorland annexed by Scots.	
950	*c.* Eastern empire called in assistance of Russia to check Bulgarian ambitions in Balkans. *c.* Lapps probably entered Norway at about this period.	*c. Merseburger Zaubersprüche*, manuscript of "Charms"; original much older, German. *c.* Constantinus Cephalas assembled *The Greek Anthology* of some 6,000 items (called *Palatine Anthology*).
954	Expulsion of Eric Bloodaxe, last Danish king of York.	
956	Dunstan exiled by Edwy of Wessex.	
957	North revolted against Edwy and made Edgar king. Byzantine armies reached northern Syria.	
959	†Edwy; Edgar became king of all England.	
960	*c.* King Harold Gormsson of Denmark accepted Christianity and prohibited paganism. Judith gained throne of Abyssinia by murdering Royal Family. Start of Sung dynasty in China; lasted to 1279.	Period of *Hi-Khio*, Chinese plays in which principal character sings (to 1119).
961	Crete retaken from Arabs by Byzantium. Dunstan became archbishop of Canterbury.	
962	Otto I, king of Germany, crowned Emperor by Pope John XII; first Saxon Emperor.	
963		*c.* Bal'ami translated *Annals* of Tabari into Persian (almost earliest extant Persian literature).

Athelstan founded Milton Abbey, Dorset.

*Abūll-Wafā (†997), who discovered the sine formula for a spherical triangle.

Glastonbury Abbey (founded *c.* 700) became great school of learning under Dunstan.

Prince Igor followed raid on Constantinople by commercial treaty.

c. Trumpets and kettledrums reached Europe from the Arabs.
c. Erection of Augsburg Cathedral.
c. Pagoda at Daigo-ji, Kyoto; main surviving Heian building, Japan.

†Alfarabi (*c.* *870), who wrote Arabic original of *Distinctio super Librum Aristotelis de Naturali Auditu*.
c. *Book of the Prefect* described Gild organization of Constantinople.

Erection of Mosque at Nayin, central Persia; interior elaborately carved.
c. (1279) Great water-colour artists of Sung period included Wēn T'ung, Wu Wei, Fu Shan and T'ang Yin; this period was renowned also for exceptionally fine pottery.

Rebuilding of St Paul's London, after a fire.

c. Emigrants from Persian Gulf settled at Kilwa (later Quiloa); visited by Ibn Battuta (1332); described as exceptionally fine town of East Africa.

Erection of Hospice of St Bernard, in St Bernard's Pass, Switzerland.

Earliest record of existence of a London bridge.

c. Al Sûfi (*903, †986): *Book of the Fixed Stars*, containing earliest record of a nebula (Andromeda).

LITERATURE

	History	Literature
965	English invaded British (Celtic) kingdom of Gwynedd. Monastic reforms of Dunstan; celibacy enforced. King of Denmark baptized. Byzantines regained Cyprus from Arabs.	*c.* Widukind of Corvey: *Saxon History (Res Gestae Saxoniae).*
967		
968	Russia ravaged East Bulgaria.	
969	Antioch and Aleppo regained from Arabs and once more part of Eastern Empire. Fatimid caliphs of Tunisia occupied Egypt with little opposition.	
970	Russia driven out of Balkans and Tsar Boris of Bulgaria captured.	*c. The Exeter Book,* collection of Old English poetry.
972	Bulgaria reconquered by Eastern Empire.	
973	*c.* Christianity permitted in Bohemia; bishopric founded at Prague. Edgar crowned at Bath. Capital of Egypt transferred to El-Kāhira (Cairo) by Caliph Al Mo'izz.	
974		
977	Kingdom of Ghazni in eastern Afghanistan founded by former slave in bodyguard of Arab caliph.	Chinese encyclopaedia of 1,000 volumes begun (completed *c.* 984, *q.v.*).
978	Murder of Edward the Martyr at Corfe Castle.	
979	Northmen in Ireland defeated by Malachi II at Tara.	
980	*c.* Monastic rule of St Benedict translated by Ethelwold, bishop of Winchester. Valdimir, grandson of Prince Igor, of the house of Rurik, became ruler of large area around Kiev. Renewal of Danish raids on England. †Dunstan. Viking raid on Chester.	

Foundation, at Worcester, of Benedictine Church, by St Oswald; later to become cathedral (see 1084).

Otto I granted archbishop of Bremen authority to hold a market.

Lothair crystal seal, Frankish work.

Foundation of Cordova University.

Jauhar el-Kaid founded El-Kāhira (Cairo); earlier settlements go back to 525.

(to 988) Adalbéron, bishop of Rheims, rebuilt Cathedral, inserting coloured glass windows representing stories (earliest known true *pictorial* stained glass).

c. Church of St Lawrence, Bradford-on-Avon; Saxon church of rare design; short in length, but high.

c. Copper and silver mines at Goslar, Hartz mountains, reported to have been in production.

Second church of Peterborough built; burnt 1116.

c. Revival of Deccan building and sculpture, India.

Direct commercial relations opened up between Egypt and Italian cities.

Earliest accurately authenticated earthquake in Britain.

c. The Pala d'oro (retable) of St Mark's, Venice; superb jewellers' work, enriched with gems.

Earliest record of Billingsgate wharf, London.

c. *Antiphonarium Codex Montpellier*, important musical MS. containing both neumes and letter notation.
c. Huge monolithic figure of Gommatesvara (57 ft high) at Sravana Belgola, India.

981		
982	Viking raids on coasts of Dorset, Portland and South Wales.	
984		*c.* Emperor of China supervised preparation of *T'ai P'ing Yü Lan*, encyclopaedia of existing knowledge.
986	Sabuktigin of Chazni invaded India; opposed by Jaipal ruler of Kangra.	
987	Hugh Capet became king of France and ended Carlovingian line.	
988	Vladimir officially introduced Christianity into his dominions, choosing Eastern form.	
990	*c.* Danzig appeared as capital of Slav duchy of Pomerellen.	*c.* Aelfric the Grammarian: *Catholic Homilies* and *Latin Grammar*.
993	Vikings ravaged Yorkshire.	*c.* Aelfric: *Lives of Saints*, a series of sermons.
994	Olaf Trygvason of Norway and Sweyn of Denmark besieged London.	
995	Olaf of Norway, baptized in England, returned to Norway and forced acceptance of Christianity. Last independent tribe of Bohemia, the Slavnici, subdued.	*c.* *Battle of Maldon*, Old English poem concerning attack in 991 by Vikings.
998	Further raids by Danes; Isle of Wight attacked.	
999	Last expedition of Emperor Basil II against Fatimids in Syria; formal treaties of peace negotiated.	
1000	Ethelred II ravaged Cumberland and Anglesey. Viking raids on Normandy. Olaf of Norway defeated and slain by Sweyn of Denmark; Norway passed under foreign rule along with Sweden. *c.* Rhenish traders settled in London; known as "Cologne Hanse" of London. *c.* Aristocratic and hereditary nature of Japanese institutions replaced bureaucratic nature of Taikwa reform edict (654).	*c.* Sei Shonagon: *Makurano-Sōshi (Pillow Book*); diary of woman author's thoughts and experiences in the Japanese Imperial Court; first example of *Zuihitsu*, in which writer puts down unconnected thoughts and ideas.

Consecration of second Abbey Church of Cluny.

First Viking colonies established in Greenland by Eric the Red.

Hall of Kuan Yin, Tu Lo temple, Chihsien, Hopei, China.

The Khitans rebuilt Peking on massive lines (see 938).

c. Al-Azhar University, Egypt, said have been founded.

c. Development of systematic musical notation.

Arabs destroyed Monte Cassino monastery (see 1066).

Thousands of people died in Aquitaine because rye was attacked by poisonous mould.

c. Foundation of Durham Cathedral; present building mainly 12th cent. (see 1092).

First record of Yamato-e painting school (true Japanese, free of Chinese influence).

Gerbert of Aquitaine, mathematician, inventor and great thinker, became Pope Sylvester II.

c. Fine silver bowl from Halton Moor, Lancs.; monastic work, Byzantine style.
c. *Bharata Natyam* (Madras), said to be oldest existing dance.
c. Eshin Siza, Japanese priest, painted religious pictures.
c. Khandariya (Shiva), temple, Khajuraho: tall Hindu shrine.
c. Cornett (*not* cornet) known to have existed.
Climax of Mayan civilization in Yucatan Peninsula with its art, calendar, astronomy and architecture.

Frisians began to build dykes against sea invasion and to reclaim land.
c. Chinese perfected gunpowder made up of charcoal, sulphur and potassium nitrate.
Theophilus described blowing of glass cylinder, opened into flat sheet.
Coast of Nova Scotia discovered by Leif Ericson, son of Eric the Red.
c. Saxon settlement at Bristol.
c. Erection of Bridge of Ten Thousand Ages, Foochow, China.

	History	Literature
1001	Mahmud, son of Sabuktigin of Ghazni, defeated and captured Jaipal of Kangra, and took Peshawar.	
1002	Massacre of St Brice's Day: Danish settlers in England massacred by order of Ethelred II.	
1004	Second invasion of England by Sweyn.	*c.* Murasaki Shikibu: *Genji Monogatari*, one of world's earliest novels; by a Japanese woman author; illustrated by Takayoshi.
1007	Ethelred II paid 30,000 pounds of silver to Danes and gained two years' freedom from attack.	
1008	Mahmud of Ghazni defeated a confederacy of rulers of Ujjain, Gwalior, Kalinjaur, Delhi and Ajmir.	
1009	Ethelred I's fleet disbanded owing to lack of stores; Sweyn returned and wintered in Kent.	
1011		Firdousī (*c.* *941, †1020), Persian poet: *Shāhnāma*, epic completed after 35 years.
1012	Further payments made to Danes, 48,000 pounds silver.	
1013	Sweyn again attacked England.	
1014	Ethelred II fled to Normandy; Sweyn, chosen king of England, died February; succeeded by Canute; Ethelred returned, defeated Danes at Lindsay; Canute withdrew to Sandwich. Battle of Clontarf: Norse Host defeated by Brian Boru, king of Southern Ireland. Attempts to revive Bulgarian empire by Samuel, Macedonian, ended by Basil II, who ordered Bulgarian army to be blinded.	*c.* Archbishop Wulfstan: *Sermo lupi ad Anglos*.
1015	Olaf Haroldson restored Norwegian independence and Christianity.	
1016	†Ethelred II (the Unready); Edmund Ironside and Canute of Denmark disputed English crown; agreed to partition kingdom.	

Erection of Church of St Michael, Hildesheim, having two transoms.

Church of St Frideswyde, Oxford, (later, the Cathedral), partially burned by Ethelred II; later restored.

Erection (to 1135) of Church of St Michele, Pavia; Italian Romanesque style.
Emperor Henry II founded Bamberg Cathedral.

Berno, abbot of Reichenau, wrote musical theory book.

Large English fleet built by Ethelred II against Danish attacks.

Mainz Cathedral built; begun 975; originally Romanesque style.

Greensted Church, Essex, built; oldest extant timber church in England.

Introduction of sight-singing in Pomposa monastery, near Ravenna.

Worms Cathedral, double-ended church, erected.

1016 †Edmund; Canute ascended English throne.
Vladimir of Kiev succeeded by son, Yaroslav the Wise.

1017 Canute divided England into four Earldoms replacing former Saxon kingdoms; married widow of Ethelred.

1018 Canute confirmed laws of Edgar at Council of Oxford.
Malcolm II of Scotland defeated Northumbria at Carham; gained Lothian.
Bulgaria organized as part of Eastern Empire.
Sacred Indian city of Muttra pillaged by troops of Mahmud of Ghazni.

Thietmar, bishop of Merseburg (*975, †1018): *Chronicon*, German chronicle from 908 to 1018.

1020 *c*. Faroes, Shetlands and Orkneys recognized Olaf Haroldson as king.

1025 Indecisive battle between Canute and Olaf Haroldson at Holy River in Sweden.

1026 Canute made pilgrimage to Rome.

1027 Norway invaded by Canute, who was accepted as king.

1028 Olaf Haroldson forced to flee from Norway by England, Denmark and rebel Norwegians.

1030 Olaf Haroldson returned to Norway and was killed at battle of Stiklestad.
Northmen settled in Naples.

1035 †Canute; English crown divided between Harold Harefoot and Hardi-canute.
Magnus I, son of Olaf Haroldson, restored independence of Norway.
William, illegitimate son of Robert of Normandy, succeeded to dukedom.

c. Yaroslav the Wise: *Russkaya pravda (Russian justice)*.

1037 Ferdinand I of Castile annexed León; asserted supremacy over Christian kingdoms of Spain; later reduced most of Moslem states to tributary kingdoms.

1039 Welsh under Gruffydd ap Llewellyn defeated Mercians at battle of Crosford.

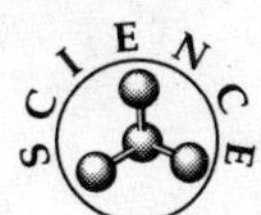

Erection of Cathedral of St Sophia, Kiev, having 13 cupolas, begun.

Brihadisvarasvamin temple, Tanjore, India, built by Rajaraja I (begun 985).

Takayoshi founded Tosa school of painting in Japan.

Erection of Castle of Alençon, France.

c. *Omar Khayyám (c.†1123), Persian mathematician, physicist and poet.

Guido d'Arezzo: *Micrologus de Disciplina Artis Musicae*, which used *neumes* for music manuscript.

c. Foundation of Benedictine Abbey of Bec; to become the home of Lanfranc's school (1045).

St Sophia, Kiev, first Russian stone-built Christian church, completed (see 1017).

†Avicenna (*980), who wrote *Khitab al-Shifa* on work of Aristotle; also wrote on (Arabic) medicine.

Lanfranc founded Law School at Avranches.

†Alhazen (*965), Arabian physicist who wrote *Octicae Thesaurus*, original (Arabic) version.

LITERATURE

Year	History	Literature
1040	Duncan, king of Scots, murdered by Macbeth, who took the crown.	Russian *Letopisi* (Chronicles), anonymous works, are extant back to this date; earlier records are traditional.
1042	Accession of Edward the Confessor, son of Ethelred the Unready, to English throne.	
1043	Magnus of Denmark defeated Slav hordes from south at Lyrskov Heath in South Jutland.	
1050	*c.* Egypt collapsed under military anarchy; rescued by Armenian general, Badr al Jamali, who with his son ruled Egypt in name of Fatimids until 1121.	*c.* Omar Khayyám, Persian poet: *Rubáiyát* (see 1859). *c. Vie de Saint Alexis*. French life of a saint. *c. The Mabinogion*, Welsh tales; later transcribed in *Red Book of Hergest* in 14th or 15th century. *c.* History of China from –500 to +1000 by Ssu-ma Kuang. *c.* Codex Zagrophenic, manuscript from Macedonia, still survives.
1052	Return of Earl Godwin and flight of Norman archbishop of Canterbury; Stigand, bishop of Worcester, made archbishop of Canterbury.	
1053	William of Normandy excommunicated by archbishop of Rouen.	
1054	Macbeth defeated by Siward of Northumbria and Malcolm at Dunsinane. Cleavage between Roman and Eastern Church became permanent. †Yaroslav of Kiev followed by series of civil wars between descendants of Rurik.	
1056	Macedonian family of Eastern Emperors ended with Empress Zoe; followed by period of anarchy.	
1057	Macbeth murdered by Malcolm; succeeded by stepson Lulach.	*Ostromir Gospel*, earliest extant Russian MS., written in Novgorod.
1058	Malcolm murdered Lulach and became king of Scots.	*c.* Humbert: *Adversus Simionacos*.
1059		
1060	Lanfranc to be Abbot of St Stephen's, Caen.	*c.* Leofric, bishop of Exeter from 1050 to 1071, presented *Exeter Book* of Old English poetry to cathedral library.

c. Virgin of Vladimir, famous icon; said to be Russian, probably came from Constantinople.

c. Petrocellus: *Practica*, important medical work of the time (school of Salerno).

Work begun on Romanesque Cathedral of Würzburg, consecrated 1189.

c. (to 1049) First printing from movable type; by Pi Cheng in China.

Earliest record of existence of Copenhagen.

c. Jōchō set up purely Japanese school of sculpture distinct from Chinese.
Earliest known work giving time-value to notes, essential for harmony, by Franco of Cologne (Paris).
Exeter Cathedral founded; present building mainly 13th cent.
c. Construction of impressive Jain temples at Mount Abu, India.

c. The astrolabe reached Europe from the Arabs (see 850).
c. Earliest reference to existence of town of Nuremburg.
c. Foundation of Christiania (Oslo, 1925) by Harold Hardrada.

Edward the Confessor commenced building Westminster Abbey; original church of St Peter 7th cent.

Hōō-dō pavilion (Phoenix Hall), Byōdō-in temple, Uji, built.

Wall-paintings of Hōō-dō of Uji; akin to Chinese style (see 1069).

Chinese observed supernova in Taurus.
Commercial relations between Cairo and Italy expanded rapidly after breach between Cairo and Constantinople.

Erection of Pagoda of Ko Fuang temple, Shansi, China.

Parma Cathedral, an Emilian church, begun (completed 1074).

c. Work began on Bonn Cathedral.

c. Christ as Ruler of the World, Byzantine mosaic in Daphni, Greece.

	History	Literature
1063	Harold of Wessex and Tostig subdued Wales. First mention of Rule of St Augustine.	
1064	Harold of Wessex shipwrecked on coast of Normandy and did homage to William of Normandy. Ferdinand I of Castile-León divided all his possessions between his sons. Seljuk Turks captured Armenia from Eastern Empire.	
1065	Seljuk Turks invaded Asia Minor.	
1066	†Edward the Confessor; accession of Harold of Wessex; Harold Hardrada of Norway invaded England to support Tostig of Northumbria against Harold; both were defeated and killed at Stamford Bridge. William of Normandy landed at Pevensey; defeated and killed Harold at the battle of Senlac or Hastings. Witan chose Edgar the Atheling as successor to Harold; he submitted to William, who was crowned in Westminster Abbey at Christmas. Outbreak of civil war in Ireland.	Norman invasion and subsequent occupation of England led to loss of prestige for English language; revived in 14th cent.
1067	Rebellion in S.W. England.	
1068	William I crushed revolt in west country. Revolt in North under Earls Edwin and Morcar crushed.	
1069	Danish invasion of England; Northumbria joined invaders; North devastated by William I.	
1070	Renewal of revolts in west of England. Hereward the Wake set up Camp of Refuge in Fens. Lanfranc became archbishop of Canterbury; set about ecclesiastical reforms.	*c.* Work begun on the *Winchester Bible* (4 vols.), magnificent ceremonial illuminated work by at least 6 artists.

Pisa Cathedral, Medieval Italian style, erected (to 1092).

Ezzolied, song of German crusaders.
Work begun on Minden Cathedral.
Wang Chen (probably): *The Island of the Immortals*, Chinese painting on silk.

Consecration of Westminster Abbey.

Abbaye-aux-Hommes, Caen (called St Etienne), vaulted Basilican church, erected by William the Conqueror (to 1077).
Rebuilding of Monte Cassino monastery.
Work begun on Fotheringay Castle, Northants.
Beginnings of Norman (Romanesque) architecture (ceased *c.* 1150).

Appearance of comet later called "Halley's comet" (see 1682).

Work commenced on Bayeux Tapestry.
William I founded Battle Abbey on site of battle of Hastings.
Building of Tower of London started.

Erection (to 1097) of Church of St Etienne, Nevers; unusual double church.
William I built York castle.

Want An-shib, prime minister under Emperor Shen Tsung of China, nationalized agricultural production and distribution.

Shōtoku Taishi Eden, oldest extant paintings of Yamato-e style (see 999).

York totally destroyed by fire.

Lanfranc undertook rebuilding of Canterbury Cathedral (destroyed by fire in 1067).
Dunster Castle, Somerset, erected.

	History	Literature
1071	Camp of Refuge suppressed. Normans conquered Bari and Brindisi, last Byzantine possessions in southern Italy. Revival of Islam under Seljuk Turks.	
1072	William I invaded Scotland; Malcolm rendered homage to William. Hereward the Wake submitted to William; English resistance over. Former possessions of Ferdinand of Castile-León reunited by his son Alfonso VI. Normans captured Palermo.	
1073	Archbishopric of York subordinate to Canterbury; Church courts outside Royal jurisdiction. Conflict between William I and Pope Gregory VII; William denied England held as a Papal Fief.	
1075	Norman earls of Hereford and Norfolk revolted against William I; suppressed; leaders executed. Godred Crovan from Hebrides conquered Isle of Man.	*c.* Adam of Bremen: *History of Hamburg Church*. *c.* Development of the saga; associated with history of colonization of Iceland.
1076	Quarrel between Gregory VII and Emperor Henry IV; latter excommunicated. Seljuk Turks captured Jerusalem and Damascus.	
1077	Emperor Henry IV submitted to Gregory VII at Canosta; received Papal pardon. Richard, second son of William I, killed in New Forest.	
1078	Revolt in Normandy led by William's eldest son, Robert; latter defeated and pardoned.	
1079	Foundation of Newcastle by Robert of Normandy.	*c.* Lanfranc: *De corpore et sanguine Domini*, defending transubstantiation.
1080	Emperor Henry IV renewed quarrel with Gregory VII and set up Anti-Pope Clement III.	

SCIENCE

c. Constantine the African (c. *1200, †1087) translated *Liber Regius*, of Haly Abbas, into Latin; brought Greek medicine to Western world.

William I built Durham castle.

No further confiscation of English lands by William I.

(to 1272) Pueblo ruins of Mesa Verde in S.W. Colorado.
c. Rajaraja II built Airavateshvara temple, Darasuram, India (begun c. 1046).

c. Cathedral of St James, Santiago de Compostela erected (to 1128); Spanish Romanesque style.
c. Robert of Marmion built Norman keep of Tamworth Castle.
c. Richard Castle, Yorkshire, erected.

Godfrey le Bossu founded Delft, Holland.

Work commenced on new St Alban's Abbey; modified 1155 *et seq*.
Bayeux Cathedral, France; developed over 400 years.
Lewes monastery, second Cluniac house in England, founded; first was at Barnstaple (date uncertain).

Bishop Gundulf began building the White Tower (Tower of London) for William I.

St Bartholomew's hospital, Rochester, for lepers, founded.

Commencement of Norman Winchester Cathedral, replacing Saxon; longest medieval church in Europe (560 ft.).

Omar Khayyám's calendar; of considerable accuracy; introduction of Jalalian era.

Consecration of Otranto Cathedral; Romanesque style.
c. Early extant stained glass in Augsberg, Germany.

Toledan table of positions of stars.

1081 Alexius I (*1048, †1118) became Eastern Roman Emperor.
Griffith-ap-Conan asserted his rule in Gwynedd after battle at Myndd Carn.
Normans, led by Robert Guiscard, invaded Balkan peninsula.

1082 Odo, bishop of Bayeux, half-brother to William I, arrested and imprisoned as Earl of Kent.
Alexius I defeated by Normans under Guiscard at Durazzo.

1083 Alexius I defeated Guiscard and Norman invaders at Larissa.

1084 Rome sacked by Normans under Guiscard; Pope Gregory VII fled to Salerno.

1085 Accession of Canute II of Denmark: invasion of England planned.
Civil war in Ireland.
Normans evacuated Balkan peninsula after †Guiscard.
Alfonso VI of Castile-León captured Toledo from Moslems.

1086 Moot of Salisbury called for fear of Danish invasion.
William I exacted oaths of allegiance from sub-tenants as well as tenants-in-chief.
Canute II assassinated; Danish invasion cancelled.
Carthusian Order founded by Bruno of Cologne.

1087 William I returned to Normandy; mortally wounded at siege of Nantes; on death-bed ordered release of Odo and Morcar; bequeathed: (i) England to second son, William; (ii) Normandy to eldest, Robert; (iii) sum of money to youngest, Henry.

1088 Revolt by Norman barons in England in favour of Robert suppressed by William II.
Urban II became Pope.

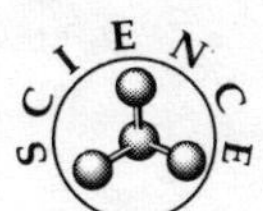

Rebuilding of Mainz Cathedral; possessing Roman basilica; repeatedly burnt down and restored, building now 12th to 14th cent. and 19th cent.

Commercial treaty established between Venice and Byzantium.

c. Japanese roll paintings of scenes from novels, lives of great men, religious stories and legends.
Benedictine Priory founded on Cuthbert's Cell, Farne Island.

Start made on Ely Cathedral (see 673).
Toba, Japanese artist, depicted priests and bureaucrats in form of birds and animals.

Printed mathematical books in China.

Wulfstan rebuilt Worcester Church as cathedral; present building mainly 13th and 14th cent.

Lincoln Cathedral burned; rebuilt 1092–1280 (see 1148).

Curfew, Forest and Games laws vigorously enforced.
Erection of The Commandery, Worcester; pre-Reformation hospital.

Nehan (Death of Buddha), great Heian painting of Japan.

Domesday Book completed: a survey of assessments for tax by William I.

St Paul's London (7th cent.) burned down and rebuilt; this cathedral was completed in 1284; destroyed yet again in 1666, *q.v.*.

(to 1118) Cluny Abbey Church rebuilt; longest in France (443 ft) in its day; one transept has survived.

1089 †Lanfranc, archbishop of Canterbury; See kept vacant by William II, who drew revenues until 1093.

1090 Norman conquest of Wales checked by Griffith-ap-Conan, Cadogan-ap-Powys and Griffth-ap-Rees of Deheubarth.
Turkish tribes made settlements between Danube and Balkans.

1091 Renewal of quarrel between William II and Robert of Normandy; invasion of Normandy; siege of Mont St Michel.
Scots under Malcolm III invaded England, but made peace with William II.

1092 William II seized Carlisle from Scots; Cumberland annexed to England.

1093 Malcolm III invaded England but slain at Alnwick; Scots throne seized by Donalbane, Malcolm's brother.
William II gravely ill; in fear, appointed Anselm (*1033, †1109) archbishop of Canterbury and recognized Urban II instead of Anti-Pope Clement III

1094 Rhys-ap-Tudor, king of South Wales, killed in battle.
Quarrel between William II and Anselm; latter exiled.
El Cid (*1043, †1099) took Valencia from the Moors.

Literature: Anselm: *Cur Deus Homo.*

1095 Revolt among Northern Barons crushed by William II.
Scotland partitioned between Donalbane and Malcolm III's second son, Edmund.
Urban II proclaimed First Crusade at Council of Clermont.
Philip I of France excommunicated for adultery.

1096 Start of First Crusade (People's Crusade); disorderly rabble, massacred in Asia Minor.
Agreement of Lyubach among Princes of House of Rurik.

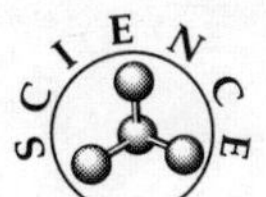

Rebuilding of Gloucester Abbey started; to 1100.

Erection of Cardiff Castle on site of Roman camp begun.
Norman Cathedral at Bath founded (see 1405).

Water-driven mechanical clock, possessing escapement, constructed in Peking.

William II ordered rebuilding of Carlisle Monastery (see 1133).
Binham Priory founded by Peter de Valoines.

(or 1092) Walcher of Malvern observed eclipse of the moon in Italy, one of first Western astronomical observations.

William II began building Carlisle Castle.
William of Carileph began Norman part of Durham Cathedral.

Hugh le Gros founded Benedictine monastery of Chester; abbey church of St. Werburgh became cathedral of Christ and St. Mary in 1541.

Completion of present St Mark's, Venice (begun 976), Byzantine style.

Early mention of gondolas in Venice.

Work started on nave of Norwich Cathedral by Bishop Herbert of Lorraine, dedicated 1101; completed *c.* 1500.

Robert of Normandy mortgaged his duchy to William II to raise money to join the First Crusade.

1097 Edgar, third son of Malcolm III, overthrew Donalbane and Edmund; reunited Scotland and ruled as vassal to William II.
Alfonso VI of Castile-León granted Portugal to Henry of Burgundy.
Crusaders, under Godfrey of Bouillon, captured Nicaea and later defeated Turks at Dorylaeum.

1098 William II invaded North Wales.
Magnus Barefoot of Norway seized Isle of Man and used it as base for raids.
Crusaders defeated Turks at Antioch.

1099 William II held Normandy; crushed revolt in Maine.
Magnus Barefoot captured Anglesey.
Crusaders, under Godfrey of Bouillon, captured Nicaea and later defeated Turks at Dorylaeum.

1100 William II killed in New Forest.
Henry, third son of Conqueror, secured English crown by system of election from elder brother, Robert of Normandy, absent on Crusade; marriage with Matilda, daughter of Malcolm III, united Norman and Saxon lines.
Establishment of feudal kingdom of Jerusalem under Godfrey of Bouillon, then Baldwin of Flanders in 1101.
Arabs expelled from Tiflis.
c. Danish Christian Church first made direct contact with Rome.

c. Chanson de Roland, earliest of French Chansons de Geste, written in Old French, describes the ambush of Charlemagne's rearguard in Pyrenees by the Saracens, and death of Roland.
Krishnamiśra: *Prabodha-Chandrodaya*, Indian allegorical play on Vishnu.
c. Middle English superseded Old English.

1101 Robert of Normandy returned from Crusade and landed in England; treaty of Walton settled on England on Henry I and Normandy on Robert.

1102 Magnus Barefoot's last expedition to Britain (against Murketagh of Ireland); killed in Ulster.
Isle of Man returned to sons of Godred Crovan.
Boleslav III became Duke of Poland; conquered Pomerania and Rügen.

Oldest known document on paper: a deed of King Roger I of Sicily.

Westminster Hall, London, erected by William II (see 1398).

Monastery of Citeaux in France, first Cistercian house, founded by St Robert.
Trani Cathedral, Italian Romanesque, begun.

Basilican Cathedral of Modena, Italy, designed by Lanfranc, begun.
Crusaders built present Church of the Holy Sepulchre, Jerusalem.

c. Erection of the Baptistry, Florence.
c. Beginnings of secular music.
(to 1150) Music school of St Martial of Limoges developed polyphonic music.
c. *The Crucifixion*, Byzantine mosaic in convent church of Daphni, Athens.
c. Rebuilding of Taunton Castle.

c. Decline in Islamic science began.
c. Third Pueblo period in S.W. North America; withdrawal from outlying parts of Utah and S.E. New Mexico; settlement in open caves on inaccessible cliff faces.
c. Period of culture under Sinchi Roca, first known Inca ruler, in Peru, South America; City of Cuzco possessed stone buildings and suntemple; influence spread.

Chapel of St Joseph built (to 1120), Glastonbury; burned down 1184.

Exchequer created by Roger of Salisbury.

LITERATURE

Year	History	Literature
1103	Murketagh of Ireland defeated by rival O'Lochlan.	
1104	War lasting until 1108 between Antioch and Byzantium.	(to 1108) Simeon of Durham: *Historia Dunelmensis Ecclesia*.
1105	War in Normandy between Henry I and Robert of Normandy.	
1106	Battle of Tinchebrai; defeat and imprisonment of Robert; Edgar the Atheling, ally of Robert, pardoned. Henry V became Emperor of Holy Roman Empire.	Abbot Daniel's account of visit to Holy Land; first Russian travel literature.
1107	Alexander I became King of Scots. Investiture question in England and Wales settled by Henry I and Anselm.	
1108	Sigurd of Norway went on Crusade to Holy Land.	*c.* Iso no Zenji *fl.*; regarded as Mother of Japanese drama.
1109	War between Henry I and France; lasted to 1113. Diocese of Ely created. Tripoli captured by Crusaders. †Anselm.	
1110	Bishopric of Greenland founded.	Earliest known record of a Miracle Play in England; at Dunstable.
1111		
1112	Robert of Belesme revolted against Henry I; imprisoned.	
1113	St Bernard joined Cistercian Order.	Gallus wrote first chronicle of Poland.
1114	Marriage of Matilda, daughter of Henry I to Emperor Henry V.	
1115	Florence became free republic in Tuscany.	Abelard teaching in Paris.
1117	War between Henry I of England and William Clito, son of Robert of Belesme; Clito allied with France, Flanders and Anjou.	Florence of Worcester (†1118) ceased chronicle *Chronicon ex Chronicis*, then continued by others until 1295.
1118	Alfonso I of Aragon (†1134) captured Saragossa, most stable of Moorish states.	

Chinese *Ying Tsao Fa Shih (Method of Architecture*) published; showed early Chinese buildings (none of which survive) similar to much later ones.

St Madeleine, Vézelay, fine Cluny-style church, erected.

c. Foundation of arsenal at Venice; extended 1304, 1325, 1473, 1539, 1564.

Angoulême Cathedral, Aquitaine, erected; French Romanesque style.

c. Candlestick made of gilt bell-metal for Gloucester Cathedral; Anglo-Norman work.

Bishop of Bremen invited Dutch farmers to reclaim and keep marshland around Bremen.

Reynelm began building new Hereford Cathedral on existing plan.

(from 1077) Bishop Gundulph rebuilt Rochester Cathedral; completed 1130.

Church of Paray-le-Monial, Burgundy; Benedictine style.
Erection of Torre Asinelli, Bologna (320 ft high).

Crypt of Canterbury Cathedral built (to 1130).

Pipe Roll, Exchequer Record, introduced into England; lasted until 1834.

c. Approximate date of Aztec Ruin.

†Al-Ghazali, whose religious teachings opposed scientific progress in Islam.

Erection of Barnard Castle, Co. Durham (to 1132).

Foundation of St Nicholas, Novgorod; early onion-domed church.

Order of Knights Hospitallers of St John of Jerusalem founded.

Foundation of Chichester Cathedral.

Foundation of Abbey of Clairvaux; St Bernard first abbot.

c. Henry I set up royal menagerie at Woodstock.

Work begun on present Peterborough Cathedral, replacing one burned down accidentally in 1116 (see 1238).

Reiner Van Huy: *Brass font* of St. Bartholomew, Liége.
Earl David founded Jedburgh Monastery.

	History	Literature
1119	Henry I defeated William Clito. †Murketagh and of O'Lochlan, his rival; anarchy in Ireland.	
1120	Peace made between Henry I and Louis VI of France. Disaster of the "White Ship"; Henry's son drowned; Matilda heiress.	*c.* Ari Fróði (*1067, †1148): *Islendingabók*, saga of Iceland to 1120.
1121	Synod of Soissons condemned Abelard's heretical teaching on the Trinity.	
1122	Concordat of Worms settled investiture question between Pope and Emperor. Patzinaks defeated by Byzantines.	
1123	First Lateran Council suppressed simony and marriage of priests.	Orderic Vitalis (*1075, †1142) began *Historia Ecclesiastica* (Bks iii, iv) (see 1141).
1124	Alexander I of Scotland succeeded by brother, David I, who became vassal to Henry I of England. Emperor John II Comnenus defeated Hungarians. Tyre captured by Christians.	*c.* William of Malmesbury: *On the Antiquity of the Church of Glastonbury*, a record of its history.
1125	†Emperor Henry V; Matilda, heiress of England, now a widow. Ch'in dynasty in China set up by Nuchens from eastern Manchuria. Displaced Khitans settled in Ili valley of Turkestan. *c.* Almohades conquered Morocco.	*c.* Tarnenari: *O-Kagami*, Japanese history of fourteen reigns, from 851 to 1036. *Yuen-Pen* and *Tsa-Ki* period of Chinese drama (to 1367).
1126	Imperial attempt at invasion of Bohemia defeated. Renewal of special trading rights granted to Venice by Eastern Empire.	*Averroes, Arab scholar, who wrote commentaries on Aristotle's works.
1127	English barons took oath of allegiance to Matilda as successor to Henry I. Sung dynasty, driven from North China by Nuchens, settled at Hangchow; thereafter known as "Southern Sung".	Earliest dated Jain manuscript, made of palm leaf, India.
1128	Order of Templars recognized by Pope Honorious II at Council of Troyes.	

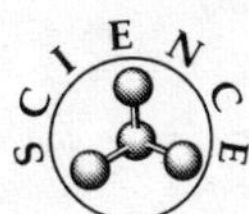

Hugh de Payns founded Order of Poor Knights of Christ and the Temple of Solomon (Knights Templars), a military order.

Norman keep of Kenilworth Castle built by Geoffrey de Clinton.
Domed church of Sainte Front, Périgueux, erected (to 1175).

c. Earliest European record of bell-founding by Theophilus the Priest.
Chinese may have invented playing-cards.

Foundation of Bolton Abbey at Embsay; removed to Wharfedale, 1150.

Bronze cross of Cong given to church of Tuam (Ireland).
Erection of chapel of Lord Leycester Hospital, Warwick.

Foundation of St Bartholomew's Hospital, London, by Rahere.

c. Bishop Ernulf completed Norman cathedral of Rochester begun by Bishop Gundulph (see also 1125).

c. First Scottish coinage struck (David I).

Nave of Tewkesbury abbey built by Benedictine monks; possesses fine 14th-cent. stained-glass windows.
Norman west front of Rochester Cathedral built; new cathedral consecrated 1130.

c. Earliest account of the preparation of alcohol.
c. Alexander Neckam: *De Utensilibus*, containing earliest authentic account of mariner's compass.

Wm. de Corbeil built keep of Rochester Castle, 11th cent.; keep still extant.

Translation of the Arabic astronomical tables of Musa al-Khowârizmî (9th cent.) into Latin.
First artesian wells (at Artois, France).

†Guillaume de Poitou (*1070), troubadour, some of whose tunes still exist.

Abbey of Holyrood founded by David I of Scotland.

1129	Matilda, heiress of England, married to Geoffrey Plantagenet of Anjou.	
1130	Roger II crowned King of Sicily at Palermo.	
1131	Gilbertine Order founded at Sempringham.	
1132		
1133	Diocese of Carlisle founded.	William of Malmesbury: *Exploits of English Kings*.
1134	Alfonso of Aragon defeated and killed by Moors.	
1135	†Henry I in Normandy; English crown and treasure seized by Stephen of Boulogne, nephew to Henry I.	
1136	Turlough of Connaught became supreme in Ireland. Emperor Lothair invaded Italy; conquered Apulia.	
1137	Creation of Bishopric of Aberdeen. Pisans captured and sacked Amalfi. Emperor John II Comnenus defeated Armenians. Antioch became vassal to Byzantium.	
1138	Civil war in England over succession: David I of Scotland invaded England on behalf of Matilda; defeated at Northallerton (Battle of the Standard).	
1139	Stephen quarrelled with bishops at Council of Oxford; Bishops of Lincoln and Salisbury arrested. Second Lateran Council. Alfonso I, Count of Portugal, used title of King and became independent ruler; defeated by Moors.	c. *Decretum Gratiani*, summarizing English ecclesiastical law.
1140	Council at Sens condemned the heresies of Abelard. Sicilian Law Code set up by Assize of Ariano.	*Cantore de mio Cid* (poem on el Cid) written; earliest Castilian literature.

Henry I presented Geoffrey of Anjou with shield bearing golden lions; beginnings of heraldry.

c. Hall of the Ambassadors, earliest section of the Alcazar (Spain).

Reclamation of Wilster Marsh, east of Elbe, carried out by Dutch settlers.

Henry I founded Dunstable Priory.
Foundation of Cefalu Cathedral, Sicily.
Rievaulx Abbey, Yorkshire, founded.

Foundation of Fountains Abbey, largest and best-preserved Cistercian retreat in England.

Henry I granted Charters of Corporate Towns protecting industry and commerce.

Adelulf persuaded Henry I to establish Carlisle Church as cathedral; largely destroyed 1292 and slowly rebuilt.

St. Bartholomew's Fair, Smithfield; was to run for 722 years; important centre for commerce and music.

Construction of west front of Chartres Cathedral started (see 1194).

Earliest record of the Chapel Royal, a body under royal patronage.

French utilized flying buttresses at Poissy.

David I of Scotland founded Melrose Abbey; destroyed 1545.

Hospital of St Cross, Winchester, earliest English alms-house.

Rochester Cathedral burnt and rebuilt.

Foundation of Forde Abbey (Cistercian); Great Hall built 1500; converted into private house.

St Zeno Maggiore, Verona; possesses simple austere façade.
c. Cappella Palatina, Palermo, built by King Roger; Christian-Saracen architecture.

Rochester Castle completed by William of Corbeil (begun 1130).
West front of Rochester Cathedral started.

c. Stamp-mill used in preparing paper.
Salt mines established at Berchtesgaden.

	History	Literature
1141	Battle of Lincoln; Stephen defeated and captured; Matilda became "Lady of England".	Orderic Vitalis: *Historia Ecclesiastica*, from birth of Christ to Norman times (Bks i, ii, vii-xiii).
1142	Stephen exchanged for Robert of Gloucester in English civil war; fighting renewed; Matilda besieged at Oxford. China made subject to the Ch'in.	†Abelard, boldest French theologian of his century; his love letters to Héloise are famous.
1143	Alfonso I of Portugal captured Lisbon.	
1144	Republican rule established in Rome.	
1145	Geoffrey Plantagenet of Anjou now master of Normandy. Roderick, son of Turlough of Connaught, defeated Munster at Moindnoe. Pope Eugene III proclaimed the Second Crusade.	
1147	Matilda left England. Eugene III decided against claim of Bishop of St David's to be independent of Canterbury. Second Crusade; Crusaders perished in Asia Minor.	*c.* Geoffrey of Monmouth (†1154): *Historia Regum Britanniae*, supposed translation of a Welsh History of Britain.
1148	Crusaders defeated at Damascus; Tunis and Tripoli subdued by Normans.	
1150	Theobald, Archbishop of Canterbury, refused to recognize son of Stephen as heir to English throne. Bishoprics of Dunblane and Brechin established. Alauddin Hussain, Sultan of Ghor, destroyed Ghazni Empire. *c.* Hamburg and Lübeck formed trading centre for area between Flanders and Novgorod.	*Salva lo vescovo santo*, earliest extant Italian composition in verse. *c. The Black Book of Carmarthen*: oldest Welsh manuscript; contains reference to King Arthur.
1151	†Geoffrey Plantagenet of Anjou; succeeded by Henry, his son by Matilda of England.	
1152	Frederick Barbarossa elected King of the Germans.	
1153	Treaty of Wallingford between Henry of Anjou and Stephen of England; Henry to succeed Stephen on English throne.	

SCIENCE

Thierry appointed Chancellor of Chartres School: set up scientific and classical studies.

Work begun on Norman church, later to become Bristol Cathedral; eastern section dates from 1306.

Foundation of Lübeck, Germany, by Adolph II of Holstein.

Gothic abbey church of St Denis, France, erected (begun 1132).

(to 1150) Building of towers of Chartres Cathedral; rebuilt 1194 (*q.v.*) after fire.
Norwich Cathedral damaged by fire but restored.

Robert of Chester: *Liber de Compositione Alchemiae*, translated from the Arabic.

c. *Antidotarium Nicolai*, a treatise on drugs.
Foundation of the important hospital of Montpellier.

Foundation of Faversham Abbey, Kent.
Lisbon Cathedral built; destroyed by earthquake 1755.

Monks used woodcuts for elaborate lettering in manuscript at Engelberg.
c. Robert of Chester translated *Al-jebr* into Latin (see 825).

Erection of Norman portals and west towers of Lincoln Cathedral.

Wooden stave-church of Borgund, Norway.
c. Gothic architecture prominent in Europe.
c. Earliest extant European tapestries; in Halberstadt Cathedral.
c. Huge pyramidal gateways in Mysore (Hoyshala dynasty).

Earliest known almanac issued by Solomon Jarchus.
c. Paper manufacture in Spain by Moors.
c. Lilāvata, Indian mathematical work, standard for many years in the East.
c. Faculty of medicine at Bologna University.
c. First appearance of European mechanical clocks.

Erection of Zemora Cathedral, Spain (to 1174).

Foundation of Easby Abbey; ruined; Premonstratensian house.

(to 1278) Erection of the Baptistry, Pisa.
Foundation of monastery of Alcobaca.
Erection of Berkeley Castle, oldest occupied castle in England.

First tax in Norway; "Peter's pence", based on English model.

Alfonso I of Portugal granted lands between Douro and Tagus to Cistercians on condition that they brought area under cultivation.

1153	Treaty of Constance: Frederick Barbarossa and Pope Eugene III allied against Arnold of Brescia.	
1154	†Stephen of England; accession of Henry of Anjou and House of Plantagenet to English throne. Nicholas Breakspear, only English man to do so, became Pope; reigned as Adrian IV (†1159).	End of the *Anglo-Saxon Chronicle;* interesting history of events since 449, but inaccurate in part because of unscientific nature of records of time.
1155	Henry II of England abolished fiscal earldoms and restored Royal demesne; received Papal Bull from Adrian IV authorizing conquest of Ireland. Roman Republic crushed by Emperor Frederick I.	*c.* Robert Wace, Anglo-Norman poet: *Roman de Brut,* rhythmical version of Geoffrey of Monmouth's History: first mention of Round Table.
1156	Austria made a Duchy with special privileges.	
1157	Thomas à Becket became Chancellor of England. Malcolm IV of Scotland and Owen of North Wales did homage to Henry II. Finland conquered by Eric of Sweden. Alfonso VII of Castile-León divided territory between his two sons, recreating kingdoms of Castile and Léon.	
1158	Rhys ap Griffith, ruler of South Wales, gave hostages to Henry II. Order of Knights of Calatrava, oldest Spanish military order, founded. Kingdom of Bohemia founded for Ladislaus II for services to Frederick I. Diet of Roncaglia defined Imperial rights in Italy.	
1159	Henry II of England accepted cash payments (scutage) in place of feudal military service.	*c.* John of Salisbury: *Policraticus.*
1160	Henry, eldest son of Henry II, married Margaret of France. Malcolm IV of Scotland subdued Galloway. Normans expelled from North Africa. Order of Alcantara, Spanish order of chivalry, founded.	*c. Tristan et Iseult,* epic by Béroul and Thomas, old Celtic story of tragic love; later became basis of Wagner's opera (1865). *Jeu de Saint-Nicolas,* dramatic poem by Jean Bodel, played at Arras on the Saint's Day.

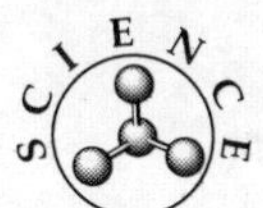

Construction of Ripon Cathedral begun (completed 1181).
Beginnings of Transitional architecture to Pointed style.
(to 1181) Choir and crypt of York Minster rebuilt.

Mohammed al Idrisi's work on geography; produced fine map of the world, at Palermo.

c. Beginnings of Paris university.

c. Aristotle's *Posterior Analytics* translated from Greek into Latin.

Cathedral of Saviour of the Transfiguration, Mirozh Monastery, Pskov, erected.

Foundation of Moscow.

Privileges granted by Henry II to German merchants in England.
Foundation of Fribourg, Swiss town, by Berchthold IV.

Construction of cathedral at Oxford, in Christ Church College (see 1002, 1478).

First attempt to stabilize English coinage into a single series for one reign (Tealby type, so-called).
Bremen merchants founded Riga; originally port store-house.
Lübeck refounded and Munich founded by Henry the Lion of Saxony and Bavaria.

c. Cathedral of St. Andrews, Scotland, founded by Bishop Arnold; destroyed 1559.

Work commenced on Soissons Abbey Church (to 1212) and Laon Cathedral (to 1350), France.
Construction of Salamanca Cathedral, Spain, begun.
Farnham Castle, Surrey, seat of bishops of Winchester.

c. Ptolemy's *Almagest* translated from Greek into Latin.

	History	Literature
1161	The "Merchants of the Roman Empire", headed by Lübeck, made trade treaty with Baltic island of Gotland. Magnus V elected king of Norway.	
1162	Thomas à Becket elected Archbishop of Canterbury. Milan destroyed by Frederick I.	
1163	Magnus V crowned in Norway; first Norwegian coronation.	
1164		*c.* Gautier d'Arras, French courtly poet: *Eracle*.
1165	Constitutions of Clarendon limited ecclesiastical jurisdiction in England; Becket fled to France, excommunicating supporters of Constitutions. Organization of Norwegian Church.	*c. Lais* by Marie de France, French; one of few women authors of Middle Ages.
1166	Assize of Clarendon set up Grand Jury system in England; travelling judges sent on circuit by Henry II—Justices in eyre. Frederick I invaded Italy for fourth time.	*c. The Song of Canute*, early English ballad (traditionally by Canute) written by a monk of Ely.
1167	Council of Albigenses at Toulouse. Romans defeated by Frederick I at Tusculum; rising in Lombardy forced return of Frederick to Italy.	
1168	Ireland invaded by barons from Wales in support of Dermot of Leinster; Wexford captured. Andrew Bogolubsky sacked Kiev; assumed title of Grand Prince but remained in Vladimir; transfer of Russian political activity from south to central Russia.	
1169	Towns represented for first time in Cortes of Castile. Saladin appointed commander of Syrian army of occupation in Egypt. Nureddin of Damascus invaded Egypt.	*c.* Giraldus Cambrensis (*c.* *1146, †1220): *Expurgatio Hibernica*, account of conquest of Ireland (to 1185).
1170	Henry II and Becket reconciled in Touraine. Becket murdered at Canterbury. "Strongbow" de Clare, Earl of Chepstow, captured Dublin and	*c.* Chrétien de Troyes, French author: *Lancelot* romance of courtly love, and *Perceval* (earliest mention of Holy Grail legend). *c.* Heinrich von Veldecke: *Eneit*, epic poem in German.

Possible use of explosives in warfare by Chinese.

Work begun on cathedral at Poitiers; completed in 14th cent.

Work begun on Nôtre Dame, Paris; superb flying buttresses at east end; spire 300 ft. high (completed 1235).

Discovery of silver mines at Freiburg led to development of the town.

Foundation of Malmesbury Abbey.

Erection of Church of the Intercession of the Holy Virgin, near Vladimir, Russia.

Saladin erected Cairo Citadel.

Military order of St Benedict of Aviz set up in Spain.
Assize of Clarendon ordered erection of gaols in all counties and boroughs of England.

Oxford University founded; English students left Paris, where they had been studying; colleges originally designed in same style as monasteries.

Plague in the army of Frederick I.

Foundation of Alessandro, Italy; so-called after Pope Alexander III.

Milan rebuilt.
Foundation of Palermo Cathedral (Basilican); stands on site of Saracen mosque (completed 1185).
c. Foundation of Carlisle Castle; keep is of

Inquest of Sheriffs in England greatly strengthened Exchequer.
c. Beginnings of famous Leipzig fairs.

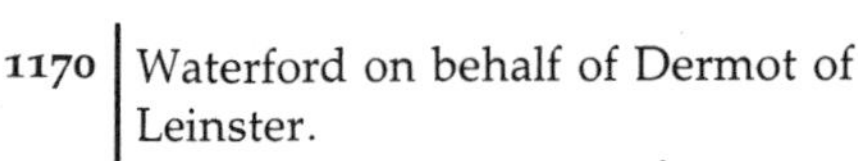

Year	History	Literature
1170	Waterford on behalf of Dermot of Leinster. Rules for canonization of saints set out by Pope Alexander III.	
1171	Henry II went to Ireland; made little progress. Strongbow, having married Dermot's daughter, became King of Leinster on †Dermot; did homage to Henry II for lands.	
1172	Reconciliation of Henry II and papacy; right of appeal to Rome from Royal courts conceded.	*c.* Wace: *Roman de Rou*, chronicle of Norman dukes from Rollo to Robert Curthose.
1173	Baronial revolt against Henry II. Saladin conquered Yemen.	*c.* Chrétien de Troyes: *Le Chevalier au Lion (Yvain)*, French poem.
1174	Henry II of England did penance at Canterbury for murder of Becket. William the Lion of Scotland captured at Alnwick; by Treaty of Falaise William did homage to Henry II for Scotland. Fifth expedition of Frederick I to Italy; *c.* Purchased Swabian and Italian possessions from Guelphs.	*c. Roman de Renard*: 27 tales in rhymed verses of Renard the Fox; many authors; written in French between 1174 and 1300. *Fabliaux* (1174 onwards), comic French short tales of simple peasants, deceitful wives and lazy priests; 150 have survived. *c.* Walter Map organized the Arthurian legends in their present shape.
1175	Henry II claimed Lordship of Ireland under Bull of 1155. Hugh de Lacy appointed Lord Deputy. Peace between Frederick I and Lombard League at Montebello. Mohammed of Ghor invaded India.	*c. Adam*, earliest extant play written in French.
1176	Assize of Northampton re-issued Assize of Clarendon; extended use of Grand Jury. Frederick I defeated by Lombard League at Legnano. Manuel I, Eastern Emperor, defeated by Seljuks at Myriokephalon.	Welsh Eisteddfod held in Cardigan Castle.
1177	Sverrir Sigurdsson, pretender, reached Norway from Faroes, posing as Royal prince.	
1178	Henry II of England and Louis VII of France met to arrange a Crusade.	

this date; outer gatehouse 13th cent.
c. Earliest *English* stained glass (in York Minster) (see 1080).

Completion of nave of Tournai Cathedral, Belgium.
c. Building of the apse of Worms Cathedral (to 1220).

Christ Church Cathedral, Dublin, rebuilt; originally founded 1038.

Saladin gained control of Southern end of profitable Indian trade route in Mediterranean.

Work begun on Campanile, Pisa (The Leaning Tower); now overhangs 13 ft. 10 in., increasing; cause is foundation subsidence.
William of Sens commenced rebuilding the choir of Canterbury Cathedral after its destruction by fire (see 1184).
The *Minnesang* in Germany, Court lyrics imbued with adoration of loved woman.
Work begun on Monreale Cathedral; Sicilian Romanesque style.

Erection of shrine to Becket at Canterbury.
c. Great hypostyle walls built around old temples in India.
c. Leonin compiled *Magnus Liber Organi de Graduali*.

Papal confirmation of Spanish military order of Knights of Santiago.
Order of Knights of St James of Compostella founded in Spain.

Foundation of Studley Priory, Benedictine nunnery near Oxford; now a hotel.

Old London Bridge, having a drawbridge and four arches, commenced; demolished 1832.

Henry II erected castle at Newcastle upon Tyne; the keep is well preserved.
Belfast originated with the building of a castle.

St Bénezèt built the famous bridge at Avignon (to 1188).

Richard Fitznigel: *Dialogus de Saccario*, account of English financial system.

1179 Grand Assize of Windsor checked power of feudal courts and enhanced authority of Royal Courts in England.
Third Lateran Council set out forms of election for popes and bishops.

1180 Judicial reforms in England begun by Ranulf de Glanville, Justiciar.
†Louis VII of France and accession of Philip Augustus (Philip II).
Henry the Lion (Duke of Saxony and Bavaria) outlawed.

1181 Crusade launched against the Albigenses.
Henry the Lion submitted to Frederick I; kept Brunswick.

1182 Jews banished from France.

1183 Peace of Constance recognized Lombard League under Imperial suzerainty.
Aleppo captured by Saladin.

1184 Diet of Mainz marked supreme power of Frederick I.
Sverrir Sigurdsson, sole King of Norway, remodelled crown and government on Anglo-Norman pattern.

1185 Philip II of France at war with Flanders; gained Amiens and Vermandois.
Frederick and the Pope revived their quarrel.
Second Bulgarian empire founded by brothers, Ivan and Peter Asen.
Minamoto family achieved control under Emperor in Japan; beginning of Kamakura Shōgunate (to 1333).

Literature: Russian epic, *Discourse on the Campaign of Igor*, a political prose-poem.

1186 English dominion in Ireland limited to "the Pale": Dublin, Waterford, Wexford, Drogheda, Cork and districts.
Bulgaria began war for freedom from Byzantium; achieved by 1188.

1187 Saladin defeated Christians at Hittin; later captured Jerusalem.
Punjab conquered by Mohammed of Ghor.

c. Conjectured date of very early Scottish silver spoon; found at Iona in 1922.
c. Foundation of Cistercian Abbey of Kirkstall, Yorkshire.

Construction of *Naviglio Grande*, which conveyed water from Lake Maggiore to irrigate large areas of land, commenced.

Commencement of present Wells Cathedral (founded 705), continued until 1333; Early English West Front.
(to 1186) Keep of Dover Castle built.

First reference to European windmill with vertical sails; earlier type was the post-mill.
Improved coinage, *Short Cross* type, introduced.
c. Glazed windows in private houses in England (see 290).

First Carthusian monastery in Britain, at Witham.
Work begun on the Alcazar, palace in Seville.

Assize of Arms in England; reorganization of militia.

Erection of Oakham Castle, Rutland, commenced.

William the Englishman completed Norman Canterbury Cathedral (see 1174), begun by William of Sens (accidentally killed 1178).
Consecration of Modena Cathedral (see 1099).

Assize of Woodstock regulated Royal Forests in England.

Great damage to Lincoln Cathedral as result of an earthquake.
Rotunda of Temple Church, London, erected (see 1240).
c. Superb Milan Candlestick, possibly by Nicholas of Verdun, created (date conjectured).

Knights Templars established in London.

Construction (to 1204) of St Hugh's choir, Lincoln Cathedral; early pointed architecture; transepts built in same period.

Completion of Verona Cathedral, possessing finely ornamented west front.
(to 1210) Extensions to Chichester Cathedral (consecrated 1108).

†Gerard de Cremona, translator into Latin of Arabic scientific works, including works of Aristotle, Avicenna, Alkindi, Al-Khowârizmî.

1188 Henry II's sons, Richard and John, allied with Philip II of France against Henry II.
Lübeck made Imperial Free City by Frederick I.

Giraldus Cambrensis began *Itinerarium Cambrense*, famous account of his journey through Wales.

1189 Henry II defeated by alliance of his sons at Angers; died at Chinon; accession of Richard I to English throne.
Henry Fitzaylwin first Mayor of London; held office until 1212.
Frederick I and Pope settled quarrel at Peace of Strasbourg.
Frederick I set out on Third Crusade.

1190 Richard I annulled Treaty of Falaise, by which Scottish kings did homage, for sum of 10,000 marks; sold Roxburgh and Berwick to William the Lion.
Frederick I conquered Iconium; later drowned in River Saleph in Cicilia; accession of Emperor Henry VI.
Great persecution of Jews in England; riots in main towns.

c. Robert Fitz-Nigel: *Dialogue of the Exchequer* (in Latin), valuable guide to civil administration of the time.

1191 Richard I captured Cyprus on way to Holy Land; sold it to Templars; Crusaders captured Acre.
Moslems under Mohammed of Ghor renewed conquest of Northern India; defeated by Hindus at Kurukshetra outside Delhi.

Richard of Devizes: *Chronicon de rebus gestis Ricardi Primi*, record of England and Holy Land during time of Third Crusade.

1192 Richard I and Saladin made truce; Richard captured by Leopold, Duke of Austria, on returning from Crusade. Cyprus sold to Guy of Lusignan, whose family ruled there until 1489.
Styria united to Austria.
Mohammed of Ghor defeated Hindu League at Tarain.

Giraldus Cambrensis: *Gemma Ecclesiastica; Vita St. Remigii* (to 1198).

1193 Richard I surrendered to Emperor Henry VI; imprisoned at Trifels.
Hubert Walter, Archbishop of Canterbury, appointed Justiciar of England in absence of Richard I.
†Saladin.
Moslems captured Bihar and Bengal.

†Benedict of Peterborough, author of *Gesta Henrici II*.

Foundation of Carlisle Grammar School; refounded in 1541.
Count Adolph III of Holstein built castle opposite bishop's town of Hamburg.

Saladin Tithe in England levied to provide funds for Third Crusade; first tax on personal property in England.

Beginnings of Early English architecture; typified by lancet-windows without mullions.
Richard I carried his coat-of-arms on his shield; first English monarch to do so.

Publication of Building Regulations, requiring improved fire-precautions in building houses.
Novgorod made treaty with German merchants.
Silver florin first minted in Florence (see 1252).
Foundation of Rostock.

c. Erection of Bell Tower, Tower of London.
c. Christ in Majesty, mosaic in Monreale, Sicily.
Foundation of Portsmouth Cathedral (present building 17th cent.) and St Patrick's Cathedral, Dublin.

Merchants of Bremen and Lübeck opened tent hospital for wounded at Acre; founded Order of German Hospitallers; became monastic order with rules similar to Knights Hospitallers (see 1198).

Consecration of Nôtre Dame Cathedral, Senlis (begun 1153).

German Hospitallers at Acre confirmed by order of Pope.

c. Work begun on present Bamberg Cathedral; consecrated 1237.

Erection of Kuwwait u'l-Islam mosque, commemorating capture of Delhi; oldest extant Mohammedan monument in India.
Work begun on present Lichfield Cathedral (to 1338).

Brazilwood and indigo imported to Britain from India for dyeing purposes.

1194	Richard I released from Austrian prison.	*c. Poetic Edda*, collection of Scandinavian mythology; also called *Elder Edda*.
1195	Armenia and Cyprus acknowledged Holy Roman Emperor as overlord.	
1196	Richard I formed league of Germany, Flanders, Champagne and Brittany against France. Mohammed of Ghor conquered Gwalior and Gujarat.	
1197	Crusaders of the Emperor captured Beirut. †Henry VI; succession disputed; civil war until 1214. Mohammed of Ghor captured Anhilwara.	
1198	Hubert Walter resigned Justiciarship because of heavy taxation levied to pay ransom of Richard I. War between Richard I and Philip II of France renewed. Innocent III became Pope.	William of Newburgh (*c.* †1198): *Historia rerum Anglicorum*, chronicle of period 1066–1198 (begun *c.* 1196).
1199	Richard I killed during war with France; accession of John. Declaration of Speyer by German princes affirmed their right to free election of their king.	
1200	John made peace with France; repudiated his Saxon wife and married Isabella of Angoulême. Anglesey seized by Llewellyn the Great of Gwynedd. Slavery extinct in Bohemia. Danzig colonized by German merchants from Lübeck and Westphalia. *c.* Aztecs established in Mexico.	*c. Carmina Burana*, collection of songs with refrains in German. *c.Nibelungenlied*, national epic of Germany, author unknown; tale of the Nibelungs and their treasure with Siegfried as hero; theme used by Wagner. *c.* Beginnings of Danish language and Portuguese literature.
1201		*c.* Roger of Hoveden: *Chronica maiora*, history of England.
1202	War between John and Philip II of France. John defeated nephew, Arthur of Brittany, in Poitou. First trial of a peer (King John of England) in France. Fourth Crusade launched against Constantinople by Venice.	

Erection of present Chartres Cathedral (completed 1260), on the site of 11th cent. church.

Portsmouth received first Charter.

Incorporation of Limerick, Ireland.

c. Roger of Salerno: *Practica Chirurgica*, early surgical textbook of importance.

La Giralda (campanile) of Seville Cathedral (at that time a mosque); erected by the Moors (see 1402).

Richard I built Château Gaillard, fine castle on the Seine.

Completion of St Demetrius's Cathedral, Vladimir (restored 1835).
Erection of Cathedral of S Maria Assunta, Spoleto; modernized by Bernini in 1634.

Venetian merchants exempted from all customs duties in Eastern Empire.
German Hospitallers converted into Knightly Order: Teutonic Knights.

c. Work begun on Siena Cathedral, which possesses unique ornamentation; many columns of striped marble (see 1325).

Foundation of Liverpool by John.
Teutonic Knights received papal approval.

c. *Ingeborg Psalter*, illuminated manuscript, French Gothic.
c. Hindu Tower of Fame, Chitorgarh.
c. Development of the *Samurai* dwelling, Japan, enclosed by ditch and palisade.
c. Work begun on Bourges Cathedral; Gothic style (to 1280).

c. Chimneys used in England.
c. Alfred of Sareshal translated Avicenna's (*980, †1037) *De Mineralibus* into Latin from Arabic; treatise on geology and alchemy.
Famous bell, *Patarina*, now in tower of Capitol, Rome; used to mourn the passing of the Pope.

Erection (to 1304) of Drapers' Hall, Ypres (destroyed 1915 and rebuilt).

Worcester Cathedral extensively damaged and subsequently rebuilt (see 1224).

Leonardo Fibonacci (*c.* *1170, *c.* †1245): *Liber Abaci*, mathematical work in which Arabic numerals were explained; source of modern system of number notation.

	History	Literature
1203	Arthur of Brittany murdered reputedly by order of his uncle, John of England. Mohammed of Ghor completed conquest of Upper India.	*c.* Wolfram von Eschenbach: *Parzival*, long German epic poem.
1204	John defeated by Philip II; English possessions north of Loire lost. Fourth Crusade; Crusaders captured Constantinople; set up Latin Empire; partitioned Greece. Michael Angelus set up independent Greek kingdom of Epirus, resisting Latin Empire.	
1205	Pope refused to recognize John de Gray as Archbishop of Canterbury. Philip II conquered John's inheritance in Anjou, Maine, Poitou and Touraine. Feudal government in Japan in hands of Hōjō family, who replaced the Minamotos; influence lasted to 1333.	
1206	Innocent III appointed Stephen Langton Archbishop of Canterbury; John refused him and quarrelled with Pope. Council of twenty-four men elected in London.	
1207	John refused Langton permission to land in England.	*c.* Geoffroy de Villehardouin: *Conquête de Constantinople*, eye-witness account of Fourth Crusade; first great literary work in French prose.
1208	Innocent III placed England under Interdict as reproof to John. Francis of Assisi (*c.* *1181, †1226) devoted himself to religion and life of rigorous poverty. Empire of Nicaea founded by Theodore Laskaris.	
1209	John invaded Scotland; peace with William the Lion. Welsh princes took oath to John at Woodstock. John excommunicated by Innocent III. Albigensian Crusade began in southern France; Simon de Montfort the elder overran Languedoc.	Illuminated book on horse-training; earliest extant Islamic work from the important school of Baghdad.

Siena University founded (doubtful).
Unkei and Kaikei made the Niō, S.Gate of Tōdai-ji, Japan; huge figures.

Foundation of Cistercian Abbey of Beaulieu; converted into private residence in 1538.
Foundation of Vicenza University.

Donnybrook Fair in Ireland licensed by John; withdrawn 1855.
Amsterdam, Holland, founded.

Erection of Palazzo Tolomei, Siena.

Declaration of Sultanate of Delhi; with Moslem conquest, Indian culture gained Islamic influence.

†Reinmar of Hagenau, minnesinger.
Solsernus: mosaic of Christ, the Virgin and St John, Spoleto Cathedral.

John granted Charter of Incorporation to Liverpool to become port for Irish trade.

Work begun on Palazzo dei Priori, Volterra; completed 1257.
Rebuilding of St Mary Overie, later (1905) Southwark Cathedral, begun.

Trade treaty between Venice and Sultan al Adil of Egypt; concessions to Venice in return for guarantee of no aid to Crusade.

A section of Oxford University moved to Cambridge and founded the university on the banks of the Cam.

	History	Literature
1210	Franciscan Order of Mendicant Friars founded by Francis of Assisi. Mongol invasion of China began with attacks on Ch'in empire, led by Jenghiz Khan.	*c.* Gottfried von Strassburg: *Tristan und Isold*. Official documentation of *Decretals*, papal pronouncements on doctrine.
1212	Pope Innocent III declared John to be deposed. War between England and France; French fleet partially destroyed. The Children's Crusade: thousands of French and German children starved while crossing Alps; survivors sold into slavery in North Africa. Crete conquered by Venice. Otakar I of Bohemia secured Golden Sicilian Bull, which recognized independence of Bohemian kingdom.	*c.* Gervase of Tilbury: *Otia Imperialia*, written for Emperor Otto IV. Kamo No Chomei (*1153, †1216): *Hojoki*, a record of Japanese author's personal experiences; written in Kamakura Period (1186 to 1332).
1213	John submitted to Innocent III and made England and Ireland Papal Fiefs. Council of St Albans: forerunner of parliament. The Assembly of Soissons.	
1214	French invasion fleet destroyed at Damme in Flanders. Philip II defeated John's forces at Bouvines. Peking captured by Jenghiz Khan.	
1215	English barons under Stephen Langton with army led by Fitzwalter forced John to accept Magna Carta. Innocent III sent foreign troops to help John against barons. Fourth Lateran Council: set out doctrine of Transubstantiation, regulated confession and forbade trial by ordeal. Dominican Friars founded by Spanish monk, St Dominic.	Best-preserved copy of *Magna Carta* is in Lincoln Cathedral.
1216	Baronial armies defeated by John; barons invited Prince Louis of France to take English throne; landed; entered London. †King John; accession of infant Henry III.	*c.* Thomas de Hales: *Love Rune*, poem on the love of Jesus. *c.* Wolfram von Eschenbach: *Willehalm*, long German epic poem.

North transept of Chartres Cathedral begun.
c. Christmas carols probably originated with Francis of Assisi.

c. Great sword of King's Lynn, Norfolk; exact date not known.

Rheims Cathedral designed as the coronation place of French kings: twin towers 275 ft. high; fine flying buttresses (to 1311).
Foundation of Puente de San Martin, fortified Moorish bridge over the Tagus at Toledo; reconstructed 1390.

To reduce fire hazard, tiles replaced thatched and wooden roofs of London houses.

Mosaic pavement in church of S Giovanni Evangelista, Ravenna.
The Angel and Royal, Grantham public-house, one of the oldest in Britain.

Foundation of St Thomas's Hospital, London; originally an almshouse; rebuilt in 1693; present building dates from 1868.

Chancellor of Oxford University appointed.

*Roger Bacon (†1294), greatest scientist of his age.

First statutes for Paris University issued.
Substantial extensions to Norman cathedral of Rochester begun.
c. Construction of nave and chapter-house of Lincoln Cathedral (to 1235).

(to 1255) Rebuilding of South transept of York Minster.

	History	Literature
1217	English baronial forces defeated Louis of France at Lincoln; French invasion fleet defeated at Sandwich; Peace of Lambeth: French left England. Dominican Friars came to England. Crusade launched against Sultanate of Egypt; failed.	Matthew Paris (†1259) became Monk of Benedictine Order at St Albans (see 1235).
1218	Peace made between England and Wales at Worcester. Jenghiz Khan conquered Kwarazm and Transoxania.	
1219	Hubert de Burgh appointed chief minister; England reduced to order. Albigensian War renewed. Valdemar II of Denmark conquered Estonia. Jenghiz Khan and Mongol forces conquered Samarkand, Bokhara and Persia.	
1220	Franciscan Order put on same basis as older monastic orders. *c.* Secular and religious centres of Hamburg united.	*c. Aucassin et Nicolete*; French medieval romance; Aucassin in love with Saracen maiden, Nicolete; written in cantefable form.
1221	Mongols invaded Sultanate of Delhi.	
1222	Council of Oxford established April 23rd, St George's Day, as National Holiday in England. Empire of Thessalonika set up.	*c.* Snorri Sturluson (*1178, †1241), Icelandic historian, compiled *The Prose Edda* (called *Younger Edda*).
1223	Henry III confirmed Magna Carta. Jenghiz Khan launched fresh attack against China. Mongol invasion of Russia; Russians defeated at River Kalka.	
1224	War between England and France; Poitou recaptured. Party of Franciscan Friars landed at Dover. Carmelite Friars, a Mendicant Order, founded by St Berthold. Latin rulers expelled from Asia Minor by Emperor of Nicaea.	Eike of Repgowe: *Saxon Law Code*.

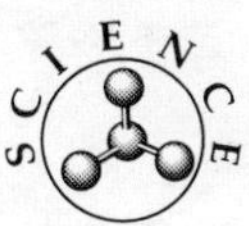

Michael Scot translated *Liber Astronomiae* (Aristotelian astronomic work) of Alpetragius from Arabic into Latin.

Amiens Cathedral burned; rebuilt (1220–1269) by de Luzarches; magnificent carving in choir stalls.
Reconstruction of Le Mans Cathedral, founded by St Julian.

c. Existence of prison at New Gate, London; destroyed 1780.
c. Denmark adopted the Danneborg (Danish Cloth) as national flag (oldest in the world).

Erection of Palazzo della Ragione, Padua; standing on arches; restored.
Oldest bell in England (at Caversfield, Oxfordshire) cast at about this time.

Tallinn (Reval) founded by the Danes.

(to 1258) Erection of present Salisbury Cathedral; early English style.
Lady Chapel added at East end of Westminster Abbey (see 1245).
Erection of Eilean Donan Castle; later rebuilt.

(to 1457) Erection of Burgos Cathedral, Spain, possessing fine openwork spires.

University of Padua founded.

Fibonacci: *Practica Geometriae,* collection of geometric and trigonometric knowledge.

Erection (to 1238) of Palazzo della Ragione, Milan; constructed of brick.

Foundation of Spanish military and religious order of Our Lady of Mercy.

Emperor Frederick II founded University of Naples (see 1258).
†Quesnes de Béthune (*1150), trouvère.
Work begun on choir of Worcester Cathedral.

Yaqut ibn Abdallah ur-Rūmī (*1179, †1229) compiled *Mu'jam ul-Buldān*, important Arabic geographical encyclopaedia.
De Materia Medica of Dioscorides (see 50) translated into Arabic and illustrated by Islamic miniatures of Mongol period.

	History	Literature
1225	England secured Gascony from France. Magna Carta issued for third time; lasting form. Status of Lübeck as Imperial Free City confirmed by Emperor Frederick II. *c.* Patrician town council set up in Bremen.	*Book of Stories* written at Lille; earliest French prose fiction (other than translations from Latin). *c.* Snorri Sturluson: *Heimskringla,* history of Norse king.
1226	Carmelite Order confirmed by Papacy. Frederick II ordered Teutonic Knights to conquer Prussia. Altamsh, Moslem ruler of Northern India, recognized as Sultan of India by the Caliph.	
1227	Henry III came of age and assumed power in England. Truce between England and France. †Jenghiz Khan, whose Empire stretched from Caspian to Pacific.	
1228	†Stephen Langton, now Cardinal Archbishop of Canterbury. Frederick II set out on Sixth Crusade; landed at Acre; captured Jerusalem. Canonization of St Francis of Assisi.	
1229	Treaty of Meaux brought area between Rivers Rhone and Narbonne under French rule. Frederick II and Sultan of Egypt made treaty; Frederick II crowned King of Jerusalem. Carmelite (White) Friars came to England.	*c.* Guido Fava of Bologna: *La Gemma Purpurea,* first Italian literary prose.
1230	Castile and Léon re-united by succession of Ferdinand III of Castile to throne of Léon.	†Walther von der Vogelweide (*c.* *1170), celebrated German lyric poet. *Alfonso et Sabo*: first example of Spanish (Castilian) prose.
1231	Hubert de Burgh replaced as Justiciar of England by Peter des Roches; beginning of illegal exactions, to raise money for Church in Rome. Three years truce between England and France. Pope Gregory IX issued new laws against heretics.	

c. Sumer is icumen in, early English round (MS. in British Museum).
c. The Coronation Spoon, kept at the Tower of London; it is still used during coronations of the monarchs of Gt. Britain.

German trading stations round Baltic made it into a "German Lake".
c. Cotton manufactured in Spain (in England 17th cent).

Completion of Laon Cathedral, begun 1115, replacing old one burnt in 1111; fine Gothic architecture.

Lawrence Vitronius, Norman glassworker, began glass-making in England.
St Gotthard pass opened.

Foundation of present Toledo Cathedral, Spain, by St Ferdinand (completed 1493).

Church of St Francis at Assisi begun; possesses monastery and upper and lower churches.
(to 1256) Rebuilding of N. transept and central tower of York Minster.

Foundation of Michelham Priory, Sussex (Augustinian priory); surrounded by great moat; gatehouse added 1385.

First commercial treaty between Grand Duke of Smolensk and German merchants.

First reference to a gigue (John Garland).
Psalter of Blanche of Castile, French Gothic illuminated manuscript.

Earliest record of the existence of Berlin.

†Folquet de Marseille, troubadour.
c. Work begun on basilican church of St Anthony, Padua; known as Il Santo (completed 1307).

Emperor Frederick II issued *augustales*, first European gold coins minted since Charlemagne abandoned gold standard (see 800).

	History	Literature
1233	Rebellion of Earl of Pembroke against Henry III; supported by Welsh.	
1235	Frederick II declared war against Lombard League. Catalan wars resulted in capture of Valencia by 1245.	Matthew Paris became chronicler of St Alban's Abbey, and continued *Chronica Maiora* (see 1201, 1259). *c.* Roger of Wendover: *Flores Historiarum,* on pagan times.
1236	Marriage of Henry III of England with Eleanor of Provence led to influx of Poitevin and other French favourites. Cordova captured from Moors by Ferdinand III of Castile. Accession of Alexander of Novgorod as Grand Duke of Novgorod.	*c. Roman de la Rose,* early French poem of 20,000 lines; allegory of courtly love; first part by Guillaume de Lorris (see 1276).
1237	Frederick II defeated Lombard League. Mongols invaded Russia second time; conquest complete by 1240.	
1238	Marriage of Simon de Montfort, Earl of Leicester, to sister of Henry III of England. Moscow captured by Mongols.	
1240	Richard of Cornwall and Simon de Montfort went on Crusade to Jaffa. Mongols destroyed Kiev and made Russia tributary. Alexander of Novgorod defeated Swedes at River Neva; won surname of "Nevski". *c.* Border line between England and Scotland fixed at roughly modern position.	*c. Gudrun,* German epic of the sea; manuscript discovered in Ambras Castle in 1820.
1241	Mongol invasion of Poland and Hungary; defeated by Silesians, near Liegnitz; Mongols never returned to the West. "Golden Horde" set up by Batu Khan at Sarai on Lower Volga.	
1242	War between England and France; Henry III defeated at Taillebourg. Alexander Nevski defeated Teutonic Knights at frozen Lake Peipus.	

Pope Gregory IX founded Toulouse university.
c. Vimala Shah temple, domed shrine, built at Mt. Abu, Rajputana.

Coal mined at Newcastle.

Work begun on St Elizabeth's Church, Marburg (completed 1283), and on Strasbourg Cathedral (see 1250), German Gothic work.
Bonaventura Berlinghiere: altarpiece of St Francis of Assisi.

Statute of Merton: regulated rights of villagers in enclosures of wastes in England.
c. Thomas of Cantimpré: *De Natura Rerum*, encyclopaedia of natural history.

c. Completion of great Kutb Minar (238 ft. high) by Sultan Altamsh, in Delhi.
Reliquary of St Elizabeth of Hungary made; German Gothic metalwork.

Gujarati manuscript painting of this date exists on palm-leaf; school of painting existed from 13th to 17th cent.
Yahya of Wasit: 90 illustrations to Schefer MS. of Hariri's *Maqamat*, Islamic work.

Teutonic Order strengthened by absorption of Brethren of the Sword.

Consecration of present Peterborough Cathedral.
Fine Chinese portrait of Wu-Chiin.

Henry III ordered six goldsmiths to supervise work of the craft to stop fraud.

c. *Cimabue, called The Father of Italian painting; there is no proof, however, that he painted the pictures attributed to him.
Choir of Temple Church erected.

Bacon returned to England from studies at Paris University.
c. Evidence that from time immemorial 24 jurymen in Romney Marsh kept watch over sea-wall and water-courses.

Completion of Rheims Cathedral Choir.
Main period of building Early English transepts of York Minster in place of Norman ones.
Siena University founded.

Commercial alliance between Lübeck and Hamburg; led to development of Hanseatic League.

Present groined roof of Gloucester Abbey Church (now cathedral) replaced Norman roof.
Bishop Jocelyn completed nave of Wells Cathedral.

Early record of ship convoy.
Kiel established as town (10th-cent. reference to port).

Year	History	Literature
1243	Five-year truce between England and France. Moorish kingdon of Murcia submitted to Castile.	
1244	Egyptian Khwarazami captured Jerusalem.	
1245	Master Martin, Papal envoy to England, expelled from country. Council of Lyons: Frederick II declared to be dethroned. Civil war in Portugal. Alexander Nevski expelled Lithuanians from Novgorod. John of Plano Carpini, Papal envoy, reached Karakoram; first of many sent to seek Mongol aid against Turks.	*c*. Wernher der Gartenaere: *Meier Helmbrecht*, earliest German example of peasant romance.
1246	Emperor of Nicaea conquered Salonika.	
1247	Innocent IV transformed Carmelite Order into one of Mendicant Friars. Georgia became vassal state to Persia.	
1248	De Montfort became Seneschal of Gascony. Frederick II defeated by Lombard League at Parma. Ferdinand III of Castile captured Seville. Genoese captured Rhodes.	
1249	Truce between England and France extended. Crusade of Louis IX hampered by 1208 treaty between Venice and Egypt. Sweden extended rule over Finland.	
1250	Gascon revolt against de Montfort; subdued 1251. †Frederick II, last Hohenstaufen Emperor. Louis IX (St Louis) captured by Saracens. Commencement of Mamluk rule in Egypt.	Bartholomaeus Anglicus: *De Proprietatibus Rerum*, encyclopaedia showing state of knowledge of his day.
1251	Austria seized by Otakar II of Bohemia. Mangu Khan became the Great Khan and Kublai Khan became Governor of China.	

SCIENCE

Salamanca University confirmed by Ferdinand III of Castile.

First competition for Dunmow Flitch.

Work commenced on present Westminster Abbey (main part finished 1269).

Erection of La Sainte-Chapelle, Paris; to 1258.

Hugo d'Oignies: shrine of St Eleutherius, Tournai Cathedral.

Foundation of Bethlehem Hospital, London, by Simon Fitzmary (see 1407).

Present Cologne Cathedral commenced; great Gothic church.
Work begun on the Alhambra, Granada; Islamic architecture.

(to 1252) Alfonsine Tables drawn up for Alfonso X of Castile.
Kiel and Tallinn joined Hanseatic League.

University College, Oxford, founded by William of Durham.

Bacon recorded existence of explosives and *may* have invented gunpower (doubtful).

Construction (to 1275) of nave of Strasbourg Cathedral.
c. Regressive Pueblo period in South-west N. America (to *c.* 1400).

First German factory at Novgorod.
c. The cog, a broad-beamed clinker-built vessel developed.
c. Walter of Henly: *Hosebondrie*, standard work on land husbandry.

Indjeminareli mosque, Konya (Turkey) built; possesses fine entrance.
Work begun on St Mary's, Lübeck.

Lübeck obtained extensive water rights for its mills.
German merchants got control of trade in Stockholm area (see 1255).

Year	History	Literature
1252	William of Rubruquis made journey to Central Asia for Louis IX; returned 1255 Alexander Nevski became Grand Prince of Vladimir.	
1253	Renewal of Anglo-French truce. Richard of Cornwall refused to accept crown of Sicily offered by Pope Innocent IV. Foundation of Ahom kingdom in Assam.	
1254	Louix IX returned to France from Palestine. Representatives of Portuguese towns sat in the Cortes for first time.	Foundation of University Library, Salamanca, Spain.
1255	Henry III accepted crown of Sicily for his son, Edmund.	
1256	Simon de Montfort assumed leadership of English barons against misrule of Henry III. Order of Augustine Hermits set up by Pope Alexander IV.	*c.* Albertus Magnus (*c.* *1206, †1280), called *doctor universalis*, completed much of his work, including *De Causis et Processu Universitatis*.
1257	Richard of Cornwall elected King of Germans. Llewellyn of Gwynedd styled himself Prince of Wales, having obtained Anglesey, Snowdon and Powys.	Sa'di (*c.* *1184, †1291): *Fruit Garden*, Persian poems; poet appears to have lived about 107 years.
1258	Welsh border troubles caused Henry II to call Council at Oxford; provisions required Henry to rule according to Magna Carta. Treaty of Corbeil between Louis IX of France and James I of Catalonia fixed Pyrenees frontier. Baghdad captured and destroyed by Mongols under Hulagu Khan.	Sa'di: *Rose Garden*. Persian poems. *The Thousand and One Nights* (Persian); series of Oriental tales first collected together about 1450.
1259	Peace established between England and Wales. Treaty of Paris defined English possessions in France for which Henry III did homage to Louis IX. Michael VIII Palaeologus crushed empire of Thessalonika; forced it to cede territory. Syria invaded by Mongols.	*Chronica maiora* ended with †Matthew Paris (see 1235).

Arts	Science
Official establishment of University of Bologna (originally founded 1116). Gold florin minted in Florence (see 1189).	Anatomical treatise by Richard of Wendover: MS. still extant. Trading privileges granted to German merchants in Bruges.
Completion, at Assisi, of Church of St Francis; famous for pilgrimages.	Linen first manufactured in England. Frankfurt-on-Oder joined Hanseatic League.
Volterra Cathedral enlarged by artists from Pisa.	Campanus of Novara issued important edition of Euclid's *Elements*, containing significant developments; standard work for 300 years.
Towers and West front of Ripon Cathedral erected; Early English style.	Birger Jarl believed to have founded Stockholm.
Robert de Sorbonne, chaplain to Louis IX, founded Sorbonne, Paris, as theological college of the university.	First meeting of "Wendish" towns of the Hanse.
	c. Bacon at work on: (i) *De Speculis*; (ii) *De Mirabili Potestate Artis et Naturae*.
Establishment of the House of Commons. Naples University refounded after temporary suppression.	First law relative to roads connecting market towns.
	First mention of Hamburg's Maritime Laws. Agreement among "Wendish" towns—Lübeck, Wismar, Rostock, Stralsund—to protect citizens against pirates and highwaymen.

	History	Literature
1260	Florentine Ghibellines defeated Guelphs at Montaperti. Hungarians defeated by Otakar II of Bohemia, who received Styria. Sultan of Egypt defeated Mongols at Ain Jalut; set himself up as Caliph in Cairo. Kublai Khan succeeded as Great Khan.	
1261	Michael VIII Palaeologus regained Constantinople; overthrew Latin Empire.	
1262	Welsh under Llewellyn carried out successful border war against English. Iceland under Norwegian rule. Moslem kingdom of Niebla annexed to Castile.	*c.* Adam de la Halle, trouvère: *Le Jeu de la Feuillée,* first French comic play.
1263	De Montfort returned from France to lead barons against Henry III. Haco of Norway made last Scandinavian invasion of Scotland; defeated; Scotland gained Hebrides. †Alexander Nevski, last Russian prince to rule from Vladimir.	
1264	Mise of Amiens: Louis IX of France, arbiter between Henry III and English barons, decided in favour of Henry; provisions of Oxford annulled. Battle of Lewes: Henry III defeated by de Montfort and English barons. Battle of Trapani: Genoese defeated by Venetians.	Thomas Aquinas (*1225, †1274), Neapolitan theologian, completed *Summa contra Gentiles* (begun 1259), great theological work of this period; Aquinas canonized 1323.
1265	De Montfort's "Parlement": archbishops, bishops, abbots, earls, barons, knights and burgesses from towns summoned to King's Council. Battle of Evesham; de Montfort defeated and killed by Prince Edward. Charles of Anjou invested with Naples and Sicily by Clement IV.	
1266	Award of Kenilworth: Barons, dispossessed for their part in the rebellion, received back lands after paying fines.	Bacon: *Opus Maius,* a summary of the current state of knowledge.

Niccola Pisano built marble pulpit of Pisa Baptistry.
Cimabue: *Madonna della Trinità*.
Erection of Charney Manor, Berkshire; earliest open-plan manor house.

Bacon explained laws of reflection and refraction of light.
c.Albertus Magnus: *De Mineralibus et Rebus Metallicus*, geological treatise.
Bremen joined Hanseatic League.

Renewal of trade treaty between Cairo and Constantinople.

John Baliol, of Barnard Castle, Co. Durham, founded Balliol College, Oxford.

c. Bacon: *De Computo Naturali*, important work of natural philosophy.

Walter de Merton, Bishop of Rochester, founded Merton College, Oxford.
A company in Rome permitted to act Christ's sufferings—Passion Play.
Foundation of Ferrara University.

c. Vincent of Beauvais (†): *Speculum Maius*, vast encyclopaedia in three parts—(1) *Speculum Naturale*, (2) *Speculum Doctrinale*, (3) *Speculum Historiale*—collating knowledge of all time.

First record of Papal *annulus piscatoris*.
c. Music of Franco of Cologne and Pierre de la Croix (to 1300) helped develop motet; Franconian reform: *musica mensurata*.

Erection of Sanjūsangendō, Kyoto; temple 384 ft. long; veranda used for Samurai archery practice.

Bacon described the use of prototype of magnifying glass (*Opus Maius*).
Introduction of "Statute of the Pillory".

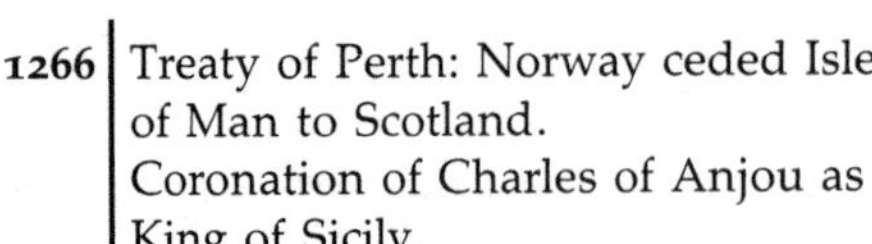

Year	History	Literature
1266	Treaty of Perth: Norway ceded Isle of Man to Scotland. Coronation of Charles of Anjou as King of Sicily.	
1267	Treaty of Shrewsbury: Henry III recognized Llewellyn as Prince of Wales. Louis IX of France prepared for a Crusade. Dispute between Portugal and Castile over suzerainty of the Algarve settled in favour of Portugal.	
1268	Antioch captured from Christians by Egyptian Moslems. Royal line of Abyssinia restored by Icon Amlac. Kublai Khan prepared for invasion of Japan.	†Henry de Bracton, who wrote *De Legibus et Consuetudinibus Angliae*, first comprehensive study of English laws and customs. Bacon: *Opus Minus*, encyclopaediae of knowledge to date.
1269	Prince Edward of England set out to join Louis IX on the Crusade. Otakar II of Bohemia acquired Carinthia, Carniola and Istria from Hungary.	
1270	Louis IX of France set out on Seventh, and last, Crusade to Tunis; died there; succeeded by Philip III.	
1271	Prince Edward landed at Acre; captured Nazareth. Toulouse and Poitou became part of French crown.	
1272	†Henry III of England; accession of Edward I, absent on Seventh Crusade. †Richard of Cornwall, King of the Germans.	Robert of Gloucester and others composed a metrical chronicle from ancient times to this date.
1273	Rudolph of Habsburg elected King of Romans. Everlasting League, or League of Uri, formed in Switzerland.	†Djelaleddin Rumi, Persian poet.
1274	Edward I returned to England. Llewellyn of Wales refused to take oath of allegiance to Edward I. Rudolph of Habsburg recognized as Emperor by Pope Gregory X. Second Council of Lyons regulated Papal Elections.	Arnold FitzThedmar (*1201, †1274): *Chronica Maiorum et Vicecomitum*, chronicle, completed.

Niccola Pisano completed Arca di San Domenico in church at Bologna.

Fierce battle in London between the Guilds of Goldsmiths and of Tailors; 500 men engaged and many were killed.

Niccola Pisano carved marble pulpit of Siena Cathedral; his finest work.

Comyn's Tower, Blair Castle, Perthshire, built.

First toll-roads begun in England.
Magnetic compass needle, previously floating on straw, now mounted on a pivot; described by Peter Peregrinus of Picardy.

St Edmund Hall, Oxford, founded.
Foundation of Academy of Fine Arts, Florence.

Wide tidal river Maas dammed, water joined Rhine round a new polder called "Holland".

The kreuzer, German coin, first struck.

Marco Polo (*c.* *1254, †1324) of Venice set out on journey to China.

Foundation of the University of Florence; refounded 1924.
Monnow Bridge, Monmouth, erected.

Mechanical process of silk winding on reels believed to have originated at Bologna.

Completion of church of Ste Gudule, Brussels (begun *c.* 1220); fine pointed Gothic.

Regulation passed prohibiting burning of coal in England.

Mingalazedi, Pagan, Burma: square-based shrine with circular top.
Niccola Pisano began work on great fountain at Perugia.

Commercial treaty between England and Flanders.

	History	Literature
1274	Kublai Khan's attempt to invade Japan failed.	
1275	Statute of Westminster: planned by Edward I to provide for correction of abuses in administration of Justice; Court of King's Bench, Chancery Common Pleas and Exchequer finally settled; wool duties granted to Crown. Statute of Bigamy. Marco Polo entered service of Kublai Khan; remained until 1292.	Completion of Swabian Law Code.
1276	First Welsh War started by Edward I. Year of three popes: Innocent V, Gregory X, Adrian V. Mongols captured Hangchow, capital of Sung empire.	Jean de Meung continued *Roman de la Rose* (see 1236).
1277	Treaty of Conway: Llewellyn, defeated by Edward I, had his power reduced. Second year of three popes: Adrian V, John XXI, Nicholas II.	Abutsu: *Izayoi No Ki*, important Japanese account of a journey to Kamakura.
1278	Edward I sent out first writs of Quo Warranto to determine rights to land holdings. Statute of Gloucester restricted feudal jurisdiction. Otakar II of Bohemia rebelled against Rudolph; defeated and killed at Durnkrut; Austria permanently possessed for Habsburgs. Emperor Rudolph renounced Romagna.	
1279	Statute of Mortmain forbade gift of land to monasteries or corporate bodies, since they could perform no feudal service.	
1280	Asen dynasty extinguished in Bulgaria; country subject to Serbs, Greeks and Mongols. Young heir to last Sung emperor captured by Mongols; murdered. Kublai Khan founded Yüan Dynasty in China (to 1368).	*c.* Rutebeuf: (*Œuvres*, French lyrical and satirical poems; edited 1839).
1281	Great Mongol attack on Japan, with Korean and Chinese fleets carrying 150,000 men; heavily defeated by Japanese.	

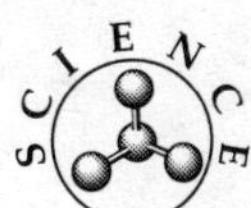

Building of Ratisbon Cathedral commenced; completed 1634.
c. Erection of Khmer temple of Angkor Wat, Cambodia; discovered by Henri Mouhot in 1861.
c. Kao K'o-Kung: *Landscape after Rain*, Chinese painting.

c. The *Carte Pisane*, earliest extant compass-chart for seamen (earliest form of medieval map, called *portolano*).
Earliest record of human dissection in *Chirurgia*, by William of Saliceto.
Glastonbury destroyed by earthquake.

Earliest extant monumental brass: Sir John d'Aubernon's grave (Surrey).
Erection of León Cathedral (to 1303); Spanish Gothic architecture.

Bacon imprisoned for heresy, until 1292.

(to 1283) Erection of Campo Santo, Pisa, by Giovanni Pisano; badly damaged in World War II.
Work begun on church of Santa Maria Novella, Florence.

278 Jews hanged in London for clipping coin; Christians, guilty of same offence, only fined.
Special liberties granted to Cinque Ports.

(to 1283) Castel Nuovo, Naples, magnificently proportioned building, erected.

c. Devorguilla's Bridge built over the Nith in Dumfries.
c. Exquisite stained-glass windows began to be widely used in Western European churches; ceased. *c.* 1550.

†Albertus Magnus, scientist and philosopher.
Invention of *glass* mirror.
Hanse formed in England by German merchants.

Year	History	Literature
1282	Revolt of Llewellyn and his brother David of Wales, against Edward I; Llewellyn defeated and killed. French expelled from Sicily. Emperor Rudolph invested sons Albert and Rudolph with Austria, Styria and Carniola. Danish nobles extorted from Eric Klipping, King of Denmark, charter promising to summon a national assembly, a "parlamentum"	
1283	Edward I set up provincial councils at York and Canterbury. David of Wales captured and executed. Rostock Alliance of Baltic towns formed for protection of peace in Baltic.	
1284	Statute of Wales regulated conquered territory; Wales divided into counties on English pattern. Genoese defeated Pisans in sea fight off Meloria; decline of Pisa followed.	
1285	Statute of Winchester dealt with problems of public order and national defence; Justices of Peace appointed. Bremen excluded from Hanseatic League because of political conflicts; re-admitted 1358. Accession of Henry II, last Christian king of Jerusalem.	Earliest completely extant Swedish literature in Latin letters (not runes), a codex.
1286	†Alexander III of Scotland; accession of his niece, Margaret, the Maid of Norway, an infant.	
1287	German National Council at Würzburg: Peace of Würzburg. Mongol invasion of Burma; fall of Pagan, capital of Burma.	†Conrad of Würzburg, main German poet of this period.
1288	Crusade against Ladislaus IV of Hungary proclaimed by Pope Nicholas IV. Foundation of Ottoman Empire by Osman I.	
1289	Treaty of Salisbury among England, Scotland and Norway. Scotland under English influence. Pope Nicholas IV ceded half of papal revenue to College of Cardinals.	

Bells used to signal "Sicilian Vespers"; name given to massacre of French in Sicily.
Hōjō Tokimune erected Shariden (Relic Hall), Engaku-ji, sole surviving Kamakura building of the period.
Construction of Albi Cathedral, France; fortress church.

Ristoro: *La Composizione del Mondo*, astrological treatise on geology, but containing a number of sound scientific ideas.
First mention of Alamania Hanse in place of Cologne Hanse marked union of Baltic and Rhenish merchants.

(to 1323) Erection of Caernarvon Castle; probably most important of those built by Edward I, who began Harlech Castle in same year.

Statute of Merchants: provision made for safeguarding of traders against loss due to debt.

Hugh de Balsham founded Peterhouse, Cambridge.
Edward I erected Conway Castle.

The Dover Seal; illustrates a 13th-cent. ship.
Venetians first coined *sequins*.

c. Adam de la Halle (*c.* *1238, †1288): *Jeu de Robin et Marion*, earliest French play with music; by the Father of *opéra comique*.
c. Erection of Orvieto Cathedral begun (to 1580).

High roads between towns widened by law, partly to reduce risk of robbery.
c. Watermarks in good-quality paper.

So-called tomb of Honorius IV, Church of Aracoeli, Rome.

c. Rufinus: *Herbal*, fine book of medical herbs and of general botany.

Erection of Palazzo Pubblico at Siena (to 1309); Gothic brick building; Torre del Mangia (bell-tower) added 1338–43.

Montpellier University confirmed by Pope Nicholas IV.

Block printing at Ravenna.

	History	Literature
1290	Treaty of Brigham between England and Scotland. Edward I annexed Isle of Man. Third Statute of Westminster. Edward I banished all Jews from England; real estate confiscated by Crown; exiles allowed to take coin and movables.	*c.* Dante Alighieri (*1265, †1321): *Vita Nuova*; early relation of author's love for Beatrice; Dante was virtually responsible for establishment of standard Italian language.
1291	Edward I called in to settle succession dispute in Scotland, between cousins Robert Bruce and John Baliol; favoured Baliol. †Rudolph I. Mamluks captured Acre; end of Christian rule in Near East; Knights of St John of Jerusalem driven from Acre settled in Cyprus.	
1292	Adolph of Nassau elected German King. †Kublai Khan.	
1293	War between England and France; Guienne lost to English. Edward I restored Isle of Man to Scotland. Adolph seized Thuringia and Meissen. First Christian missionaries in China.	
1294	Adolph of Germany joined Edward I against France. Beginning of Franco-Scottish alliance; John Baliol and Philip IV against Edward I. Church refused demand of Edward I for half of annual income of clergy. Rebellion in Wales.	
1295	Edward I summoned the "Model Parliament", first truly representative English parliament. Welsh defeated at Conway. Baliol defeated by English at Battle of Dunbar.	*c.* *The Harrowing of Hell*, one of earliest known English Miracle Plays (date doubtful).
1296	Edward I captured Berwick, Edinburgh and Stirling Castle; Baliol deposed. Papal Bull forbade clerics to pay taxes to temporal powers; opposed by Edward I and Philip IV of France.	Chou Ta-kuan described ancient Khmer city of Angkor Thom.

Lisbon University founded by King Dinis (see 1308); refounded 1911.
c. Beautifully carved oak stalls of Winchester Cathedral; earliest English woodwork (to 1300).

c. Invention of spectacles (see 1303).

*Philippe de Vitri (†1361), important musician, who developed notation and time values.
Erection of York Minster nave.
Erection of Charing Cross, London, and Waltham Cross, Hertfordshire, by Edward I in memory of Eleanor.

Erection of Hellens, Herefordshire, begun; ancient manor house.

Torgils Knutsson erected castle at Viborg; formed nucleus of city.
Foundation of King's College, Taunton; boys' public school.

Arnolfo di Cambio began work on S. Croce at Florence.
Work begun on Cathedral of San Gennaro, Naples; completed 1323; western façade 1906.

Peace of Tonsberg confirmed economic control of Norway by Hanse.

Triumph of Mary, mosaic by Turriti in S. Maria Maggiore, Rome.
c. Erection of great mosque of Kilwa, E. Africa (rebuilt *c*. 1430).
(to 1298) Edward I built Beaumaris Castle.

Letters of Marque granting licence to seize any enemy's property; discontinued 1856.
Marco Polo returned to Venice from the East.

Florence Cathedral: building started by Arnolfo di Cambio.
Earliest dated bell in Britain.
Edward I took Scottish crown, sceptre and "Stone of Destiny" (Stone of Scone; see –700) to England.

Lanfranchi: *Chirurgica Magna*, surgical textbook.
Guild of Merchant Adventurers began at Brabant.

	History	Literature
1297	Confirmation of Magna Carta and Charter of Forests. Parliament invested with sole right of raising money apart from feudal claims. Truce between England and France. English defeated by Sir William Wallace at Stirling. Genoese defeated Venetians in sea battle off Curzola.	
1298	Edward I defeated Wallace at battle of Stirling. Emperor Adolph deposed by Electors; defeated and killed at Gollheim; Albert I of Austria elected King of Germans.	Marco Polo: *Travels*, account of Venetian traveller's journeys through Asia.
1299	Confirmation of Charters again renewed by Edward I. Anglo-French truce made at Montreuil. Alliance between Philip IV of France and Albert I of Germany.	
1300	Edward I invaded Scotland. Pope Boniface VIII claimed right to arbitrate quarrel between England and Scotland. Wenceslas II of Bohemia elected King of Poland. Metropolitan of Russian Church made Vladimir his official see.	*c.* Robert of Gloucester: history of England; in Old English rhymed couplets (from Brut to 1272). *c.* Jewish *Zohar* (Book of Splendour) compiled.
1301	English parliament rejected papal interference between England and Scotland. Edward I's son created Prince of Wales. Osman I defeated Byzantine forces at Baphaion.	
1302	The Flemings defeated an army of French knights at Courtrai. First meeting of the French Estates General. Papal Bull declared papal authority supreme (*Unam Sanctam*). Bordeaux evicted French and admitted English. Malik Kafur, former Hindu slave, conquered Southern India.	

Work begun on fine cloisters of Norwich Cathedral (completed 1430).
c. Giotto di Bordone (*1267, †1337) painted four frescoes in Lower Church at Assisi.

Dutch reclamation farmers drained land and founded town of Prussian Holland in Vistula delta.
Earliest reliable record of Chinese possessing marine compass (see 270).

Giovanni Pisano carved bas-relief in S. Andrea church, Pistoia.
Giotto: *Navicella*, mosaic of Christ saving St Peter.

Riot involving bloodshed between the university and city of Oxford.

(to 1301) Erection of Palazzo Vecchio, Florence.
Giovanni di Cosma: tomb of Cardinal Rodriguez, Rome.
En-I: *Ippen Shōnin* scroll painting (in 12 rolls); Japanese.

Parliament in England passed a law to suppress bad coinage.
Lübeck adopted Hamburg's Maritime Laws.
Commercial treaty between Venice and the Turks.

c. Earliest madrigals, for unaccompanied voices.
c. The "Guardians" of the Goldsmiths Guild assayed all silver articles with a leopard's head (hall-mark).
Foundation of Academy of Fine Arts, Palermo.
Coronation Chair, Westminster Abbey, made.

c. Commissioners of sewers appointed in S. English counties to supervise protective and reclamation work on S. coast.
c. *Liber Ignium*, Latin MS., contained earliest Western reference to *manufacture* of gunpowder (see 1249).

Giovanni Pisano carved the fine pulpit of S. Andrea at Pistoia; earliest of his pulpits in Tuscany.

Completion of Chapter House of Wells Cathedral (begun 1290); octagonal plan.
Palazzo dei Papi, Orvieto (begun 1264) completed.
Giovanni Pisano carved the pulpit of Pisa Cathedral (to 1310).

Bartolommeo da Varignana: first detailed record of a *post mortem* examination.
Charles II of Anjou began construction of Porto Grande, extension of Naples harbour.

Year	History	Literature
1303	Gascony restored to England by Treaty of Paris. French Estates General supported Philip IV against claims of papacy to supremacy. Last Mongol invasion of Syria defeated at Damascus.	
1304	Confirmation of Charters again extorted from Edward I by barons. Capture, trial and execution of Wallace. Philip IV again defeated Flemings by sea and land.	*c.* Dante: *Convivio (Banquet)*, uncompleted philosophical study.
1305	Execution of Sir William Wallace in London. Treaty of Athis between France and Flemings. Clement V elected Pope.	
1306	Scots revolted under Robert Bruce; latter crowned at Scone; defeated by English at Methven. Clement V declared *Unam Sanctam* invalid in France. Philip IV expelled Jews from France.	
1307	English forces defeated by Bruce at Loudon Hill. †Edward I on way to invade Scotland; accession of Edward II. Piers Gaveston, favourite of Edward II in power at intervals to 1312. Clement V ordered arrest of Templars. Archbishopric of Peking set up under John of Pontecorvine.	*Red Register of Lynn*, one of earliest paper books in existence; municipal records of King's Lynn.
1308	Edward II of England married Isabella of France. Edward II seized all Templar property. English barons insisted on banishment of Piers Gaveston. Henry VII of Luxembourg elected King of Germans.	†Duns Scotus, Scottish theologian, founder of a scholastic system; the word "dunce" came from his name.
1309	Robert Bruce joined by the Douglases against England. Clement V fixed papal residence at Avignon: start of "Babylonian Captivity". Henry VII recognized the Swiss League.	Jean de Joinville (†1317): *Histoire de Saint Louis*, life of saintly Louis IX of France by his intimate friend.

Foundation of University of Rome.

Bremen adopted Hamburg's Mercantile Laws.
Bernard of Gordon: first medical reference to spectacles.
Edward I granted privileges to foreign merchants in England: *Carta Mercatoria*.

All Saints' Day flood in N. Germany; did enormous damage.
Pietro de Crescenzi: *Opus ruralium commodorum*; start of modern agriculture.

c. Giotto: *The Mourning of Christ*, wall-painting, Capella dell'Arena, Padua.

Edward I standardized certain units of measurement, e.g. the yard, the acre.

Erection of Broughton Castle, Oxfordshire; extended in 16th cent.
Giotto: *Faith*, wall-painting, Capella dell'Arena, Padua.

Erection of Palazzo Chiaramonte, Palermo, begun; now used as Court of Justice.
Beginnings of Geometrical Pointed architecture.
Completion of Lincoln Cathedral tower (271 ft.).

Incorporation of Bakers' Company in London.

Lisbon University moved to Coimbra.

(to 1424) Doge's Palace, most impressive secular building of the period, built on site of earlier palaces in Venice.
Foundation of Orleans University.

Foundation of the Free Counter at Bruges.

1309 Union of Aragon and Valencia. Danzig came under Teutonic Knights when latter seized Polish Pomerania.

1310 Edward II forced to appoint Lords Ordainers for better ruling of England. Scots recaptured their towns held by English. Henry VII gave Bohemia to his son, John of Luxembourg. Moslems, under Malik Kafur, captured Mysore.

c. Queen Mary's Psalter, finely illuminated manuscript.

1311 Lords Ordainers transferred government from Edward II to his barons. Scots plundered North of England. Moslems captured Madura, Pandya capital.

Raymond Lully persuaded Council of Vienne to establish university faculties of foreign languages.

1312 Revolt of English barons against Edward II; execution of Piers Gaveston. Scots under Bruce invaded England. Treaty of Vienne: Lyons became part of France.

Dante: *De Monarchia*, expressing his political views, in three books.

1313 Scots recaptured Perth. †Henry VII, German king and Holy Roman Emperor.

1314 Edward II invaded Scotland; defeated by Bruce at Bannockburn. Edward II to dismiss friends from council and replace them by Lancaster's nominess. Jacques de Molay, Grand Master of Templars, burned at stake in Paris. Frederick of Austria and Lewis IV of Bavaria elected Kings of Germany.

c. Dante: *La Divina Commedia* begun; visionary journey through Hell, Purgatory and Paradise; cantos in terza rima; greatest literary work of Middle Ages; this time virtually marks the beginning of the Italian Renaissance.

1315 Leopold of Austria defeated at Morgaten; Swiss League renewed.

1316 Earl of Lancaster in almost absolute power in England. Edward Bruce, brother of Robert, crowned King of Ireland. Election of Pope John XXII after vacancy of 27 months. Accession of Grand Duke Gedimin, founder of Lithuanian empire.

(to 1320) Kariye Camii, Constantinople, Byzantine church with two ante-chambers, erected.
c. Giotto: *The Ascension*, Italian fresco.
Erection of Chirk Castle, Wrexham; unaltered.

John Maudith known to have used the tangent of an angle, in trigonometry.

Foundation of the Guild of Master-singers at Mainz.
Duccio di Buoninsegna (**c.* 1255, †1319), Italian painter, finished masterpiece *Maesta* (panel painting) for Siena Cathedral.

Earliest extant dated portolano, a type of navigational chart.

c. Giotto: *The Madonna of the Ognissanti*, huge altarpiece (9 ft high).

Order of Knights Templars dissolved by papal decree; property transferred to Hospitallers.

*c.*Invention of cannon attributed to Berthold Schwartz, German Grey Friar.

Walter de Stepeldon, Bishop of Exeter, founded Exeter College, Oxford.
Completion of Old St Paul's Cathedral, London.

The Hereford *Mappa Mundi*, symbolic type map.

Simone Martini (†1344): *Virgin in Majesty*, fresco at Palazzo Pubblico, Siena.

c. Silk industry developed in Lyons by Italian immigrants.

Erection of Loggia degli Ossi, Milan, palace of black and white marble.
John XXII began work on Avignon papal palace (completed 1370).

Anatomia, textbook of anatomy completed by Mondini of Luzzi (*c.* *1275, †1326), who used corpse dissection for teaching purposes.

1317 Salic Law barring women from succession to French Throne.
John XXII claimed imperial powers for papacy in Italy.
Order of Templars suppressed in Spain; James II of Aragon founded Order of Montesa and endowed it with Templar estates.

1318 Treaty of Leek between Edward II and his barons.
Edward Bruce killed in battle; Scots recaptured Berwick.
Truce between Swiss League and Habsburgs.
Portuguese military and religious Order of Christ founded and endowed with confiscated Templar property.

1319 English defeated by Scots at Myton.
Despensers (banished 1321) in power as favourites of Edward II.
Accession of Magnus VII united Sweden and Norway under one ruler.

1320 Scots ravaged northern English counties until 1321.
Black Parliament at Scone tried 70 people for plots against Bruce.
France and Flanders settled differences at Peace of Paris.
Kiev conquered by Gedimin of Lithuania.
Sultan of Delhi murdered; accession of Tughlak dynasty brought period of waste, ferocity and famine.

Literature:
c. *Guy of Warwick*, long romance in verse form.
c. *The Lay of Havelock the Dane*, verse romance.

1322 Abortive invasion of Scotland by Edward II.
Despensers recalled by Edward II.
Thomas of Lancaster revolted; defeated and executed.
English parliament enacted that all legislation required consent of both King and Parliament.
Lewis IV captured Frederick of Austria at Mühldorf.

1323 Truce between Edward II and Robert Bruce.
Escape of Roger Mortimer, supporter of Lancaster, to Paris.

c. Mosaics of New Testament in Kariye Camii, Constantinople.

Matthaeus Sylvaticus: *Pandectae*, dictionary of medical herbs.
German trading privileges restricted to Hanse in England by Edward II.

Angelus ad virginem, early English popular song.

c. Issue of *Speculum Morale*, originally thought to be fourth section of *Speculum Maius* of Vincent of Beauvais.

Completion of La Ghirlandina, bell-tower, 282 ft high, in Modena; begun 1224.

Cannon may have been used at the siege of Berwick (see 1346), which Edward II failed to retake.

(to 1330) Giotto carried out famous frescoes in Bardi and Peruzzi chapels, including *St Louis of Toulouse* and *Dance of Salome*.
Pietro Lorenzetti (*c.* *1280, †1348), brother of Ambroglio: altarpiece at S. Maria della Piere, Arezzo.

The Steelyard, London factory of the Hanse, occupied premises between Upper Thames Street and the River Thames.
Richard of Wallingford constructed an astronomical clock of considerable interest.

Completion of Octagon of Ely Cathedral by Alan of Walsingham.
Consecration of choir of present Cologne Cathedral (begun *c.* 1248), largest N. European Gothic church.

c. Reinvention of saw-mill for timber.

Caernarvon Castle completed (begun 1283).

1324 Charles IV of France recovered Gascony.
Moors recaptured Baza from Castile.
Germany resisted papal claims to supremacy.
Lewis IV excommunicated.

1325 Lewis IV accepted Frederick of Austria as co-regent.
Muhammad Adil became Sultan of Delhi.
Russian Metropolitan, Peter, made Moscow his official residence.

Ramon Muntaner (*1265, †1336), Catalan chronicler and soldier, began *Chrónica*.
c. Horne Childe, a verse romance.
c. Development of the Nō play in Japan, by adding dialogue to form of music and dancing called *Kagura*.

1326 Isabella, wife of Edward II, and Mortimer, now her lover, invaded England; Despensers captured and executed; Edward II a prisoner.
Ottoman Turks captured Brussa.

1327 Edward II deposed by Parliament; accession of Edward III; government in hands of Isabella and Mortimer; Edward II murdered at Berkeley Castle.
Scots invasion of England.
Charles IV restored Guienne to England.

Francesco Petrarca (*1304, †1374) (called Petrarch), Italian poet, first saw Laura who inspired his poems (see 1366).

1328 Treaty of Northampton between England and Scotland; Robert Bruce recognized as King of Scotland.
†Charles IV, last of Capet kings of France; accession of Philip VI.
Louis IV crowned Emperor in Rome; declared John XII deposed for heresy and lèse-majesté.

1329 †Robert Bruce and accession of David II to Scottish throne.
Compact of Pavia: separation of Bavaria and Palatine.

1330 Edward III assumed power in England; Mortimer hanged as traitor.
Treaty of Hagenau gave Habsburg recognition to Lewis IV on death of Frederick of Austria.

1331 Danes defeated by Gerard (the Great) of Holstein at Danewerk.
Accession of Stefan IV, Dushan founder of Greater Serbia.

Consecration of Burgos Cathedral.

Siena Cathedral and Baptistry of San Giovanni largely completed; West front built *c.* 1377–80.
c. Classical period of Hokoham culture, along Colorado River and parts of Arizona and Mexico, superseded Sedentary period.
c. Jean Pucelle illustrated the *Breviary of Belleville*, French Gothic work.

c. The Luttrell Psalter, important illustrated manuscript showing many details of everyday life and many machines in use.
c. Construction of famous clock of Glastonbury (now vanished; once believed to have been clock now at Wells).

Oriel College, Oxford, founded by Edward II; Clare College, Cambridge, founded in same year.

Manuscript illustrating an English gun called *pot de fer* (Walter de Milemete).
Mineral springs discovered at Spa, Belgium; hence adaptation of name.

Jean Pucelle, first important French painter to make birds, animals and flowers look real, illustrated Bible now in Bibliothèque Nationale.
Beginnings of Decorated architecture.

Guild of London Goldsmiths incorporated by Royal Charter; and Skinners' Company in same year.
Traditional date (or 1325) for establishment of Mexico City by Aztecs.

Martini: *Guidoriccio da Fogliano*, fresco, Palazzo Pubblico, Siena.

Thomas Bradwardine (*1290, †1349): *Tractalis Proportionum*, early investigation into kinematics, using algebra.
c. John of Milano: *Flos Medicinae*, illustrated herbal.
Incorporation of Merchant Taylors' Company, London.

Completion of S. Maria della Spina, white marble church at Pisa (begun 1325).

Visconti erected (to 1336) San Gottardo Church, now incorporated in Palazzo Reale, Milan.
Emperor Lewis IV founded monastery of Ettal, Bavaria.

Erection of Wiesenkirche, Soest (to 1376); German Gothic architecture.
Goffredo da Viterbo illuminated the *Liber Pantheon*.

At York, first record of weaving in England.

1331 Disputed Imperial succession in Japan led to civil war against Hōjō regents.

1332 Parliament in England provisionally divided into two Houses for first time.
Civil war in Scotland.
Denmark lost Schonen to Sweden.

1333 Renewal of war between England and Scotland; Edward II defeated Scots at Halidon Hill; recaptured Berwick.
Edward Baliol became vassal king of Scotland.
Gibralter retaken from Castile by Moors.
Accession of Casimir III, the Great, in Poland.
Accession of last Mongol emperor in China heralded period of civil war led by Chu Yüan-chang, of peasant stock.
Overthrow of Hōjō regency in Japan; Muromachi period (to 1573).

1334 Accession of Jaques Fournier as Pope Benedict XII.

1335 Invasion of Scotland by Edward III.
Lewis IV as Emperor invested Habsburgs with Carinthia.

1336 Edward III occupied Scotland.
Philip VI of France attacked Isle of Wight and Channel Islands.
Jan van Artevelde led rebellion against Louis II, Count of Flanders.

1337 Edward III of England, claiming throne of France, took title of "King of France"; retained by English kings until 1801.
English defeated Flanders, ally of Philip VI, at Cadsand.
Start of Hundred Years War.
Orkhan of Turkey captured Nicomedia.

1338 Edward III landed in France and allied with Artevelde and Flemings.
French burned Portsmouth.
Lewis IV allied with Edward III and annulled papal verdict against himself; issued laws against papal interference in German affairs.

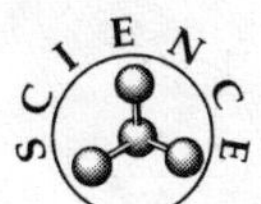

Formation of group of mastersingers at Toulouse.

Probable date of the origin of the Black Death (bubonic plague) which seems to have started in India.

Lippo Memmi and Simone Martini altarpiece of the *Annunciation*; in the Uffizi.
Erection of Kapell Brücke, famous bridge at Lucerne.
Königsberg Cathedral build; restored 1856.

Accession of Yussef I as Caliph of Granada indicated peak of Moorish civilization in Spain.

Erection of Palace of the Popes, Avignon (to 1362).

First public striking clock, San Gottardo, Milan.

Andrea Pisano (*c.* *1270, †1348), Italian sculptor, completed bronze south door of Baptistry, Florence (begun 1330).

Louis II stopped commerce with England; Edward III prohibited export of English wool to Flanders and moved Staple from Bruges to Antwerp.

Ugolino da Siena fabricated great silver reliquary of Orvieto; designed to hold the Holy Corporal from Bolsena.

(to 1344) William Merlee kept monthly weather records for Oxford; attempted to forecast using somewhat dubious symbols.
Thomas Blanket established looms at Bristol.

c. Ambroglio Lorenzetti (*c.* *1300, †1348): *Good* and *Bad Government, Tyranny, Effects of Tyranny,* four frescoes at Siena.
Work begun on Maria Gloriosa dei Frari, great Gothic church at Venice.
Foundation of University of Pisa.

Light cannon may have been mounted in English ships.

Year	History	Literature
1339	Edward III invaded France from Flanders. Venice conquered Treviso and gained first mainland possession.	Petrarch: *Africa*, epic on Scipio Africanus.
1340	English defeated French at sea battle of Sluys. French occupied Guienne. Truce between Edward III and Philip VI. Robert de Bouchier appointed first lay Chancellor of England. Portugal and Castile united to defeat Moslem invasion of Rio Salado. Epirus and Acarnania re-incorporated into Byzantine empire. Gerard of Holstein murdered by Danish nobles.	*Dafydd ap Gwilym, Welsh lyric poet (†1370). *c.* Kitabatake Chikafusa (*1293, †1360): *Jīnkoshotoki*, Japanese history designed to prove that Southern Mikados were rightful sovereigns of Japan.
1341	Truce between England and France. Actual division of Parliament into two separate Houses, of Lords and Commons respectively. Edward III removed all sheriffs. David II restored to Scots throne; captured fortresses retaken. Alliance between Philip VI and Lewis IV. Succession war in Brittany between John de Montfort and Charles de Blois.	Petrarch crowned Poet Laureate in Rome.
1342	Edward III supported John de Montfort in Brittany; defeated Charles de Blois at Morlaix. Election of Pope Clement VI. Accession of Louis I (the great) of Hungary.	
1343	Truce between Edward III and Philip VI. Parliament set aside Royal Acts of 1341. Treaty of Kalisz: Poland ceded Pomerellen and Kulm to Teutonic Order. King of Aragon conquered Mallorca.	
1344	German Electors deserted Lewis IV in favour of Charles of Moravia, grandson of Emperor Henry VII; rejected papal interference in their elections.	

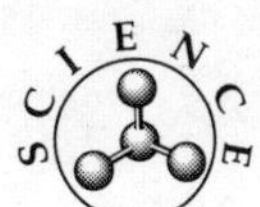

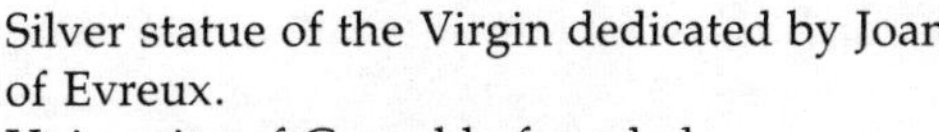

Silver statue of the Virgin dedicated by Joan of Evreux.
University of Grenoble founded.

Guillaume de Machaut (*1300, †1377) *fl.*; greatest musician of his day; associated with *ars nova*.
Pietro Lorenzetti: *Madonna with Angels*, Sienese painting, for S. Francesco Church, Pistoia.
Queen's College, Oxford, founded by Robert de Eglesfield.

The Black Death in China.
First European paper mill set up at Fabriano, Italy:
Blast furnaces with water-powered bellows introduced at Liége.

Penshurst Place, Kent; fine manor house, well preserved, possessing hall with minstrels' gallery.

A. Lorenzetti: *Presentation at the Temple*, Sienese panel painting.
P. Lorenzetti: *Nativity of the Virgin*, Sienese panel painting.

The cross-staff, for astronomical observation, introduced by Levi ben Gerson (invented earlier).

Church of San Giovanni a Carbonara, Venice, erected; enlarged 1400 by King Ladislaus (see 1428).

Edward had gold florins, worth 6s, struck.
First Commission on Public Health (Venice).
German merchants at Bergen given special privileges by Magnus VII of Norway.

Cathedral of St Guy, Prague, started by Matthew of Arras.
Edward III rebuilt Round Tower of Windsor Castle (founded by William I).

LITERATURE

	History	Literature
1345	Lewis IV obtained Holland, Hainault, Zeeland and Frisia. Jan van Artevelde murdered.	*Hexabiblos*, Byzantine adaptation of Roman civil laws.
1346	Edward III defeated French and allies at battle of Crecy. David II of Scotland invaded England; defeated and captured at Neville's Cross. Charles of Moravia elected Charles IV of Germany. Lewis IV excommunicated and dethroned by Clement VI.	
1347	Calais captured by English. Truce between England and France; lasted to 1355. Hassan Bahmani set up Kingdom of Kulbarga in Deccan in India.	
1348	Pope Clement VI purchased town of Avignon. Kingdom of Epirus conquered by Serbia under Stefan Dushan.	*c.* Ulrich Boner: *Der Edelstein*, 100 fables written in Middle High German.
1349	Dauphine and Montpellier added to French crown by Philip VI. Large-scale persecution of Jews in Germany.	Serbian Law Code issued by Stefan Dushan.
1350	Statute of Labourers in England: attempt to check labour problems left by Black Death; regulated wages in England. English sea victory over Spaniards off Winchelsea. Accession of John II of France. Brandenburg and Tyrol ceded by Charles IV to Wittelsbachs in recognition of their support.	(*et seq.*) Meistersingers in Germany: Burgher poets aspirant to poetic honours; started as "Schüler" (pupil) under a "Meister". English replaced French in the schools of England. *c. Sir Gawayne and the Green Knight*, Middle English poem.
1351	Statute of Treasons in England. Statute of Provisors forbade applications to Rome for any English benefice. Zürich joined Swiss League. Accession to Delhi Sultanate of Firoz Shah (†1388), liberal ruler centuries ahead of his time.	Petrarch: *Epistle to Posterity*, Italian autobiography.

Guido da Vigevano: *Anatomia*, fine illustrated treatise on anatomy.

Erection of Kumesu Shinto shrine, Matsue, Japan.
Foundation of the old university of Valladolid.

Use of cannon at battle of Crecy (see 1319).
Estonia sold by Denmark to Teutonic Order.

Pembroke College, Cambridge, founded.
Chapel of St Stephen, Westminster, completed; under Edward VI became House of Commons.

Black Death reached Europe from China; lasted until 1352.
Hanse merchants set up organization at Bruges.
Importation of wheat into England.

Edward III established the Most Noble Order of the Garter, originally known as Order of St George (according to Froissart, 1344).
Gonville and Caius College, Cambridge, founded.
Charles IV founded Prague University, first university East of the Rhine.

Egypt ravaged by the Black Death; in the same year, Weymouth became the first English town to be ravaged by the disease.
Giovanni de Dondi's astronomical clock (completed 1362); unfortunately no longer extant.

Mutō Shūi painted Musō Kokushi, a priest; fine Japanese picture of Muromachi period.

Black Death reputed to have killed one-third of population of England.

Trinity Hall, Cambridge, founded by Wm. Bateman, Bishop of Norwich.
Erection of Thurstaton Hall, Cheshire, ancient manor house.
c. Icon painting flourished at Novgorod (to *c.* 1450).
c. Italian maiolica ware, earthenware coated with tin glaze, developed.

c. The *Gough Map* (Bodleian library), fine early map of England; cartographer unknown.
Conrad von Megenburg: *Der Buch der Natur*, first important German naturalist work (see 1475).
Black Death in Scotland.

Between 1347 and 1351 it is estimated that 75,000,000 people died of the Black Death, the most dreadful scourge in history.
Groat (4*d* piece) first minted; finally discontinued 1856.

1352	English-supported claimant in Brittany defeated French. Glarus and Zug joined Swiss League; Zürich at war with Austria.	Ranulph Higden: *Polychronicon*, standard historical work of 14th and 15th cents.
1353	Statute of Praemunire forbade appeals to Rome by English clergy; outlawry for anyone appealing to Rome in law case already settled in English court. Re-establishment of papal authority in Papal States. Berne joined Swiss League. Turkish invasion of Europe began.	*c.* Giovanni Boccaccio (*c.* *1313, †1375): *Decameron*, a hundred tales in Italian supposed to be told by ten storytellers during the plague at Florence in 1348.
1354	Renewal of alliance of Scots and French. Turks captured Gallipoli.	
1355	Renewal of war among England, France and Scotland; English defeated Scots at Nesbit. Charles IV crowned Emperor at Rome. Norway and Sweden divided between two sons of Magnus V—Haakon VI and Eric. Iliyas Shah established independent kingdom of Bengal.	
1356	Battle of Poitiers: English defeated French; John II of France and his son captured. Peace between Austria and Zürich. Charles IV issued Golden Bull at Nuremberg and Metz: regulated election of German kings until 1806. Chu Yüan-chang and rebels captured Nanking from Mongols.	
1357	Anglo-French truce at Bordeaux; John de Montfort established as Duke of Brittany by English. Turks captured Adrianople.	Petrarch: *The Triumphs*, Italian allegorical poem. Law Code of Papal States; lasted until 1816.
1358	Revolt of French peasants—Jaquerie—suppressed by Dauphin. Peace between Habsburgs and Swiss League. Genoese defeated Venetians, who were forced to cede Dalmatia to Hungary.	*c.* Original French compilation of classic of travel literature, translated into English early 15th cent. as *Sir John Mandeville's Travels*.

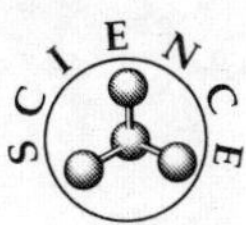

Foundation of Corpus Christi College, Cambridge.
Work begun on Antwerp Cathedral, largest Belgian church.

Black Death reached Russia.
Early form of spectacles illustrated in portrait of Cardinal Ugone.

(to 1370) Erection of the Rathaus, Aachen, on the ruins of Charlemagne's palace.

Edward III moved wool staple from Bruges to England.
Bristol created a staple town.

Erection of Wakefield Tower (housing Crown Jewels), Tower of London.

The Strasbourg clock, incorporating a mechanical cockerel; the latter has survived, although the clockwork has been lost.

Work begun on St Mary's, Nuremberg.

Windsor Castle virtually rebuilt by Edward III

Intense earthquake virtually destroyed city of Basle, including cathedral (consecrated 1019), rebuilt in 14th cent.

Andrea Orcagna: altar of the Strozzi Chapel in Church of Santa Maria Novella, Florence.
Erection of Merchant Adventurers' Hall, York.

First use of term "German Hanse" indicated earlier union of Baltic and Rhenish towns to give political backing to trading agreements.

1359 Treaty of London between England and France: restored Henry II's French territories to England; rejected by French Estates; Edward III invaded northern France, Champagne and Burgundy.

1360 Treaty of Bretigny ended first phase of Hundred Years War; Edward III retained western France south of Loire, Calais and Ponthieu. Valdemar IV of Denmark regained Schonen from Sweden.

c. Bartholomew de Glanville, English Franciscan friar: *De proprietatibus rerum,* popular Latin encyclopaedia in 19 volumes.

1361 Valdemar IV of Denmark at war with Hanseatic League; captured Visby in Gottland. Murad I, Emir of Turks, captured Demotika and Seres.

1362 Urban V became Pope. Valdemar IV of Denmark defeated Hanseatic merchants off Helsingborg.

c. Piers Plowman, long poem in Middle English ascribed formerly to Wm. Langland, a cleric at Malvern.

1363 Austria obtained the Tyrol. Haakon VI of Norway married Margaret, daughter of Valdemar IV of Denmark. Timur the Lame (Tamerlaine) began conquest of Asia.

1364 †John II of France, in prison in London (captured at Poitiers). Family pact of succession between Luxembourgs and Habsburgs. Crete revolted against Venetian rule.

1365 Charles IV crowned king of Burgundy; allied with France. Alexandria captured by Peter I of Cyprus; later abandoned.

1366 English Parliament refused to pay feudal dues to Pope in Rome. Wyclif became prominent through attacks on papal claims to supremacy. Statutes of Kilkenny forbade Anglo-Irish marriages, Irish language and laws. Amadeus of Savoy captured Gallipoli from Turks, Varna from Bulgarians; later had to give them up.

Petrarch: *Canzoniere* (full title *Rime in Vita e Morte di Madonna Laura*), his famous Italian love-poems; he was first great poet to use the sonnet.

Work on the nave of St Stephen's Cathedral, Vienna, begun.
Erection of St Nicholas's Cathedral, Newcastle upon Tyne; Gothic style.
Orcagna completed masterpiece, Tabernacle of Orsanmichele, Florence.

Edward III granted self-government to English traders in Netherlands.

City of Jaunpur founded by Firoz Shah.

Francs first coined in France (John II).

Pavia University refounded by Galeazzo II (see 825 and 1490).
Sacrificial silver bowl shaped like hollow tree trunk; Chinese (Chih Cheng period).

Black Death reappeared in England.
c. Nicole Oresme: *Lattitudes of Forms*, early throught on coordinates (see Descartes, 1637).

Sultan Hassan mosque, Cairo, erected; cruciform design.
c. Arca di S. Agostino, Pavia, tomb holding remains of S. Augustine of Hippo.

English Staple fixed at Calais.
First English apothecary.
Reference, in *Piers Plowman*, to practice of alconomye (alchemy).

Statute of Apparel "to restrain the outrageous and excessive apparel of divers persons against their estate and degree".
Consecration of Magdeburg Cathedral.
Every English goldsmith ordered to put his individual mark on his work after it had been assayed.
The Ascension, fresco at Volotovo, Russia.

Guy de Chauliac (*1300, †1368) wrote principal work on surgery of Middle Ages, *Chirurgia magna*; first printed at Lyons in 1478; de Chauliac performed operations for cataract and hernia.

Cracow University founded.
Aztecs of Mexico built their capital at Tenochtitlan.

Normans reached and settled at mouth of River Senegal, West Africa.
Ponte delle Torri, huge bridge, part of aqueduct of Spoleto, erected.

Rudolf IV of Austria founded Vienna University; a fine portrait of Rudolf (of about this year) exists—artist unknown.

John of Burgundy: *Treatise on the Epidemic Sickness* (plague).
Incorporation of Drapers' Company, London.

Meier Abdeli completed El Transito Synagogue in Toledo.
Completion of choir of Cracow Cathedral.
Beginnings of Bruges School of Flemish painting, lasting until mid 16th cent.

1367 Edward, Black Prince, led army into Spain; Battle of Najara; defeat of Henry of Castile; restoration of Peter I.
First Scottish Parliamentary Committee set up.
Hanseatic towns formed Confederation against Valdemar IV.

1368 Emperor Charles IV extended Imperial territory by treaty.
Habsburgs gained Breisgau.
Mongols driven from Peking.

Hafiz: *The Diwan*; the Persian poet sang of love, wine, flowers and nightingales.
Casimir III issued Central Law Code for Poland.

1369 †Philippa of Hainault, wife of Edward III; King passed under evil influence of mistress, Alice Perrers.
Charles V of France declared war on England.
14–year truce between England and Scotland.
Timur the Lame ascended throne of Samarkand.

Geoffrey Chaucer (*1328, †1400) greatest Middle English poet: *The Book of the Duchesse*; East Midland dialect in which he wrote became basis of standard English of modern times.

1370 French successful against English in Gascony and Maine.
Sack of Limoges by Black Prince.
Denmark defeated by Hanse; Peace of Stralsund confirmed economic and political hegemony of Hanse in Baltic.
Teutonic Order defeated Lithuanians at Rudau.
†Casimir III; Louis I of Hungary became also King of Poland; beginning of elective Polish monarchy.

c. The Pistill of Suete Susan, oldest Scottish (or English, perhaps) alliterative poetry; attributed to Huchown.
c. The Shahnāma (Book of Kings), epic poem of the School of Tabriz, illustrated with Islamic miniatures (see 1011).

1371 English defeated Flemings off Bourgneuf.
Turks defeated Serbians at Chirmen.
Accession of House of Stewart to Scottish throne.

1372 English defeated off La Rochelle by French and Castilians; French captured Poitiers, La Rochelle and Angoulême.
Treaty of Vincennes: Franco-Scottish alliance.
Owsen-ap-Thomas, self-styled Prince of Wales, aided by French, captured Guernsey.

c. Construction of sixty-two stalls of Lincoln Cathedral; finest extant Early Perpendicular tabernacle work.

Beginning of Ming period in China renowned for exquisite porcelain; lasted until 1644.

Guild of Master-Surgeons of London.

Completion of Exeter Cathedral, Gothic style; nave begun about 1280 (see 1050).
*John Dunstable (†1453), composer.

Urban V confirmed Order of Brigittines.
c. Heralds first appeared at tournaments.
Erection of Gate House of Westminster; used as prison; demolished 1776.
Carthusian monks built the Charterhouse, London.
Erection of the Bastille, Paris, then a fortress; later a prison; destroyed 1789.

Steel crossbow used as a weapon of war.
c. Charles V of France ordered all Parisian churches to ring the hours and quarters, based on the time indicated by Henri de Vick's clock, first reasonably accurate timepiece.

Francesco de Volterra: *Last Judgment*, fresco in Campo Santo, Pisa.

The Refectory of Worcester Cathedral, Decorated style, erected; now a part of King's School.

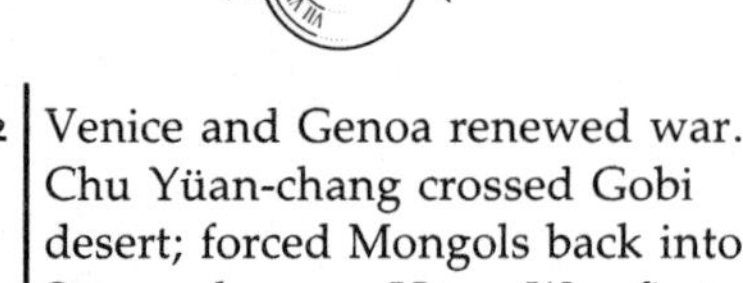

	History	Literature
1372	Venice and Genoa renewed war. Chu Yüan-chang crossed Gobi desert; forced Mongols back into Steppe; became Hung Wu, first Ming emperor.	
1373	English invasion of France by John of Gaunt. Brittany allied with France. Anglo-Portuguese treaty of friendship.	
1374	Truce between England and France; only Bordeaux, Bayonne and Calais remained of English conquests. Peace between Aragon and Castile.	
1375	Switzerland invaded by English, French and Welsh mercenaries. †Valdemar IV of Denmark; succeeded by grandson, Olaf. †Last Duke of Holstein of Royal Danish line. Sis, capital of Armenia, captured by Mamluks; end of Armenian independence.	John Barbour (*1316, †1395), Scottish poet: *The Bruce*, on war of Scottish independence. John Wyclif became Rector of Lutterworth.
1376	"Good Parliament"; impeached incompetent ministers; banished Alice Perrers; work undone by John of Gaunt. † Edward, Black Prince. Swabian towns formed League.	
1377	†Edward III; accession of grandson, Richard II (of Bordeaux). Hanse privileges confirmed by Richard II. Formation of Lollards, group taking up Wyclif's views on Church. French attacks on English coast. Pope Gregory XI returned to Rome; end of "Babylonian Captivity".	Compilation of Laurentian version of oldest extant Russian chronicle (see 1040).
1378	Renewal of English war with France, Spain and Scotland; English captured Brest and Cherbourg. Owen of Wales slain. Start of Great Schism: Urban VI elected Pope in Rome, Clement VII at Fondi.	Wyclif: *Schism of the Popes*, anti-papal tract; John of Gaunt protected Wyclif, who urged that "Peter's pence" should not be paid to Rome.
1379	Brittany revolted against Charles V. Hapsburg territories divided between Albert III and Leopold III of Austria.	

Francesco Pizigani illustrated church of St Mark's and Campanile, Venice, on a portolano chart.

Early form of lock for canals devised by the Dutch.
Tunnage and poundage imposed on English and foreign merchants.

Ni Tsan (*1301, †1374), Chinese painter: *Autumn Landscape*.
Erection of Worcester Cathedral tower.

Louis I of Hungary and Poland granted nobles immunity from taxation.

c. *The King John Cup* (so-called), embossed and enamelled; magnificent medieval silver-gilt cup of Borough of King's Lynn.

The *Catalan Atlas* produced for Charles V of France by the Majorcan cartographers; it incorporated Marco Polo's knowledge of the East.

(to 1421) Erection of the Belfry and Town Hall, Bruges: Flemish tower containing fine carillon.

Erection of Scotney Castle, Kent.
Work begun on French tapestries of the Apocalypse.
(to 1417) Erection of Ulm Cathedral, Germany (spire 529 ft).
Choir and cloisters of Gloucester Cathedral built; Perpendicular style.
Court of Lions, Alhambra, Granada, built.

Isolation of visitors to Ragusa, who might have been in contact with plague, for 30 days (see 1383); first quarantine in Europe.
Malays founded settlement of Malacca.
Poll tax levied in England.

Completion of fine Gothic town hall of Tangermünde; begun 1373.
(to 1411) Nave and transepts of Canterbury Cathedral again rebuilt.

William of Wykeham (*1324, †1404) founded New College, Oxford.
c. Peter Parler the Younger: *Self-Portrait*, a

Wendish currency union among Lübeck, Hamburg and Wismar with several other Low German towns.

1379	Clement VII moved to Avignon. Ferdinand of Portugal renewed claim to throne of Castile.	
1380	Franco-Castilian fleet defeated by English off Irish coast. †Haakon VI of Norway; succeeded by his son, Olaf IV, already King of Denmark; union of Norway and Denmark lasted more than 400 years. Mongols defeated by Dmitri IV of Moscow at Kulikov. Leadership of Golden Horde seized by Tokhtamish, protégé of Timur.	Wyclif's translation of the Bible into the vernacular. Earliest Malayan metrical verse on Pasai tomb.
1381	Anglo-French truce. Peasants Revolt in England; Wat Tyler, main leader, killed. Sudbury, Archbishop of Canterbury, murdered by rebels. Wyclif denounced doctrine of transubstantiation at Oxford. Rhenish towns formed a League.	Wyclif: *De eucharista*. *c.* Chaucer: *Hous of Fame*, poem linked with proposed royal marriage.
1382	Richard II of England married Anne of Bohemia. Wyclif expelled from Oxford; persecution of Wyclifites and Lollards. Leopold III of Austria acquired Trieste. Sofia captured by Turks.	Wyclif: *Trialogus*, summarizing his views on philosophy and doctrine of religion; his greatest work; printed 1525.
1383	Portuguese crown passed to John II of Castile through marriage; unrest in Portugal. †Ivan Sisman, last native Tsar of Bulgaria.	*c.* John Gower (*c.* *1330, †1408): *Vox Clamantis*, Latin poem on peasant rising in 1381.
1384	Truce arranged among England, France and Scotland; Scotland refused to recognize truce; Anglo-Scottish war resumed. †John Wyclif.	*c.* Chaucer: *The Parlement of Foules*, lively, humourous poem.
1385	Anglo-French war renewed; French sent men and money to Scotland to facilitate invasion of England; Richard II advanced into Scotland; forced to retreat from lack of supplies.	*c.* Chaucer: *Troilus and Criseyde*, a tragic tale of young love and betrayal; his first great work.

bust in Prague Cathedral; one early identifiable self-portrait.
Master Bertram: *Grabow Altarpiece* of gilded wood.

Graduated Poll tax in England.

c. *The Studley Bowl*, late medieval silver drinking-bowl.
Browsholme Hall, Lancashire, of Parker family; rebuilt 1507; new façade 1604.
Gold and emamelled cup of the kings of France; now in British Museum.

Parliament forbade sending of revenues from English benefices to absentee foreign holders.
Establishment of Ravensburg Trading Company.

Egypt again ravaged by Black Death.
Earliest record of small arms, known as *bastons-á-feu*, having no trigger.

Rebuilding of St Mary's, Stralsund.
Loggia dei Lanzi, Florence, completed.

Construction of Dulle Griete, great bombard (early gun) of Ghent; 25-inch calibre.

Quarantine (i.e. 40 days) instituted at Marseilles for ships arriving from plague-infected areas.

Pietà from St Elizabeth's, Breslau; Gothic painting in Expressionist style.

Incorporation of Fishmongers' Company, London.

(to 1495) St Giles's Cathedral, Edinburgh, built.
Heidelberg University founded by Rudolph I, Elector Palatine.

	History	Literature
1385	Portuguese deposed John II of Castile and declared John I, illegitimate son of Pedro I, to be king; defeated Castile at Aljubarrota; ensured Portuguese independence. Alliance of Rhenish and Swabian Town Leagues.	
1386	English Lords and Commons removed from power Earl of Suffolk, favourite of Richard II. Treaty of Windsor between Richard II and John I of Portugal. Swiss defeated and killed Leopold III of Austria at Sempach. Schleswig granted to Counts of Holstein by Margaret, Regent of Denmark.	
1387	Council at Nottingham: Richard II restored Suffolk. Lords Appellants attempted to restrict powers of Richard II.	Jean d'Arras: *L'histoire de Lusignan*, old French prose romance.
1388	English defeated by Scots at Otterburn (battle of Chevy Chase). Heavy persecution of Lollards in England. Leopold IV of Austria defeated by Swiss League at Näfels. Swabian League defeated at Döffingen; Rhenish League defeated at Worms.	*c.* Chaucer: *Canterbury Tales*, twenty-four tales told by a band of pilgrims on their way to Canterbury.
1389	William of Wykeham made Chancellor. Truce among England, France and Scotland. Sweden defeated by Danish-Norwegian force. Leagues of Towns within the Empire forbidden; Public Peace of Eger. Serbians defeated by Turks at Kosovo.	
1390	Statute: no one, on pain of death, to bring into England any summons or sentence of excommunication. †Robert II of Scotland; accession of infant Robert III. Turks captured last Byzantine possession in Asia Minor.	Writings of John Wyclif reached Bohemia. *c.* Gower: *Confesio Amantis*, in praise of courtly love; written in English.

Work begun on Milan Cathedral, mainly of Gothic style and built of marble; capable of holding 40,000 people, this great church was completed in 1813.
Erection of Bodiam Castle, Sussex; medieval moated castle.

Salisbury Cathedral clock, earliest surviving twin-drive striking clock, constructed.

William of Wykeham founded Winchester College.

Foundation of Cologne University, through the efforts of the Dominican order.
Erection of monastery of St Mary of the Victory, Batalha (to 1416); Portuguese Gothic style.

First Sanitary Act passed in England.

Embargo on Flanders by Hanseatic League.

Fan vaulting of timber of Winchester College carved.
c. Erection of Powderham Castle, Devonshire; partly destroyed in Civil war; later modifications.

1390 Tartars overcome by Timur the Lame.

1391 Statute of Mortmain (Edward I) reinforced and enlarged.

c. *Book of Ballymote*, Irish manuscript of poetry and prose.

1392 Statute of Praemunire, supported by full Parliament, asserted supremacy of Crown in management of Church affairs in England.
Succession dispute in Japan: Ashikagas gained supremacy; became Shoguns of Muromachi, near Kyoto.
Baghdad sacked by Timur the Lame.

1393 Swiss League formed first military organization.

1394 Revolt in Ireland quelled by Richard II.
Court of Chancery in England made permanent.
Anglo-French truce extended for four years.

1395 Irish rulers did homage to Richard II; amnesty for Irish.
Tokhtamish and Golden Horde routed by Timur the Lame; Golden Horde broke up into Khanantes of Kazan, Astrakhan and Crimea.

1396 Marriage of Richard II and Isabella of France; Anglo-French truce extended to 28 years.
Christian army defeated at Nicopolis by Turks under Bajazet.
Vidin, last Bulgarian stronghold, fell to Ottoman Turks; Bulgaria under Turkish rule for next 500 years.

1397 House of Commons claimed right of impeachment.
Issue of John of Gaunt and mistress, Katherine Swynford, legitimized; important in later Tudor claims to throne.
Union of Kalmar: Eric of Pomerania crowned king of Denmark, Norway and Sweden.

1398 Richard II in complete control of England; Dukes of Hereford and Mowbray banished.
Prince David, son of Robert III of Scotland, made Regent.

John Huss (*1369, †1415), Bohemian reformer who renovated and stabilized Czech language, began lecturing on theology at Prague university; preached Wyclifism.

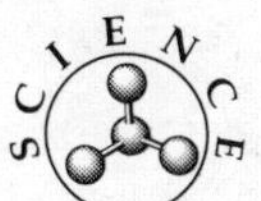

Erfurt University founded (suppressed 1816).
Porch and banqueting hall of Kenilworth Castle built (see 1120, 1571).
Lord Berkeley's brass; portraying English livery.

Construction of Wells Cathedral clock; possesses two separate striking mechanisms.
Aliens in England forbidden by Statute to retail goods.
Commercial treaty between Hanse and Novgorod.

Claus Sluter: *Daniel and Isaiah*, Moses fountain, Dijon.

Incorporation of Mercers' Company, London.

Rebuilding of nave of Winchester Cathedral begun.

c. Statue of Alfred the Great, London—probably oldest statue in the City.

Incorporation of Saddlers' Company, London.

Foundation of the Carthusian monastery of Pavia by Visconti; completed by 1507; superb Renaissance architecture.

Painting of Wilton diptych.

Confrérie de la Passion created at Paris to act religious plays.
Richard II enlarged Westminster Hall (see 1097).

	History	Literature
1398	Visby conquered by Teutonic Knights. Timur the Lame overran northern India; Khizr Khan, one of Timur's officers, left in charge; descendants ruled in Delhi (to 1450).	
1399	†John of Gaunt; Richard II seized his possessions; provoked invasion of England by Gaunt's son, Henry of Lancaster (Hereford), who deposed Richard II and usurped throne as Henry IV. Mongols defeated Lithuanians at River Vorskla.	Henry IV addressed Parliament in English for the first time.
1400	Hamburg began to acquire territory along the Elbe and to the north, still traceable in Greater Hamburg. Supposed murder of Richard II. War between England and Scotland. Welsh War of Independence under Owen Glendower. Suppression of conspiracy of the Four Earls in England.	Jean Froissart (*c.* *1337, *c.* †1410): *Chronicles*; the French historian described events of Hundred Years' War (translated into English 1525). Earliest known literature written in Cornish tongue; language ceased by 1800.
1401	Marriage of Henry IV to Joan of Navarre. Statute of *Heretico Comburendo*: Sawtrey (a Lollard) burned; Lollards were persecuted until 1413. Welsh rebellion spread; Glendower assumed title of Prince of Wales. Formal union of Poland and Lithuania. Conquest of Damascus and Baghdad by Timur the Lame.	In this year a 14th-cent. Icelandic manuscript of the Lives of the Apostles was given to the Church of Skare, Iceland; MS. fetched £36,000 in 1965 (at Sotheby's).
1402	Glendower defeated English force under Sir Edmund Mortimer; Henry IV invaded Wales. Scots defeated at Nesbit and Homildon Hill; Duke of Albany declared Regent of Scotland. Timur the Lame defeated and captured Bajazet at Ankara.	
1403	Anglo-Portuguese Treaty ratified by Henry IV. Rebellion of the Percys; battle of Shrewsbury; Percys defeated; Henry Percy (Hotspur) killed. Henry IV made second expedition against Glendower. Plymouth sacked by French ships. Valais joined Swiss League.	*c.* Compilation of *Yung Lo Ta Tien*, huge Chinese encyclopaedia in 22,937 volumes; defied printing; three copies made, two being destroyed at fall of Ming dynasty, the third during the Boxer rebellion.

(to 1419) Tower of Strasbourg Cathedral built.
Construction of hammerbeam roof, Westminster Hall, completed.
Perpendicular architecture widely established by this time.

c. First mention of the dulcimer.
c. Chapel of Bramall Hall, Cheshire, Tudor manor house, erected.
c. Development of Middle Mississippi and Upper Mississippi phases of mound-builders, N. America.

c. Primitive cord-driven turning-lathes used in Nuremberg trade.

*Nicolaus Cusanus (†1464), who was to perform experiments with growing plants which he observed to absorb weight from the atmosphere.
Timur the Lame carried off all craftsmen from Damascus and ended famous steel industry there.

Work commenced on Brussels Town Hall.
(to 1519) Erection of cathedral of Santa Maria de la Sede, Seville; 414 ft long, 271 ft wide; Spanish-Gothic architecture (see 1196).

Lorenzo Fhiberti (*1378, †1455) commenced work on porches of Florence Baptistry (see 1424).
Rebuilding of St Mary's, Danzig, commenced.

Yung Lo re-established Peking as capital of China, south of Ta-tu (earlier capital of Kublia Khan).
Quarantine hospital in Vienna.
Beginning of period of great progress in China.

	History	Literature
1403	Alliance between Manuel II and Suleimann, Emir of Turkey.	
1404	"Unlearned Parliament" at Coventry; attacked wealth of Church. Glendower captured Harlech Castle; Welsh Parliament held at Machynlleth; Welsh alliance with France. John the Fearless became Duke of Burgundy. Verona and Vicenza acquired by Venice.	*Pi-Pa-Ki (Story of the Lute)*, important Chinese play of 13th cent., improved by Mao-Tseu.
1405	Revolt in North England under Scrope defeated. Welsh received support from French; landings in South Wales; Welsh defeated at Grosmont and Usk. Jalayid rulers returned to Baghdad.	
1406	Parliament reorganized financial system, county elections and control of Privy Council and regulated succession to Crown. Treaty of Aberdaron among Percys, Glendower and Mortimer; partition of England proposed. Welsh defeated by Henry, Prince of Wales. †Robert III of Scotland. Florence overthrew Pisa.	
1407	Anglo-French truce. Duke of Orleans murdered by Burgundians; start of civil war in France. Republic of Genoa assumed control of Corsica.	
1408	Defeat of Percy's at Bramham Moor; †Earl of Northumberland. Capture of Aberystwyth (under siege since 1406). Duke of Burgundy, aided by Scots force, defeated French at Liège. Rome captured by Ladislaus of Naples. Cardinals of Avignon and Rome met in attempt to end Schism.	Earliest extant manuscript of *Bogurodzica* song, sung by Poles in battle, beginnings of Polish poetry.

Altar paintings, Niederwildungen, by Conrad of Soest.
Foundation of University of Turin.
Record of existence of clavichord.

City walls of Baghdad rebuilt.
(to 1499) Erection of Bath Abbey, replacing Cathedral (see 1090).

Konrad Kyeser: *Bellifortis*, book of military knowledge.

c. Erection of mausoleum of Timur the Lame (†1405) in Samarkand; Islamic domed building with twin towers.
St Peter's Church, Riga, erected (to 1409); tower 412 ft high.
Bartolino da Novara erected Castello di Corte, Mantua (begun 1395).

Giacomo d'Angelo translated Ptolemy's *Geographia* and had fine maps redrawn; beginnings of accurate cartography.
The Mistery of Free Brewers constituted.

Bethlehem Hospital (see 1247) became an institution for the insane; gave rise to the word "bedlam".
Henry IV granted charter to Merchant Adventurers.

c. Andrew Rublev (*c*. *1370, †1430): *The Descent into Hell*, Russian icon; Rublev was principal (Russian) artist of his period.
Donatello (*c*. *1386, †1466): (i) *David*, (ii) *St John the Evangelist*; marble statues.
Erection of Norwich Guildhall; flint Perpendicular style; completed 1413.

Construction of "Dance of Death" bridge at Lucerne; made of covered timber.

	History	Literature
1409	English regained Harlech Castle from Welsh. Council of Pisa to end Schism; deposed two rival popes and elected a third; now three rival Popes. War between Venice and Sigismund of Hungary.	
1410	English Parliament again attacked wealth of clergy. Ladislaus II of Poland overthrew Teutonic Knights at Tannenberg. †Pope Alexander V, elected at Pisa; Council of Pisa elected John XXIII.	
1411	Plot to depose Henry IV; Henry, Prince of Wales, involved along with Beauforts. English force supported Burgundy faction and with Parisian Guilds defeated Orleanists at St Cloud. Highland invasion defeated at Harlaw. Peace between Portugal and Castile.	*c.* Thos. Occleve: *De Regimine Principum,* English poem outlining responsibilities of a prince. Huss ecommunicated by Pope John XXIII.
1412	Henry IV repudiated Burgundian alliance and joined Orleanists.	*c.* John Lydgate (*1373, †1450), poet: *Troy-book.*
1413	†Henry IV of England; accession of Henry V. Lollards, led by Sir John Oldcastle, persecuted; Oldcastle imprisoned in Tower; escaped. Accession of Mohammed I as Emir of Turkey.	Wyclif's writings condemned by Pope John XXIII.
1414	Henry V made treaty with Burgundian faction in France. Lollard rising in England failed. Council of Constance considered problems of reunion and reform.	*c. Imitatio Christi (The Imitation of Christ),* devotional Latin work ascribed to Thomas à Kempis (certainly written between 1380 and 1425).
1415	Renewal of war between England and France; Henry V invaded France and defeated French at Agincourt. Southampton plot against Henry V by Earl of March failed. Council of Constance deposed Pope John XXIII; Gregory XII, Pope in Rome, resigned. Huss burned at stake in Constance as a heretic. Ceuta conquered by Portuguese.	Charles d'Orléans (*1391, †1465), French noble, captured by English; wrote best poems in England.

Leipzig University founded by refugees from Prague.
c. Rublev: *The Old Testament Trinity*, Russian icon.
School of Theology and Laws at Aix became university.

Commercial treaty between England and Teutonic Order.

c. Paul and Jean de Limbourg: *May*, illustration in the Duke of Berry's *Book of Hours*.
Completion of tomb mosque of Sultan Barkuk, Cairo.

Benedetto Rinio: *Liber de Simplicibus*, important herbal reference work.

Foundation of the Guildhall (principal building of the Guilds, London); rebuilt on various occasions.
Tomb of Philip the Bold, Burgundian work.
Foundation of St Andrews University by Henry Wardlaw, Bishop of St Andrews.

Donatello sculpted *St Peter, St George* and *St Mark*, originally for Or San Michele (to 1416); *St George* is famous.

Yung Lo designed the nine-story Porcelain Pagoda (destroyed 1864), Nanking.

Henry V began building large ships (up to 1,000 tons) for his fleet.

Erection of Church of Sant'Anna dei Lombardi, Naples.
Foundation of Durham School.
St Andrew's Church, Cologne, holding tomb of Albertus Magnus, founded.

Medicis of Florence became bankers to Papacy; remained so until 1476.

Agincourt Song, commemorating English victory over the French; earliest copy at Trinity College, Cambridge.

Parliament granted Henry V tunnage and poundage for life.

LITERATURE

1415	Frederick VI of Nuremberg received Electorate of Brandenburg.	
1416	Henry V of England made alliances with Sigmund of Germany and Duke of Burgundy. Franco-Genoese fleet active in Channel. Amadeus VIII, Count of Savoy, became first Duke of Savoy. Eric of Pomerania acquired Copenhagen from See of Roskilde. Turks defeated off Gallipoli by Venetian fleet.	Alain Chartier (*c.* *1392, †1430), French poet: *Livre des Quatres Dames*, written after Agincourt.
1417	Henry V launched second invasion of France. Oldcastle burned as heretic. Council of Constance deposed Benedict XIII, Pope at Avignon; Martin V elected in Rome; end of Great Schism.	John Capgrave (*1393, †1464), Augustinian friar: *Chronicle of England* to this date.
1418	John, Duke of Burgundy, entered Paris. Close of Council of Constance. Lübeck entrusted with permanent conduct of Hansa affairs.	Pope Martin V condemned writings of Wyclif and Huss.
1419	Rouen captured by Henry V of England. John, Duke of Burgundy, murdered by agents of Dauphin at Montereau. Alliance between England and Burgundy. †Wenceslas IV of Bohemia; Czechs refused to accept Sigismund as king.	
1420	Treaty of Troyes brought peace between England and France; marriage of Henry V of England to Katherine of Valois. Four Articles of Prague set out principles of first national protestant Church; members called Utraquists.	*Dafydd Nanmor, Welsh bard (†1485). *c.* Lydgate: *The Siege of Thebes*, poem published *c.* 1500.
1421	England and France again at war: Henry V's third invasion of France. Florence acquired Leghorn. †Mohammed I and accession of Murad II as Emir of Turkey.	

*Piere della Francesca (†1492), Renaissance painter from Umbria.
Eric of Pomerania built castle on sound opposite Helsingborg.

Dutch fishermen used drift nets.
Incorporation of Cutlers' Company, London.

Introduction of Garter King of Arms (in Heraldry).
c. Silver nef (model ship) used at table of French king.

Gowhar Shad Mosque (part of a large complex of buildings), dedicated to Iman Riza, erected by Queen Gowhar Shad.

Foundation of Rostock University.
Foundling Hospital, Florence, early Renaissance architecture; designed by Filippo Brunelleschi (*1377, †1446), to whom the development of the Renaissance is attributed and who was a pioneer in using perspective.

Portuguese sailors rediscovered Madeira, first discovered in 14th cent., and claimed it for Portugal.

Church of San Lorenzo, Florence, built by Brunelleschi.
Erection of the Great Temple of the Dragon, Peking, an aggregate of buildings, mainly circular.
Stone fan-vaulting at Gloucester.

J. Fontana referred to a kind of velocipede, early attempt at mechanical transport.

Maas Polder, known as Holland, collapsed in one night; 65 villages lost; 10,000 people drowned.

Year	History	Literature
1422	†Henry V of England at Vincennes; accession of baby son, Henry VI; Bedford, brother to Henry V, Regent. †Charles VI of France; accession Charles VII, Henry VI proclaimed king of England and France at Paris. Constantinople besieged by Turks.	Thomas Walsingham: *Historia Anglicana* (from 1272). Beginning of the *Paston Letters* (see 1509). Chartier: *Quadrilogue-invectif*, among France and three State orders, expounding the evils of the day.
1423	Earl of Salisbury defeated French and Scots force at Crevant. James I of Scotland, prisoner in England since 1406, released; returned to Scotland. Council of Pavia. Margrave of Meissen became Elector of Saxony.	James I of Scotland: *The Kingis Quair*, written in prison, possibly for Jane Beaufort.
1424	Duke of Bedford routed French and Scots at Verneuil; English invaded Hainault. Beaufort now Chancellor of England. Anglo-Scottish truce. Election of anti-Pope Clement VIII. Smyrna captured by Turks. †Jan Zizka, leader of Utraquists in Bohemia; struggles between Utraquists and radical "Taborites".	
1425	Earl of Salisbury captured Le Mans. Flanders and France sent emissaries to Scotland to try to renew the alliance against England.	*c.* Chartier: *La Belle Dame sans Merci*, French poem.
1426	"Parliament of Bats" met at Northampton; rivalry between Beaufort and Gloucester nearly caused civil war; Bedford patched up quarrel. Brittany declared war on England; Philip of Burgundy defeated Gloucester in Hainault. Beaufort became a Cardinal; made Crusade against Hussites. Utraquists and Taborites, united under Prokop the Bald, repelled Saxon invasion at Usti.	
1427	English force under Bedford defeated by French under Dunois at Montargis. Hussites in Bohemia defeated Sigismund, at Mies, and crusading army, organized by Beaufort, at Tachov.	

Erection of the Ca D'Oro, Venice, of Gothic design; façade richly ornamented with gold; completed 1440 for Marino Contarini.

Feuerwerksbuch, military technical book.

Wood block print of St Christopher, now in Manchester.
Wood engraving carried out at Memminingen, Germany.
Gentile da Fabriano (*1370, †1427): *The Adoration of the Kings*, Italian painting.

Goldsmiths in York, Newcastle upon Tyne, Norwich, Coventry, Lincoln, Salisbury and Bristol were awarded different assay marks for silver and gold plate.

Chang-ling tomb of Yung Lo (Ming dynasty), Peking.
The Green mosque of Bursa commenced.
Ghiberti completed North bronze doors for baptistry at Florence: motif *Abraham and Isaac* (see 1403).

c. Carpenter's brace known to have been used.

Church of St. Mary the Virgin, Chelmsford, built; became cathedral in 1914.
Erection of Ratchapurana Monastery, Aryth. Siamese work, now a ruin.

c. Fra Angelico da Fiesole (*1387, †1455): *Virgin enthroned*, Italian tempera work.
c. Stephan Lochner (*c.* *1400, †1451): famous triptych in Cologne Cathedral.

European printing commenced.
Act to improve River Lea for passage of ships (see 1767).

Foundation of Louvain University, Belgium; closed 1797; re-established 1817.
c. Masaccio (*1401, †1428), earliest perspective painter: *Expulsion from Eden*, Florentine work.
(to 1435) Hsuan-Te period of rich ruby-red porcelain in China.
Tomb of Cardinal Brancaccio, work of Donatello and Michelozzo (in Naples).

Donatello *Herod's Feast*, gilt bronze relief on font at Siena.
c. Masaccio: (i) four paintings based on St Peter; (ii) *The Tribute Money*, fresco in S. Maria del Carmine.

	History	Literature
1427	Eric of Denmark defeated Hanse off Copenhagan.	
1428	Peace between England and Flanders at Delft. Beaufort returned and resumed Chancellorship. Salisbury began the siege of Orleans; Joan of Arc led French armies against English. Peace between Milan and Venice.	
1429	Henry VI crowned at Westminster. English defeated French at Rouvrai (battle of the Herrings). Joan of Arc, Dunois and La Hire relieved Orleans. English defeated by the French at Jargeau and at Patay. Eric of Denmark attempted to recover Schleswig for Denmark; war until 1435.	*c.* Chartier: *Traité d'Espérance,* attack on clergy and nobles by the French poet and political writer.
1430	Right of voting in England fixed on 40s. freeholder. Henry VI went to France. Joan of Arc captured by Burgundians at Compiègne. Murad II captured Yanina.	*c.* Modern English developed from Middle English. *c.* Lydgate: *The Fall of Princes,* a poem.
1431	Henry VI of England crowned king of France at Paris. Truce between England and Scotland extended to 1433. Joan of Arc burned at Rouen on charge of witchcraft. Bohemian Hussites again defeated crusading army of Beaufort at Domazlice.	
1432		*c. Mystère du Concile de Bâle,* French historical morality play.
1433	Sigismund crowned Holy Roman Emperor by Pope Eugen IV. Cosimo di Medici exiled from Florence; ban removed in 1434 and until 1464 virtual ruler of Florence. Ladislaus II of Poland granted his nobles *habeas corpus*.	

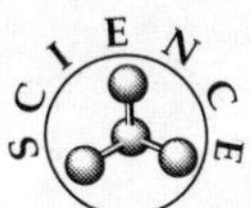

Andrea da Firenze created great tomb of King Ladislaus, in Church of San Giovanni a Carbonara, Naples.

Incorporation of Grocers' Company, London.

Brunelleschi at work on the Pazzi Chapel in cloister of Santa Croce, Florence.
Richard Fleming, Bishop of Lincoln, founded Lincoln College, Oxford.

c. Work begun on the Divinity School building, Oxford; completed 1466 (or a little later, perhaps 1479).

Great cast-iron gun, "Mad Marjorie" (16 ft long), now at Ghent, constructed.
c. Introduction of first genuine matchlock; earliest trigger mechanism for small arms.

Caen University founded by Henry VI.
Poitiers University founded by Charles VII of France.

First English almanack issued.

Jan van Eyck (*c.* *1384, †1441) completed *Adoration of the Lamb at Ghent*, Flemish altarpiece, begun by his brother.

Gonzalo Cabral, Portuguese sailor, discovered the Azores.

Altar-front of Teramo, by Nicola da Guardiagreli, Abruzzi goldsmith.
c. Donatello: *David*, first free-standing bronze to be cast since Classical times.

LITERATURE

	History	Literature
1434	Emperor Sigismund recognized as King of Bohemia. Revolt in Rome; Pope fled to Florence. Accession of Ladislaus III to Polish throne. Internal confict between Utraquists and Taborites in Bohemia ended at battle of Lipany; Utraquists defeated Taborites and killed Prokop.	
1435	English defeated by French at Gerberoi. Congress of Arras: Duke of Burgundy abandoned English alliance and united with Charles VII of France. Peace of Vordinborg: Eric of Denmark ceded Schleswig to Adolph VIII of Holstein. Swedish Riksdag (Parliament) met for first time.	
1436	English forced to abandon Paris. Siege of Calais by French; raised by Edmund Beaufort. Scots defeated English force near Berwick. Compact of Iglau: between Council of Constance and Hussites-Utraquists; Hussites recognized Sigismund as King of Bohemia.	Niccolo Nicoli founded a library in Florence.
1437	Henry VI began to rule in his own right. Talbot, Earl of Shrewsbury, successful against French. James I of Scotland murdered at Perth; accession of James II; nine years truce with England. Albert of Austria, son-in-law of Emperor Sigismund, appointed King of Bohemia.	
1438	Albert of Austria elected King of Germans. Pragmatic Sanction of Bourges asserted Gallican liberties against Papacy. Diet of Nuremberg set about reform of Empire's government.	

J. van Eyck: *Giovanni Arnolfini and his Wife*, Flemish painting.
Florence Cathedral completed by Brunelleschi (started 1420).
Caister Castle built by Sir John Fastolf.

João Diaz, Portuguese explorer, rounded Cape Bojador.

Consecration of Uppsala Cathedral.
c. Rogier van der Weyden (*c.* *1400, †1464): *The Descent from the Cross*, Flemish altarpiece in the Chapter House of the Escurial.

Eric of Denmark confirmed privileges on Hanse in his dominions.

Erection of church of San Marco, Florence.
Erection of funerary mosque for Qait Bey at Cairo (to 1480); decorated with horizontal stripes.

First attempts to drain the Fens.

Fra Angelico painted (to 1445) fresco in San Marco, Florence.
c. Michelozzo di Bartolommeo (*1396, †1472): sculptures for Aragazzi tomb, Montepulciano.
c. John Dunstable developed counterpoint in music.
Caen University received its charter.

Henry the Navigator founded important Colonial and Naval Institute at Sagres.
Henry VI confirmed Hanse privileges in England.
(to 1441) Poole, outlaw, occupied cavern, named after him, at Buxton; length 569 yds.
Incorporation of Vintners' Company, London.

Henry Chichele, Archbishop of Canterbury, and Henry VI founded All Soul's College, Oxford; College is exclusively for dons.
Erection (to 1478) of Jamma Musjid, great mosque of Husain, Jaunpur.

Laurens Koster (real name Janssoen) (*c.* *1370, †1440), Dutch, probably used movable wooden blocks in printing at Haarlem (see 1447).
Incorporation of Brewers' Company, London.

LITERATURE

Year	History	Literature
1439	Truce between England and Burgundy made at Calais. Eric of Pomerania deposed by Danish and Swedish Diets; Christopher (of Bavaria) elected as king. †Albert II of the Germans and Bohemia. Pope Eugene IV deposed (see 1443).	
1440	Richard, Duke of York, appointed Lieutenant General in France. Earl of Douglas murdered at Edinburgh. Frederick, Duke of Styria, elected King of Germans as Frederick III. Ladislaus III succeeded to throne of Hungary.	*c*. Frederick III founded Imperial Library of Vienna. Cusanus: *De docta ignorantia*; indicating all knowledge as conjectural.
1441	Trial of Duchess of Gloucester for sorcery. French took Pontoise from English. Pope Eugene IV declared monopoly of means of grace to Roman Catholic Church. Peace at Copenhagen between Holland and the Hanse.	Huss: *De Orthographia Bohemica* posthumously published; advocated Czechoslovak standardized spelling.
1442	Marriage of Isabel, youngest daughter of James I of Scotland, to eldest son of John, Duke of Brittany. Eric of Pomerania expelled by Norwegians; Christopher of Denmark succeeded.	
1443	English armies invaded Maine and Anjou; Dieppe relieved by Dauphin. William Douglas gained control in Scotland. Pope Eugene IV returned to Rome. Epirus joined Albania against Turks; Epirus overrun by Turks; Turks defeated at Nish by Hunyady Janos.	
1444	Truce between England and France for two years; England to surrender Maine and retain Normandy. Swiss League defeated by Armagnacs at St Jacob near Basle. Ladislaus III of Poland and Hungary defeated and killed by Turks at Varna. Viceroy of Timurid emperors in Baghdad set up own empire in Iraq and Kurdistan.	

J. van Eyck: *Madonna of the Fountain*, Flemish painting.
Porta della Carta, great gateway of ducal palace, Venice, erected (to 1443).

Incorporation of Cordwainers' Company, London.
French Estates General met at Orleans and set up permanent tax for a standing army.

van Eyck: *The Lucca Madonna*, Flemish painting.
Foundress's Cup, Christ's College, Cambridge; silver-gilt.
Foundation of Eton College; Public School.
Erection of Tattershall Castle, Lincolnshire.
c. Earliest sketch (MS. at Weimar) of keyed instrument (clavichord).

Foundation of King's College, Cambridge, by Henry VI.
Completion of the Confessor's Chapel, Westminster Abbey.

Opening of the City of London School.
(to 1458) Western towers of Burgos Cathedral erected by John of Cologne.
Castagno: frescoes in vaults of San Zaccaria, Venice.

Renaissance Arch at Naples erected in memory of Alfonso I of Aragon.
(to 1453) Erection of Palace of Jacques Cœur, Bourges.
(to 1464) Beauchamp Chapel, Warwick, built; Perpendicular style; remainder of St Mary's Church rebuilt after fire in 1694.

John II of Castile made trade treaty with Hanse.
First English plague order concerning quarantine and cleansing.

Laurentine Library, Florence, founded by Cosimo (the Elder) di Medici.
Michelozzo di Bartolommeo began building Palazzo Riccardi, Florence, for Cosimo di Medici (completed 1452).
Bernardo Rossellino: Tomb of Leonardo Bruni, in S. Croce.
Central tower of York Minister again rebuilt.

Incorporation of Leathersellers' Company, London.

LITERATURE

	History	Literature
1445	Marriage of Henry VI to Margaret of Anjou. Charles VII of France created standing army. Eugene IV dissolved Council at Rome.	
1446	Eugene IV deposed Archbishops of Cologne and Triers opposed to him; German Electors stood against papal interference in matters of the Empire. Hunyady Janos elected Regent of Hungary.	
1447	Renewal of Anglo-French truce. †Gloucester and Beaufort, rivals in English Council. Casimir IV elected King of Poland and Lithuania. †Pope Eugene IV; succeeded by Nicholas V. Turks under Murad II defeated by Scanderberg. India, Persia and Afghanistan gained independence on break up of Timur's Empire.	
1448	Renewal of English war with France. Rival political groups in England: Somerset and Suffolk (Lancaster) opposed York, Salisbury and Warwick (York). War between England and Scotland; English force defeated; English burned Dunbar and Dumfries. Christian of Oldenburg elected King of Denmark. Knutson Bonde elected King of Sweden as Charles VIII. Accession of Constantine XI, last Eastern Roman Emperor. Turks under Murad II defeated Hunyady Janos at Kossovo.	*c.* Capgrave completed *Liber de Illustribus Henricis*, a record of lives of German emperors from 918 to 1198, English kings named Henry, and others.
1449	England ceded Rouen to France; Salisbury forced to yield most of Normandy. Marriage of James II of Scotland to Mary of Guelders. War between towns and princes in Germany; lasted to 1553. Felix V, last anti-Pope, resigned.	

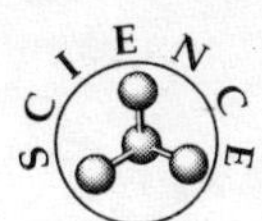

Jean Fouquet (*1420, †1480), French miniaturist and painter: *Portrait of Charles VII.*

Outbreak of plague in England.
Diniz Diaz, Portuguese explorer related to João Diaz (see 1434) discovered Cape Verde.

Building of King's College Chapel, Cambridge (to 1515): exceptionally fine perpendicular vaulting.
Erection of Church of St Francis, Rimini, to design of Alberti; eight remarkable side-chapels; ready 1450.

Foundation of University of Palermo. Fra Angelico painted (i) *Christ as Judge,* (ii) *Prophets,* in cathedral at Orvieto.

Margaret of Anjou founded Queen's College, Cambridge.
Introduction of bar lines in music.
Fra Angelico began painting frescoes representing lives of SS. Lawrence and Stephen, in Chapel of Pope Nicholas V, Vatican.
Work begun on Louvain Town Hall; completed 1463.

Incorporation of Haberdashers' Company, London.
Hanse town of Berlin subdued by Frederick II, who made it his capital.

Van der Weyden: *Entombment*, Flemish painting executed in Italy.
Aix Annunciation, fine French painting, completed.

1450	Jack Cade's rebellion in England; caused by high taxation and anger at mismanagement of war in France. Suffolk murdered. English defeated French at Formigny; French regained Cherbourg. Hunyady Janos recognized as Regent of Hungary by Frederick III. Christian of Oldenburg, king of Denmark, crowned King of Norway. Bohemian and Moravian Communion of Brethren formed.	*c.* Appearance in Germany of first *Volksbücher*, popular sagas in prose. Vatican library started by Pope Nicholas V. *c. The Red Book of Hergest*; four ancient Welsh tales; date speculative.
1451	English lost Guienne to French. Cardinal Nicholas of Cues appointed Legate to organize reform of German Church. Mohammed II became Emir of Turkey. First Pathan king established in Delhi.	Eisteddfod held at Carmarthen; Dafydd ap Edmwnd (*1425, †1500) most distinguished poet.
1452	Talbot, Earl of Shrewsbury, defeated and killed by French at Castillon; English recaptured Bordeaux. William Douglas murdered by James II of Scotland. Frederick III, King of Germans, crowned Emperor in Rome.	
1453	Hundred Years War between England and France came to end; England gave up all conquests except Calais. Henry VI became insane. Republican conspiracy in Rome against Papal rule. Mohammed II and Turks captured Constantinople; end of Eastern Roman Empire. Metropolitan of Moscow assumed headship of Orthodox Church on fall of Constantinople.	
1454	Richard, Duke of York, named "Protector" of England during insanity of Henry VI; Edward, son of Henry VI, named Prince of Wales. Peace of Lodi between Venice and Milan; Venice secured Brescia, Bergamo, Crema and Treviglio.	Indulgences bearing *printed* date produced at Mainz.

SCIENCE

Modern keyboard for the organ.
c. The *Giant Salt*, crystal salt cellar, supported by elaborately worked silver mountings.
c. Fouquet painted early miniature (self-portrait) in enamel.
Erection of Adlington Hall, Cheshire; half-timbered black-and-white section added 1581.
Foundation of University of Barcelona.

c. Hamburg began to mark the lower Elbe with buoys and beacons as far as the river mouth.
The Ethiopians used coffee.
Purbach first *printed* an almanack.
Basil Valentine made early reference to bismuth (under name *wismut*).
Period of finest Chinese enamel work (to 1456).
c. Gold used for filling teeth; earlier fillings known (temp. Middle Ages) were of wax or gum.

Pope Nicholas V founded Glasgow University.
Gloucester Abbey Church refounded as a cathedral.
Fouquet painted the Melun diptych.

Fall of Jacques Cœur, French financier.
Flanders-Burgundy engaged in trade war with Hanse.

Conrad Paumann (*1410, †1473): *Fundamentum organisandi*, treatise on the organ; he was born blind but became famous for his playing.
Ghiberti completed Gate of Paradise in the Florentine Baptistry (begun 1425).

Metal plate known to have been used for printing.

Fra Angelica: *Lives of St Stephen and St Lawrence* and *Four Evangelists*, paintings in Chapel of Nicholas V, the Vatican.

Incorporation of Company of Armourers and Braziers, London.

Turks converted Hagia Sophia (see 532) into mosque.
Donatello completed *Gattamelata*, equestrian statue at Padua.

Wm. Austen: fine bronze effigy of Richard Beauchamp; at Warwick.
Andrea Mantegna (*1431, †1506), of Paduan school of art: (i) *St Luke and other Saints*; (ii) *St Euphemia*.

Johann Gutenburg (*c.** 1398, †1468) began printing, using movable punches and copper type; discovery independent of Chinese (see 1042), but European invention may have been in 1440, *q.v.*

LITERATURE

Year	History	Literature
1455	Henry VI recovered sanity; York replaced by Somerset and excluded from Royal Council. Civil war in England; York defeated Royal army at St Albans; York again Protector. War between England and Scotland. Alfonso Borgia elected Pope as Calixtus III.	Mazarin Bible, first book printed by movable type; issued at Mainz by Gutenberg; called 42–line Bible as it had 42 lines on each page.
1456	Verdict and trial of Joan of Arc annulled. Athens captured by Turks; Acropolis held out. †Hunyady Janos after repelling Turks at Belgrade.	François Villon (*1431), celebrated French criminal and poet of late Middle Ages: *Le Petit Testament*.
1457	French attacked Sandwich and burned Fowey. Christian of Denmark and Norway crowned King of Sweden. Marienburg, headquarters of Teutonic Order captured by Poland; moved to Königsberg.	Mainz Psalter, by Fust and Schoeffer, first book to carry printer's name, date and place of manufacture, issued; was also first to be printed in colour.
1458	Naples established as kingdom. George Podiebrady, Regent of Bohemia, elected king. Fall of Acropolis at Athens to Turks.	*Mystère du Vieil Testament*, famous French religious play, produced at Abbeville.
1459	Renewal of Civil War in England; Yorkists defeated Queen Margaret at Bloreheath; Yorkists scattered at rout of Ludford. Parliament met at Coventry; attainder of York. Decision to make Crusade against Turks taken at Congress of Mantua under Pius II. Serbia overrun by Turks.	
1460	London captured for Yorkists by Warwick; Henry VI defeated and captured at Northampton; York defeated and killed by Queen Margaret at Wakefield. James II of Scotland killed at Siege of Roxburgh. Agreement of Ribe: Schleswig and Holstein passed to Danish Crown and declared to be indivisible. Turks captured Morea.	

Van der Weyden: *Portrait of a Lady*, Flemish painting.
da Settignano: Tomb of Carlo Marsuppini, in S. Croce.
Erection of Palazzo Venezia, one of finest palaces of Rome, Renaissance architecture.

Cadamosto, Venetian sailor, explored River Senegal and went beyond Cape Verde to Gambia.

Thos. Bouchier built Knole, great house in Kent; substantial extensions *c.* 1603.

Early type of instrument, the sea quadrant, used for nagivation; a primitive quadrant was used by Ptolemy for astronomy.
Cadamosto discovered Cape Verde Islands.

Foundation of Freiburg University.
Psalter of Fust and Schoeffer, containing printing in two colours.

Records of Portuguese voyages of exploration sent by Henry the Navigator to Fra Mauro, Venetian monk and cartographer, who produced a new map of the world.

Wm. of Waynflete, Bishop of Winchester, founded Magdalen College, Oxford.
San Zaccaria, Venice; Medieval-Renaissance church by Pietro Lombardi (vaults, see 1442).

Mantegna completed triptych *Madonna Enthroned* (begun 1457) for church of St. Zeno, Verona.
Benozzo Gozzoli (*1420, †1497): *The Journey of the Magi to Bethlehem*, Florentine fresco in Medici chapel.

Completion of Winchester Cathedral.
c. Mantegna: *The Adoration of the Magi*, Italian tempera.
Foundation of Basle University.
St. George's Chapel, Windsor, erected (to 1483).

†Henry the Navigator.
c. First lessons in dentistry by barbers; previously dentistry independent of surgery, sometimes carried out as punishment.
c. Magnetic variation (angle between magnetic and geographic N. pole) known.

	History	Literature
1461	Warwick defeated at second battle of St Albans. Edward of York victorious at Mortimer's Cross and Towton; became King of England as Edward IV. Scots captured Berwick. †Charles VII of France; accession of Louis XI.	Villon: *Le Grand Testament*, French poetry on the vanity of human nature.
1462	Henry VI of England in refuge in Scotland; Queen Margaret of England and Edward of Wales in France. Lancastrian uprisings suppressed. Aragon ceded Roussillon to France. Gibraltar captured by Castile from Arabs.	Publication of first dated edition of the *Vulgate, Cent Nouvelles Nouvelles*, gay French prose stories.
1463	Truce between England and Scotland. Truce between England and France made at Hesdin. Lancastrian revolts crushed. Bosnia captured by Turks; Venice declared war on Turks. Pope Pius II proclaimed Crusade against Turks under his own control.	*c.* Sir John Fortescue: *De Natura Legis Naturae*, authoritative Latin work on the monarchy.
1464	Lancastrian defeated by Warwick at Hedgeley Moor and by Montague at Hexham. Anglo-Scottish truce made a permanent peace; Henry VI brought to London and imprisoned in Tower. Marriage of Edward IV to Elizabeth Woodville; later alleged to have been bigamous.	*c. La Farce de Maistre Pierre Pathelin*, celebrated French comedy with a roguish hero; author uncertain.
1465	Burgundy and League of Public Weal in France defeated Louis XI at Montlhery; Peace of St Maur followed.	*Kalender*, early book containing metal engravings.
1466	Influence of Warwick in Yorkist affairs declined. Alliance between Louis XI and Warwick. Teutonic Order lost West Prussia and only able to retain East Prussia as fief of Poland, at Peace of Thorn.	First German Bible printed at Strasbourg by Johann Mentel.

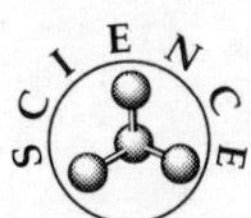

First book printed in German (*Der Edelstein*: see 1348); containing 101 wood-engravings.
c. Mantegna: *Agony in the Garden*, Italian painting.

Manufacture of gunpowder in England restricted to Tower of London for safety.
Barbers first incorporated by Edward IV.

*Piero di Cosimo (†1521), who painted vivid imaginative pictures, e.g. *Death of Procris*.
Rebuilding of Hever Castle, Kent, fortified manor house with a moat.

John de Castro discovered alum mines at Tolfa.
Pedro de Cintra, Portuguese, discovered Sierra Leone, to which he gave this name.

Construction (to 1470) of Sultan Mohammed II's mosque at Constantinople: rebuilt 1768.
First English musical degrees; at Cambridge.
Fra Filippo Lippi (*1406, †1469): *The Annunciation*, Italian painting.

Incorporation of Ironmongers' Company, London.
Monte di Pietà, money loaned at low interest rate to poor people, introduced at Orvieto.
Regiomontanus (*1436, †1476), German astronomer, completed *Epitome in Ptolemaei Almagestum*, mathematical work begun by Puerbach.

Stone Masons and the King, pictured in Jean Colombe's *Story of Troy*.

Louis XI of France established French Royal Mail.
Regiomontanus: *De triangulis omnimodus*, complete introduction to trigonometry; printed in Nuremberg, 1533.

Earliest printed music published.
First appearance of angel-noble; coin worth 6*s*. 8*d*.

First printing press set up in Italy at Subiaco by Pannartz and Sweynheym.

Luciano Laurana began work on the enormous Ducal Palace, Urbino, for Frederico Montefeltro.
Embroideries worked for baptistry of Florence (to 1487).

Development of the carrack, an advanced type of carvel-built sailing vessel.

LITERATURE

Year	History	Literature
1467	Quarrel between Edward IV and Warwick became open rupture. Charles the Bold became Duke of Burgundy; captured Liége. Herzegovina conquered by Turks. Outbreak of civil war in Japan; spread to Provinces *c.* 1500.	*c.* Ballad of about this date first gives story of William Tell.
1468	Outbreak of war between England and France. Margaret of York, sister to Edward IV, married Charles the Bold; Edward, Duke of Clarence, brother to Edward IV, married Isobel Neville, daughter of Warwick. Orkney and Shetland Islands mortgaged to Scotland; James III annexed them in 1471.	*Troan Chronicle,* first printed Czechoslovak book, issued.
1469	Yorkists led by Edward IV defeated by Warwick at Edgecote. Marriage of Ferdinand of Aragon to Isabella of Castile. Lorenzo di Medici, the "Magnificent", became leader of Florentine Republic.	
1470	Edward IV fled to Flanders; Warwick and Clarence, in league with Margaret of Anjou, restored Henry VI. Turks recaptured Negroponte from Venice.	Earliest extant "block book", i.e. printed from engraved wood blocks; process earlier in use for pictures.
1471	Edward IV defeated and killed Warwick at Barnet and defeated Queen Margaret and Prince Edward of Wales at Tewkesbury; Edward murdered; Henry VI murdered in Tower. Swedes defeated Christian I of Denmark at battle of Brunkeberg. Sea war between Hanse towns and England. Portuguese under Alfonso V took Tangier from Moors. †King George of Bohemia; succeeded by Ladislaus II.	*c.* First printing of *Imitatio Christi,* at Augsburg (see 1414).
1472	St Andrews, Scotland, made into Archbishopric. Ivan III, Grand Prince of Moscow, married Sophia Paleologue, niece of last Eastern Emperor.	Dante's *La Divina Commedia* (see 1314) first printed at Foligno.

Behzâd of Herat, great Persian artist, illustrated *History of Timur*.
Completion of Liebfrauenkirche, fine Gothic church outside Worms.

Roman Academy abolished by Pope Paul II.
Work begun on St Mary's Munich.
Hans Memlinc (*1432, †1494): The *Donne Triptych*, at Chatsworth; Flemish work.

c. Woodwose (Wild Man) silver spoon, the only one in existence.

Andrea del Verrocchio (*1435, †1488), whose true name was Cioni: *David*, Italian bronze sculpture.
† Fra Filippo Lippi, still engaged on decorating Spoleto Cathedral with scenes of the Virgin's life.

Alberti designed St Andrea's Church, Mantua; nave, 338 ft long, begun 1472.
Palace of Knights of Rhodes, Rome, completed.

First French printing press set up at Sorbonne.

Francesco di Giorgio Martini (*1439, †1501): *Coronation of the Virgin*, altarpiece at Siena.
c. Jacob Obrecht (*c*. *1430, †1500), Dutch composer: *St Matthew Passion*, having a Latin text; he also created eight masses, including *Fortima Desperata* (dates conjectural).

First European observatory (Nuremberg), designed by Regiomontanus.
Portuguese sailors reach the Gulf of Guinea.
Printing introduced into Holland.
Incorporation of Dyers' Company, London.
Destruction of Khmer civilization, Cambodia (see 860, 1275, 1296).

Teaching began at Ingoldstadt University.
c. Memlinc: *Last Judgment*, altarpiece, at Danzig.
Sophia brought to Moscow foreign architects who built stone churches and palaces.

Regiomontanus observed Halley's comet; beginning of modern astronomy of comets.
Claims by Deitrich Pining, a Dane, to have discovered Newfoundland (see 1497).
Fernão do Po, Portuguese, discovered Fernando Po, West Africa.

Year	History	Literature
1473	Burgundy enlarged by acquisition of Gelderland and Zutphen. Cyprus came under rule of Venice. Albert Achilles, the Elector, declared indivisibility of Electorate of Brandenburg. Mohammed II styled himself Sultan of Turkey, no longer an Emir.	
1474	Edward IV made alliance with Charles the Bold. Treaty of Utrecht between Edward IV and Hansa merchants. Isabella succeeded as Queen of Castile. Habsburgs recognized independence of Swiss League. Novgorod incorporated into Grand Duchy of Moscow.	William Caxton (*1422, †1491) printed first book in English, *Recuyell of the Historyes of Troye*; printing probably done at Bruges.
1475	*c.* Steelyard, London H.Q. of Hanse, enlarged by Edward IV. Edward IV invaded France; Peace of Piéquigny between England and France. Queen Margaret released from Tower of London.	*Gesta Romanorum* printed at Utrecht; popular tales in Latin with morals attached.
1476	Swiss defeated Charles the Bold at Grandson and Morat. Papal Bull authorized King of Spain to administer all military orders in Spain. Uzun Hasan overthrew Timurid emperors and installed his own governor in Baghdad. Bahlol Lodi deposed Husain, last King of Jaunpur.	*c.* Fortescue: *The Governance of England*, in English. Masuccio (*c.* (*1415, *c.* †1477): *Novellino* printed at Naples; five books each of ten stories.
1477	Charles the Bold of Burgundy defeated and killed at Nancy by French; Louis XI seized Artois. Marriage of Maximilian, son of Emperor Frederick III, to Mary of Burgundy, heiress of Charles the Bold; Estates of Netherlands received great privileges from Mary.	Caxton printed *Canterbury Tales* (see 1388) and other works at his new press in Westminster.
1478	†George, Duke of Clarence, imprisoned in Tower for treason. Pazzi conspiracy in Florence against Lorenzo and Giuliano di Medici; Giuliano assassinated. Peace of Olomouc between Bohemia	

Robert Wodeclarke founded St Catherine's College, Cambridge.
Giovanni dei Dolci built Sistine Chapel of the Vatican for Sixtus IV.
Martin Schongauer (*c.* *1445, †1491): altarpiece for St Martin's, Colmar.

*Nicolas Copernicus (†1543), mathematician, physicist, classics scholar: he was to propound rotation of the earth once in 24 hours and refute the idea that the earth is the centre of the universe.
Incorporation of Pewterer's Company, London.

Tinctoris: *Terminorum Musicae Diffinitorum*, first musical dictionary (Naples).
Mantegna: frescoes in Camera degli Sposi, Mantua.
c. Erection, to 1509, of Palais de Justice, Rouen.

All earlier Hanse privileges in England confirmed.
Silver drinking-horn of Oldenburg.
Regiomontanus: *Ephemerides*, nautical almanack for years 1474–1506, introducing method of lunar distances for longitude.

Erection (to 1479) of cathedral of the Assumption (Uspensky Sobor), Kremlin, on site of ruined church of 1325.

Das Buch der Natur (see 1350) first printed: contained first woodcuts of plants.

The Game and Playe of the Chesse printed by Caxton, contains the earliest English woodcuts.

Caxton began printing in Westminster, London, at the "Red Pale" in the Almonry.
L. van Berquen, Bruges, developed lapidary's wheel for faceting diamonds.

Sandro Botticelli (*1444, †1510), Florentine painter who worked for the Medici family: *Primavera*.
Foundation of the University of Uppsala and of the University of Tübingen.

Incorporation of Company of Carpenters, London.
Early record of gun with rifled barrel; in Italy; in general, rifling developed early in 16th cent.

Verrocchio at work (until 1480) on bronze group, *Unbelief of St Thomas* for Or San Michele, Florence.
Choir of Christ Church Cathedral, Oxford, added; perpendicular vaulting.
Foundation of Copenhagen University.

Important printing of Celsus's *De Medicina*.
An apostle spoon bears the date letter apparently belonging to this year; the earliest exactly datable English silver; leopard's head hallmark *crowned* (till 1829).

	History	Literature
1478	and Matthias of Hungary; Bohemia ceded Moravia, Silesia and Lusatia. Ivan III, Grand Prince of Moscow, subdued Novgorod.	
1479	Intrigues of Albany and Mar against James III of Scotland. Battle of Guinegate; French defeated Maximilian of Habsburg. Union of Aragon and Castile under Ferdinand and Isabella. Peace of Constantinople: Venice ceded territory in Albania and Lemnos to Turks.	
1480	†Réné of Lorraine; Louis XI acquired Anjou, Maine and Provence. Ferdinand and Isabella of Spain authorized by Pope Sixtus IV to appoint Inquisitors against heresy. Treaty of Toledo; Spain recognized Portuguese conquest of Morocco; Portugal ceded Canaries. Turks captured Otranto. Ivan III, of Moscow, threw off Mongol allegiance and styled himself "Tsar".	Caxton printed *Chronicle of England*. Angelo Poliziano (*1454, †1494): *Favola di Orfeo*, first dramatic pastoral produced in Italy.
1481	Anglo-Scottish war broke out; Richard of Gloucester supported Albany against James III. Fribourg and Solothurn joined Swiss League. †Mohammed II; succeeded by Bajazet II. Turks evacuated Otranto.	Elio de Lebrija (*1441, †1522), Spanish scholar: *Introductiones Latinae*, study of Latin grammar.
1482	Richard of Gloucester entered Edinbrgh; English captured Berwick; James III a prisoner. Peace of Arras between France and Maximilian: Burgundy partitioned; Netherlands, Luxembourg and Franche-Comté to Maximilian. War between Papal States and alliance of Ferrara, Venice and Naples. †Mohammed Shah III and end of Bahmani kingdom of Deccan. Franciscan Mission received in Abyssinia.	

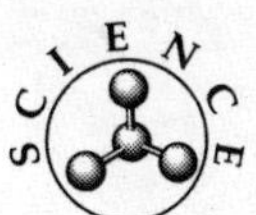

Memlinc: *The Marriage of St Catherine*, Flemish painting, at Bruges.

Nettlecombe chalice, earliest silver cup with a date letter.

Giovanni Bellini (*1430, †1516), central figure of the Venetian school: *St. Francis in Ecstasy*, painting on wood.
Memlinc: *Madonna and Child with Angels*, Flemish painting.
c. Foundation of Scottish Order of the Thistle by James III.
The *Warden's Grace Cup*, silver-gilt, New College, Oxford.

Leonardo da Vinci (*1452, †1519), engineer, tactician, architect, painter, sculptor and musician—genius of his day—experimented with small parachutes.
Islamic spherical astrolabe made (3¼ in. diameter); now at Oxford.
Mittelalterliches Hansbuch, military handbook.

Pietro Perugino (*1450, †1524) and Pinturicchio (*1454, †1513), Italian painters, at work on frescoes in Sistine Chapel of the Vatican.

The *Anathema Cup* of Pembroke College, Cambridge.

**c.* Botticelli: *Adoration of the Magi*, Italian painting.
c. Filippino Lippi (*1457, †1504): *Madonna kneeling before the Child*, Florentine painting.
(to 1490) Mantegna: *Triumphs of Caesar*, nine paintings (restored).
Erection of Oxburgh Hall, Norfolk; moated house.

Portuguese established settlements on Gold Coast.
First *printed* Latin text of Euclid's geometry.

	History	Literature
1483	†Edward IV of England; accession of son Edward V; doubts cast on legality of marriage of Edward IV and Elizabeth Woodville. Richard of Gloucester proclaimed king as Richard III. Disappearance of Edward V and his brother, Richard of York. Revolt and execution of Duke of Buckingham. Albany deposed from office of Lieutenant General of Scotland. †Louis XI of France; accession of Charles VIII. Spanish Inquisition under direction of Church and State.	Caxton printed Jacobus de Voragine's *Golden Legend*, a history of the saints. The *Sarum Breviary*, basis for prayer books of Edward VI, printed in Venice.
1484	Richard III summoned only Parliament of his reign; benevolences declared to be illegal. James III, supported by Richard III, suppressed revolt by Albany. Peace of Bagnolo: Ferrara ceded Polesina to Venice. Papal Bull issued against witchcraft.	First Parliamentary Statutes set out in English and printed.
1485	Richard III defeated and killed by Henry Tudor at battle of Bosworth; accession of Henry as Henry VII; start of Tudor dynasty. Brittany revolted against Charles VIII of France. Vienna captured by Matthias of Hungary. Murder of Pedro de Arbues, Spanish Inquisitor. Diet at Knuttenberg: Utraquists in Bohemia granted equal rights with Roman Catholics; rights of all Bohemian burgesses in the Bohemian Diet restricted.	Caxton printed Sir Thomas Malory's *Morte d'Arthur*, a finely written collection of the legends of Arthur and his knights.
1486	Marriage of Henry VII to Elizabeth of York ended succession question in England. Revolt of Lord Lovel suppressed. Cardinal Moreton became Archbishop of Canterbury. Anglo-French truce for three years. Maximilian of Habsburg elected King of Germans.	†Erik Olai, Father of Swedish historical writing, who wrote *Chronica Regni Gothorum*. *The Book of St Albans* printed; on heraldry and blood-sports.

Richard III incorporated the College of Arms (concerned with genealogy and armorial bearings).
Fischbrunnen (fountain) at Freiburg, Baden; still extant.
(to 1511) Palazzo della Cancellaria, fine Renaissance building, Rome, erected.

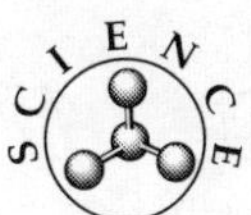

Theodore of Gaza translated Theophrastus's *Historia Plantarum* (*c.* –300) into Latin.
Incorporation of Waxchandlers' Company, London.
Russians began to explore Siberia.

Botticelli: *Birth of Venus*, Florentine painting.
Pinturicchio: frescoes in chapel in Ara Coeli on the Capitol.
Antonio Rizzo constructed great Renaissance staircase of inner court of Doge's Palace, Venice.

Diego Cam, Portuguese seaman, discovered mouth of the R. Congo, which is more than 4800 km long.
Thaler (now corrupted as *dollar*) introduced by Sigismund of Tirol.
Richard III's reforms in law, trade and tax collection.

c. Coconut cups, silver-mounted, at New College, Oxford.
(to 1539) Erection of Cotehele House, Cornwall.
c. Rare mazer (drinking-bowl) mounted in silver-gilt, of Holy Trinity, Colchester.
Verrocchio began work on bronze equestrian statue of Bartolommeo Colleoni; completed by Leopardi 1496.

De re aedificatoria, work on building construction by Alberti, published posthumously.
Navigation Act passed under Henry VII.
Bordeaux wines limited to English ships.
Henry VII renewed Hanse privileges in England.
First appearance of sweating-sickness in England; not to be confused with the plague.
Establishment of Yeomen of the Guard.

Sesshū (*1420, †1506) painted famous Japanese landscape scroll, 50 ft. long.
Josquin des Près (*1445, †1521), early French composer, joined papal chapel in Rome, which became the home of European music.

Portuguese discovered Angola.
Incorporation of Barbers' Company, London.
Rediscovery of *De Architectura Libri Decem*, great work by Vitruvius, Roman architect; *fl.* –90, *q.v.*

	History	Literature
1487	Rebellion of Lambert Simnel; John de la Pole supported Simnel; defeated at Stoke near Newark. Court of Star Chamber established. Tsar Ivan III subdued Khanate of Kazan.	
1488	Anglo-French truce renewed. Rebellion in Scotland; James III defeated at Sauchieburn; murdered after battle; truce between England and Scotland. Charles VIII of France defeated Brittany at St Aubin. Formation of Swabian League in Southern Germany. Treaty of Reval between Teutonic Order and Sweden. Revolt of Flemish towns against Maximilian I.	Duke Humphrey's library opened at Oxford.
1489	Alliance between England and Brittany. Alliance between Henry VII and Emperor Frederick III—Treaty of Dordrecht. Queen of Cyprus ceded island to Venice. Yasuf Adil Shah, former Georgian slave, became first independent ruler of Bijapur.	Philippe de Commynes: *Mémoires*, memoirs of a French noble of the reigns of Louis XI and Charles VIII (completed 1498). Poliziano: *Miscellanea*.
1490	Anglo-Danish treaty of peace: English ships admitted to Iceland. Sigismund of Tyrol ceded his lands to Maximilian I. Crusade against Turks decided upon at Congress in Rome. †Matthias of Hungary; Ladislaus of Bohemia elected to Hungarian throne. *c*. Bahmani kingdom broke up; Ahmadnagar and Bijapur leading Deccan states.	
1491	Anglo-Scottish truce for five years concluded at Coldstream. Brittany united to France by marriage of Charles VIII of France to Anne, Duchess of Brittany. Treaty of Pressburg: Ladislaus of Bohemia and Hungary recognized Habsburg right of succession in these territories.	Grocyn taught Greek at Oxford. Publication of *Schatzbehalter*, containing fine wood-cuts.

SCIENCE

Bellini: *Madonna degli Alberetti,* Italian painting.
Foundation of Stockport Grammar School.

Bartholomew Diaz sailed round the Cape of Good Hope, then called Cape of Storms.
Statute of Livery and Maintenance passed by Parliament.

(to 1496) Collegio di San Gregorio, Valladolid, erected: possesses curious Spanish decoration.
Mantegna painted frescoes, Chapel of Innocent VIII, Vatican.
Cristoforo Rocchi began building Cathedral of San Martino, Pavia.

Bartholomew Diaz landed at Mussel Bay and went to mouth of the Great Fish River.
Trading concessions granted by Henry VII to Italian merchants.
Construction of Henry VII's famous ship: the *Great Harry*.

Church of the Annunciation, Kremlin, built (begun 1484).
c. Bellini: S. Giobbe altar.
Memlinc: *Shrine of St Ursula,* Flemish painting.
Benedetto da Maiano began work on Palazzo Strozzi, Florence.

Symbols + (plus, originally *surplus*) and − (minus) in use.
Trade treaty between England and Spain.
Regulation for importation of Bordeaux wine made permanent.

Eton College manuscript, book of early English music, produced for the college.
Present buildings of Pavia University begun by Lodovico il Moro (see 1361).
c. Warden Hill's Salt, silver-gilt standing salt cellar at New College, Oxford.

da Vinci observed capillary action of liquids in small-bore tubes.
Bonardo translated Galen's complete Greek medical works into Latin (see 1525)
c. Colourless glass superseded earlier type, usually blue, green or violet.

Erection of Spasskiye Vorota (Gate of Salvation) of Kremlin, Moscow.
Old Lincoln's Inn Hall, London, erected; rebuilt 1928.
Domenico Ghirlandaio: *Birth of the Virgin,* wall painting in church of Santa Maria Novella, Florence.

Portuguese expedition to Angola.

Year	History	Literature
1492	Revolt of Perkin Warbeck against Henry VII; Warbeck claimed to be Richard, Duke of York, son to Edward IV; recognized by Margaret, Duchess of Burgundy, and kings of France and Scotland. Henry VII's mock invasion of France; Treaty of Etaples. France abandoned Warbeck. Ferdinand of Aragon conquered Moorish province of Granada and ended Mohammedan era in Spain. Jews expelled from Spain. Roderigo Borgia elected Pope as Alexander VI. †Casimir IV of Poland and Lithuania; succeeded, in Poland, by John Albert and, in Lithuania, by Alexander.	*c.* Elio de Lebrija: *Arte de la Lengua castellana,* first modern language grammar book (of Castilian). Latin writings of St Brigitta (*1303, †1373) of Sweden, concerning her visions, printed.
1493	Peace between France and Spain at Barcelona. Treaty of Senlis between France and Emperor by which France ceded Netherlands to Burgundy. †Frederick III; Maximilian I of Germany succeeded as emperor. Pope Alexander VI divided newly discovered lands between Spain and Portugal. Peasants revolted in Alsace. Husain Shah became King of independent Bengal.	
1494	Warbeck recognized as King of England by Maximilian I. Poynings Laws: passage of two laws which made Irish Parliament subservient to English Parliament. Treaty of Tordesillas: Spain and Portugal shared the New World. Ludovico Sforza of Milan invited Charles VIII of France to invade Italy; Piero di Medici supported Charles's claim to Naples; driven out of Florence.	Aldo Manuzio (*1450, †1515) established the Aldine Press at Venice; famous for fine books. Sebastian Brant: *Narrenschiff,* in Swabian dialect (see 1509). Johann Reuchlin (*1455, †1522): *De Verbo Mirifico,* supporting Jewish writings.
1495	Warbeck attempted landing in Kent; failed; welcomed to Scotland by James IV. Portugal expelled the Jews.	*c.* Manuzio, printing at Venice, introduced *italic* lettering. First book printed in Denmark: a rhymed history.

(to 1498) Donato Bramante (*c. 1444, † c. 1514), Italian architect and painter, erected cupola and choir of S. Maria delle Grazie, Milan.
Erection of Knebworth House, Hertfordshire; Gothic exterior added 1843.
Pinturicchio painted frescoes (to 1495) in the Borgia apartments.

da Vinci designed a flying machine.
Christopher Columbus, Genoese navigator in service of Spain, crossed Atlantic and discovered the West Indies; landed at San Salvador, observed that magnetic compass North differed from true North but was subject to change (the difference is known as *variation*; see 1460).
Martin Behaim of Nuremberg constructed first modern globe of the Earth.

The Nuremburg Chronicle, news-sheet illustrated with woodcuts.
Erection of Buckden Palace, Huntingdonshire, tower and gatehouse; residence of Bishops of Lincoln from 12th cent.
(to 1526 Gran Guardia, loggia in Padua, erected.

Fasciculo di Medicina, Italian medical work with fine illustrations.
Merchant Adventurers moved headquarters from Antwerp to Calais.
Trade war between England and Flanders; Flemings evicted from England.
Steelyard attacked by London mob hostile to Hanse.
Columbus discovered Antigua and Puerto Rico.

King's College, Aberdeen University, founded by Bishop Elphinstone (charter 1498).
(to 1515) Erection of Riga Castle; since rebuilt.
c. Giovanni Mansueti: *The Miracle of the True Cross*, Venetian painting.
Completion of Arras town hall (belfry 1554).

Luca Pacioli (*1450, †1520): *Summa de Arithmetica*, important textbook of arithmetic and algebra.
Paper manufacture in England.
Mercury used in treatment of venereal disease.
St. Peter's Court, headquarters of Hanse merchants in Novgorod, closed by Ivan III.

Early reference to the trombone, then called a sackbut.
Perugino: *Pietà*, Italian painting.
Tidal wave removed wooden building

Grave outbreak of syphilis at Naples.
Fra Mauro, monkish cartographer, completed fine world map (begun 1493) for Alfonso of Portugal.

LITERATURE

1495 Charles VIII of France entered Naples; Holy League, formed of Pope, Emperor, Spain, Venice, Milan, forced Charles to withdraw.
Savonarola, preacher of penitence in Florence, summoned to Rome; refused to attend.

1496 Henry VII joined Holy League against France.
Border warfare; James IV of Scotland invaded England.
Magnus Intercursus: trade treaty between Henry VII and Philip the Fair (son of Maximilian I) of Burgundy.
Marriage of Philip the Fair to Joanna, heiress of Spain, ensured his accession as Philip I.

John Colet (*1467, †1519), divine and educationist, began to lecture on the Pauline epistles, at Oxford.
Juan del Encina (*c.* *1469, †1529), founder of Spanish drama: *Cancionero*.

1497 Warbeck landed in Cornwall; Cornish insurgents defeated at Blackheath; Warbeck later captured.
Anglo-Scottish truce.
Pope Alexander VI conferred on Ferdinand and Isabella of Spain title of "Most Catholic Majesties".
Battle of Brunkeberg: John II of Denmark invaded and defeated Sweden; became joint king of Denmark, Norway and Sweden for a short time.
Law enacted in Bohemia which strictly bound peasants to land of masters.

Aldine Press, Venice, issued fine edition of *Horae Beatae Mariae Virginis*.
Tsar Ivan III of Russia issued *Sudebnik*, Code of Laws.

1498 †Charles VIII of France; succeeded by Louis XII, who divorced his wife and married Anne of Brittany, widow of Charles, to keep Brittany for French Crown.
Grisons joined Swiss League.
Savonarola burned at stake in Florence.
Columbus deprived of Governorship of West Indies and brought back to Spain in chains.

Desiderius Erasmus (*1469, †1536), Dutch philosopher of the Reformation, settled at Oxford.
Aldine Press issued nine comedies of Aristophanes.

1499 Warbeck executed for attempt to escape from Tower; Earl of Warwick, last male Yorkist in direct line of succession, executed for aiding Warbeck.
Switzerland became independent Republic by Peace of Basle.

Celestina, immensely successful Spanish novel in dialogue form, printed.
Printing of *De Modis Significandi sive Grammatica Speculativa*, by Duns Scotus (see 1308).

surrounding Great Buddha of Kamakura (*c.* 1250), which has remained out-of-doors ever since.
c. Exceptional brass of Bishop Bell, Carlisle Cathedral.

Giorgio Martini, Italian engineer and artist (see 1471), invented military mines.
Imperial Diet of Worms imposed "Common Penny", general tax throughout Empire.

Earliest extant English silver beaker.
Bellini: *Procession on Piazza San Marco,* Venetian painting.
(to 1498) Pinturicchio painted altarpiece for S. Maria de'Fossi, Perugia.
Erection (to 1532) of present St David's Cathedral, Bangor, Wales.

Henry VII gave Royal Patronage to the Cabots in their voyage to North America.
Magnus Intercursus encouraged export of English wool to Netherlands.
Dockyard established at Portsmouth.
Bartholomew Columbus founded Santo Domingo, first European town in America.

da Vinci: *The Last Supper,* famous painting.
Jesus College, Cambridge, founded.
Michelangelo Buonarroti (*1475, †1564): *Cupid,* marble statue by the great Italian.
Erection of monastery and church of Belem, Lisbon.
Old Royal Palace (of Elizabeth I) near site of Hatfield House (built 1607, *q.v.*).

Standard yard and other measurements of Henry VII established; based on earlier systems of Edward I.
Venetian sailors, John and Sebastian Cabot, in ships fitted out by Bristol merchants, discovered Newfoundland (probably known earlier) and Nova Scotia.
Vasco da Gama sighted Natal (Terra Natalis), South Africa.

Botticelli: *Calumny of Apelles,* Florentine painting.
The Apocalypse, fifteen fine woodcuts of Albrecht Dürer (*1471, †1529), German etcher, engraver, painter.
East wing of the Château de Blois added to 13th cent. building.
Michelangelo: *Pietà,* famous marble statue.

Vasco da Gama, Portuguese seaman, followed route of Diaz and reached Calicut in India; first European to find Indian sea-route.
Mozambique discovered by da Gama's fleet.
Cabot discovered Hudson Bay (see 1610).
Columbus discovered Trinidad and mainland of S. America (coast of Venezuela).

c. Dürer: *The Great Passion,* seven woodcuts; four added later (1510).
Foundation of Alcala University.
The *Leigh Cup* of the Mercers' Company, London.
c. da Vinci: *Madonna with St Anne,* cartoon.

Amerigo Vespucci (*1451, †1512) and Alonso Hojeda discovered Venezuela and Guiana; America was so named after the former.
Abbot Trithemius (*1462, †1516): *Polygraphia,* first work on cryptography (see 1518).

LITERATURE

	History	Literature
1499	Cesare Borgia, son of Pope Alexander VI, conquered Romagna. Henry VII of England attempted to form trading alliance with Riga; prevented by Hanse influence.	
1500	Louis XII of France, descendant of Viscontis of Milan, conquered Duchy of Milan. Treaty of Granada: France and Spain agreed on partition of Italy. Pope Alexander VI proclaimed Crusade against Turks. *Charles of Ghent, son of Philip the Fair and Joanna of Spain, future Emperor Charles V. Peasants of Ditmarschen revolted against Danes; defeated Hans of Denmark. Sweden revolted against Denmark. Anti-Danish disturbances in Norway. Assembly of Diet of Augsburg.	*c. Till Eulenspiegel (Owl-glass)* first published; collection of Low German folk tales. Manuzio founded the Venice Academy for the study of Greek classics. Erasmus: *Adagio*, study of classical proverbs. *c.* Renaissance spread from Italy through Western Europe during this century.
1501	Marriage of Arthur, Prince of Wales, to Katherine of Aragon linked fortunes of England with those of Spain and Austria against France. France and Spain conquered Naples; conquest, together with French conquests in North Italy, recognized by Empire at Treaty of Trento. Basle and Schaffhausen joined Swiss League.	Aldine Press issued fine edition of Virgil.
1502	Marriage of Margaret, daughter of Henry VII of England, to James IV of Scotland; led in 1603 to Stuart succession. Rebellion of peasants in Bishopric of Spires. Safayid dynasty established in Persia.	*Mendoza Codex* (beginning 1324) terminated in this year; Aztec pictorial MS. of Mexican history. Aldine Press published fine editions of works of Herodotus, Sophocles and Thucydides.
1503	Export of more than 6*s*. 8*d*. worth of bullion to Ireland forbidden by Henry VII of England. Piero di Medici drowned fighting for Charles VIII at Garigliano. Bavaria and Palatinate at war over Bavarian succession.	William Dunbar (**c.* 1460, †*c.* 1520): *The Thrissil and the Rois*, Scottish poem on politics. Erasmus: *Enchiridion Militis Christiani*, guide to faith.

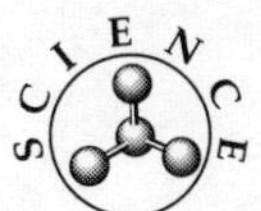

Luca Signorelli (*c.* *1450, †1523) frescoes (to 1504), Orvieto Cathedral.

Trading agreement with Burgundy; English cloth allowed into Burgundian territories, except Flanders, free of controls.

c. Bellini: (i) *Pietà*, (ii) *Madonna and Child in a Landscape*, Venetian paintings.
Piero di Cosimo (*1462, †1521): *The Visitation with two Saints*, Italian painting.
Dürer: *Self-Portrait*.
Michelangelo: *Madonna and Child with the young St John*, marble relief, Florence.
c. Introduction of the virginals, earliest form of harpsichord.
c. Violin family appeared; of separate origin from the viols; for a time both sets of instruments were used concurrently.

Brazilian coast discovered by Pedro Cabral, who claimed it for Portugal.
Vicente Pinzon, Spanish explorer, discovered the Amazon mouth.
c. Dutch used pumping machinery to help drain and reclaim land.
c. Peter Henlein, of Nuremberg, invented coiled spring to drive a clock.
c. Goldfish reached Japan from China.
Wynkyn de Worde established press in Fleet Street; first connection of the latter with printing.
c. The *Richmond Cup*, silver-gilt, was constructed.

Publication of the first hymnbook (Bohemia).
The Campion Cup, made of silver-gilt.
Pinturicchio: frescoes in S. Maria Maggiore, Spello.
Holyrood House, royal residence at Edinburgh, first built.

Anglo-Portuguese Syndicate made first voyage to N. America.
João de Nova discovered Ascension Island.
Incorporation of Company of Coopers, London.

King's School, Macclesfield, founded by Sir John Percyvale (see 1552).
Foundation of Wittenburg and Seville Universities.
Bellini: *Doge Leonardo Loredano*, Italian painting.

Fourth voyage of Columbus to the West Indies; explored Gulf of Mexico; discovered Nicaragua.
Vespucci sailed down Eastern seaboard of S. America; Portuguese knew of Seychelles; João de Nova of Portugal discovered St Helena.

da Vinci: *Mona Lisa (La Gioconda)* famous Italian painting begun.
Michelangelo: *David*, great Italian sculpture, 14 ft high.
Mathias Grünewald: *Flagellation*, German painting by artist with intense religious motivation.

Pedro Navarro (*c.* *1460, †1528) successfully mined Naples castle; first military engineering of this period of history.
First gold sovereigns struck; value, originally 22*s.* 6*d.*, varied from time to time.

Year	History	Literature
1504	Treaty of Blois: peace between France and Empire. Treaty of Lyons: France ceded Naples to Spain. Church Council in Moscow condemned "Judaizers", who denied divinity of Christ and Trinity. Albert IV of Bavaria defeated Rupert of Palatinate so re-uniting two principalities. Kabul captured by Mogul, Babur.	Jacopo Sannazzaro: *Arcadia*, a romance, early pastoral prose-poem.
1505	Martin Luther entered Augustine monastery at Erfurt. †Tsar Ivan III; accession of Vasily III, last of "collectors" of territory in central and northern Russia.	Jakob Wimpfeling: *Epitome Rerum Germanicarum*, first Teutonic history, published.
1506	King Hans of Denmark sent son and heir, Christian, to Norway as Regent until 1512. First national Italian troops—Florentine militia—embodied by Niccolo Machiavelli (*1469, †1527). Marriage of Firoz Shah Bahmani and princess of Vijayanager.	*c.* Dunbar: *The Dance of the Sevin Deidly Synnis*, Scottish poem.
1507	Anglo-Venetian treaty renewed by Henry VII only when Venetians agreed to abandon carrying trade between England and Flanders. Pope Julius II proclaimed Indulgence to help building of St Peter's. Diet of Constance: Imperial Chamber established. Territorial taxation according to fixed Roll introduced.	
1508	League of Cambrai, Empire, France and Aragon against Venice. Ismail of Persia entered Baghdad and made Iraq into a Persian province. Martin Luther appointed Professor of Divinity at Wittenburg University.	*Amadis de Gaula*, first printed in Spanish; prose romance written by Lobeira, Montalvo and others; immensely popular story.

SCIENCE

Raphael (Raffaello Sanzio); (*1483, †1520): *The Marriage of The Virgin*, Italian painting.
Giorgione (da Castelfranco) (*1478, †1510): *Madonna*, Italian painting.
Michelangelo decorated hall of Palazzo Vecchio.

English Cordwainers barred from practising trade of tanners by State.
Gilds and Companies in England placed under State control by Henry VII.
Henry VII confirmed Hanse privileges only if similar privileges granted to English merchants in Hanse areas.
First silver shilling minted.

Lady Margaret Beaufort founded Christ's College, Cambridge.
Raphael: (i) *St. George and the Dragon*; (ii) *The Madonna della Granduca*, Italian paintings.
Bellini: S. Zaccaria altarpiece, *Madonna with Saints*.
Erection (to 1509) of Archangel Cathedral, Kremlin.
Grünewald: *Crucifixion*, German painting.

Henry VII granted Charter to Merchant Adventurers of All England.
Francesco de Almeida, Portuguese, first European explorer to reach Ceylon.
Mascarenhas, Portuguese, discovered Mauritius, previously uninhabited.
Francis, Count of Thurn and Taxis, set up first regular mail service between Vienna and Brussels.
First artificial hand manufactured.

Rebuilding of the world's greatest cathedral, St Peter's, Rome, commenced; completed 120 years later.
Raphael: (i) *Madonna del Giardino*; (ii) *Ansidei Madonna*, Italian paintings.
University of Frankfurt-on-Oder, founded.

Henry VII secured retail and wholesale cloth trade of Flanders for English merchants (*Malus intercursus*).
†Christopher Columbus in poverty.
Medal of Pope Julius II, by Francia; first *engraved* medal.

Raphael: *Entombment*, Italian painting.
da Vinci: *Virgin of the Rocks*, Italian painting.
c. Giorgione: *The three Philosophers*, Italian painting.
Early form of musical suite published in Venice.

Martin Waldseemüller: map of world showing S. America separated from Asia—first time the name *America* was used in a book; made early globe in same year.
Philip of Burgundy revoked *Magnus intercursus* (see 1496).

Michelangelo painted (to 1512) curved ceiling of Sistine Chapel, Vatican; Raphael summoned by Pope Julius II to help decorate Vatican.
Giorgione: *The Tempest*, Venetian painting.
Wooden stall-work of Amiens Cathedral carved.

First book printed in Scotland.

LITERATURE

1509 †Henry VII and accession of Henry VIII, who married Katherine of Aragon, widow of his elder brother, Prince Arthur.
Pope Julius II joined League of Cambrai.
Venice defeated by League at Agnadello; lost Faenza, Rimini and Ravenna to Pope; Otranto and Brindisi to Aragon.
Spaniards conquered Oran.
Portuguese naval victory over Egypt and Gujarat at Diu.

Paston Letters ended (1422–1509); collection of letters written by the Norfolk family of the Pastons; shed valuable light on customs of the time.
Erasmus: *The Praise of Folly*, his best known book.
Jewish books burned by Imperial Order.
Alexander Barclay (*c.* *1475, †1552): *The Ship of Fools*, English verse translation of *Narrenschiff* (see 1494).

1510 Empson and Dudley, unpopular tax-collectors of Henry VII, executed by Henry VIII.
Treaty between Pope Julius II and Venice.
Luther in Rome as delegate of Augustinian Order.
Portuguese under Albuquerque took Goa from Sultan of Bijapur.
War between Denmark and Hanse; ended 1512.

1511 Henry VIII of England joined Holy League of Julius II, Aragon and Venice against France; invaded France; failed to recover Guienne.
Albert of Hohenzollern became Grand Master of Teutonic Order.
Vasily III of Moscow appointed new Patriarch of Moscow on his own authority.

Peter Martyr: *De Orbe Novo*, history of Spanish exploration (trans. into English 1555).
Erasmus appointed professor of Greek at Cambridge.

1512 French driven from Milan by Swiss, who restored a Sforza puppet as Duke.
Medicis, supported by Holy League, restored to Florence.
Battle of Ravenna; French driven out of Italy.
Spaniards invaded Navarre.
Fifth Lateran Council.
Diet of Cologne set up ten Circles in the Empire as basis of Imperial Government.
Outbreak of war between Russia and Poland; ended 1522.

Erasmus: *De ratione studii*, a study of language.

Giorgione: *The Rustic's Concert*, Italian painting.
Foundation of Brasenose College, Oxford, by William Smyth.
Lucas Cranach the Elder (*1472, †1553): *Venus*, German painting.
St Paul's School, London, refounded by Dean Colet; kept free from clerical influence.
c. Grünewald: Isenheim triptych.

First attempt to restrict the right to practise medicine to licensed and qualified men; previously surgery was carried out by barbers.
Watch invented by Peter Henlein of Nuremberg (*Nuremberg Egg*).
Tapestry-weaving works established at Barchester.
Louis XII of France founded Havre.
Sumatra first settled by Europeans (Portuguese).

Giorgione: *The Adoration of the Shepherds*, Italian painting.
Girard David (*1460, †1523): *The Rest on the Flight into Egypt*, Flemish painting.
Dürer: *Death of the Landsknecht*, woodcut with verses.
First use of word "architecture".
c. Hieronymus Bosch (*c*. *1460, †1516): *Hell*, fantastic visionary painting by the Dutch artist.

da Vinci expounded the principles of water-turbine; also drew anatomical studies in same year.
Discovery of the East coast of America as far as the neighbourhood of what is now Charleston.
Silk industry established in Spain and Italy.
Parliament granted Henry VIII tunnage and poundage for life.

Dürer: *Reunion of the Saints*, German painting; also *St Jerome*, woodcut.
Lady Margaret Beaufort founded St John's College, Cambridge.
The Jew's harp illustrated in a woodcut of Virdung; instrument is of earlier origin; earliest mention also of the virginals and of the xylophone.

Waldseemüller of Strasbourg made very accurate maps of the Rhine valley; invented polymetrum, prototype of the theodolite.
Portuguese traders reached Malacca and Spice Islands.
Earliest known record of the Bermudas.

Michelangelo completed *The Creation of Adam*, part of the decoration of the Vatican.
Dürer: *Madonna and Child*, German painting.
c. Chapel of Henry VII, Windsor, commenced.
Torregiano commenced work on tomb of Henry VII at Westminster Abbey (completed 1518).
Raphael: *Madonna with Fish* and *Julius II*, Italian paintings.

No one allowed to practise as physician or surgeon in London without licence of Bishop of London.
Act of Parliament against deceitful working of woollen cloth.
Stobnicza: *Introduction to Ptolemaic Cosmography*.
Vintners ordered not to assess price of wine.
Importation of foreign caps forbidden by Parliament.

1513 Henry VIII defeated French at Guinegate (battle of Spurs); captured Terouenne and Tournai; withdrew from Holy League.
For services in organizing French campaign, Thomas Wolsey received Bishopric of Tournai; admitted to King's confidence; rise began.
Battle of Flodden: Scotland, in alliance with France, invaded England when Henry VIII invaded France; Scots defeated; James IV killed.
Giovanni di Medici elected Pope as Leo X.
Peasants of Breisgau revolted.
Inquisition introduced into Sicily.

Machiavelli: *The Prince*, treatise by the Florentine statesman to show that rulers have a right to be cunning to uphold their power.
Sir Thomas More (*1478, †1535), historian, humanist and lawyer: *History of Richard III* (printed 1557).

1514 Treaty of alliance between England and France; sealed by marriage of Mary, sister of Henry VIII, to Louis XII of France; recognition of Spain as chief rival to England.
Sale of Indulgences commenced by Johann Tetzel.
Treaty of Gmunden: alliance between Emperor Maximilian I and Vasily III of Moscow.
Smolensk captured from Poland-Lithuania by Vasily III.
Principality of Moldavia became Turkish.
War between Turkey and Persia.

1515 Thomas Wolsey created Cardinal and Archbishop of York and appointed Chancellor of England.
Battle of Marignano: Francis I of France defeated Sforza puppet Duke of Milan.
Treaty of Bologna: Pope Leo X surrendered Parma and Piacenza to France.
Navarre incorporated with Castile.
Vienna Treaties settled succession of Habsburgs and Jagellons in Austria, Poland and Hungary.
Battle of Chaldiran: Selim I of Turkey overthrew armies of Shah of Persia.

Giangiorgio Trissino: *Sofonisba*, first blank-verse play; the Italian wrote in unrhymed iambic pentameter.
John Skelton (*c.* *1460, †1529): *Magnificence*, morality play.
First publication of *Epistolae Obscurorum Virorum* (Letters of Lowly Men).

Early English woodcut on a news-sheet (*Trewe Encounter*) issued after the battle of Flodden.
Bellini: S. Giovanni Crisostomo altar, Venetian work.
Raphael and his pupils: *Meeting of Attila*, fresco in the Vatican.
Dürer: *Knight, Death and the Devil*, German copper engraving.
Pinturicchio (†): *Christ bearing His Cross*, Italian painting.

da Vinci appears to have flown small figures filled with hot air.
Vasco Balbao (*c.* *1475, †1517) crossed the Isthmus of Panama and discovered the Pacific Ocean.
Florida discovered for Spain by Ponce de Leon.
Mascarenhas discovered Réunion.
Portuguese set up trading factory at Diu.
First Commissioners of Sewers to deal with drainage problems.

Titian (Tiziano Vecelli, *1447, †1576), famous for mythological and religious pictures: *The Tribute Money*.
Dosso Dossi (*1479, †1541): *Circe and her Lovers*, Italian painting (completed 1516).
Raphael: (i) *Liberation of St Peter*; (ii) *The nymph Galatea*, frescoes.
Dürer: *Melancholy*, German print.

Henry VIII chartered Trinity House as Corporation of London Pilots.

Raphael: *The Sistine Madonna*, Italian painting (completed 1519).
Free Grammar School, Manchester, founded by will of Hugh Oldham, Bishop of Exeter.
Bellini: *Girl arranging her Hair*, Venetian painting on wood.
Torregiano: Tomb of Henry VII, Westminster Abbey.
Hampton Court Place erected by Wolsey; presented to Henry VIII in 1526; later extended by Wren for William III.

Latin translation of *Almagest* by Gerard de Cremona printed in Venice.
Legislation against enclosures in England; reconversion of pasture to tillage and rebuilding of decayed houses ordered.
Diaz de Solis, Spanish captain, discovered River Plate.
Introduction of German wheel-lock pistol.
Fees charged by London watermen fixed by Parliament.

	History	Literature
1516	Concordat between France and Papacy confirmed Gallican Liberties. Pope Leo X reaffirmed Bull of *Unam Sanctum*. †Ferdinand of Aragon; succeeded by grandson Charles, who united under his rule Burgundy, Netherlands, Spain, Sicily and Spanish America. †Ladislaus II of Bohemia; succeeded by his son, Lewis, King of Poland and Hungary. Sultan al Ghawri defeated by Sultan Selim I of Turkey near Aleppo; end of Syrian independence.	More: *Utopia*, description in Latin of an imaginary island where everything is perfect. Ludovico Ariosto: *Orlando Furioso*; the Italian poet wrote this epic of Charlemagne's Paladin in his struggles against the Saracens. Erasmus published New Testament in Greek.
1517	Wolsey appointed Papal Legate to England. Luther made his protest against sale of Indulgences. Christian II of Denmark sailed to Sweden to enforce peace between Regent, Sten Sture, and Archbishop Gustavus Trolle. Ottoman Turks under Selim I entered Cairo: end of Mamluk Empire; Turks appeared in Red Sea area and seized Massawa; provoked war with Portugal.	Reuchlin: *De Arte Cabbalistica*. Luther nailed his ninety-five Theses to the door of Wittenberg Castle church.
1518	Peace of London: Wolsey allied England, Empire, France, Spain and Papacy, nominally against Turkey. Luther, interrogated at Augsburg, refused to recant. Treaty between Portugal and kingdom of Kotte (suburb of modern Colombo).	Daniel Romberg completed Rabbinical Bible. First recorded copyright awarded to Richard Pynson, the King's Printer. Publication of *Polygraphia*, by John Trithemius of Spanheim (see 1499).
1519	Henry VIII of England and Francis I of France candidates for Imperial throne. †Emperor Maximilian I; succeeded by Charles of Spain as Emperor Charles V. Luther's disputations at Altenburg and Leipzig.	
1520	Field of Cloth of Gold: Francis I failed to obtain alliance of Henry VIII against Empire.	*c.* Francis I founded Royal Library, Paris, later to become the Bibliothèque Nationale. Publication in Venice of first complete

Michelangelo: *Moses*, Italian statue of world fame.
Completion of St George's Chapel, Windsor.
Hans Holbein the Younger (*1497, †1543): *Burgomaster Meyer and his Wife*, German painting.

Discovery of large silver deposits at Joachimsthal (Bohemia).
Portuguese merchants and traders reached China.
Establishment of first Master of the Post (private mail service for Henry VIII).
Court of Star Chamber forbade craftsman to engage in mercantile activities unless he first abandoned his craft.

Richard Fox, bishop of Winchester, founded Corpus Christi College, Oxford.
Cranach the Elder: *A Prince of Saxony*, German painting.
Raphael: *Lo Spasimo*, Italian painting; and *Incendio del Borgo*, in the Vatican.
Andrea del Sarto (*1486, †1530): *John Baptizing*, Italian painting.
Grünewald: Maria Schnee chapel altarpiece.
Prior Goldstone II's central tower of Canterbury Cathedral.

Seventeen Commissioners appointed by Wolsey to enquire into lands enclosed since 1488 and contrary to 1515 Act.
Coffee first introduced into Europe.
Spanish expedition from Cuba discovered Yucatan peninsula.
English merchants granted trading concessions in Andalusia.
Evil May Day riots in London against alien merchants.

c. Veneto Bartolommeo: *Portrait of a Gentleman*, tempera on wood.
Titian: *Assumption of the Virgin*, Italian painting in Baroque style.
Cranach: *Madonna*, German painting.
Raphael: *The Holy Family*, Italian paintings.

Thomas Linacre, physician to Henry VIII, founded Royal College of Physicians.
Daubers and rough masons at Coventry forbidden to form a Craft Guild on their own.
Trading fort erected at Kotte.
Grijalva, Spanish sailor, discovered mainland opposite Cuba.
Notification of epidemic diseases required in England.

Dürer: *The Emperor Maximilian*, German painting.
Holbein the Elder (*c.* *1460, †1524): *Fountain of Life*, German painting.
Titian: *Madonna, Saints and Pesaro family*, Venetian painting.

Kratzer of Nuremberg appointed horologist to Henry VIII.
Ferdinand Magellan, Portuguese seaman, set out on voyage of discovery from San Lucar.
Hernando Cortes landed in Mexico at Vera Cruz and marched into interior.

Dürer: drawing of Erasmus.
(to 1534) Michelangelo designed tombs of the Medici princes in Florence.

Chocolate known to have been eaten in Spain (imported from Mexico).
Petrus Apianus published the first map to

LITERATURE

1520 Henry VIII and Charles V met at Gravelines.
Secret treaty of Calais: alliance between England and Empire aimed at France.
Coronation of Charles V as Emperor at Aachen.
Luther declared excommunicated in Papal Bull; Luther burned Bull.
Christian II of Denmark invaded Västergötland; Sten Sture defeated and killed; Stockholm "Blood Bath"; Christian II crowned King of Sweden.
Accession of Suleiman the Magnificent as Sultan of Turkey; empire extended from Baghdad to Hungary.

Talmud, the Jewish code; divided into Mishna, oral traditions, and Gemara, commentaries.

1521 Mexico City captured by Cortes.
Habsburg territories in Austria given to Ferdinand, brother of Emperor Charles V.
Martin Luther condemned as heretic at Diet of Worms before Charles V; Anabaptist movement founded at Wittenberg.
Tartars from Crimea invaded southern Russia as far as Moscow.
Sinhalese kingdom established at Avissawella in Ceylon.

(to 1532) Luther's translation of the Bible into German gave nation a normal language in place of many dialects in use; he chose dialect of Meissen, the language of the Saxon "Kanzlei" or chancellery; "official" language of Saxony became literary language of the German-speaking world.
Henry VIII's *Golden Book* written to refute Luther's ideas in *Babylonish Captivity*.

1522 War between England and France; latter in alliance with Scotland.
French and Swiss defeated by Spanish and Germans at Bioocca.
Francesco Sforza restored to Duchy of Milan.
Reformation teachings introduced into Bremen.
Partition of Habsburg territories between Charles V and Ferdinand, ratified by Treaties of Brussels.
Knights Hospitallers driven from Rhodes by Suleiman.

Luther's *New Testament* first published.
Henry VIII given title *Fidei Defensor* by Pope Leo X for his *Golden Book*.
Ludovico Arrighi (Vicento): *La Operina*, first writing-manual; printed from woodblocks; explained art of writing in *cancellaresca* style; Italian.

1523 Empire, England and Charles of Bourbon invaded France.
Diet of Nuremberg: Pope Hadrian VI promised reform of abuses.
Philip of Hesse joined Reformation.
†Pope Hadrian VI, last non-Italian Pope.
Administration of Spanish Military

Eisteddfod held at Caerwys; foremost poet was Tudur Aled (*c.* *1470, †1526).
Hans Sachs: *The Wittenberg Nightingale*, German poem on Luther.
Arrighi: second book on handwriting; illustrating various styles, including those suitable for Papal Bulls, notary's work and commercial purposes.

Erection of the Palais de Justice, Bruges.
Titian: *Bacchanalia,* Italian painting.
Completion of cathedral of St Machar, Aberdeen; made of granite.
Cranach: *Luther,* copper engraving.

include America.
Magellan discovered Chile and the strait which bears his name; entered Pacific Ocean, which he so named; Nuno Garcia de Torino at work on 21 charts of Magellan's voyage.
Cappers' Guild, Coventry, forbade journeyman to make caps for any but their masters.
c. A. Kotter, of Nuremberg, developed J. Zoller's invention of gun-barrel rifling (see 1477).

Wynkyn de Worde printed *Boar's Head Carol,* in first collection of carols.
Michelangelo designed the Medici Chapel, Florence; also created statue *Christ.*
Holbein the Younger: *The Dead Christ,* German painting.
c. *Philippe de Mons (†1603), great madrigal composer.
(to 1577) Cathedral of Segovia, Spain, built.

Magellan killed in fight with natives in Philipine Islands.
Portuguese traders in Moluccas.
Silk industry introduced into France.
Termination of *Academia Platonica;* Platonic school founded by Cosimo di Medici in Florence (1459).
Spaniards from Santo Domingo visited S. Carolina; settled in 1526.

Antonio Allegri Correggio (*1494, †1534): *Night,* Italian painting of the Nativity.
Oldest existing harpsichord dates from this year.
Holbein the Younger: *Madonna and Child with two Saints,* German painting.
Titian: *Bacchus and Ariadne,* Italian baroque painting.

Magellan's ship, *Victoria,* under Sebastian del Cano, returned to Seville having been first to circumnavigate the world.
Gil González de Avila, first European to explore Nicaragua, landed in Chiriqui area.
Books began to be printed at Cambridge (see 1583).
Chia-Ching period in China; magnificent sky-blue porcelain.

Albrecht Altdorfer (*1480, †1538) *Nativity,* Swiss painting on wood.
Holbein the Younger: *Erasmus,* German portrait.
First introduction into America of European music.
Correggio: *Noli me tangere,* Italian painting.
Perugino: *The Adoration of the Shepherds,*

Publication of handbook on agriculture, *Husbandry,* by John Fitzherbert.
Statute forbade alien craftsmen in England from employing aliens.
Supervision of Norwich worsted trade.
English sale of broad white woollen cloths to aliens for dyeing abroad regulated.
Act of Parliament made London physicians

1523 Orders finally annexed to Spanish crown by papal bull.
Surrender of Stockholm to Gustavus Vasa, later elected king of Sweden.
Oslo attacked by Swedes.
Christian II deposed in Denmark and Norway; replaced by uncle, Frederick of Holstein; end of Scandinavian Union.
Expulsion of Europeans from China.

1524 Siege of Marseilles; Spaniards and Germans driven off.
Revolt of peasants in parts of Empire; claimed the teachings of Luther justified their actions.
Frederick I of Denmark forced to accept Norwegian self-government; later re-established Danish control.
Portuguese fort at Kotte, in Ceylon, destroyed; only factory remained.

c. Machiavelli: *Mandragola,* Italian comedy.
G. A. Tagliente: *Opera che a Scrivere,* popular Italian writing-book.

1525 Peace between England and France.
Francis I of France defeated and captured by Charles V at Pavia in attempts to regain Milan.
Frederick I of Denmark supported spread of Lutheranism in Denmark.
Free peasantry in Germany ended with severe suppression of rebellions.
Teutonic Order secularized in Prussia.
Capuchin Order founded by Matteo di Bassi.

Huldreich Zwingli (*1484, †1531), Swiss reformer who started Reformation in Switzerland: *Commentarius de Vera et Falsa Religione.*
Machiavelli: *Florentine Histories.*
Wm. Tyndale (*1484, †1536) completed translation of the Bible into English; forced to leave England, he printed his work at Cologne and Worms (1526).

1526 Treaty of Madrid between Francis I of France and Charles V.
League of Cognac: France, Florence, Venice, Milan and Papacy allied against Charles V.
Increase of Anabaptist movement in S. Germany.
Diet of Spires.
Lewis of Bohemia, Poland and Hungary, defeated and killed by Suleiman at Mohacs; succeeded by brother-in-law, Ferdinand of Habsburg, Archduke of Austria.
Rebellion of Austrian peasants suppresed.
Papal nominee for Archbishopric of Lund set aside; end of papal confirmation in Denmark.

Hector Boece (*c.* *1465, †1536): *History of Scotland,* in Latin.
Publication of Tyndale's New Testament by Peter Schoeffer, at Worms.
Luther published Order of Service in German.
New Testament translated into Swedish; led to rapid spread of Lutheran doctrines.
Francisco de Sáde Miranda founded important Italianate school of literature in Portugal.

Italian painting, now in the National Gallery.
Titian: *Entombment of Christ*, one of greatest paintings of the Italian master.

into a corporate body; doctors' position more secure.
Portuguese mission of Alvarez received in Abyssinia.

First Lutheran hymn-book published.
Michelangelo began construction of Biblioteca Laurenziana in Florence.
Correggio completed frescoes in San Giovanni, Parma (begun 1520).
Enrique de Arfe: silver monstrance in Toledo Cathedral.

Apianus: *Cosmographicus Liber*; work on map construction.
Giovanni da Verrazano led French expedition along part of East coat of N. America.
Francisco Pizarro sailed from Panama, explored S. American coast, landing in modern Ecuador.

c. Altdorfer: *Virgin and Child in Glory*, Swiss painting on wood.
The Howard Grace Cup, ivory, silver-gilt, gem-mounted.
Wolsey founded Cardinal College, Oxford (see 1546).
del Sarto: *Madonna del Sacco*, Italian fresco; his finest work.

Introduction of square root sign (√) by Rudolf.
Earliest mention of the fusee for spring-driven clockwork.
First publication of Galen's medical works in original Greek (see 1490).
c. J. C. Scaliger recorded metal, which could not be fused, mined in Mexico and Darien; possible reference to platinum.

Correggio: (i) *Jupiter and Antiope*, (ii) *Madonna della Scala*, (iii) *Madonna della Scodella*, Italian paintings, Dürer: *St John and St Peter*, and *St Paul and St Mark*, famous panels at Munich.
c. Giulio Romano commenced Palazzo del Té, Mantua (completed 1535).
Foundation of Nuremberg Gymnasium, removed to Altdorf as university in 1575.
Holbein: (i) *Madonna of Burgomaster Meyer*, (ii) *Lais*, German paintings.
Lucas van Leyden (*1494, †1533), called Lucas: *Last Judgment*, Dutch painting.
del Sarto: *Birth of the Baptist*, Italian painting.
Erection of Château of Chambord begun.

Paracelsus (*1493, †1541), Swiss physician, greatly extended the uses of medicine; also believed to have discovered zinc.
English proclamation ordering casting down of hedges and opening up of enclosed lands.
Garcia visited Plate Estuary and found Sebastian Cabot with small settlement; later abandoned.
First publication of Greek version of Hippocrates's work; 16th cent. revival of ancient learning.
Francisco Pizarro reached Peru.
Famous diamond, Koh-i-Noor, taken from Agra by Babur.
Jorge de Menesis probably landed on New Guinea.

1526 Battle of Panipat: Ibrahim Lodi, last Delhi Sultan, defeated and killed by Babur, first of Mogul rulers in India.

1527 Henry VIII sought annulment of marriage to Katherine of Aragon.
Treaty of Amiens: Anglo-French alliance negotiated by Wolsey.
Florence overthrew Medici rulers; declared Republic.
Troops of Charles V sacked Rome and took Pope Clement VII prisoner; Wolsey used incident to break Anglo-Spanish alliance.
Frederick I of Denmark declared right of every man to decide his own religious faith.
Reformation effected in Sweden, Denmark and Luneburg.

1528 England at war with Empire.
Andrea Doria seized Genoa in name of Emperor.
Disputation at Berne between Catholics and Reformers prepared way for Swiss acceptance of Reformed doctrines.
Hubmaier, leader of Austrian Anabaptists, burned at stake in Vienna.

Baldassare Castiglione (*1478, †1529): *Il Cortegiano (The Courtier)*; book gave the rules for the dress, behaviour, conversation and morals of a gentleman; had a wide influence; translated, 1561, into English.
Luther: *Smaller Catechism*.

1529 Wolsey dismissed from Chancellorship for failure to obtain King's divorce from Katherine of Aragon; More appointed Chancellor.
Henry VIII summoned "Reformation Parliament".
Peace of Cambrai: ended war between France and Spain; Treaty of Barcelona reconciled Emperor Charles V and Pope Clement VII.
Hamburg accepted Reformation.
Vienna besieged by Turks.
Civil war between Catholic and Reformed cantons in Switzerland; Catholics defeated.
Colloquy of Marburg: between Luther and Zwingli; differences over Eucharist hindered union.
Second Diet of Spires.

More: *The Dialogue concerning Heresies*, controversial discussion.
Christian Pedersen (*1480, †1554), Father of Danish literature; translated the New Testament into the vernacular.
Synod of Örebro ordered Bible in Swedish to be read daily in Swedish cathedrals.
Luther: *Larger Catechism*.
Sir David Lindsay (*1486, †1555): *Complaynt to the King*, Scottish poem.

Correggio: *Day*, Italian painting of St Jerome.
Holbein the Younger: *Thomas More*, German painting.
Diego de Riano and Martin designed the Ayuntamiento (town hall), Seville; completed 1532.
Titian: *The Venus of Urbino*, Italian painting.
Marburg, first protestant university, founded by Philip the Magnanimous.
Foundation of Faversham Grammar School.

Voyage in search of North West Passage by John Rut.
First discovery of Hawaiian Islands by westerners; rediscovered by Cook 1778 (*q.v.*).
Dürer published a book on fortifications.

Holbein the Younger: *The Artist's Family*, German painting.
Le Breton designed Palais de Fontainebleau for Francis I; externally plain, internally ornate, surrounded by fine gardens; 12th cent. origin.
Diego de Silöe began Granada Cathedral, Spain.

Spanish sailor, Grijalva, reached New Guinea; possibly visited two years earlier by Dom Jorge de Menesis.
Cocoa beans first imported into Europe.
Incorporation of Clothworkers' Company, London.
English merchants arrested in Spain and Flanders as reprisal against English wool-trade policy.

Altdorfer: *The Battle of Arbela*, Swiss painting.
Famous mazer (wooden drinking-bowl, silver mounted), All Souls' College, Oxford.
del Sarto: *The Holy Family*, Italian painting.
Titian: *Pessaro Madonna*, Italian painting.

Importation of linen cloth forbidden in interest of London linen drapers.
Diego Ribero's accurate map of Pacific Ocean.
All alien merchants to swear allegiance to English king; statute of 1523 made perpetual.
Michelangelo made overseer of fortifications at Florence.
Treaty of Saragossa defined frontier between Spanish and Portuguese territories in Pacific.

1530

†Wolsey.
Charles V crowned Emperor by Clement VII at Bologna; last such coronation by a pope.
Protesting states in Empire formed League of Schmalkalden.
Charles V gave Malta to Knights Hospitallers; most of remaining lands of Order confiscated.
Clement VII, using Imperial forces, defeated Florentine Republic.
Alassandro Medici created Duke of Florence; married Margaret of Habsburg.
Catholic mission to Abyssinia failed to impress Coptic Church.
Assembly at Copenhagen accepted Hans Tausen's (Danish Luther) Confession of Faith.
†Babur, founder of Mogul dynasty in India.

Zwingli: *De providentia dei*.
Thos. Berthelet appointed first King's Printer.
Philipp Melanchthon (*1497, †1560), German reformer, prepared *Augsburg Confession* on Protestantism for the Diet.
Tyndale published English version of the *Pentateuch*.

1531

Statutes ordered unlicensed beggars in England to be whipped.
Reformed teachings prohibited in Netherlands by Charles V.
Free cities of Southern Germany joined League of Schmalkalden.
Ferdinand of Bohemia elected King of Romans.
Inquisition set up in Portugal.
Pizarro imprisoned and executed Inca, Atahuallpa; captured Inca capital, Cuzco.
Second civil war in Switzerland; Protestants defeated at Kappel; Zwingli killed.

Sir Thomas Elyot (*c.* *1499, †1546): *The Governour*, a treatise on education and politics.
Issue of Swedish Mass Book; embodied teachings of Luther.
Pedersen translated the Psalms into Danish.
Zwingli: (†): *Christianae Fidae Expositio*.

1532

Act of Annates forbade payment of first year's income from newly appointed English bishop to the Pope.
Alliance of France, Bavaria, Saxony and Hesse against Ferdinand of Austria.
John Calvin (*1509, †1564) began Reformation movement in Paris.
Suleiman's invasion of Hungary defeated at Güms.
Religious Peace of Nuremberg caused by Turkish invasion.

Clément Marot (*1496, †1544), lyric poet, one of the first poets of French Renaissance; *Adolescence Clémentine*.
François Rabelais (*1494, †1553): *Pantagruel*, story of giant Pantagruel, by a French scholar, humanist and physician; burlesque in which author satirizes politics, pedantry and religion.

Titian: (i) *St Peter the Martyr*, (ii) *Madonna del Coniglio*, Italian paintings.
(to 1580) Production of Limoges painted enamels on copper.
Correggio: *Assumption of the Virgin*, Italian painting.
Henry VIII took over and rebuilt Whitehall Palace, formerly residence of Archbishops of York.
(to 1598) Erection of Speke Hall, Liverpool; half-timbered manor.
c. Michelangelo: *The Virgin and the Child Jesus*, marble; Medici Chapel, Florence.
Jacopo Sansovino (*1486, †1570) built Libreria Vecchia, Venice.

c. The flyer, devised by da Vinci for winding and spinning silk, generally utilized.
William Hawkins made first of three voyages to Brazil.
Portuguese began to colonize Brazil.
Empire adopted Police Regulations.
Georg Agricola (*1490, †1555) began work on *De Re Metallica*, first modern study of metallurgy; written at Venice (see 1556).
The infectious disease hitherto known by various names (lepra, the pox, French disease) renamed syphilis.
Foundation of Amsterdam Exchange (for currency).

Correggio: *The Holy Night*, Italian painting.
(to 1612) Erection of Heidelburg Castle.
Lucas: *The Healing of the Blind Man of Jericho by Jesus Christ*, Dutch triptych.
c. Church of St Andrew Undershaft, London, rebuilt.

Parliament fixed cost of bridge repairs.
Act regulating construction of London sewers.
Butchers forbidden to be tanners of hides in England.
Pizarro crossed Andes to Inca town of Caxamarca.
Site of Rio de Janeiro discovered by Villegagnon.
Earthquake at Lisbon.
Sebastian Münster (*1489, †1552) of Basle: *Horologiographia*, on sundials; he also invented a moon-dial.

Holbein the Younger: (i) *Noli me tangere*, German painting at Hampton Court; (ii) *Georg Gisze*, portrait of a merchant.
Erection of St James's Palace Chapel, now used for Chapel Royal (see 1135).
Correggio: *Leda and the Swan*, Italian painting.
Church of the Ascension, Kolomenskoie, Russia, erected.

Hessus referred to important rolling mills at Nuremberg, for soft metals.
Avoirdupois weight in use.
English brewers prohibited from being coopers as well.
Penalties imposed on persons who wound wool unwashed or mixed it with sand and stones to increase weight of fleece.
English government regulated wholesale price of wine.

Year	History	Literature
1533	No more "Flanders Galleys" to be sent to England. Act of Appeals forbade appeals to Rome from England regarding wills, marriage and divorce. Secret marriage of Henry VIII and Anne Boleyn; Henry excommunicated by Pope Clement VII. Thomas Cranmer appointed Archbishop of Canterbury. Ferdinand of Hungary, Bohemia and Austria made peace with Suleiman. †Frederick I of Denmark; Norwegians regained self-government. Christian III acceded to Danish throne; completed Reformation in Denmark. Accession of three-year-old Ivan IV (The Terrible) to principality of Moscow on †Vasily III.	Marot: French translation of the Psalms begun (published 1541). John Heywood (*c.* *1497, *c.* †1580): *Play of the Weather,* allegory. More: *An Apologie of Syr Thomas More.*
1534	Henry VIII Supreme Head of Church in England; end of English and Roman church unity (began 564); future bishops in England to be appointed by the Dean and Chapter. All payments of money to Rome from England forbidden. Ignatius Loyola founded Society of Jesus (Jesuits). Anabaptist rule in Münster put into practice communistic principles; suppressed by both Catholic and Protestant princes. Lübeck and Holstein at war with Denmark and Sweden. Suleiman captured Baghdad; Iraq Turkish for nearly 400 years.	Rabelais: *Gargantua,* the life of Pantagruel's father, a giant who picks his teeth with an elephant's tusk. Luther finished his translation of the complete Bible. Heywood: *A Play of Love.*
1535	Thomas Cromwell appointed Vicar General by Henry VIII; devised measure which brought Church directly under Crown control. Sir Thomas More and Bishop Fisher of Rochester executed for refusing to accept Act of Supremacy. Statute of Uses in England restricted right of landowners in demise of their lands.	Miles Coverdale (*1488, †1568): first complete Bible in English; printed at Marberg, in Germany. John Bellenden: *Chronicles of Scotland,* translation of Boece's *History of Scotland.* Francesco Pegolotti: *Practica della mercatura,* a valuable record of commerce and customs of the times.

Cranach: *Adam and Eve,* German painting.
Holbein the Younger: (i) *The Ambassadors,* (ii) *Portrait of Thomas Cromwell,* (iii) *Dirk Tybis,* fashionable German portraits, leading to his position at the English court.
Titian: (i) *Charles V,* (ii) *St John the Almsgiver,* Italian paintings.
John Leland (*c.* *1506, †1552) became Henry VIII's antiquary; first modern one.
Completion of Ghent Town Hall.

Earliest printed exposition on triangulation in surveying, by Gemma Frisius.
Regiomontanus: *De triangulis,* German trigonometry work.
Growth of flax made compulsory in England for all tillage farmers; to check unemployment caused by importation of linen cloth.
Meat ordered to be sold in England by weight, seller producing scales, at fixed Government prices.
Sugar plantations developed in Brazil.

(to 1545) Palazzo Farnese, Rome: important house constructed by Michelangelo and da Sangallo.

Titian: *Landscape with Sheep,* Italian painting.
Holbein the Younger became court-painter to Henry VIII.
Construction of wall round Kitai Gorod, Moscow, formerly merchants' residence.
Johann Walther helped in publication of Luther's first protestant hymn book.

Manufacture of wool cloth in Worcestershire: limited to county's five towns.
Worsted makers forbidden to act as calenderers.
First voyage of Jaques Cartier (*1491, †1557), French seaman, to Gulf of St Lawrence.
Parliament regulated number of sheep per farmer to 2,000 to limit enclosure for pasture.

The Boleyn Cup, silver-gilt, at Cirencester Church.
Holbein the Younger completed the 51 plates of *Dance of Death* (commenced 1523).
Baldassare Peruzzi (*1481, †1536), Italian architect, began Palazzo Massimi, Rome.
Richly carved wood choir stalls in Church of S. Pietro dei Cassinensi, Perugia.

Niccolo Tartaglia (*c.* *1506, †1559): solution of the cubic equation; derived from Ferro (†1525).
Francisco Orellana, starting from Peru, traced course of the Amazon.
Almagro, Spanish explorer, travelled South from Peru to Chile.
Discovery of Galapagos Islands, then uninhabited.
Spaniard, Mendoza, established colony

	History	Literature
1535	Lübeck defeated in plans to re-impose commercial control on Scandinavian countries; end of Hanseatic League.	
1536	†Katherine of Aragon. Henry VIII executed Anne Boleyn and married Jane Seymour. Statute of Union between England and Wales; uniform system of government. Pilgrimage of Grace: revolt of Northern counties against religious changes and economic effects of enclosures. Act of Ten Articles kept Mass and Roman Catholic doctrine in England. Invasion of Provence by Charles V. First Helvetic Convention issued by Swiss Protestants. Christian III established as King of Denmark after Civil War. Franco-Portuguese naval treaty against Spain at Lyons. French conquered Savoy and Piedmont.	Calvin: *Institution of the Christian Religion* (in Latin), published in French in 1541, first theological treatise in French; Calvin's radical Protestant views and his theological doctrines had immense influence. Tyndale, at instigation of Henry VIII, burned at the stake in Vilvorde, near Brussels.
1537	*Prince Edward to Henry VIII and Jane Seymour; †Jane Seymour. France and Turkey acted together in Mediterranean against Charles V. Succession agreement between Hohenzollerns of Prussia and Piasts of Silesia. Christian III recognized as King of Norway, which lost independence for nearly 300 years.	Luther: *Articles of Schmalkald.* *Lexicon Symphonicum*, first Czechoslovak scientific dictionary, produced. First Roman Catholic hymn-book issued.
1538	Destruction of Becket's shrine at Canterbury. Francis I of France and Emperor Charles V made Truce of Nice. Catholic German princes formed League of Nuremberg.	Elyot introduced word "encyclopaedia", explained in his Latin dictionary.
1539	Act of Six Articles asserted Roman Catholic doctrine in England; breaches of Act punishable by burning at stake. Truce between France and Empire converted into peace at Toledo. Truce of Frankfurt between Charles V and Protestant princes. Cuba annexed by Spain.	Great Bible; translation combining Coverdale's and Tyndale's work, with preface by Cranmer, licensed by Henry VIII; copies ordered to be placed in every parish church; private persons allowed to have copies.

which later became city of Buenos Aires.
Pizarro founded Lima.
c. Development of wallpaper in China and Europe (early 15th century).

Earliest book of song with accompaniment (Milan).
Rare set of 12 Apostle Spoons and a Master Spoon, silver (London).
Sansovina erected (to 1553) St Mark's library, Venice.
The *Cordonata*, great flight of stairs to Capital, designed by Michelangelo for triumphal entry of Charles V.
First Act of Suppression of smaller monasteries in England; by 1539 all monastic houses virtually destroyed.

*Felix Platen (†1614), who first understood the working of the lens and retina of the eye.
Hore attempted to find the North West Passage.
Second voyage of Cartier: Canada claimed for France.
Law introduced in England for relief of poor: sought to distinguish between the impotent and those able to work.
Foundation of Valparaiso, Chile, by de Saavedra.
c. Fine clock of Henry VIII and Anne Boleyn.

Earliest Portuguese university, previously alternating with Lisbon, established at Coimbra.
Holbein the Younger: *Jane Seymour*, German painting of English queen.
Erection of Castle of S. Elmo, Naples; completed 1546.
Rebuilding of Bergen Cathedral; originally founded 1248.
Titian: *Francis I of France*, Italian painting.

Tartaglia: *Nuova scienzia*, study of ballistics.
Gerardus Mercator, otherwise Gérard de Cremer (*1512, †1594), Flemish geographer, issued his first map (of Palestine).
Severe eruption of Mount Etna.
Caroline Islands first seen by Portuguese sailors.

Holbein the Younger: *Prince Edward*, German painting.
Johann Sturm founded school in Strasbourg (see 1621).
Verdelot: first five-part madrigals.

Libellus de re herbaria, first English work on botany.
Use of diving bell in Europe.
Quesada, Spaniard, explored River Magdalena; founded city of Bogota (in Colombia).

Invention of the bassoon in Italy.
Holbein the Younger: *Anne of Cleves*, German portrait of English queen.
Completion of Church of Madonna della Steccata, Parma, in form of Greek cross (begun 1521).

c. Printing began in Mexico City; probably first transatlantic press.
Aurelio Paparo and Leonardo di Palma founded the Bank of Naples.

1540

Marriage of Henry VIII and Anne of Cleves negotiated by Cromwell to strengthen Protestant princes in Germany; Henry disapproved of his wife, the "Flanders Mare", and secured divorce.
Thomas Cromwell executed on charge of "treason".
Marriage of Henry VIII and Catherine Howard.
Statute of Wills modified 1535 Statute of Uses.
John III of Portugal sent Jesuit missionaries to Far East.
Emperor Charles V invested his son Don Philip with Duchy of Milan; until 1713 Milan remained part of Spanish Empire.
Attempt by Cardinal Contarini to reconcile Protestants and Catholics failed.

Amadis of Gaul translated into French; see 1508.
Publication of *The Birth of Mankind*, which contains the earliest English line-engravings.
Lindsay: *Ane Pleasant Satyre of the thrie Estaits*, morality play.
Henry VIII founded first Cambridge Regius Professorship. (see 1546).

1541

Henry VIII assumed title of King of Ireland and Head of Irish Church.
Wales given representatives in English parliament.
Charles V failed to conquer Algeria.
John Calvin established at Geneva.
John Knox (*1505, †1572) began Reformation in Scotland.
Ignatius Loyola elected first General of Jesuit Order.
Hungary conquered by Turks; remained Turkish province until 1688.

Marot translated the Psalms into French.
Sebastian Franck (*1499, †1542): Collection of German Proverbs, one of the earliest in the language.

1542

War between England and Scotland; small Scots force defeated at Solway Moss; †James V fortnight later.
Execution of Catherine Howard; marriage of Henry VIII and Catherine Parr.
Renewal of war between France and Empire.
Archbishop Wied failed in attempt to introduce Reformation into Cologne; deposed; Inquisition established.
Brunswick became Protestant state.
Pope Paul III established Inquisition in Rome.
Abolition of Indian slavery in Spain's American colonies.

Bartolomé de las Casas, Spanish historian: *Very Brief Account of the Ruins of the Indies*, protest against Spanish ruthlessness in America.

Publication of *Psalter-Songs* (Dutch) in use for some 70 years.
Michelangelo: *Brutus*, Italian marble bust.
Titian: *Portrait of a Young Man*, Venetian painting.
Holbein the Younger (to 1541): *Catherine Howard*, German portrait of English queen.
Erection of Palazzo Spada, Rome.
Erection of Stirling Palace begun by James V of Scotland.

Biringuccio of Siena: *De re pyrotechnica*, first practical book of mining and technology.
Michael Servetus (*1511, †1553) discovered circulation of the blood through lungs but did not know the purpose.
Barbers and surgeons amalgamated as one Guild.
Spaniards developed heavy two-man musket from arquebus.
c. Manufacture of artistic stoneware at Cologne.
Spaniards discovered California.
Closure of Free Counter at Bruges.

Holbein the Younger: *Portrait of a Young Merchant*, German painting.
Michelangelo completed *The Last Judgment*, Italian fresco; great sensation at the time.
Cathedral school of Worcester founded.
Henry VIII founded King's School, Chester, and King's School, Worcester.
John Marbeck appointed organist at St George's Chapel, Windsor.
Southwell Minster refounded: original foundation pre-Norman.

Roger Barlow (*1526, †1554) produced English nautical tables.
Orellano, having sailed *down* the Amazon, reached mouth and Trinidad.
Valdivia explored Chile beyond Atacama desert and conquered Chile; Santiago founded.
Third voyage of Cartier down St Lawrence halted at Lachine Rapids.
De Soto explored Arkansas.

*Wm. Byrd (†1623), a founder of the English Madrigal School.
Laurentine Library, Florence, designed by Michelangelo.
Baron Audley founded Magdalene College, Cambridge.
Pisa University refounded.
Jesuits founded theological college in University of Coimbra, Portugal.

Robert Recorde (*1510, †1558): *Ground of Artes*, first of a series of mathematics books in English; all previous works had been in Latin.
Henry VIII increased weight of base alloy in coins while leaving price of bullion and weight of coins unchanged.
Sher Shah introduced rupee in India.
Portguese sailors and merchants forced ashore in Japan for first time.
First pharmacopoeia issued; at Nuremberg.

	HISTORY	LITERATURE
1543	Treaty of Greenwich ended Anglo-Scots war; Prince Edward of Wales to marry Mary, Queen of Scots; Scots repudiated Treaty. Ferrer's Case: House of Commons compelled Sheriff of London to release arrested member named Ferrers; action upheld by Henry VIII. Alliance of Henry VIII with Charles V against Francis I of France. Portuguese influence reduced King of Jaffna, in Ceylon, to position of tributary.	
1544	English invaded Scotland; captured Leith and Edinburgh. Henry VIII and Charles V invaded France; threatened Paris; Henry VIII captured Boulogone. Diet of Spires: Imperial support for Charles V against France and Turkey. Division of Schleswig-Holstein among Christian III of Denmark and his two brothers. Act of Hereditary Settlement fixed Swedish succession in male line.	Litany issued in English. G. B. Palatino: *Libro nel qual s'insegna a scrivere*, detailed Italian book of handwriting.
1545	English defeated by Scots at Ancram Moor; English again invaded Scotland. Emperor Charles V and Suleiman made Truce of Adrianople. Opening of Council of Trent. Palatinate became Protestant. Knights Hopsitallers in Brandenburg continued as Lutheran body.	Publication of first complete edition of works of Martin Luther. Services for morning and evening prayer issued in English. Establishment of a Book-Fair at Leipzig.
1546	Peace of Ardres ended Anglo-French war; Boulogne to remain English for 8 years. Cardinal Beaton murdered in Scotland; start of Scottish revolt against Rome. Alliance of Empire and papacy against Protestants. †Martin Luther. Portuguese trade mission to Kandy, Ceylon; retained independence until 1815.	Roger Ascham tutuor to Elizabeth: *Toxophilus*, treatise on archery; advocating physical education. *Yn y Llyvyr hwnn*, the first book to be printed in Welsh. Council of Trent declared *Bel and the Dragon* (apocryphal writings) to be canonical.

Benvenuto Cellini (*1500, †1571) goldsmith, constructed famous gold salt-cellars for Francis I.
Titian: *Ecce Homo*, Italian painting.
School of Music founded at Cracow, Poland.
University of Verona founded.

Copernicus's treatise on heliocentric solar system, *De revolutionibus orbium coelestium*, published; superseded Ptolemaic system; banned by R.C. Church until 1758.
Andreas Vesalius (*1514, †1564), called the Father of Modern Anatomy: *De Humani Corporis Fabrica*, great work issued at Padua.
Parliament conferred on York monopoly of coverlet manufacture.

The "lion passant" first regularly stamped on English silver.
Königsberg University founded by Albert III, Margrave of Brandenburg.
Holyrood House, Edinburgh, destroyed in attack by English; immediate re-erection.

Georg Hartmann of St Petersburg, discovered magnetic dip.
Discovery of silver mines at Potosi in Peru.
Stifel improved notation in algebraic equations.
Münster: *Cosmographia universalis*, his principal work (on cosmography).
Georg Agricola (*1490, †1555): *De ortu et causis subterraneorum*, groundwork of physical geology.

Jacopo Tintoretto (*1518, †1594): *Ascension of Mary*, Italian painting.
Archbishop Parker's silver ewer (octagonal) and basin.
Completion of Tomb of Sher Shar, at Sarasam; Pathan architecture (begun 1540).

G. Cardano (Italian; *1501, †1576) published solution of cubic equation, cribbed from Tartaglia (see 1535), in *Ars Magna*.
Botanical garden at Padua; oldest in Europe.
Needles manufactured in Britain.
Counter at Bruges moved to Antwerp.

Rebuilding, by Pierre Lescot, of the Louvre, Paris, which now houses many famous paintings.
Cardinal College, Oxford, renamed Christ Church College.
Henry VIII founded Trinity College, Cambridge; also founded Oxford Regius Professorships, except one (see 1540).

Henry VIII established English Navy Board.
Agricola: *De veteribus et novis metallis*, treatise on minerals.
Silver mines discovered at Zacatecas, Mexico.
Girolamo Fracastoro (*1483, †1553): *De Contagione*, early study of contagious disease.
Wm. Stumpe, clothier, bought Malmesbury Abbey from Henry VIII and installed large number of looms employing 500 people.
Commercial exchanges set up at Toulouse and Lyons.
First accurate map of Britain; produced in Rome.

Year	History	Literature
1547	†Henry VIII accession of Edward VI, a minor; Duke of Somerset, Protector. English invasion of Scotland; Scots defeated at Pinkie Cleugh; Mary, Queen of Scots, sent to France. John Knox exiled to France from Scotland. Charles V defeated League fo Schmalkalden at Mühlberg. †Francis I of France; succeeded by Henry II. Council of Trent transferred to Bologna. Revolt of Utraquists in Prague. Coronation of Ivan the Terrible as Tsar of Russia.	First issue of *Book of Homilies* for use of clergy, prepared under the direction of Cranmer. *c.* John Bale (*1495, †1563): *King John*, first English historical play.
1548	Heresy Laws in England abolished. Government of Netherlands separated from Empire. "Interim' of Augsburg granted laity right to Chalice at Communion and Matrimony to priests pending final decision of General Council. Bohemian Brethren, Protestant sect, expelled from Bohemia; went to Poland.	Knox: *Epistle on Justification by Faith.* Sir Thomas Gresham founded seven professorships at London, but University not established until 1828 (*q.v.*).
1549	Mass abolished in England along with use of Latin in English church services. Kett's rebellion in Norfolk; revolt in West of England suppressed. Outbreak of war between England and France. End of Council of Bologna. End of controversy between followers of Calvin and Zwingli over Holy Communion. First Jesuit missionaries in South America. Francis Xavier landed at Kagoshima and began to preach with full permission of Japanese government.	Joachim du Bellay (*1522, †1560): *Défense et Illustration de la Langue française*; the French poet advocated the use of French for serious literature instead of Latin; member of the Pléiade movement. Act of Uniformity: Prayer book form of service enforced; issue of first *English Book of Common Prayer*, mainly the work of Cranmer.
1550	Somerset arrested; Duke of Northumberland became Protector. Peace of Boulogne between England and France and between England and Scotland; England gave up	John Marbeck: *Concordance* of the Bible in English; and *Boke of Common Prayer noted,* attempt to standardize the chant of Church of England; his early Calvinism almost led to his burning at the stake.

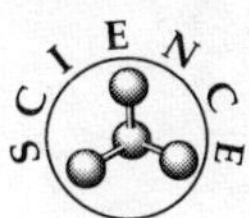

Michelangelo appointed chief architect at St Peter's, Rome.
Tintoretto painted the *Last Supper* in S. Marcuola Church.
Henricus Glareanus: *Dodecachordon*, in which he proposed 12 modes, instead of 8, in music.
Completion of Beauvais Cathedral; begun 1225; tower collapsed 1573.
Léonard Limosin: 12 enamel apostles in St Pierre Abbey Church, Chartres.

First Poor Rate levied in London.
Three Acts of Edward VI to combat evils of enclosure.
Vagrants found wandering in England without employment to be branded with letter V; for second offence, branded S and enslaved for life.
c. Nostradamus (*1503, †1566), French astrologer began to make predictions.

Work begun on Palazzo Pitti, Florence; façade 660 ft. long.
Erection of Christchurch Mansion, Ipswich; modified in 16th–18th cents.
Tintoretto: four paintings, including *Miracle of the Slave*.

Abolition of Craft Guilds in England; London Guilds spared because too dangerous to molest; Chantries Act abolished Guild and Chantry chapels.

Crowley published first book of versified psalms (plainsong).
c. Erection of Lindisfarne Castle, Holy Island.
Foundation of Somerset House, formerly home of Protector Somerset; demolished 1775; rebuilt as headquarters for Inland Revenue and Registry; East wing (1883) constitutes King's College, London.

Rebellion in England caused by opposition to enclosures and dislike of new religious policies.
c. Discovery of mercury in Peru; known much earlier to Chinese, Egyptians and Hindus (see –1500).
Price-rings, formed by provision-merchants, made illegal; unfortunately for the public, price-rings have continued in various fields (e.g. auction sales) into the 20th cent.

Giorgio Vasari (*1511, †1574), Italian painter and architect, wrote his great *Lives of the Painters*.
Michelangelo completed two frescoes in Pauline Chapel, Vatican: (i) *Conversion of*

Hollerius prescribed spectacles for myopic people.
K. von Gesner (*1516, †1565) began *Historia animalium*, basis of modern zoology; vols. I-IV (on animals, birds and fish) published

1550	Boulogne, Tsar Ivan IV summoned first "Assembly of the Land" and introduced reforms in local government to curb power of local governors.	
1551	Second Session of Council of Trent. Charles V recognized Don Philip as his sole heir. Tsar Ivan IV summoned council of higher clergy which reformed educational standard of priests and restricted right of Church to acquire land.	More's *Utopia* translated into English.
1552	Execution of Duke of Somerset. Acts passed in England to organize voluntary collection of funds in churches for assistance of poor. Treaty of Chambord between Henry II of France and German Protestants; Metz, Toul and Verdun ceded to France. War between Maurice of Saxony and Emperor Charles V; Maurice captured Augsburg; Peace of Passau ended war. "Interim" of Augsburg; Lutherans granted freedom of worship. Khanate of Kazan completely subjugated to Moscow by Tsar Ivan IV.	Pierre de Ronsard (*1524, †1585), greatest French poet of his day: *Les Amours de Cassandre*. Etienne Jodelle (*1532, †1573): *Cléopâtre captive*, first French tragedy written according to classical rules. Second Prayer Book, more protestant than first, issued (withdrawn 1553 on accession of Mary).
1553	Duke of Northumberland forced Lady Jane Grey, in line of succession, to marry his son, Lord Guildford Dudley. †Edward VI; Northumberland forced succession of Lady Jane Grey, who ruled for nine days; accession of Mary I (Tudor), daughter of Henry VIII and Katherine of Aragon; execution of Northumberland. England reconciled with Rome. Serious illness of Ivan IV of Russia; boyars refused to swear allegiance to his heir; beginning of long struggle between Ivan and boyars.	Sachs: *Tristant und Isalde*. Nicholas Udall (*1505, †1556): *Ralph Roister Doister*, earliest English comedy; written by Headmaster of Eton for a performance by his scholars. *c.* Gavin Douglas (*1474, †1522): *The Palice of Honour*, dream allegory, first printed.
1554	Sir Thomas Wyatt's rebellion against Mary I. Execution of Lady Jane Grey and Lord Dudley.	Agostino de' Beccari: *Il Sagrifizio*, played at court of Ferrara; early sentimental Italian pastoral. *c.* Matteo Bendello (*1480, †1561): *Novelle*;

St Paul; (ii) *Crucifixion of St. Peter*.
Refounding of Sherborne School; originally founded 705.

1551–8; vol. V (on snakes) published posthumously 1587.
Gustavus Vasa of Sweden founded Helsinki.

Charles V signed decree establishing San Marcos University, Lima.
c. Tintoretto: *Susanna and the Elders*, Venetian painting.

c. Coach introduced into Britain by W. Rippon.
Mercator constructed a pair of globes.
Tartaglia set out method of raising sunken ships.

Melford Hall, Suffolk, built.
Thomas Tallis (*c*. *1515, †1585), Father of English cathedral music: *Service in the Dorian Mode*, first published in 1641.
Foundation of Christ's Hospital, London, blue coat school; on site of Franciscan monastery founded 1224; removed to Horsham 1902.
Foundation of Shrewsbury School.
De l'Orme began work on Château d'Anet.

Bartolommeo Eustachio (*1524, †1574) discovered Eustachean tubes and valve.
c. Commercial hop-growing began.
First "Bridewell" established in London in Old Bridewell Palace (see 1576).
Termination of Hanse privileges in England.

Erection of Sawston Hall, near Cambridge.
Foundation of Tonbridge School.
Inauguration of University of Mexico; closed 1865 as such, although certain faculties continued; re-established 1910.

Pierre Belon (*1517, †1564), French naturalist: *De Aquatilibus*, foundation of study of marine animals.
English trader, Syndham, first Englishman to sail specifically for Africa. G. F. Ingrassia, of Italy, first described scarlet fever.
Sir Hugh Willoughby and Richard Chancellor set out to find trade route with Russia via North Cape.
The *Great Harry*, largest ship of the day, accidentally burned.

c. G. P. da Palestrina (*1525, †1594), Italian composer of unaccompanied part-songs and church music: *Missa Ecce sacerdos* and other masses.

Mines and forges in Saxony regulated by State.
John Locke sailed to Guinea.
Cardano isolated absolute alcohol.

	History	Literature
1554	Marriage of Mary I of England to Philip of Spain, son and heir of Charles V. Act of Supremacy repealed. Cardinal Pole admitted to England as Papal Legate. Richard Chancellor received in Moscow by Ivan IV. Henry II of France invaded Netherlands.	214 Italian stories of great popularity. First Roumanian book, a catechism.
1555	Commencement of Mary's persecution of Protestants in England; Bishops Ridley and Latimer burned at Oxford. Departure of Philip of Spain from England. John Knox returned to Scotland from French exile; united Scottish Protestants. Religious Peace of Augsburg; confirmed toleration to Lutherans. Charles V handed Spain and Netherlands to his son, Philip, as Philip II. Siena captured by Spaniards. Accession of Akbar the Great; climax of Mogul rule in India. Union of Bohemian Brethren and Polish Calvinists strengthened Polish Reformation.	Olaus Magnus 1490, †1558), Swedish historian: *Historia de Gentibus Septentrionalibus*, telling of lives of the Norsemen. Gesner: *Mithradates de differentiis linguis*, Swiss account of 130 languages. Ronsard: *Hymmes*, French poetry of the Pléiade movement.
1556	Cranmer, Archbishop of Canterbury, burned at the stake; succeeded as Archbishop by Cardinal Pole. Truce of Vaucelles between Henry II of France and Philip II of Spain. Abdication of Emperor Charles V; resigned Imperial title to his brother Ferdinand I of Austria, Bohemia and Hungary. †Loyola, founder of Jesuits. Akbar the Great defeated Hindus at Panipat.	Ronsard: *Les Amours de Marie*, poems. *Les Amours de Francine*, by Baïf, a disciple of Ronsard. (to 1601) Period covered by James Melville's (*1556, †1614) *Diary*, ecclesiastically important; early part of work autobiographical. Incorporation of Stationers' Hall.
1557	Anglo-French war broke out; French defeated at St Quentin. Disputation at Worms: final attempt by Empire to reconcile Lutheran and Catholic viewpoints. Catholic Mission to Ethiopia under Barreto and Oviedo failed to win Ethiopians from Coptic Church.	Georg Wickram: *Der Goldfaden*, early German novel. George Cavendish: *Life and Death of Thomas Wolsey*, early English biography (printed 1641). Publication of *Songes and Sonettes (Tottel's Miscellany)*, containing 40 of Sir Thos. Wyatt's (†1542) poems.

Cellini: *Perseus holding the head of Medusa*, bronze group, completed.
Dillingen University founded (closed 1804).
Sir Martin Bowes's cup, silver-gilt, mounted crystal.

Jean Fernel (*1497, †1558), "Father of Pathology": *Pathologia*, study of morbidity.

Sir Thomas White founded St John's College, Oxford.
Building of Gray's Inn Hall, London, commenced.
Palestrina: *Missa papae Marcelli*, six-part Mass.
c. Baltazar de Beaujoyeaux: musical dances, first named ballet.
Foundation of Gresham's; Public School.
c. Fine woodcarving in Japan, spread from temples to palaces of shōguns.
c. Tintoretto: *St. George's fight with the Dragon*, Venetian painting.
Sir Thomas Pope founded Trinity College, Oxford.

P. Belon: *Histoire Naturelle des Oiseaux*, which included some classification of birds.
Formation of Muscovy Trading Co. to develop Anglo-Russian trade; first of great Chartered Joint Stock trading companies.
Gesner: *Descriptio Montis Fracti sive Montis Pilati*, Swiss account of early mountaineering.
Christophe Plantin (*1514, †1589), French printer, established works at Antwerp; his type design is still used.

Old Hundredth, great psalm tune; found in Knox's Psalter, but probably older.
Rare silver tankard with bulbous body known.
Jesuits given control of theological and philosophical faculties at Prague University of Ferdinand I.

Posthumous publication of Agricola's *De re metallica* (see 1530).
Stephen Burrough (*1525, †1584) set out to find North East Passage: reached Bay of Petchora before being forced back.
In Shensi Province, China, on 24th Jan. occurred the most violent known earthquake; 830,000 people perished.
First trucks run on rails (in Germany).
Tartaglia: *Trattato generale di numeri e misure*, mathematical treatise, published.

The Mosque of Suleiman I, Constantinople, built; example of Turkish Saracen architecture.
Foundation of Repton College, public school.
Gonville and Caius College, Cambridge, refounded by Dr Caius.
(to 1560) Building of city walls at Naples.

Recorde: *Whetstone of Witte*, algebra text-book in which sign of equality (=) appeared.
Thomas Tusser: *Hundreth good pointes of husbandrie*, on farming; he introduced the growing of barley.
First venture of Muscovy Trading Co. under Antony Jenkinson.
Portuguese merchants and traders settled in Macao, S. China.

1558	England lost Calais, last English foothold in Europe, to the French. †Mary I of England; accession of Elizabeth I, daughter of Henry VIII and Anne Boleyn. William Cecil appointed Secretary of State. Marriage of Mary, Queen of Scots, to Dauphin Francis. †Emperor Charles V; Ferdinand I assumed Imperial title. Battle of Gravelines: French defeatd by Egmont in Netherlands. Diet of Frankfurt failed to settle differences between groups of German Protestants. Geneva gained independence from Berne. Tsar Ivan IV invaded Livonia; involved in long war with Sweden and Poland. Akbar the Great conquered Gwalior.	Marguérite d'Angoulême: *The Heptaméron*; a collection of stories supposed to have been told in seven days. Du Bellay: *Antiquités de Rome* and *Les Regrets*. (to 1561) Sachs issued collected writings in three volumes; German meisterlieder and drama. Knox: *First Blast of the Trumpet against the Monstrous Regiment of Women* directed against Mary I.
1559	Acts of Supremacy and Uniformity in England restored Protestant Church and severed England from Rome; beginnings of Puritanism. Properties of English Knights Hospitallers confiscated. Henry II of France killed in tournament; Guise faction seized government for Francis II; Mary of Scotland Queen of France. Treaty of Câteau-Cambrésis ended struggle between Spain and France. Peasant Republic of Ditmarschen seized by Denmark. Margaret of Parma appointed Regent in Netherlands.	Revised Prayer Book of Elizabeth I issued; less extreme than predecessors. Pope Paul IV issued preliminary *Index Expurgatorius* for R.C.s; listing unapproved books (see 1564). *Acts and Monuments* published in Latin at Strasbourg; later as Foxe's *Book of Martyrs* (see 1563).
1560	Treaty of Edinburgh signed; Council of Regents set up; French troops evacuated; treaty denied by Francis II and Mary of France. Scottish Parliament sanctioned establishment of Reformed Church; Papal authority abolished and Protestant faith only recognized. †Francis II of France; succeeded by brother, Charles IX, with his mother Catherine di Medici, as Regent.	*c*. *Robert Greene (†1592), English poet. Publication of Geneva ("breeches") Bible by reformers. Knox: (i) *Treatise on Pre-destination*; (ii) *The Book of Discipline*, this latter forming the framework of Scottish Presbyterianism.

c. Pieter Brueghel the Elder (*1525, †1569): *The Alchemist at Work,* Flemish painter who had a love of humorous, grotesque or fantastic scenes.
John Blahoslav (*1523, †1571); *Musica,* first Czech music theory book.
Charlecote Park, Warwickshire, built by Sir Thomas Lucy.
Establishment of Lutheran University of Jena.

Printing of Petrus Petregrinus's work on magnetism.
Jenkinson set out to find overland route to China; reached Bokhara.
First Russian trade delegation to England reached London.
Hamburg Exchange set up.
Firearms first manufactured at Ferlach in Carinthia.
French entered Senegal River area in West Africa.

Titian: *Diana and Actaeon,* Italian painting.
Foundation of Geneva Academy; university in 1876.
Erection of Little Moreton Hall, Cheshire; moated house.
Erection of Llanvihangel Court, Monmouthshire, façade; alterations 1660 internally.

Realdo Colombo (*c.* *1516, †1559): *De re Anatomica,* proposed and tested theory of pulmonary circulation (theory suggested earlier).
Ferdinand I tried to standardize Imperial coinage.
Jenkinson travelled overland to Moscow.
c. Earliest plane tables in use for surveying.

Brueghel the Elder: *Children at play,* Flemish painting.
Westminster School, which was originally attached to the Abbey, was founded by Elizabeth I.
(to 1574) Vasari erected Palazzo degli Uffizi, Florence.
Formal gardens of Penshurst Place, Kent, laid out.
Erection of Sulgrave Manor, Northamptonshire, home of Washington's ancestors.

c. Burroughs persuaded Muscovy Co. to publish Cortes' *Art of Navigation;* made knowledge of Spanish School of Seamanship available to English seamen.
Gresham set about reforming currency; Gresham's Law.
Tobacco imported into France by Jean Nicot.
Academia Secretorum Naturae, scientific society at Naples, founded.

	History	Literature
1560	†Gustavus Vasa of Sweden and accession of Eric IV. Tsar Ivan IV blamed boyars for death of his wife, Anastasia.	
1561	Mary, Queen of Scots, now widowed Queen of France, returned to Scotland. John Knox established Scottish Church Constitution. Colloquy of Poissy attempted reconciliation between French Catholics and Protestants. Philip II of Spain declared Madrid to be capital of Spain. Baltic States of Teutonic Order secularized; Courland made into Duchy, Livonia ceded to Poland, Estonia ceded to Sweden. Eric IV of Sweden compelled his brothers to recognize his authority by Articles of Arboga. Catholic Archbishopric of Prague restored by Emperor Ferdinand I.	Julius Caesar Scaliger (*1484, †1558): *Poetics*, literary criticism of the Italian scholar published posthumously. Thomas Sackville and Thomas Norton: *Gorboduc*, or *Ferrex and Porrex*, first historical play and tragedy in English, produced.
1562	Second Act of Uniformity in England; Court of High Commission set up to deal with breaches of church law. Treaty of Hampton Court between Elizabeth I and Huguenots; English occupied Le Havre. Edict of St Germain gave formal recognition to French Protestants; massacre of Huguenots at Vassy; religious wars between Catholics and Protestants began in France. Revolts against Spanish rule in Netherlands. Council of Trent re-opened. Frederick III of Palatinate gave hospitality to refugees from Netherlands. Truce between Emperor Ferdinand I and Turks for eight years. Maximilian, son of Ferdinand I, crowned King of Bohemia and elected King of Romans. Rajah of Jaipur submitted to Akbar the Great.	Cellini: *Autobiography*, written between 1558 and 1562 by the famous Florentine goldsmith. Lope de Vega Carpio (†1635): founder of Spanish drama, wrote many plays, together with pastorals, sonnets, odes and novels. Torquato Tasso (*1544, †1595), Italian poet: *Rinaldo*, narrative poem. Gerard Legh: *Accedens of Armory*, work on heraldry.

Titian: *Jupiter and Antiope,* Italian painting.

(to 1572) Construction of Antwerp Town Hall.
Sterling standard silver coinage finally established and lasted until 20th cent., except for 1697 to 1719.
Foundation of Merchant Taylors' School by the London livery company of the same name.
Blahoslav co-ordinated production of Czech Hussite hymnal.
c. Brockhall, Elizabethan manor house, erected.

Second trade journey of Jenkinson; this time to Persia via Russia.
Forerunner of hand grenade made.
Roy López, great Spanish chess player, developed modern chess strategy.
Gabriel Fallopius (*1523, †1562), Italian anatomist who discovered tubes named after him and carried out important research on female reproductive organs: *Observationes anatomicae.*

*John Bull (†1628), fine composer for the virginals.
Tintoretto: *Christ at the Sea of Galilee,* Venetian painting.
Psalter of Sternhold and Hopkins, principal 16th cent. work on sacred songs.
Bologna University, founded in 11th cent., built by Borromeo.
Paolo Veronese (*1528, †1588) began *The Marriage at Cana,* Italian painting.
Erection of Loseley Hall, Guildford, Elizabethan mansion.
Archbishop Parker's Salt, silver-gilt, at Corpus Christi College, Cambridge.

Aulnegers (government agents) established at Manchester to stamp woollen cloth.
Trade in West African slaves began.
French attempted to colonize Florida; Huguenot settlers massacred by Spaniards.
Plague in Paris.
First voyage of (Sir) John Hawkins (*1532, †1595) to West Indies.

1563 French regained Le Havre from English. Edict of Amboise; granted some toleration to Huguenots; end of first Huguenot War.
Maximilian of Bohemia elected King of Hungary.
Commendone, Papal Legate to Poland, persuaded Sigismund II to accept decrees of Council of Trent and forbid Poles to receive Reformed doctrine.
End of Council of Trent; did much to win back countries which had accepted Protestantism and reformed abuses at Papal Court.
Calvinism organized in Netherlands.
Frederick II of Denmark, in alliance with Poland, Saxony and Lübeck, started Seven Years War with Sweden.

John Foxe (*1516, †1587): *The Book of Martyrs*, the story of religious persecution in England (see 1559). *The Thirty-Nine Articles*, setting out doctrine of Anglican Established Church, were evolved.
Second *Book of Homilies* issued (see 1547).
Barnabe Googe (*1504, †1594): *Eclogs, Epytaphes and Sonnetes*, containing first English pastorals.

1564 First Puritan opposition to Anglicanism in England.
Anglo-Spanish war broke out.
Peace made between England and France at Troyes.
†Emperor Ferdinand I; succession of Maximilian II.
Danish ships and those from Lübeck defeated Swedish fleet off Gotland.
Counter Reformation began in Poland.
Tsar Ivan IV deserted by Prince Kurbsky, who joined king of Poland; Period of Terror introduced by Ivan. Akbar the Great annexed Malwa.
Alliance of Bijapur, Ahmadnager, Golkonda and Bidar against Vijayanager; latter defeated at Talikot; empire and city destroyed.

First complete *Index Librorum Prohibitorum* published (see 1559).
Creed of Pope Pius used in R.C. Church.
The Apostle, first printed book in Russia, on French paper.
Frederick III, Elector Palatine, accepted Heidelberg Catechism as statement of his State's religious belief.
Tridentene Creed promulgated.
*William Shakespeare (†1616).

1565 Marriage of Mary, Queen of Scots, to Lord Darnley, her cousin.
Religious Edict of Philip II in Netherlands aroused opposition of William I of Orange, Egmont and Admiral Hoorne.
Attack on Malta by Turks repulsed by La Valette.

Cinthio: *Hecatomiti*, Italian prose love stories.
Ronsard: *Abrégé de l'art poétique français*, one of his major works.

Erection (to 1584) of the Escorial, 30 miles from Madrid; huge block of buildings, including palace, church, monastery and college.
c. Tintoretto: *Finding of the Body of St Mark,* Venetian painting.
John Shute: *First and Chief Groundes of Architecture.*
(to 1566) Michelangelo constructed Church of St Mary of the Angels of materials from one of Baths of Diocletian.
Giovanni da Bologna (*1524, †1608): great fountain of Bologna (to 1566).

Statute of Apprentices in England attempted to solve problem of unemployment and poverty by ensuring that everyone had trade in his hands.
Further Act of Parliament against evils of enclosure; ordered permanence of tillage if under plough in 1528 and 1563.
Ambroise Paré (*1509, †1590): *Five Books of Surgery,* development of French surgery.
Bernard Palissy (*1510, †1589), French potter, began making his fine dishes and plaques.

Delorme began work on the Tuileries, Paris, originally designed for Catherine di Medici; Palace destroyed by the Commune in 1871.
Building of The Hague Town Hall.
Michelangelo worked on the *Rondanini Pietà,* unfinished sculpture, up to his death.
Jesuits gained control of higher education in Poland.
Foundation of Felsted; public school.
(to 1566) Tintoretto: *The Flight into Egypt,* Venetian painting.

Introduction of horse-drawn coach into Britain from Holland (see 1551). New Charter granted to Merchant Adventurers of England.
Second voyage of Hawkins to W. Indies and S. America.
English trading centre established at Emden.
Hamburg merchants invited English merchants to trade in Hamburg under same conditions as native citizens.
Eustachio: *Opuscula Anatomica.*
Spain seized the Philippine Islands and built Manila.
Printing first reached Moscow.

Brueghel the Elder: *Autumn* and *Winter* (hunters in the snow), Flemish paintings.
Titian: *Toilet of Venus,* Italian painting.
Tintoretto: *Crucifixion,* Italian painting.

Pencils first mentioned (by Gesner of Zurich).
Dutch merchants founded settlement in Kola Peninsula, Lapland.
Tobacco introduced into England (or 1586?).
Hawkins introduced *sweet* potatoes into England.
Garcia de Orta, Portuguese, described Indian diamond mining.

1566	Elizabeth I forbade English parliament to discuss prospect of her marriage. Murder of David Rizzio, favourite of Mary of Scotland, in her presence at Holyrood House at instigation of Lord Darnley. †Suleiman.	*Notizie Scritte*, one of the first newspapers, issued officially, in Venice. George Gascoigne (*c.* *1539, †1577): *Supposes*, oldest surviving prose comedy in English. Archbishop Parker: *Book of Advertisements*, aimed at uniformity of church service and vestments.
1567	Lord Darnley killed at Kirk o' the Field House, near Edinburgh; arranged by Earl of Bothwell at Queen's instigation. Marriage of Mary, Queen of Scots, to Lord Bothwell; Mary forced to abdicate. †Shan O'Neill in Ireland in rebellion against Elizabeth I. Conspiracy of Meaux by Huguenots; started Second Civil War in France. War between Spain and Dutch; Duke of Alva sent to Netherlands. Monastery Council established by Maximilian II to supervise clergy. Akbar the Great conquered Chitor. Nobunaga became supreme in Japan; deposed Shogunate and centralized Government.	William Salesbury and Richard Davis translated into Welsh the New Testament and Prayer Book. Gruffydd Robert's *Welsh Grammar* published in Milan. Elizabeth I recognized Eisteddfod, which originated much earlier. Sir Geoffrey Fenton (*c.* *1539, †1608): *Tragicall Discourses*, popular translations of Matteo Bandello's romances.
1568	Bothwell's forces defeated at Battle of Langside; Mary of Scotland fled to England. Treaty of Longjumeau ended Second Civil War in France and confirmed terms of Edict of Amboise; outbreak of Third Civil War in France between Catholics and Huguenots. Spanish Inquisition condemned all inhabitants of Netherlands to death as heretics. Spanish ships carrying pay to Alva's troops in Netherlands seized by orders of Elizabeth I. Swedish Parliament deposed Eric IV; succeeded by John III. Jesuit missionaries given friendly reception in Japan.	Eisteddfod held at Caerwys in Flint. Pope Pius V issued modern R.C. breviary; modified version of 11th cent. breviary. Archbishop Parker issued *Bishop's Bible*.
1569	Rising of Northern Earls in England against Protestantism of Elizabeth I; Mary, Queen of Scots, to replace Elizabeth; revolt quelled by Sussex.	

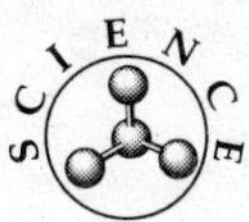

Brueghel the Elder: *The Wedding Dance*, Flemish painting.
St. Andrew's Psalter, illuminated manuscript.
(to 1580) Erection of Longleat House, Wiltshire, on site of a priory.

Establishment of Exchanges at Rouen and Cologne.
Foundation of Royal Exchange, London, by Sir Thomas Gresham; burned down 1666; rebuilt 1668; again burned down 1838 and rebuilt 1840.

Palestrina: *Missa Papae Marcelli*, church music.
Tallis's Canon, famous tune.
*Michael Mierevalt (†1641), who painted *Portrait of a Lady*.
Titian: *Ecce Homo* and *Self-Portrait*, Italian paintings.
Rugby School founded by Lawrence Sheriff.
Helmstedt University founded; chartered 1575.
Erection of Ancient House, Ipswich.
Giovanni da Bologna: *Mercury*, Florentine bronze.

Ten-year trade treaty between Hamburg and England.
Foundation of Rio de Janeiro, Brazil.
Third voyage of Hawkins to the West Indies; accompanied by Francis Drake (knighted 1581), who commanded the *Judith*.
Construction of elegant Santa Trinità bridge over the Arno, Florence.

Primaticcio designed Aile de la Belle Cheminée, Fontainebleau.
Brueghel the Elder: *The Blind Leading the Blind*, Flemish painting.
School for English Jesuits established at Douai in Netherlands.
(to 1575) Floris erected tomb of Christian II, at Roskild.
Vignola began Church of Jesus, Rome; completed by Giacomo della Porta.

Jacques Besson: *Theatrum Instrumentorum et Machinarum*, technological work illustrating machinery.
Hawkins's flotilla attacked by Spaniards when on slave run.
Incorporation of Company of Bricklayers and Tylers, London.
c. Alvaro de Mendaña reached Solomon Islands.
c. Sebastian of Portugal abolished Indian slavery in Brazil.

c. El Greco (Domenikos Theotokopoulos) (*1541, †1614), of Cretan descent: *Coronation of a Saint or a King*, Modena polyptych.

Invention of Mercator Chart, widely used in navigation; it was based on rectangular orthomorphic projection (constant longitude scale; latitude scale porportional

LITERATURE

	History	Literature
1569	Frederick III of Palatinate proposed union of German, English and Scandinavian Protestants; failed, due to opposition of Brandenburg. Union of Lublin: Lithuania united to Poland. Cosimo di Medici of Florence obtained Siena from Emperor and created Grand Duke of Tuscany. Ottoman Turks captured the Yemen. Fitzmaurice's rebellion in Ireland; lasted until 1574.	
1570	Elizabeth I excommunicated by Pope Pius V; declared usurper. Peace of St Germain: amnesty granted to French Huguenots. Peace of Stettin: end of Seven Years War between Sweden and Denmark. John III of Sweden, in alliance with Stephen Batory of Poland, declared war on Ivan IV of Russia. Lutherans joined with Bohemian Brethren, Calvinists and Moravians in Bohemia; failed to give unity to Bohemian Protestant movement.	Ascham: *The Schoolmaster*: author gave his views on education; in favour of physical exercise and against foreign schooling. Early Deccani MS.: *Nujum al'Ulum* of Bijapur, India.
1571	Ridolfi plot against Elizabeth I; uncovered by Cecil's spies. Parliament prohibited importation of Papal Bulls into England. Convocation in England sanctioned the Thirty Nine Articles of Faith. Turks took Cyprus from Venice and Tunis from Spain; battle of Lepanto; combined fleet from Mediterranean states under Don John of Austria defeated Turks.	Revision of the Thirty-Nine Articles, in form now printed in the Prayer Book. Foundation of Mediceo Laurenziana Library in Florence. John de Beauchesne and John Baildon: *A Booke Containing Divers Sortes of Hands*, first English writing-book.
1572	Duke of Norfolk executed for part in Ridolfi plot. Drake's attack on Nombre di Dios. Massacre of St Bartholomew; most Protestants in Paris for marriage of Henry of Navarre and Margaret de Valois murdered on St Bartholomew's eve. William I of Orange elected Stadholder; Dutch war of liberation from Spain began. William de la March and his "Sea Beggars" captured Brill; led to rising	Ronsard: *La Franciade*, uncompleted epic of Francus, son of Hector of Troy, founding French monarchy. Guillaume de Salluste, Seigneur du Bartas (*1544, †1590): *Judith*, dramatic epic. Luis de Camoëns (*1524, †1580): *The Lusiad*, Portuguese epic poem, mainly on exploits of Vasco da Gama. Henri Estienne (*1531, †1598): *Thesaurus Linguae Graecae*. Thos. Cartwright: *Admonition to Parliament*, advocating Presbyterian form of government.

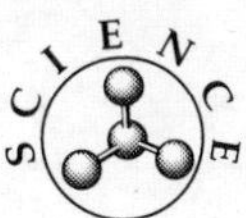

to secant of latitude).
Mercator: *Cosmographia* in same year.
Caesar Fredericke, Venetian, visited Burma.

Andrea Palladio (*1518, †1580): *Treatise on Architecture*, fine work on building, published in Venice.
*David de Heem the Elder (†1632), who had two sons, nephew and grandsons, all fine painters.
Thibaut (musician) and de Baïf (poet) founded an Academy of Poetry and Music in Paris.
Painting of the *Prajnapivamita sutra*, illustrated manuscript on palm-leaf; art of Nepal.
Earliest known musical festival to St Cecilia; in Normandy.

Early reference to sulphuric acid.
A map in Paris gives considerable information on mouth of Hudson river. (see 1609).
First voyage of Francis Drake to West Indies.
Abraham Ortelius of Antwerp (*1527, †1598): *Theatrum Orbis Terrarum*, first modern atlas.
Platen attempted to systematize treatment for the insane.
Establishment of Whitechapel bell foundry.

Harrow School founded by John Lyon.
Br. Hugh Price (and Queen Elizabeth I) founded Jesus College, Oxford.
The gatehouse of Kenilworth Castle built.
Erection of Trerice, Elizabethan house in Cornwall.
c. Titian: *Christ crowned with Thorns*, Italian painting.

Leonard Digges constructed theodolite and is *recorded* (doubtful) as having made one of the first telescopes; more probable date 1608 (*q.v.*).
Royal Exchange, London, opened by Elizabeth I.
Incorporation of Blacksmiths' and of Joiners' Companies.

Foundation of the Society of Antiquaries; dissolved 1604; reformed 1717; chartered 1751.
Middle Temple Hall, London, erected (begun 1562).

Drake's first sight of the Pacific.
First Parish Poor Rate; compulsory levy on each parish to relieve poor.
Rafael Bombelli used imaginary numbers in his book, *Algebra*, without understanding their significance.
G. Braun and F. Hogenberg, Flemish, began *Civitates orbis terrarum*, fine studies of cities of the world; illustrated by Joris Hoefnagel (*1542, †1600).

Year	History	Literature
1572	of Northern Provinces of Netherlands under William of Orange. †Sigismund II of Poland, last Jagellon king; Polish monarchy became elective. Gujarat annexed by Akbar the Great.	
1573	Fourth Huguenot War ended by Pacification of Boulogne. Spaniards captured Haarlem after seven-month siege; inhabitants massacred. Henry of Anjou elected King of Poland. Treaty of Constantinople between Venice and Turkey.	François Hotman: *Francogallia,* a political work. Tasso: *Aminta,* Italian shepherd romance.
1574	Roman Catholic Mission to reconvert England. Fifth Religious Civil War in France. †Charles IX of France; succeeded by Henry of Poland, who became Henry III of France. Relief of Leyden, after siege of eleven months, by "Sea Beggars", who cut dykes and sailed over land to city.	Burbage received licence to open theatre (see 1576).
1575	Elizabeth I offered sovereignty of Netherlands; refused. English Parliament successfully claimed freedom from arrest for members and their servants. Henry III, king of France and Poland, refused to return to Poland; deposed by Polish nobles; Emperor Maximilian II elected King of Poland; large Polish group refused to accept German king and elected Stephen Batory. Akbar the Great conquered Bengal.	*Gammer Gurton's Needle,* author unknown; early English comedy first acted at Christ's College, Cambridge. Tasso: *Jerusalem Delivered,,* Italian epic poem about the Crusades.
1576	Peter Wentworth, M.P., attacked Elizabeth I's interference with rights of House of Commons. Edict of Beaulieu permitted reformed religion in France, with exception of Paris. Antwerp sacked by Spaniards; Catholics and Protestants in	First theatre in England opened at Shoreditch (see 1574).

Work begun on Mexico City Cathedral, Spanish-American architecture; completed 1813.
Medieval house of Althorp, Northamptonshire; modified later.

Hawkins made Treasurer of Navy Board; introduced greater efficiency.

Federigo Zuccaro (*c. 1542, †c. 1609): Italian portraits of (i) *Elizabeth I*, (ii) *Mary, Queen of Scots*, during visit to England.
c. Titian: *Pietà*, Italian painting.
Church of St Lorenzo, Milan, last rebuilt.

Portuguese colonized Angola.
Conrad Dasypodius built famous clock of Strasbourg Cathedral; astronomical clock since rebuilt but containing some original parts.

Foundation of Leyden University by William of Orange.
Cantiones Sacrae, 16 motets by Tallis and 18 by Byrd.
Veronese: *Martyrdom of St Giustina*, Italian painting.
Abd al-Samad and Sayyid 'Ali: 1,500 Indian pictures on cloth illustrating romance of Amir Hamza.

Paré applied massage to invalids.
Sir Humphrey Gilbert (c. *1539, †1583), navigator, in his *Discourse* advocated development of English colonization.
Turberville: *Book of Falconry*.
Abolition of child labour in Hungarian mines.
c. First known genuine European imitation of oriental porcelain; at Venice.

Sir Richard Grenville (*c. 1541, †1590) rebuilt Buckland Abbey, 13th cent. Cistercian monastery.

Tycho Brahe (*1546, †1601), Danish astronomer, established remarkable observatory at Uraniborg.
Cardano described typhus fever.
Early treatise on flowers of Spain and Portugal, by Clusius, distinguished botanist – beginnings of modern botany.
Act concerning the Poor: materials to be

	History	Literature
1576	Netherlands united against Spain at Pacification of Ghent. †Emperor Maximilian II; accession of incompetent Rudolph II. John Casimir invaded France in support of Huguenots. Infallibility Edict of Akbar the Great.	
1577	Archbishop Grindal suspended until 1582 for failing to oppose non-conformist meetings of clergy. Cuthbert Mayne, Jesuit missionary from Douai, executed in England. Sixth War of religion in France; Peace of Bergerac confirmed Edict of Beaulieu. Perpetual Edict issued by Don John of Austria to settle dispute between Dutch and Spain; rejected by William I of Orange. John III of Sweden supported Catholic reaction in Sweden. Stephen Batory captured Danzig.	Raphael Holinshead; *Chronicles of England, Scotland and Ireland*, famous history often used as a source book by Shakespeare for his plays. Jean Bodin (*1530, †1596), French political philosopher: *De la République*, political work concerned with constitutional monarchy.
1578	James VI of Scotland assumed personal government. Protestant preachers expelled from Vienna. John Casimir of the Palatinate supported extreme Calvinists at Ghent. Sebastian of Portugal led crusade against Moors in Morocco; defeated at Al Kasr al Kebir and disappeared.	Du Bartas: *La Semaine*, French account of the creation in seven days. Ronsard: *Les Amours d'Hélène*.
1579	Outbreak of rebellion in Ireland under Earl of Desmond. Union of Utrecht; seven northern provinces (Protestant) of Netherlands joined together against Catholics; became "United Provinces", later kingdom of Holland. Peace of Arras: Southern Netherlands acknowledged Philip II of Spain.	John Lyly (†1606): *Euphues*, a prose romance noted for its elaborate style which has led to the word euphemism. Sir Thomas North: translation of Plutarch's *Lives* from the French. Edmund Spenser (*1552, †1599): *The Sheapheardes Calandar*, eclogues for each month of the year. Johann Fischart: *Bienenkorb*, early German novel.
1580	Fresh campaign of R.C. missionaries opened against England. Smerwick, Ireland, captured by Lord Grey; all Spaniards supporting Desmond slain. Seventh civil war of religion in France; ended with Peace of Felix. †Cardinal Prince Henry, who had	Michel de Montaigne (*1533, †1592): *Essais, personal essays of a French scholar and noble.* Jan Kochanowski (*1530, †1584): *Treny*, Polish dirges. Augustus of Austria authorized *Book of Concord*, summary of protestant works of 16th cent. Foundation of Edinburgh University Library.

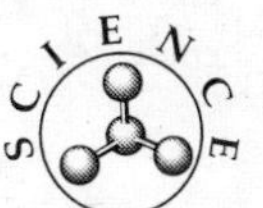

provided for able-bodied poor and houses of correction (Bridewells) for vagabonds (see 1552).
Martin Frobisher (*c. 1535, †1594) sailed for North West Passage.

Greek College founded in Rome.
(to 1580) Robert Wynne built Plas Mawr, Conway.
Veronese: *The Finding of Moses*, Venetian painting.
Tintoretto: *The Doge Mocenigo*, Venetian painting.
Consecration of Milan Cathedral by Cardinal Borromeo.
El Greco completed *The Assumption of the Virgin*, Graeco-Spanish painting for S. Domingo Church, Toledo.

Complaints in England of enclosure of commons for breeding and feeding of cattle, because of over-population.
Frobisher's second voyage in search of North West Passage.
Drake set out in the *Pelican* (later called *The Golden Hind*) on voyage which was to take him round the world.
Portuguese monopoly of colonial trade abolished.
Tycho Brahe made observations of a bright comet.

Scottish Order of Thistle dormant as result of Reformation.
Nicholas Hillyarde (*c. 1547, †1619): miniature of Elizabeth I.
English College at Douai removed to Rheims.
Foundation of Polish University of Vilna.
Work begun on Pont Neuf, oldest bridge over River Seine at Paris.

Levant Trading Company founded in London for trade with Turkey.
Frobisher made his third voyage.
The Conrade brothers established faience pottery at Navers.
Ortelius: *Synonymia geographica*.
Gilbert, granted general patent of colonization, set out for the North-West (returned 1579).

English College removed from Rheims to Rome.
Martini Longhi erected Capitoline Tower, Rome.
El Greco: *The Espolio*, Graeco-Spanish painting.
Azuchi, great fortress of Azuchi-Momoyama period (1573–1603), completed for Nobunaga of Japan; no longer extant.

Elizabeth I granted Charter to Eastland Trading Co, with monopoly of English trade in Baltic.
Failure of Gilbert's attempt to colonize West Indies.
Drake claimed English sovereignty over New Albion (California).
Portuguese merchants set up trading station in Bengal.
First national atlas (British); survey by Christopher Saxton.

Earliest reference to song *Greensleeves*.
Robert Smithion designed Woolaton Hall, Nottinghamshire.
(to 1600) Renewed work on Somerset House.
Borromeo established Sunday Schools in Milan.
Palladio and Scamozzi: Teatro Olimpico, Vicenza; classical Greek theatre.

Muscovy Trading Co. sent Arthur Pet and Charles Jackman in search of North East Passage: failed to penetrate Kara Sea.
Sir E. Osborne and R. Stoper, London merchants, sent Wm. Harborne to court of Murad III of Turkey: granted English merchants freedom of trade in Turkish Empire.

	History	Literature
1580	ruled Portugal since disappearance of nephew Sebastian; resulted in Succession War. Philip II of Spain invaded Portugal; proclaimed king; united colonial empires of Spain and Portugal; lasted to 1640.	Last Miracle Play performed at Coventry.
1581	Discussion of proposed marriage of Elizabeth I of England and Francis, Duke of Anjou. Penalties of High Treason imposed by law in England on converts to Roman Catholicism. Pope Gregory XIII attempted to reconcile Roman and Orthodox churches; failed. Netherlands proclaimed independence from Spain. Sweden and Poland overran Livonia. Tsar Ivan IV murdered his heir with his own hands. Russians began conquest of Siberia. Akbar the Great conquered Afghanistan.	Sir Philip Sidney (*1554, †1586): *Defence of Poesy*, written. *c.* George Peele (*c.* *1557, †1596): *The Arraignment of Paris*, pastoral play presented by the children of the Chapel Royal.
1582	"Raid of Ruthven"; James VI of Scotland kidnapped by Protestant nobles to ensure his safety from Esmé Stuart, Catholic. Poland engaged in successful war against Russia; Livonia ceded to Poland; Russia excluded from Baltic coastline. First Jesuit Mission to China. Jesuit missionaries claimed 150,000 converts in Japan. Nobunaga of Japan killed; suceeded by Hiedyoshi, who carried on work of breaking feudal power.	Publication of English edition of New Testament authorized for Catholic use. George Buchanan (*1506, †1582): *Rerum Scotiarum Historia*; important work on Scottish history in Latin.
1583	Throckmorton plot against Elizabeth I by Spanish Ambassador, Mendoza, and Cheshire gentleman, Francis Throckmorton. John Whitgift appointed Archbishop of Canterbury to check Puritanism and ensure conformity. Earl of Desmond slain in skirmish; end of rebellion. Münster reduced to desert; 30,000 people died of starvation in last six months of war.	Robert Garnier (*1545, †1590): *Les Juives*, one of earliest French tragi-comedies. Joseph Justus Scaliger (*1540, †1609), French scholar: *De Emendatione Temporum*, work suggesting investigation of accuracy of ancient history records. First Cambridge University Press printer commenced duties (see 1522).

Coffee imported into Italy.
Earthquake in London on 6th April.
c. Potatoes *may* have been introduced into Spain from Peru (see 1586).

Ballet Comique de la Reyne, said to be the first dramatic ballet, performed at Versailles, under the direction of Baltasar de Beaujoyeux.
Early reference to English lutes; instrument of much greater antiquity in Europe and Asia.
c. El Greco: *The Martyrdom of St Maurice,* Graeco-Spanish painting.

Robert Newman: *The Newe Attractive*: independently described magnetic dip (see 1544).
Drake returned to England after sailing round the world.
Sedan chairs introduced into England.
William Burrough, younger brother of Stephen (see 1556): *Discourse of the Variation of the Compas.*
Galileo Galilei (*1564, †1642), one of the greatest men of his age, discovered isochronous property of the pendulum by observing a swinging lamp in Pisa Cathedral.

Edinburgh University founded by James VI.
Würzburg University founded by Bishop Julius.
Establishment of Accademía della Crusca, Florence.
Work begun on Malaga Cathedral, Spain: never completed.
Erection of Corsham Court, Wiltshire; Georgian State Rooms added 1760.
Teatro Olimpico, Vicenza, world's oldest theatre, completed.

Revision of weights by Elizabeth I: standards remained unaltered until 1824.
Gregorian calendar introduced into Italy and other Catholic countries.
First London waterworks established.
Gilbert founded first English colony in Newfoundland.
Richard Hakluyt (*c.* *1552, †1616: *Divers Voyages touching the Discovery of America,* account of English exploration.

*Orlando Gibbons (†1625), organist and composer of church music.
Hans Vredeman de Vries: *Différents Pourtraicts de Menuiserie, à sçavoir Pourtaux, Bancs, Tables Escabelles, Buffets,* Flemish work on furniture design.
Hideyoshi founded castle of Osaka, Japan.

A form of life assurance policy known to have been issued.
Galileo experimented with falling bodies dropped from Leaning Tower of Pisa (doubtful); discovered parabolic nature of trajectories.
Gilbert drowned on second voyage to Newfoundland.
Osborne and Stoper sent overland expedition under R. Fitch and J. Newbery to India. Fitch reached Malay peninsula; returned 1594.

1583	Conflict between Catholics and Protestants for Archbishopric of Cologne; Catholics won.	
1584	"Enterprise of England" launched by Pope to restore Roman Catholicism in England. Alliance between Elizabeth I and James VI of Scotland in defence of their religion. Assassination of William I of Orange by Balthasar Gerard. †Duke of Anjou; succession open to Henry of Navarre,Protestant leader in France (see 1589). League of Joinville; Philip II of Spain and Guise faction in France against Huguenots. †Tsar Ivan IV; accession of incompetent son Fyodor; power in hands of Boris Godunov. Stephen Batory set out to conquer Russia as preliminary to driving Turks from Europe.	*Casket Letters*, concerned with Darnley's murder (1567), disappeared. Adam Bohoric wrote first Slovene Grammar. Albericus Gentilis: *De Legationibus*, Latin work on diplomatic privilege, by Italian lawyer.
1585	Elizabeth I sent Earl of Leicester to Netherlands to aid Dutch and made open war on Spain in revenge for murder of William I of Orange. Parliament, by expelling Dr Parry for opposing Bill against Jesuits, asserted right to expel elected members. Drake, sent by Elizabeth I to plunder West Indies, sacked Cartagena, Santiago and Domingo; returned unscathed. Duke of Parma sacked Antwerp, which lost its importance in international trade.	Giovanni Guarini (*1537, †1612): *Il Pastor Fido* Italian pastoral drama. Cervantes (Miguel de Cervantes Saavedra) (*1547, †1616), Spanish novelist: *Galatea*, a pastoral, published. Court of Star Chamber suppressed all printing offices outside London.
1586	Babington Plot to kill Elizabeth I revealed; complicity of Mary, Queen of Scots, proved. Mary, Queen of Scots, arrested and tried before Commissioners at Fotheringhay Castle, Northamptonshire. War of Three Henries in France (Henry III, Henry, Duc de Guise and Henry of Navarre). Battle of Zutphen: †Sir Philip Sidney. *c.* Abbas the Great became Shah of Persia.	Publication of "Martin Marprelate's" tracts attacking Episcopacy. (to 1593) Cesar Baronius: *Annales Ecclesiastici*, important work on the history of the Roman Catholic church. William Camden (*1551, †1623), antiquary: *Britannia*, a comprehensive guide to the counties of Britain; translated from Latin into English, 1610. Knox: *History of the Reformation in Scotland*.

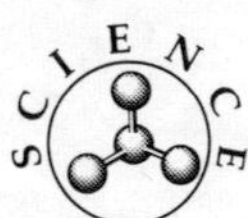

Sir Walter Mildmay founded Emmanuel College, Cambridge.
c. Erection of Oakwell Hall, Yorkshire.
Palestrina: setting of the *Song of Solomon*, in 29 motets.
Erection, at Cordonan, of oldest extant lighthouse; completed 1611.
Foundation of Uppingham; Public School.

Von Grafenberg introduced artificial respiration.
Raleigh discovered Virginia.
Ortelius: *Nomenclator Ptolemaicus*.
c. Establishment of Banco di Rialto, in Venice; beginnings of European public bank system.
Posthumous publication of *Opera genuina omnia*, collected works of Fallopius, Italian anatomist.

Michelangelo de Caravaggio, known as Caravaggio (*1573, †1610), leader of Naturalist Movement: *The Young Bacchus*, Italian painting.
c. Hermon Pietersz's fine pottery began to be manufactured at Delft.
Domenico Fontana (*1543, †1607), Italian architect, built the Quirinal Palace, Rome.
Landini created Fountain of the Tortoises, Rome.
Foundation of Franeker University.

c. Bartholomew Newsam constructed a travelling clock and a standing clock; earliest surviving authentic English spring-driven clocks.
Paddle-boats illustrated by Ramelli.
Raleigh attempted to found colony in Virginia: abandoned 1586.
c. Decimal point seems to have come into general use; very limited use earlier, perhaps from 12th cent.
John Davis, searching for North West Passage, discovered Davis Strait.

Earliest date attributed to Sonata; Scarlatti wrote 500 single-movement sonatas, whereas Beethoven's smaller number have three or four movements.
Foundation of Graz University.
Sixtus V rebuilt Lateran Church of St John, Rome.
El Greco: *Funeral of the Conde de Orgaz*, Graeco-Spanish painting.

Simon Stevinus (*1548, †1620) *Statics and Hydrostatics* in which he evolved the theory that pressure on a body in liquid depends only on its depth and is independent of its shape and size; also enunciated theorem of triangle of forces.
Thomas Cavendish (*c*. *1555, †1592) sailed from Plymouth; returned 1588, having been the third man to circumnavigate the world.

1587 Elizabeth I's absolutism in Church affairs challenged.
Execution of Mary, Queen of Scots.
Return of Leicester to England after failure of Dutch expedition.
Drake raided Cadiz and destroyed Spanish fleet there; delayed Armada against England for twelve months.
Sigismund Vasa, son of John III of Sweden, elected King of Poland as Sigismund III.
Akbar the Great annexed Kashmir.
Hideyoshi broke power of great Shimadzu house of Satsuma.
Hideyoshi: Edict banishing all missionaries from Japan but allowing traders to remain; not strictly enforced.

c. Christopher Marlowe (*1564, †1593): *Tamburlaine*, blank verse tragedy.

1588 Defeat of Armada sent against England by Philip II of Spain by English fleet composed of Queen's ships (under Lord Howard of Effingham) and numerous merchant ships.
Assassination of Henri, Duc de Guise, and his brother Cardinal de Guise.
†Frederick II of Denmark and accession of Christian IV to powerful and prosperous kingdom.

Bishop William Morgan: *The Welsh Bible*: he revised Salesbury's translation of the New Testament and added his translation of the Old Testament:created the Welsh language as it is known today.
c. Jan Blahoslav: his Czech translation of the New Testament incorporated into Bible of Kralice.

1589 House of Commons set up first Standing Committee on Privileges.
James VI of Scotland married Anne of Denmark-Norway.
†Catherine di Medici, Queen Mother of France and main opponent of Huguenots; accession of Henry of Navarre as Henry IV of France; start of Bourbon Dynasty.
Metropolitan of Moscow became Patriarch of Russian Church.
c. Invasion of Abyssinia by primitive Galla pagans; never racially absorbed.

Thomas Nashe (*c.* *1567, †1601): *Anatomie of Absurdities*, criticism of contemporary literature.

1590 Grenville killed in fight of *Revenge* with larger Spanish force.
League of Joinville defeated by Henry IV of France at Ivry.
Duke of Parma attacked Henry IV of France.
John III of Sweden recognized claims of his brother Charles to independent authority in Södermanland.

c. Marlowe: *The Jew of Malta*, blank verse tragedy.
Sidney: *Arcadia*, pastoral romance in prose, published posthumously.
Spenser: *Faerie Queene*, Bks I-III, allegorical romance of chivalry of knights at court of Queen Gloriana (representing Elizabeth I).

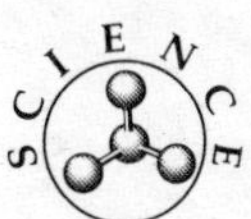

Publication of *Zemiroth Israel*, early collection of Jewish songs.
Completion of Osaka Castle, Japan, built to withstand earthquake and attack.
Claudio Monteverdi (*1567, †1643), Italian, composed his first book of madrigals.
Cobham Hall, Kent, built; later work by Inigo Jones and Adam brothers.

New attempt to colonize Virginia failed.
English Merchant Adventurers settled at Stade on Lower Elbe: remained until 1611.
Hakluyt: *Notable History, containing four Voyages made by certain French Captains into Florida*.
Construction (to 1591) of Rialto Bridge over the Grand Canal, Venice, by Antonio da Ponte.

Vatican Library opened in Rome; built by Domenico Fontana (see 1450).
(to 1590) Cupola and lantern of St Peter's Rome, construted.
Thoinot Arbeau: *Orchésographie*, book of contemporary dances.
Elizabeth I presented Armada Jewel to Sir T. Heneage.

Use of coffer-dam to assist work on river beds.
Elizabeth I built original Chatham Dockyard (moved 1662).
Formation of short-lived English Gambia Trading Co.
Waghenaear: *Mariners' Mirrour*, navigational work containing charts by Hondius (see 1606).
Opening of Billingsgate, London, as landing-stage (see 1699).

c. Caravaggio: *Boy with a Basket of Fruit*, Italian painting.
Arbeau composed earliest surviving march.
University of Kiev founded.

Rev. William Lee made the first English knitting machine.
London merchants applied to the Privy Council for permission to send trading expedition to India.
Hakluyt: *The Principal Navigations, Voyages and Discoveries of the English Nation*, account of journeys of contemporary explorers.

El Greco: *St Jerome*, Graeco-Spanish painting.
Caravaggio: *Matthew and the Angel*, Italian painting.
(to 1597) Constrution of Hardwick Hall, Derbyshire.
Monteverdi's second madrigal book; he served at ducal court of Mantua from this year until 1612.

Z. Janssen invented the compound microscope; of little value until the 18th cent., when the achromatic lens appeared.
Galileo: *De Motu*, in which experiments on dropping different bodies are described.
Ruhr coal mining first developed.
First English paper mill, at Dartford.

LITERATURE

Year	History	Literature
1590	Akbar the Great conquered Orissa. Hideyoshi defeated rivals at Odawara and became master of Japan.	
1591	Liberties of Aragon suppressed by Philip II. League of Torgau formed by German Protestants. Dmitri, youngest son of Ivan IV, murdered; Boris Godunov accused; charge never proved.	Sidney: *Astrophel and Stella* published posthumously. Spenser: *Complaints*, a collection of his minor poetry; and *Colin Clouts Come Home Again*, a poem published 1595.
1592	Establishment of Presbyterian system of government in Scotland. †John III of Sweden; succeeded by son Sigismund III of Poland; strong Catholic Regency in Sweden under Charles of Södermanland (protestant). Marriage of Sigismund III of Poland to Anne of Austria secured Habsburg support against both Turks and Protestants. Akbar the Great conquered Sindh. Hideyoshi's invading army in Korea reached Tumen River but had to withdraw.	*c.* William Shakespeare (*1564, †1616), greatest of English playwrights: *Henry VI*, *Richard III* and *Venus and Adonis*. *c.*Marlowe: *The Tragicall History of Dr Faustus*, a drama. Juan de Mariana (*1536, †1623): *Historia General de España*, first modern Spanish history; written in Latin; translated into Spanish 1601.
1593	Elizabeth I defined freedom of speech in Parliament as "Not to speak every one what he listeth . . . your privilege is *Aye* or *No*". All absentees over sixteen from church in England to be imprisoned. Henry IV of France became a Catholic: "Paris is worth a Mass." Swedish Diet of Uppsala accepted Luther's Catechism. Renewed war against Turks in Hungary; Wallachia won independence from Turks.	*c.* Shakespeare: *Richard II*, an historical play. Nashe: *Christ's Tears over Jerusalem*. Drayton: *Idea, the Shepheards Garland*, eclogues, and *Piers Gaveston*, historical ode. Marlowe: *Edward II*, a play: the playwright was killed in same year.
1594	English sacked Portuguese colony of Pernambuco. Henry IV of France entered Paris. Philip II closed port of Lisbon to Dutch shipping. Sigismund III of Sweden and Poland compelled to accept Uppsala Resolution as condition of coronation; crowned by Protestant Bishop. Turks recaptured fortress of Raab.	Thomas Kyd: *The Spanish Tragedie*, a play. *c.* Shakespeare: *Love's Labours Lost*, *Titus Andronicus* and *The Rape of Lucrece*. Nashe: *The Unfortunate Traveller*, early adventure novel. Micael van Isselt: *Mercurius Gallobelgicus*, German biannual summary of events (in Latin).

Elizabeth I founded Trinity College, Dublin (see 1742).
c. Maderno designed S. Andrea della Valle, Rome.
John Farmer: forty canonical accompaniments to *Miserere*.
Michael Drayton (*1563, †1631): *Harmonie of the Church*, paraphrased Old Testament prayers.

François Vieta (*1540, †1603): *In artem analyticam isagoge*, important French work on algebra, using letters for algebraic quantities and introducing marked improvement.
James Lancaster, seaman, took three ships via Cape of Good Hope to Sumatra, Malacca and Borneo: first Englishman to reach East Indies: returned 1594.

Erection, to 1598, of Palazzo del Senatore, Rome; begun by Michelangelo, continued by Ramaldi; beautiful Renaissance building.
The Vyvyan Salt, made of silver-gilt and painted glass.
Evidence of ruins of Pompeii discovered.
Monteverdi: third madrigal book.

Galileo: *Della Scienza Meccanica*, summarizing many of his principles of mechanics.
Juan da Luca discovered British Columbia.
Edward Wright and Emery Molyneux constructed first English globes.
John Davis discovered Falkland Islands.
Levant Trading Co. received its charter.

Thomas Morley (*1557, †1603), organist of St Paul's, wrote five books of madrigals.
c. El Greco: *The Crucifixion* and *The Resurrection*, Cretan paintings.
Chu-tsai-ya of China first developed the twelve equal temperament semitones in an octave; the problem was solved in Europe in 1691 (*q.v.*).

First French botanical gardens established by University of Montpellier.
Gervase Markham (*1568, †1637): *A Discourse of Horsemanshippe*, by a man keenly interested in horses and veterinary work.

Schifardini designed great church of S. Maria di Provenzano, Siena.
Jacopo Peri (*1561, †1633): *La Dafne*, first Italian opera; music lost (see 1597).

Giordano Bruno, philosopher, impounded by R.C. Church for supporting Copernican theory of the universe (see 1600).
Lancaster broke Portuguese trade monopoly in India.
Fitch returned to England after covering overland journey to India, Ceylon, Malacca, started in 1583.
William Barents, Dutch, sailed from Amsterdam and reached Novaya Zemlya and Kara Sea.

	History	Literature
1595	Widespread rebellion in central and northern Ireland led by Earl of Tyrone; supported by Spain; lasted to 1603. Henry IV of France declared war on Spain. Protestant Charles of Södermanland made Lieutenant-governor of Sweden in defiance of Catholic Sigismund III of Poland and Sweden. Peace of Teusin between Sweden and Russia recognized Swedish rights to Narva and Estonia. Peasants revolted in Upper Austria. Warsaw became capital of Poland.	*c.* Shakespeare: *A Midsummer Night's Dream.* Sidney: *Apologie for Poetrie (Defence of Poesie)*, an essay written to defend poetry from its critics, published posthumously. Spenser: *Epithalamion*, lyric poem written to celebrate his marriage, published. Robert Southwell, Jesuit poet hanged: his *St Peter's Complaint and other Poems* published anonymously in same year.
1596	English force sacked Cadiz. Rising of peasants in South Oxfordshire against agrarian conditions; checked by military preparations of Privy Council. End of French League against Protestants. France, England and Netherlands allied against Spain; Spaniards captured Calais. Erlau conquered by Turks.	*c.* Shakespeare: *The Merchant of Venice, Romeo and Juliet* and *Taming of the Shrew*, plays. Spenser: *Hymns (Heavenlie Love and Heavenlie Beauty)*. Thos. Danet translated Philippe de Commines's chronicles of Louis XI and Charles VIII into English.
1597	Storms destroyed second Armada sent by Philip II of Spain against England. English raiders devastated Portuguese Azores. Transylvania ceded to Emperor Rudolph II by Sigismund Bathory. Re-Catholicization of Upper Austria, Styria, Carinthia and Carniola; effected by force. Second Japanese edict banishing missionaries; more strictly enforced. Hideyoshi again attempted Japanese invasion of Korea; forces withdrawn in 1598.	Francis Bacon (*1561, †1626): *Essays* (also 1612, 1625). Shakespeare: *Henry IV* (1 and 2), historical play. Drayton: *England's Heroicall Epistles*, versified imaginary letters by famous personages. Richard Hooker (*c.* *1554, †1600): *Of the Laws of Ecclesiasticall Politie* (in 5 vols.), a case for the English Church. James VI: *Demonologie*, book on witchcraft.
1598	English force in Ireland defeated at Blackwater; uprising in Ireland under Hugh O'Neill and Earl of Tyrone. Edict of Nantes issued by Henry IV of France gave French Protestants right to worship according to their beliefs.	Benjamin Jonson (*1572, †1637): *Every Man in his Humour*, a comedy by the great dramatist. *c.* Acting of the *Parnassus Plays* at St John's College, Cambridge; satires on poverty of university scholars. Spenser: *Veue of the Present State of Ireland*:

Caravaggio: *Narcissus*, Italian painting.
c. Development of crayoning at about this period, possibly by Guido Reni (*1575, †1642), Italian artist; date uncertain.
Zuccaro, Italian painter of huge frescoes, founded Academy of St. Luke, Rome.
c. First appearance of heels on shoes.

Final abolition of bow and arrow as weapons of war.
Raleigh voyaged to Guiana in search of *El Dorado*: explored River Orinoco; described curare (poison) on native arrow-heads.
First Dutch trader, Ericks, in Guinea; colonies established in E. Indies.
Mendaña discovered Marquesas Islands.
Galileo may have invented thermometer (uncertain).
†Hawkins at sea, near Porto Rico.

Caravaggio: *Basket of Fruit*, Italian painting.
*Jan van Goyen (†1656), painter of flat river scenes.
Foundation of Sidney Sussex College, Cambridge (will of Lady Francis Sidney).
Erection of Harvard House, Warwickshire, home of John Harvard's mother.
Whitgift School,Croydon, founded.

John Harrington designed early water-closets installed at the Queen's Palace, Richmond; two centuries later idea came into general use (see 1778).
Publication of the trigonometric tables of G. J. Rheticus (*1514, +161576), containing all six ratios.
†Drake at sea in W. Indies.
Barents discovered Spitzbergen and Barents Sea.
Tomatoes introduced into England.

First book of English airs, accompanied by lute, by John Dowland.
Morley: *Plaine and Easie Introduction to Practicall Musicke*, authoritative work on 16th cent, music.
Erection of Culross Palace, Fife.
Shakespeare bought "New Place", Statford-on-Avon.
Ottavio Rinuccini: *La Dafne*, first real opera.
Peri: *Euridice*, Italian opera; performed in 1600, it is oldest opera of which the complete music survives.
Gresham's College, London, founded.

Andreas Libavius: *Alchymia*, which gives a lucid account of medical chemistry; described a metal from India—apparently zinc.
Act restating 1576 provision for poor relief in England and Workhouses erected; beggars punished.
Dutch founded Batavia in Java and started trading with Bali.
Three survivors of Barents'1596 expedition returned to Amsterdam from Novaya Zemlya in two open boats.
Dean of Durham complained that enclosure of tillage had reduced 8,000 acres to 160 in a few years.
Hanse League excluded English merchants from Empire.

Jan Brueghel (*1568, †1625): *The Adoration of the Kings*, tempera.
(to 1610) Erection of Burton Agnes Hall, E. Yorkshire, unmodified Elizabethan house.
First reference to game of cricket.
c. El Greco: *The Baptism of Christ*, Graeco-Spanish painting.

*François Mansart (†1666), French architect, whose name is given to a special kind of roof (mansard); this type of roof is, in fact, of earlier origin.
G. de Baillou, of France, described whooping cough.
Steelyard, headquarters of London Hanse merchants,

1598 Peace of Vervins ended Franco-Spanish war.
†Philip II of Spain.
Civil war in Sweden between followers of Sigismund III and Charles of Södermanland, "Peasant King"; Sigismund III routed at Stangebro.
†Tsar Fyodor ended Rurikovich dynasty; Godunov elected Tsar by Assembly of Land; ruled until 1605.
†Hideyoshi, from his death bed, ordered withdrawal of Japanese forces from China and Korea; campaign ended; Tokugawa Iyeyasu nominated successor.

publication refused until 1633.
Lope de Vega Carpio, Spanish poet and dramatist: *La Dragontea*, fanciful account of Drake's adventures; in verse form.

1599 Earl of Essex, having failed to crush Tyrone's rebellion, banished by Elizabeth I on return.
Assembly of Convention of States in Edinburgh.
Basilikon Doron published by James VI of Scotland asserted Divine Right of Kings.
Swedish Diet deposed Sigismund III and proclaimed Charles of dermanland ruler as Charles IX.
Transylvanis conquered by Michael of Wallachia.
Subjugation of Deccan commenced by Akbar the Great.

Shakespeare: *As You Like It, Henry V, Much Ado About Nothing* and *Twelfth Night*, plays.
Mateo Alemán: *Guzmán de Alfarache*, early Spanish picaresque novel.
Jonson: *Every Man out of his Humour*, satirical comedy.

1600 Essex succeeded in Ireland by Lord Mountjoy, who systematically ravaged each district, starving it into surrender.
Persecution of Catholics in Sweden under Charles IX.
Execution of Swedish nobles who had opposed Charles of Södermanland.
Spanish force, sent by Philip III to support Tyrone, landed at Kinsale.
Maurice of Nassau gained victory over Spain at Nieuport.
Iyeyasu defeated rivals at battle of Sekigahara; three years later, he was appointed Shogun, with military and administrative capital at Yedo (later Tokyo); Imperial capital still at Kyoto; thus began 250 years of Tokugawa Shogunate and exclusion of foreigners.

Thomas Dekker (*1570, +161632): *The Shoemaker's Holiday*, a play showing the craftsmen of Elizabethan London, published.
c. Shakespeare: *The Merry Wives of Windsor*, a comedy.
*Calderon de la Barca (†1681), Spanish playwright; he wrote more than 100 plays.
Sir Edward Fairfax: *Godfrey of Bulloigne, or the Recoverie of Jerusalem*, English translation of *Gerusalemme Liberata* (see 1574).
c. Introduction of Black Letter type, Gothic style.
Dekker: *Old Fortunatus*, a comedy.

Sir Thomas Bodley (*1545, †1613) began rebuilding of Library at Oxford.

closed; all privileges withdrawn.
(to 1601) van Noort became fourth man to circumnavigate the world.
French attempted colonization of Nova Scotia.
Admiral Yisunsin of Korea invented world's first iron-clad warships (tortoise-ships) and defeated Hideyoshi's Japanese forces.

El Greco *The Virgin with St Ines and St Tecia,* Graeco-Spanish painting.
Erection of the Globe Theatre, Southwark, where Shakespeare's plays were acted; finally destroyed 1644.
Morley edited series of pieces for six instruments.

Ulisse Aldrovandi (*1523, †1605) produced the first three volumes of his *Natural History* (these books being devoted to ornithology—see 1602): he and Gesner (see 1550) laid foundations of modern zoology; earlier works were less scientific.
First postal charges fixed in Germany.

Foundation of Scottish College at Rome.
Sethus Calvisius (*1566, †1615), German musician: *Exercitationes Musicae Duae,* the first history of music (completed 1611).
Godunov ordered erection of Kremlin belfry, Moscow.
Royal Palace of Naples begun: extended by Ferdinand II (1837).
c. El Greco: *St Joseph with the Child Jesus,* painting of Spanish school.
c. Harps used in orchestras.
c. Popularization of the recorder (flute-à-bec), mainly in England; after dying out, it was revived in 1930s.

William Gilbert (*1544, †1603)' *De Magnete,* work on magnetism; introduced names electricity, magnetic pole, etc,; believed that theories should be checked by experiment; described magnetic induction and earth's magnetic field.
Bruno burned for heresy (see 1594); such incidents in the name of Christianity, were frequent in the history of science.
Vieta: *Apollonius Gallus,* French mathematical work, introducing centre of similitude.
Elizabeth I granted Charter of Incorporation to the East India Trading Co.
Wm. Adams, English seaman, landed in Japan: became adviser to Ieyasu on shipbuilding and navigation.
c. Unsuccessful attempt by Dutch to found settlement on Amazon.
c. Caspar Lehmann, jewel-cutter to Rudolph II, began cut-glass process.

1601	Insurrection and execution of Essex. Spaniards fortified Kinsale. Poor Law Act: codification of all previous Tudor Poor Laws. Dutch expelled Portuguese from Malacca. Matteo Ricci, Jesuit missionary, admitted to Peking.	*c.*Shakespeare: *All's Well That Ends Well*, a comedy, and *Julius Caesar*, historical play. Morley edited *The Triumphes of Oriana*. Foundation of Library of Trinity College, Cambridge. John Donne (*c.* *1571, †1631), poet: *Progress of the Soul*, unfinished satire.
1602	Spanish force in Ireland routed by Lord Mountjoy; O'Neil submitted and was pardoned by Elizabeth I. Dutch fleet arrived at Kandy in Ceylon; welcomed as aid against Portuguese. Emperor Rudolph II suppressed meetings of Moravian Brethren.	*c.*Shakespeare: *Hamlet*, a tragedy. Cardinal Borromeo founded Ambrosian Library, Milan; opened 1609. Bodleian Library, Oxford, opened. Samuel Rowlands: *'Tis Merry when the Gossips Meet*, character-sketch.
1603	†Elizabeth I and accession of James VI of Scotland as James I of England. Millenary Petition expressing Puritan desire for reforms in Church of England presented to James I. Bye-Plot against James I to force concessions to Puritans and Roman Catholics. Main Plot against James I to set Arabella Stuart on English throne; Raleigh implicated; imprisoned in Tower. Tyrone submitted on promise of restoration of title and lands.	*c.* Shakespeare: *Troilus and Cressida*, a play. Thomas Heywood: *A Woman Killed with Kindness*, a play. Alexandre Hardy: *Didon*, play by the precursor of French Classical tragedy. Nudozersky issued standard Czech grammar leading to modern language. Jonson: *Sejanus*, a tragedy.
1604	Hampton Court Conference summoned to consider Church reform: Puritan proposals rejected. Proclamation ordering Roman Catholic priests to leave England. Inception of Gunpowder Plot. First Parliament of James I; Godwin's case vindicated Parliament's right to control its own elections; prorogued. Peace between England and Spain. Puritan ministers ejected from livings. Henry IV of France made judicial offices hereditary; created "Noblesse de la Robe". Maurice of Nassau captured Sluys from Spain; Spaniards under Spinola captured Ostend. Charles IX officially proclaimed king of Sweden; Protestantism ensured.	*c.*Shakespeare: *Measure for Measure* and *Othello*, plays. Drayton: *The Owl*, a satire. Dekker: *The Honest Whore* (part I), a play. Robert Cawdrey: *Table Alphabetical*, earliest English dictionary. Thos. Middleton (*1580, †1627), dramatist and satirist: *The Black Booke* and *Father Hubbard's Tales* attacks on sordid aspects of London life. Nicholas Breton: *The Passionate Shepheard*, pastoral writings.

Caravaggio: *The Conversion of St Paul*, Italian painting.
Edward Phelips completed Montacute House, Somerset (started 1588).
Foundation of University of Parma; reconstituted 1768.
Earliest piece of English faience pottery.
Hillyarde: *Treatise on the Art of Limning*.

*Pierre Fermat (†1665), French who laid foundations of theory of numbers; stated famous last theorem, $a^n + b^n c^n$, where a, b, c and n are integers ($n > 2$).
First trading venture of East India Co,; five ships, under Lancaster and Davis, sailed from Torbay for Sumatra and Bantam.
Abolition of Monopolies after debate in Parliament.

Construction of Long Gallery at Haddon Hall, Derbyshire (15th cent.): original decoration survives.
Akbar the Great built Buland Darwaza, great gateway at Fathpur Sikri, India.
Abu'l Fazl: *Akbar-nama*, illustrated chronicle of Akbar, completed.

Foundation of Dutch East India Company: captial £540,000.
Establishment of Amsterdam Stock Exchange.
Gosnold explored area of Massachusetts, U.S.A.
Aldrovandi's 4th volume of *Natural History* (this one on insects).

Flaminio Ponzio erected Rospigliosi Palace, Rome.
Monteverdi: fourth madrigal book.
Erection of Audley End House, Essex, great mansion, on site of Benedictine Abbey.

Johann Bayer's star catalogue.
H. Fabrizio, Italian: first accurate drawings of valves in veins.
Plague in England.
Samuel de Champlain explored Saguenay tributary of St Lawrence River.
Foundation of scientific society, Accademia dei Lincei, Rome.
c. Establishment of first English bank by Francis Child.

Negri: *Inventioni di Balli*, dance tunes.
Incorporation of Company of Musicians, London.
Foundation of Blundell's, public school at Tiverton.
Caravaggio: *The Deposition* (in the Pinacoteca Vaticana), Italian painting.

Second trading voyage of East India Company.
Beginnings of silk manufacture in England.
Conic sections arranged systematically in order: from line-pair to circle.
Johann Kepler (*1571, †1630), German astronomer, realized that crystalline centre of the eye is a lens projecting image (inverted) on back of eye (retina); findings published in his *Astronomiae pars optica*.
Foundation of French East India Co.; ceased operation 1770.
Incorporation of Turners' Company, London.

	History	Literature
1605	Discovery of Gunpowder Plot: capture of Guy Fawkes. Sir Arthur Chichester appointed Lord Deputy in Ireland. Attempted settlement in Ireland on English legal lines. Decrees of Council of Trent adopted for Bohemia; Protestant opposition. Stephen Bocskai, Pretender to Hungary and Transylvania, allied with Turks against Austria. †Akbar the Great; succeeded by son, Salim, as Jahangir.	*c.*Shakespeare: *King Lear*, a tragedy. Bacon: *The Advancement of Learning*, criticism of traditional methods of learning. Cervantes: *Don Quixote*, Pt. I; Spanish novel of an eccentric knight. Drayton: *Ballad of Agincourt*. François de Malherbe (*1556, †1628), French poet who advocated simplicity: *Poésies* (to 1628).
1606	Execution of Gunpowder Plotters. Impositions levied at ports; merchant, Bates, refused payment of extra duties; Courts held these to be part of Royal Prerogative. Combined Spanish and Portuguese fleets routed by Dutch in East Indies. Reconciliation of Emperor and Stephen Bocskai. Peace of Sitvatorok between Emperor and Sultan. Pretender claimed to be Tsar Dmitri; secured throne but murdered; Boyar Vasili Shuiski elected Tsar; opposed by second false Dmitri. Ieyasu issued decrees against Christians in Japan; not enforced.	*c.* Shakespeare: *Macbeth*, a tragedy. Jonson: *Volpone*, comedy of a rich nobleman who pretends to be dying in order to extract presents from his would-be heirs.
1607	Union of England and Scotland rejected by English Parliament. Courts affirmed common citizenship of English and Scottish persons born after accession of James VI of Scotland to English throne. Complete defeat of Spanish fleet off Gibraltar by Dutch under Heemskerk. Ban of the Empire pronounced against Donauworth, where Protestants tried to stop Catholic processions; Protestantism abolished. War between Sweden and Poland; Swedish rule restored in Estonia.	*c.* Shakespeare: *Timon of Athens*, a play. Honoré d'Urfé: *L'Astrée*, French pastoral romance set in 4th cent. France with the shepherdess Astrée and her lover Céladon; this book had many imitators. Francis Beaumont (*1584 †1616): *The Woman Hater*, a comedy. John Marston (*c.* *1575, †1634): *What You Will*, a comedy. Middleton: *Michaelmas Term*, a comedy.
1608	Confiscated clan lands in Ireland given to English and Scottish settlers. New Book of Rates issued by Salisbury regulated Customs Duties based on Court decision in Bates's case.	*c.* Shakespeare: *Pericles* and *Antony and Cleopatra*, plays. Jonson: *The Masque of Beauty*. Middleton and Dekker: *The Roaring Girl*, a comedy.

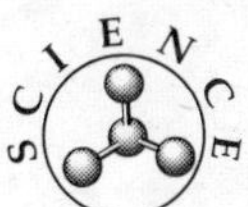

Monteverdi: fifth madrigal book.
c. El Greco: (i) *View and Plan of Toledo*, (ii) *St Bartholomew*, (iii) *St Ildefonso writing at the Virgin's dictation*, Graeco-Spanish paintings.

Port Royal in W. Indies founded by French.
Dutch captured Amboyna from Portugal; set up trading posts in Moluccas.
Incorporation of Butchers' Company and of Shipwrights' Company, London.

*Rembrandt van Ryn (†1669), famous for portraits and pictures of enormous size; altogether produced some 2,000 drawings, paintings and etchings.
Peter Paul Rubens (*1577, †1640), called "The Fleming," painted *The Circumcision*, altarpiece at Genoa, and *Virgin in a Glory of Angels*, Rome.
El Greco: *The Feast in the House of Simon*, painting of the Spanish school.

Jodocus Hondius (*1563, †1612) published famous *Mercator-Hondius Atlas*, so-called.
Royal Charter granted to Virginia Company.
Torres, Spanish explorer, discovered Strait between Australia and New Guinea.
de Quiros, Spanish explorer, discovered several islands of New Hebrides group.
Foundation of Society of Apothecaries and Grocers.
Incorporation of Company of Fruiterers', London.

Thos. Ford: *There is a Lady Sweet and Kind*, madrigal.
(to 1611) Hatfield House, Hertfordshire, built by Robert Cecil, Earl of Salisbury.
Discovery of *Aldobrandini Nuptuals*, antique fresco now in Vatican.
Monteverdi: *La Favola d'Orfeo (Orpheus)*, Italian opera, and *Scherzi Musicali*.

Colony of Virginia inaugurated at Jamestown; John Smith (*1580, †1631), president, 1608, explored Chesapeake Bay.
Henry Hudson (†1611), navigator and explorer, found Jan Mayen Island in the Arctic Sea (doubtful); possibly seen by Jan May in 1614.
de Quiros discovered Tahiti.
Markham: *Cavelariee, or the English Horseman*.
Early reference to the use of forks in Italy; the knife dates back to the Stone Age; the spoon, although later than the knife, existed thousands of years ago.

Monteverdi: *Arianna*, Italian opera.
Sir Walter Cope began building Holland House, Kensington; completed 1610.
El Greco: *Cardinal Taverna*, Spanish portrait.

Hans Lippershey, of the Netherlands (or Janssen in 1609), appears to have first constructed a practical telescope; doubt as to exact origin of instrument.

1608	German Lutherans and Calvinists formed Evangelical Union to resist Habsburgs; supported by Henry IV of France. Protestant States of Rhineland formed Protestant Union under Elector Palatine.	St François de Sales (*1567, †1622), Bishop of Geneva: *Introduction à la Vie dévote.*
1609	Truce between Spain and United Provinces; latter recognized as free States; treaty favoured Spanish colonies at expense of Portuguese. Turkish fleet destroyed by Spaniards at Tunis. Maximilian of Bavaria formed Catholic League in answer to Protestant League. †John William, Duke of Cleves; posed succession problem involving Protestant and Catholic interests.	Shakespeare: *Coriolanus*, a tragedy, and *Sonnets* published. Beaumont and Fletcher, who collaborated in many plays: *The Knight of the Burning Pestle.* *Avisa Relation oder Zeitung* and *Relation*, the first real newspapers; former published at Augsburg and the latter at Strasbourg. Bacon: *De Sapienta Veterum.* Jonson: *Epicoene, or the Silent Woman*, a comedy.
1610	Commutation of Feudal dues for annual grant of £200,000 refused by Parliament; Great Contract. Assassination of Henry IV of France by Ravillac; 18th attempt on king's life. Dutch supported Protestant succession to Jülich and Cleves; Maurice of Nassau captured Jülich. Followers of Jacobus Arminius (*1560, †1609) issued Remonstrance setting out religious views. Moriscos, Christianized Moors, driven out of Spain. Sweden seized Novgorod. Tsar Vasili Shuiski overthrown; Ladislaus of Poland elected Tsar.	*c.* Shakespeare: *Cymbeline*, play. Jonson: *The Alchemist*, comedy of an alchemist and his rich dupes. Foundation of Academy of Poetry at Padua. Publication of English edition of Old Testament authorized for Catholic use (Douai). Stationers' Company began to send to Bodleian Library a copy of every book printed in England.
1611	Dissolution of first Parliament of James I. Imprisonment of Arabella Stuart. Matthias, brother of Emperor Rudolph II elected King of Bohemia; concessions to Protestants. War of Kalmar: Denmark at war with Sweden. †Charles IX of Sweden; accession of Gustavus Adolphus.	The Authorized Version of the Bible, made by a number of scholars working for James I, published. *c.* Shakespeare: *The Winter's Tale* and *The Tempest*, comedies. George Chapman: Translation of Homer's *Iliad* completed. Beaumont and Fletcher: *Philaster*, tragedy. Thos. Coryate (c. *1577, †1617): *Coryats Crudeties*, story of his travels.

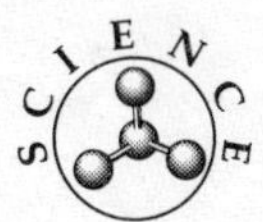

Champlain's second visit to Canada: founded Quebec.
Plantation of Ulster.
Stevinus: *Hypomnemata Mathematica*, applied mathematics.
Krabbe: *Newes Astrolabium*, on use of astrolabe.

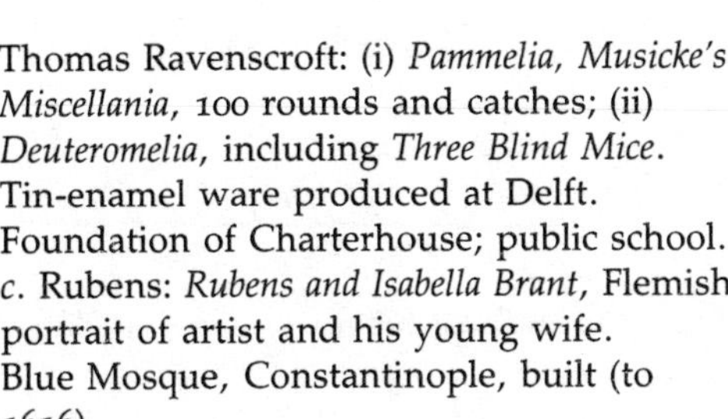

Thomas Ravenscroft: (i) *Pammelia, Musicke's Miscellania*, 100 rounds and catches; (ii) *Deuteromelia*, including *Three Blind Mice*.
Tin-enamel ware produced at Delft.
Foundation of Charterhouse; public school.
c. Rubens: *Rubens and Isabella Brant*, Flemish portrait of artist and his young wife.
Blue Mosque, Constantinople, built (to 1616).

Galileo constructed his telescope, *concave* eyepiece and *convex* object-glass; observed craters on moon; his later instruments gave magnification of 30 times.
Kepler defined first two of his three Laws of Planetary Motion, on which much of Newton's work depended (see 1618).
Hudson entered the bay and river named after him.
Virginia Company's Charter amended.
Amsterdam Bank founded (dissolved 1796).

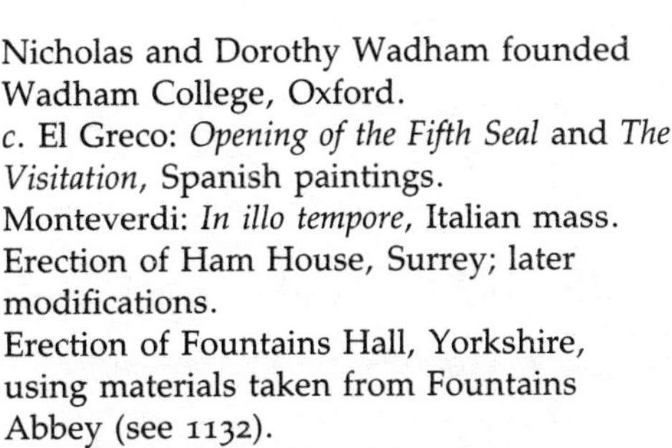

Nicholas and Dorothy Wadham founded Wadham College, Oxford.
c. El Greco: *Opening of the Fifth Seal* and *The Visitation*, Spanish paintings.
Monteverdi: *In illo tempore*, Italian mass.
Erection of Ham House, Surrey; later modifications.
Erection of Fountains Hall, Yorkshire, using materials taken from Fountains Abbey (see 1132).
c. Rubens: *Mulay Ahmed*, Flemish portrait.

Galileo: *Siderius Nuntius*, in which he recorded Saturn's rings and the four moons of Jupiter; also discovery of sunspots.
Nicholas Pieresc (*1580, †1637), French scientist, discovered Orion nebula.
English bond in brickwork to this date: one row headers, one row stretchers.
Dutch introduced tea into Europe from China.
Commons complained against Book of Rates.
Spanish industry and agriculture adversely affected by expulsion of Moriscos.

Ravenscroft: *Melismata*, 21 pieces, chiefly madrigals.
University of Rome founded.
Order of Baronets introduced by James I as means of raising money.
Erection of Masjid-i-Shah, Isfahan, Persia; elaborately decorated Royal mosque.

Kepler: *Dioptrice*, described advantages of convex lens.
Scheiner described sun-spots.
Hudson cast adrift in Hudson Bay; perished.
Merchant Adventurers now settled in Hamburg.
Dutch began trading with Japan.
John Speed (*1552, †1629): *Theatre of the Empire of Great Britaine*, 54 maps of England.
Marco de Dominis (*1566, †1624) published scientific explanation of rainbow.

Year	History	Literature
1612	Henry, Prince of Wales, refused to marry Catholic princess; †in November; Charles, aged eleven, Heir Apparent. Last recorded burning of heretics in England. Rudolph II ousted by brother Matthias of Bohemia, who ruled until 1619. Turks regained Moldavia from Sigismund III of Poland. Treaty between Dutch and King of Kandy in Ceylon.	*c.* Shakespeare: part of *Henry VIII*, historical play. John Webster: *The White Devil*, a tragedy of violence. Publication of an Italian dictionary by the Accademia della Crusca.
1613	Marriage of Elizabeth, daughter of James I, to Frederick V, Elector Palatine. Gondomar appointed Spanish Ambassador to England; gained influence over James I. Essex divorce scandal: marriage of Lady Essex to Earl of Somerset, chief Minister to James I. Treaty of Knarod ended War of Kalmar. Michael Romanov secured throne of Russia; founded Romanov dynasty.	Bodley left bulk of his fortune to Bodleian library. Drayton: *Polyolbion*, poem describing the beauty of England (completed 1622). Middleton: *A Chaste Maid in Cheapside*, play on sordid London life. Donne: *Epithalamium*, based on wedding of the Elector Palatine.
1614	Second Parliament (Addled Parliament) of James I met; refused to discuss finance until grievances considered; first appearance of Thomas Wentworth. Chief Justice Coke resisted pressure of Crown in judgments. Marie, Queen Regent of France, summoned States General of France to counteract power of nobility; failed; next meeting 1789. Treaty of Xanten divided government of Duchies of Jūlich and Cleves between John Sigismund of Brandenburg (Calvinist) and William of Neuburg (Catholic). Gustavus Adolphus of Sweden captured Novgorod from Russians.	Webster: *The Duchess of Malfi*, a grim tragedy. Raleigh: *History of the World*. Chapman translated Homer's *Odyssey*: thereby later gaining much praise in a poem of Keats. (see 1816) Jonson: *Bartholomew Fayre*, a farce.
1615	Murder of Sir Thomas Overbury made public; fall of Somerset; George Villiers became favourite of James I. Embassy of Sir Thomas Roe to Mogul Jahangir. Failure of Gustavus Adolphus to capture Russian Pskoff.	Cervantes: *Don Quixote* (part II) (see 1605). Geo. Ruggle (*1575, †1622): *Ignoramus*, Cambridge University farce.

Gibbons: *Fair is the Rose,* madrigal.
Rubens: *The Conversion of St Bavo* and *Descent from the Cross,* Flemish paintings.
c. El Greco: *The Laocoon,* Graeco-Spanish painting.
Mosque of the King of Isfahan, Persia (to 1637); Safavid period.

Simon Marius (*1573, †1624) rediscovered Andromeda nebula (see 963).
Neri of Florence: *De Arte Vetraria,* first book on glass-making.
East Indian Company introduced Joint Stock principle for series of voyages instead of for single voyage.

Amsterdam Exchange built (see 1602).
Cerone: *El Melopeo,* musical history.
Monteverdi appointed as *maestro di cappella* at St Mark's, Venice, until (†) 1643.
Reni: *The Dawn,* Italian ceiling painting.

Early English domestic water reservoir at Clerkenwell; new river water supply for London opened.
First issue of copper farthings; silver ones known as early as *temp.* Edward I.
Galileo: *Historia e Dimostrazioni intorno alle Macchie Solari,* treatise supporting Copernican system.
East India Co. established settlement at Surat.

El Greco: *The Apostles, Peter and Paul,* Spanish painting.
The Hulse carpet (Jacobean design).
(to 1628) Solari built Salzburg Cathedral; Baroque architecture.
Zampieri Domenichino (*1581, †1641): *Communion of St Jerome* Italian painting.
Foundation of Groningen University.
Monteverdi: sixth madrigal book; first madrigals with *basso continuo.*
(to 1624) Erection of Blickling Hall, Norfolk; altered in 1765.

John Napier (*1550, †1617): *Canonis Descriptio,* in which he developed natural logarithms (to base *e*).
Santorio Santorio (*1561, †1636): *De Medicina Statica,* in which study of metabolism and perspiration first appeared.
A submarine appears to have been constructed and sailed on Thames.
Foundation of Danish East India Company.
c. Sir Robert Mansell developed glass industry substantially in England.
Incorporation of Founders' Company, London.

Inigo Jones (*1573, *c* †1652), originally a painter, became England's chief architect; brought Renaissance to England.
Salomon de Brosse commenced the Palais de Luxembourg.

c. Spaniards made minor use of rubber in S. America; known to natives much earlier.
c. Marin le Bourgeoys designed first flintlock (perhaps later: 1630).
Champlain reached the Great Lakes of Canada.

1615 Tokugawa family began 250-year dominance in Japan.

1616 Dismissal of Coke.
Richelieu appointed French Secretary of State.
Britain returned "Cautionary Towns", taken as pledge of repayment of money advanced by Elizabeth I for aid against Spain, of Brill and Flushing to Dutch for £215,000.
Struggle between Arminians and religious opponents, Counter-Remonstrants, led to political conflict in Holland between States General of United Provinces and Provincial States.
†Ieyasu of Japan; successor, Hidetada, made suppression of Christianity matter of national policy.

Théodore D'Aubigné (*1551, †1630): *Les Tragiques*; the French Protestant poet who took refuge in Geneva from religious persecution, wrote glorification of Protestants and bitter invective against Catholics.
c. Middleton: *The Witch*, sombre Italian-set play.
One of the first reliable English dictionaries printed.
Jonson: *The Devil is an Ass*, a comedy.

1617 James I revisited Scotland.
States General of Holland summoned National Synod to resolve dispute between Arminians and Counter-Remonstrants; Provincial States refused to attend.
Ferdinand of Styria elected King of Bohemia at bidding of Emperor Matthias; Catholic, but promised tolerance.
Russia surrendered parts of Baltic coast to Sweden; Peace of Stolbova.
War between Sweden and Poland; lasted to 1629.

James I appointed Ben Jonson first poet laureate (to royal family).
John Selden (*1585, †1654) lawyer: *De Diis Syris*, important work on Middle East.

1618 Five Articles of Perth: attempt of James I to modify Presbyterianism in Scotland.
Francis Bacon appointed Lord Chancellor.
Maurice of Nassau occupied Utrecht; National Synod agreed; arrest of Oldenbarneveldt and Grotius, leaders of Arminians; meeting of Synod of Dort included representatives from England, Scotland, Geneva and Brandenburg.
John Sigismund secured Duchy of Prussia.
"Defenestration of Prague": incident led to outbreak of Thirty Years War.

John Fletcher (*1579, †1625), dramatist: *The Loyal Subject*, a drama, first acted.
Latham's Falconry completed.
Edmund Willis: *An Abbreviation of Writing by Character*, a system of shorthand; although not the first chronologically, it was one of the earliest useful styles.

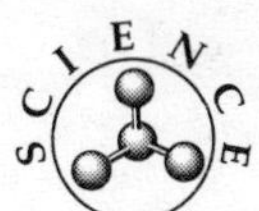

Inigo Jones built Queen's House, Greenwich.
Rubens: *The Last Judgment* and *The Abduction of the Daughters of Leucippus*, Flemish paintings.
Collegium Musicum at Prague.
Erection of Dorfold Hall, Nantwich, and of Cefntilla Court, Monmouth.
Frans Hals (*1580, †1666), Dutch artist: *Banquet of the Civic Guard of Archers of St George*, his earliest dated painting; of his works, some 200 portraits and 8 group pictures are still extant.

Sir William Harvey (*1578, †1657) lectured on circulation of blood, at Royal College of Physicians.
Galileo prohibited by Roman Catholic Church from further scientific work: threat of imprisonment for "heresy".
First rounding of Cape Horn: by Willem Schouter in the *Hoorn* and Jacob Lemaire in the *Eendracht*.
William Baffin (*1584, †1622), navigator and explorer, discovered Baffin Bay.
Release of Raleigh from Tower of London to lead expedition to Guiana in search of *El Dorado*; departure 1617.
Foundation of Bermudas (Somers Islands) Co.
Foundation of Dutch Guiana.

Changes in decoration of Chapel at Holyrood House aroused alarm among Presbyterians.
c. Anton Van Dyck (*1599, †1641), originally Flemish painter (see 1632): study of four Negro heads.
Rubens: *The Lion Hunt*, Flemish painting.

Napier: *Rabdologia*, in which was described method of logarithms using "Napier's bones".
W. Snell (*1591, †1626), Dutch, developed triangulation method of measuring land.
Dutch settlement established at Goree; later led to important gains on Gold Coast.
Dutch settlement at Surat aroused English hostility.

James I issued his *Book of Sports*.
Birde set *Non Nobis Domine* to music, as a grace.
(to 1635) Erection of Aston Hall, Birmingham, fine Jacobean house.
Rubens: *Perseus rescuing Andromeda*, Flemish painting.
Erection of Teatro Farnese, Parma; wooden theatre in Palazzo della Pilotta.
Van Dyck became fully fledged member of Antwerp gild of painters.

Kepler: *Harmonices Mundi*, containing third Law of Planetary Motion.
First record of gas being burned; obtained from heated crushed coal in a container, but potential not realized until much later (see 1792).
English trading company of African Adventurers formed in London.
Failure of Raleigh's Guiana expedition; on return Raleigh executed for treason.
Cysatus of Lucerne studied nebula of Orion and first saw a comet with a telescope.
College of Physicians, London, issued a pharmacopoeia for apothecaries (see 1542).
Mineral spring at Epsom used; town became spa (see 1695).

Year	History	Literature
1618	Ladislaus of Poland invaded Russia; defeated; Smolensk ceded to Poland by Russia.	
1619	Villiers created Marquis of Buckingham. James I refused to assist son-in-law, Elector Palatine, elected King of Bohemia. Representative government in Virginia. Execution of Oldenbarneveldt, Arminian leader. Philip III of Spain supported Catholics against Protestants in Bohemia. †Emperor Matthias; election of Ferdinand of Styria and Bohemia as Ferdinand II. Accession of George William, Elector of Brandenburg-Prussia.	Fletcher: *The Humorous Lieutenant*, a comedy, first acted. Honorat Racan: *Les Bergeries*, a pastoral poem, written.
1620	Negotiations with Spain for marriage of Prince Charles and Infanta. Dutch seized Pularoon in East Indies from British. Spanish forces under Spinola overran Palatinate. Spaniards seized Valtelline; ensured communications between Milan and Netherlands. Battle of the White Mountain; Fredrick of Bohemia's Protestant army routed outside Prague; Frederick fled to The Hague.	Bacon: *Novum Organum Scientiarum*, philosophical treatise in Latin showing Bacon's inductive method of interpreting knowledge gained. Publication of first English corantos (news-sheets). Fletcher: *Women Pleased*, a comedy, first acted.
1621	This Parliament of James I; appearance of Pym and Sir John Eliot. Attack on Monopolies: revival of right of impeachment, in abeyance since 1452; Mompesson and Bacon impeached. Protest on Foreign Affairs torn from Journal of Commons by James I. Twelve Years' Truce between Spain and United Provinces ended; hostilities between Maurice of Nassau and Spinola. Protestant armies under Mansfield driven out of Upper Palatinate and Alsace by Tilly. Iraq re-occupied by Persia.	Robert Burton: *The Anatomy of Melancholy*; all phases of melancholy discussed with many examples. Edmwnd Prys: *Salmau Cân*, metrical psalms in Welsh. Fletcher: *The Wild-Goose Chase*, a comedy, first acted.

(to 1625) Inigo Jones built new Palace of Whitehall: probably his finest work.
Foundation of Dulwich College, London, by Edward Alleyn.
Giovanni Lorenzo Bernini (*1598, †1680): *David with his Sling*, Italian sculpture.
Monteverdi: seventh madrigal book.
Muchall's Castle, Kincardineshire, built by Burnetts of Leys.
Rubens: *Portrait of his son, Nicholas*, Flemish painting.

Hamburger Bank founded to improve "desolate state of the currency".
Batavia renamed Djakarta by Dutch traders in Java.
Start of Dutch attacks on English factories in East Indies.
Napier: *Mirifici Logarithmorum Canonis Constructio*, his second work on logarithms; also in the book appears first systematic use of decimal point, based on Stevinus's work (*La Disme*, 1585).

Diego Velazquez (*1599, †1660), great Spanish painter: (i) *St John in the Wilderness*; (ii) *Water Seller of Seville*.
Van Dyck: *The Three Graces*, Dutch painting.
Erection of Winton House, East Lothian, by Geo. Seton.
Erection of Gladstone's Land, Edinburgh, possessing painted wooden ceilings.

Edmund Gunter (*1581, †1626) proposed names for tigonometic ratios *cosine* and *contangent*.
Voyage of the *Mayflower* to New World.
English trading expedition to Gambia.
c. First settlement by Dutch in British Guiana.

Butcher's Guildhall, Hereford (called the Old House).
Scots Parliament ratified charter of Edinburgh University.
Sturm's School in Strasbourg (see 1538) received university status.
Ravenscroft: *The Whole Book of Psalmes*.

Invention of ribbon-loom in Holland.
Dutch engineer, Cornelius Vermuyden, appointed by James I to drain Royal Park at Windsowr.
British attempt to colonize Newfoundland and Nova Scotia.
Foundation of Dutch West Indies Company; later acquired coasts of N. America from Chesapeake Bay to Newfoundland.
Friedrichstadt built on reclaimed land in Schleswig.
Kepler: *The Epitome of the Copernican Astronomer*, banned by R.C. Church.
Oxford University Botanical Gardens, oldest in Britain, laid out.

	History	Literature
1622	Third Parliament of James I dissolved. Renewed negotiations for Anglo-Spanish marriage. Richelieu created a Cardinal. Huguenot revolt against Catholic rule ended by Peace of Montpellier but lost all guaranteed towns except La Rochelle; first step in destruction of Huguenot power. Spaniards besieged Bergen-op-Zoom; relieved by Maurice of Nassau. Baden routed by Tilly at Bad Wimpfen. Protestant army of Christian of Brunswick routed by Hochst. Tilly captured Heidelberg and Mannheim.	Charles Sorel: *Francion,* first French burlesque novel; hero mixed with all sorts of men; reaction against pastorals and romances. Nicholas Bourne issued *Weekly Newes;* pamphlet successor of the corantos; in same year, Nathaniel Butler issued *A Currant of Newes.* Bacon: *History of Henry VII.*
1623	Prince Charles and Buckingham visited Madrid to woo Infanta but failed; returned eager for war with Spain. Bahia captured from Spain by Dutchman, Piet Hein. Emperor's authority restored in Bohemia; Protestant worship forbidden. Ferdinand II replaced Elector Frederick of Palatine by Maximilian, Elector of Bavaria. Jägerndorf seized by Emperor Ferdinand II.	First folio edition of Shakespeare: containing 10 histories, 12 tragedies and 14 comedies. Bacon: *De Augmentis,* virtually an expansion of *Advancement of Learning* (see 1605). Wm. Drummond of Hawthornden (*1585, †1649); *The Cypresse Grove,* sombre prose.
1624	Fourth Parliament of James I assembled; voted supplies for Spanish war. Impeachment of Middlesex, Lord Treasurer. Proposed marriage alliance between Prince Charles and French princess. Alliance between James I and France against Spain after expulsion of Frederick from Palatinate. Richelieu became Minister and virtual ruler of France. Treaty of Compiègne between French and Dutch. Spaniards under Spinola captured Breda.	Martin Opitz (*1597, †1639): *Buch van der deutschen Poeterey,* the *Ars poetica* of German poetry. Edward Herbert of Cherbury: *De Veritate,* standard theological work. Bacon: *Apophthegms Old and New.* Philip Massinger (*1583, †1640), dramatist: *The Bondman,* a play. Saruwaka Kanzaburō opened first Japanese theatre at Yedo.

Rubens: 24 pictures of life of Marie de'Medici, now in Louvre (finished 1625); also painted *Le Chapeau de Paille* (in which *Paille* indicates a "canopy" and not "straw").
Bernini: *Apollo and Daphne*, Italian sculpture.

William Oughtred invented the slide-rule.
Snell formulated Law of Refraction of Light at boundary of two transparent media.

East India Company founded factory at Masulipatam.
Moors, expelled from Portuguese areas in Ceylon, settled in Kandyan territory on east coast of island.

Velazquez painted an equestrian portrait of Philip IV of Spain.
Rubens: *The Landing of the Medicis*, Flemish painting.
Foundation of Benedictine University of Salzburg; suppressed in 1810.

Gaspard Bauhin (*1560, †1624): *Pinax Theatri Botanici*, systematic work on some 6,000 plants.
German silver mines at Kongsberg, Norway.
English merchants at Amboyna massacred by Dutch.
*Blaise Pascal (†1662), French mathematician and philosopher, who developed modern treatment of conics and helped to lay foundation of calculus.
Patents Law to protect inventors.

Van Dyck: *Portrait of a Young Warrior*, Flemish painting.
Pembroke College, Oxford, founded.
Hals: *The Laughing Cavalier*, famous Dutch painting.
Lettered stone parapet of Castle Ashby, Northampton, Elizabethan house, Inigo Jones façade.
(to 1633) Great bronze canopy (baldachin) by Bernini, in St Peter's; Baroque style.

Henry Briggs (*1566, †1630): *Arithmetica Logarithmica* published; used logs to base 10 instead of base *e*; called "common" or "Briggian" logs (pilot scheme in 1617).
Gunter invented surveyor's chain (22 yards long).
Monopolies forbidden by Act of Parliament.
Abolition of Virginia Company; Virginia became Crown Colony.
Van Helmont, Dutch, coined the name *gas* for compressible fluid.
Dutch began to colonize Formosa.

1625 †James I and accession of Charles I.
Marriage of Charles I and Henrietta Maria of France.
Failure of English expedition against Cadiz.
First Parliament of Charles I, angered by Richelieu's attack on Protestant La Rochelle, withheld supplies; dissolved.
Ferdinand II appointed Wallenstein Com. in Chief of Imperial Armies.
Tilly occupied Lower Saxony.
†Maurice of Nassau; succeeded as Stadholder and Prince of Orange by brother, Frederick Henry.
United Provinces supported Richelieu and sent fleet to assist blockade of La Rochelle.
Spaniards recaptured Bahia from Dutch.

Hugo Grotius (*1583, †1645): *De Jure Belli et Pacis*, great work by Dutch jurist on international law.
Fletcher: *Rule a Wife and have a Wife*, a comedy, first acted.
Jonson: *The Staple of News*, a comedy.

1626 Second Parliament of Charles I persisted in impeachment of Buckingham; dismissed.
Case of the Five Knights, refused writs of Habeus Corpus because they were "Detained at His Majesty's Pleasure".
Treaty of Monzon between France and Spain.
Mansfield defeated by Wallenstein at Bridge of Dessau.
Peace of Pressburg between Ferdinand II and Bethlen Gabor, leader of Hungarian Protestants.
Christian IV routed by Tilly at Lutter.
Battle of Wallhof; Swedes defeated Poles.

Geo. Sandys translated Ovid's *Metamorphoses*.
Thomas May (*1595, †1650), dramatist: *Cleopatra*, a tragedy, first acted.
Bacon: *New Atlantis*, political philosophy in story form; account of imaginary island with philosophical state cultivating natural sciences.

1627 War between England and France; failure of Buckingham's expedition to Ile de Rhé.
La Rochelle in revolt.
Revolt in Languedoc under Rohan.
Wallenstein conquered Silesia.
Tilly subjugated Brunswick and with Wallenstein invaded Holstein.
Imperial forces seized Mecklenburg; invaded Jutland.
†Jahangir: succeeded by son, Shah Jahan.

Gundulic (*in Dubrovnik): *Osmun*, an epic.
Don Luis de Góngora y Argote (*1561, †1627), Spanish poet with stilted precious style; *Sonnets*.
Sorel: *Le Berger extravagant*, French burlesque novel.

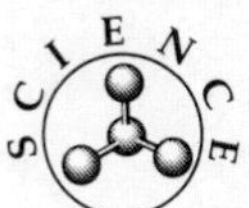

Bacon wrote important contemporary essay *Of Masques and Triumphs*; the English masque was precursor of English opera.
Erection of the Pellerhaus, Nuremberg; early German Renaissance architecture.
c. Rubens completed portrait of *Marie di Medici* and painted *Albert and Nicolas* (the artist's sons).
Famous peal of bells installed in Gate of Salvation, Kremlin (see 1491).

*G. D. Cassini (†1712) first of four generations of scientists who advanced knowledge of astronomy, mathematics, geography and botany.
Johann R. Glauber (*1604, †1670) discovered his salts (sodium sulphate), made from vitriol and common salt
First fire-engines in England.
Hackney coaches appear on London streets.
Plague prevalent in England.
Caribbean buccaneers tried to found colony on St Christopher as base for attacks on Spanish-held San Domingo.
French founded Cayenne in Guiana.

Mansart, French architect, designed Château of Balleroy.
c. Erection of Townend, Troutbeck, Westmorland.
Rubens painted *Assumption of the Virgin*, altarpiece for Antwerp.
Façade of basilica (St Peter's) in Vatican completed to Carlo Manderna's design; consecrated by Pope Urban VIII.
Richelieu reconstructed the buildings of the Sorbonne.

Forced loans, tunnage and poundage illegally collected.
Dutch colony of New Amsterdam (New York, see 1664) founded on Hudson River, Peter Minuit having purchased Manhattan Island from the Indians for the princely sum of about 60 guilders' worth of cloth and baubles.

H. Schütz: *Daphne*, first German opera, libretto by Opitz.
Discovery of Parian Chronicle, marble tablet, on island of Paros; gives outline of Greek history to –264.
c. Rubens: *Mystic marriage of St Catherine*, Flemish painting.

Publication of *Rudolphine Tables*, standard set of astronomical tables, by Kepler.
Incorporation of Company of New France (Canada) by Richelieu.
Swedish South Sea Company founded.

	History	Literature
1628	Petition of Right passed by Third Parliament of Charles I. Assassination of Buckingham by John Felton. William Laud appointed Bishop of London. Thomas Wentworth appointed President of Council of North. Richelieu starved La Rochelle into surrender. Ferdinand II captured Wismar, Rostock and coast of Pomerania. Treaty of Stuhmsdorf between Gustavus Adolphus of Sweden and Christian IV of Denmark.	Juan Ruiz de Alarcón: *La Verdad Sospechosa*, play by Spanish dramatist; imitated by Corneille in *Le Menteur* (1643). Patriarch of Alexandria and Constantinople presented *Alexandrian Codex* (5th cent. MS.) to Charles I.
1629	Parliament passed three Resolutions against innovations in Church and State; dissolved. Eliot and other opponents of Charles I imprisoned. Quebec captured by English from French. Richelieu invaded Languedoc; Rohan surrendered; Peace of Alais, which gave liberty of worship to Huguenots but broke their political power. Peace of Lübeck between Christian IV of Denmark and Emperor; all hereditary territories of Denmark returned. Edict of Restitution: Emperor ordered return of Church property secularized since Peace of Augsburg, 1555; Edict opposed by Wallenstein.	*Mélite*, comedy by the great French dramatist, Pierre Corneille (*1606, †1684). John Milton (*1608, †1674): *On the Morning of Christ's Nativity*, probably his first great poem. Abraham Cowley (*1618, †1667): *Pyramus and Thisbe*, epic romance written at very early age. Sir Wm. D'Avenant (*1606, †1668): *The Tragedy of Albovine*, his first drama.
1630	Court of King's Bench upheld imprisonment of Eliot. Peace between England and France and between England and Spain. Large sums collected from English gentry by *Distraint of Knighthood*. Richelieu raised siege (begun 1627) of Casale; captured Pinerolo. *Day of Dupes* in France; failure by Queen Mother to overthrow Richelieu. Dutch took Olinda from Portugal. Wallenstein dismissed from Imperial Command.	Lope: *Laurel de Apolo*, Spanish narrative poem. D'Avenant: *The Cruel Brother*, a tragedy. Dekker: *The Honest Whore* (part II); see 1604. Massinger: *The Renegado*, a play. Johann Heinrich Alsted (*1588, †1638): *Encyclopaedia septem tomis distincta*, a careful study superseded by vernacular works a few years later.

Velazques: (i) *Christ on the Cross*, (ii) *The Merrymakers*, Spanish paintings.
Braemar Castle, Aberdeenshire, built by Earl of Mar; burned 1689 by the Black Colonel; later repaired.
Rubens: *Miracles of St Benedict*, Flemish painting.

Harvey's work *Exercitatis anatomica de motu cordis et sanguinis* on blood circulation published (see 1616).
Construction, at Le Havre, of first harbour having sluices.
Duties of Lord High Admiral of England taken over by Lords Commissioners (Board of Admiralty).
Spanish treasure fleet captured in Matanzas Bay by Dutch.

Rubens: *Isabella of Spain* and *Adam and Eve*, Flemish paintings.
*Pieter de Hooch (†1683) of Delft, who painted courtyard scenes and interiors, e.g. *The Lace Maker, Woman Sewing*.
Velazquez: *The Topers*, Spanish painting.
Van Dyck: *Rinaldo and Armida*, Flemish painting, one of his finest works.

Albert Gerard (Dutch, *1595, †1632) used brackets and other abbreviations in mathematics; he stated that equation of degree *n* has *n* roots.
J. Bontius (see 1642) studied cholera in Dutch East Indies.
Colony of Massachusetts founded.
Charles I granted charter to Guild of Spectacle Makers.
John Parkinson (*1567, †1650), herbalist to Charles I: *Paradisi in sole Paradisus terrestris*, on flowers.

Bernini: *Constanza Buonarelli*, Florentine bust.
c. Daniel Seghers (*1590, †1661): *Landscape with Tree Stumps*, very early modern style painting.
Inigo Jones built Stoke Park Pavilions, Towcester.
Giuseppe Ribera (*1588, †1652), naturalist artist: *Martyrdom of St Bartholomew*, Spanish painting.
Velazquez: *Forge of Vulcan*, Spanish painting.

Drainage of Hatfield Chase (20,000 acres of Fenland) proposed (see 1634, Vermuyden).
Flemish bond in brickwork: alternate header and stretcher along a row.
Buccaneers seized small island of Tortuga and converted it into a fort.
Christoph Scheiner recorded constructing a telescope of type proposed by Kepler (1611).
First colonization of Dutch Guiana.
c. Lambeth pottery first manufactured.

	History	Literature
1630	Gustavus Adolphus of Sweden invaded Empire.	
1631	Treaty of Cherasco: ended Duchies dispute in favour of Duke of Nevers; France retained Pinerolo. United Provinces joined confederation formed by Gustavus Adolphus against Empire. Dutch destroyed Spanish fleet on the Slaak. Treaty of Bärwalde: France and Sweden agreed to co-operate in invasion of Germany. Swedish garrison at Neu Brandenburg massacred by Tilly; Gustavus massacred garrison at Frankfort in reprisal; Tilly sacked Magdeburg. Alliance of Sweden, Brandenburg, Hesse and Saxony. Tilly routed at Breitenfeld by Gustavus. Protestants under Elector of Saxony seized Prague, Mecklenburg, Magdeburg and Brunswick. Wallenstein re-appointed Com. in Chief of Imperial Armies; besieged Magdeburg.	Publication of first French newspaper, the *Gazette*; later called *Gazette de France*. May: *Antigone*, a tragedy. James Shirley (*1596, †1666), dramatist: *Love's Cruelty* and *The Traitor*, tragedies. Johann Amos Comenius (*1592, †1670), authority on education: *Gate of Languages Unlocked*; he believed in the use of topical ideas in teaching languages.
1632	Eliot died in Tower. Quebec returned to France. Richelieu broke power of French nobles. Frederick Henry of Orange captured Maestrich. Gustavus Adolphus captured Mannheim; routed Tilly on the Lech. Junction of Imperial armies under Wallenstein and Maximilian of Bavaria. Wallenstein captured Dresden. Gustavus Adolphus returned to Saxony; captured Erfurt and Naumberg; defeated Wallenstein at Lützen, but killed in battle. Accession of infant Christina to throne of Sweden.	Shirley: *Hyde Park*, a comedy. All corantos suppressed because Spain took offence at published articles; no news sheets for six years. Massinger: *The Maid of Honour*, a romantic drama.
1633	Ulster settlements of City of London confiscated by Court of Star Chamber, for alleged mismanagement. Wentworth appointed Lord Deputy	Donne: collected poems published. George Herbert (*1593, †1633), metaphysical poet: *The Temple* published. Massinger: *A New Way with Old Debts*, Jacobean drama.

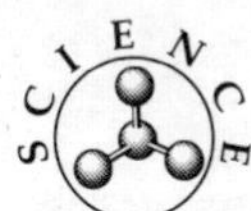

Inigo Jones laid out Square of Covent Garden Market.
D. Mazzocchi: *The Plaint of St Mary Magdalene*, Italian oratorio, performed at Rome.
Erection of New Palace, Kew, in Dutch style.
Baldassare Loghena began work on Santa Maria della Salute, Venice, fine domed church of Renaissance style.
c. Rubens: *The Kermesse*, Flemish pastoral painting of a frenzied dance.
Velazquez: *Infanta Maria, Queen of Hungary*, Spanish portrait.

Vernier invented auxiliary scale used in scientific measurement.
Oughtred proposed symbol × for multiplication.
William Petty: *Political Arithmetic*, work on economics.
Earthquakes at Naples.
Incorporation of Clockmaker's Company, London.
First settlement in Maryland, U.S.A. (so-called in tribute to Queen Henrietta Maria), by W. Claiborne, who opposed Lord Baltimore's colony (see 1634).

Van Dyck: *Philip, Lord Wharton*, painting; became English court painter in this year.
Rembrandt: *The Lesson in Anatomy of Dr Tulp*, Dutch painting.
Mansart began fine circular church of Ste Marie de la Visitation.
Monteverdi: *Scherzi Musicali*.
Foundation of Municipal University of Amsterdam.
Rubens: *The Garden of Love*, large Flemish painting, an allegory of love (completed 1634); also *The Ildefonso Altar*, three wood panels.
Shah Jahan built (to 1648) the Taj Mahal, Agra, beautiful mausoleum for his favourite wife.

Jean Ray, French, constructed water thermometer; inaccurate, but better than earlier air thermometers.
Yakutsk, great Siberian fur-trading centre, founded.
Galileo: *Dialogues on the Ptolemaic and Copernican Systems* (see 1633).
Opening of first London coffee shop.

Van Dyck: (i) *Portrait of Charles I*, (ii) *Queen Henrietta with Dwarf Hudson and Monkey*, paintings.
Post and van Campen began Mauritshuis, The Hague.

Galileo taken before Inquisition for not obeying decree of 1616 (*q.v.*).
Colony of Connecticut founded.
Development of trading post at Orissa, India.

Year	History	Literature
1633	in Ireland; Laud appointed Archbishop of Canterbury. Refoundation of Bishopric of Edinburgh. Coronation of Charles I in Edinburgh. Portuguese expelled from Abyssinian territory. Imperial Circles of Franconia, Swabia and the Rhine united as Protestant League of Heilbronn. Heidelberg taken by Protestants. Lorraine forced to admit French garrison to Nancy. Wallenstein negotiated with Saxony and Sweden proposals for withdrawal of Edict of Restitution. Protestant forces invaded Bavaria and captured Ratisbon. Wallenstein drove Swedes from Silesia; invaded Brandenburg.	Milton: *L'Allegro*, poem expressing gaiety; and *Il Penseroso*, poem celebrating contemplation. John Ford: *Love's Sacrifice* and *'Tis Pity She's a Whore*, plays. William Prynne (*1600, †1669), pamphleteer: *Histrio-Mastix: The Players Scourge*, for which Star Chamber ordered his ears to be cut off.
1634	Emperor Ferdinand II dismissed Wallenstein and replaced him by his son, Ferdinand, King of Hungary; Wallenstein murdered. Ferdinand of Hungary regained Ratisbon and Donauworth; routed Swedes at Nördlingen; regained Franconia and Swabia. Protestants defeated at Nördlingen obtained aid from France; Imperial armies forced to raise siege of Heidelberg. Ladislaus of Poland renounced claim to Russia; Treaty of Polianovka gave him money and confirmed Smolensk as Polish.	Milton: *Comus*, masque first presented at Ludlow Castle. Jean Mairet: *Sophonisbe*, first French classical tragedy. First performance of Passion Play at Oberammergau, in Germany, to commemorate termination of plague of 1633; re-enacted every 10 years. Thos. Carew: *Coelum Britannicum*, a masque.
1635	Council of New England dissolved. Alliance between United Provinces and France against Spain and Empire. Peace of Prague between John George of Saxony and Emperor; acceptance of peace by Brandenburg led to Dutch invasion of Cleves. Imperial armies captured Philipsburg and over-ran Palatinate. France declared war on Spain; supplied four armies against Imperialists. Treaty of Stuhmsdorf between Poland and Sweden.	Louis XIII, advised by Richelieu, established the *Académie française* (which began as a literary society in 1629) to give exact rules for the French language (40 members). Corneille: *Médée*, French tragedy. Francis Quarles (*1592, †1644), *Emblems*, devotional poems. Shirley: *The Lady of Pleasure*, a comedy.

Rembrandt: *Shipbuilder*, Dutch painting.
Hals: *Pieter van der Broecke*, Flemish-Dutch painting.
Rebuilding of present Kiyomizu (Pavilion) of Seisuiji, near Kyoto, Japan.
J. Callot: *The Miseries and Sufferings of War*, French engravings.
Restoration of Stapleford Park, Leicestershire; old wing dated 1500.

Enquiry into extent of encroachments on Royal Forest by English landowners ordered by Charles I.
Robert Fludd: *Clavis Philosophiae et Alchymiae*.
Erection of a wind saw-mill near the Strand, London.
Establishment of the Royal Scots, oldest *regular* regiment in the British Army.

Rubens received 920 florins for *Adoration of the Magi* (sold in June 1959 for £275,000).
Rembrant: (i) *Portrait of Martin Daey*, (ii) *Old Woman*, (iii) *Balshazzar's Feast*, Dutch paintings.
Erection of Bateman's at Burwash, Sussex: home of Rudyard Kipling from 1902 to 1936.

Philip White had early patent for manufacturing iron chain.
Thos. Mouffet: *Theatrum Insectorum*, compilation of work on insects by various scientists.
Ship Money levied on English maritime counties to provide fleet against pirates.
Colony of Maryland founded (see 1631).
Wisconsin explored by Jean Nicolet.
Vermuyden began drainage work on Gt. Level in Fens; opposed by Cromwell; dykes destroyed; eventually 680,000 acres reclaimed.
Opening of Covent Garden Market.

Velazquez: *Prince Baltasar Carlos*, Spanish painting.
c. Hals: *Willem van Heythuisen*, Flemish-Dutch painting.
Ribera: *Conception,*, Spanish painting.
Jacques Lamercier designed Church of the Sorbonne.
Rubens' Baroque ceiling for Whitehall.
Original foundation of Budapest University.
Casting of the Tsar Kolokol (king of bells) for Kremlin.

First Inland public Post Service set up in Britain between Edinburgh and London (see 1516).
Fixed speed limit, 3 m.p.h., on hackney coaches in London and Westminster.
Strafford tried to raise revenue by fines against farmers for enclosures contrary to Tudor Acts of Parliament.
Second Writ for Ship Money extended tax to inland towns and counties.
Portugal lost trading posts on Formosa to Dutch.

Year	History	Literature
1636	Juxon, bishop of London, appointed Treasurer. Spanish forces under Cardinal Infant Ferdinand successful against United Provinces. Anthony van Diemen Governor General of Dutch East Indies; treaty with King of Kandy established Dutch in Ceylon. Imperial armies invaded Burgundy; forced to retire. Spaniards invaded Northern France; forced to retire. Brandenburg declared war on Sweden but failed to obtain Pomerania.	Corneille: *Le Cid,* French classical play; tragic love story of Rodrigue and Chimène. First Italian weekly news-sheet issued. D'Avenant: *The Platonick Lovers,* a play, and *The Wits,* a comedy. Massinger: *The Great Duke of Florence,* a romantic comedy.
1637	Introduction of new Liturgy into Scotland caused riots. Destruction of Pequod Fort, Connecticut. Intendants, Royal Officers with control of French provinces, appointed by Richelieu. French invaded Netherlands; Cardinal Infant Ferdinand retreated South. Breda captured by Frederick Henry of Orange. Dutch ousted Portuguese from Elmina on Gold Coast. †Emperor Ferdinand II; succeeded by son, Ferdinand of Hungary. Spanish invasion of Languedoc repelled. Imperial armies failed to secure Pomerania.	Milton: *Lycidas,* famous elegy for friend drowned at sea. Heywood: *The Royal King and the Loyal Subject,* a play. Prynne, Bastwick and Burton condemned by Star Chamber for seditious writings.
1638	Scottish Covenant drawn up and signed. Charles I abandoned Liturgy and Canons in Scotland. Meeting of General Assembly at Glasgow abolished Episcopacy; Covenanters prepared for war. Counts William and Henry of Nassau defeated by Spain. Spanish fleet crushingly defeated by Dutch in Downs. *Cornelius Jansen, who later founded Jansenism, opposed to Jesuits and Protestants.	Cowley: *Naufragium Joculare,* comedy in Latin, and *Love's Riddle,* pastoral play. D'Avenant: *The Unfortunate Lovers* first performed (published 1643). Thos. Randolph (*1605, †1635): *The Muses' Looking Glass,* a play in favour of plays. William Rowley: *Shoomaker a Gentleman,* a play. Cornelius Jansen (*1585, †1638): *Augustinus* completed after 20 years' work; condemned by R.C. Church (see 1853).

Rubens: *Judgment of Paris,*, Flemish painting.
Harvard, first American University, founded (so-named 1639).
Utrecht University founded.
Schütz: *Kleine Geistliche Concerten*, collection of motets with figured bases.
Rembrandt: *Danae*, Dutch nude painting.
Van Dyck: *Children of Charles I*, painting.

Rhode Island colony founded.
Tea first reached Paris.

Opening of the Opera House, Venice.
Rembrandt: *Angel Raphael leaving Tobias* and *The Carpenter's Family*, Dutch paintings.
Ribera: *The Pietà*, Spanish painting.
c. Rubens: *Landscape with Rainbow* and *Allegory of War*, Flemish paintings.

René Descartes (*1596, †1650): *Discours de la Méthode*, important French work on philosophy; *Dioptrique; Météoris; La Géometrie*, published in the same year; all important; developed analytical geometry.
East India Co. set up factories at Canton.
Courteen Association of London Merchants to trade with China; failed.
Maurice of Nassau established himself at Recife (Pernambuco) Portuguese trading area.
Judges declared Ship Money legal form of tax; John Hampden condemned for refusing to pay.
Star Chamber restricted number of typefounders in England to three.

Van Dyck: (i) *Prince of Orange*, (ii) *Lord John and Lord Bernard Stuart*, paintings.
Gothic Hall stairway of Christ Church, Oxford.
c. Rubens: *The Three Graces*, Flemish painting.
Monteverdi: eighth madrigal book.
Erection of Swakeleys, Middlesex; transitional style.
Rembrandt: *Marriage of Samson*, Dutch painting.
Velazquez: *Christ on the Cross*, Spanish religious painting.

Galileo: *Dialogues concerning Two New Sciences*, important work on mechanics.
Newhaven, North America, founded.
Dutch occupied Mauritius.
Printing press established at Cambridge, Massachusetts; first in America.
Incorporation of Glaziers' Company, Glovers' Company, Distillers' Company, London.
Dublin assay office began to use date letters.

	History	Literature
1638	Imperial army routed at Rheinfelden by Bernard of Saxe-Weimar. Sultan Murad V recaptured Iraq from Persia. Massacre of Shimabara: remaining Christians in Japan exterminated.	
1639	Scottish Covenanters in arms against introduction of "Popery"; Charles I levied troops for use against Scots; Covenanters seized Edinburgh and Dumbarton; Charles I advanced to York and Berwick; First Bishops' War ended with Pacification of Berwick. Scots Parliament prorogued for abolishing Episcopacy and proposing acts against Royal power. Giulio Mazarin entered service of Cardinal Richelieu. Dutch captured Trincomalee from Portuguese.	May: *Julia Agrippina,* a tragedy. Massinger: *The Unnatural Combat,* a play. Milton: *Epitaphium Damonis,* Latin poem.
1640	Short Parliament in England; sat from April to May. Renewal of war with Scotland; Second Bishops' War; Treaty of Ripon with Scots. Long Parliament assembled. Last Session of Court of High Commission. Canons passed by Convocation in 1640 declared illegal. Japanese actions cut country off from rest of world. Malacca conquered by Van Diemen. Portuguese revolt against Spanish rule; John of Braganza became king of independent Portugal. Revolt of Catalonia against Spain; admitted sovereignty of Louis XIII. Accession of Frederick William to Electorate of Brandenburg Prussia (The Great Elector).	Carew: *Poems,* love poems by a courtier of Charles I. Corneille: *Horace, Cinna,* French tragedies. John Evelyn (*1620, †1706) diarist and dilettante: *Diary* (1640–1706), of great historical value (published 1818). First American (now U.S.) book, The Bay Psalm Book, printed at Cambridge, Mass.; in use until 1773. Charles I: *Eikon basilike,* in support of divine rights of kings (now thought to be written by Dr Gauden).
1641	Triennial Act passed. Trial and execution of Wentworth. Courts of Star Chamber and High Commission abolished by Parliament. Marriage of William, son of Frederick Henry of Orange, to Mary, daughter of Charles, averted	Descartes: *Meditationes de Prima Philosophia.* Freedom of the Press resulted from suppression of Court of Star Chamber; *Diurnal Occurrences,* weekly periodical issued. *c.* Edward Hyde, Earl of Clarendon (*1609, †1674), benefactor of University Press, Oxford: *History,* concerned with civil wars

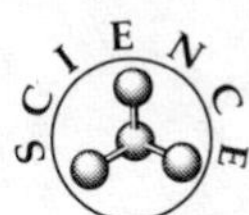

Rembrandt: *Death of the Virgin*, Dutch etching.
Velazquez: *The Surrender of Breda*, great Spanish historical painting.
Jones and Wren designed Greenwich Hospital (later Royal Naval College).
First patent issued for Drury Lane Theatre.
Erection of Church of the Three Saints, as Jassy; Roumanian architecture.
c. Rubens: *Self Portrait*, Flemish painting.
Van Dyck: (i) *Countess of Portland* (ii) *Arthur Goodwin*, portraits.

Gérard Désargues (*1593, †1662) issued book of modern geometry: studied triangles in perspective.
Jeremiah Horrocks (*1619, †1641) observed transit of Venus.
Foundation of colonies of Maine and New Hampshire.
East India Company founded trading post at Fort St. George, Madras.
William Gascoigne invented micrometer.
Russian Cossack advance over Urals, begun in 1589, reached Pacific at Okhotsk.
Pascal laid foundations of modern analytical geometry by age of 16.

Louis le Vau designed the Hôtel Lambert, Paris.
Abo University founded.
Rembrandt: *Self-Portrait*, Dutch painting (National Gallery, London).
Completion of Barberini Palace, Rome, now housing Italian National Gallery.
Pietro da Cortona: *Triumph of Divine Providence*, Italian fresco.
c. Rubens: *Diana and Callisto*, large Flemish painting.
Completion of Copenhagen Exchange (begun 1619).

Coke first made from coal.
Eight postal lines running in England.
Stage-coaches introduced into England.
East India Company founded trading post on River Hooghli.
Buccaneers settled in Barbados.
27 lakes north of Amsterdam pumped dry and land below sea-level reclaimed by use of wind-driven pumps; Bedford Level, in England, also drained.
Portuguese ambassadors on trade mission to Japan executed.
Parkinson: *Theatrum botanicum*, important herbal.

Claude Lorraine (*1600, †1682): *The Embarkation of St Ursula*; French painting by artist who spent much time in Italy.
Rembrandt: *Manoah*, Dutch painting.
Hals: *Regents of the Company of St Elizabeth*, Dutch painting.
Monteverdi: *The Holy Apostle*, Italian opera.
Barnard published ten books of cathedral

First mention of *cotton* goods being manufactured at Manchester.
Preparation of arsenic explained.
Louis d'or coined in France; discontinued 1795.
First settlement in Michigan, U.S.A., by French.
Commission issued by Commons to deface

1641 war between England and United Provinces.
Outbreak of rebellion in Ireland.
Grand Remonstrance: list of acts of misrule by Charles I, passed by Commons with majority of eleven votes.
Moderate opponents of King joined Royal supporters.
Parlement of Paris compelled to register all Royal Edicts in future.
Treaty of Peace between Portugal and Holland.
Frederick William of Brandenburg made treaty with Swedes.

in England; proceeds provided press with new building.

1642 Charles I attempted arrest of five Members of Parliament; failed and left London.
Militia Bill took control of militia and fortified places against King; Royal Assent refused.
Preparations for war in England; Earl of Essex Captain-General of Parliamentary forces; Charles I established force at Shrewsbury; Essex garrisoned line of towns from Northampton to Worcester.
Indecisive battle between King and Parliament at Edge Hill.
Royalist attack on London foiled at Turnham Green.
Imperial forces routed at Kempten; Electorate of Cologne and Duchy of Cleves occupied by Protestants under Guébriant.
Torstenson defeated Imperial armies with Swedes at Breitenfeld.
†Richelieu.
Treaty between Portugal and England.

Corneille: *Polyeucte*, French tragedy.
Regulation prohibiting printing of author's works without his agreement; beginnings of copyright.

1643 Battle of Atherton Moor: Fairfaxes, father and son, defeated by Royalist, Newcastle.
Battle of Roundway Down; Parliamentarians defeated.
Bristol sacked by Prince Rupert.
Oliver Cromwell won battle at Gainsborough.
Agreement between Parliament and Scots; Solemn League and Covenant.

Corneille: *Le Menteur*, French comedy.
Antoine Arnauld "the great Arnauld" (*1612, †1694): *Fréquente Communion*, attacked methods of confession and absolution.
Royalist newspaper *Mercurius Aulicus* appeared.
First Norwegian printed book: an almanack at Christiana.
Sir Thomas Browne (*1605, †1682), physician and author: *Religio Medici*,

music; only extant composite set at Christ Church, Oxford.
Ribera: *St Agnes*, Spanish painting.
(to 1701) Erection of the Potala, Lhasa, Tibet.

and demolish images, altars and monuments.

Mansart began *Château de Maisons*.
Monteverdi: *The Coronation of Popaea*, Italian opera.
Parliament's proclamation against popular sports and pastimes.
University of Ancona founded.
(to 1660) All theatres closed in England during the Commonwealth.
Rembrandt: *The Night Watch* (renamed *Sortie of the Banning Cocq Company*), huge Dutch painting.
Paul Potter (*1625, †1654): *Abraham entering into Canaan*, Dutch painting mainly of animals.

*Sir Isaac Newton (†1727), one of the world's greatest mathematicians.
Portuguese ceded Gold Coast to Dutch.
Ludwig von Siegen (*1609, †1676) discovered mezzotint process.
Foundation of Montreal, Canada.
First Income Tax and Property Tax introduced.
J. Bontius gave earliest description of cholera.
Abel Tasman (*c.* *1603, †1659) sighted Tasmania (which he named Van Diemen's Land) and New Zealand (which he named Land of the States).

Velazquez: *Venus and Cupid*, Spanish painting.
Rembrandt: *Saskia*, Dutch painting of his wife (who died in 1642).
Charles I issued first English medals for gallantry.

Torricelli (*1608, †1665) invented barometer; experiment performed by Viviani, a pupil.
Russian pioneers reached mouth of Amur River.
Colonies of New England formed "New England Federation"
Tasman discovered Tonga (Friendly) Isles and reached Fiji and New Guinea.

1643 Royalist forces of Newcastle defeated at Winceby.
Cessation of war in Ireland negotiated by Ormonde.
Mazarin became Chief Minister in France.
Renewal of alliance between France and United Provinces.
Insurrection in China: last Ming Emperor hanged himself; Shun Chih established Manchu dynasty.

philosophical work justifying his profession.

1644 Scottish army captured Newcastle.
Charles I summoned Parliament at Oxford.
Battle of Nantwich: Irish contingent defeated by Fairfax.
Parliamentarians under Waller defeated at Copredy Bridge.
Cromwell defeated Prince Rupert at Marston Moor; turning-point in Civil War.
Charles I defeated Essex at Lostwithiel.
Self-Denying Ordinance to remove all M.Ps except Cromwell from military commands.
Attainder of Laud.
Covenanters defeated by Montrose at Tippermuir.
Turenne and Enghien defeated Imperial forces at Freiburg; captured Mainz and Worms.
Torstenson conquered Jutland; later defeated Imperial army.

Milton: *Areopagitica*, famous pamphlet for the freedom of the Press; and *Tractate on Education*, in same year.
Corneille: *Rodogune*, French tragedy.
Descartes: *Principia Philosophiae*.

1645 Execution of Laud.
Sir Thomas Fairfax and Cromwell defeated Charles I at Naseby.
Montrose defeated Covenanters at Inverlochy, Aldern and Kilsyth, but was defeated at Philiphaugh.
Royalists defeated at Langport and Bristol.
Treves captures by Turenne; pro-French Elector restored.
Denmark forced to make humiliating peace with Swedes at Brömsbro.
Saxony made peace with Sweden.
Battle of Jankow.

Edmund Waller (*1606, †1687): *Poems*, published in London.
Revised Prayer Book of Elizabeth I suppressed until the Restoration; replaced by *The Directory for the Public Worship of God in Three Kingdoms* (see 1662).

*Antonio Stradivarius (†1737), great violin manufacturer; some 800 of his instruments have survived.
Rembrandt: *Woman taken in Adultery*, Dutch painting (National Gallery, London.)
Ribera: *Descent from the Cross*, Spanish painting.
Bernini: *The Vision of St Theresa*, altar of Santa Maria della Vittoria, Rome.
Ch'ing dynasty in China (to 1912); last age of fine Chinese porcelain—K'ang-hsi, Yung-cheng, Ch'ien-lung (1644–1795).

Tasman charted parts of Northern and Western coasts of Australia, then called *New Holland*.
Dutch and Portuguese sugar plantations established in Surinam.
William Lily (*1602, †1681) began yearly astrological almanack (to 1681).
Swedish 10 daler coins, weighing 20 lb., minted; world's heaviest.

Hals: *Balthasar Coymans*, Flemish painting.
Rembrandt: *Young Girl at an Open Half-Door*, Dutch painting.
(to 1652) Bernini: *St Theresa in Ecstasy*, Baroque sculpture.
University of Palermo founded.
Velazquez: *King Philip IV on a Boar Hunt*, Spanish painting.
Carlisle Cathedral extensively damaged by Parliamentary forces.

c. Beginnings of wall-papering of rooms in England.
Dutch occupied St. Helena.
c. Preliminary regular meetings of scientists (natural philosophers) of London; was to lead to foundation of Royal Society in 1660 (charter 1662, *q.v.*).
Foundation of Medical Academy at Palermo.

1646

Surrender of Charles I to Scots at Newark.
Negotiations between King and Parliament at Newcastle broke down on questions of Militia and Church.
Second plot against John IV of Portugal from Spain crushed.
Wrangel and Turenne invaded Bavaria and forced Elector to submit.

In *Fragmenta Aurea* appeared lyrics of Sir John Suckling (*1609, †1642), Cavalier poet.
Richard Crashaw, English poet who lived in Italy: *Poems*.
Henry Vaughan (*1622, †1695), metaphysical poet: *Poems*, his secular poems.
Jean Rotrou, French dramatist: *Saint Genest*.
Paul Scarron (*1610, †1660) began *Le Roman Comique*, French burlesque novel (published 1648).

1647

Scots, promised £400,000, withdrew over Border and surrendered Charles I to English Parliament.
Charles I captured from Parliament by Cornet Joyce at Holmby House.
Heads of Proposals: negotiations between Army and Charles I failed.
London occupied by Army; escape of Charles I from Hampton Court to Carisbrooke Castle; "Engagement" between Charles I and Scots revived Civil War in England.
†Frederick Henry of Orange; succeeded by son, William II of Orange.
Revolt in Spanish Naples, caused by Fruit Tax, suppressed.
Truce of Ulm.
Condé defeated in Spain at Lerida.

Cowley: *The Mistress*, cycle of love poems.
Claude Vaugelas, grammarian of French Academy: *Remarques sur la langue française*, first detailed treatise on prose.
Matthew Hopkins, notorious witch-hunter: *Discovery of Witches*; he was hanged in same year.

1648

Royalist insurrections in Kent and Wales suppressed.
Scots invaded England; defeated by Cromwell at Preston, Wigan and Warrington.
Presbyterian majority expelled from Commons by Colonel Pride ("Pride's Purge").
Decision to try Charles I before special High Court of Justice.
First War of Fronde in France; Mazarin agreed to demands of Parlement.
Wrangel and Turenne ravaged Bavaria.
Peace of Westphalia ended Thirty Years War.
Treaty of Münster: Spain recognized independence of United Provinces.
Siege of Candia by Turks.

Savinien Cyrano de Bergerac (*1620, †1655): *Histoire comique des Etats de la Lune* (published 1656).
Robert Herrick (*1591, †1674), country vicar: *Hesperides*, great collection of his poetry.
Clarendon ceased work on his *History* (see 1646) until 1671 (when exiled in France).

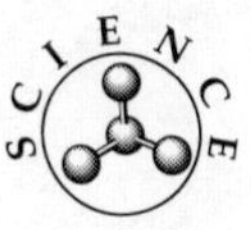

Rembrandt: *Winter Landscape*, Dutch painting.
Clarendon, in exile in the Scilly Isles, commenced his *History of the Rebellion and Civil Wars in England* (see 1648, 1702).

*Baron G. W. von Leibnitz, German (†1716), who invented calculus independently of Newton; a bitter and unseemly dispute was to arise between the two.
Baliani correctly enunciated law of falling bodies.
First colonization of Bahamas.
A. Kircher, German mathematician, made first projection lantern (probably).

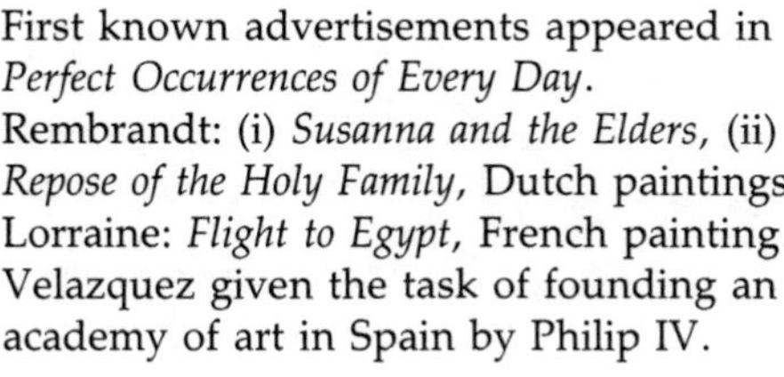
First known advertisements appeared in *Perfect Occurrences of Every Day*.
Rembrandt: (i) *Susanna and the Elders*, (ii) *Repose of the Holy Family*, Dutch paintings.
Lorraine: *Flight to Egypt*, French painting.
Velazquez given the task of founding an academy of art in Spain by Philip IV.

Pierre Gassendi (*1592, †1655): (i) *Institutis Astronomica*, important account of contemporary science, (ii) *De Vita Epicuri*, philosophical work.
Johann Hevelius (*1611, †1687), German astronomer: *Selenographia*, finely illustrated and detailed work on the moon; foundation of selenography.
Establishment of Swedish African Company.
Pascal: *Nouvelles expériences sur le vide*.
Earliest reliable account of yellow fever; in Barbados.

Jakob van Kampen built Amsterdam Royal Palace (formerly the Town Hall).
Foundation of Royal Academy of Arts at Paris by Mazarin.
Rembrandt: *Pilgrims at Emmaus*, Dutch painting (Louvre).
Potter: *Bull and Cows*, Dutch painting.
Bamberg University opened.

Glauber developed chemical distillation process.
Publication, posthumously, of complete works of Brahe, Danish astronomer.
Dezhnev first navigated the Bering Strait.

1649

"Agreement of People", basis for new constitution, drawn up by Levellers in Army.
Trial and execution of Charles I; monarcy and Lords abolished; proclamation of England as Commonwealth.
Royalists led by Ormonde defeated at Rathmines; Cromwell invaded Ireland; sacked Drogheda and Wexford.
End of Westminster Assembly.
Peace of Ruel ended war of Fronde.

Richard Lovelace (*1618, †1658), Cavalier poet: *Lucasta*.
Madeleine de Scudéry: *Le Grand Cyrus,* French historical novel in ten volumes.
D'Avenant: *Love and Honour,* a play (first performed 1634) published.
Eikon Basilike (see 1640), alleged thoughts of Charles I, replied to by *Eikonoklastes* of Milton.

1650

Montrose defeated at Corbiesdale and executed.
Charles II landed in Scotland.
Cromwell invaded Scotland; Scots under Leslie defeated at Dunbar; Edinburgh Castle surrendered to Cromwell.
Outbreak of civil war in Barbados; lasted to 1652.
Start of second war of Fronde (The Noble Fronde); easily suppressed.
William II of Orange succeeded in setting up supremacy of States General over Provincial States of Holland.

Vaughan: *Silex Scintillans,* religious poems.
Jeremy Taylor: *Holy Living,* religious prose work.
Corneille: *Nicomède.*
Joose van der Vondel: *Manual of Dutch Poetry.*
Anne Bradstreet (*1612, †1672): *The Tenth Muse, lately sprung up in America,* early American poetry.
Andrew Marvell (*1621, †1678), *Horatian Ode upon Cromwell's Return from Ireland,* poem in praise of Protector.

1651

Charles II crowned King of Scotland at Scone; invaded England; defeated by Cromwell at Worcester; fled to France.
Mazarin failed to keep promise made to Parlement; union of Old and New Frondeurs under Condé returned to Paris; Mazarin fled.
Louis XIV declared of age; revolt against Mazarin became rebellion against King.
John Casimir V of Poland defeated Cossacks and Tartars.

Christen Bang (*1580, †1678) *Description of Christiana,* early Norwegian work.
Unofficial publication of *Olor Iscanus,* second book of secular poems by Vaughan.
D'Avenant: *Gondibert,* romantic epic peom.
Hobbes: *Leviathan,* political treatise on the power of the State.
Taylor: *Holy Dying.*

1652

Outbreak of first Anglo-Dutch war; Dutch defeated off Dover; Van Tromp defeated Blake off Dungeness.
Perpetuation Bill to make all existing M.P.s perpetual members introduced.
Cromwellian settlement of Ireland.
Eight months war of Fronde in

*Sor Juana Inés de la Cruz, Spanish poetess, in Mexico
c. Marvell: *The Garden* and *Appleton House,* poems.
c. Hayashi Shunsai (*1618, †1680): *O-Dai-Ichi-Ran,* a history of Japan.

Velazquez: *Pope Innocent XIII*, Spanish painting.
(to 1656) Van Bassen and Novrwits designed New Church, The Hague.
Pietro Cavalli (*1602, †1676); *Jason*, Italian opera.

Construction of first British frigate for the Navy, the *Constant Warwick*.

St Giles House, Dorset, built for Earl of Shaftesbury.
Earliest known rules of billiards printed.
c. Introduction of overture to operas; two types: (i) French; (ii) Italian.
c. Country dances took on definite form; almost died out in 19th cent.; revived by English Folk Dance Society.
c. Development of musical modulations and corresponding division of scale into twelve semitones; beginnings of modern harmony (also see 1722).

Thomas Hobbes (*1588, †1679): *Human Nature*, first book on modern psychology.
c. Leather upholstery used for furniture.
c. All continents except Antarctica known.
Tea first drunk in England.
Opening, at Oxford, of first coffee-house.
c. Development of textile printing in Europe.
Otto von Guericke (*1602, †1686), German, natural philosopher, invented the air pump (see 1654).

Rembrandt: *Girl with a Brook* and *Descent from the Cross*, Dutch paintings.
John Playford: *English Dancing Master*; describes many country dances.
Erection of Lanhydrock, Cornwall, possessing long picture gallery.

Riccioli's map of the moon introducing many of the modern names of lunar features.
Christian Huyghens (*1629, †1695): *Theoremata de Quadratura Hyperbolae, Ellipsis et Circuli*, geometry of the conics.
Navigation Act aimed by English against Dutch merchant shipping.
Dutch settled at Cape of Good Hope; colony governed from Batavia.

Jean-Baptiste Lully (*1632, †1687), later to become the founder of French opera, popularized the Minuet, important dance at the French Court.

Horrebow discovered aberration of light from fixed stars.
*Casper Thomeson Bartholin (†1738), Danish anatomist who was to describe lymphatic glands in the human body.
Foundation of Cape Town by the Dutch.
Pascal constructed first simple calculating machine for addition and subtraction.

LITERATURE

Year	History	Literature
1652	France; Frondeurs under Condé, Royal forces under Turenne. Louis XIV entered Paris; punished Frondeurs; deprived Parlement of power; Condé entered service of Spain. Catalan revolt suppressed by Philip IV at surrender of Barcelona after 15–month siege.	
1653	Parliament expelled by Cromwell; New Council of State appointed. Barebones Parliament: members selected by Council of State from lists submitted by independent ministers. Parliament of Saints. Cromwell appointed Lord Protector by Instrument of Government. Mazarin returned to Paris; surrender of Bordeaux ended Fronde. Condé, with Spanish troops, invaded Northern France; compelled to retreat by Turenne. John de Witt appointed Grand Pensionary of Holland. Van Tromp defeated by Blake and Monk off Portland; later, Monk defeated and killed Van Tromp off Texel. Cossacks took oath of allegiance to Tsar Alexis.	Izaac Walton (*1593, †1683): *The Compleat Angler*, discourse on pleasures of fishing. Richard Brome: *The City Witt (or the Woman wears the Breeches)*, a comedy. Pope Innocent X declared Jansen's *Augustinus* (see 1638) heretical; the followers of the teachings of this book were called Jansenists by R.C. Church. Shirley: *Cupid and Death*, notable English masque.
1654	Board of Triers: to examine character of ministers appointed by patrons of livings. Peace concluded between England and Holland. Discovery of Vowell and Gerard's plot against Cromwell. First Protectorate Parliament met; M.P.s from the three kingdoms. Republicans debated "government by a single person", supporters excluded by Cromwell. French forced Condé to raise siege of Arras. War between United Provinces and Portugal. Christina of Sweden abdicated; succeeded by Charles X. Alexis of Russia invaded Poland.	Comenius: *Orbium Sensualium Pictus*, first illustrated book for children. Madame de Scudéry: *Clélie*, French novel of chivalry.

Fine jewellery found in the tomb of Childeric (see 481).
Nicolas Poussin (*1594, †1665): *The Holy Family*, French painting; artist's work included romantic landscapes, biblical pictures and classical compositions.
Rembrandt: *The Three Crosses*, Dutch etching.
Borromini and Rainaldi designed Santa Agnese in Piazza Navona, Rome.
Jacob van Ruisdael (*c.* *1628, †1682), Dutch landscape artist: *Castle of Bentheim*.

Commercial treaty made between Britain and Portugal.
Johann Schultes (*1595, †1645), German surgeon: *Armamentarium chirurgicum*, celebrated posthumous work on contemporary surgical instruments and procedures.

Foundation of Duisburg University.
Rembrandt: *Portrait of Jan Six, an Amsterdam Patrician*, Dutch painting.
De Hooch became a member of the painters' gild of Delft (to 1657).

*Jacques B. Bernoulli (Swiss; †1705), first of three mathematicians; brother Jean (*1667, †1748) discovered exponential functions; Daniel (*1700, †1782), son of Jean, said to have founded mathematical physics: studied hydrodynamics.
Von Guericke's remarkable experiment with 30 horses pulling two halves of metal spheres from which air evacuated (see 1650).
Great explosion at Delft.
Publication of Timothy Pont's maps of Scottish Counties, drawn much earlier.

1655 Parliament dissolved by Cromwell.
Penruddock's rising against Cromwell suppressed.
William Penn and Venables took Jamaica from Spain.
Cromwell divided England into eleven military districts.
Anglo-French Treaty against Spain; Prince Charles excluded from France.
John Casimir V of Poland refused to recognize Charles X as King of Sweden; latter captured Warsaw and Cracow.

First Berlin newspaper issued.
Hobbes: *De Corpore,* Latin philosophical work (trans. 1656).
Marchmont Nedham issued the *Publick Intelligencer* periodical (to 1660).

1656 Second Protectorate Parliament met; more than 90 Republicans and Presbyterians excluded.
Treaty of Königsberg; Brandenburg recognized Swedish suzerainty over East Prussia.
Second invasion of Poland by Charles X; Russian invasion of Finland forced Charles X to return home.
Treaty of Labiau; Sweden recognized Frederick William of Brandenburg as ruler of East Prussia.
Moncenigo, Venetian admiral, routed Turks in Dardanelles.
Mohammed Kiuprili, Albanian, appointed Grant Vizier to Mohammed IV, with absolute power.

Jansenist Antoine Arnauld expelled from the Sorbonne for heresy; led to publication by Pascal of *Lettres Provinciales,* theological controversy.
Jansenists produced widely used textbooks of grammar and logic.
Cowley published *Fifteen Pindaric Odes;* became (erroneous) pattern for many would-be imitators.

1657 Cromwell refused title of king offered by Parliament but accepted new constitution; new House of Lords appointed.
Treaty of Paris: Cromwell and Mazarin allied for English aid against Spain.
Treaty of Wehlau: Brandenburg allied with Poland against Sweden.
Denmark declared war on Sweden; Charles X crossed frozen sea in winter of 1657–8 and threatened Copenhagen.
Turks, organized by Kiuprili, defeated Venetians.
Failure of Shah Jahan's health; contest for supremacy between his sons.

In Holland was printed *Killing No Murder,* a sheet proposing the murder of Oliver Cromwell.
Middleton: *No Wit, No Help like a Woman's,* a play, and *Women beware Women,* a tragedy.

Rembrandt: *The Artist's Son, Titus*, Dutch painting.
Festival of Sons of the Clergy, originally simple Commonwealth ceremony, became musical in character after Restoration; believed to have originated English musical festivals.
(to 1777) Erection of St Sulpice, Paris, Classical style church.

John Wallis (*1616, †1703): *Arithmetica Infinitorum*, laid foundation of "limit"; infinity sign (∞) introduced.
Huyghens identified largest Saturn moon and true nature of Saturn's rings; published findings in *Systema Saturnium* (1659).
Jamaica became Caribbean base for buccaneers.
Isaac Barrow (*1630, †1677): *Euclidis Elementa*; he was tutor to Newton, giving up his Chair of Mathematics at Cambridge in favour of the latter.

Velazquez: *Las Meninas* (Maids of Honour), Spanish painting.
De Hooch: *A Dutch Courtyard*, painting.
Opening of the Opera House in London.
Rembrandt: *Jacob blessing the Sons of Joseph*, Dutch painting.
Jan Vermeer (*1632, †1675): *Woman and Soldier*, Dutch painting.
Bartolomé Murillo (*1617, †1682): *Vision of St. Anthony*, Spanish painting in Seville Cathedral.
Foundation of Academy of Painting at Rome.

Foundation of Copenhagen observatory.
Formation of Regiment of Grenadier Guards.
Stockings manufactured in Paris (but stocking loom believed to have been invented *temp*. Elizabeth I).
Beginnings of Dutch commerce with China.
Blake captured part of Spanish treasure fleet.
Rembrandt declared bankrupt; all his property put up for sale.

c. Rembrandt: *The Apostle Paul*, and *Old Man with a Grey Beard*, Dutch paintings.
Durham University founded by Cromwell, but dissolved three years later (see 1832).
Pietro da Cortona began building façade of Santa Maria della Pace, Rome.
Le Vau began Château de Vaux-le-Vicomte.
Comenius: *Great Didactic*, theory of education of the period.

Huyghens designed first pendulum for clock.
Hautsch of Nuremberg designed special fire-fighting machine.
East India Company introduced permanent non-returnable Joint Stock system.
First manufacture of fountain pen at Paris.
Foundation of Accademia del Cimento, Florence, as an academy of experiment.

LITERATURE

	HISTORY	LITERATURE
1658	New Parliament, including new Lords, met; soon dissolved. English and French defeated Spaniards at battle of Dunes; England gained Dunkirk. †Oliver Cromwell; succeeded as Lord Protector by son, Richard Cromwell. End of Portuguese rule in Ceylon. Treaty of Roskild; Danes gave up territory in South Sweden and Trondheim in Norway. Second Swedish invasion of Denmark; Copenhagen besieged; Swedes driven off in 1659. Aurangzeb became Great Mogul; Shah Jahan state prisoner in Agra fort.	May: *The Old Couple*, a comedy. Hobbes: *De Homine*, philosophical work. Massinger: *The City Madam*, a comedy.
1659	Parliament summoned by Richard Cromwell; differences with Army; dissolved; remains of Long Parliament, the Rump, restored by Army; Cromwell left Whitehall. Royalist and Presbyterian rising in Cheshire under George Booth; suppressed by John Lambert; Lambert dismissed by Rump; Lambert marched to Westminster and expelled Rump; Monk marched into England from Scotland; Lambert sent against him. Treaty of Pyrenees ended war between France and Spain. Convention of The Hague: France, England and Holland agreed to enforce Treaty of Roskild.	Jean Baptiste Molière (*1622, †1673), France's greatest dramatist: *Les Précieuses Ridicules*, comedy. Foundation of Royal Library at Berlin. John Dryden (*1631, †1700): *Heroic Stanzas*, on Cromwell's death. Henry Muddiman (*1629), great journalist, issued *Mercurius Publicus* and *The Parliamentary Intelligencer*.
1660	Fairfax met Lambert at Marston Moor and persuaded Army not to oppose Monk; Monk entered London and declared for Free Parliament; Long Parliament dissolved itself after calling a Convention; Declaration of Breda by exiled Charles II set out terms of Restoration; Convention Parliament invited Charles to return; Charles II restored to English throne. May 29th. Act of Indemnity and Oblivion.	Dryden: *Astraea Redux*, poem celebrating Charles II and intended to compensate for his work on Cromwell (see 1658). Samuel Pepys (*1633, †1703), diarist who was to become Secretary to the Admiralty, began his celebrated *Diary*.

Rembrandt completed painting *Head of Christ*.
Bernini erected church of St Andrew at the Quirinale.
De Hooch: *Mother and Child Indoors*, Dutch painting.

Jan Swammerdam (*1637, †1680) first observed red blood corpuscles (see 1675).
Fromanteel made first English spring pendulum clock.
Evelyn translated *The French Gardener*, in which mushroom-growing appears.
Robert Hooke (*1635, †1703), natural philosopher, invented balance-spring for watches.
De Ruyter, Dutch admiral, blockaded harbours of Portugal and ruined that country's trade.
Groseilliers and Radisson explored Minnesota, U.S.A.
Fermat's theory of numbers published.

Vermeer: *Young Girl with a Flute*, Dutch painting.
Early reference to organs to accompany musical evenings in taverns—forerunner of Music Hall.
Velazquez: *St. Anthony the Abbot and St Paul the Hermit*, Spanish painting.

Huyghens improved telescope by using eye-piece corrected for spherical aberration (achromatic lens free from colour fringes); saw Mars.
Rahn first used division sign (÷).
Heriot's Hospital, Edinburgh, completed; probably designed by Inigo Jones.
Typhoid fever first described; by T. Willis.

Albert Cuyp (*1620, †1691): *The Maas at Dordrecht*, Dutch painting.
Rembrandt: *St Joseph's Dream*, Dutch painting.
Sir Peter Lely, portrait painter to Charles II: *The Ladies of the Lake*.
First actresses appeared on English stage.
Rainaldi designed church of St. Mary in Campitelli.
Sir Roger Pratt built Kingston Lacy, Dorset.
Van Ruisdael: *The Inn*, Dutch painting.
Creation of post of Master of the King's Musick.

Von Guericke observed severe storm followed sudden drop in barometric pressure; invented static electricity machine in same year.
Bayonets first made (at Bayonne).
Establishment of Vauxhall glass mirror factory.
Military tenures and feudal dues abolished.
Foundation of Royal Society (see 1662).
Prince Rupert introduced mezzotint process into England.
Re-enaction of 1651 Navigation Laws restricting transhipment of goods to

	History	Literature
1660	Louis XIV married Maria Theresa, daughter of Philip IV of Spain; important in later Spanish succession question. †Charles X of Sweden. Treaty of Oliva ended war between Sweden, Poland, Brandenburg and Empire. Treaty of Copenhagen ended war between Sweden and Denmark. M. Kiuprili deposed Ragotsky, slain at Grosswarden.	
1661	Savoy Conference in London between bishops and Presbyterian ministers failed. Cavalier Parliament met: confirmed Acts of Convention Parliament. Corporation Act required all holders of municipal office to renounce Covenant. Act of Settlement restored some lands to Irish. Episcopacy re-established in Scotland. Lambert tried and executed for treason. Louis XIV assumed absolute power in France. Treaty between Holland and Portugal: Ceylon, Malacca, the Moluccas ceded to Holland; Dutch renounced claims on Brazil. Treaty of Kardis; peace between Swedes and Russia. †M. Kiuprili; succeeded by son, Achmet Kiuprili.	Molière: *L'École des Maris*, and *Les Fâcheux*, French plays. Dryden: *Panegyric*, concerning the Restoration. Evelyn: *Fumifugium or the Inconvenience of the Air and Smoke of London dissipated*, an attack on air pollution.
1662	Marriage of Charles II to Catherine of Braganza; Tangier and Bombay ceded to Britain. Dunkirk sold to French. First Declaration of Indulgence by Charles II; withdrawn. Act of Uniformity passed: non-conforming ministers ejected from livings. Law of Settlement; removed to parishes of birth persons who became chargeable to Poor Law in parish of Residence. Treaty of Paris; temporary alliance between France and Netherlands;	Molière: *L'École des Femmes*, French play. François, duc de La Rochefoucauld (*1613, †1680): *Mémoires*. Jacques B. Bossuet (*1627, †1704), French bishop and orator: *Sermons on the Duties of Kings, Death, Providence, Ambition*. Michael Wigglesworth: *The Day of Doom*, New England puritanical poetry. Revised version of Prayer Book again issued; little modification since. Marie-Madeleine, Comtesse de La Fayette (*1634, †1693): *Princesse de Montpensier*, first real novel in French.

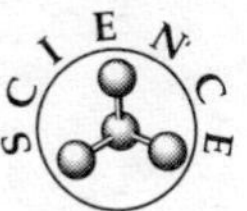

Vermeer: *The Cook*, Dutch painting.

Americas to English vessels.
Export of wool from Britain prohibited; did great harm to the trade; law revoked 1825.

Foundation of *L'Academie Nationale de la Danse* (Louis XIV), whence arose modern ballet.
Van Ruisdael: *Landscape with Watermill*, Dutch painting.
Le Vau began Collège des Quatre Nations, now the Institut.
The Palais de Versailles built (to 1756) for Louis XIV.
Rembrandt: *The Syndics of the Cloth Hall*, Dutch painting.
Edward Lowe: *Short Direction for the Performance of Cathedral Service*, to revive organ accompaniment suppressed during Commonwealth.

(Hon.) Robert Boyle, Irish (*1627, †1691): *The Sceptical Chymist*, handbook of chemistry in which chemical elements were defined.
Marcello Malpighi (*1628, †1695) observed blood flow through capillaries of lung of frog: completion of Harvey's theory of blood circulation.
French revenue showed deficit of 22 million francs.
Huyghens invented the manometer.
Glauber: *Opera omnia*, his principal work on chemistry (written in German).
Bank of Sweden issued world's first banknotes.

Rembrandt: *Famly Portrait*, Dutch painting.
French government took over Gobelin factory for tapestries and industrial arts (see 1697).
Sir Christopher Wren (*1632, †1723), architect, designed Sheldonian Theatre, Oxford.
Wing added to Rufford Old Hall, Lancashire, medieval house with Great Hall possessing hammer-beam roof.

Grant of Royal Charter to Royal Society by Charles II; many great men, including Newton, have presided; letters F.R.S. (Fellowship), highest scientific honour obtainable.
Hooke invented compound microscope.
Wren made first English rain-gauge.
Boyle: famous law of expansion of gas under isothermal conditions; known as "Father of Chemistry", he wrote one of earliest books on statistics, then called Political Arithmetic; earlier statistical records (1563) less detailed.
Royal Adventurers trading into Africa set up by Charles II under Royal Charter.

LITERATURE

	History	Literature
1662	Louis XIV hoped to distract Dutch from interfering with plans against Spanish Netherlands. Frederick William of Brandenburg in conflict with towns of East Prussia. K'ang Hsi succeeded Shun Chih as second Manchu Emperor of China.	
1663	First Turnpike Act passed by Parliament. Convocation granted last subsidy to Crown. Achmet Kiuprili attacked Austria; overran Transylvania; invaded Hungary; captured Neuhäsen.	(to 1678) Samuel Butler (*1612, †1680): *Hudibras*, satiric poem of quixotic Hudibras who tries to reform fellow citizens. Molière: *La Critique de l'Ecole des Femmes*, and *L'Impromptu de Versailles*.
1664	Conventicle Act forbade religious assemblies other than those of Church of England. Triennial Act of 1641 repealed. Outbreak of second Anglo-Dutch war. Renewal by France of membership of League of Rhine. Dutch seized part of Guiana from England; English seized Dutch Goree and Guinea in Africa, New Amsterdam in North America; latter renamed New York. Austrians under Montecuculi, aided by French, defeated Turks at St Gothard on River Raab. Treaty of Vasvar between Emperor Leopold I and Sultan; Turkey kept all recent conquests.	Dryden: *The Rival Ladies*, play in verse, first performed. Molière: *Le Tartuffe*, French play. Sir George Etherege (*1635, †1691): *The Comical Revenge*, a play by the inventor of the comedy of intrigue.
1665	Duke of York defeated Dutch fleet off Lowestoft. †Philip IV of Spain; succeeded by imbecile Charles II; Louis XIV of France led to claim Spanish Netherlands.	Molière: *Dom Juan* and *L'Amour Médecin*, French plays. La Rochefoucauld: *Maximes*, psychological and moral study of man. Jean de la Fontaine (*1621, †1695) *Contes et Nouvelles* tales in verse drawn from Boccaccio and Ariosto. Pierre de Brantôme (*1540, †1614): *Dames Galantes*, reflections on women, published. Dryden: *The Indian Emperor*, a play.

Hugh May designed Eltham Lodge, now golf club house.
Opening of first Drury Lane Theatre.

First wire-mill in Britain (Mortlake).
J. Gregory (*1638, †1675) *designed* but failed to construct reflecting telescope (see 1668); he is noted for series for $\pi = 1 - /1/3/ + /1/5/ + /1/7/ + \ldots$ and for distinguishing between convergent and divergent series.
Charles II established Sheerness Dockyard.
Foundation of colony of North Carolina.
First minting of the guinea in England.
Introduction of Hearth Tax in England.

Schültz: *Christmas Oratorio*, performed at Dresden.
Introduction of large periwig style from France.
Erection of Burlington House, London; modified in 1716, *q.v.*
Lully began composing music for Molière's ballets.
Jan Steen (*1626, †1679): *The Christening Feast*, Dutch painting.

First coach-springing fitted.
Hooke: *Micrographia*, great early work on crystallography, chemistry, botany and optics; used condenser and projection lenses for lantern.
Beginnings of mechanical separation of wood and fibre of flax in linen industry.
French East and West Indies Companies founded by Jean Baptiste Colbert to rival English companies; Colbert appointed Superintendent of Buildings.
Work commenced on Canal du Midi (completed 1681).
First Royal Marine regiment established.
Descartes: *De l'homme*, first work on physiology from point of view of mechanics of the body.

Five Mile Act forbade ejected ministers to live within 5 miles of corporate towns or to teach in schools.
De Hooch: *Boy bringing Pomegranates*, Dutch painting.
Vermeer: *The Artist's Studio*, Dutch painting.
Bernini completed High Altar of St Peter's Rome (begun 1656).
Foundation of Kiel University by Christian Albert of Schleswig.

Newton's famous experiments on gravitation; he evolved binomial theorem in same year; and discovered differential calculus, then called direct method of fluxions; had needed analytical geometry to pave the way (see 1637).
Hooke discovered that plants need to breathe; also found living cells in plants.
First publication of Royal Society's proceedings.
Great Plague of London at its height.
Colony of New Jersey founded.

Year	History	Literature
1666	France declared war on England in support of United Provinces. De Ruyter outmanoeuvred Monk in Four Day Battle of Downs; Monk defeated Dutch off North Foreland and later destroyed Dutch merchant fleet in Terschelling Roads. French captured Antigua and Montserrat. Dutch captured Surinam. Louis XIV issued Edict weakening Huguenots. Treaty of Cleves between Brandenburg and Neuburg. Frederick William of Brandenburg joined Quadruple Alliance against France. Hungarian nobles rose in revolt against Emperor. †Shah Jahan.	Molière: *Le Misanthrope* and *Le Médecin malgré lui*, French plays. Antoine Furetière: (*1619, †1688): *Roman Bourgeois*, French realist novel of middle-class life. *London Gazette*, formerly called *Oxford Gazette* (1665), established as official government paper; has remained so ever since. John Bunyan (*1628, †1688): *Grace abounding to the Chief of Sinners*, a religious work written during 12 years in prison.
1667	Treaty of Breda: peace between England and Dutch. Clarendon, architect of Restoration Settlement, dismissed by Charles II; Cabal Ministry appointed. Louis XIV made treaty with Portugal; latter to continue war with Spain. France invaded Flanders: War of Devolution. Secret agreement between Charles II and Louis XIV for non-interference if France attacked Netherlands. Treaty of Andrusoff ended Russia-Poland struggle.	Milton: *Paradise Lost*, epic poem on the fall of man "with loss of Eden". Dyrden: *Annus Mirabilis*, description in verse of Great Fire of London and victories over the Dutch. Jean Racine (*1639, †1699): *Andromaque*, early play by great French dramatist.
1668	Secret Treaty between Emperor Leopold I and Louis XIV for partition of Spanish Empire. French conquered Franche-Comté. Treaty of Aix-la-Chapelle ended war between Spain and France. Spain ceded 12 strong fortresses in Netherlands. Triple Alliance of England, United Provinces and Sweden to protect Spanish monarchy. Treaty of Lisbon: Spain finally recognized independence of Portugal.	Dryden: *Essay of Dramatic Poesy*. Molière: *Amphitryon*, *George Dandin* and *L'Avare*, French comedies. Racine: *Les Plaideurs*, his only comedy. La Fontaine: *Fables* (also 1678, 1679, 1694) in French verse with homely morals.

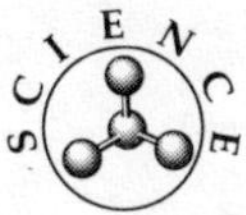

Destruction of Gothic St Paul's Cathedral, London, in Great Fire; as a result of the same fire, Wren was to build 51 parish churches in London.
(to 1670) Erection of colonnade of east front of the Louvre.
Stradivarius began to label his violins.
Foundation of University of Lund.

Newton discovered integral calculus, then called inverse method of fluxions; developed theory of colours in same year, separating colours of the rainbow in a prism.
Cassini observed polar caps on Mars.
Otto Tachenius: *Hippocrates Chimicus,* on chemistry, proposed all salts as arising from acid + base.
Great Fire of London.
Foundation of the Académie Royale des Sciences, Paris.
Early reference to cheddar cheese.

c. Murillo: series of 22 Spanish paintings for Church of Capuchins.
c. Rembrandt: *Family Group* and *Jewish Bride,* his last great works.
Agostino Barelli built Theatinerkirche, a Neapolitan church, in Munich; completed 1675.
Marcantonio Cesti (*1618, †1669): *Pomo d'Oro,* early Italian opera.

Hooke proposed systematic weather recording; beginnings of meteorology.
Picard added a telescope to the quadrant, astronomical instrument (see 1456).
French known to have used hand-grenades.
French revenue now showing credit of 30 million francs; Colbert appointed Controller General of Finance to Louis XIV.
Incorporation of Feltmakers' Company, London.

Tintinnalogia published by Fabian Stedman, authority on campanology (bell-ringing).
(to 1687) Guarino Guarini designed San Lorenzo, Turin.
*Francois Couperin (†1733), greatest of French family of musicians; wrote harpsichord works in form of Programme Music.

Newton constructed highly efficient (Gregorian) reflecting telescope; made even more efficient telescope (38 diameters) in 1671.
Hevelius: *Cometographia,* systematic German record of all known comets.
Charles II handed Bombay to East India Company, who founded Fort William, now Calcutta, in same year.
Antoni van Leeuwenhoek (*1632, †1723) developed Malpighi's work (1661, *q.v.*) on blood capillaries.
First trading station set up by French in India.

	History	Literature
1669	James, Duke of York, publicly acknowledged conversion to Roman Catholicism. Pope Clement IX reconciled Jansenists and opponents in "Clementine Peace". Last meeting of Hanseatic League with only nine represented out of former estimated 166 member towns. Candia capitulated to Turks after siege lasting from 1648. Freedom of worship in India rejected.	Pepys' *Diary* ended. Molière: *Le Tartuffe* performed in public. Racine: *Britannicus*, French tragedy. Bossuet: *Funeral Oration on Henriette de France*. *Codex Argentaeus* presented to Uppsala University (see 350).
1670	Secret Treaty of Dover between England and France. Alliance between France and Bavaria for joint action on death of either Emperor Leopold I or Charles II of Spain. Cossacks of Ukraine, subject to Poland since 1667, rebelled; crushed by Jan Sobieski.	Molière: *Le Bourgeois Gentilhomme*, French comedy. Racine: *Bérénice*, French play. Pascal: *Pensées*. Dryden: *The Conquest of Granada*, play in rhymed couplets. Mme de La Fayette: *Zaÿde*, early novel by famous authoress.
1671	Sir Henry Morgan, former buccaneer, made deputy Governor of Jamaica by Charles II. Louis XIV made treaties with Hanover, Osnabrück, Brunswick and Lüneburg; secured neutrality of Empire in war with Dutch. Alliance of Spain and United Provinces against France. Hungarian revolt crushed; reign of terror in Hungary. Cossacks of Ukraine appealed to Turkey for aid against Poland; Turks declared war on Poland.	Milton: *Paradise Regained*; and *Samson Agonistes*, verse drama of the death of Samson. William Wycherley (*1640, †1716): *Love in a Wood*, early play by cynical Restoration dramatist. Mme de Sévigné (*1626, †1696) started famous correspondence with daughter. Molière: *Les Fourberies de Scapin*, French comedy.
1672	Second Declaration of Indulgence by Charles II. Outbreak of Third Anglo-Dutch War. Treaty of Stockholm between France and Sweden. Turks and Cossacks invaded Poland. French and English fleets defeated by De Ruyter in Sole Bay. French invaded United Provinces.	Molière: *Les Femmes Savantes* and *Le Malade imaginaire*, French comedies. Racine: *Bajazet*, French play. Foundation of the Clarendon Press, official press of Oxford University. Thomas Shadwell (*c.* *1642, †1692), playwright and poet: *Epsom Wells*, one of his best plays.

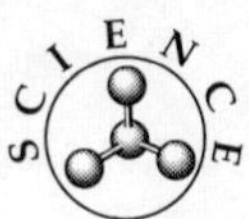

Work begun on Royal Opera House, Paris,
Aurangzeb, Mogul emperor, ordered destruction of all non-Islamic temples and schools.
Rembrandt: *Self-portrait.*
Vermeer: *Girl at the Spinet,* Dutch painting.

Nicolaus Steno (*1638, †1689), Danish, gave first accurate exposition on fossil origin.
J. J. Becher (*1635, †1682) suggested idea of inflammable earth; led to Stahl's *phlogiston* theory (see 1702).
Outbreak of cholera in China.
Colbert made Secretary of French navy.
Hennig Brandt, of Hamburg, first isolated phosphorus.

*O'Caloran (†1738): Irish harpist; many of his tunes are still played.
Moor Park Mansion House built for Duke of Monmouth; two wings added 1727.

Hooke probably invented anchor-escarpement for clocks.
Giovanni A. Borelli (*1608, †1679), Italian scientist, endeavoured to use artificial wings for flying.
Francisco Lana designed aerial ship but did not construct it.
Colony of South Carolina founded.
Hudson Bay Trading Company incorporated by Royal Charter.
British colonies set up in Bahamas.

Edward Jerman erected Royal Exchange building, London.
Sir Wm. Bruce began rebuilding Holyrood House, Edinburgh (completed 1679).
Wren commenced the Monument, London, 200 ft high, commemorating the Great Fire (1666).
Académie de la Musique (the Opera), Paris, founded.
Weston Park, Shropshire, fine Restoration mansion, erected.

Foundation of Paris observatory.
Cassini discovered more satellites of Saturn (see 1655 and 1898) in this year and next.
Sir Henry Morgan led buccaneers across Gulf of Panama to Pacific.
Malpighi: *Anatome plantarum,* a study of plant tissues.
Leibnitz defined existence of the aether.
French naval strength now 196 vessels, due to work of Colbert.

John Banister, violinist, gave first concerts in the world for which people paid admission (at Whitefriars, London).
Jules Hardouin, called Mansart (*1646, †1708), began work on Château de Clagny.
Erection of Porte Saint-Denis, Paris; triumphal arch.
Wren erected Temple Bar; gateway; removed to Hertfordshire (1888).
Kao Ts'en: *Autmn Landscape,* Chinese Indian-ink picture.

Newton presented account of his colour experiments to Royal Society.
Vanderheide produced flexible fire hose.
Cassini estimated sun's distance as 87 million miles.
Baltic trade, hitherto controlled by Eastland Trading Company, thrown open to all English merchants.
African Trading Company, ruined by Dutch wars, surrendered Charter; replaced by Royal African Company of England.

	History	Literature
1672	William III of Orange appointed Captain General of Union despite Eternal Edict. John and Cornelius de Witt murdered by Orange mob in Gevangenpoort; William III protected murderers. Emperor joined Brandenburg and Dutch in new alliance against France. Treaty of Buczacz: Poles surrendered Podolia and Ukraine to Turkey.	
1673	Parliament forced Charles II to withdraw Declaration of Indulgence; Test Act excluding all Non-Conformists from office. End of Cabal Ministry. English took St. Helena from Dutch. Louis XIV extended "Regale" to all France. Great Elector defeated by Turenne; forced to make pace with France. De Ruyter defeated French and English fleets at Schooneveld and Kykduin. Emperor, Lorraine, Spain and United Provinces formed new alliance against France.	Wycherley: *The Gentleman Dancing-Master*, a comedy, published. Archpriest Avvakum (*c.* *1620, †1681): *Life of Himself*, important Russian work. Dryden: *Amboyna*, a tragedy, and *Marriage à la Mode*, a comedy. Racine: *Mithridate*, French play.
1674	Treaty of Westminster ended Third Dutch War. Agitation to exclude Duke of York from succession. William III of Orange made hereditary Stadholder of Holland. Empire declared war on France; formed alliance with Spain; joined by Frederick William Brandenburg. Turenne devastated Palatinate. Brandenburghers and Imperial Army occupied Alsace. Denmark, Palatinate and Brunswick joined coalition against France. Sobieski elected King of Poland; Franco-Polish alliance.	Racine: *Iphigénie*, French tragedy. Nicolas Boileau-Despréaux (*1636, †1711), *L'Art Poétique*; laid down the literary principles of French classical period; and *Le Lutrin*, mock-epic, continued 1683. Nicolas Malebranche (*1638, †1715): *De la Recherche de la Vérité*, major work on philosophy.
1675	Charles II received 500,000 crowns from Louis XIV and prorogued Parliament for 15 months. Turenne defeated Great Elector at Türckheim, but was killed at	Wycherley: *The Country Wife*, a comedy, published. Benedictus de Spinoza (*1632, †1677), Dutch philosopher, completed his great work *Ethics*, begun 1662 (see 1677).

Palace of Charlottenborg erected in Copenhagen; later passed to the Academy of Arts.

Stop of Exchequer applied; no principal of Government loans to be repaid, only interest.
Cassegrain constructed a reflecting telescope (see 1668).

Lully: *Cadmus and Hemoine*, first French opera, performed at Paris.
Erection of Lindridge Mansion, Devonshire; possesses Italian and water gardens.
Edward Pierce: *Sir Christopher Wren*, marble bust.

Huyghens: *Horologium Oscillatorium*, work on time-measurement, including use of improved pendulums (see 1657).
Jacques Marquette (*1637, †1675), French explorer, reached head waters of Mississippi.
French East India Company founded factory at Chandernagori on Hooghli.
Establishment of Chelsea Physic Garden.
Discovery of stalactite grotto of Antiparos.

Publication of *The Compleat Gambler*, book of instruction for gamesters.
Second Drury Lane theatre opened.
Matthew Locke (*c.* *1630, †1677): incidental music to Shakespeare's *Tempest*.
Erection of Porte Saint-Martin, Paris; (second) triumphal arch.
Lully: *Alceste*, French opera.

John Mayow (*1640, †1679), chemist and physiologist, carried out experiment with burning candle in bell-jar over water.
Company of New France (Canada) abolished.
Boyle verified that metals increase in weight when oxidized.
Evelyn: *Navigation and Commerce*.

Lully: *Thésée*, French opera.
Murillo: *Girl and her Duenna*, Spanish painting.
Wren began present St Paul's Cathedral; completed 1710.

Newton demonstrated experiments on static electricity (amber and glass); effect known far earlier but not scientifically explained.
George Ravenscroft's flint glass (hard,

1675 Sassbach; France fell back but was held by Condé in Alsace; Duke of Lorraine routed French at Saarbrück.
Frederick William claimed Dukedom of Liegnitz under agreement of 1537; Emperor Leopold I denied treaty and seized Liegnitz.
Turks defeated Sobieski at Lemburg.
Christian V of Denmark declared war on Sweden, captured Landskrona and recovered Scania.
Swedes invaded Brandenburg; defeated at Fahrbellin where Frederick William earned title of "Great Elector".

c. Development of Haiku poetry, still popular in Japan, largely as result of work of Matsuo Basho (*1644, †1694); style has three lines, of 5, 7, 5 syllables.

1676 Secret treaty between Charles II and Louis XIV.
War against Indians in New England ended.
Dutch fleet routed by French off Palermo; †De Ruyter.
Duke of Lorraine captured Philipsburg.
Austrian party in Spain overthrown by Don Juan.
Danish and Dutch fleets seized Gotland.
Swedes routed Danes at Lund.
Peace of Zurawno; Turkey received part of Podolia and Ukraine.
†Achmet Kiuprili.

Thomas Otway (*1652, †1685): *Don Carlos, Prince of Spain*, play in rhymed verse by Restoration dramatist.
Dryden: *Aurangzebe*, a tragedy in rhyme.
Etherege: *The Man of Mode*, a comedy.

1677 Parliament recalled; Shaftesbury and Buckingham sent to Tower.
Marriage of Mary, daughter of James, Duke of York, to William III of Orange.
French defeated William III of Orange at Cassel.
French under Créqui captured Freiburg.
Brandenburg under Great Elector captured Stettin.
Charles XI of Sweden defeated Christian V of Denmark at Landskrona.
Swedish fleet defeated Danes at Rostock.

Racine: *Phèdre*, French tragedy.
(to 1681) Aphra Behn (Mrs) (*1640, †1689): *The Rover*, a play in two parts concerning adventures of Royalists abroad.
Publication posthumously, of Spinoza's greatest work: *Ethics*.
Wycherley: *The Plain Dealer*, a comedy, published.

Jacob van Ruisdael: *The Jewish Cemetery*, Dutch painting.
Locke composed music for Shadwell's *Psyche*, earliest extant English opera.
c. Development of English crystal-glass work.

compared with soft soda-glass).
Leeuwenhoek discovered protozoa (one-celled organism) and accurately described red blood corpuscles.
Huyghens made balance-wheel and balance-spring for watches.
Nicolas Lemery, French (*1645, †1715): *Cours de Chymiée*, important chemistry textbook in modern style.
Olaus Roemer (*1644, †1710), Danish, estimated by astronomical methods the speed of light.
Royal Observatory built at Greenwich: John Flamsteed (*1646, †1719), first astronomer royal.
Ogilvie: *Book of Roads*, earliest road-atlas.

J. Smith: *The Art of Painting in Oyle*; described wood graining.
Lully: *Atys*, French opera.
c. Murillo painted two self-portraits.

Barlow invented repeating-clock.
Edmond Halley (*1656, †1742), astronomer and scientist, catalogued Southern stars.
Wiseman: *Seven Chirurgical Treatises*, works on modern surgery.
Western trading with Amoy began.
Bethlehem Hospital moved to Moorfields.

Lully: *Isis*, opera first performed in Paris.
Foundation of Innsbruck University: suspended between 1782 and 1792 and again between 1810 and 1826, in which year it was refounded.

Halley observed transit of Venus.
Leeuwenhoek observed spermatozoa in dogs and in other animals.
Incorporation of Company of Masons.
Dutch merchants hostile to William III's marriage.
Fryer gave an account of shagreen.

1678

Murder of magistrate Sir Edmund Godfrey.
Titus Oates revealed "Popish Plot"; trials of many leading Roman Catholics.
Louis XIV revealed secret treaty with Charles II (1676).
Commons impeached Danby.
Public opinion in England forced Charles II to make alliance with United Provinces against French.
Peace of Nymwegen ended Franco-Dutch war.
Rügen and Stralsund captured by Brandenburg from Sweden.

Bunyan: *The Pilgrim's Progress* (written in prison), the life of a Christian.
Dryden: *All for Love,* tragedy of Cleopatra.
La Fayette: *La Princesse de Clèves,* first French analytical novel.
Vaughan: *Thalia Rediviva.*

1679

Charles II dissolved Cavalier Parliament; Third Parliament summoned.
Bill to exclude Duke of York from Succession rejected by Lords.
Royal Assent to Habeas Corpus Act.
Parliament prorogued and then dissolved; Fourth Parliament elected.
Revolt of Covenanters crushed by Monmouth at Bothwell Bridge.
Peace signed between France and Empire at Nymwegen.
Treaty of St Germain en Laye: Louis XIV restored Cleves to Great Elector; latter restored all conquests to Sweden.
†Don Juan.
Christian V of Denmark made peace with France at Fontainebleau.
Treaty of Lund: peace between Sweden and Denmark.

Gilbert Burnet (*1643, †1715), bishop and historian, published the first volume of his *History of the Reformation in England*; vol. 2 (1681); vol. 3 (1714).

1680

Petitions sent to Charles II to assemble elected Parliament (1679): supporters called Petitioners, opponents Abhorrers, later known as "Whigs" and "Tories".
Exclusion Bill passed by Commons, rejected by Lords.
Bombay mutineers pardoned by Charles II.
Caribbean buccaneers crossed Isthmus of Darien, seized Spanish ships at Panama and scourged South Sea.

Bunyan: *Life and Death of Mr Badman,* an allegory.
Otway: *The Orphan or the Unhappy Marriage,* a tragedy.
Marvell: *Poems.*

Thomas Britton organized concerts at Clerkenwell.
Opening at Hamburg of first German opera house.
Henry Purcell (*1658, †1695), composer noted for songs and church music: music for Shakespeare's *Timon of Athens*.

Hooke expounded law "Extension of elastic string (or spring) is proportional to its tension".
G. Ceva, Italian (*1647, †1734): geometrical theorem on concurrency.
Ban on importation of French merchandise into England (lifted 1685).
Chrysanthemums reached Holland from Japan.
Roemer constructed an automatic planetarium.

Elias Ashmole (*1617, †1692) founded Ashmolean Museum Oxford.
Purcell became organist at Westminster Abbey, in succession to John Blow.
Alessandro Scarlatti (*1659, †1721): *Gli Equivoci nell' Amore*, his first opera, produced at Rome.
Lully: *Bellérophon*, French opera.

Johann Knuckel (*1630, †1703) *Ars Vitraria*, treatise on glass.
Mutiny of East India Company's garrison at Bombay, led by Robert Keigwin.
Niagara Falls discovered by Father Louis Hannepin, French Jesuit missionary explorer.
Colbert issued decree to test all merchants in commercial knowledge.
Publication posthumously of Fermat's work on analytical geometry.
Denis Papin (*1647, *c.* †1712), French physicist, invented "steam digester", enabling boiling point of water to be raised.

Present building of temple of the Queen of Heaven (founded in 12th cent.), Ningpo, erected.
Erection of Ragley Hall, Warwickshire.
Emperor K'ang Hsi developed factories for revival of art industries in China.

Clement, horologist of London, appears to have used (Hooke's?) anchor-escapement for clocks (see 1670).
Hanckwitz produced first phosphorus matches.
c. The dodo became extinct because of persecution for food and for its feathers.
Borelli: *On the Motion of Animals*, study of muscles and skeleton, published posthumously.
Newton's drawing for steam-propelled vehicle; an abortive locomotive.

1680 Swedish Estates forced *Reductio* on nobles and declared that king was subject to God alone.

1681 Charles II refused to consent to Exclusion Bill: Commons withheld supplies; dissolved.
Third Exclusion Bill: New Parliament summoned to Oxford; refused Charles' offer of Regency of William III of Orange for James; dissolved.
French successes led to formation of League to maintain treaties of Westphalia and Nymwegen.
Prestige of boyars in Russia reduced by Tsar Feodor.
Akbar, rebellious son of Aurangzeb, fled to Deccan; action made excuse for subjugation of country by Aurangzeb.

Jean Mabillon (*1632, †1707), Benedictine monk: *De Re Diplomatica*, important text on archives.
Dryden: *Absalom and Achitophel*, (part one) satirical poem; Absalom stands for Duke of Monmouth, Achitophel for Shaftesbury.
Thomas Burnet (*1635, †1715), divine: *Sacred Theory of the Earth*, entirely imaginary ideas of the earth's evolution.
Bossuet: *Discours sur L'Histoire universelle*, history with religious motif.

1682 Duke of Monmouth, illegitimate son of Charles II and Lucy Walters, made progress through England in Royal State.
Shaftesbury, charged with treason, fled the country.
Assembly of St Germain recognized right of Louis XIV to exercise "Regale" over all France; also limited papal power in France.
58,000 Huguenots "accepted" conversion.
France raised siege of Luxembourg after Anglo-Dutch protests.
Empire and Spain joined Defensive League against France.
Brandenburg's short-lived African empire set up.
†Tsar Feodor; succeeded by Ivan V and Peter as co-tsars with half-sister Sophia as Regent.
Peace between Russia and Turkey.

Bunyan: *The Holy War*.
Dryden: *The Medal, a Satire against Sedition*.
Otway: *Venice Preserved, or A Plot Discovered*, very popular play.
Foundation of Advocates Library, Edinburgh; later to become Scottish National Library.
Mrs Behn: *The City Heiress*, a comedy.
Dryden: *MacFlecknoe; Absalom and Achitophel* (part two); and *Religio Laici*.

1683 Rye House Plot to murder Charles II and James, Duke of York; leader, Rumbold, escaped to Holland; Lord William Russel and Algernon Sydney executed for complicity.
Penn's Treaty of Peace with Indians in North America.
Spain declared war on France.
France compelled Bey of Algiers to submit.

Penn: *General Description of Pennsylvania*.

c. Earliest surviving example (in England) of flocked wallpaper (Worcester).

Foundation of Comédie Française (dramatic as opposed to operatic), by amalgamation of three theatre companies.
Purcell: *Swifter, Isis, swifter flow,* musical ode.
Edinburgh assay office began to include date letters; office in use 1485.

First street lamps (oil) in London.
Work finished on Languedoc Canal, France: vast project 150 miles long (see 1664).
Charles II granted Wm. Penn patent for territory in N. America.
La Salle, French, explored Mississippi from source to mouth, claimed territory for France and named it Louisiana.
Huguenots in France excluded from trade gilds, financial posts and King's Household.
Wren elected President of the Royal Society.

Universities founded at Brest and Toulon.
Henry Somerset, first Duke of Beaufort, erected Badminton; Palladian mansion.
Lully: *Persée,* French opera.
Chelsea Hospital for disabled soldiers built by Wren; completed 1694.
Foundation of Royal Academy of Nîmes.

Halley observed comet bearing his name (also seen 1066, 1531, 1607, 1682, 1759, 1835, 1910, 1986).
"Machine of Marly", great waterwheel supplying fountains of gardens of Versailles.
Borough Charters remodelled in interests of Court.
Large weaving-mill established at Amsterdam by Pierre Baille.
Hudson Bay Company's fort at Port Nelson captured by French; returned at peace.

Sadler established, in N. London, Sadler's Wells at a mineral spring; in due course clients were entertained at theatre, opened 1765; led to foundation of opera and ballet company of that name; fell into disuse early in 20th cent.; rebuilt 1926.
Lully: *Phaëton,* French opera.

Cassini observed Zodiacal Light.
Wm. Dockwra proposed penny postal system in London: post office did *not* help him (see 1840).
Halley published first comprehensive map of winds.
Newton explained mathematical theory of tides under gravitational attraction of sun, moon and earth.

Year	History	Literature
1683	Turkey, under Kara Mustafa, accepted Hungarian suzerainty and invaded Austria; Vienna, besieged for two months, relieved by Imperial army under Sobieski; Kara Mustafa executed at Belgrade for failure.	
1684	Monmouth banished to Holland. Duke of York restored to all offices. French invaded Spanish Netherlands. Truce of Ratisbon between France and Emperor Leopold I, acting on behalf of Spain. Marriage of Louis XIV and Madame de Maintenon. Revolts of Huguenots in Cevennes led to "Dragonnades". Holy League formed against Turkey among Empire, Poland and Venice, supported by Pope Innocent XI.	Dryden: *Miscellany Poems*.
1685	†Charles II and peaceful accession of James II. Titus Oates punished for "Popish Plot". Persecution of Dissenters. Earl of Argyle rebelled in Scotland on behalf of Monmouth; executed; Monmouth landed in West; defeated at Sedgemoor; executed; "Bloody Assize" of Chief Justice Jeffreys followed. Catholics appointed as army officers regardless of Test Act; Parliament refused to repeal Test Act; prorogued. Revocation of Edict of Nantes by Louis XIV; Huguenot migration from France to British N. America and to Britain to avoid persecution; Edict of Potsdam offered Huguenots refuge in Brandenburg. Defeat of Spanish fleet by Caribbean buccaneers. French captured Genoa. †Elector Palatine.	Waller: *Divine Poems*. La Fontaine: *Philémon et Baucis*. Printing of *Reliquiae Wottonianae*, containing fifteen fine poems of Sir Henry Wotton (*1568, †1639). Gilbert Burnet began work on his *History of My Own Times* (published posthumously: 1724 vol. 1; 1734, vol. 2).
1686	James II claimed power to dispense with Parliamentary laws. Case of Godden *v.* Hales: collusive action to test validity of Crown to dispense with Test Act to permit Hales, a Catholic, to hold military commission.	Dryden: *Ode to the Memory of Mrs Anne Killigrew*, one of his finest poems.

SCIENCE

Brandenburg factories established on Gold Coast.
Dutch merchants gained entry to Canton.
Leeuwenhoek, Dutch scientist, first drew bacteria.
Wild boar became extinct in Britain.

815 Huguenot churches reduced to 245 by closure.
Pelle: *Charles II*, marble bust.
Lully: *Amadis et Gaule*, French opera.

Claude Perrault (*1613, †1688), French, devised efficient force-pump.
Charter of Massachusetts colony annulled.
Hudson Bay Company dividend 50%.
Hooke invented the heliograph.
The Bermudas became Crown Colony.

*Domenico Scarlatti (†1757), son of Alessandro (see 1679), famous for his sonatas.
Erection of Belton House, Lincolnshire, possibly by Wren; fine carvings by Grinling Gibbons (*1648, †1721).
Construction of Place des Victoires, Paris.
J. Mansart erected the Orangery at Versailles, 508 ft long.
Lully: *Roland*, French opera.

Construction of Pont Royal, Paris, finely engineered bridge.
Huguenots began silk manufacture in Britain.
c. Camera obscura (pin-hole type) developed; principle understood as early as 1000.
East India Company received new Charter from James II; outbreak of war between East India Company and Emperor Aurangzeb.
Wm. Dampier, sailor and buccaneer, visited Philippines, East Indies and New Holland.
Menno van Coehoorn (*1641, 1704): *Nieuwe Vestingbouw*, treatise on fortifications by Dutch military engineer.
Chinese ports opened to foreign merchants.
Newton discovered gravitational attraction theory associated with inverse square law.
French settled in Texas.

First mention of tune *Lilliburlero*.
A Roman Catholic was appointed Dean of Christ Church, Oxford.
(to 1696) Rebuilding of Petworth House, Sussex; 13th-cent. chapel; 19th cent. reconstructions by Solvin. Daniel Marot (†1752), French architect, designed

Halley explained trade winds, monsoons and salinity of sea.
Willoughby and Ray: *Historia Piscium*, a treatise on fishes.
All Hudson Bay Company's trading forts except Fort Nelson captured by French.
Newton: *De Motu Corporum*, first book of

	History	Literature
1686	New Court of High Commission. League of Augsburg formed by William III of Orange among Empire, Spain, Sweden, United Provinces against France. Buda captured from Turks by Imperial force under Charles of Lorraine. Denmark failed in last attempt to conquer Hamburg. Bijapur destroyed by Aurangzeb.	
1687	Protestant Clarendon replaced as Lord Deputy of Ireland by Roman Catholic Tyrconnel. Declaration of Indulgence issued by James II. Lords Lieutenants asked to supply lists of Nonconformists and Catholics suitable for election to Parliament; many resigned; Parliament dissolved. Publication of Fagel's letter in which William III and Mary declared for toleration and Tests. Turks routed by Lorraine at Mohacs; Crotia and Slavonia secured; mutiny in Turkish army and accession of Suleiman II. Diet of Pressburg recognized Hungary as hereditary possession of Habsburgs. Corinth and Athens captured by Venetians under Morosini. Aurangzeb captured Golkonda.	Dryden: *The Hind and thePanther*, allegorical poem in defence of his religion;Panther, the Church of England; Hind, the Church of Rome. Bossuet: *Funeral Oration on the Prince de Condé.* François Fénelon (*1651, †1715): *L'Education des Filles,* French pedagogical work.
1688	Second Declaration of Indulgence by James II; clergy ordered to read it; Canterbury and six other bishops declined; tried but acquitted. William III of Orange invited to restore liberties of England; landed at Torbay; James II fled. William summoned members of parliaments of Charles II, who advised a Convention Parliament. Louis XIV invaded Palatinate. Transylvania and Belgrade captured by Charles of Lorraine. †Great Elector; succeeded by Frederick III.	Mrs Behn: *Oroonoko*, popular novel. Jean de La Bruyère, French (*1645, †1696): *Les Caractères*, vivid character portrait of his contemporaries. Shadwell: *The Squire of Alsatia*, a play.

audience chamber of The Hague.
Maison de Saint Cyr founded by Madame de Maintenon for impoverished girls of high birth.

the great *Principia* (1687, *q.v.*) presented to Royal Society.

Erection of Grand Trianon, Versailles.
Lully and Colasse: *Archille et Polyxène*, French opera.
Order of Thistle revived by James VII of Scotland (James II of England).
University refounded at Bologna.
Venetian bombs wrecked Propylaea and Parthenon.
(to 1707) Erection of Chatsworth, Derbyshire, by Talman; additions by Wyatville in 1820–30; great home of Dukes of Devonshire.

Newton: *Philosophiae Naturalis Principia Mathematica* (in three books), basis of modern mathematics; laws of motion form foundation of dynamics; one of greatest mathematical works of all time.
East India Company transferred its headquarters from Surat to Bombay.
Huguenots established at Cape of Good Hope.

Erection of Wallington, Northumberland; modified in 18th cent.; Central Hall added in 19th cent.

Hudson's Bay Company's dividend maintained at 50%.
Abraham Thevart manufactured plate-glass.
Parker: *Treatise on Japanning and Varnishing*.
Destruction of Smyrna by earthquake.
William Dampier (*1652, †1715), buccaneer, explored Australia, sighted on various earlier occasions by different explorers.

1689 Convention Parliament met; Declaration of Rights; William III and Mary II proclaimed King and Queen.
James II landed in Ireland; siege of Londonderry.
Rebellion in Scotland; battle of Killiecrankie.
Secession of Non-jurors from Church of England.
Scottish Convention Parliament accepted William and Mary; abolished Episcopacy.
Toleration Act gave rebellious freedom to all who accepted 36 out of 39 Articles of Religion in Book of Common Prayer.
Louis XIV declared war against Spain and England.
Massacre at Lachine.
Alliance between Russia and Imperial forces against Turkey.
Peter I (later called the Great) of Russia assumed control of government.
Treaty of Nerchinsk between China and Russia.

Racine: *Esther*, French biblical tragedy.
John Locke (*1632, †1704): *On Civil Government*.
Shadwell: *Bury Fair*, dramatic work giving insight into customs of the times.

1690 Dissolution of Convention Parliament; election of Tory-dominated parliament.
William III crossed to Ireland to deal with revolt.
Battle of Beachy Head: French defeated English and Dutch fleets and burned Teignmouth.
Battle of Boyne: James II defeated and returned to France.
French under Luxembourg defeated Waldeck at Fleurus.
Victor Amadeus of Savoy defeated by French under Catinat at Staffarda.
Belgrade, Nish and Widdin recaptured by Mustafa Kiuprili.
Mogul conquests in Southern India complete except for fort of Jinji.

John Locke: *Essay concerning Human Understanding*, enquiry into the essence of the intellect, applying Baconian ideas.
Antoine Furetière, French lexicographer: *Dictionaire universel*.
Nathaniel Lee: *Massacre of St Bartholomew*, a play. *Worcester Postman*, later *Borrow's Worcester Journal* first weekly English provincial paper issued; oldest in the world to be in continuous production.

1691 Viscount Preston convicted of plotting against Government.
Battle of Aughrim; General Ginkel defeated Jacobites in Ireland.

Racine: *Athalie*, a biblical tragedy.
Kasper Stieler (*1632, †1707): *Der Teutschen Sprache Stammbaum und Fortwachs*, important work on German language.

c. Purcell: *Dido and Aeneas*, first English opera, produced.
Meindert Hobbema (*1638, †1709): *The Avenue, Middleharnis*, Dutch landscape painting.
Work begun on Kensington Palace, London.
Order of Thistle again dormant because of Catholic connections.

Hudson's Bay Company's dividend fell to 25%.
Mutiny Act: Army legalized annually.
Bill of Rights completed work begun by Magna Carta (1215).
Foundation of English factory at Calcutta.
Abolition of duty on corn exported from England.
Issue of gun-money by James II; debased coins partly minted from discarded cannon.
William III built first Devonport naval dockyard.

Hobbema: *The Mill*, Dutch painting. *c.* Clarinet probably developed by Denner of Nuremburg from early instrument of simple construction (the chalumeau).
c. M. A. Charpentier: *The Denial of St Peter*, French oratorio.
Purcell: *Diocletian*, an opera.
Erection of present Stamford Hall, Leicestershire, begun.

Huyghens: *Traité de la Lumière*, treatise on study of light (theory of undulation) published at Leyden (written 1678).
Calico (name derived from Calicut, India) printing introduced into Britain from France.
Hudson Bay Company's stock trebled without any call being made on shareholders.
Foundation of mathematical academy at Bologna.
East India Co. set up factory at Calcutta (see 1689).
Introduction of Land Tax.
Second Turnpike Act applied for.
c. Turnip first cultivated in England.

c. Fischer von Erlach began building great Schönbrunn Palace, Vienna.
(to 1697) Villa Palmieri at San Domenico, Renaissance style.

J.P.s appointed Surveyors of Highways for each parish to levy fines for failure to keep up roads and for Highway Rate to be charged on each parish.

	History	Literature
1691	Siege of Limerick (begun 1690) successful. Test of Limerick ended revolt in Ireland. Mons captured by French. Nice taken from Savoy by French under Catinat. Mustafa Kiuprili invaded Hungary; defeated and killed Margrave of Baden at Szcelankemen; Transylvania conquered by Imperial forces.	Issue of the *Compleat Library*, one of the first periodicals to be published in Britain.
1692	Duke of Marlborough (*1650, †1722), suspected of treason, dismissed. Massacre of Glencoe. Louis XIV and James II planned invasion of England; French fleet utterly defeated at La Hogue. French captured Namur and defeated William II at Steinkirk. Edict of Toleration for Catholics in China.	William Congreve (*1669, †1729): *Incognito*, his first literary work, a novel.
1693	Louis XIV reconciled with Papacy largely through efforts of his wife, Madame de Maintenon. William III defeated at Neerwinden by Luxembourg. Victor Amadeus of Savoy defeated by French under Catinat at Marsiglia. Tourville captured greater part of Smyrna fleet off Lagos; serious blow to British shipping.	Congreve: *The Old Bachelor*, first play of brilliant Restoration dramatist. Locke advocated use of Direct Method of learning foreign language; now fairly widely practised.
1694	Marlborough restored to employment. Triennial Act limited duration of Parliament to three years. †Mary II, wife of William III. Failure of British naval attack on Brest blamed on Marlborough's treachery. Barcelona saved from French attack under Noailles by English fleet.	Congreve: *The Double Dealer*, a comedy. *Dictionnaire de L'Académie française*, first edition of major work of the French Academy. Dryden: *Love Triumphant*, tragi-comedy.
1695	Namur recaptured from French by William III; regarded as his finest military achievement. Russia at war with Turkey; Peter the Great built fleet for attack on Azoff.	Congreve: *Love for Love*, a comedy. Leibnitz: *New System of Nature*. Freedom of Press established by non-renewal of Licensing Act.

Purcell: *King Arthur*, an opera; libretto by Dryden.
Andreas Schlüter: relief decoration of Krasinski Palace, Warsaw.
Andreas Werkmeister solved the problem, in Europe, of the 12 equal temperament semi-tones in one octave (also see 1593).

Plymouth Colony absorbed by Massachusetts.
Creation of another East India Co. which amalgamated with first in 1708.
c. John Clayton demonstrated lighting power of coal gas (see 1792).

Dyrham Park, Gloucestershire, built for Blathwayt, Secretary of State to William III; frontage by Talman *c.* 1700.
Purcell: *The Libertine*, containing the song *Nymphs and Shepherds*.

Lloyd's coffee-house established as headquarters of marine insurance.
Bank, later known as Coutts and Co., first opened; in the Strand.
Earthquake in Jamaica (7th July).
Nehemiah Grew (*1641, †1712): *Anatomy of Plants*, botanical work.

Erection, to 1706, *q.v.*, gilded dome of Hôtel des Invalides, Paris, for pensioners, and Eglise Royale, by Mansart.
Purcell: *The Fairy Queen*, an opera.
Erection of Fenton House, London.
Discovery of Alfred jewel at Athelney.

Wallis: *Algebra*; used notation of fluxions devised by Newton.
National Debt originated in loan raised by Montagu.
East India Company obtained new Charter as result of bribery.
Foundation of Kingston, Jamaica.

University of Halle founded by Frederick III of Brandenburg.
Purcell: *Jubilate* and *Te Deum*, religious music.
Redesigning of Kimbolton Castle, Huntingdonshire; Tudor mansion.

Rudolf Camerarius, German botanist (*1665, †1721), published work explaining plant sexes.
Bank of England established, with government backing, by Wm. Paterson.
Bribery scandal of East India Company's new Charter exposed.
Indian trade thrown open to all English subjects.
Opening of Chelsea Royal Hospital for invalid soldiers.

Bishop Ken: *Awake, my Soul*, a hymn.
First public concert in Edinburgh.
Wren designed Morden College, Blackheath.
Purcell: *Indian Queen*, music for the play.

Grew isolated magnesium sulphate (Epsom salts) from North Downs springs.
Brown glaze stoneware made at Nottingham by John Morley.
Foundation of Academy of Sciences, Naples.

LITERATURE

	History	Literature
1695		
1696	New Act regulated Treason Trials in England; improved conditions for accused. Plot by Sir George Barclay to murder William III discovered. Treaty of Turin between Savoy and France; French possession of Nice, Savoy, Casale and Pinerolo confirmed. William III accepted mediation in war of Grand Alliance offered by Sweden. †Jan Sobieski of Poland; weakened French influence there. Surrender of Turkish Azoff to Russians. †Ivan V left Peter the Great as sole Tsar.	John Aubrey (*1626, †1697), English antiquary: *Miscellanies*. Sir John Vanbrugh (*1664 †1726): *The Relapse*, a riotous comedy by famous Restoration dramatist. Colley Cibber (*1671, †1757): *Love's Last Shift*, a comedy.
1697	Execution of Sir John Fenwick for treason. Capture of Cartagena by Caribbean buccaneers: final event in their story. French under Vendôme captured Barcelona. Treaty of Ryswick signed between France and Grand Alliance. Frederick Augustus of Saxony elected King Augustus II of Poland. Accession of Charles XII of Sweden; declared of age to rule. Peter the Great, travelling as "Peter Michailoff", worked in dockyards of Saardam and Deptford. Mustafa II attacked Transylvania; routed at Zenta.	Congreve: *The Mourning Bride*, a play. Vanbrugh: *The Provok'd Wife*, a play; a fine study of an ill-treated wife. Pierre Bayle (*1647, †1706): *Dictionnaire historique et critique*, major work of French philosopher. Charles Perrault (*1628, †1703): *Contes du Temps Passé*, immortal French fairy-tales. Dryden: *Alexander's Feast*.
1698	Attempts by Scots to establish settlements on Isthmus of Darien; failed. First Partition Treaty: England, United Provinces, France and Empire agreed on Spanish succession and partitioned Spanish Empire. Charles II of Spain made his first will, leaving territories to infant Electoral Prince of Bavaria. Revolt of Streltsi, Praetorian Guard of nobles founded by Ivan the Terrible; Streltsi exterminated.	Foundation of S.P.C.K. (Society for Promoting Christian Knowledge) with intention of cultivating literacy and scriptural knowledge of children.

Act of Parliament established the Bank of Scotland.
Davis, a pirate, appears to have discovered Easter Island.

Henry Winstanley built first Eddystone Lighthouse.
New coinage issued under management of Somers, Montagu, Locke and Newton.
Academy of Arts founded at Berlin.
(to 1704) Carshalton House, Surrey erected.

Jacques B. Bernoulli (*1654, †1705), proposed calculus of variations: brachistochrone problem, path of quickest descent.
Fifty Russian youths sent to study shipbuilding, fortifications and languages in England, Holland and Venice.
Quaker workhouse set up at Bristol.
Establishment of Board of Trade.
Introduction of Exchequer Bill.
Foundation of first Insurance Company in England (for property).
Window tax introduced in England; abolished 1851.

Silver articles ordered to be manufactured at Britannia standard (11 oz, 10 dwt. = 1lb troy): regulation introduced to stop the melting down of silver coins.
Gobelin factory exclusively produced tapestries from this date.
Grinling Gibbons carved stalls and Mayor's Chair, St Paul's Cathedral, London.
Whitehall Palace burned down, with exception of banqueting hall.

Abraham Demoivre (*1667 †1754) mathematician, elected F.R.S.; during his career he produced fundamental theorem on complex numbers and was arbiter in wrangle between Newton and Leibnitz about invention of calculus.
Parliament withdrew trading monopoly of Royal African Company of England.
All Hudson Bay Company's forts, except Fort Albany, ceded to France.
Earliest date for which U.K. National Debt figures are known.

Schülter built Royal Palace, Berlin, for Frederick I.
Opening of Mrs White's Chocolate House, which later became White's famous club.
Russians ordered not to wear beards.
Erection of Bramham Park, Yorkshire; possesses fine gardens.

Newton calculated speed of sound.
First insurance company used firemen.
Thos. Savery made practical steam engine, for raising water, using principle of atmospheric pressure thrusting after steam was condensed (not force of expanding steam, as in later engines).
New East India Trading Company, called General Society, founded in England; members traded as individuals, not as a company.

1699

Dutch Guards sent home from England; William III's grants of land to Dutch favourites attacked; cancelled in 1770.
Accession of Frederick IV to Danish throne.
Denmark, Russia and Poland in alliance against Sweden.
Treaty of Carlowitz ended war between Holy League and Turkey.

George Farquhar (*1678, †1707): *Love and a Bottle*, Restoration comedy.
Fénelon: *Télémaque*, a novel full of satire and political ideas written by a tutor for the heir to the French throne.
Dryden: *Fables, Ancient and Modern*, paraphrases.

1700

Second Partition Treaty, on Spanish question, between William III and Louis XIV.
†Duke of Gloucester, only surviving child of Anne, created Succession problem in England.
Second will of Charles II of Spain left possessions to Philip of Anjou, grandson of Louis XIV.
†Charles II of Spain; accession of Philip of Anjou as Philip V in contravention of Second Partition Treaty.
Kontractat between Emperor Leopold I and Frederick III of Brandenburg against France in Spanish succession problem.
Peace between Peter the Great and Turkey.
State control over Church in Russia strengthened by abolition of Patriarchate.
Poland invaded Swedish Riga and Denmark invaded Schleswig.
Charles XII of Sweden sailed against Copenhagen.
Denmark withdrew from alliance with Poland and Russia; made Peace of Travendal with Sweden.
Swedes defeated Russians at Narva.

Congreve: *The Way of the World*, a comedy.
Samuel Sewall (*1652, †1730): *Selling of Joseph*, American condemnation of slavery.
Tom Brown (*1663 †1704): *Amusements*.
c. Development of *Kabuki Shibai*, popular theatre, as opposed to the more intellectual *No Shibai* in Japan.

1701

Act of Settlement established Hanoverian and Protestant Succession.
Tory ministers impeached Whig ministers.
†James II of England; Louis XIV recognized "James III" contrary to Treaty of Ryswick.
Philip of Anjou entered Madrid as Philip V of Spain.

Foundation of Biblioteca Casanatense, Rome.
Yale College Library established, U.S.A.
Sir Richard Steele (*1672, †1729): (i) *The Christian Hero*, arguing that religious principles only will help to create great men; (ii) *The Funeral*, a comedy, first produced.
Arai Hakuseki (*1675, †1725): *Hankampu*, history of the noble families of Japan from 1600 onwards.

(to 1707) de Cotte and J. Mansart built the Royal Chapel, Versailles.
Feuillet: *Choréographie*.
(to 1726) Castle Howard, Yorkshire, erected to design of Vanbrugh.

Dampier appointed captain of H.M.S. *Roebuck*; sent to explore New Holland by way of Cape of Good Hope.
Russian calendar reformed by Peter the Great.
c. Newton appointed Master of the Mint to solve government currency problem (see 1697).
Billingsgate became a market (see 1588).

Peter the Great issued ordinances regarding types of clothes which Russians might wear.
Sir Robert Bruce Cotton's (*1571 †1631) collection of MSS and early coins given to nation; now in British Museum.
Berlin Royal Academy founded.
Gunby Hall, Lincolnshire, built.
Palace of Forty Pillars, Isfahan, redesigned.
c. The horn came into use in orchestras; perfected in France.
c. Establishment of string orchestras.
c. First appearance of the commode (chest of drawers).

Francis Moore (*1657, †1715): *Vox Stellarum*, later published as *Old Moore's Almanack*.
Howland Great Wet Dock, Rotherhythe, commenced.
Dampier visited New Guinea after New Holland; on return voyage wrecked off Ascension Island.
c. Earliest accurate metal-working lathes.
Leibnitz founded Prussian Akademie der Wissenchaften, Berlin.
c. First bonded warehouses in Britain; first intended to hold oriental silks awaiting re-export.

Foundation of Collegiate School of America, at Saybrook; later Yale University (see 1718).
University of Venice founded.
Erection of Mompesson House, Salisbury; Queen Anne town house.
Henry Playford: *Musical Companion*; by musical publisher who did much to promote Catch Clubs.

Quaker workhouse set up in Clerkenwell.
Antoine Cadillac founded settlement at Detroit (name is corruption of Ville d'Etroit).
Jethro Tull (*1674, †1741), agricultural reformer, invented horse-drawn drill for planting seeds in rows.
Newton thought of idea of using sextant for measuring altitudes of stars at sea (see 1731).

Year	History	Literature
1701	France seized Barrier fortresses in Spanish Netherlands. Alliance of United Provinces and Empire against France. Sweden invaded Polish Courland. Frederick III of Brandenburg crowned himself King of Prussia at Königsberg.	
1702	William III dismissed Tory ministers. Outbreak of War of Spanish Succession. †William III, following fall from a horse; accession of Anne. English Parliament increased Army and Navy to 40,000 men each. Failure of English attack on Cadiz; Franco-Spanish fleet routed at Vigo Bay. Battles of Cremona, Luzzara, Friedlingen. Russians defeated Swedes at Errestfer. Swedes entered Warsaw; deposed Augustus II; entered Cracow.	*The Daily Courant,* first English daily newspaper in London, issued. Clarendon's *History of the Rebellion and Civil Wars in England* published posthumously. J. Kersey: *New English Dictionary.* Brown: *Letters from the Dead.* Nicholas Rowe (*1674 †1718): *Tamerlane,* "key-tragedy".
1703	Anglo-Portuguese Methuen Treaty. Charles XII routed Saxons at Pultusk; captured Thorn.	Ellis Wynne (*1671, †1734): *Y Bardd Cwsc* (Visions of the Sleeping Bard), life of Wales at close of 17th cent. First Russian newspaper, *Vyedomosti,* issued.
1704	Bill of Security reserved to Scottish Parliament right to refuse to recognize Successor named by England. British fleet captured Gibraltar. British and allied forces under Marlborough defeated French at Blenheim. Assembly in Warsaw deposed Augustus II and elected Stanislaus Lesczinski King of Poland. Russia secured Ingria by capturing Dorpat and Narva.	Jonathan Swift (*1667, 1745): (i) *The Battle of the Books,* literary controversy; (ii) *A Tale of a Tub,* satire on excesses in religion. *Weekly Review,* first American newspaper, started by Defoe at Boston. Jean-François Regnard (*1655, †1709): *Les Folies amoureuses,* French comedy of manners. First publication of *Vossiche Zeitung* in Berlin; last edition in 1933.
1705	Further meeting of Commissioners to attempt Union between England and Scotland. †Emperor Leopold I; accession of Joseph I.	Bernard de Mandeville (*1670, †1773): *The Grumbling Hive,* satirical verse on human greed. John Philips (*1676, †1709): *The Splendid Shilling* published; burlesque poem.

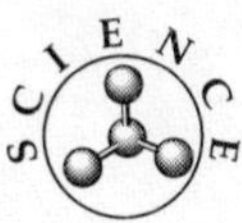

John Arbuthnot (*1667, †1735): *Essay on the Usefulness of Mathematical Learning.*

Early English form of pantomime at Drury Lane: pantomime in various forms dates back over 2,000 years.
Haymarket Theatre first opened.
(to 1713) Erection of Church of St Peter, Vienna.
Jesuit College established at Breslau; later university (see 1811).

Halley's chart of magnetic declination for world.
Asiento Guinea Co. created to develop Slave Trade between Africa and America.
French settled in Alabama.
Stahl propounded phlogiston theory of combustion; refuted by Lavoisier in 1774.
Abolition of serfdom in Denmark.

Schlüter: monument to the Great Elector, in Berlin.
Work begun on Buckingham Palace for the then Duke of Buckingham; George III purchased it in 1762 (also see 1825).
Order of the Thistle revived in Scotland by Queen Anne.

Peter the Great founded St Petersburg; fortified Kronstadt to defend city.
First Eddystone lighthouse destroyed by storm.
Newton became President of the Royal Society (until his death).

Jeremiah Clarke (*1673, †1707) became organist at Chapel Royal.
Commencement of influence of Beau Nash at Bath.
University of Mantua founded.
(to 1715) Erection of Wotton House, Buckinghamshire; remodelled 1820.
George Frideric Handel (*1685, †1759), German-born composer who became British: *St John Passion.*

Newton: *Opticks*, one of his great works; in which he enunciated corpuscular theory of light.
Use of jewelled bearings for watches.
Newcomen built his first steam engine.
Development of the landau.
Queen Anne's Bounty introduced for relief of impoverished clergymen.
Leibnitz: *Nouveaux Essais sur l'Entendement humain*, principal work of German philosopher.
John Harris (*c.* *1667, †1719): *Lexicon technicum*, first alphabetical encyclopaedia.

Handel: *Almira*, an opera.
Opening of His Majesty's Theatre, London; new building 1897.
(to 1722) Vanbrugh built Blenheim Palace; baroque style; presented to Marlborough.

Halley predicted return of his comet in 1758 (see 1682).
Introduction of ship's wheel to replace tiller.
Thomas Newcomen (*1663, †1729)

Year	History	Literature
1705	Revolt of Camisards suppressed by Louis XIV.	
1706	French forces routed by Allies under Marlborough at Ramilies. French opened Peace negotiations. Swedes invaded Saxony; forced latter to renounce Russian alliance.	Farquhar: *The Beaux' Stratagem* and *The Recruiting Officer*, comedies. Evelyn's *Diary* ended. Rowe: *Ulysses*, a play, produced.
1707	Act of Union united Scottish and English Parliaments; Scotland ceased having separate Great Seal. Perpetual Alliance of Sweden and Prussia; latter refused to join Sweden in Great Northern War. †Aurangzeb at Ahmadnagar; last of great Mogul rulers.	Edward Lhuyd (*1660, †1709): *Archaeologia Britannica*, information relating to Celtic languages. Alain René Lesage (*1668, †1747): (i) *Le Diable boiteux*, French novel of manners; (ii) *Crispin rival de son Maître*, a comedy.
1708	Robert Walpole (*1676, †1745) appointed Secretary of War. Marlborough and Eugene routed French at Oudenarde. Old Pretender made abortive expedition to Scotland. Peter the Great divided Russia into eight regional governments.	Regnard: *Le Légataire universel*, a comedy describing the social corruption of his day. Bernard de Montfaucon (*1655, †1741): *Palaeographica Graeca*, study of ancient Greek writings. Philips: *Cyder*, blank verse.
1709	Marlborough and Eugene captured Tournai and defeated French army at Malplaquet. Failure of French peace proposals at The Hague. Charles XII of Sweden routed by Peter the Great at Poltava; Denmark, Saxony, Russia form Second Coalition against Sweden.	Lesage: *Turcaret*, a play of manners; bitter attack on financiers and "les nouveaux riches". Alexander Pope (*1688, †1744): *Pastorals*; early work of the great poet published; said to have been written when he was 16. Steele launched *The Tatler* a paper giving news and essays.
1710	Impeachment of Dr Sacheverell; Tory reaction and riots; Whig ministry dismissed; replaced by Tories under Harley and St. John. Jansenist centre at Porte Royal attacked and nuns expelled. Peace negotiations between France and Allies failed. Tallin (Reval) annexed by Peter the Great; conquest of Livonia completed.	First English Copyright Act came into force. Congreve: *Works*, including poems. Berkeley: *Treatise on the Principles of Human Knowledge*, philosophical work.

Ange-Jacques Gabriel designed École Militaire, Paris.

inventor, made steam engine by separating the boiler and the cylinder; improvement on Savery's (1698, *q.v.*).

Filippo Juvarra began building La Superga, domed church on square plan at Turin.
Completion of l'Hôtel des Invalides, Paris.

Henry Mill invented carriage springs.
Abruzzi destroyed by earthquake.
First insurance company (see 1696) adopted name, *Hand-in-Hand* (to 1905).
Rudyerd's Eddystone lighthouse (the second) begun; completed 1709; destroyed 1755.

(to 1717) Sir James Thornhill created Painted Hall, Greenwich; excellent example of baroque work.
Isaac Watts (*1674, †1748): *Hymns and Spiritual Songs*.
Gottfried Silbermann, best-known of family of organ builders, constructed his first organ.

Denis Papin invented a steamboat; destroyed by a mob.
Cornelius Meyer and his son drained the Pontine Marshes; works destroyed by local inhabitants.
Last eruption of Mt Fujiyama.

New figures of Gog and Magog (Guildhall) to replace earlier ones destroyed in Great Fire.
First permanent German theatre founded in Vienna.
Carlyle's House, Chelsea, built; home of Thos. and Jane Carlyle.

Wall compared lightning with electric spark.
Amalgamation of New East India Co. and old Company into single Trading Company.
Royal African Co. of England declared insolvent; traded until 1750.
Early excavations at Pompeii and Herculaneum (see 1748).

Bartolomeo Cristofori of Florence (*1655, †1731) produced first piano; two of his instruments still exist.
The Old Rectory, Epworth, home of John and Charles Wesley, erected.
Work begun on St Margaret's Abbey Church, Brevnov, near Prague.
Peter the Great built Peterhof, oldest of the summer palaces of the tsars.
False hips introduced as women's fashion.

Secrets of Chinese porcelain discovered at Dresden by Johann Böttger (*1682 †1719).
Abraham Darby produced coke and used it to smelt iron ore in England.
Postage rates in England regulated by mileage.
George Berkeley (*1685, †1753): *New Theory of Vision*; ideas offered to our senses are sole reality.
Johann Maria Farine (*1685, †1766), Italian, produced eau-de-cologne in the city of that name.

Foundation of University of Lyons.
Kaibara Yekken (*1630, †1714): *Dojikun*, Japanese treatise on education.
Completion of the present St. Paul's Cathedral, London.
Establishment of Academy of Ancient Music, London; continued until 1792.
Handel became Kapellmeister to Elector of Hanover.

First successful attempts to produce Chinese hard-paste porcelain in England.
Formation of English South Sea Trading Co.
Three-colour printing invented by J. C. Le Blon (*1667, †1741).
c. Bartholomeo de Gusmão designed a hot-hair balloon (impracticable).
Leibnitz: *Theodicée*, philosophical work (see 1714).

1711 Marlborough dismissed from Command by Tory Government.
Guiscard's attempt to assassinate Harley at Privy Council meeting.
Act against occasional conformity passed by creation of twelve peers.
Walpole imprisoned in Tower on charge of peculation.
†Louis the Dauphin, his heir (Duke of Burgundy), the Duchess and their eldest son within twelve months.
†Emperor Joseph I; accession of Archduke Charles, claimant to Spanish throne; balance of power in Europe endangered.
Establishment of Administrative Senate in Russia.
Turkey declared war on Russia; Russians defeated at River Pruth; Treaty of Pruth forced Peter the Great to return Azoff and withdraw from Poland.

Pope: *Essay on Criticism*, statement in verse of principles in literature.
Joseph Addison (*1672, †1719) founded *The Spectator*, a daily paper famous for its essays and papers referring to Sir Roger de Coverley, a genial country squire.
Swift: *Conduct of the Allies*, attacking war policy of Whigs.

1712 Marlborough replaced as Com. in Chief by Ormonde, a Jacobite.
Separate truce made between England and France; troops withdrawn from Prince Eugene.
Franco-Dutch truce.
Denmark seized Bremen and Verden from Sweden.
Slave revolt in New York.

Pope: *The Rape of the Lock*, mock-heroic poem inspired by cutting of lock of hair from head of Miss Fermor by Lord Petre.
Arbuthnot: *History of John Bull*, satire in prose with John Bull, Lewis Baboon of France and Lord Strutt of Spain as characters.

1713 Harley and St John plotted for accession of Old Pretender.
Treaty of Utrecht among England, France and Holland ended War of Spanish Succession in favour of Philip V.
Renewal of Russo-Turkish war: Maritime powers intervened: Peace of Adrianople settled Russo-Turkish differences.
Great Northern War: Swedes invaded Denmark, defeated at Oldenburg; Russians and Saxons captured Stettin.
Accession of Frederick William I of Prussia.

Clement XI condemned Jansenist *Moral Reflections* in Bull *Unigenitus*.
Anthony Hamilton (*1646, †1720): *Memoirs of Count de Gramont*, story of French nobleman in reign of Louis XIV.
Addison: *Cato*, a classical tragedy showing the last Roman republican.

Early reference to *rondo*, music in form ABACA, in work of Jeremiah Clarke for harpsichord.
London Academy of Arts established under Sir Godfrey Kneller.
(to 1721) Sir William Carey built Antony House, Cornwall; unaltered since.
Work begun on Birmingham Cathedral by Thomas Archer.
Handel: *Rinaldo*, an opera, written during visit to London.
Queen Anne established Ascot races.

Newcomen constructed successful steam engine for pumping water (see 1698, 1705); in use for 60 years.
John Shore, trumpeter at Chapel Royal, invented tuning fork.
South Sea Co. took up £9,000,000 of uncovered portion of National Debt.
J. J. Partels made first mine ventilator.
Leibnitz first president of Berlin Academy of Sciences.

Concerto (in classic form) gained recognition in twelve *Concerti Grossi*, by Corelli; J. S. Bach composed in this style; later concertos (e.g. Beethoven, Mendelssohn) more romantic and massive.
Handel returned to England and produced operas: (i) *Il pastor fido;* (ii) *Teseo*.
University of Madrid founded.

Cultivation of East Friesland moorlands commenced.
Newspaper Stamp Act passed in England; duty on advertisements introduced.
Last English execution for witchcraft.
John James (*1672, †1751), great silversmith, began his career.

†Arcangelo Corelli (*1653), great Italian violinist.
Lucas von Hildebrandt (*1668, †1745) built Kinsky Palace, Vienna.
Scarlatti: *St Francis Neri*, oratorio on man responsible for oratorio.
Handel: *Te Deum* for Peace of Utrecht.

South Sea Co. took over whole National Debt, receiving 8% interest and monopoly of all extra-European trade from Government.
Peter the Great founded naval harbour at Tallinn (Reval).
Foundation of Spanish Academy of Sciences.
Posthumous publication of *De Arte conjectandi*, by Jacques Bernouilli, in which his numbers appeared and in which first proof of binomial theorem was given.

LITERATURE

	History	Literature
1714	Harley dismissed from office; succeeded by Shrewsbury; Hanoverian Succession assured. †Electress Sophia of Hanover; Electoral Prince George invited to England; †Queen Anne; end of Stuart dynasty; accession of George I. Treaty of Rastadt between France and Austira; Treaty of Baden between France and Empire; ended War of Spanish Succession. Marriage of Philip V of Spain and Elizabeth Farenese. Turkey confirmed Peace of Carlowitz with Poland. Charles XII of Sweden deported from Sultan's territory; returned to Sweden. Tripoli gained independence from Turkey. Philip V destroyed Catalonian political liberties. Great Northern War; Swedes routed by Russians at Storkyro; Russia secured Finland.	John Gay (*1685, †1732): *Shepherd's Week*, a pastoral. James Quin (*1693, †1766), great actor, first appeared on stage, at Dublin. Rowe: *Jane Shore* produced at Drury Lane. Mandeville: *Fable of the Bees* (1st part), based on verse, *The Grumbling Hive* (see 1705); (2nd part, 1723); political satire.
1715	St John and Ormonde retired to France; attainted of Treason; Harley impeached and committed to Tower. Walpole appointed Chancellor of Exchequer. Jacobite rebellion in North; defeated at Preston. Habeas Corpus Act suspended; Riot Act passed. †Louis XIV; accession of Louis XV, a minor; Orléans Regent. Third Coalition against Sweden; Allies captured Stralsund. Spanish Netherlands (Belgium) ceded to Emperor Charles VI. Turks renewed war against Empire; recaptured Morea from Venice.	Pope: translation of Homer's *Iliad* (to 1720), in poetic form. Lesage: *Gil Blas* (to 1735), a novel full of adventures, with Spain as the scene. Matthew Prior (*1664, †1721): *Solomon, or the Vanity of the World*, a poem. Rowe: *Lady Jane Grey*, a play, produced. Gay: *What d'ye Call It*, his first play, a satirical farce.
1716	Septennial Act limiting life of Parliament to seven years (1911). Old Pretender landed in Scotland; joined Earl of Mar; retired. Leaders of 1715 revolt in England executed.	*William Williams of Pantycelyn, Welsh hymn writer; author of *Guide me, O thou great Redeemer*. Gay: *Trivia*, poem on London. Hakuseki: *Ori-Taku-Shiba*, Japanese autobiography.

Schism Act prevented Dissenters from being schoolmasters in England unless licensed by Bishop.
Musical *Inventions*, short suite, by Bonparti; term later used by J. S. Bach in slightly different way.
Handel: *Silla*, an opera, and *Water Music*.
*Carl Philip Emanuel Bach (†1788, Hamburg) at Weimar; son of J. S. Bach; originated sonata and symphony forms of composition, in contrast to suite and fugue.
Important concerts at Hickford's Room, Piccadilly.
Foundation of Worcester College, Oxford, by Sir Thos. Cookes.
(to 1720) John Greame built Sewerby Hall, Yorkshire.
Giovanni Buononcini (*1672, †1750): *Astarte*, Italian opera.
Gibbons became master wood-carver to George I.

Daniel Gabriel Fahrenheit, German (*1688, †1736): mercury thermometer with temperature scale: 32° freezing point, 212° boiling point, of water.
Publication of works of Eustachio, Italian anatomist (see 1552), some of which concerned the tube, now bearing his name, connecting ear and mouth.
Leibnitz: *Monadologie*, philosophy of the "monad" and the "pre-established harmony" of the universe.
Mill took out patent for a typewriter but venture was unsuccessful.
Parliament offered reward of £20,000 to first explorer who discovered North West Passage; many attempts made, some ending in tragedy; passage actually navigated by Amundsen (1903–5).

Watts wrote first children's hymnal.
Nicholas Hawksmoor designed quadrangle of All Souls College, Oxford.
Von Erlach began Karlskirke, Vienna.
Palladio's *Architecture* translated into English (see 1570).
c. Thos. Archer designed Hale Park, Hampshire; modified 1770.
Stradivarius made the Alard, one of his best-known violins.
Handel: *Amadigi*, an opera.

Brook Taylor (*1685, †1731): *Methodus incrementorum directa et inversa*, calculus of finite differences.
Magnetic iron-filing maps known.
East India Co. set up trading post at Canton.
First Liverpool Dock opened.
Thos. Doggett awarded coat and badge for waterman's race; continued annually.
George Graham designed compensating pendulum for clocks.
John Lethbridge's practical leather diving equipment.

Couperin: *Art de toucher le Clavecin*, keyboard technique.
G. M. Oppenord (*1672, †1742) developed rococo design; used for French regent's palace.
Erection of Beningbrough Hall, Yorkshire; possibly by Giacomo Leoni.

East India Co. obtained trading concessions from Mogul Empire.
Court set up in France to try dishonest financiers during crisis.
John Law, Scottish exile, founded joint-stock bank in Paris.

LITERATURE

	History	Literature
1716	Second visit of Peter the Great to Western Europe (to 1717). Allies captured Wismar from Sweden. Turks routed by Prince Eugene at Peterwardein. Emperor K'ang Hsi of China repealed Edict of Toleration and prohibited Christian teaching.	Publication of great K'ang Hsi dictionary of 40,000 characters, of which many were obsolete or rare (Chinese).
1717	Townsend, Walpole and Pulteney forced to leave Government; Ministry of Stanhope. Harley tried and acquitted. Triple Alliance of Britain, France and Holland. Treaty of Amsterdam; provided for French mediation in Great Northern, War; entry of Russia into general European system. Spaniards seized Sardinia. Austrians defeated Turks at Belgrade. Cardinal Alberoni urged Sweden to invade Britain in Jacobite interests.	Cardinal de Retz, French (*1614, †1679): *Mémoires*, memoirs covering period of the Fronde. Viscount Henry St J. Bolingbroke (*1678, †1751): *Letter to Sir Wm. Wyndham.* Publication of collection of Pope's poems, including *Eloise to Abelard.* *Three Hours after Marriage*, a comedy written by Gay and Pope.
1718	Occasional Conformity and Schism Acts repealed. Quadruple Alliance: Britain, France, Austria and Holland against Spain. British fleet routed Spaniards off Cape Passaro. Bahamas pirates suppressed. Abolition of Six Councils for State Affairs in France. Aland Conference: peace negotiations between Russia and Sweden; failed. Sweden attacked Norway; Charles XII killed in trenches at Friedrichshall. Spain captured Sicily. Treaty of Passarowitz ended Austro-Turkish war; marked zenith of territorial expansion of Habsburgs.	Voltaire (pseudonym of François-Marie Arouet) (*1694, †1778): *Oedipe*, French tragedy written in the Bastille, published. Cibber: *The Nonjuror*, play directed against Jacobites. Allan Ramsay (*1686, †1758), Scottish poet, extended ancient poem *Christ's Kirk on the Green*.
1719	Peerage Bill restricting number of peers: passed by Lords, rejected by Commons. Statute enabling English Parliament to legislate for Ireland.	Daniel Defoe (*1661, †1731): *Robinson Crusoe*, a novel based on adventures of Alexander Selkirk on the Island of Juan Fernandez.

Burlington House, London, rebuilt.
Japan relaxed interdict against Western culture.
(to 1740) John Aislabie laid out Studley Royal Gardens, Yorkshire.

French constructed naval base at Louisburg, Cape Breton.
Homann published World Atlas.
Mineral waters discovered at Cheltenham.
Royal Regiment of Artillery founded.

School attendance made compulsory in Prussia.
Mother Grand Lodge of Freemasonry inaugurated in London.
Antoine Watteau (*1684, †1721): *Setting Sail for Cythera*, French painting by artist famous for scenes of revelry.
Refounding of Society of Antiquaries (see 1572).
James Gibbs commenced work on St Mary-le-Strand, London.
Will of Sir George Downing provided for a college at Cambridge (see 1800).
Erection of Lockley's Hertfordshire; brick mansion.
J. S. Bach: 46 organ chorales collected in *Orgelbüchlein*.

Lady Mary Wortley Montagu (*1690, †1762) introduced practice of inoculation against smallpox into England.
Law founded French Mississippi Co. with monopoly of trade with Louisiana.
Prussian colonies in Africa sold to Dutch.
Value of golden guinea fixed at 21*s*.

Early Georgian façade of cut and moulded brick at Willmer House, Surrey.
Colin Campbell designed Ebberston Hall, Yorkshire; Palladian style.
Jacob Sutton made great brass Eagle Lectern of St Paul's, London.
Erection of Elysée, Paris.
Watteau: *Fête in a Park*, French painting.
Foundation of London Society of Antiquaries.
Collegiate School of America transferred to present site at New Haven; renamed Yale University in recognition of benefactor, Elihu Yale.

Halley discovered true motion of fixed stars.
J. Law's bank made into Royal Bank of France.
First appearance of bank-notes.
Mississippi Co. gained control of French Mint and Senegal Co.; New Orleans founded as part of Mississippi Co. project.
Leopold of Dessau invented iron ramrod; increased efficiency of infantry fire.
Henry Portal became paper-maker to Bank of England; Laverstoke mill still manufactures paper for this bank.
Jai Singh II built Jaipur observatory (to 1734).

Handel: *Chandos Anthems* (11 in number) completed.
Neumann designed Würzburg Residenz, episcopal palace (completed 1744).

Repeal of Britannia silver standard; sterling standard resumed.
Foundation of Westminster Hospital.
Mississippi Co. secured control of French East India Co.

	History	Literature
1719	Spanish invasion of Scotland in support of Jacobites; defeated at Glenshiel. France declared war on Spain. Hanover received Bremen and Verden from Sweden; Treaty of Stockholm. Liechtenstein independent principality within Empire. Maria Josepha, niece of Charles VI, renounced claims to Habsburg dominions on marriage with Elector of Saxony. Accession of Mohammed Shah as Great Mogul.	Thos. D'Urfey (*1653, †1723): *Wit and Mirth, or Pills to Purge Melancholy*, songs and ballads.
1720	Townshend and Walpole returned to office. Orléans exiled Parlement of Paris to Pontoise. Peace between Spain and Quadruple Alliance. Treaties of Stockholm ended war between Sweden and Prussia, Poland, Denmark. Tibet became tributary to China.	Christian Wolff (*1679, †1754): *Rational Thoughts on God, the World and the Human Soul*. Defoe: *Adventures of Captain Singleton*, a novel. Voltaire: *Artémise*, French tragedy. Thos. Hearne published *A Collection of Curious Discourses*, papers of an antiquarian society of 1572 to 1604.
1721	Walpole appointed Chancellor of Exchequer and First Lord of Treasury. Defensive alliance among Britain, France and Spain. Peace of Nystädt: Sweden and Russia came to terms; end of Great Northern War. Proclamation of Russian Empire and Peter the Great as Emperor of all the Russias.	Pierre de Marivaux (*1688, †1763): *Arlequin poli par l'Amour*, one of the numerous comedies of the Parisian writer. Charles de Montesquieu (*1689, †1755): *Lettres persanes*, a criticism of French society; letters written by two "Persians" giving their impressions of Europe.
1722	Jacobite Bishop of Rochester, Atterbury, banished for conspiracy. Habeas Corpus Act suspended. Maria Amelia, niece to Charles VI, renounced Habsburg rights on marriage to Charles of Bavaria. Hungary accepted Charles VI's Pragmatic Sanction in favour of his daughter, Maria Theresa.	Defoe: (i) *Moll Flanders*, a novel written in the form of an autobiography of a harlot who repents; (ii) *Journal of the Plague Year*, supposed first-hand account; the author was five years old at the time of the events. Mattheson: *Musica Critica*, earliest journal devoted to music; German work.

Erection, at Berwick-upon-Tweed, of oldest extant barracks in England.

Emperor Charles VI founded Oriental Co. in Vienna.
Thos. Lombe established water-powered silk factory on island in River Derwent at Derby.

Handel: (i) 5th Harpsichord Suite; (ii) *Acis and Galatea*, choral work; (iii) *Radamisto*, an opera; (iv) *Esther*, an oratorio.
Cavendish Square, London, built.
University of Lisbon founded.
Colin Campbell built Mereworth Castle, Kent; replica of Villa Rotunda.
Leoni designed Palladian front of Lyme Park, Cheshire; Elizabethan house.
Von Hildebrandt designed the Belvedere, Vienna.
Earliest record of clarinet in orchestral use.

Zinc smelted at Swansea; 20 years later at Bristol.
John Astbury's salt-glazed pottery, Staffordshire.
Austrian East India Co. founded at Ostend.
National bankruptcy in France; flight of Law; failure of Mississippi Co.; Royal Bank ceased payment.
"South Sea Bubble" in London; Government took over National Debt.
c. Cork Harbour Club, first yachting club, established.
First colonial settlements in Vermont, New England.

Gibbs began to build St Martin's-in-the-Fields, London.
Johann Sebastian Bach (*1685, †1750), greatest musician of a famous family: *Brandenburg Concertos*, six Concerti Grossi.
Earliest English organ-pedals; at St Paul's.

Graham: cylinder escapement for watches.
Establishment of regular postal service between London and the North.
Johann Jablonski (*1654) of Danzig: *Allgemeines Lexicon*, short standard encyclopaedia.
Directors of South Sea Co. prosecuted.
Last Prussian trading factories in Africa purchased by Holland.
Swiss immigrants introduced rifle into America.

Jean Philippe Rameau (*1683, †1764) laid foundations of modern musical harmony.
J. S. Bach: (i) *Das Wohltemperiertes Klavier* (Vol. 1), the 48 preludes and fugues for piano (Vol. 2 in 1744); (ii) the *Anna Magdalena* suites.
(to 1727) Campbell and Kent built Houghton Hall, Norfolk (Palladian mansion), for Walpole.

Workhouse Act: private practice towards the Poor made general.
Thos. Guy (*1644, †1724), bookseller, founded Guy's Hospital, London, for which purpose he allocated the sum of £300,000.
Foundation, on estate of Count Zinzendorf in Saxony, of Herrnhut as Moravian settlement.

LITERATURE

Year	History	Literature
1722	Frederick William I of Prussia centralized government in General Directory under his control.	
1723	St John, Viscount Bolingbroke, allowed to return from exile. Charles VI settled all Habsburg dominions on daughter, Maria Theresa.	Steele: *The Conscious Lovers*, a play.
1724	Henry Carteret appointed Lord Lieutenant of Ireland. Congress of Cambrai failed to settle differences between Spain and Empire. Abdication of Philip V; accession of Louis, who died after two months; return of Philip V. Treaty of Stockholm between Russia and Sweden. Alliance of Russia and Turkey against Persia. Austria accepted Pragmatic Sanction ensuring succession of Maria Theresa to Habsburg dominions.	Defoe: *Roxana*, a novel. Publication of Swift's *Drapier's Letters*, opposing British Government's decision to offer contract for manufacture of Irish copper coins to Wm. Wood of Wolverhampton. Foundation of oldest British publishing house, Longman's, still extant.
1725	Pulteney, former supporter of Walpole, joined Opposition. Marriage of Louis XV of France and Maria Lesczinski, daughter of former king of Poland. †Peter the Great of Russia; accession of widow as Catherine I. Treaty of Vienna united Spanish Bourbons and Austrian Habsburgs; led to Treaty of Hanover among Britain, France, Prussia, Sweden, Denmark and Holland.	Ramsay: *The Gentle Shepherd*, dramatic pastoral. Publication of Mme de Sévigné's letters (also 1726). James Thomson (*1700, †1748): *The Seasons*, descriptive nature poem in blank verse (to 1730).
1726	War between England and Spain. Cardinal Fleury appointed chief minister in France. Austro-Russian treaty of alliance against Turkey. Treaty of Wusterhausen; Prussia supported Pragmatic Sanction.	Allan Ramsay opened first circulating library in Edinburgh. Defoe: *The Four Years Voyages of Captain George Roberts*, adventure. Pope translated Homer's *Odyssey*. Swift: *Gulliver's Travels*, adventures in Lilliput, Brobdingnag, Laputa and Houyhnhnms; social and satire, frequently considered a children's book.

Capesthorne, Cheshire, built; major alterations by Blore and Salvin.
Erection of Peckover House, Cambridge; rococo decoration.

(to 1727) Wm. Kent designed part of Kensington Palace.
Bonnet: *Histoire de la Danse sacrée et profane*.
J. S. Bach defined his musical *Inventions* for students; composed *St John Passion*.

Duty on tea reduced by Walpole.

Three Choirs Festival (Gloucester, Hereford and Worcester), oldest English musical festival, began.
Erection of Chillington Hall, Staffordshire; additions 1785; gardens laid out later by Lancelot ("Capability") Brown (*1715, †1783).
Von Hildebrandt completed the Belvedere, Vienna.

Passion for gin-drinking developed among English public.
Official opening of Paris Bourse.

Military Order of Bath revived and instituted by Letters Patent.
J. J. Fux (*1660, †1741): *Gradus ad Parnassum*, important treatise on counterpoint.
A. D. Philidor founded the *Concerts Spirituels*, Paris; lasted until 1791.
Lord Burlington and Wm. Kent built Chiswick House, London.
Foundation of Prague opera house.
Wm. Adam built wings of Mellerstain, Berwickshire; Robert Adam built main block later.
c. Antonio Canaletto (*1697, †1768): *The Grand Canal seen from the Ca'Foscari*, Italian topographical painting.

Posthumous publication of *Historia Coelestis Britannica*, great star catalogue of Flamsteed; vols. 1 and 2 on observations at Derby and Greenwich; vol. 3, catalogue of 3,000 stars..
Catherine I founded the Russian Academy of Sciences in St Petersburg.
c. Greengage introduced into England by Sir Wm. Gage.
c. Serious agrarian distress in Japan reduced agricultural population.

Ballerina Marie-Anne de Cupis de Camargo (*1710, †1770) rose to fame, to last until 1751; she introduced the short skirt for ballet-dancers.
Erection of church of St Martin's-in-the-Fields, London.
Foundation of Universities of Cortono and Marseilles.

To avoid silicosis, flint ground under water during manufacturer of pottery.
Introduction of money economy into Japan.
Spaniards first settled on site of Montevideo, Uruguay.
General George Wade began 250-mile road-construction in Scotland (to 1737).

Year	History	Literature
1727	†George I; accession of George II. Spencer Comptom proposed as Prime Minister; Walpole retained post; increased Civil List. First Annual Act removing disabilities of Protestant Dissenters in England. Anglo-Spanish war; Spain blockaded Gibraltar. Treaty of Kiachta: Russia and China rectified Amur frontier. †Empress Catherine I; accession of Peter II (†1730).	Gay: *Fables*; first series. Pope, Swift and Arbuthnot issued *Miscellanies*, satirical periodical. *Stabat Mater* embodied in Roman Missal; later set to music by various composers (see, e.g., 1736). *c.* Translation of fairy tale, *The Sleeping Beauty*, from French into English.
1728	Publication of Parliamentary debates declared breach of privilege. Parliamentary enquiry into cruelties practised by Thomas Bambridge, Governor of Fleet Prison. Convention of Prado ended Anglo-Spanish war, but Congress of Soissons failed to secure peace.	Pope: *The Dunciad*, fierce verse satire on the dunces; anonymously issued. Voltaire: *La Henriade*, epic poem on Henry IV of France. Cibber: *The Provoked Husband*, a comedy. Ephraim Chambers (†1740): *Cyclopaedia*.
1729	North and South Carolina established as Crown Colonies. *Dauphin assured Bourbon succession in France; ended dynastic rivalry between Spain and France. Treaty of Seville ended war among France, Britain, Holland and Spain. Succession of Don Carlos, son of Philip V of Spain, recognized to duchies of Parma and Piacenza.	Muro Kiuso (*1658, †1734): *Shundai Zatsuwa*, collection of Japanese notes on philosophy, politics, war and poetry.
1730	Quarrel between Walpole and Townshend; latter forced to leave Government. John and Charles Wesley founded Methodist Society at Oxford. Dupleix appointed Governor of Chandernagore; extended French influence. Proposed marriage alliance between Prussia and Britain failed; Prussia embittered. Attempted flight of Crown Prince Frederick of Prussia to England failed; imprisoned at Cüstrin. †Emperor Peter II of Russia; accession of Empress Anne, niece of Peter the Great.	de Marivaux: *Le Jeu de l'Amour et du Hasard*, a comedy; Silvia and Dorante disguise themselves to test their love. Gottsched *Versuch einer Kritischen Dichtkunst*, a guide to the writing of German poetry. Thomson: *Sophonisba*, verse tragedy. Matthew Tindal (*1656, †1733): *Christianity as Old as the Creation*, nicknamed the "Deist's Bible".

Johann C. Gottsched (*1700, †1766) founded German Society at Leipzig.
Horatio Walpole built Wolterton Hall.
c. Canaletto: *The Mole and the Ducal Palace,* Italian topographical painting.
J. S. Bach: *Trauer-Ode,* funeral cantata.
c. Development of sonata form with two motifs.
Thomas Coram (*1688, †1751), philanthropist, created Foundling Hospital.

Stephen Hales (*1677, †1761) first isolated oxygen but did not recognize what it was; published *Vegetable Staticks,* foundations of plant physiology, in same year.
Foundation of Royal Bank of Scotland.
Austrian East India Co. at Ostend disbanded.
Coffee first planted in Brazil.
Foundation, at Philadelphia, of American Philosophical Society.

Gay and Pepusch's *Beggars' Opera,* early form of ballad opera, first performed; produced by John Rich.
John Wood the Elder built Queen Square, Bath; possesses Palladian façade.
Havana university originally founded; refounded 1900.

B. F. de Belidor: *La Science des Ingénieurs,* important engineering treatise.
Vitus Bering discovered Straits between Asia and America, to which his name is given.
Gibbs planned rebuilding of St Bartholomew's Hospital, London (work begun 1729).
James Bradley (*1692, †1762) discovered aberration of light of fixed stars.
*F. Bartolozzi (†1815) of Florence, fine engraver.

J. S. Bach: *St Matthew Passion,* German oratorio.
D. Scarlatti, principal Italian harpsichord composer, was at Madrid court until (†)1757.
Cibber: *Love in a Riddle,* ballad opera.
Handel: Six Oboe Concertos.
Gay: *Polly,* to succeed *Beggars' Opera;* stage production forbidden (see 1777).

Stephen Gray (*1670, †1736): list of electric conductors and insulators.
Emperor Yung Ch'eng issued edict forbidding public sale of opium.
Foundation of Baltimore, now in the U.S.A.; incorporated 1797.

Gibbs erected Senate House at Cambridge.
Garthewin, Denbighshire, built; possesses 18th cent. barn converted into theatre.
Canaletto: *Scuola di San Rocco,* Italian painting.
Scottish Grand Lodge of Freemasonry established.
Johann Adolph Hasse (*1699, †1783): *Artaserse,* German opera in Neapolitan style.
Handel: *Partenope,* an opera.

G. Brandt (*1694, †1768), Swiss, isolated cobalt.
Wm. Gad, of Edinburgh, made stereotype plates.
Abraham de Moivre (*1667, †1754): *Miscellanea Analytica de Seriebus et Quadraturis,* major work including his famous theorem on complex numbers.
Foundation of Edinburgh Royal Infirmary.
Townshend retired to estate at Rainham; introduced Four Year Rotation of Crops.
Diamonds found in Brazil.
Robert Gillow began to manufacture furniture in Lancaster; later in London.
René Réaumur (*1683, †1757): alcohol thermometer with graduated scale (0°–80°).

Year	History	Literature
1730	*c.* Reduction of slavery in China brought about by Emperor Yung Ch'eng.	
1731	First and Second Treaties of Vienna among Britain, Holland, Spain, Austria and Empire; Maritime Powers guaranteed Pragmatic Sanction. French built fort at Crown Point on Lake Champlain to check British expansion. Protestants expelled from Archbishopric of Salzburg. Spanish coast guards seized English ship *Rebecca;* her captain, Jenkins, lost an ear in engagement (see 1739).	L'Abbé Prévost (*1697, †1763): *Manon Lescaut,* tragic French tale of the love of Chevalier des Grieux for Manon. Voltaire: *Histoire de Charles XII,* history of Charles XII of Sweden. Pietro Metastasio (*1698, †1782): *Adriano,* Italian play. First publication of *The Gentleman's Magazine* (to 1914). Franklin founded free public library of Philadelphia.
1732	Moors of Oran routed Spaniards; cannon and powder supplied by British. Don Carlos of Spain secured Parma and Piacenza. Pragmatic Sanction guaranteed by Empire except Saxony, Bavaria and Palatinate. Salzburg Protestants settled in East Prussia.	Voltaire: *Zaïre,* French tragedy, classical in form. James Hammond: *Love Elegies.* Benjamin Franklin (*1706, †1790) published *Poor Richard's Almanack,* in America.
1733	Walpole introduced Excise Scheme; unpopular, so withdrew it. First "Family Compact" between France and Spain against England. War of Polish Succession: Augustus III of Saxony, supported by Russia and Austria, against Stanislaus Lesczinski, supported by France and Spain. Treaty of Turin: France and Sardinia guaranteed succession of Don Carlos to Naples and Two Sicilies. Conscription introduced in Prussia.	(to 1734) Pope: *Essay on Man,* optimistic philosophy in verse; also began *Imitations of Horace,* a series of satires.
1734	France at war with Empire. Stansilaus expelled from Poland by Russians. Salzburg protestants emigrated to Georgia. Battles of Guastalla, Parma and Bitonto; Lorraine overrun; Philipsburg captured. Naples returned to importance as captital of kingdom of Naples.	Voltaire: *Lettres sur les Anglais,* Frenchman discusses aspects of English life. Emanuel Swedenborg (* 1688, †1772): *Prodromus Philosophiae,* mystical work by the Swedish philosopher.

Earliest reference to concerts in America; at Boston and Charleston.
Prime Minister first resided at 10 Downing Street.
(to 1751) Building of State House, Philadelphia, later Independence Hall, designed by Andrew Hamilton.
(to 1735) Clandon Park, Surrey, built by Leoni in Palladian style.
Cassels designed Powerscourt House, Co. Wicklow; fine Italian gardens.

Original Covent Garden Opera House, London, opened; present one is the third.
William Adam built Haddo House, Aberdeenshire, on site of earlier house.
Giustini: earliest published piano music (sonatas).

Rameau: *Hippolyte et Aricie*, French opera, first produced.
First German Masonic Lodge (at Hamburg).
Paine designed Nostell Priory; additional wing (1766) by Robert Adam.
Handel: *Athalea* and *Deborah*, oratorios
Tsar Kolokol, world's heaviest bell (193 tons), cast at Moscow.

Dilettanti Society founded in London.
Erection of Holkham Hall, Norfolk, Palladian mansion, by Wm. Kent.
J. S. Bach: *Christmas Oratorio*, six cantatas.
Foundation of University of Göttingen by George II of Gt. Britain.

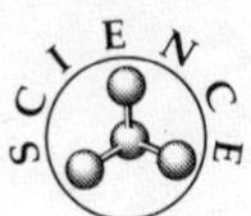

John Hadley, mathematician, invented navigational sextant; appears to have been designed independently by Godfrey at about same time; Hadley's instrument was an octant (eighth of circle) increased to one-sixth by Campbell in 1757.
Arbuthnot: *An Essay concerning the Nature of Ailments*, in which he advocated dieting in combating diseases.
Johann Zedler (*1706, †1760), German bookseller, produced great encyclopaedia in 64 volumes (1732–60), *Grosses vollständiges Universal Lexicon*.

Carl Linnaeus (*1707, †1778), Swedish botanist, visited Lapland; formed Linnaean collection.
H. Boerhaave: *Elements of Chemistry*, established science of organic chemistry.
James Oglethorpe founded Georgia, last British colony in America.
Anglo-Russian commercial treaty.

*J. C. Borda (†1799), French mathematician; partly responsible for metric system.
Hales: *Haemostaticks*, work on measurement of blood pressure.
Chester More Hall made achromatic lens, free from colour fringes.
John Kay's flying shuttle loom patented.
Molasses Act: American trade with W. Indies forbidden.
Corvée, compulsory road, bridge and public works service, instituted in France by Fleury.

First issue of *Lloyd's List* forerunner of *Lloyd's Register of Shipping*; oldest daily paper.
(to 1786) Trade treaty beteween Russia and Britain.
Swedenborg, Swedish mystic and scientis: *Opera philosophica et mineralia*.

Year	History	Literature
1735	William Pitt became M.P. for Old Sarum, family "Rotten Borough". France agreed to peace with Empire.	Pope: *Epistle to Dr Arbuthnot*, a satirical poem (on Addison). Freedom of Press established in New England. Thomson: *Liberty*, poetry (to 1736). Bolingbroke: *A Dissertation upon Parties*, against the Whigs. Wm. Somerville (*1675, †1742): *The Chase*, blank verse, on hounds.
1736	Porteous Riots in Edinburgh Marriage of Maria Theresa, daughter of Charles VI, to Francis Stephen of Lorraine. Austria and Russia at war with Turkey; Russians captured Azoff and Koslov; retired to Ukraine. Accession of Nadir Khan as Shah of Persia. Accession of Ch'ien Lung as Emperor of China; adding Sinkiang and Tibet to empire.	Marivaux: *Le Legs*, French comedy. Joseph Butler (*1692, †1752): *Analogy of Religion*. Henry Fielding (*1707, †1754): *Pasquin*, a satire. John Wesley (*1703, †1791): *Journal* diary of the famous preacher.
1737	Frederick, Prince of Wales, became centre of opposition to Walpole. †Queen Caroline, wife of George II, main supporter of Walpole. End of Medici rule in Tuscany; Grand Duchy passed to Francis Stephen of Lorraine. Russians captured Ochakoff, occupied Moldavia and ravaged Crimea.	Alexander Cruden (*1701, †1770): *Concordance to the Bible*. Marivaux: *Les fausses Confidences*, French comedy. Lady Mary Wortley Montagu: *The Nonsense of Common Sense*. Wm. Shenstone (*1714, †1763): *The Schoolmistress*, poem on a village school.
1738	Peeresses, led by Duchess of Queensberry, forced entry into House of Lords' debate. Third Treaty of Vienna: Lorraine separated from empire and taken by France. Semindria and Orsova captured by Turks from Austria.	Pope Clement XII: *In Eminenti*, bull attacking Freemasonry. Posthumous publication of Gay's second series of *Fables*. Pope: *One Thousand Seven Hundred and Thirty-Eight*, satirical work.
1739	Walpole yielded to demand for war with Spain: "War of Jenkins's Ear"; Admiral Vernon captured Porto Bello, base of Spanish revenue vessels. John Wesley developed society known as Methodists in London. Execution of Dick Turpin, highwayman (*1705). Peace of Belgrade: ended Austro-Russian war with Turkey.	*Obradovitch (†1811), Serbian poet, who created modern literary language of his country. David Hume (*1711, †1776): *Treatise on Human Nature*, first two vols.; third vol. 1740; together with *Enquiry Concerning Human Understanding* (1748) and *Enquiry concerning the Principles of Morals* (1751) they form a remarkable philosophy. *Twm O'r Nant (†1810), author of Welsh plays and interludes.

Foundation of Russian Imperial Ballet School of St Petersburg.
J. S. Bach: piano concerto in Italian style,
Construction of façade of St John in the Lateran, Rome.
Salvi built the Fountain of Trevi, Rome.
William Hogarth (*1697, †1764), engraver, illustrator, satirist of gin drinking: *A Rake's Progress* (8 pictures, begun 1733).

John Harrison's (*1693, †1776), first chronometer (see 1761).
Manufacture of carpets at Kidderminster.
French East India Co. established sugar industry in Mauritius and Réunion.
Probable date of foundation of Ste. Genevieve, Missouri, U.S.A.
Linnaeus: *Systema naturae* begun (see 1768).

Giovanni Pergolesi (*1710, †1736): *Stabat mater*, Italian church music for singers, organ and orchestra.
Handel: *Alexander's Feast*, choral work.
Act passed to raise money by lottery to provide a stone bridge over the Thames at Westminster.

Leonhard Euler (*1707, †1783), Swiss mathematician: *Mechanica*, foundation of analytical mechanics and study of geodesics.
A. C. Clairaut (*1713, †1765), French mathematician, calculated length of meridian degree.
Statutes against witchcraft in England.
Claudius Aymand (*1680, †1740): first known successful operation for appendicitis.
India-rubber brought to Europe.

Rameau: *Castor and Pollux*, French opera, first produced in Paris.
Lord Chamberlain's censorship of plays established by Act.
(to 1749) Gibbs built Radcliffe Library, Oxford.
John Wesley: *Collection of Psalms and Hymns* published in Georgia.

Richmond, Virginia, founded.
Measurements made in Lapland and in Peru demonstrated the flattening of the Earth, towards the Poles, indicating its form to be an oblate spheroid.
Linnaeus published *Flora Lapponica* (see 1732); also *Genera Plantarum* the beginning of modern botany.

G B. Sacchetti began work on Royal Palace at Madrid.
Clement XII issued bull *In Eminenti*, against Freemasonry.
Handel: *Xerxes*, an opera, and *Saul* an oratorio.

Daniel Bernoulli (*1700, †1782) enunciated important hydrodynamical law: static plus dynamic pressure energy of fluid particle is constant.
c. Iron rails began to replace wooden ones.
Lewis Paul invented and patented spinning machine using rollers; also John Wyatt of Birmingham.

Charles Wesley (*1707, †1788): *Hark the Herald Angels Sing*, a hymn.
Rameau: *Dardanus*, French opera, first produced.
Handel: *Israel in Egypt*, an oratorio, and 12 Concerti Grossi.
Erection of Nanteos, Cardiganshire; Georgian mansion.
J. B. S. Chardin (*1699, †1779): *Le Bénédicité*, French painting.
Peacock Throne of Shah Jahan taken to Persia.

Harrison's second chronometer.
Foundation of Queen Charlotte's Hospital (for lying-in).
Foundling Hospital, London, received its charter.
French explorers reached Colorado.
Foundation of Swedish Scientific Academy.
Establishment of Royal Society of Edinburgh; Fellows take the letters F.R.S.E.

1739

Marriage of Don Philip, second son of Philip V of Spain, to daughter of Louis XV; strengthened Franco-Spanish alliance.
Delhi sacked by Persians under Nadir Shah.

1740

Growth of opposition to Walpole led by Pulteney, Carteret and Sandys.
Famine in Paris; Louis XV's carriage mobbed.
Franco-Swedish alliance against Russia.
Accession of Frederick II (the Great) of Prussia who abolished torture.
†Emperor Charles VI, last Habsburg Emperor; accession of Maria Theresa and Habsburg-Lorraine to Austria, Bohemia and Hungary.
Frederick II of Prussia repudiated Pragmatic Sanction; invaded Silesia; began War of Austrian Succession.
†Empress Anne of Russia; accession of Ivan VI, a baby.

Samuel Richardson (*1689, †1761): *Pamela,,* the novel of an innocent servant girl who resists temptation and is rewarded for her virtue by marrying the young squire.
Liberty of the Press introduced in Prussia.
Apology for the Life of Colley Cibber, an autobiography.
Thomson: *Alfred* verse tragedy.

1741

Motion for dismissal of Walpole defeated.
Dupleix appointed Governor General of French possessions in India.
Charles Albert of Bavaria recognized as King of Bohemia.
Treaties of Nymphenburg and Breslau: France and Prussia supported Bavarian claim to Empire and Habsburg territories.
Austrians defeated by Prussia at Mollwitz.
Saxony joined allies against Austria.
Sweden declared war on Russia; defeated at Vilmanstrand.
Infant Ivan VI deposed and imprisoned (murdered 1764); accession of Elizabeth, daughter of Peter the Great.
Convention of Klein-Schnellendorf between Prussia and Austria: broken by Prussia.

Voltaire: *Mahomet*, a French tragedy.
First appearance on London stage of David Garrick (*1717, †1779), pioneer in natural and expressive acting, in Shakespeare's *Richard III*; Garrick wrote *The Lying Valet*, a farce, in same year.
Hume: *Essays Moral and Political* (to 1742).

1742

Resignation of Walpole; succeeded by Lord Wilmington and Carteret.
Charles Albert of Bavaria elected Emperor with title Charles VII.

Edward Young (*1683, †1765): *Night Thoughts*, a religious poem in blank verse (to 1745).
Fielding: *Joseph Andrews*, his first novel and

c. Canaletto: *The Square of St Mark's* and *The Quay of the Piazzetta*, Italian topographical paintings.
Rule Britannia; words by James Thompson, music by Thomas Arne (*1710, †1778), contained in Arne's masque *Alfred*.
François Boucher (*1723, †1770): *The Triumph of Galatea*, French painting.
Handel: *Water Music* published.
Peg Woffington, Irish actress, noted for her male parts, made her début at Covent Garden.

Commercial production of sulphuric acid.
Harrison founded the London Hospital (and incidentally gave it all he had).
Benjamin Huntsman (*1704, †1776) of Sheffield produced crucible steel; process used 1870.
c. Inoculation against smallpox in general use in England (see 1717).
Whatman established the manufacture of paper at Maidstone.
Wm. Stukeley (*1687, †1765), a founder of Society of Antiquaries: *Stonehenge*.
Charles Bonnet (*1720, †1793), published his findings on parthenogenesis.

Handel: (i) *Samson*, an oratorio; (ii) *Deidamia*, his last opera.
University or Stockholm founded.
Christoph Gluck (*1714, †1787), great German opera composer: *Artaxerxes*.
Rameau: *Pièces de clavecin en concerts*, French piano trio-sonatas.
Pietro Longhi (*1702, †1785): *The Apothecary's Shop*, Venetian painting.
First use of wrought iron in bridge construction; chain cables of Wynch suspension bridge over the Tees.

Nicholas Andry, Parisian physician, invented word *orthopaedics* (Gk. straight child), specially devoted to correction of physical deformities.
Highway Act attempted to improve English roads.
Frederick II introduced horse artillery into Prussian army.
Russian navigator Tchivikov landed in California.
†Bering, after discovering Alaska and the Aleutian Islands in the same year.
Violent earthquake at Leghorn.
Royal Military Academy, Woolwich, founded.
Linnaeus became Professor of Botany at Uppsala University (until †).

Wm. Kent designed Horse Guards Parade, Whitehall.
Boucher: *Diana resting*, French painting.

Thos. Bolsover discovered plating of silver on copper (annealing, not electro-plating); Sheffield plate.
c. Cotton factories established in

LITERATURE

Year	History	Literature
1742	Treaty of Berlin: Austria and Prussia ended First Silesian War.	a parody of *Pamela*; Joseph remains virtuous despite temptation. Thomas Gray (*1716, †1771): (i) *On Spring,* (ii) *On a Distant Prospect of Eton College,* poems.
1743	†Wilmington; Henry Pelham Prime Minister. Pragmatic Army under George II defeated French at Dettingen. Second Family Compact between France and Spain: Treaty of Fontainebleau. Visit of Voltaire to Frederick II of Prussia. Treaty of Worms: Austria ceded Parma and Piacenza to Sardinia. Peace of Abo: Russian and Sweden reconciled.	Voltaire: *Mérope,* French tragedy. Fielding: *Jonathan Wild the Great,* a novel; Wild was a famous criminal hanged at Tyburn. Carlo Goldoni, Italian (*1707, †1793): *La Donna di Garbo,* one of the author's two hundred plays. Pope's *Dunciad* reissued complete in four books.
1744	Formal declaration of war on Britain and Austria by France. Frederick II invaded Bohemia; Second Silesian War. Indians and French invaded Nova Scotia but failed to take Annapolis; Louisberg captured by colonial force from Massachusetts. Prussia acquired East Friesland on death of last ruler.	Samuel Johnson (*1709, †1784): *Life* (of poet, Richard Savage). Thos Osborne published (to 1746) *Harleian Miscellany,* reprints of sections of famous Harleian MSS., acquired for British Museum by Act of 1754.
1745	Jacobite rebellion in England and Scotland led by Prince Charles Edward. Madame de Pompadour gained influence over Louis XV; retained until death in 1764. Austro-Russian alliance against Prussia. Treaty of Warsaw: Britain, Holland, Poland supported Maria Theresa. †Emperor Charles VII; succeeded in Bavaria by son, Maximilian II; Francis Stephen of Habsburg-Lorraine elected as Francis I. Legal reforms begun in Prussia; completed 1755. Treaty of Füssen: Bavaria renounced claims on Habsburg dominions. Battles of Fontenoy and Hohenfriedberg.	Publication in Amsterdam, of *Mémoires secrets pour servir à l'histoire de Perse;* drew attention to the case of *The Man in the Iron Mask,* a Bastille prisoner (*c.* 1698 to 1703. Julien Offray de La Metrie (*1709, †1751): *L'Histoire naturelle de l'Âme,* French psychological work which was burned. †Dolly Pentreath, last person to speak Cornish naturally; miracle plays still exist in the tongue. Thomson: *Tancred and Sigismunda,* a tragedy.

First Methodist hymn tunes published by John Wesley.
Trinity College, Dublin, became university.
Handel: *The Messiah*, an oratorio.
J. S. Bach: *Goldberg Variations* (in *Clavierübung*).

Birmingham and Northampton.
Construction of canal linking the Elbe and Havel.
Jean Malouin, French chemist, invented process of galvanizing iron.
Foundation of Royal Danish Academy of Sciences and Letters.

Handel: *Joseph*, an oratorio; also *Dettingen Te Deum*.
Foundation of Universities of Copenhagen and Erlangen.
First performance of *Messiah* in London: George II and audience rose in a body, profoundly overcome during *Hallelujah Chorus*; the custom is still observed (see 1742).
Neumann designed church at Vierzehnheiligen, near Banz (completed 1772).
Hogarth: *Marriage à la Mode* (to 1745); six satirical pictures.

Christin de Lyons produced present Centigrade scale: O° freezing point, 100° boiling point, of water; the one hundred divisions had been proposed a year earlier by Celsius.
Clairaut: *Théorie de la figure de la terre*, containing his well-known theorem.
East India yarns imported into Lancashire for manufacture of finer goods.
French explorers reached foothills of Rocky Mountains.
First settlements in South Dakota.

J. S. Bach: *Das Wohltemperiertes Klavier* (Vol. 2: see 1722).
Foundation in London of the Madrigal Society.
Tune of *God Save the King* appeared almost in present form: evolved from earlier tune, having rhythm of galliard.

Survey of France by triangulation, commenced by C. F. Cassini; completed 1783.
Robert Clive (*1725, †1774) arrived in Madras as East India Co. clerk.
George Anson (*1697, †1762) returned home after voyage round the world.
Berlin's first cotton factory established.
c. India-rubber by now widely used in Europe.

Jean-Baptiste Perronneau (*1715, †1783): *Girl with a Kitten*, French pastel.
First printing of *The Campbells are Coming* and of *God Save the King*; latter probably composed by Henry Carey in 1740.
Publication of folk-tunes in Ireland.
Earliest record of Manchester's "Gentlemen's Concerts"; lasted until 1914.
Wordsworth House, Cumberland, built; birthplace of the poet.
Foundation of Philadelphia Academy, later Pennsylvania University (see 1789).
Quadrille, French dance, believed to have developed from dance in *Fêtes de Polymnie* by Rousseau.
Rameau: *Platée*, French ballet-bouffon.

Edward J. von Kleist (*1702, †1748), German invented Leyden jar (electric condenser) at Leyden University; developed later by Benjamin Franklin, U.S.A.
Robert Bakewell (*1725, †1795), of Leicestershire, began improved methods of sheep breeding.
Dissolution of Barber-Surgeons union: dentists thereafter learned privately and practised without licence.
Foundation of the Middlesex Hospital.
Lemery: *Treatise on all Sorts of Foods*.
W. Cooke invented steam heating.
Fort George, Inverness-shire, built; now used as barracks.
Admiral Vernon introduced seamen's ration of grog (rum and water) in R.N.; name derived from grogham cloak he wore.
Linnaeus: *Flora Suecica*.

LITERATURE

	History	Literature
1745	Marriage of Peter, heir to Russian throne, to Sophia of Anhalt-Zerbst, later Empress Catherine II. Nawab of Carnatic refused to allow British to bombard French at Pondicherry.	
1746	Pelham resigned ministry because George II refused to accept Pitt; returned with Pitt as Paymaster of Forces. Final defeat of Jacobites at Culloden Moor; Highlands subjugated. †Philip V of Spain; accession of Ferdinand VI. Austrians occupied Genoa; driven out by rising led by boy called Ballila. Period of persecution of Christians in China; lasted to *c.* 1784.	William Collins (*1721, †1759): *Odes* poems by a pre-Romantic. Denis Diderot (*1713, †1784), French encyclopaedist: *Pensées philosophiques,* written in four days at Easter. Establishment of Princeton University Library, U.S.A.
1747	Execution of the Lords of Kilmarnock, Lovat and Balmerino for part in 1745 rising. British naval victories at Finisterre and Belle Isle. Revolution in Holland; William IV of Orange appointed Stadholder. Treaty of St Petersburg between Russia and Britain; precipitated Aix-la-Chapelle. Nadir, Shah of Persia, murdered. Ahmed Shah Durani founded Afghan throne independent of Persia.	*Edward Williams (Iolo Morganwg), inventor of Gorsedd and bardic druidism (†1826). Voltaire: *Zadig*, a philosophical tale; the hero, Zadig tries in vain to improve mankind. Garrick: *Miss in her Teens*, a farce. *c.* Gray: *Ode on the Death of a Favourite Cat* (Walpole's Selima).
1748	Treaty of Aix-la-Chapelle ended War of Austrian Succession. Don Philip of Spain received Duchies of Parma and Piacenza. Punjab invaded by Ahmed Shah of Afghanistan. Dupleix repulsed British naval attack on Pondicherry.	Richardson: *Clarissa Harlowe*, a novel told in the form of letters. Tobias Smollett (*1721, †1771): *Roderick Random*, a novel of sea life. Thomson: *The Castle of Indolence*, an allegorical poem. Montesquieu: *L'Esprit des Lois*, analysis of the relations between each country and its own peculiar laws. Friedrich Gottlieb Klopstock (*1724, †1803): *Messias*, German religious poem dealing with the life of Christ.

Boucher: *Mme Bergeret*, French portrait.
Handel: *Judas Maccabaeus*, oratorio, and *Occasional Oratorio*.
Gluck claimed to have invented musical glasses, but instrument known earlier.
Princeton University founded at Elizabethville (see 1748, 1756).
(to 1782) Wearing of tartan forbidden.

Euler supported wave theory of light.
Earliest investigations into hogging and sagging of ships (longitudinal bending between wave crests and troughs) by Pierre Bouguer, Frenchman.
French captured British factory at Madras.
Destruction of old city of Callao, Peru, by earthquake.
Gianfrancesco Pivati (*1689, †1764): *Nuovo dizionario scientifico e curioso sacroprofano*, Venetian encyclopeadia in 10 vols, with fine copper engravings.
G. E. Hamburger (*1697, †1755) described duodenal ulcer.

Handel: *Joshua* and *Alexander Balus*, oratorios, the latter containing music for mandolin.
Hogarth: *Industry and Idleness*, satirical prints.
c. Flitcroft redesigned Woburn Abbey in style of Inigo Jones.
Knobelsdorff completed Sans Souci Palace at Potsdam (begun 1745); for Frederick the Great.

Andreas S. Margraff (*1709, †1782), German, discovered the existence of sugar in beetroot.
Construction of Swinemünde harbour started.
Bradley discovered variation of the earth's axis.
Hannah Glasse: *The Art of Cookery Made Plain and Easy*.

Handel: *Solomon* and *Susanna* oratorios.
Thos. Gainsborough (*1727, †1788): *View of Charterhouse* (at Foundling Hospital), a painting.
Opening of Holywell Music Room, Oxford, oldest European concert hall; still operative.
Princeton University moved to Newark from Elizabethville (see 1756).
Opening of Opera House at Beyreuth.

Abbé Nollet (*1700, †1770) recognized osmosis, tendency of fluids, separated by membrane, to mix.
First machines for wool carding using revolving cylinder, by Lewis Paul.
Establishment of Berlin's first silk factory.
Royal Navy adopted indigo-dyed cloth.
Euler: *Introductio in Analysin Infinitorum*, mathematical analysis.
Foundation of the Ohio Co. in Virginia and Maryland.
J. Jannsen made first steel pen (in Germany).
c. Introduction of platinum into Europe from South America.
Larger-scale excavations at Pompeii undertaken (see 1708).

1749	Georgia became Crown Colony. Treaty of Aquisgran: Spain confirmed Britain's commercial rights. Kaunitz, chief minister in Austria, submitted memorandum on foreign policy to Maria Theresa on Austria's natural friends and enemies.	Fielding: *Tom Jones,* one of the first great English novels. Johnson: *The Vanity of Human Wishes,* his best poem.
1750	Britain gave up *Asiento* of Negro slaves. Chiltern Hundreds first granted to M.P.s as grounds for resignation. Britain joined Austro-Russian alliance against Prussia; refused support to war preparations against Prussia. Failure of Franco-British Commission to settle boundaries in N. America. Kaunitz appointed Ambassador to France; failed to secure Austro-French alliance. Pombal in power in Portugal.	Gray: *Elegy Written in a Country Churchyard,* a reflective poem. Johnson: *The Rambler,* essays (to 1752). Publication of adventures of Hannah Snell (*1723, †1792), the "female soldier". *c.* Afrikaans developed its modern form as spoken language in S. Africa (see 1875).
1751	†Frederick, Prince of Wales, and Henry St John, Viscount Bolingbroke. Clive captured Arcot from French; turning-point in British power in India. Accession of Adolphus Frederick to Swedish throne strengthened French influence in Sweden.	Smollet: *Peregrine Pickle,* a picaresque novel. Voltaire: *Le Siècle de Louis XIV,* French history. *Encyclopédie* (1st vol.), in which Voltaire, Diderot, Montesquieu and Rousseau collaborated; completed in 1780, it ran into 35 vols. Fielding: *Amelia,* his last novel.
1752	Trichinopoly captured from French by Clive. Augustus III of Saxony won over to French policies in Europe. Duquesne appointed Governor of Quebec. Treaty of Aranjuez recognized *status quo* in Italy.	First two volumes of *Encyclopédie* suppressed in France for attacks on clergy. Hume: *Political Discourses.* Bolingbroke: *Letters on the Study and Use of History,* published posthumously. Fielding issued *Covent Garden Journal* twice weekly.
1753	Marriage Act attempted to prevent clandestine marriages. Louis XV exiled Parlement of Paris for its Jansenist sympathies. French seized Ohio valley in N. America.	Goldoni: *La Locandiera,* Italian play in which the mistress of an inn trounces her suitors to marry the man of her choice. Smollett: *Ferdinand Count Fathom,* a novel.

Handel: *Theodora,* oratorio; also *Firework Music,* in which he used a curious instrument, the serpent.
c. Giovanni Battista Tiepolo (*1692, †1769): *Giovanni Querini,* Italian portrait.
J. S. Bach: *The Art of the Fugue.*

*Sir G. Blane (†1834), who was to insist on lime-juice during long voyages to combat scurvy.
Halifax, Nova Scotia, founded.
George de Buffon (*1707, †1788): *Histoire naturelle,* in 36 vols.; completed in 1788.

Boucher: *The Sleeping Shepherdess,* French painting.
Horace Walpole (*1717, †1797) designed Strawberry Hill, in Gothic form.
Introduction of clarinet into a French orchestra.
c. Development of *modern* sonata and symphony.
c. (to 1830) Principal of Glee singing.
c. 18th-cent. French nursery rhyme, *Malbrouck*: gave rise to 'For He's a jolly good Fellow.

Nicolas de Lacaille (*1713, †1762) catalogued 10,000 southern stars.
Anthoine Thiout designed tool carriage for lathes.
Muschenbrock constructed a pyrometer.
Erection of Ackworth School, only remaining building of London Foundling Hospital.
Interest on British National Debt reduced to 3%.
East India Co's trade activities in China severely restricted.
First Westminster Bridge completed.
Colonization of Labrador.

Hogarth: (i) *Four Stages of Cruelty,* (ii) *Gin Lane,* (iii) *Beer Street,* satirical prints.
University of Genoa founded.
Handel: *Jephtha,* an oratorio.
Royal Worcester porcelain works established.
c. Antonio Guardi (*1698, †1760) and Francesco Guardi (*1712, †1793) jointly painted *The Convent Parlour* and *The Ridotto,* Venetian paintings.

A. F. Cronstedt isolated nickel.
Linnaeus: *Philosophia botanica,* followed (1753) by *Species plantarum,* gave detailed nomenclature of plants.
Chaumette: breech-loading gun.
Natal clinic at Göttingen.
Frederick II of Prussia founded Emden Trading Co.
First mental asylum in London.
N. American frontier markers Mason and Dixon at work.

La Guerre des Bouffons: Paris divided into pro-Italian and pro-French opera; the fracas reached a grand scale.
Gililei began the construction of the Royal Palace, Caserta.
(to 1769) Erection of Claydon House, Buckinghamshire.

Benjamin Franklin invented lightning conductor; demonstrated identity of lightning and electric spark.
Gregorian calendar, proposed by Pope in 1582, adopted in Britain; eleven days dropped from calendar to correct it led to riots, as people thought they had been deprived of part of their lives.
Establishment of Manchester Infirmary.

Erection of Potsdam Town Hall, Germany.
Erection of Tomb of Nawab Safdar Jang, Delhi; last Mogul funeral monument.
*Utamaro (†1806): fine Japanese colour-printer.

Euler's mathematical variation of parameters.
France declared National Bankruptcy for second time in century.
Parliament made grant enabling creation of British Museum out of private collections (see 1757, 1759).
Vienna Stock Exchange established.

1754

†Pelham; ministry of Newcastle.
Albany Congress of New England colonies rejected union plea of Franklin.
Anglo-French war in N. America. Virginian militia under George Washington defeated at Great Meadows.
Parlement recalled to Paris.
French abandoned conquests in India.
Wall became chief minister in Spain.

Hume: *History of Great Britain*; work continued until 1762.
Richardson: *Sir Charles Grandison*, a novel whose hero is an ideal gentleman.
John Almon: *A New Peerage*, later taken over by John Debrett as *Debrett's Peerage and Baronetage.*

1755

Dismissal of Pitt for opposing treaties with Russia and Hesse for defence of Hanover.
English force under General Braddock defeated by French near Fort Duquesne.
D'Armenoville attempted to reorganize French navy.
Corsican revolt against Genoa led by Paoli.
Frederick II refused to defend French territory in America.
Admiralty took over marines and established Royal Marines in present form.

Johnson: *Dictionary of the English Language*, first standard one.
Voltaire: *La Pucelle d'Orléans*, French poem on Joan of Arc.
Jean-Jacques Rousseau (*1712, †1778): *Discourse sur l'Origine de l'Inégalité parmi les Hommes*, attacking private property and the political state.
Morelly (life unknown), *Code de la Nature* published.
Johnson: *Letter to Chesterfield*, famous letter which hastened end of "patrons".

1756

Resignation of Newcastle; ministry of Devonshire and Pitt; latter raised Highland regiments.
Treaty of Westminster: alliance of Britain and Prussia.
First Treaty of Versailles: France allied with Austria; completed "Diplomatic Revolution".
Start of Seven Years War by Prussian invasion of Saxony; Britain declared war on France.
Richelieu captured Minorca from Britain; Byng, failing to relieve it, was court-martialled and executed in 1757.
French prepared to invade Britain.
Calcutta captured by Surajadowlah; Black Hole of Calcutta.
Maritime union between Sweden and Denmark against Britain.

Voltaire: *Poème sur le Désastre de Lisbonne*, French poem on earthquake disaster at Lisbon.
Salomon Gessner (*1730, †1788): *Idylls*, Swiss pastoral prose poems.
Thos. Amory (*c.* *1691, †1788): *The Life of John Buncle, Esq.*, sequel to *Memoirs of Several Ladies of Great Britain* (1755); curious fictional work containing confused but interesting information on various topics.

Thos. Chippendale: *The Gentleman and Cabinet Maker's Directory*, famous work on furniture design.
Foundation of Society for Encouragement of Arts.
George II founded King's College, New York, now Columbia University.

John Canton (*1718, †1772) enunciated principle of electrostatic induction; invented electroscope.
Henry Cort invented iron-rolling process; set up mill at Fareham.
Joseph Black (*1728, †1799) identified carbon dioxide ("fixed air").
Admission fee to Levant Trading Co. reduced.
Fort Duquesne built by French in Ohio Valley.

c. Gainsborough: *Joseph Gibbs*, a portrait.
University of Mannheim founded.
c. Canaletto: *The Vegetable Market*, Italian painting.
Johann J. Winckelmann (*1717, †1768), *Gedanken über die Nachahmung der Griechischen Werke in Malerei und Bildhauerkunst*, on Greek painting and sculpture.

Thomas Mudge: lever escapement for watches, superior to cylinder escapement (see 1721).
Saverien: first physical dictionary.
Richard Cantillon issued first major work on economics.
Earthquake at Lisbon; some 30,000 deaths.
Euler: *Institutiones Calculi Differentialis*, earliest complete work on differential calculus.
Alompra founded Rangoon, Burma.
Erik Pontoppidan (*1698 †1764), a Dane: *Natural History of Norway*, referred to mythical kraken.
Manufacture of carpets at Axminster (to 1835); re-established 1936.

(to 1757) Rebuilding of Lisbon Cathedral after earthquake.
Princeton University (see 1746 and 1748) moved to Princeton and Newark, U.S.A.
C. P. E. Bach (*1714, †1788), third son of J. S. Bach: *Easter cantata*.

John Smeaton (*1724 †1792) discovered advantages of hydraulic lime cement.
Cotton velvets first made at Bolton by Jeremiah Clarke.
Joseph Lagrange (*1736 †1813) developed *calculus of variations* (see 1696).
First chocolate factory opened in Berlin.
Launching of the *Royal George*, flagship of Admiral Kempenfelt; sank in Portsmouth Harbour in 1782.
Foundation of famous porcelain factory at Sèvres.
Louis XV suppressed two chambers of Parlement for refusing to register laws for taxes for war against England.

1757 Pitt dismissed by George II; Newcastle failed to form ministry without Pitt; Pitt directed Seven Years War.
Calcutta retaken; Battle of Plassey; Clive secured Bengal for East India Co.
Cumberland defeated at Hastenbeck; capitulated at Klosterseven.
Russia joined France and Austria against Prussia and Britain.
Treaty of Stockholm; Sweden joined alliance against Prussia and Britain.
Battles of Rossbach and Leuthen.
Attempted assassination of Louis XV by Damiens.

Nibelungenlied edited.
Diderot: *Le Fils Natural*, French play advocating social reform to get rid of injustice.
Hume: *Natural History of Religion*.
Gray: *The Bard*, a pindaric ode.

1758 Treaty of London guaranteed annual subsidy of £670,000 to Frederick II.
Choiseul became chief minister in France.
French lost Louisburg, Cape Breton and Fort Duquesne.
British naval victories off Cartagena, Basque Roads and Cherbourg.
Russians invaded Prussia; repulsed at Zorndorf.

Rousseau: *Lettre à M. d'Alembert sur les Spectacles;* tried to prove that Geneva would be better without a theatre.
Diderot: *Le Père de Famille*, French bourgeois drama.
Claude-Adrien Helvétius (*1715, †1771): *De l'Esprit*, philosophy by a Parisian writer.

1759 Trial of Eugene Aram, York murderer.
Wolfe captured Quebec from French.
Revival of French plan to invade Britain; French fleets defeated at Lagos and Quiberon Bay.
Accession of Charles III of Naples to throne of Spain.
Pitt refused offer of Charles III to mediate between England and France.
British maritime policy forced Spain to join forces with France.
Battles of Minden and Kunersdorf.
Russo-Swedish alliance to exclude all foreign vesels from Baltic.
Jesuits expelled from Portugal.

Johnson: *Rasselas, Prince of Abyssinia*, philosophical romance, written to meet costs of his mother's funeral.
Voltaire: *Candide*, philosophical tale of a young man who discovers that this is not "the best of all possible worlds".
Gotthold Lessing (*1729, †1781), Nicolai, Mendelsson and von Kleist: *Briefe die neueste Literatur betreffend (Letters on Modern Literature*); in 24 volumes (to 1765).
Edmund Burke (*1729, †1797) began *Annual Register*, of political and literary events.

1760 †George II; accession of grandson, George III.
Execution of Earl Ferrers; last English peer executed as felon.

Laurence Sterne (*1713, †1768): *Tristram Shandy* (completed 1767), a humorous novel introducing Uncle Toby.
James Macpherson (*1736, †1796):

(to 1765) Kedleston Hall built by Robert Adam, on site of 12th cent. manor house; possessed unique marble hall.
Tiepolo: *Cleopatra's Banquet*, fresco in Palazzo Labia, Venice.
Handel: *The Triumph of Time and Truth*, an oratorio.
(†) Nicolo Pasquali, Italian violinist and composer: *Thoroughbass Made Easy*.

Sankey Navigation, Lancashire, first British canal, constructed.
Harrison's third chronometer.
Physiocrats founded by F. Quesnay (*1694, †1774), economist and physician to Mme de Pompadour.
Old Royal Library passed over to British Museum (see 1759).
Clairault calculated masses of Venus and the Moon.
State-coach of Lord Mayor of London constructed.

Jean-Baptiste Greuze (*1725, †1805): *The Wool Winder*, French painting.
First British book on guitar-playing published: guitars popular in 17th to early 19th cent.
Boucher: *Madame de Pompadour*, French portrait.
Hogarth: *Parliamentary Elections*, paintings (begun 1755).

John Dollond (*1706, †1761), optician, marketed first achromatic telescope.
Jedediah Strutt (*1726, †1797), invented his ribbed hosiery machine.
Quesnay: *Tableau Économique* published.
Macquer and Baumé first melted platinum.

British Museum opened at Montagu House (see 1823).
Germain Soufflot began Panthéon at Paris: pseudo-Grecian (completed 1790).
William Boyce (*1710, †1779): music for *Harlequin's Invasion*, including song *Hearts of Oak*.
Robert Adam began building Harewood House, great country mansion in Yorkshire, containing Chippendale furniture.

Johann H. Lambert (*1728 †1777), German physicist, produced textbook of geometrical projection (to 1774).
(to 1761) James Brindley (*1716, †1772) constructed Bridgewater Canal from Worsley to Manchester.
Smeaton's Eddystone Lighthouse (the third) officially opened.
Establishment of Carron Iron Works, originally to make carronades, short guns of large calibre; later for general cast-iron work; oldest extant British ironworks.
Hally's Comet returned as predicted.
Meteorite weighing 56 lb fell near Scarborough.

J. G. Noverre (*1727, †1810): *Lettres sur la Danse*, important work on ballet.
Josiah Wedgwood's early pottery began to be produced at Etruria, Staffordshire.

Black began the study of calorimetry: latent heat and specific heat.
Lambert formulated fundamental law of photometry.

1760	Eyre Coote defeated French and Indians at Wandewash. Montreal capitulated to British. Robert Clive returned to England. Failure of Choiseul's plan for peace between Britain and France. French invasion force defeated at Kinsale, Ireland. Denmark joined Russo-Swedish Baltic alliance. Battles of Lanshut, Leignitz, Torgau and Warburg.	*Fragments of Ancient Poetry Collected in the Highlands*; a literary fraud, the so-called translation of an early Gaelic poet, Ossian, was the work of Macpherson himself.
1761	Earl of Bute, favourite of George III, opposed Pitt's policy of war with Spain; Pitt resigned. Treaty of Ildefenso renewed Franco-Spanish Family Compact. Portugal refused to close ports to British shipping; invaded by Spain. Battles of Grüneberg and Villingshausen.	Rousseau: *Julie, ou la Nouvelle Héloise*, a novel of passion; Julie falls in love with her tutor Saint-Preux. Gray: *The Descent of Odin*, poem on Scandinavian mythology.
1762	Financial assistance to Frederick II withdrawn; resignation of Newcastle; ministry of Bute. Britain declared war on Spain. Failure of Spanish invasion of Portugal. †Elizabeth of Russia; acession of Peter III removed threat to Prussia; Tsar Peter murdered by Guards; accession of widow as Catherine II. Battles of Burkersdorf and Freiburg.	Rousseau: (i) *Le Contrat social*; the state must be based on a contract which guarantees each citizen his rights and liberty; (ii) *Émile, ou de l'éducation;* how to educate children by freeing individuals from traditions of society; a novel. John Wilkes (*1727, †1797) founded the *North Briton*, radical newspaper. Macpherson: *Fingal*, an epic (see 1760). Smollet: *Sir Launcelot Greaves*, a novel.
1763	Resignation of Bute; ministry of George Grenville. Peace of Paris among Britain, France, Spain and Austria ended Seven Years War. Peace of Hubertsburg; deserted by Britain, Frederick II made own terms with Saxony and Austria. Wilkes imprisoned, under General Warrant, for attack in *North Briton* on Government; released under Habeas Corpus Act. Frederick II began series of far-reaching reforms in Prussia.	Lady Mary Wortley Montagu: *Letters*, lively and amusing. Voltaire: *Traité sur la Tolérance*. Macpherson: *Temora*, an epic (see 1760). Christopher Smart (*1722, †1771): *Song to David*, religious poem. Rousseau's *Contrat Social* publicly burned in Geneva.

University of Haarlem founded.
c. (to 1830) Period of classical sonata.
c. Canaletto: *Piazza San Marco seen through an Archway*, Italian painting.
Edmund Hoyle (*1672, †1769) issued established rules of Whist.

Matthew Boulton (*1728, †1809) established hardware factory.
Lawrence Childs printed first banker's cheques.
Kew Botanical Gardens first opened, privately; extended 1841; now 300 acres.

Foundation of "Noblemen and Gentlemen's Catch Club" for singing.
Gluck: *Don Juan*, a ballet.
Gainsborough held his first exhibition of paintings.
Arne: *Judith*, first oratorio to require women singers in England.

B. G. Morgagni (*1682 †1771): *On the Causes of Diseases, based on Anatomical Reasons*; true beginnings of pathological anatomy (see 1554).
Harrison's fourth chronometer for determination of longitude; awarded government prize (£20,000): payment long held up.
Mikhail V. Lomonosov (*1711, †1765), Russian scientist and poet, discovered atmosphere of Venus.

Arne: (i) *Love in a Village*, ballad opera; (ii) *Artaxerxes*, an opera.
Franklin invented harmonica: word originally referred to drinking-glasses (see 1746); but since applied to various instruments, e.g. mouth-organ.
Gluck: *Orpheus and Euridice*, opera of French school.

Bradley catalogued 60,000 stars.
G. C. Fuchsel: textbook of stratigraphy, first work on geological formulation.
Foundation at Lyons of first veterinary college by St Bel.
Carsten Niebuhr's expedition began exploring Arabia (to 1764).

The Petit Trianon, French Renaissance style built for Mme Dubarry by Louis XV.

M. A. Plenciz suggested that each disease had its associated organism.
c. The solitaire flightless bird of Rodriguez Island, became extinct.

Wolfgang Amadeus Mozart (*1756, †1791), German "classical school" composer, began his grand tour (with his sister Maria Anna and his father) as child prodigy.
Walpole: *Catalogue of Engravers in England*.

General introduction of cloth-bleaching.
British muslins first made at Alderton.
Earliest use of pit ponies.
First English Chambers of Commerce; Jersey and New York.
John Canton demonstrated compressibility of water.
Robert Orme (*1728, †1801): *History of the Military Transactions of the British Nation in Indostan* (to 1778).

Year	History	Literature
1764	Wilkes expelled from Commons. Archduke Joseph, son of Maria Theresa, elected King of Romans. Treaty of Alliance between Russia and Prussia. Stanislaus Poniatowski elected King of Poland. Murder of Ivan VI, Tsar of Russia, imprisoned since infancy.	Horace Walpole: *The Castle of Otranto*, a romantic novel. Oliver Goldsmith (*1728, †1774): *The Traveller*, a poem; also *History of England in a series of Letters*. Voltaire: *Dictionnaire philosphique*. Foundation of *The Club*, which included Boswell, Burke, Garrick, Goldsmith, Johnson and Reynolds.
1765	Stamp Act operative in North American Colonies. Regency Act in England. Resignation of Grenville; Rockingham Prime Minister. Accession of Leopold of Habsburg as Grand Duke of Tuscan; his enlightened reforms failed to win support of Florentines. †Emperor Francis I; accession of Joseph II; co-regent with Maria Theresa of Habsburg dominions. Start of Manchu invasions of Burma; to 1769; repelled.	Thomas Percy (*1729, †1811): *Reliques of Ancient English Poetry*, collection of old ballads, including *Sir Patrick Spens* and *Chevy Chase*. Sir William Blackstone (*1723, †1780): *Commentaries on the Laws of England*. Michel Sedaine (*1719, †1797): *Le Philosophe sans le Savoir*, French drama with a social problem.
1766	Stamp Act repealed by Parliament; followed by Declaratory Act. Withdrawal of British troops from Boston. William Pitt, now Earl of Chatham, formed ministry. Parliament following Wilkes' case, declared General Warrants illegal. †Frederick V of Denmark; accession of lunatic Christian VII. Prussian system of Customs and Excise reorganized by Frenchman, de Launay.	Goldsmith: *The Vicar of Wakefield*, novel describing misfortunes of country clergyman, published. Swift: *Journal of Stella*, letters to Miss Esther Johnson, published posthumously. Johann Herder (*1744, †1803): *Fragmente über die neuere deutsche Litteratur*, influential German work. Christoph Wieland (*1733, †1813): *Agathon*, first German psychological novel.
1767	American Import Duties Act. Jesuits expelled from Spain by Charles III. †Empress Josepha, heiress of Elector of Bavaria, through whom Joseph II hoped to acquire Bavaria for Austria.	Lessing: (i) *Minna von Barnhelm*, first masterpiece of German comedy, (ii) *Die Hamburgische Dramaturgie*, an attack on French dramatic theory and pseudo-classic drama of Corneille and Voltaire. Rousseau settled in England; received pension from George III.

Robert Adam, who attended excavations at Pompeii and published folios on Roman remains, built Ken Wood.
Franz Joseph Haydn (*1732, †1809), called Father of the Symphony: Symphony No. 22 in E♭ (*The Philospher*).
Mozart created his first symphony at age of eight.

Tavern keeper William Almack founded Whig gaming club in Pall Mall.
Spinning Jenny made by Thos Highs; named after his daughter (see 1767).
Trésaguet's method of road construction in France.
Practice of numbering houses introduced in London.
First permanent settlement at St Louis.

Robert Adam designed Lansdowne House.
Gainsborough: *Sunset*, a painting.
Haydn: Symphonies in D minor (*Christmas S.*), in C (*Hallaluja S.*) and in D (*S. with the Horn Signals*).

De Bernières, French invented unsinkable boat; not utilized.
Frederick II established Bank of Prussia.
Spallanzani proposed used of airlock for safety in certain circumstances.
James Watt (*1736, †1819) invented separate condenser for steam engine; patented 1769 (see 1775, 1776).
Launching of H.M.S. *Victory*, Nelson's flagship; now in Portsmouth dockyard.
Foundation of Frieberg *Bergakademie*, famous mining academy.

Haydn: *Great Mass with Organ*, in E♭.
Gotthold Ephraim Lessing (*1729, †1781): *Laokoon*, critical treatise in which German dramatist defined the boundaries of various arts.
Jean Honorê Fragonard (*1732, †1806), Rococo artist often with erotic subject interpretation: *The Swing*, French painting.
Opening of Theatre Royal, Bristol, oldest in Britain to be in continuous use.

Anglo-Russian treaty of friendship, commerce and navigation.
Louis Antoine de Bougainville (*1729, †1811) set out on exploration (until 1769) to take him as far as Tahiti.
Henry Cavendish (*1731, †1810), physicist, identified hyrdrogen as an element and analysed air; science laboratories at Cambridge named after him.
Mason-Dixon Line marked boundaries between Pennsylvania and Maryland; separated free and slave regions.
Paved footpaths laid in City of Westminster.
Jesse Ramsden (*1735, †1800), astronomical instrument maker, designed his first screw-cutting machine; second, more efficient, 1775.

Gluck: *Alcestis*, German opera to Italian libretto produced in Vienna.
Rousseau: *Dictionary of Music*, standard textbook of 18th cent.
Maria Theresa and Joseph II introduced educational reform in Austria.
(to 1769) John Wood the Younger built

James Hargreaves (*1720, †1778) of Lancashire, greatly improved spinning jenny; only suitable for spinning *weft* (see 1764).
Nevil Maskelyne (*1732, †1811) first published *Nautical Almanack*.
Arthur Young (*1741, †1820), agricultural

LITERATURE

1767 Russia tried to exchange Holstein for Oldenburg.
Russo-Danish Treaty.
Catherine II of Russia unsuccessfully appointed Commission to codify Russian Laws based on popular election.
Ali Bey seized Cairo; aimed to restore Mamluk empire.
Outbreak of First Mysore War (to 1769).

1768 Wilkes elected M.P. for Middlesex; rejected by House of Commons.
Resignation of Chatham; Grafton's ministry.
Corsica ceded to France.
Pact of Gottorp between Denmark and Hamburg recognized latter city's independence.
New Criminal Code on liberal lines introduced in Austria.
Turkey, urged on by France, declared war on Russia.

Sterne: *A Sentimental Journey*, French travels and experiences by English novelist and clergyman.
James Boswell (*1740, †1795): *An Account of Corsica*, a country in which he took profound interest.
Goldsmith: *The Goodnatur'd Man*, a play, first produced.
Priestley: *Essay on the First Principles of Government*, advocating consideration of well-being of the people.
Walpole: *The Mysterious Mother*, a tragedy.
First numbers of *Encyclopaedia Britannica* issued; intention was to have 100 weekly parts.

1769 *Napoleon Bonaparte at Ajaccio, Corsica.
Austria seized Polish territory of Zips; actual beginning of partition of Poland.
Frederick II of Prussia proposed partition of Poland to Catherine II of Russia.
Russia invaded Turkish provinces of Moldavia and Wallachia.

Letters of Junius: anonymous attacks on men in public life; exposed corruption of political life.

Johann Wolfgan von Goethe (*1749, †1832): *Neue Lieder*, early poems of Germany's greatest writer.
Burke: *Observations on the Present State of the Nation*.

1770 Attacks of Junius brought down Grafton's ministry; Lord North, Prime Minister.
Boston 'Massacre" following snow-balling of British troops.
Marriage of Louis, the Dauphin, and Marie Antoinette of Austria.
Spanish troops expelled British sailors from Falkland Islands.

Thomas Chatterton (*1752, †1770), the boy poet, committed suicide.
Goldsmith: *The Deserted Village*, a poem of a traveller returning to a ruined native village.
Johannes Ewald (*1743, †1781): *Rolf Krage*, first original Danish tragedy.
Burke: *Thoughts on the Present Discontents*.
Goethe began work on *Faust*, famous

Royal Crescent, Bath; developed idea of making whole perimeter of square into façade of house.
Earliest record of piano in England.

pioneer, set out on travels through England and France.
Lea Navigation opened up substantially for canal work.
Joseph Priestley (*1733, †1804), great chemist: *The History and present State of Electricity*.
Carteret discovered Pitcairn Island.

Adam brothers built Adelphi Terrace.
Arne's Innovation, first known explanatory concert programme.
First piano solo in England; by J. C. Bach.
Francesco Guardi (*1712, †1793): *The Bucentaur leaving the Lido*, Venetian painting.
Foundation of Royal Academy of Arts, London, under patronage of George III; Sir Joshua Reynolds (*1723, †1792), fashionable portrait-painter, first President.
Haydn: Symphony No. 49 in F minor (*La Passione*).

Black determined latent heat of ice and steam (see 1760).
Capt. James Cook's (*1728, †1779) first voyage to the Antipodes in the *Endeavour*; Sir J. Banks (*1743, †1820), naturalist, joined him.
Euler (to 1770): *Institutiones calculi integralis*, first complete work on integral calculus.
Lambert indicated that π is incommensurable.
Linnaeus: *Systema naturae*, Swedish natural history in three parts: (i) animals, (ii) plants, (iii) minerals.
John Baptiste le Prince (*1734, †1784), French, invented aquatint process.
Work begun on Forth-Clyde Canal (opened 1790).

Fragonard: *The Study*, French painting.
Old Blackfriars Bridge built; demolished 1869.

Three universities set up in Malta.

Sir Richard Arkwright (*1732, †1792) put first water-powered spinning mill into operation; first mechanical spinning of cotton *warp*; domestic system replaced by factory system.
Cook explored East coast of Australia.
Nicholas Cugnot's three-wheeler steam carriage; speed 4 m.p.h.; not really successful.
Distance from Earth to Sun measured.
Mahadji Sindhia founded Gwalior, India.

Fragonard: *The Love Letter*, French painting.
Guardi: (i) *The Doge appearing in St Mark's*. (ii) *The Piazza*, (iii) *View on the Cannareggio*, Venetian paintings.
Haydn: *Little Mass with Organ*, in B♭, *Paride ed Elena*, German opera.
Mozart: *Mitridate*, an opera.
Reynolds: *Miss Mary Hickey*, a portrait.
Visiting cards introduced into England.

James Bruce (*1730, †1794), explorer, discoverd source of Blue Nile.
Cook discovered Botany Bay, Australia.
P. M. Hahn constructed multiplication machine.
Antoine Lavoisier (*1743, †1794), great French chemist, proved that water could not be transmitted into earth, confounding longstanding theory.

	HISTORY	LITERATURE
1770	John Frederick Struensee chief minister of Denmark; issued 600 reform decrees. Austria seized further territory from Poland. Russians captured Bender, Ismail and Akerman from Turkey. Troops of Ali Bey captured Mecca.	dramatic poem; not completed until the year of the author's death, the work engaged him regularly. Henry Brooke (*1703, †1783): *The Fool of Quality* (from 1766), unusual novel.
1771	Right to report Parliamentary debates acquired. †Adolphus Frederick of Sweden; accession of Gustavus III; attempt to restore monarchal rule. Russia agreed with Prussia to partition of Poland. Austro-Turkish treaty to compel Russia to evacuate Moldavia and Wallachia. Russia secured Crimea and crushed Turkish fleet. Damascus seized by troops of Ali Bey.	Smollett: *Humphry Clinker*, a novel; the adventures of a workhouse boy. *Encyclopaedia Britannica* (first edition), in 3 vols., completed (see 1768). James Beattie (*1735, †1803): *The Minstrel* (first part; second part 1774), Scottish descriptive poem. Samuel Foote (*1720, †1777), actor and playwright: *The Maid of Bath*, a play lampooning elderly Squire Long. Henry Mackenzie (*1745, †1831): *The Man of Feeling*, sentimental sketches round one hero.
1772	Old Age Pensions first proposed by Francis Maseres (see 1787). Royal Marriages Act: to prevent undesirable royal marriages. Struensee murdered by "Danish" Party. Gustavus III of Sweden broke power of Diet; imposed new Constitution; checked Sweden from partition among Russia, Prussia and Denmark. First partition of Poland between Russia and Austria. Ali Bey driven into exile by revolt among his troops.	*Sandor Kisfaludy, Hungarian poet (†1801). *Letters of Junius* ceased; author, unknown, may have been Philip Francis or Lord Shelburne. Newspaper *The Morning Post* first issued; ceased 1937. Garrick: *The Irish Widow*, a farce. Lessing: *Emilia Galotti*, German tragedy.
1773	North's Regulating Act brought political activities of East India Co. under control of British Government. General Turnpike Act. Boston Tea Party; protest against tea duty by Bostonians. Expulsion of Jesuits from Imperial dominions by Joseph II. Polish Diet, well bribed, accepted Partition Treaty.	Goldsmith: *She Stoops to Conquer*, sentimental comedy; Miss Hardcastle pretends to be a barmaid to win the bashful Marlow. Gottfried August Bürger (*1747, †1794): *Lenore*, famous German ballad, which hastened on the Romantic movement. Goethe: *Götz von Berlichingen*, romantic drama based on story of famous German knight. Herder: *Von deutscher Art und Kunst*, the manifesto of the "Sturm und Drang".

c. Gainsborough: *Margaret Gainsborough*, a portrait.

Discovery, in Hungary, of opal of 2,975 carats.
Repeal of American Import Duties apart from duty on tea.
Famine in Bengal.
Glasse: *The Complete Confectioner*.
Thos. Pennant (*1726, †1798): *British Zoology*, formerly a standard work on the subject.

Clément: *Principes de Choréographie*.
Johann Zoffany (*c*, *1734, †1810): *Life School at the Royal Academy with portraits of leading artists including Reynolds*, a painting.
Discovery of 6th cent. Kingston brooch, in Kent.
Opening of Assembly Rooms, Bath (see 1942).
c. Fragonard: *A Game of Hot Cockles*, French painting.
c. Gainsborough: *Blue Boy*, famous portrait.
c. Haydn: Symphony in E♭ (*The Mercury*) and *Sun Quartets* (Op. 20 Nos. 1–6).

John Hunter (*1728, †1793), surgeon: *Treatise on the Natural History of the Human Teeth* (to 1778), basis of modern dentistry.
C. W. Scheele (*1742, †1786), German, discovered oxygen (independently found by Priestley 3 years later, *q.v.*) and fluorine.
Foundation of New York Hospital.
Bougainville: *Voyage autour du Monde*, account of first French circumnavigation of the world.
Pennant: *History of Quadrupeds*, classical study of the subject.
J. B. B. D'Anville (*1697, †1782); *États formés en Europe*, typical of his accurate modern geography.

Haydn: Mass in G (*Sechsviertelmesse*: 6/4 mass) and Symphonies in F♯ minor (*The Farewell*) and C (*Maria Theresa*).
Firm of Flights, London, advertised barrel-organs.
c. Gainsborough: *Ralph Schomberg*, a portrait.
Mozart: *Lucio Silla*, an opera.

Bougaineville, French explorer, visited Tasmania and New Zealand.
Cook departed on second voyage of discovery.
Romé de l'Isle studied crystals; further work by Abbé Hauy led to foundation of crystallography (see 1819).
Priestley, by publishing his findings, laid foundations of modern chemistry; produced soda-water and isolated nitrous oxide (laughing gas) during this year.
D. Rutherford (*1749, †1819) discovered nitrogen.
Hunter began to lecture on the theory and practice of surgery.

Education in Czechoslovakia under State Control with German as main language.
Haydn: *Stabat Mater*, choral work, and *Philemon and Baucis*, singspiel.
Reynolds: *Lady Cockburn and her Children*, fashionable family portrait.
Foundation of Brussels University.
The waltz became popular in Vienna (see 1791).
Offices opened at Birmingham and Sheffield to assay silver and gold articles.

Cook sighted the islands named after him; crossed Antarctic Circle this year; first man to do so.
Samuel Crompton (*1753, †1827) designed spinning mule; perfected 1779; for warp *and* weft.
Rouelle discovered urea in urine (see 1828).
Sheet glass introduced into England from France.
Parliament regulated wages in Spitalfields silk trade; repealed 1824.

LITERATURE

1773 Turks rejected Russian peace proposals at Bucharest.
Dissolution of Jesuit Order in China.

1774 Quebec Act became law: toleration to Canadian Roman Catholics; angered Puritan New Englanders.
Wilkes elected Lord Mayor and M.P.
Parliamentary "Intolerable Acts" suppressed colonial opposition to tea duty.
First Congress of Colonies at Philadelphia.
†Louis XV of France; accession of Louis XVI; Maurepas, First Minister; Parlements recalled.
Revolt among Austrian peasants over failure of Maria Theresa to improve conditions.
Don Cossack revolt under Pugacheff against Catherine II.
Turks forced to accept Russian-dictated Treaty of Kutchuk-Kainjardi.
Warren Hastings appointed Governor General of India.

Earl of Chesterfield (*1694, †1773): *Letters to his Son*, advice on how a gentleman should behave, published; letters begun 1737.
Voltaire: *Sophonisbe*, a tragedy; the heroine is the daughter of a Carthaginian general, Hasdrubal.
Goethe: *Die Leiden des jungen Werthers*; Werther the student takes his life because his love for Lotte is unrequited; "Werther" fever soon affected all Europe.
Sir William Jones (†1748, †1794): *Poeseos Asiaticae Commentariorum Libri Sex*, books on oriental poetry.

1775 War of American Independence: battle of Bunker's Hill; "Olive Branch" petition from Colonists rejected by British government; ride of Paul Revere from Charleston to Lexington; battle of Lexington.
Government of Portuguese Goa reorganized by Pombal, Portuguese dictator.
Austria exploited Turkish weakness to seize Bukhovina.
Catherine II divided Russia into Provinces, sub-divided into Circles and Districts.
Basra captured by Shah of Persia.
Outbreak of First Maratta War; lasted until 1782.

Richard Brinsley Sheridan (*1751, †1816): *The Rivals*, a comedy with Mrs Malaprop as one of the characters.
Pierre-Augustin Caron de Beaumarchais (*1732, †1799): *Le Barbier de Séville*, French comedy of rascal barber Figaro and his master, County Almaviva.
Vittorio Alfieri (*1749, †1803), Italian tragic dramatist: *Cleopatraccia*.
Sarah Siddons first appeared on the stage.
Johnson: *Journey to the Western Islands of Scotland*, made with Boswell.

1776 War of American Independence: Colonies issued Declaration of Independence, drawn up in Independence Hall (1735),

Adam Smith (*1723, †1790): *An Enquiry into the Nature and the Causes of the Wealth of Nations*, famous economic treatise on nature of national wealth.

Muzio Clementi (*1752, †1832) published his first three sonatas (Op. 2).

Gluck: *Iphigenia in Aulis*, German opera.
Haydn: Symphony No. 55 in E♭ (*The Schoolmaster*).
c. Gainsborough: *Viscount Kilmorey*, a portrait; the artist removed from Bath to London in the same year.
Completion of the Radcliffe Camera, Oxford, from funds left by Dr Radcliffe, court physician (begun 1771).
Rules of cricket first drawn up, although the game had been played earlier; possibly developed from 13th-cent. bat and ball games.

C. P. E. Bach: *The Israelites in the Wilderness*, German oratorio.
Charles Dibdin (*1745, †1810): *The Quaker*, an opera.
c. Haydn: Symphony in A (*Fire S.*) and *The Return of Tobit*, an oratorio.
Mozart: Five violin concertos.
Reynolds: *Miss Bowles and her Dog*, a portrait.
Toplady: *Rock of Ages*, a hymn.
c. Fragonard: *The Washerwoman*, French painting.
First Thames Regatta.
Adam brothers erected Portland Place.
(to 1778) Le Camus erected Pagoda of Chanteloup, Forest of Amboise.
Lowestoft china became popular.

Sir William Chambers erected Somerset House; 600 ft long; holds records of population statistics.

Foundation of Philadelphia Museum.
c. Johann Elert Bode (*1747, †1826) enunciated his Law (distance law of planets): $4,\ 3.2^n + 4$ ($n = 0, 1, 2, 3, \ldots$).

Lavoisier helped to develop modern chemistry (see 1772).
F. A. Mesmer (*1734, †1815), Austrian physician, used hypnosis (known to Paracelsus) for health purposes.
Mastoid operation successfully performed by Petit in France.
Priestley prepared ammonia gas and oxygen.
Scheele described preparation of chlorine (gas probably known in 13th cent.).
J. G. Gahn isolated manganese.
John Wilkinson, iron-master, constructed boring-mill.
Export of cotton-making machinery from Britain prohibited.
Bode founded *Astronomisches Jahrbuch*, German year book of astronomy.

Thos. Jeffreys: *The American Atlas*.
Maskelyne, astronomer royal: experiment to determine effect of mountain on plumb-line (gravitational attraction).
Priestley discovered hydrochloric and sulphuric acids.
Watt and Matthew Boulton set up partnership to manufacture steam engines designed by the former (see 1776).
Preparation of soda.
English took over Indo-Chinese opium trade from Portuguese.
Completion of Bromberg canal, connecting Oder and Vistula (started 1772).
First British Bank Clearing-house established at Lombard Street.
Vaucanson founded Conservatoire des Arts et Métiers, technical school and museum of machinery.

Cook set out on third voyage of discovery.
Lassone investigated properties of carbon monoxide.
Tobias Mayer's lunar map.

1776	Philadelphia, from Britain; British forced to evacuate Boston; captured New York; Battle of Trenton; British repulsed at Charleston; unsuccessful colonial attack on Canada. Parlement of Paris opposed to reform; dismissal of Turgot.	Edward Gibbon (*1737, †1794): *Decline and Fall of the Roman Empire*; completed 1788. Last public appearance of Garrick, great actor (see 1741).
1777	War of American Independence: surrender of General Burgoyne at Saratoga; Colonists defeated at Brandywine Creek; British captured Philadelphia. Jacques Necker appointed Finance Minister in France. Perpetual Alliance between Spain and Portugal. †Joseph I of Portugal; banishment of Pombal. †Elector of Bavaria; succession of Charles Theodore, Elector Palatine, led to disputes involving Austria, Prussia and German States; reunion of Palatinate with Bavaria; separated since 1294.	Chatterton: *Poems* (the author pretended these were the work of a 15th cent. monk) exposed posthumously by Tyrwhitt (see 1770). Mackenzie: *Julia de Roubigné*, a novel. Hannah More (*1745, †1833): *Percy*, a tragedy produced at the Garrick.
1778	†William Pitt, Earl of Chatham. France allied herself to the American Colonists against Britain. War of American Independence: Battle of Monmouth, New Jersey. War of Bavarian Succession between Prussia and Austria; "Potato War" a bloodless campaign. Russian forces under Suvaroff entered Crimea. French settlements in India captured by British.	Fanny Burney (*1752, †1840): *Evelina*, a novel whose heroine is a young girl; after many difficulties she discovers she is of noble birth and there is a happy ending. Sheridan: *The School for Scandal*; his greatest comedy, with the famous characters Lady Teazle and Charles Surface.
1779	Anglo-French naval engagement off Flamborough Head. Liberation of Royal serfs in France. Charles III of Spain joined France and American colonies in war against Britain; commencement of siege of Gibraltar. Peace of Teschen ended bloodless Austro-Prussian war over Bavarian Succession.	Lessing: *Nathan der Weise*, a drama of Nathan, the wise Jew who thinks that all religions are forms of the same truth. Wieland: *Oberon*, long German epic poem. Publication of the *Olney Hymns*, which included several by Wm. Cowper (*1731, †1800), e.g. *God moves in a mysterious way*. More: *The Fatal Falsehood*, a tragedy. Sheridan: *The Critic*, a play and satire on other plays of the time.

Gainsborough: *Lady Brisco* and *Miss Robinson*, portraits.
Mozart: *Haffner Serenade*, so-called.
Charles Burney (*1726, †1814): *A General History of Music* (4 vols., completed 1789), first such work in English.
Antient Music Concerts, supported by George III, in London (to 1848).

Bode: *Sammlung astronomischer Tafeln*.
Watt and Boulton produced first commercial steam engine.
Wilkinson, iron-master, used steam engine to operate bellows for blast furnace.
First St Leger (horse race) run at Doncaster.

Burney published eight pianoforte sonata duets.
Gluck: *Armide*, German opera.
c. Guardi: *Santa Maria della Salute*, Venetian painting.
Haydn: Symphony in C (*La Roxolane*).
Device of Stars and Stripes adopted as Continental Congress Flag in America; then 13 stars and 13 stripes.
First performance of ballad opera *Polly* by John Gay (written 1729).

Cook discovered Sandwich Islands.
John Howard: *The State of the Prisons in England and Wales*, an early social study.
Lavoisier showed that air consisted (mainly) of oxygen and nitrogen (the latter was called azote at the time).
Scheele observed the effect of light of different colours on silver compounds; a step towards photography.

Jean Antoine Houdon (*1741, †1828), French sculptor: *Voltaire*, a bust.
Mozart: (i) *Paris Symphony* (in D), so-called; (ii) Double Concerto for Flute and Harp; (iii) *Sinfonia concertante*, for bassoon, clarinet, horn and oboe.
First performance of *Les Petits Riens*, ballet with music by Mozart, choreography by Noverre.

Robert Barron made double-acting lock.
Joseph Bramah (*1748, †1814), Yorkshireman, invented water-closet (see 1596).
Thos. Coke, of Holkham, Norfolk, commenced experiments in new farming techniques.
Cook discovered Hawaii and was murdered there in 1779.
Benjamin Thompson (Lord Rumford, *1753, †1814) made first investigation into heat generated by friction in firing gun.

Gluck: *Iphigenia in Tauris*, German opera, produced in Paris; made early use of piccolo in the work.
Mozart: (i) *Coronation Mass*, incorrectly named; (ii) *Sinfonia concertante*, for violin and viola.
Foundation, at St Petersburg, of the Imperial Ballet School.
Foundation of Birmingham Library.
Construction, across the Severn at Broseley, of first cast-iron bridge in the world.

Blanchard and Magurier: four-wheeled velocipede.
James Emerson manufactured brass from copper and zinc.
Ingenhousz, Dutch, noted that plants absorb carbon dioxide during the day but give it out at night.
Pope Pius VI began draining Pontine Marshes.
Scheele prepared glycerine; chemistry of fats founded.
Schroter founded Lilienthal observatory.
First children's clinic; in London.

1780	William Pitt the Younger entered Parliament. "No Popery" riots in London; led by Lord George Gordon. Foundation of Cartwright's Constitutional Society. Spanish fleet defeated by Rodney off Cape St Vincent. Armed Neutrality of North formed against Britain by Holland, Denmark, Sweden and Russia; protest against R.N. searching neutral ships at sea. †Maria Theresa of Austria; succession of Emperor Joseph II. End of Alliance between Prussia and Austria. Suleiman the Great assumed Pashalik of Baghdad. Outbreak of Second Mysore War; lasted to 1784. Start of Peruvian rebellion against Spanish rule; lasted to 1783.	*c.* Johnson: *Lives of the Poets*, collection of biographies and analysis of their works. John Nichols (*1745, †1826), author and printer: *Royal Wills*. Charles Panckoucke (*1736, †1798) began immense task of revising and enlarging *Encyclopédie* as collection of separate works under generic titles.
1781	War of American Independence: British forces under Cornwallis surrendered to Washington at Yorkstown. Ratification of Articles of Confederation and Perpetual Union by all States of North America. Necker: *Compte Rendu au Roi*; led to his dismissal. French attack on Jersey failed. Dutch surrendered Barrier Forts to Joseph II. Edict of Toleration issued by Joseph II; authority of Papacy in Austria reduced. Austro-Russian Alliance formed against Turkey.	Rousseau: *Confessions*, the frankest of autobiographies. Johann Christoph Friedrich Schiller (*1759, †1805): *Die Räuber*, a stirring drama full of revolutionary feeling and challenge to political tyranny. Johann Heinrich Pestalozzi (*1746, †1827): *Lienhard und Gertrud*, social novel by Swiss educationalist. Immanuel Kant (*1724, †1804): *Critique of Pure Reasoning*; German treatise laying foundation of modern philosophy.
1782	Younger Pitt appointed Chancellor of Exchequer. Resignation of North: Rockingham in office, followed by Shelburne. Gilbert's Act allowed parishes in England and Wales to administer Poor Law. Admiral Rodney defeated French at Isle of Saints; British naval supremacy restored. Loss of *Royal George*.	Choderlos de Laclos (*1741, †1803): *Les Liaisons dangereuses*, a novel of depraved French aristocrats. Burney: *Cecilia*, a novel. Eight satires of Cowper published: (i) *Charity*, (ii) *Conversation*, (iii) *Expostulation*, (iv) *Progress of Truth*, (v) *Retirement*, (vi) *Progress of Error*, (vii) *Table Talk*, (viii) *Hope*. Peter Pindar (John Wolcot) (*1738, †1819): *Lyric Odes to the Royal Academicians*, satirical verse (to 1785).

Sebastian Carezo invented *bolero*, Spanish dance, 3 beats in bar; Chopin and Ravel wrote piano music in this style.
Francisco de Goya (*1746, †1828), Spanish artist famous for nude women and grotesque tragic pictures: *The Doctor*, painting for tapestry-work.
Haydn: Symphony in C (*The Toy S.*).
Robert Raikes, of Gloucester, opened his first Sunday School.
Gainsborough: *Miss Haverfield*, a portrait.
Thos. Turner (*1749, †1809), potter, introduced Willow pattern design.

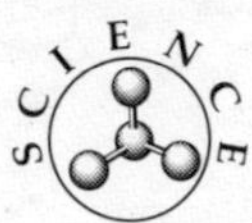

Felice Fontana produced water-gas.
Gervinus invented circular saw.
Rush, of Philadelphia, accurately described dengue fever.
Scheller made first fountain pen.
Watt invented a letter-copying press.
Commercial manufacture of muslins commenced (see 1763).
Aquatint process in Britain (see 1768).
Derby flat race first run; established by 12th Earl of Derby.
American Academy of Sciences founded at Boston.

Jacques-Louis David (*1748, †1825), counter-Rococo artist: *Belisarius*, French painting.
Gainsborough: *Mrs Robinson*, a portrait.
Haydn: Symphony in D (*La Chasse*) and *Russian String Quartets*, six in number, so-called.
Mozart: (i) *Idomeneo*, an opera in Italian style; (ii) sonata for two pianos.
George Romney (*1734, †1802), fashionable artist: *Miss Willoughby*, a portrait.

Sir Frederick William Herschel (*1738, †1822) discovered planet Uranus; used 7 ft reflecting telescope.
Jonathan C. Hornblower (*1753, †1815), inventor, patented compound two-cylinder steam engine.
Charles Messier (*1730, †1817): catalogue of nebulae and star-clusters.
Construction of Siberian highway commenced.
Franciscan fathers established settlement at Los Angeles.
First Building Society set up; in Birmingham.

Haydn: *Mariazell Mass* in C, so-called.
Mozart: *Haffner Symphony* in D, so-called; and *Abduction from the Seraglio*, opera, originally in German, of Spanish girl abducted to Turkey.
*Niccolo Paganini (†1840), great violinist, at Genoa; his *compositions* were of little merit.
Romney: *Lady and Child*, a painting.

*Joseph Arnold (†1818, in Sumatra), botanist, who was to discover world's largest flower, *Rafflesia arnoldi*, 3 ft across.
Edmund Burke's Economic Reform Act.
Adrien Marie Legendre (*1752, †1833): *Trajectories in Resisting Media*, French mathematical work.
Joseph Montgolfier constructed fire-balloon; first sent up empty.
Richenstein discovered tellurium.
Scheele manufactured hydrocyanic acid

Year	History	Literature
1782	Siege of Gibraltar raised. Irish Parliament secured legislative independence; partial removal of Irish Roman Catholic disabilities; congress of Irish Volunteers at Dungannon; Meeting of Gratton's Free Irish Parliament. Franco-Spanish force captured Minorca from British. British seized Trincomalee from Dutch; retaken by French, allies of Dutch.	
1783	Coalition ministry under Portland. Fox's India Bill. Fall of Portland ministry; Younger Pitt's "Mince Pie" Administration. British Honduras acquired. War of American Independence ended by Treaty of Versailles; Britain recognized independence of American Colonies; Britain restored Minorca and Florida to Spain, but retained Gibraltar. United Empire Loyalists, who had supported Britain in American War of Independence, driven out of the U.S.A.; settled in Canada. Calonne appointed Controller-General in France. Catherine II of Russia introduced Imperial Governors and strengthened direct power of Crown over Baltic Provinces. Serfdom introduced into Little Russia. Russians annexed Crimea. Trincomalee restored by French to Britain and by her to Dutch.	William Blake (*1757, †1827): *Poetical Sketches*, by famous English mystic poet and engraver known as the Cockney visionary. Cowper: *John Gilpin*, a ballad of a draper unable to control his horse. George Crabbe (*1754, †1832): *The Village*, a poem dealing with a Suffolk village. Thomas Day (*1748, †1789): *Sandford and Merton*, a tale of a good boy and a bad boy; Merton is rich and selfish, Sandford, a farmer's son, commands our respect.
1784	Younger Pitt victorious at General Election. Government of India Act by Younger Pitt: Government control over East India Co.'s rule in India. Appointment of first Anglican colonial bishop. Dutch refused demand by Joseph II that they should open Scheldt to free navigation. Reforms of Joseph II aroused great opposition in Hungary.	Cook: *Voyages of Discovery* published. Beaumarchais: *Le Mariage de Figaro*, a comedy in which Figaro reappears as a cunning barber; banned for six years for its attacks on the aristocracy. Young started *Annals of Agriculture;* important farming journal. Cowper, *The Task*, a poem in six books; his chief work in which he recommends rural life.

from Prussian blue (hence name *prussic acid*).
Watt invented double-acting rotary steam engine.
Wedgwood developed pyrometer; needed for temperature checking in pottery furnace (see 1750).
Establishment of Bank of North America, at Philadelphia.
P. J. Helm isolated molybdenum.

Broadwood patented piano pedal.
Moses Mendelssohn gave first careful exposition on ancient Hebrew musical instruments.
c. Mozart: *Linz Symphony* in C, so-called.
Reynolds: *Captain Bligh*, a painting.
Foundation of first London Glee Club.
Order of St Patrick founded in Ireland by George III.
David: *The Grief of Andromache*, French painting.
Servandoni built St Sulpice Church, Paris.

Bell invented process of using copper cylinders for printing cotton and linen fabrics.
Leger, French, invented flat ribbon-wick for oil lamps.
J. M. and J. E. Montgolfier, French brothers, successfully ascended in fire balloon; first ascent in hydrogen balloon in same year by brothers Charles.
Horace B. de Saussure (*1740, †1799), Swiss physicist and climber, invented hair-hygrometer.
Retort-production of charcoal in England.
Establishment of Bank of Ireland.
Foundation of North West Trading Co. as rival to Hudson Bay Trading Co.
Oldest Chamber of Commerce in Britain; incorporated at Glasgow.
First working paddle-steamer, the *Pyroscaphe*, French; not really successful (see 1787 for steamship and 1807 for paddle steamship).

Etienne-Louis Boullée designed cenotaph to Newton in shape of a planetarium.
Gainsborough: *Baillie Family*, a painting.
Goya: *Don Manuel de Zuniga*, Spanish painting.
Romney: *Mrs Davenport*, a portrait.
Work begun on Brighton Pavilion, for Prince Regent, completed 1827.
Haydn: Six symphonies (Nos. 82–87), composed for the Paris *Concerts Spirituels*.
Thomas Bewick (*1753, †1828), famous for his wood-blocks: *Select Fables*.

Aimé Argand (*1755, †1803) Swiss: first scientifically designed oil burner.
George Atwood (*1746, †1807) accurately determined acceleration of a freely falling body.
Bramah designed safety locks.
Henry Cort introduced puddling process for conversion of pig iron into wrought iron.
Goethe discovered intermaxillary bone.
Pierre S. Laplace (*1749, †1827): *Théorie du mouvement et de la figure des planets*, first of

1784 Convention of Constantinople between Russia and Turkey; Turkey agreed to Russian annexation of Crimea.

1785 Younger Pitt introduced Bill to reform Parliament; defeated.
Irish Trade Bill rejected by Irish Parliament.
Resignation of Warren Hastings as Governor General of India.
Treaty of Fontainebleau between France and republican estates in Holland; opposed to Stadholder William V of Orange.
Arrest of Cardinal de Rohan; affair of Diamond Necklace.
Formation of Fürstenbund by Frederick II of Prussia to check Austria.

Cowper: *Tirocinium*, against Public Schools.
Wolcot: *The Lousiad*, a mock-heroic poem.
Boswell: *Journal of a Tour of the Hebrides*, by the biographer of Dr Johnson.
John Walter founded *The Daily Universal Register*, renamed *The Times* in 1788, by which name it has been known ever since.

1786 Lord Cornwallis, Governor General of India (to 1793), founded Indian Civil Service.
Penang purchased by British Government.
Calonne's proposed reforms in France.
Assembly of Notables in France.
Dutch Estates suspended by Stadholder.
Royal extravagance in Sweden caused great distress.
†Frederick II (the Great) of Prussia; accession of nephew, Frederick William II.
Ottoman Turks re-occupied Cairo for short time.
Japanese famine since 1780 reduced population by a million; great discontent; Shogunate losing support; revival of Imperialist sentiment.

Robert Burns (*1759, †1796): *Poems chiefly in the Scottish dialect.*
Necker: *Administration of Finance in France.*
William Beckford (*1759, †1844): *Vathek*, oriental romance of a wicked caliph.
Schiller: *Philosophische Briefe*, German philosophical work.
Mrs Sarah Trimmer (*1741, †1810): *The History of the Robins*, book for the young.
Kant: *Metaphysical Rudiments of Natural Philosophy.*

1787 Old Age Pension scheme proposed by Mark Rolle.

Bernardin de Saint-Pierre (*1737, †1814): *Paul et Virginie*, tragic French story of two

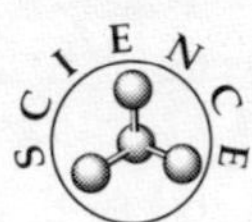

Introduction of duty on silver articles; special hall-mark (monarch's head) stamped on silver; duty abolished 1890.

four great works by French mathematician.
Vincent Lunardi made first balloon ascent in England.
John Palmer: first official mail coach; operated between Bristol and London.
United Empire Loyalists founded Ontario and New Brunswick.

David: *The Oath of the Horatii*, French painting which caused sensation by its unusual style.
Dibdin published *The Bells of Aberdovy*, song; not Welsh as popularly believed.
Gainsborough: *Mrs Siddons*, a portrait.
Haydn: seven orchestral adagios for Cadiz Cathedral; and instrumental music based on the *Seven Last Words of the Saviour on the Cross* (see 1796, when work modified for voices).
Emerald Buddha Chapel, Bangkok, erected.
Foundation of New Brunswick University, Canada.
Charles III of Spain founded Real Museo de Pintura del Prado, famous picture gallery.

Claude Louis de Berthollet (*1748, †1822) developed chemical bleaching using chlorine.
Edmund Cartwright (*1743, †1823), took out patent for power-loom.
Charles Augustin de Coulomb (*1736, †1806), French physicist, discovered inverse-square law; designed torsion-balance.
Earliest form of life-boat built by Lionel Lukin.
Solsano invented seismograph for measuring earthquakes.
Withering used digitalis (extracting *digitalin*) for heart disease.
Introduction of word *chiropody*; originally referred to *hands* and feet.
First Channel crossing made by balloon by Blanchard and Jeffries (January 7th).

Gainsborough: *Miss Linley*, a portrait, and *The Market Cart*, a painting.
Goya: *The Seasons*, Spanish tapestry painting.
Haydn: Symphonies in C (*The Bear*); in G minor (*The Hen*); in B♭ (*La Reine*) and in D; four of the six Paris symphonies.
Mozart: *The Marriage of Figaro*, German opera produced in Vienna (1787); and *Prague Symphony* in D, so-called.
Reynolds: *The Duchess of Devonshire and her small Daughter*, a painting.
Joseph II established seminary at Louvain; ordered all candidates for ministry to attend.

F. W. Herschel propounded disc theory of shape of Galaxy.
Martin Heinrich Klaproth (*1743, †1817), German chemist, discovered uranium.
Potemkin founded Dniepropetrovsk.
Earliest attempts at gas-lighting in Germany and in England.
Financial reforms introduced by younger Pitt: reduction of import duties; reconstruction of Board of Trade; creation of Sinking Fund; commercial treaty with France (Pitt-Vergennes Treaty).
Balmat and Paccard first climbed Mont Blanc.
James Rumsey, U.S.A., designed mechanically driven boat.

C. P. E. Bach: *The Resurrection and Ascension of Jesus*, an oratorio.

Bennet invented gold-leaf electroscope.
Ernst Chladni (*1756, †1827) experimented

1787 Federal Government established in the U.S.A.
Pennsylvania admitted to statehood in the U.S.A.
Dissolution of Assembly of Notables in France.
Parlement of Paris opposed to Stamp Tax; exiled; France declared herself bankrupt.
Wilhelmina, wife of Stadholder William V, imprisoned by insurgents; Prussia, supported by Britain, invaded Gelderland to assist William V, who was restored.
Joseph II reduced powers of Estates in Austrian Netherlands; outcry forced him to withdraw scheme.
Turkey, fearing seizure of Caucasus region, declared war on Russia.

children in Mauritius who fall in love; Virginie returning from France is shipwrecked near the island.
Schiller: *Don Carlos,* a drama; the love of the Spanish heir-apparent for his stepmother.
Goethe: *Iphigenie auf Tauris,* a play; version of the Greek legend.
Jeremy Bentham (*1748, †1832): *Defence of Usury,* written in Russia.

1788 George III's first attack of illness; Regency crisis in England.
Impeachment of Warren Hastings.
Triple Alliance (among England, United Provinces and Prussia) guaranteed constitution of Holland.
First Federal Congress of the U.S.A. in New York.
Gustavus III of Sweden declared war on Russia without sanction of Estates; Battle of Hogland; mutiny of Swedish officers.
Danes invaded Sweden; Treaty of Uddevalla ended Danish-Swedish war.
Austria declared war on Turkey in support of Russia; overran Moldavia; Transylvania refused to support Joseph II.
Meeting of Four Years Diet in Poland.
Russian fleet defeated Turks; Suvaroff captured Ochakoff.

Duc de Saint-Simon (*1675, †1755): *Mémoires,* recollections of French aristocrat.
Goethe: *Egmont,* historical tragedy; the Flemish Count Egmont is executed for opposing Philip II.
Religious Edict by Frederick William II limited freedom of speech in Prussia.
Kant: *Critique of Practical Reason,* philosophical work.

1789 British vessels seized by Spanish in Nootka Sound; hostility between Britain and Spain.
First American National Election; George Washington first President of the U.S.A.
French Estates General met at Versailles; Third Estate adopted

Blake: *Songs of Innocence,* poetry.
Gilbert White (*1720, †1793): *Natural History of Selborne,* by the curate of Selborne in Hampshire.
First large-scale Eisteddfod held at Corwen.
Bentham: *Introduction to Principles of Morals and Legislation* published.

Kiyonaga (*1742, †1815): *Sudden Shower at Mimeguri Shrine*, Japanese wood-block print.
Mozart: (i) *Don Giovanni (The Rake Punished)*, opera first performed in Prague; (ii) *Ein Musikalischer Spass*, miniature symphony in F, lampooning inferior composers; (iii) *Eine Kleine Nachtmusik* for string orchestra.
Reynolds: *Heads of Angels*, a painting.
Marylebone Cricket Club (M.C.C.) established at Thos. Lord's ground, Dorset Square; removed 1815 to St John's Wood.

with sound patterns on vibrating plate.
John Fitch, American, made first practical steamboat.
Ramsden constructed a 3 ft theodolite; capable of measuring spherical excess.
Saussure climbed Mont Blanc and took weather observations.
Watt introduced centrifugal governor (wrongly named).
Wilkinson demonstrated feasibility of iron ships.
English settlement founded at Sierra Leone for freed slaves.
Dollar currency first introduced in the U.S.A. (see 1792).
Jacques Charles (*1746, †1823) enunciated his gas law; independently propounded by Gay-Lussac (1802).

David: *Love of Paris and Helen*, French painting.
Haydn: *Oxford Symphony* in G major; so-called when composer visited city in 1791.
George Hepplewhite (†1786): *The Cabinet-makers' and Upholsterers' Guide* (to furniture of fine design) published.
Mozart: *Jupiter Symphony* and symphonies in E♭ and G minor, his three greatest; also *Bastien and Bastienne*, an opera.
Roman baths at Bath found, but not excavated until later.
Council of Brabant refused to agree to Joseph II's Louvain seminary.

Lagrange, French mathematician, who did major work on vibrations and degrees of freedom in dynamics: *Mécanique analytique*, in which he utilized virtual velocities.
A. Meikle designed a threshing-machine.
Sir James E. Smith founded Linnaean Society for science of natural history (see 1751).
Foundation of New South Wales as convict settlement.
Abolition of serfdom in Denmark.
Food scarcity and bread riots in France.
Opening, in Hamburg, of first cigar factory.

Burney completed his *History of Music*.
David: *Lictors bringing Brutus the bodies of his sons*, French painting.
Dibdin: *Tom Bowling*, an opera.
Christopher Potter introduced porcelain painting in France.
Ça Ira, revolutionary song during "The Terror" in France.

Patent granted to Henry Greathead for design of life-boat.
Herschel constructed 40 ft telescope: discovered 6th and 7th moons of Saturn.
Klaproth discovered zirconium in sand in rivers of Ceylon.
Lavoisier gave formal enunciation of conservation of matter.

	History	Literature
1789	name of National Assembly; Oath of Tennis Court; Union of Three Estates; Committee of Constitution; Fall of Bastille; march to Versailles; King and Assembly returned to Paris; National Guard formed in Paris under Lafayette; risings in French provinces. Act of Union in Sweden; Gustavus III changed constitutional monarchy to despotism. Estates of Brabant suppressed by Joseph II; revolt of Austrian Netherlands; Joseph II declared deposed; Belgian Republic established. Joseph II forced to withdraw all Hungarian reforms except abolition of serfdom. Austrians captured Belgrade, overran Serbia. Turkish overthrow prevented by alliance of Britain, Prussia and Holland.	
1790	Nootka Sound Convention: to solve Anglo-Spanish dispute. First meeting of Supreme Court of the U.S.A. French Revolution: Civil Constitution of Clergy in France; resignation of Necker; naval mutiny at Brest; foundation of Order of Cordeliers. Peace of Varala ended Russo-Swedish war. Austrian forces destroyed Belgian Republic. †Emperor Joseph II; accession of Leopold II. Truce between Turkey and Austria. Convention of Reichenbach between Prussia and Austria. Russians captured Ismail; Turkish fleet defeated at Sebastopol. Alliance of Prussia and Turkey. (to 1792) Third Mysore War.	Burns: *Tam o'Shanter*, a narrative poem. Burke: *Reflections on the French Revolution*. French Revolution: National Assembly abolished *Lettres de Cachet*. Blake: *Marriage of Heaven and Hell*, attacking established ideas of authority and religion. Kant: *Critique of Judgment*, philosophical work.
1791	Pitt's Canada Act: gave Canada representative government. Church and King Riots in Birmingham.	Thomas Paine (*1737, †1809): *Rights of Man* (first part), political work in defence of French Revolution.

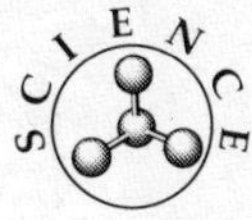

(to 1790) Mozart: *Prussian Quartets*, three string quartets for Frederick William.
State University of Pennsylvania created by charter, out of Philadelphia Academy (founded 1745).
†*Eclipse*, famous racehorse, unbeaten throughout its career.

First steam-driven cotton factory in Manchester.
Preliminary work, in France, on metric system of measurement, now used in progressive countries (see 1791, 1795, 1801).
Assignats, paper money, issued in France.
Reform of slave trade advocated by younger Pitt.
Mutineers from H.M.S. *Bounty* settled on Pitcairn Island.
United States Post Office established.
Evans, U.S.A., patented first amphibious vehicle.
Chrysanthemums, known 2,000 years earlier in the Orient, introduced into Britain.

Bewick: *A General History of Quadrupeds*, containing fine wood-blocks.
Guardi: *Gondola on the Lagoon*, Venetian painting.
Mozart: (i) *Cosi fan tutti*, German opera with Italian libretto: (ii) *Adagio and Allegro* in F minor, for piano.
Thomas Sheraton (*1751, †1806): *Cabinet Makers' and Upholsterers' Drawing Book* (to 1794), of fine furniture designs.
First musical competition in America.

Luigi Galvani (*1737, †1798), Italian scientist, carried out electrical experiments which led to discovery of galvanic battery (see also 1800).
Lavoisier: first table of chemical elements (31 listed).
William Nicholson invented the rotary-press.
T. Sanit constructed sewing machine for shoes (hand sewing machine later).
First steam-powered rolling mill in England.
Construction of Forth-Clyde Canal completed.
Foundation of Washington, capital of the U.S.A. since 1800.

*Carl Czerny (†1857) at Vienna, pianist famous for his studies.
Haydn: Symphony in G (*The Surprise*) called *Kettledrum (Paukenschlag*, in German) third

Galvani published results of experiments on muscular reactions in frogs to passage of electric current.

1791

Pro-French group founded in Ireland: led by Wolfe Tone and Lord Edward Fitzgerald.
U.S. Congress ratified Bill of Rights.
Vermont admitted to membership of United States.
French Revolution: Louis XVI accepted Constitution; massacres at Paris and Avignon; decrees against émigrés; Louis XVI and family attempted flight, captured at Varennes, brought back to Paris as prisoners; Lafayette resigned command of National Guard.
Rising of natives in San Domingo.
Treaty of Friendship and Union between Sweden and Russia.
Peace of Sistova between Austria and Turkey.
Circular of Padua issued by Leopold II.
Stanislaus of Poland introduced reforms; supported by Leopold II; opposed by Prussia and Russia.
Declaration of Pillnitz.
Turkey defeated by Russia.

Boswell: *The Life of Samuel Johnson*, great biography, published.
First Gorsedd Beirdd Ynys Prydain (Session of the Bards of the Isle of Britain) held on Primrose Hill, London.
Allgemeines Landrecht, codified laws of Prussia, issued.
Bentham: *Panopticon*, letters on prison organization.
Blake: *The French Revolution*.
Cowper: *Yardley Oak*, a poem.
William Bartram (*1739, †1823), American naturalist: *Travels through North and South Carolina*.

1792

Foundation of Baptist Missionary Society.
Kentucky became State in the U.S.A.
French Revolution: France declared a Republic; Revolutionary Tribunal set up; France declared war on Austria; September Massacres in Paris prisons; Battles of Valmy and Jamappes; flight of Lafayette.
Treaty of Berlin between Austria and Prussia.
Duke of Brunswick's *Manifesto*.
†Leopold II; accession of Francis II, last Holy Roman Emperor.
Gustavus III assassinated in Stockholm Opera House.
Attempt at Convention of Targowice to restore old Polish constitution; Russian invasion defeated Poles in six weeks.
Treaty of Jassy ended Russo-Turkish war.

Young: *Travels in France*; described conditions in France just before the Revolution.
Paine: *Rights of Man* (second part).
Johann Paul Richter, German novelist (Jean Paul), (*1763, †1825): *Hesperus*, fictitious biography.
Samuel Rogers (*1763, †1855): *Pleasures of Memory*, popular poetry.

London symphony; and symphony in D (*The Miracle*.
Mozart: (i) *Die Zauberflöte (The Magic Flute)*, ever popular German opera; (ii) *La clemenza di Tito*, an opera; (iii) *Fantasia* in F for piano duet; (iv) *Requiem*, written on his death-bed; he was buried in an unmarked pauper's grave.
Introduction of the waltz into England.

Rev. William McGregor discovered titanium, rare metal.
Leblanc, French, developed soda-making process which was to lead later to development of heavy chemical industry.
William Rushton established first institution for the blind (at Liverpool).
Wilberforce's *Motion for Abolition of Slave Trade* carried through Parliament.
French Academy of Sciences defined metre as 10^{-7} of Earth's polar quadrant through Paris.
School of veterinary surgery established in London.
Completion of canal (begun 1784) linking Baltic and North sea; superseded (1886) by Kiel Canal.

Domenico Cimarosa (*1749, †1801): *The Secret Marriage*, Italian opera produced in Vienna.
Haydn: *The Creation*, oratorio performed in Vienna.
Claude Rouget de Lisle (*1760, †1836): *La Marseillaise*, war song composed for the Army of the Rhine; now the French National Anthem.
Carmagnole, revolutionary song in Marseilles.
Ye Banks and Braes, a song; words by Burns.
Tuileries invaded by Paris mob.

Claude Chappé, French, invented mechanical semaphore system; erected 22 stations from Paris to Lille; *idea* of semaphore signalling dates back to 1666.
Mackenzie travelled across Canada to the Pacific.
William Murdoch first successfully illuminated a home by coal-gas; at Redruth, Cornwall.
Last year in which England had exportable surplus of wheat.
Mint established in the U.S.A.; dollar currency developed (see 1787).
French revolutionary calendar established.
Slave trade abolished in Danish colonies.
Guillotine erected in Paris.
Russian ships attempted to enter Japanese waters; failed.

1793

Outbreak of war between Britain and Revolutionary France.
Aliens Act restricted liberty of foreign visitors to Britain.
Scottish Treason Trials: Muir and Palmer transported for advocating Parliamentary Reform.
Irish Catholics received right to vote.
French Revolution: execution of Louis XVI; Reign of Terror lasting 15 months; 2,596 victims in Paris; revolt in La Vendée; Marie Antoinette and Madame Dubarry guillotined; execution of Charlotte Corday for assassination of Marat (*1743); fall of Girondins; Revolutionary Army formed.
Toulon occupied by British forces for 4 months.
Battles of Hondschoote, Kaiserslautern, Wattignies and Weissenburg.
Polish Diet met at Grodno; Second Partition of Poland between Russia and Prussia.
Outbreak of second Kaffir War.

William Godwin (*1756, †1836): published *Political Justice*.
William Wordsworth (*1770, †1850): *An Evening Walk* and *Descriptive Sketches*.
Schiller: *Geschichte des dreissigjährigen Krieges*, history of the Thirty Years' War.
Seditious Publications Act limited liberty of the Press.
Kant: *Religion within the Boundaries of Pure Reason*, for which he was censured.
Paine: *The Age of Reason*, an outspoken book advocating deism, it did him no good in England or America.

1794

Habeas Corpus Act suspended in Britain until 1801.
Acquittal of Hardy and Horne Tooke on treason charges.
British naval victory at Battle of First of June.
Earl Fitzwilliam, Viceroy of Ireland, planned reforms; recalled.
St. Lucia captured from French.
French Revolution: Execution of Danton; Festival of Supreme Being; Robespierre executed; Commune of Paris replaced by Commissioners; reversal of policy of Terror; leaders of Cordeliers guillotined.
British captured Corsica from French.
Poles revolted against Partition; suppressed by Russia, Prussia and Austria.

Blake: *Songs of Experience*.
Mrs Ann Radcliffe (*1764, †1823): *The Mysteries of Udolpho*, sensational novel; scene laid in old castle where the heroine is subjected to supernatural horrors.
Goethe: *Reineke Fuchs*, a satirical poem.
Publication of *Auld Lang Syne* (by Burns, *c.* 1791) in its present form.

1795

Treasonable Practices and Seditious Meetings Act.
Acquittal of Warren Hastings.

Matthew Gregory Lewis ("Monk Lewis") (*1775, †1818): *The Monk*, a novel.
Marquis de Sade (*1740, †1814): *La*

David: *Death of Marat*, French painting mourning his friend.
Foundation of Institut National de Musique, Paris.
Song *The Girl I left behind me* first appeared.
Les Jardins des Plantes, Paris, opened for the study of natural history.

John Dalton (*1766, †1844): *Meteorological Observations*, early work on meteorology by the renowned chemist.
Herschel discovered binary motion of double stars.
Hope and Klaproth discovered strontium; isolated by Davy (see 1808).
Friedrich H. A. von Humboldt (*1769, †1859): *Flora Subterranea Friberginsis*, botanical work.
Lord Macartney's Mission to China to attempt to remove restrictions on Anglo-Chinese trade; failed.
Pitt established Board of Agriculture.
Christian Sprengel (*1750, †1816) discovered process of pollination of flowers by insects.
Financial crisis caused by canal speculation.
Catherine II of Russia introduced policy of protection in regard to commerce.
Permanent Revenue Settlement in Bengal.
Alexander Mackenzie first to cross Canada from coast to coast.

Blake: *The Ancient of Days*, engraving to his poem *Europe, a Prophesy*.
Goya: *Procession of the Flagellants*, Spanish painting.
Haydn: Symphonies in D (*The Clock*) and in G (*The Military*).
James Hewitt: *Tammany*, probably first American opera.
John Trumbull (*1756, †1843), American, completed painting *Declaration of Independence*.
Wren's Drury Lane Theatre pulled down and re-erected.

Dalton described colour-blindness.
Gadolin discovered first rare-earth element.
Execution of Lavoisier, great French chemist, on trumped-up charge; he had been closely associated with development of metric system.
Maudsley constructed bar lathe of metal.
Eli Whitney, of the U.S.A., invented cotton-gin for extracting cotton seed.
Creation of Manchester Chamber of Commerce.
Establishment of U.S. Navy.
Foundation (in Paris) of first Technical College (École Polytechnique).
France first used observation balloons in war.

*Pedro Albéniz (†1855), founder of modern piano style, in Spain.
Ludwig van Beethoven (*1770, †1827), great

François Appert's preserving jar for foods.
Bramah invented hydraulic press.
Mungo Park (*1771, †1806) explored West Africa.

	History	Literature
1795	British took Cape of Good Hope and Ceylon from Dutch. French Revolution: Paris mob attacked Convention; defeated; White Terror in S. France; National Guard reorganized; destruction of Jacobin party; second rising in Paris, dispersed by Bonaparte; Convention proclaimed General Amnesty; †(?)Louis XVII; end of revolt in La Vendée; Convention replaced by Directory; Bonaparte Com. in Chief in Italy; Quiberon Bay expedition, under R.N., failed. Austrian Netherlands absorbed into France. Franco-Austrian Armistice at Weissenburg. France regained Luxembourg from Spain. Prussia forced to accept Treaty of Basle with France. Austro-Russian alliance against either Prussia or Turkey. Final Partition of Poland.	*Philosophie dans le Boudoir*, novel by an infamous French author, whose name gave rise to the word "sadism". Robert Southey (*1774, †1843): *Poems*. André Chénier (*1762, †1794): *La Jeune Captive*; French poem published after the author had been guillotined during the French Revolution. Stamp Duty on newspapers increased. Lindley Murray (*1745, †1826): *English Grammar*, widely used in schools.
1796	Failure of British peace talks with Directory in France. Guiana captured by British. French invasion attempt in Ireland at Bantry Bay under Hoche; failed. Corsica returned to France. Tennessee joined the U.S.A. French Revolution: Paris divided into 12 municipalities; Armistice at Cherasco; establishment of Cispadane Republic in Modena, Bologna and Ferrara. Outbreak of war between Spain and Britain. †Catherine II (the Great) of Russia; accession of Paul I. Teheran became capital of Persia. Dutch possessions in Ceylon occupied by Britain.	Thomas Morton (*c.* *1764, †1838): *The Way to get Married*, a comedy. Joseph Strutt (*1749, †1802), antiquary: *Dresses and Habits of the English People* (to 1799). Wordsworth: *The Borderers*, a tragedy.
1797	Mutiny in the Royal Navy at Spithead and Nore. French invasion of Fishguard repulsed. British naval victories at	Samuel Taylor Coleridge (*1772, †1834): *The Ancient Mariner*, a poem. Friedrich Hölderlin (*1770, †1843): *Hyperion*, German romance in form of letters (also 1799).

German composer: Piano Concertos in B and C.
Blake: (i) *God creating Adam*, (ii) *Nebuchadnezzar*, (iii) *Newton*, prints finished in water-colour.
Haydn: Symphony in E♭ (*Drum-Roll*), 8th London Symphony.
Sir Henry Raeburn (*1756, †1823): *Miss Eleanor Urquhart*, a painting.
Foundation of Conservatoire de Musique, Paris.

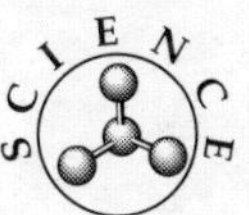

Adoption of metric system in France.
First settlements made in New Zealand.
Chemical bleaching powder introduced.
A Naturalist's Calendar, extracted from the papers of the late Rev. Gilbert White published posthumously.
Compulsory use of lime-juice in R.N. as antidote for scurvy; resulted from work of Blane.
John Playfair (*1748, †1819): *Elements of Geometry*; enunciated Playfair's Axiom.
Speenhamland system of Poor Relief (to 1834; see 1832 and 1834).

B. Carr: *The Archers of Switzerland*, opera, produced in New York.
Haydn: *Holy Mass* in B♭ and *Kettledrum Mass* in C, so-called; *Passion Music* based on *The Seven Last Words* (see 1785).
Thomas Jefferson (*1743, †1826) designed Monticello, Virginian classical building.
Edward Savage (1761, †1817): *The Washington Family*, American painting.

G. L. C. Cuvier (*1769, †1832), French naturalist, laid foundations of animal palaeontology.
Edward Jenner (*1749, †1823) vaccinated against smallpox, using cowpox; idea of cowpox giving immunity known earlier but not utilized.
Laplace propounded his Nebula Hypothesis.
Johann T. Lowitz (*1757, †1804) prepared pure ethyl alcohol.
J. Parker patented Roman cements, prepared by burning argillaceous limestone.
Dispensary for relief of poor children; did not survive.
Foundation of Royal Technical College, Glasgow.
Assignats (see 1789) recalled; replaced by *mandats*, which soon lost value.
Edict of Peking forbade importation of opium into China.

Bewick: *History of British Birds* (Vol. 1) containing outstanding wood-engravings; Vol. 2 in 1804.
Haydn: Music for *Emperor's Hymn*, used in string quartet in C.

Lagrange: *Théorie des Fonctions Analytique*, mathematical work on analytical functions.
John MacArthur (*1767, †1834) introduced merino sheep into Australia.

1797 Camperdown and St. Vincent; Texel blockaded.
Trinidad captured from Spain by Britain.
French Revolution: revival of religious prohibitions; Royalist revolt crushed; Bonaparte master of Austrian Lombardy following victories at Rivoli and Mantua; Treaty of Tolentino between Bonaparte and Papacy; French invasion of Austria; Bonaparte defeated Austrians at Neumarkt and Unzmarkt; Veronese Vespers—400 sick French soldiers massacred at Verona; French occupation of Venice; Treaty of Milan; Venice submitted to France.
Bonaparte established Ligurian Republic at Genoa; Austrian Lombardy became Cisalpine Republic; Franco-Austrian Treaty of Campo Formio.
Congress of Rastadt for peace terms between France and Empire.
Final Partition of Poland removed it from map.

Goethe: *Hermann und Dorothea*, German pastoral poem with a simple sentimental tale.
Morton: *A Cure for Heartache*, a comedy.
Radcliffe: *The Italian*, novel based on the Inquisition.

1798 Rebellion in Ireland led by Emmet and Wolfe Tone; suppressed.
British naval riot in Mediterranean; Nelson's victory over French at Aboukir Bay (Battle of Nile).
French invaded Switzerland; established Helvetic Republic.
French troops under Berthier looted Rome; established Roman Republic; Pope Pius VI left Rome.
French invasion of Piedmont; abdication of Charles Emmanuel of Savoy.
French entered Naples; set up Parthenopean Republic.
Directory in France annulled elections.
Bonaparte's Egyptian campaign: Malta captured; Alexandria occupied; Mamluks defeated at battle of Pyramids.
Lord Wellesley, Governor General of India; Tippoo Sahib of Mysore renewed war in Carnatic.

Wordsworth and Coleridge: *Lyrical Ballads.*
Thomas Malthus (*1766, †1834): *Principle of Population*.
*Giacomo Leopardi (†1837), Italian poet of the *Canti*.
Printing of Parliamentary Reports by Luke Hansard.
Morton: *Speed the Plough*, a comedy in which character, Mrs Grundy, first appeared.
Charles Lamb (*1775, †1834): *The Old Familiar Faces* in blank verse.

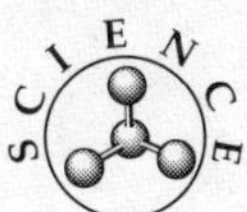

Discovery of 4th-cent. graves containing treasure, at Szilagy, Transylvania.
Blake completed 537 water-colours for *Night Thoughts*, by Young.

William Smith (*1769, †1839) laid down time-basis for geological eras.
Garnerin made first parachute descent from a balloon, but parachutes had been used earlier.
First copper pennies minted; earlier pennies (silver) mainly maundy money.
Pound notes issued by Bank of England.
Spode organization made modern English porcelain, by adding felspar to boneash.
In France "Bankruptcy of the Two-Thirds", whereby two-thirds of the public debt was cancelled and replaced by bonds which became worthless.
Financial crisis in Britain; payments suspended by Bank of England; resumed 1821.
Louis N. Vauquelin (*1763, †1829), French chemist, discovered chromium.

Goya: *The Bewitched*, Spanish picture of man haunted by Satanic spirits.
Haydn, *The Creation*, an oratorio, and *Nelson Mass* in D, so-called.
Joseph Lancaster (*1778, †1838) opened elementary school in Borough Road, London.
John Soane: *Sketches in Architecture*, book of designs, published.
Extinction of the ancient universities of Cologne and Mainz.

Bass and Flinders circumnavigated Tasmania.
Cavendish performed experiment to determine mean density of Earth.
Legendre: *Theory of Numbers*, French mathematical work.
Gaspard Monge (*1746, †1818) developed representative geometry.
Count Rumford (*1753, †1814) surmised that heat is a form of motion (see 1843).
Vauquelin isolated beryllium.
Beginning of Irish emigration to Canada.
Kleingert of Breslau developed modern diving apparatus.
First weaving mill opened at Bradford.
Thos. Robert Malthus (*1766, †1834): *An Essay on the Principle of Population*, re effect of unchecked population increase.
Alois Senefelder (*1771, †1835), German, invented lithography; printing from flat stone bed.
Earl Stanhope: wooden printing press replaced by metal one.

1798	Ceylon became British Crown Colony.	
1799	Combination Laws prohibited trade unionism; Corresponding Societies suppressed. Capture of Seringapatam by British forces under Baird; †Tippoo Sahib; end of Mysore War. †George Washington. Bonaparte forestalled Turkish invasion of Egypt by advance into Syria; repulsed at Acre; Turks defeated at Aboukir. Austria declared war on France, supported by Britain, Russia, Naples and Portugal; Cisalpine, Roman and Parthenopean Republics overthrown. Directory unpopular through corruption and defeat; Bonaparte returned from Egypt; landed at Fréjus; overthrew Directory in *coup d'état* of 18th Brumaire; Consulate established. Third Kaffir War; London Missionary Society began work in South Africa.	Thos. Campbell (*1777, †1844): *The Pleasures of Hope*, poetry. Mungo Park (*1771, †1806): *Travels in the Interior of Africa*. Schiller: (i) *Wallenstein*, monumental trilogy of German plays with background of Thirty Years' War; (ii) *Das Lied von der Glocke*, a poem describing the making of a bell, an allegorical epitome of human life. Freedom of the Press again restricted. L. Murray: *Reader* widely used in schools.
1800	Act of Union with Ireland united Parliament of England and Ireland. Laws against Combinations of workpeople extended to include employers. Game Law passed. Malacca Provinces (Straits Settlements) annexed by Britain. Republican party in power in the U.S.A. Negotiations by Sir Sidney Smith to permit evacuation of French army of Egypt repudiated by British government; French defeated Turks at Heliopolis; reoccupied Cairo; assassination of French Com. in Chief Kléber. French defeated Austrians at Marengo and Hohenlinden. Tsar Paul I became friend of France; left coalition and revived Armed Neutrality of North against Britain. Malta surrendered to British.	Maria Edgeworth (*1767, †1849): *Castle Rackrent*, her first novel; it deals with Ireland. Schiller: *Mary Stuart*, a play dealing with intrigues of Mary and Elizabeth. Wordsworth: *Michael*, a poem. Friedrich von Schelling (*1775, †1854): *System des transcendentalen Idealismus*, German philosophical work.

Beethoven: Symphony No. 1 in C, and Sonata in C minor (*Pathétique*).
Blake: *The Adoration of the Magi*, tempera.
Goya: *Caprichos*, satirical etchings.
French troops digging trenches near Rosetta, Egypt, unearthed engraved stone, Rosetta Stone (now in Britain Museum), from which it proved possible to translate Egyptian hieroglyphics.

Cuvier laid groundwork of comparative anatomy.
Sir Humphry Davy (*1778, †1829), great scientist, used nitrous oxide as anaesthetic for easing toothache (not for extractions).
Laplace: *Mécanique céleste* (to 1825).
French applied mathematics work.
Lebon took out patent for coal-gas.
Income Tax first introduced by Younger Pitt, as war-time financial measure (see 1815).
Louis Robert invented continuous sheet paper-making machine.
Stanhope constructed iron printing-press.
Benjamin Thompson founded Royal Institution.
Discovery in Siberia of mammoth perfectly preserved in ice.
Serfdom in Scottish mines abolished.
Standard metre length of platinum adopted in France (see 1889).
French foundation of Egyptian Institute in Cairo.

Beethoven: 3rd piano concerto, in C minor, and string quartet, op. 18 (Nos. 1–6).
François Boïeldieu (*1775, †1834): *The Caliph of Baghdad*, French opera which won composer instruction from Cherubini.
Cherubini, Marla Luigi C. Z. S. (*1760, †1840), Italian composer, mainly of church music: *The Water Carrier (Les Deux Journées)*, opera produced in Paris.
Clementi founded music firm, known later as Collard and Collard of London.
David: *Portrait of Mme Récamier*, French painting.
Goya: Portrait of his wife, Spanish painting.
Downing College, Cambridge received its charter (see 1717).
c. Modern style Punch and Judy shows developed.

Carlisle and Nicholson: electrolysis of water; name given to process later by Faraday.
Herschel discovered infra-red band (warm radiation region) of spectrum.
Mawdsley's improved screw-cutting lathe.
Robert Owen (*1771, †1858) took over New Lanark mills.
Eli Terry made first U.S.A. clock.
Alessandro Volta (*1745, †1827), Italian physicist, made first battery (Volta's *pile*) of zinc and copper plates; the *volt* is named after him.
Jenner: *Complete Statement of Facts and Observations* (concerning vaccination, see 1796).
Joseph Marie Jacquard (*1752, †1834) invented his improved loom for figured material; exhibited 1801.
c. Franz J. Gall (*1758, †1828), German physician, proposed phrenology (skull and brain measurement) to assess ability; not generally accepted as scientific.

1800	Bonaparte appointed committee of lawyers to draw up Civil Code.	
1801	Resignation of Younger Pitt following refusal of George III to agree to Catholic emancipation: Addington Prime Minister. General Enclosure Act; simplified method of enclosing lands. Bill introduced to prevent marriage of women with their seducers. British force landed at Aboukir; French defeated at battle of Alexandria. British occupation of Madeira. British naval victory at Copenhagen. France concluded Peace of Lunéville with Austria; terms hastened breakup of Holy Roman Empire. Treaty of Madrid between France and Spain. Treaty of Florence between France and Naples. Treaty of Badajoz between France and Portugal. Haiti declared itself a republic. Turkish forces aided by British held French in Egypt; French army surrendered; repatriated. Murder of Tsar Paul of Russia; accession of Alexander I.	Chénier: *La Jeune Tarentine*, a poem, posthumously published. François René de Chateaubriand (*1768, †1848): *Atala*, a novel by the great French Romantic. Schiller: *Die Jungfrau von Orleans*, German drama retelling story of Joan of Arc. Edgeworth: *Belinda*, a novel of 18th century society. First edition of collected works of Goldsmith. Southey: *Thalaba, the Destroyer*, a poem.
1802	Health and Morals of Apprentices Act; passage secured by elder Peel; first attempt to relieve conditions of pauper apprentices. Peace of Amiens ended war between Britain and France; British possession of Ceylon confirmed. Bonaparte became President of Cisalpine Republic renamed Italian Republic; France annexed Elba; Piedmont incorporated into France; Parma seized by French. Napoleon Bonaparte appointed First Consul for life. Concordat between France and Roman Catholic Church. Wahabis sacked Kerbala in Iraq without interference from Suleiman. Second Maratta War (lasted to 1803).	Sir Walter Scott (*1771, †1832): *Minstrelsy of the Scottish Border*, collection of works. François René de Chateaubriand: (i) *Le Génie du Christianisme*, criticism upholding superiority of Christian faith; (ii) *René* (1802–5), a novel with a melancholy hero. Hölderlin: *Hymnen*, poetry. Akerblad, Swedish diplomat, published demotic alphabet based on work on Rosetta Stone. Publication of Debrett's *Peerage*.

Corporation of Surgeons became Royal College of Surgeons.
Royal Institution (founded 1799) received royal charter.

Union Jack became flag of United Kingdom.
Beethoven: *Sonata quasi una fantasia (Moonlight sonata)* in C♯ minor.
Goya: *The Naked Maja* and *The Clothed Maja*, Spanish paintings.
Haydn: *The Creation Mass* in B♭, so-called (not to be confused with oratorio of same name—1798) and *The Seasons*, an oratorio.
Foundation of University of Breslau.
Strutt: *Sports and Pastimes of the People of England*.
Johan H. Pestalozzi (*1746, †1827), Swiss educationalist. *Wie Gertrud ihre Kinder lehrt*, (How Gertrude Teaches her Children), explaining his method of educating needy children.

F. K. Achard (*1753, †1821), German, opened first sugar-beet factory, having discovered earlier extraction process of obtaining sugar.
Chaptal developed metric system in France; based on earlier ideas (see 1791, 1795).
Dalton enunciated laws of saturated vapour pressure; also suggested all gases could be liquefied by compression and cooling.
Karl F. Gauss (*1771, †1855): *Disquisitiones arithmeticae*, great German work on modern theory of numbers.
Hare, U.S.A., invented oxy-hydrogen blow-lamp.
Discovery of Ceres through Piazzi led to knowledge of asteroids.
J. J. Lalande catalogued 47,390 stars.
Richard Trevithick (*1771, †1833) invented a steam road-carriage.
First paddle-steamer *Charlotte Dundas*; used as tugboat in Scotland.
Opening of Grand Union Canal.
Surrey Iron Railway, from Wandsworth to Croydon, opened; horse-drawn trucks on double-track railway carried farm produce and coal.
First decennial census in Britain.

Beethoven: 2nd Symphony, in D.
Haydn: Mass in B♭ (*Harmoniemesse*).
Order of the Legion of Honour instituted by Bonaparte as First Consul.

Bramah invented wood-planing machine.
Ekeburg discovered tantalum, rare metal.
Johann W. Ritter (*1779, †1859) discovered ultra-violet rays.
William H. Woolaston (*1766, †1828) observed dark lines in sun's spectrum; later tabulated by Joseph von Fraunhöfer (*1787, †1826), German physicist, to which he gave his name.
Treviranus introduced word *biology*.
Thos. Wedgwood (*1771, †1805) described effect of light on silver nitrate; beginnings of photography.
West India Docks, London, built.
Chambers of Commerce reorganized in France by government.

1803

Renewal of war with France; Napoleonic Wars to 1815.
Execution of Emmet, Irish patriot.
Poaching in England made capital offence if capture resisted.
Withdrawal of British army from Egypt.
Capture of Tobago.
U.S.A. purchased Louisiana from France; "Louisiana Purchase".
Ohio admitted as State of the U.S.A.
French recovered San Domingo from Toussaint l'Ouverture, who had revolted and set up republic.
Civil War in Switzerland; intervention by Bonaparte; new constitution set up, weakening federal government and strengthening French influence.
Cape Colony restored to Holland.
British expedition to Kandy in Ceylon; failed completely.

Anne Louise Germaine de Staël (*1766, †1817): *Delphine,* French novel incorporating feminist views.
Schiller: *Die Braut von Messina,* a play in verse with a chorus, concerning two brothers in love with a girl, later revealed as their sister.
Wm. Cobbett (*1762, †1835) began publishing the *Weekly Register*.

*Libri, the Book Thief (†1869), Florentine nobleman who became notorious for stealing valuable literary works; he was also a fine mathematician; real name Guglielmus Libri-Carucci dalla Somaja.
Jane Porter (*1776, †1850): *Thaddeus of Warsaw,* historical novel.

1804

Resignation of Lord Addington; younger Pitt returned to Prime Ministership.
Castle Hill "Rising" in New South Wales.
Alexander Hamilton, American statesman, killed in duel.
Coronation of Bonaparte as Emperor Napoleon in France.
Kidnapping of Duc d'Enghein from neutral Baden; executed in Paris.
Napoleon introduced tax on liquors in France.
Haiti declared itself independent of France.
Russia broke off diplomatic relations with France; allied with Britain and Austria.

Blake: *Jerusalem,* mystical poem.
Schiller: *Wilhelm Tell,* a popular play of the Swiss national hero.
Richter: *Flegeljahre,* German novel.
Foundation of British and Foreign Bible Society.
L. Murray: *Spelling Book,* standard school book.

1805

Third Coalition against France.
French/Spanish fleets defeated by English under Nelson at Trafalgar; Nelson mortally wounded.

Scott: *The Lay of the Last Minstrel,* romantic poem.
*Hans Christian Andersen (†1875), Danish writer known for his fairy tales.

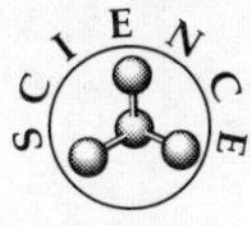

*Adolphe Adam (†1856), composer of ballets and operas.
Beethoven: *Christ on the Mount of Olives*, oratorio produced in Vienna; and *Kreutzer Sonata* in A (Op. 47).
First award of *Prix de Rome* for outstanding work in music.
Lancaster: *Improvements in Education*; led to establishment of voluntary elementary schools (to 1870).
Joseph M. W. Turner (*1775, †1851), who produced over 20,000 pictures and sketches: *Calais Pier*.
Sheraton: *Cabinet Directory*.

Berthollet: *Essai de statique chimique*, pioneer French work on chemical physics.
Jöns J. Berzelius (*1779, †1848), Swedish scientist, discovered cerium.
Dalton commenced work on his atomic theory, which led to systematic arrangement of chemistry; atoms making up an individual element are identical in size and weight but atom characteristics vary in different elements. (see 1808, 1810).
Davy gave lectures on agricultural chemistry.
Wm. Freemantle patented "grasshopper" stationary steam engine.
Horrocks invented improved power-loom.
Thomas Telford (*1757, †1834) began construction of roads in Scotland.
Trevithick built first successful railway locomotive; it ran from Penydarran ironworks to Glamorganshire coast.
Lyceum Theatre experimentally lit by gas.
Income Tax reimposed: Schedule A, B or C, according to origin of income.
First settlement in Tasmania (then Van Dieman's Land).
Thousands of meteorites fell at l'Aigle, France; people first convinced they came from outer space.

Beethoven: *Eroica Symphony* (No. 3 in E♯) probably composed; also *Waldstein Sonata*, in C, for piano forte (Op. 53).
Bewick, renowned for wood-engravings, completed *History of British Birds*.
Royal Horticultural Society presented first English flower show.
Extinction of Bamberg, Dillingen and Duisburg Universities.

Sir George Cayley, "Father of Gliding", carried out gliding experiments.
Oliver Evans, American, made experimental tour through Philadelphia in a steam car (began experiments earlier).
J. B. Richter isolated pure nickel.
Telford commenced construction of Caledonian Canal.
Smithson Tennant (*1761, †1815) discovered iridium and osmium.
W. H. Wollaston discovered rare metal palladium.
Dahlias introduced into England.
Second attempt by Russian ships to force Japan to open ports to Western trade: failed.
Joseph Louis Gay-Lussac (*1778, †1850), French scientist, made balloon ascents to study weather.

Beethoven: *Fidelio*, his only opera, produced at Vienna; dissatisfied with its overture, he wrote three, all great; in present form opera dates from 1814; also

A. J. Forsyth invented percussion lock (see 1820).
F. W. A. Sertürner (*1783, †1841) discovered morphine.

1805	Napoleon crowned himself king of Italy; Ligurian Republic added to France. Austria joined Russia, Britain, Naples and Sweden against France; Austrian army defeated by Ney; surrendered to Napoleon at Ulm; combined Russian and Austrian force defeated by Napoleon at Austerlitz. Peace of Pressburg between Austria and France. Treaty of Schönbrunn between Prussia and France ceded Hanover to Prussia. Napoleon deposed King of Naples; added Venice to his kingdom of Italy; seized Ancona from Papacy. Mehemet Ali nominated Pasha of Egypt by people of Cairo; modern Egypt established.	Southey: *Madoc*, a poem. Wordsworth completed *The Prelude* (published 1850), long autobiography in poetic form.
1806	†Younger Pitt: succeeded by William Grenville's "Ministry of all talents". Sepoy mutiny at Vellore. Cape Colony captured from Dutch. Abolition of Holy Roman Empire by Napoleon; all Habsburg estates made into Empire under former Francis II now Francis I of Austria. Conquest of S. Italy by French; Joseph Bonaparte, brother of Napoleon, made King of Naples. Louis Bonaparte, brother of Napoleon, made King of Holland. Napoleon offered to return Hanover to George III in peace negotiations with Britain; led to Franco-Prussian war; Prussian army defeated at Auerstädt and Jena; French entered Berlin; Napoleon created Confederation of Rhine; under his own control. Napoleon occupied Warsaw. Sultan of Turkey agreed to maintain Mehemet Ali in Cairo for annual tribute of 2 million piastres.	Heinrich von Kleist (*1777, †1811): *Der zerbrochene Krug*, famous German comedy, a village trial over a broken jar. German became the official language of new empire of Francis I. Jane (*1783, †1824) and Ann (*1782, †1866) Taylor: *Rhymes for the Nursery*, in which "Twinkle, twinkle, little star" appeared. Antoine Barbier (*1765, †1825), French librarian: *Dictionnaire des ouvrages anonymes et pseudonymes* (to 1809), standard work.
1807	British Orders in Council replied to Napoleon's Berlin Decrees. Portland formed ministry with Castlereagh and Canning. War between France and Portugal: escape of Prince Regent to Brazil;	Lord George Gordon Noel Byron (*1788, †1824): *Hours of Idleness*, poetry. Crabbe: *The Parish Register*, poetry. Mary (*1764, †1847) and Charles (*1775, †1834) Lamb: *Tales from Shakespeare*, an attempt to make Shakespeare's works

composed, in this year, Piano Concerto in G and Kreutzer Violin Sonata.
Haydn's catalogue of his enormous list of compositions.
Turner: *Shipwreck*, a painting.

London Docks opened.
First factory to be illuminated by gas at Manchester.
French Revolutionary Calendar abandoned by Napoleon.
Mungo Park explored course of River Niger.
Wollaston discovered rhodium in crude platinum.
Rockets reintroduced as weapons by British; used in Napoleonic wars; based on work of Sir William Congreve (1801).
Royal Military Canal (Hythe-Winchelsea) constructed.

Beethoven: 4th Symphony in B, and Violin Concerto in D.
John Cotman (*1782, †1842) water-colour artist: *Gretna bridge* and *Mumbles*, paintings.
(to 1836) Chalgrin built l'Arc de Triomphe de l'Étoile, Paris, for Napoleon I.
East India Co. founded Haileybury College, boys' Public School.
Institut de France created by combining Académie Français and another academy.

Berzelius: *Lectures on Animal Chemistry*, Swedish groundwork of bio-chemistry.
Thaer founded, on his estate in Prussia, the first agricultural training college.
East India Docks opened in London.
Commencement of building of Dartmoor Prison.
Napoleon forced to issue licences to French merchants to bring British goods into France.
Napoleon imposed tax on salt.
Pius VII refused Napoleon's demand to close ports to British trade.
Napoleon's Berlin decrees against trade with Britain.
Sir Francis Beaufort (*1774, †1857) designed his scale of numbers, 0–12, to indicate wind strength.

Beethoven: 5th Symphony in C minor (theme adopted by Allies in World War II); also Mass in C.
Thomas Hope: *Household Furniture*, illustrating strictly classical revival styles.
Jean-Dominique Ingres (*1780, †1867),

Davy discovered, using electrolytic method, alkaline metals potassium and sodium.
Robert Fulton (*1765, †1815), of the U.S.A., constructed P. S. *Clermont*, one of the first commercially successful paddle-steamers.

1807 Treaty of Fontainebleau among France, Spain and Portugal.
Grand Duchy of Warsaw, created by Napoleon, given to King of Saxony.
Prussian land west of Elbe given by Napoleon to brother, Jerome; new kingdom of Westphalia.
British fleet bombarded Copenhagen; seized Danish fleet; Franco-Danish alliance.
Anglo-Swedish alliance; Sweden refused to apply Berlin Decrees.
Battle of Eylau between French and Russians indecisive.
Treaty of Bartenstein: Russia, Prussia, Sweden and Britain to continue war against France.
Battle of Friedland; Napoleon routed Russians.
Danzig became free city under French protection.
Napoleon and Tsar Alexander I, by Treaty of Tilsit, broke Prussian power.
Stein became Minister of Home Affairs in Prussia.
Restoration of order in Egypt supported by British expedition.

intelligible to children.
Wordsworth: *Poems*.
Kleist: *Amphitryon*, German comedy, after Molière.
Georg Wilhelm Friedrich Hegel (*1770, †1831): *Die Phänomenologie des Geistes*, German philosophy.
Johann Gottlieb Fichte (*1762, †1814), professor of philosophy at Jena: *Reden an die deutsche Nation*, advocating German patriotism through national education.
Lamb: *Mrs Leicester's School*, ten stories.
Staël: *Corinne*, French novel.

1808 French under General Miollis occupied Rome; Papal States annexed.
Gustavus IV of Sweden deposed; accession of Charles XIII; Bernadotte, Marshal of France, elected Crown Prince of Sweden.
Abdication of Charles IV of Spain after being lured to France; surrender of Madrid; Joseph Bonaparte made King of Spain; succeeded in Naples by Murat; Order of Alcántara deprived of its property by Joseph Bonaparte.
Madrid revolt against French occupation began Peninsular War.
Russians invaded Finland; Alexander I became Grand Duke of Finland; promised to maintain rights.
Franco-Russian Conference at Erfurt.
Stein established local self-

Scott: (i) *Marmion*, a story in verse; (ii) *Life*, of Dryden.
Lamb: *The Adventures of Ulysses*.
Adam Gottlob Oehlenschlaeger (*1779, †1850); *Hakon Jarl*, Danish tragedy.
Goethe: *Faust*, first part completed (see 1770); also *Wahlverwandtschaften*, a romance.

French, head of "Classical Movement" after David's death, began painting *La Source*, finished 51 years later; now in Louvre (see 1858).
I. G. Pleyel (*1757, †1831) founded famous pianoforte manufacturing works.
Gasparo L. P. Spontini (*1774, †1851), Italian composer: *The Vestal Virgin*, opera, produced in Paris; this work led to widespread use of orchestral bass drum.
Turner: *Sun rising through Vapour*, a painting.
Altdorf University joined to Erlangen.

Lukin designed standard life-boat of Suffolk type (see 1785).
Mawdsley's table engine, compact direct-action machine having vertical cylinder.
Air pump for mines introduced.
Trading privileges of South Sea Co. withdrawn by Parliament.
Abolition of Slave Trade in Jamaica and in British ships.
French government stock reached maximum price of 93.4.
Napoleon's Milan decrees reinforced his trade war with England.
Preparations along English coast against expected Napoleonic invasion.
Drainage of Fens completed.
Stein abolished serfdom in Prussia.
Erection of Bell Rock (Inchcape) tower begun; completed 1811 by R. Stevenson.
Oliver Evans, U.S.A., proposed use of conveyor-belt; later essential to mass-production.

Beethoven: 6th Symphony (*The Pastoral*) in F; contains spectacular thunderstorm music.
Ingres: *La Grande Baigneuse*, French nude picture.
Foundation of Royal Lancasterian Society to further educational ideas of Joseph Lancaster.
Establishment of Imperial University in France; all of that country's teachers had to have degrees from here.
Disappearance of pig-tail in men's hairdressing.
Establishment of Théâtre St. Philippe, New Orleans; early American opera house.

Captain S. Brown, R.N., patented ships' iron anchor-chains.
Dalton extended his atomic theory to molecular theory of compounds (see 1803).
Davy isolated barium, calcium, magnesium and strontium.
Gay-Lussac formulated law of Volumes of Gases.
Etienne Louis Malus (*1775, †1812) discovered polarization property of light (see 1816).
Newberg invented bandsaw; not successful until 1860.
N. T. de Saussure (*1746, †1845) determined composition of alcohol.
Trevithick exhibited his locomotive, *Catch me who can*, on circular railway track at Euston.
Webb discovered source of River Ganges.
Code of Criminal Procedure decreed in France.
Importation of slaves into the U.S.A. forbidden by Federal Government..

1808 government in Prussia; Napoleon compelled Frederick William III to dismiss Stein; Prussian army limited by Napoleon to 42,000 men, but Scharnhorst trained 150,000 men by 1812.
H.M.S. *Phaeton* forced entry into Nagasaki.

1809 Resignation of Canning and Castlereagh from Portland ministry; new ministry under Percival.
British expedition to Walcheren failed.
Rome added to French Empire; Pope Pius VII excommunicated Napoleon: Pope imprisoned at Savona.
Austria renewed war with France; French took Vienna; Napoleon defeated by Austrians under Archduke Charles at Aspern; Austrians defeated at Wagram; Peace of Schönbrunn, or Vienna, ended Austro-French war.
Metternich (*1773, †1859), chief minister in Austria; followed reactionary policy at home and subservience to France abroad.
All property of Teutonic Order, except that in Austria, confiscated.
English army in Portugal: battle of Corunna; †Sir John Moore, succeeded by Wellesley; French defeated at Talavera.
Ecuador became part of republic of Colombia (see 1830).

Quarterly Review started.
Byron: *English Bards and Scotch Reviewers,* poetry and a vigorous satire.
Chateaubriand: *Les Martyrs,* a prose epic, inspired by religious faith.
August Wilhelm von Schlegel (*1767, †1845): *Über dramatische Kunst und Literatur;* lectures on dramatic art by German poet.
More: *Coelebs in search of a Wife,* a novel.

1810 Durham miners' strike.
Mauritius and Seychelles annexed by Britain.
French Senate decreed that all future Popes must accept Gallican Liberties of 1682.
Marriage of Napoleon and Marie Louise, daughter of Emperor Francis I.
Duke of Oldenberg dethroned by France.
French occupied Hamburg; absorbed Bremen into Empire.
Holland united with France; abdication of Louis Bonaparte.

Scott: *The Lady of the Lake,* a poem.
Staël: *De l'Allemagne,* an attempt to make Germany and German literature known to her French contemporaries.
Kleist: *Michael Kohlhaas,* outstanding German tale.
Penal Code of *Code Napoléon* authorized by decree.
Crabbe: *The Borough,* a poem portraying life in a country town.
Southey: *The Curse of Kehama,* a poem.

Beethoven: *The Emperor Concerto* No. 5 in E♭, so-called for its brilliance; also String Quartet in E (Op. 74).
Raeburn: *Mrs Spiers*, a portrait.
Second Drury Lane Theatre burned down.
Karl W. von Humboldt, Prussian Minister of Public Instruction, reformed Prussian educational system; classical languages replaced by thoroughness and efficiency.
Foundation of Friedrich Wilhelm University in Berlin, for the purpose of warfare training as well as academic learning.
Spontini: *Fernand Cortez*, opera written for Paris.
Extinction of Helmstedt University.

Gauss: *Theoria Motus Corporum Coelestium*, celestial mechanics.
John Heathcoat (*1783, †1861) invented lace-making machine.
L. B. Antoine de Lamarque (*1744, †1829), *Philosophie Zoologique*, important French work on evolution.
Vauquelin identified nicotine (named after J. Nicot; see 1560).
Wollaston invented goniometer for measuring angles of crystals.
Publication of *Description d'Egypte*, in 20 vols. begun; influenced French interest in Egypt in 19th cent.
As result of British blockade, French used chicory as substitute for coffee.
Dartmoor Prison opened for clients.
Construction of Bristol harbour.
†Daniel Lambert (*1770), gaoler of Leicester, who weighed 739lb.; his coffin was mounted on wheels.

Beethoven: String Quartet in F minor (Op. 95).
*Frederick Chopin in Poland (†1849, in Paris), pianist and pianoforte composer of études, impromptus, mazurkas, nocturnes, polonaises.
c. Goya: *Majas on a Balcony*, Spanish painting.
*Robert Schumann (†1856) in Saxony, composer of pianoforte music, four symphonies and a piano concerto.
University of Berlin opened (see 1809): Fichte, Savigny, Wolf and Niebuhr influenced German thought.
Extinction of Salzburg University.

Berzelius discovered element silizium.
Dalton: *New System of Chemical Philosophy*, in which he explained atomic theory (see 1803, 1808).
Davy produced carbon electric arc.
Peter Durand discovered how to preserve food in cans.
Samuel Hahnemann (*1755, †1843): *Organon of Rational Healing*; laid foundations of homoeopathy (similia similibus curantur).
John L. Macadam (*1756, †1836) began road construction in England (see 1819).
Opening of St Quentin Canal.
Trianon Tariff: permission for British and

1810	Battle of Busaco in Portugal and Lines of Torres Vedras; Wellesley held French advance. Napoleon forced Frederick William III of Prussia to dismiss Scharnhorst; Knights Hospitallers in Brandenburg Bailliewick suppressed by King of Prussia. Charles XIII named Bernadotte as heir to Swedish throne. Buenos Aires, Chile and Mexico overthrew Spanish rule.	
1811	Prince of Wales became Regent. British occupied Java. Pius VII refused to approve French National Council's order that Sees should be filled by nomination by Metropolitan of France if vacant for more than six months. French finally driven out of Portugal by Wellesley; invasion of Spain; victories at Fuentes d'Onoro and Albuera. Massacre of Mamluks; relieved Mehemet Ali of obstacle to pacification of Egypt. Outbreak of Fourth Kaffir War. Russians again failed in attempt to force Japan to open trade with west. Paraguay declared her independence from Spain.	Jane Austen (*1775, †1817): *Sense and Sensibility*, a novel of two sisters, published. Goethe: *Dichtung und Wahrheit*, autobiography. Barthold Georg Niebuhr (*1776, †1831): *Römische Geschichte*, Roman history in German. Three remaining Paris newspapers ceased to appear; French Press almost defunct. Completion of *Conversations-Lexicon* of Friedrich Brockhaus (*1772, †1883), German publisher.
1812	Assassination of Spencer Percival, Prime Minister, by John Bellingham; Lord Liverpool Prime Minister, Castlereagh Foreign Secretary. Louisiana became State in the U.S.A. War between the U.S.A. and Britain arising out of British naval policy towards neutral shipping. Pius VII brought to Fontainebleau. Napoleon seized Swedish Pomerania; Sweden replied by Treaty of Abo, alliance with Russia. Treaty of Orebro among Sweden, Russia and Britain. Treaty of Bucharest ended Russo-Turkish war. Napoleon invaded Russia; Russian retreat; battle of Borodino, bloody and indecisive; French entered	Byron: *Childe Harold* (first two cantos), a poem of a man who travels to escape from himself. Jacob Ludwig Carl (*1785, †1863), Wilhelm Carl (*1786, †1859) Grimm: *Kinderhund Haus-Märchen*, fairy tales collected by the famous German brothers. Goethe: *Gedichte*, German poems. Hegel: *Logik*, treatise on logic in connection with metaphysics. Crabbe: *Tales*, a collection of twenty-one stories. Edgeworth: *The Absentee*, story of an Irish absentee landlord. Nichols: *Literary Anecdotes of the Eighteenth Century* (to 1815), important collection in 9 vols.

Colonial goods to be smuggled into Europe on payment of 50% tariff.
Fontainebleau Decrees ordered burning of all British manufactured goods found on French territory.
Sale of tobacco in France made monopoly of French government.

Ingres: *Cordier*, French painting.
Vincent Novello published first book of church music with organ part in full; previously figured bass only appeared.
(to 1814) Sir John Soan built Dulwich Art Gallery.
National Schools Society founded.
Opening of Prague Conservatory of Music.
Incorporation of University of Breslau and foundation of University of Christiana (Oslo).

Avogadro (*1776, †1856) propounded hypothesis of gas molecules; also stated that each substance consists of molecules, which are smallest particles of that substance which can exist.
Gauss illustrated complex numbers of form $a + ib$, where a and b are real and $i = \surd(-1)$.
Friedrich Krupp (*1787, †1826) founded great Krupp ironworks at Essen; later to gain world renown for armaments manufacture.
Heinrich W. M. Olbers (*1758, †1840), German astronomer: theory of comet tails.
Sir Chas. Bell (*1774, †1842), anatomist: *New Idea of Anatomy of the Brain*.

Beethoven: 7th Symphony in A, and 8th Symphony in F; also *Ruins of Athens*, an overture.
J. Burckhardt discovered Great Temple of Abu-Simbel, possessing superb rock-carvings.
Goya: *Dona Antonia Zarata*, Spanish portrait.
John Nash (*1752, †1835), architect, built York Gate, Regent's Park, London.
The *Elgin Marbles*, work of Pheidias, brought to England.
Erection of present Drury Lane Theatre.
Royal Yacht Squadron founded.
University of Philadelphia founded.
Foundation of Gesellschaft der Musikfreunde, Vienna, by Joseph von Sonnleithner.

Henry Bell (*1767, †1830) constructed early steamship *Comet*, which operated on the Clyde.
John Blenkinsop designed locomotive using gear-wheel engaging toothed track alongside rails.
John Common invented a reaping-machine.
Courtois, of Paris, discovered iodine.
Cuvier: *Recherches sur les Ossemens fossils des Quadrupèdes*, great French work on animal palaeontology.
Laplace: *Théorie analytique des probabilités* (to 1820), advanced work on general probability.
F. A. Winsor developed Gas Light and Coke Co.
Red River Settlement, Manitoba, Canada, founded.
Baron Larrey, Napoleon's surgeon,

1812

Moscow; retreated; out of army of 550,000 only 20,000 survived.
Convention of Tauroggen; Prussian forces agreed not to interfere with Russian pursuit of retreating French.
Battle of Salamanca: Wellesley advanced to Madrid but forced to retreat.
Constitution of Cadiz.
Ali Pasha of Janina defeated Turks.
Chinese Edict against Christianity.

1813

Lord Hastings appointed Governor General of India.
Fiume captured by British.
Concordat of Fontainebleau between Napoleon and Pius VII; latter repudiated treaty later.
War of Liberation in Prussia, begun by people; Frederick William III finally called Prussia to arms; Landwehr formed; Treaty of Kalisch: Russia and Prussia agreed to war on France; French forces retreated to Elbe.
Sweden joined Russia and Prussia.
Army of Allies defeated by Napoleon at Lützen and Bautzen.
Austria joined Allies against Napoleon; renewal of war; Napoleon defeated at Leipzig – "Battle of Nations"; agreed to Armistice of Plestwitz; refused terms of peace at Conditions of Frankfort.
Wellington's victory at Vittoria drove French from Spain.
Throne of Holland returned to House of Orange.

Austen: *Pride and Prejudice*, her best known novel.
Owen published *New View of Society*.
Southey: *Life of Nelson*.
Percy Bysshe Shelley (*1792, †1822): *Queen Mab*, a philosophical atheistic poem.
James Hogg (*1770, †1835), known as "Ettrick Shepherd": *The Queen's Wake*, a poem.
Scott: *Rokeby* and *The Bride of Triermain*, poems.

1814

Britain restored Madeira to Portugal.
Mauritius and Malta ceded to Britain by France.
Missionary work in New Zealand.
Washington, D.C., burned by British troops.
Treaty of Ghent ended Anglo-U.S.A. war.
Pius VII returned to Rome; Murat forced to restore Papal authority.
Allied invasion of France; Congress

Wordsworth: *The Excursion*, long didactic poem.
Austen: *Mansfield Park*, a novel of a poor lady educated among her rich cousins.
Byron: *The Corsair* and *Lara*, narrative poems.
Scott: *Waverley* (anon), his first historical novel, which gave the name to all his others.
Pierre-Jean de Béranger (*1780, †1857): *Chansons*, popular and patriotic French songs.

introduced local analgesia; amputated limbs painlessly during Moscow retreat, by first freezing them.
Sir Stamford Raffles began series of secret reports to East India Co. outlining scheme for commercial and political domination of Japan (continued to 1816).
Commencement of "Luddite Riots", machine-breaking by unemployed hand operatives.
First English savings bank (at Bristol).

Foundation of London (later Royal) Philharmonic Society; meetings held in Argyll Rooms.
Franz Peter Schubert (*1797, †1828), prolific composer of beautiful music, created his first symphony.
Blake: *The Day of Judgment*, one of a collection of mystical drawings.
Turner began series of 40 drawings for Cooke's *Southern Coast*; completed 1826.
James McGill founded McGill University, Montreal, which received its status in 1821.

Davy: *Elements of Agricultural Chemistry*; showed diamonds to consist of carbon, in same year.
Wm. Hedley built *Puffing Billy*, oldest extant locomotive.
East India Co.'s Charter revised; monopoly in Indian trade abolished.
Repeal of wage assessment clauses in Elizabethan Statute of Apprentices.
Guinea coins (gold) last issued in England.
Manufacture of "shoddy" started in West Riding.
G. W. Evans discovered and named Macquarie River, Australia; explored Murray Basin.
Foundation of Sunderland Society for prevention of mining accidents.
Two British ships forced way into Nagasaki Harbour hoping to dislodge Dutch traders.

Goya: *King Ferdinand VII*, Spanish court painting famous for its merciless appraisal of the monarch's character, also *Señora Sabasa Garcia*.
Ernst T. W. Hoffmann (*1776, †1822), German writer and music critic: *Phantasiestücke in Callots Manier*, collected stories, used by Offenbach.
Ingres: *The Odalisque*, French painting.
Schubert completed his first opera, a Mass, and numerous songs, including *The Erl King* and *Gretchen and her Spinning Wheel*.

Fraunhöfer discovered spectrum of sun produced by prism has distinct lines (see 1802).
Madersperger constructed hand sewing-machine; not efficient (see 1851).
Orfila systematically studied poisons.
George Stephenson (*1781, †1848) constructed first really efficient steam locomotive at Killingworth Colliery, near Newcastle.
Steam cylinder-press printing developed.
St Margaret's, Westminster, became first

1814 of Châtillon: Napoleon again refused Allied terms.
Treaty of Chaumont: Allies not to make separate peace with Napoleon.
Allies captured Paris; Provisional Government with Talleyrand as President; abdication of Napoleon I; Treaty of Fontainebleau; Napoleon to retain title, principality of Elba, pension of 2 million francs.
Restoration of Bourbons; Louis XVIII, brother of Louis XVI.
First Treaty of Paris between Allies and France.
Charter granted to France; secured revolutionary advantages as Royal Grant; contract between Crown and People denied.
Congress of Vienna to settle peace terms.

Adalbert Von Chamisso (*1781, †1838): *Peter Schlemihl*, German tale of a man who sold his shadow.
Southey: *Roderick, the last of the Goths*, a poem.

1815 British occupation of Ascension.
Napoleon escaped from Elba; landed at Fréjus; entered Paris within month; Louis XVIII fled to Ghent; Murat rose against Austrians in Italy; defeated at Tolentino; Congress of Vienna dispersed.
Waterloo Campaign: Napoleon successful at Ligny against Prussians under Blücher; Ney defeated by Wellington at Quatre Bras; French defeated at Waterloo.
Napoleon abdicated in favour of son; Provisional government in Paris under Fouché; Louis XVIII returned.
Napoleon tried to escape to America; failed; surrendered to Captain Maitland on board H.M.S. *Bellerophon*.
Second Treaty of Paris: Napoleon banished.
Execution of Ney and Murat.
Reassembly of Congress of Vienna; Luxembourg set up as state within former Empire; former Holy Roman Empire reconstituted as German Confederation under presidency of Austria; Brazil declared kingdom

Johann Ludwig Uhland (*1787, †1862): *Gedichte*, German poems.
James Sheridan Knowles (*1784, †1862): *Caius Gracchus*, a tragedy.
c. Nichols: *The History and Antiquities of Leicester*, an important work of reference.
Scott: (i) *Guy Mannering*, a novel; (ii) *The Lord of the Isles*, a poem.
Mrs Mary M. Sherwood (*1775, †1851): *Little Henry and his Beaver*, children's book.

Turner: *The Frosty Morning,* a painting.
British and Foreign Schools Society founded.

district to be illuminated by gas.
Repeal of Apprentices Statute of 1563; compulsory apprenticeships ended.
Berzelius: *Theory of Chemical Proportions and the Chemical Action of Electricity,* Swedish electro-chemical theory.

John Constable (*1776, †1837): *Boat Building,* a painting by the landscape artist.
Goya: *Self Portrait* and *Hexensabbat,* Spanish painting.
Nash rebuilt Brighton Pavilion in outrageous pseudo-oriental style.
Turner: (i) *Dido building Carthage,* (ii) *Crossing the Brook,* paintings.
Wittenberg university joined to Halle.
Schubert: 3rd Symphony in B (*The Wanderer*), two symphonies, many songs including *Heidenröslein,* four singspiels and his first piano sonata.
Establishment of Universities of Ghent and Liége and foundation of University of New York.

Trial by Jury established in Scotland.
Edwards developed compound steam engine.
Evans discovered Lachlaw River, Australia.
Gay-Lussac prepared cyanogen.
Olber discovered comet bearing his name.
Corn Law passed by Parliament; prohibited importation of foreign corn until British corn reached 80s. per quarter.
Regular London to Margate trips by S.S. *Marjory.*
Bianconi began car service from Clonmel, Ireland; opened country to travellers.
Income Tax ceased (see 1842).
Apothecaries' Company permitted to license and examine apothecaries in England and Wales.
Malthus: *Enquiry into the Nature and Progress of Rent,* economic work.
Great Britain purchased Cape of Good Hope for £6m.
Davy discovered value of double wire gauze to stop flame; led to use of safety lamps in mines.

	History	Literature
1815	under Braganza rule; kingdom of Kandy annexed to Ceylon. Establishment of Lombardo-Venetian kingdom under Austrian rule. Holy Alliance: attempt by Tsar Alexander I to outlaw war.	
1816	Acute distress in England; Spa Fields Riot; Game Law offenders liable to 7 years' transportation. Bootle's Act attempted to limit apprenticeship to London children. Napoleon landed as prisoner on St Helena; †1821. British occupied Ascension. Final suppression of Barbary Pirates. U.S.A. introduced protection against British imports. Indiana made State in the U.S.A. Diet of German Confederation met at Frankfurt. Grand Priory of Rome restored to Knights Hospitallers. Argentina declared independence from Spain.	Austen: *Emma*, a novel of an heiress. Byron: *The Prisoner of Chillon*, a poem: Bonnivard imprisoned near Lake Geneva. John Keats (*1795, †1821): sonnet on Chapman's 'Homer' published. Cobbett's *Twopenny Register* appeared. Coleridge: (i) *Kubla Khan*, a poem; (ii) *Christabel*, unfinished poem. Benjamin Constant (*1767, †1830): *Adolphe*, French novel inspired by love for Mme de Staël. Leopardi: (to 1836) Italian poems. Alessandro Manzoni (*1785, †1873): (to 1825) Italian poems. Thomas Love Peacock (*1785, †1866): *Headlong Hall*, a novel. Scott: (i) *The Antiquary*, (ii) *Old Mortality*, novels. *Blackwood's Magazine* founded. American Bible Society founded.
1817	Continued distress and unrest in England; attack on Prince Regent; Habeas Corpus suspended; "Derbyshire Insurrection"; march of Manchester "Blanketeers". †Princess Charlotte, heiress to English throne. Trial and acquittal of William Hone for treason. Revolt against British rule in Kandy, Ceylon, suppressed. Mississippi became State in the U.S.A. Wartburg Festival, Reformation anniversary celebration, used by German students to demonstrate against absolutism. Serfdom in Russian Estonia abolished. Revolt of Greeks against Turkish rule. Accession of Da'ud Pasha, last Georgian ruler, to Pashalik of Baghdad.	Byron: *Manfred*, a drama. Coleridge: *Biographia Literaria*, essays on literary criticism. Franz Grillparzer (*1791, †1872): *Die Ahnfrau*, Austrian tragedy. Wm. Hazlitt (*1778, †1830): *Characters of Shakespeare's Plays*. John Keats: *Poems*. Robert de Lammenais (*1782, †1854): *Essai sur l'Indifférence*, French denunciation of spiritual inertia. Thos. Moore(*1779, †1852): *Lalla Rookh*, poems with Eastern Setting. Papal Bull disapproving of Bible Societies.

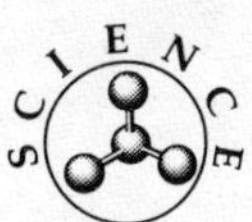

Establishment of London musical firm of Boosey; joined with Hawkes 1930.
†Viscount FitzWilliam (*1745), leaving *FitzWilliam Virginals Book* of 17th-cent. music to Cambridge University.
Robert Owen opened school at New Lanark cotton mill.
Gioacchino Rossini (*1792, †1868): *The Barber of Seville*, Italian comic opera, first performed at Rome.
Schubert: (i) 4th Symphony (*The Tragic S.*) in C minor; (ii) 5th Symphony in B major.
Introduction of quadrille into England from France.
Group of French painters invited to settle in Brazil to develop art there.
Erfurt University ceased to exist.
University of Warsaw founded by Alexander I.
Foundation of Ghent University.

Sir David Brewster (*1781, †1868) invented kaleidoscope.
Augustin Fresnel (*1788, †1827), French, explained polarization of light (see 1808).
R. T. Laennec (*1781, †1826), French, invented the stethoscope.
Commencement of transatlantic packet service.
Carriage Act.
British founded Bathurst, Gambia.

Constable: *Flatford Mill*, landscape painting.
Jefferson designed University of Virginia.
c. Théodore Géricault (*1791, †1824): *Horse held by Slaves*, painting by a French artist devoted to horses; he was to die in a riding accident.
Opening of Waterloo Bridge, built by John Rennie; replaced 1945, *q.v.*

Berzelius, Swedish, found selenium and lithium; he introduced terms: halogen, allotropy, catalytic action, in chemistry.
Cuvier: *La Règne Animal distribué d'après son Organisation*, classification of animals (4 vols.).
Karl F. von Drais (*1785, †1851), German, constructed the hobby-horse, precurser of the bicycle.
P. N. Johnson commercially produced rare metals.
James Murray, Irish, manufactured superphosphates (important fertilizers).
David Ricardo (*1772, †1823): *Principles of Political Economy and Taxation*, in which was defined theory of distribution.
Richard Roberts constructed first planing-machine for metal.
Sadler crossed St. George's Channel in a balloon.
Construction of Erie Canal commenced (see 1824).

Year	History	Literature
1818	Burdett's resolution on Annual Parliaments and universal suffrage rejected by House of Commons. Outbreak of Fifth Kaffir War. Illinois admitted State in the U.S.A. Congress of Aix-la-Chapelle; Allied army of occupation left France. Accession of Bernadotte, former Napoleonic Marshal, to Swedish throne as Charles XIV.	Austen: *Northanger Abbey*, satire on the "novel of terror": *Persuasion*. Grillparzer: *Sappho*, Austrian classical drama. Keats: *Endymion*, a poem and allegory. Peacock: *Nightmare Abbey*, a novel. Scott: (i) *The Heart of Midlothian*, (ii) *Rob Roy*, novels of Scottish history. Mary Shelley (*1797, †1851): *Frankenstein*, a novel.
1819	Peterloo Massacre at Manchester; Six Acts ("Gag Acts") passed. Allotments Act, Poor Law measure. Alabama became State in the U.S.A.; Spain ceded Florida to the U.S.A. Java restored to Dutch. Tariff treaty between Prussia and Schwartzburg-Sonderhausen; start of German Customs Union. Carlsbad Decrees; peak of Austrian influence in Germany; postponed constitutional reform for 20 years.	Byron: (i) *Don Juan* (to 1824), poem with a young Spanish aristocrat as hero: (ii) *Mazeppa*, poem of Cossack page lashed to a wild horse. Shelley: *The Cenci*, a tragedy. Chénier: *Poésies* (posthumous). Arthur Schopenhauer (*1788, †1860): *Die Welt als Wille und Vorstellung*, German philosophy.
1820	† George III; accession of Prince Regent as George IV. Cato Street conspiracy in London; failed. Failure of George IV's divorce action against Queen Caroline. American Colonizing Society	Keats: (i) *Hyperion*, (ii) *Lamia*, poems. Scott: *Ivanhoe*, a novel of reign of Richard I. Shelley: *Prometheus Unbound*, poetry; a lyrical drama. Alphonse de Lamartine (*1790, †1869): *Méditations*, French poems inspired by tragic love.

Gaetano Donizetti (*1797, †1848): *Enrico, Conte di Borgogna*, Italian opera; his first.
Rossini: *Moses in Egypt*, Italian opera.
Foundation of London Theatre later known as the *Old Vic*.
Order of St Michael and St George instituted by Prince Regent.
Foundation of Bonn University by Friedrich Wilhelm III.

First iron passenger ship on Clyde.
George III offered £20,000 for first man to make the North West Passage; Sir John Ross (*1777, †1856) and Parry made unsuccessful expedition; in later exploration was joined by Sir James R. Ross (*1800, †1862), nephew of Sir John.
Berzelius published molecular weights of 2,000 chemical compounds.
Friedrich Wilhelm Bessel (*1784, †1846): *Fundamenta Astronomiae*, German catalogue of 3,222 stars.
Thos. Blanchard, U.S.A., constructed machine for mass-production of gunstocks; basis of "American system" of 19th cent., i.e. making machines with interchangeable parts.
Rumford medals awarded to Brewster for work on polarization of light.
J. B. Caventou and P. J. Pelletier named green plant pigment *chlorophyll*.
Coindet used iodine in treatment of goitre.
Jeremiah Chubb's detector lock.
Johann F. Encke (*1791, †1865) computed orbit of his comet.
Establishment of Institution of Civil Engineers.

Géricault: *The Raft of the Medusa*, French romantic painting.
Jacques F. Halévy (*1799, †1862): *Le Dilettante d'Avignon*, French comic opera.
Mehemet Ali presented Cleopatra's Needle (see – 1475 and 1878) to Britain.
Schubert: Piano Quintet in A major.
University of St. Petersburg founded by Alexander I.
Opening of Burlington Arcade in London.

Brewster noted refraction of light through crystals; development of crystallography (see 1772).
First macadam roads laid, utilizing stones of approx. equal size; named after Macadam (see 1810).
Photography: Sir John F. Herschel (*1792, †1871) improved Wedgwood's method of copying pictures on glass.
S.S. *Savannah* crossed Atlantic in 26 days.
Peel and Robert Owen: Factory Act for children in cotton mills.
Singapore founded by Raffles.
c. David Napier; flat-bed cylinder-press for printing.

Daniel F. E. Auber (*1782, †1871): *La Bergère Châtelaine*, French opera; his first real success.
Constable: *Dedham Mill*, a landscape painting.
Nash designed Cumberland Terrace, Regent's Park, London.

Frederick Accum: *Treatise on Adulterations of Food*, outcry against sale of bad food.
Thomas Hancock: factory in London for rubber-proofed materials.
Hans C. Oersted (*1777, †1851), Danish physicist, discovered effect of electric current on magnetic needle.

	History	Literature
1820	founded Liberian Republic for freed Negro slaves. Maine became State in the U.S.A. Assassination of Duc de Berri, sole hope of Bourbon succession in France. Liberal revolution in Naples under Morelli and Salvati. Military revolt in Spain; Liberal Constitution of 1812 proclaimed; meeting of Spanish Cortes (to 1822); Inquisition finally abolished. Rebellion in Lisbon and Oporto; Portuguese Cortes set up Liberal Constitution. Revolt of Ali Pasha of Janina against Turks; crushed. Congress of Troppau to consider Spanish revolt. Diet of German Federation accepted "Final Act of Vienna" which destroyed Liberal Constitutions granted in German States except Bavaria, Baden and Würtemberg. Alexander I of Russia returned to reactionary policies after revolt of Seminowsky regiment of Guards.	Augustin Thierry (*1795, †1856): *Lettres sur l'Histoire de France*. Hegel: *Grundlinien der Philosophie des Rechts*, German philosophy. Robert Jones (*1745, †1829): *Drych yr Amseroedd*, reminiscences; showing contemporary Welsh life. Washington Irving (*1783, †1859): *Sketch Book*, with Rip van Winkle as hero.
1821	*Report to County of Lanark* by Robert Owen, social reformer, (see 1819). Gold Coast became Crown Colony. Congress of Laibach; Austria authorized to crush Neapolitan revolt. Piedmontese revolt against Austrian rule crushed at Novara; plots against Austrian rule crushed in Lombardy. John VI of Portugal left Brazil; returned to Portugal. Revolt of Greeks against Turks; under Hypsilanti at Jassy, crushed at Dragashan; successful in the Morea; Greek independence declared. Nobility abolished in Norway. Mexico and Peru declared independence from Spain. Netherlands Government's meat and corn taxes hit Belgian peasantry. Witchcraft Act repealed in Ireland.	James Fenimore Cooper (*1789, †1851): *The Spy*, North American novel. Kleist: *Der Prinz von Homburg*, a play with a gallery of military types, his masterpiece, which gained fame 10 years after the author committed suicide in 1811. Thomas de Quincey (*1785, †1859): *Confessions of an Opium-Eater*, the author's early life. Scott: *Kenilworth*, a novel of the reign of Elizabeth I. Shelley: *Adonais*, a lament on Keats' death.

Opening of Union Chain Bridge, near Berwick; first large British suspension bridge.
Discovery of the *Venus de Milo* on the island of Melos.

André Marie Ampère (*1775, †1836), French physicist, expounded electromagnetic theory in much greater detail than Oersted.
Foundation of Royal Astronomical Society.
Opening of Regent's Canal, London: partly subterranean.
Merchants began movement for free trade.
British immigrants settled in Cape Colony; foundation of Port Elizabeth.
c. Henry Derringer of Philadelphia used percussion lock (see 1805) to make pistols.

Constable: *The Hay Wain*, a painting which created a sensation when shown in Paris.
Géricault: *Derby Day*, French painting of English scene.
Carl M. F. E. von Weber (*1786, †1826), German opera composer: *Der Freischütz*, romantic opera, first produced at Berlin.
Rauche: *Goethe*, German marble bust.
Ahorn, Swiss sculptor, carved the Lion of Lucerne out of solid rock; monument commemorates the Swiss Guards massacred at the Tuileries in 1792.

London Co-operative Society founded.
Michael Faraday (*1791, †1867) expounded principle of electric motor; published *Chemical Manipulation* in same year.
Fraunhöfer (probably) invented diffraction grating for spectroscopy.
Gay-Lussac and Arago made electromagnet.
Schweigger invented the galvanometer.
Seebeck, using copper and bismuth, discovered electric current generated by thermocouple.
Sir Charles Wheatstone (*1802, †1875) demonstrated sound reproduction, using boards connected by rod.
Union of Hudson Bay Trading Co. and rival North West Trading Co.
Bank of England resumed cash payments abandoned in 1797.

	History	Literature
1822	Suicide of Lord Castelreagh, Foreign Secretary: resignation of Lord Sidmouth, Home Secretary; Liverpool ministry reconstructed. Suppression of military risings in France. Civil war on Northern Spain between Liberal and Royalist forces. John VI of Portugal accepted Constitution of 1820; Queen Carlotta rejected it. Brazil declared an Empire under Portuguese Prince. Fall of Janina; †Ali Pasha. Turks massacred whole population of Chios (30,000 Greeks). Costa Rica declared independence from Spain. New Corn Laws improved Colonial Preference.	Heinrich Heine (*1797, †1856): *Gedichte*, German poems. Charles Nodier (*1780, †1844): *Trilby*, French novel of woman haunted by a goblin. Scott: *Fortunes of Nigel*, a novel. Alfred de Vigny (*1797, †1863): French poems. Dutch declared official language of New Kingdom of The Netherlands.
1823	British fiscal policy reformed under Huskisson and Goderich, to 1827. Reciprocity of Duties Act. Peel, Home Secretary, began series of Penal reforms. Formation of Catholic Association in Ireland. First Ashanti War (to 1866). Independence of South American Republics recognized by Britain. Monroe Doctrine promulgated by U.S. President Monroe. Congress of Verona; Britain withdrew from Congress. French troops under Angoulême entered Spain to restore Ferdinand VII's absolutism; Liberal generals defeated; absolutist reaction to 1825. Military revolt in Portugal; John VI forced to dismiss Cortes and annul Constitution. Frederick William III established Provincial Diets in Prussia. British recognized Greek War of Independence.	Lamb: *Essays of Elia*, a collection of whimsical essays which had appeared in the *London Magazine*. *Sandor Petöfi, Hungarian poet (†1849). Scott: *Quentin Durward*, a novel. Stendhal (*1783, †1842): *Racine et Shakespeare*, early French romantic manifesto.
1824	Repeal of 1662 Settlement (Poor Law) Act. Master and Servant Act. Repeal of Combination Laws of 1779 and 1800.	Mary R. Mitford (*1787, †1855): (to 1832) *Our Village*, sketches about Three Mile Cross, near Reading. Scott: *Redgauntlet*, a novel. Adolphe Thiers (*1797, †1877): *Histoire de la*

(to 1825) Nash built All Souls'Church, London.
Schubert: 8th Symphony, in two movements (*The Unfinished S.*).
Royal Academy of Music founded in London.
Secret Societies and Masonic Lodges suppressed in Russia.

Louis Jacques Mandé Daguerre (*1784, †1851) and Bouton invented *diorama*: paintings illuminated in dark room to give impression of realism.
Jean B. J. de Fourier (*1768, †1830): *Théorie analytique de la Chaleur*, French study of heat flow in which Fourier analysis appears.
J. V. Poncelet's work on projective geometry.
Roberts's improved power loom.
First iron paddle-steamer, *Aaron Manby*; incorporated early oscillating engine.
First British railway to use locomotives for haulage; at Hetton, County Durham.

Henry R. Bishop (*1786, †1855) composed song *Home, Sweet Home* in his opera, *Clari*.
Cotman: *Dieppe Harbour*, a water-colour.
c. Géricault: *The Plaster Kiln*, French painting of Montmartre.
Sir Thomas Lawrence (*1769, †1830): *The Calmady Children*, a painting.
Present buildings of British Museum erected (to 1847), designed by Sir R. Smirke (see 1759).
Schubert: *Rosamunde* music.
Waldmüller: *Beethoven*, German portrait.
Weber: *Euryanthe*, German opera on medieval chivalry.
Foundation of Birkbeck College, London, later to be part of University.
Foundation of Royal Thames Yacht Club.
Rugby football originated at Rugby School.

Charles Babbage began work on a calculating machine; unfinished, but similar to machines of a century later.
Faraday liquefied chlorine.
Von Leonhard made earliest attempts at petrology (rock classification).
Charles Macintosh developed rubberized waterproof material bearing his name.
Introduction of medical journal *The Lancet*.
Mechanics Institutes founded in Glasgow and London.
Baltic Club (for trade) established in London.
Khartoum founded by Mehemet Ali.
Stephenson built world's first iron railway bridge; for Stockton and Darlington railway.

Beethoven: 9th Symphony, *The Choral*, for choir and orchestra; and *Missa Solemnis*, his great mass.
Blake: *Beatrice addressing Dante*, a water-colour.

Joseph Aspdin produced Portland cement at Wakefield; roasted lime and clay.
Bessell explained his mathematical functions.
Nicholas L. Sadi Carnot (*1796, †1832),

1824 Gaols Act brought about some prison reform.
Catholic Association levied "Catholic Rent".
British acquired Singapore; occupied Melville Island; First Burmese War; Rangoon captured.
†Louis XVIII; accession of brother, Charles X.
Leading Portuguese Liberals arrested by Dom Miguel; forced to release captives by British fleet sent to aid John VI.
Würtemberg forced to accept Carlsbad Decrees by Austria; Decrees made permanent.
Failure of Allied Conference over Greek Question.

Révolution française.
Thomas William, Welsh hymn writer (*1762, †1844): *Dyfroedd Bethesda.*
†Byron at Missolonghi.

Irish Catholic Association
1825 suppressed (Gouldburn's Act).
Hobson's Factory Act.
Northumberland and Durham Miners' Union formed.
Britain acquired Malacca.
Portugal recognized Brazilian independence; Dom Pedro first Emperor.
Prussian law on mixed religious marriages extended to Rhine province; R.C. bishops appealed to Pius VIII.
Old Hungarian Constitution recognized by Emperor Francis I; dualism re-established.
†Alexander I at Taganrog; accession of Nicholas I; Decembrist conspiracy at St Petersburg and Moscow; suppressed.
Ibrahim, son of Mehemet Ali, devastated the Morea; declaration of British neutrality in Greek War of Indpendence.
Foreign vessels to be driven from Japanese ports.
Bolivia declared her independence.

Scott: *The Talisman,* a novel.
Thierry: *Histoire de la Conquête de l'Angleterre,* French account of the Norman conquest.
Publication of *Diary* of Samuel Pepys (17th cent.); manuscript at Magdalene College, Cambridge.

1826 †John VI of Portugal; accession of grand-daughter Maria Gloria; succession disputed by Dom Miguel.
Missolonghi captured by Turks; final revolt of Janissaries in Turkish army; dissolved.

Burke's Peerage first issued.
Fenimore Cooper: *The Last of the Mohicans,* North American novel.
Joseph von Eichendorff (*1788, †1857); *Aus dem Leben eines Taugenichts,* German novel.
Heine: *Die Harzreise,* account of journey through the Harz mountains.

Ferdinand Victor Eugène Delacroix (*1798, †1863), esoteric artist noted for lion and tiger paintings: *The Massacres at Chios*, French picture.
Lawrence: *Master Lambton*, famous portrait.
Telford erected St Katherine's Dock warehouses.
Establishment of National Gallery for the collection of pictures for the British people.
François Pascal Gérard (*1770, †1837): *Daphnis and Chlöe*, French painting.
Foundation of Athenaeum Club, London.

French physicist: *Puissance motrice*, on the potential power of heat machines.
Hume discovered Murray River (1,600 miles long), Australia.
Act abolished earlier standard liquid measure; established Imperial gallon.
Macintoshes in production in Manchester.
French voyages of exploration in Southern Ocean.
Opening of Polytechnic at Berlin.
Durban, S. Africa, founded as Port Natal.
Foundation of the Royal Society for the Prevention of Cruelty to Animals (R.S.P.C.A.).

William I of Holland made candidates for priesthood study for two years at his college in Louvain.
Beethoven: Great Fugue in B major.
Constable: *The Leaping Horse*, a painting.
Goya: *Tauromaquia*, in which he used lithography.
Thos. Hamilton built Edinburgh Royal High School.
Lawrence: *King Charles X*, a portrait.
Nash reconstructed Buckingham Palace for George IV; extended by later monarchs.
c. Etienne Bouhot (*1780, †1862): *St Peter's Church, Montmartre*, French painting.
Introduction into Europe from China of the tea-rose.

Faraday discovered benzene; important in later development of drugs and dyes.
Sir Goldsworthy Gurney (*1793, †1875) invented oxy-hydrogen lime-light.
Oersted produced aluminium; costly for many years.
Stephenson constructed *The Rocket*, famous locomotive (see 1829).
Sturgeon made *efficient* electromagnet (see 1821).
Taylor and Martineau made first horizontal direct-action stationary steam engine.
Opening of Stockton-Darlington railway; first passenger line; built by Stephenson.
Commercial crisis in England.
S.S. *Enterprise* sailed to Calcutta.
Turkish trade of Levant Co. open to all English merchants.
Erie Canal opened (see 1817).
New Zealand Colonization Co. formed.

Last State Lottery held in England.
Hector Berlioz (*1803, †1869), French composer whose unstable disposition is reflected in his music: *Symphonie Fantastique* (final form 1830).
Richard Bonington: *Piazza San Marco, Venice*, a painting.

A. J. Balard (*1802, †1876) found bromine in sea water.
Biela's comet appeared.
Pierre Bretonneau (*1778, †1862), French epidemiologist, published his work on diphtheria.
Sturm measured speed of sound in water.

LITERATURE

	History	Literature
1826	Protocol of St Petersburg between Russia and Britain concerning Greece. Russo-Swedish amicable settlement of Finmark frontiers.	Hölderlin: *Gedichte*, German poems. Victor Hugo (*1802, †1885): *Bug-Jargal*, French novel of Negro revolt in W. Indies. Vigny: (i) *Cinq-Mars*, historical French novel; (ii) *Poèmes antiques et modernes*. Bible Society finally suppressed in Russia.
1827	Resignation of Lord Liverpool as Prime Minister; succeeded by Canning, who died; Viscount Goderich, Prime Minister. National Guard disbanded in France. Extreme Spanish royalists proposed to make Don Carlos king in place of his brother Ferdinand VII; origin of Spanish Carlists. Acropolis at Athens captured by Ibrahim; Greeks destroyed a Turkish fleet at Salona; combined French, Russian, British fleets under Codrington destroyed Turkish fleet at Navarino.	John Clare (*1793, †1864) peasant poet: *The Shepherd's Calendar*. François P. Guizot (*1787, †1874): *Histoire de la Révolution d'Angleterre*. Heine: *Buch der Lieder*, popular German poems. Hugo: (i) *Cromwell*, a drama; (ii) *Préface de Cromwell*, manifesto of French Romanticism. John Keble (*1792, †1866) Anglican clergyman: *The Christian Year*. Manzoni: *I promessi Sposi*, Italian novel. Jules Michelet (*1798, †1874): *Précis d'Histoire moderne*.
1828	Canningites seceded from ministry; Wellington Prime Minister; repeal of Test and Corporation Acts. Daniel O'Connell elected for County Clare; debarred because Roman Catholic. Liberal-Catholic Union formed to oppose Dutch government in Belgium; States General of Netherlands rejected Budget. Establishment of three Customs Unions in Germany: (i) North German States and Prussia; (ii) Middle German States; (iii) South German States.	Lord Edward Bulwer Lytton (*1803, †1873): *Pelham*, a novel. Giovanni Casanova (*1725, †1798): *Mémoires*, of Venetian adventurer. Adam Mickiewicz (*1798, †1855). Polish poet: *Konrad Wallenrod*. Charles-Augustin Ste-Beuve (*1804, †1869): *Tableau historique et critique de la Poésie française au XVIe Siècle*: French critic re-introduced forgotten authors. First publication of Webster's *Dictionary*.

Constable: *The Cornfield*, a painting.
Samuel Palmer: *The Hilly Scene*; he used oil, tempera, water-colour, sepia and indian ink for paintings of Kentish countryside.
Felix Mendelssohn-Bartholdy (*1809, †1847): Overture for *Midsummer Night's Dream* (Op. 21).
Schubert: String Quartet in D minor (*Death and the Maiden*).
Weber: *Oberon*, German opera.
University transferred from Ingoldstadt to Munich.

Unverdorben obtained aniline from indigo.
Opening of Menai Bridge, designed by Telford (begun 1818).
Anti-Power Loom riots in Lancashire.
Settlement of Western Port in Australia.
N. I. Lobatschewski developed his non-Euclidean geometry.
J. Ressel, of Trieste, designed ship's screw propeller; built 60 ft boat power-driven at 6 knots.

Nash designed Carlton House Terrace, London.
Karl Baedeker began publishing his travel guide.
Introduction of weekly payment of 2*d*. by children attending Church schools.
John James Audubon (*1785, †1851), American naturalist, published first sections of *Birds of North America*, famous for beautiful colour plates.

Settlement founded at King George's Sound, later Albany.
Richard Bright (*1789, †1858), physician, described *Bright's disease*.
Brown noted movement of particles in colloidal liquids ("Brownian movement").
Gurney's steam coach in use.
J. F. Herschel proposed use of contact lens; not manufactured until some 60 years later.
G. S. Ohm (*1787, †1854), German, defined current, potential and resistance: propounded law, $I = E \div R$.
Joseph N. Niepce (*1765, †1833) made photographs on a metal plate (see 1829).
Rev. R. Stirling invented air-engine using regenerative process.
James Simpson constructed sandfilters for purification of London water-supply.
Walker: frictional sulphur matches.
Friedrich Wöhler (*1800, †1882): aluminium extracted from clay-earth; commercial proposition.
Machine constructed for tongued-and-grooved floor-boards.

Auber: *Masaniello (La Muette de Portici)*, French opera.
Constable: (i) *A View of the Stour at Dedham*; (ii) *Salisbury Cathedral*, paintings.
Ingres: *La Petite Baigneuse*, French painting.
Schubert: 7th Symphony in C major (*The Great S.*).
Foundation of University College, London (see 1836).
Foundation of Société des Concerts du Conservatoire, Paris.
Non-sectarian college, calling itself London University, opened in Gower St (see 1829 and 1836).

Berzelius discovered thorium and silicon.
William R. Hamilton (*1805, †1865), Irish mathematician: *Theory of Systems of Rays*, on optics.
Henry James: typesetting and casting.
John Thorpe, U.S.A., invented ring-spinning frame.
Wöhler: first synthesis of an organic chemical (urine); led to differentiation between organic and inorganic chemistry; destroyed theory of *vital force*.
Portland cement used for engineering (see 1824).
St Katherine Docks opened.
Sliding Scale Corn Law introduced.

LITERATURE

1828 Dom Miguel appointed Regent of Portugal; usurped throne; internal war to 1834.
War between Russia and Turkey to 1829; Russo-Persian treaty of Turkmanchay gave Russia Erivan; start of peasant revolts in Russia, averaging 23 per year to 1854.
Turks under Ibrahim evacuated Greece; Greek Independence guaranteed by Powers.
Uruguay declared her independence.

1829 Catholic Emancipation Act.
Metropolitan Police Force established by Peel.
O'Connell re-elected for County Clare after Catholic Relief Bill.
Dogherty's National Association for Protection of Labour formed.
Grand General Spinners' Union formed.
Fremantle took possession of Western Australia; colonization commenced.
Abolition of Suttee in British India.
Fourth marriage of childless Ferdinand VII of Spain; to Maria Christina of Naples.
Cadiz made free port.
Mahmoud, Sultan of Turkey, acknowledged independence of Greece.
Treaty of Adrianople; ended Russo-Turkish war; Russia gained free navigation of Bosphorus and Dardanelles.

Honoré de Balzac (*1799, †1850): (i) *Les Chouans*, French novel, his first success; (ii) *Physiologie du mariage*.
Alexandre Dumas (*1802, †1870): *Henri III et sa Cour*, French Romantic drama.
Prosper Mérimée (*1802, †1870): (i) *Chronique du Règne de Charles IX*, French historical novel; (ii) *Mateo Falcone*, short story on Corsica.
Alfred de Musset (*1810, †1857): *Contes d'Espagne et d'Italie*, French poems by the poet, novelist and playwright.

1830 †George IV; accession of Duke of Clarence as William IV.
Resignation of Wellington; Earl Grey Prime Minister.
Agricultural labourers' riots in S. England; 10 executed, 450 transported.
Birmingham Political Union formed.
Rev. John Nelson Darby founded Plymouth Brethren.
Protocol of London proclaimed Greece an independent kingdom.
"July Revolution" in Paris;

William Cobbett (*1762, †1835): *Rural rides*, descriptions of English countryside.
Auguste Comte (*1798, †1857), French founder of Positivism: *Cours de Philosophie positive*.
Hugo: *Hernani*, French historical drama.
Lamartine: *Harmonies*, French poetry.
Mérimée: (i) *Tamango*, (ii) *L'Enlèvement de la Redoute*, French short stories.
Richard Oastler: *Letters on Yorkshire Slavery*, political.
Silvio Pellico (*1788, †1854): *Le mie Prigioni*, Italian record of imprisonment.

Act regulating conditions in Emigrant ships.
Royal Menagerie transferred to the Zoological Gardens, Regent's Park, under control of Royal Zoological Society.

Rossini: *William Tell*, Italian opera, first performed at Paris.
Mouth organ and concertina probably invented by Wheatstone, physicist, the latter instrument being an improvement on the accordion invented, probably, by Buschmann of Berlin (not Damian of Vienna).
First Oxford and Cambridge Universities' Boat Race.
Louis Braille (*1809, †1852), French, completed system of finger-reading for the blind; begun 1825 (not the only system but the best for young people).
Katsushika Hokusai (*1760, †1849): 36 views of Mount Fuji, remarkable series of Japanese prints.
Opening of King's College, London, originally Anglican (see 1836).

Braithwaite constructed first steam fire-engine.
Cammell Laird began shipbuilding at Birkenhead.
Joseph Henry (*1797, †1878), U.S.A.: electro-magnetic motor.
Neilson's improved Hot Air Blast Furnace for iron; at Glasgow.
Niepce joined Daguerre to perfect photographic process.
The Rocket locomotive won Rainham trials (max. speed 29 m.p.h.; later reached 53 m.p.h. after modification).
George Shillibeer: horse-drawn omnibuses in London; operated from Marylebone to the Bank; carried 22 passengers.
Registration of Friendly Societies.
J. J. Parrot: first ascent of Mount Ararat.

Auber: *Fra Diavolo*, French comic opera.
Jean-Baptiste C. Corot (*1796, †1879): *Houses at Honfleur*, French painting.
Daguerre: *General View of Paris from Montmartre*, French painting by a pioneer of photography.
Mendelssohn: *Reformation Symphony* (No. 5, wrongly numbered).
Thomas Rice, original Negro minstrel, sang *Jim Crow*.
Ludwig Spohr (*1784, †1859): *Der Alchymist*, German opera, based on a Washington Irving story.

Bessel: *Tabulae Regiomontanae*, modern star catalogue.
F. J. Hugi studied glaciers.
Charles Lyell did important geological work.
Opening of Liverpool-Manchester railway, begun in 1825 by Stephenson, by Duke of Wellington; Huskisson, Liverpool M.P., killed; Stephenson constructed locomotive *Northumbrian*. Zinc amalgam used in primary batteries.
Foundation of Royal Geographic Society.
Beer Act: removed restrictions on sale of beer.

1830

Charles X overthrown; Orléanist Louis Philippe elected king.
Revolt against Dutch rule in Brussels; Provisional Government declared Belgium independent; National Congress to draw up Constitution.
Conference of London: Powers considered Belgian Question.
Ferdinand VII issued "Pragmatic Sanction" setting aside Spanish Salic law; *Maria Isabella; declared heiress.
Dom Miguel compelled to abdicate from Brazilian throne.
Algiers captured by France.
Uster meeting of Zürich demanded representative democracy in Switzerland.
Democratic Reds in Poland seized Warsaw; failed to gain full advantage.
Leopold of Saxe-Coburg accepted Greek throne, February; resigned May; terms made task impossible.
Milosh Obrenovich, former pig dealer, recognized by Sultan as ruler of Serbia.
Ecuador gained independence.

Alfred, Lord Tennyson (*1809, †1892): *Poems*.
Publication of *Book of Mormon*.

1831

Struggle for Reform Bill in the Commons; rejected by Lords; riots in Bristol, Nottingham and Derby.
National Union of Working Classes formed.
Cotton Mills Act: 12–hour working day under 18 years of age.
Revolt of Jamaican Negroes.
First Mormon Church at Kirkland, Ohio, U.S.A.
Leopold of Saxe-Coburg elected first King of Belgium; Dutch invasion; Leopold appealed for aid to France.
Italian revolt at Bologna; National Congress to establish Italian unity; crushed by Austria.
Austria, Russia and Britain recognized Greece as independent kingdom.
Hesse-Cassel joined Prussian Zollverein; Central Customs Union broken.

Balzac: *La Peau de Chagrin*, French novel.
Hugo: (i) *Nôtre Dame de Paris*, French novel; (ii) *Les Feuilles d'Automne*, poems; (iii) *Marion Delorme*, drama.
Alexander Pushkin (*1799, †1837): *Boris Godunov*, Russian tragedy.
Stendhal: *Le Rouge et le Noir*, French novel.
Vigny: *La Maréchale d'Ancre*, French drama.

Clara Wieck (*1819, †1896), great German pianist, gave her first recital.
c. Romantic Period of Music, as composed with the earlier Classical Period, developed; lasted until *c.* 1912; concurrently Romanticism in Art in France took form as a reaction to Classicism.

Gibbon Wakefield founded Colonization Society.
Landers explored River Niger.
Charles Sturt traced Murray River to its mouth.
J. F. Herschel, astronomer: *On the Study of Natural Philosophy*.
Barthelemy Thimonier, French, designed machines to sew seams; his machines were later destroyed by rioters.

Louis J. F. Hérold (*1791, †1833): *Zampa*, French opera (his most important work) produced at Paris.
Giacomo Meyerbeer (*1791, †1864): *Robert le Diable*; of German birth, Meyerbeer wrote operas in Italian style and later (from 1830) in French style.
Opening of London Bridge (demolished and re-erected in U.S.A. 1968, *q.v.*). Grand Priory of Knights Hospitallers re-established in England, not recognized by Grand Master in Rome.

Faraday discovered change in magnetic field produces electric current (electromagnetic induction); basis for development of dynamo.
Bickford invented safety-fuse for blasting-powder.
Charles Robert Darwin (*1809, †1882) was naturalist on board the *Beagle*; five-year survey to 1836; investigations into coral formation.
Justus von Liebig (*1803, †1873), German chemist, discovered chloroform.
Sir James R. Ross discovered *South* magnetic pole in North polar region; wrongly named magnetic North, it has never been corrected.
Foundation of British Association for Advancement of Science.
Cholera reached England.
Truck Act and Allotments Act.
Sadler's Committee on employment of children in factories.

Year	History	Literature
1831	Start of German Nationalist movement in Schleswig and Holstein. Rising in Poland against Russia; failed. Mehemet Ali sent son, Ibrahim, to invade Syria.	
1832	First Parliamentary Reform Act in England. Irish "Tithe Strike". Operative Builders' Union formed. Anti-Slavery Abolitionist Party in Boston, U.S.A. Risings in France (Republican in Paris: Legitimist in La Vendée); suppressed. France, Britain, Austria, Prussia and Russia to guarantee independence of Belgium. †Napoleon I's son, King of Rome. Swiss Cantons in two groups: (i) League of Seven; (ii) League of Sarnen. Further revolt in Bologna against Papal rule; defeated at Casena. Liberal demonstration at Hambach; used by Metternich as sign of revolutionary plot; Diet at Frankfort passed repressive measures. Polish Constitution (1815) abolished; Poland became Russian province. Ibrahim victorious in S. Palestine; main Turkish army defeated. Falkland Islands occupied by Britain.	Balzac: (i) *Le Curé de Tours*, French novel; (ii) *Contes drolatiques* (to 1837), licentious short stories. Hugo: *Le Roi s'amuse*, French drama which inspired *Rigoletto*. *Islwyn (William Thomas), great Welsh 19th-cent. poet. Nicolaus Lenau (*1802, †1850): *Gedichte*, German poems of Romantic despair. Musset: *Le Spectacle dans un Fauteuil*, French drama. Mérimée: *Contes et Nouvelles*, French short stories. George Sand (*1804, †1876): *Indiana*, French authoress's early novel. Vigny: *Stello*, French novel in dialogue form.
1833	First session of reformed Commons; Irish Coercion Bill passed; Althorp's Factory Act; Abolition of Slavery Act; Scottish Burgh Reform Act. Irish bishoprics reduced from 22 to 12. First meeting of Judicial Committee of Privy Council. Tories adopted name "Conservative". Indian Civil Service opened to Indian subjects. Falkland Islands became Crown Colony. Kandy amalgamated with Ceylon. Armistice between Dutch and Belgians.	Balzac: (i) *Le Médecin de Campagne*, French novel about a doctor; (ii) *Eugénie Grandet*, novel about a miser. Thomas Carlyle (*1795, †1881): *Sartor Resartus*, philosophical satire (to 1834). *Ceiriog, Welsh lyric poet (†1887). Hugo: *Lucrèce Borgia*, French drama. Lamennais: *Les Paroles d'un Croyant*, French attempt to unite Catholicism and Liberalism. Michelet (to 1844): *Histoire de France*. Musset: (i) *Les Caprices de Marianne*, French drama; (ii) *Rolla*, poem. Beginning of Oxford Tractarian movement.

Donizetti: *L'Elisir d'Amore,* Italian comic opera.
Foundation of Durham University; received charter 1837; college there as early as 1300.
First performance, in London, of Mendelssohn's *Fingal's Cave;* having been twice revised by the composer it was now in its final form.

Coffey patented his still; led to fine standard of alcoholic spirits.
Faraday proposed pictorial representation of electric and magnetic lines of force.
Legendre: *Treatise on Elliptic Functions,* French mathematical work, completed.
Oakes further improved blast-furnace design.
Beginnings of geological survey of Britain.
Creosote found in wood-tar; so-named by Reichenbach.
Some 30 services in London amalgamated to form Fire Engines Establishment.
Horse-drawn tramway in New York; construction of first U.S. railway.
Completion of Gotha Canal, Sweden (240 miles long).
Royal Commission to enquire into English Poor Law.
Hodgkin described the disease (of the lymphatic glands) named after him.

Donizetti: *Lucrezia Borgia,* Italian opera.
Konradin Kreutzer (*1780, †1849): *Melusine,* German opera (he composed 30 operas).
Mendelssohn: *Italian Symphony* (No. 4) first performed.
Schumann, German composer, founded *Neue Zeitschrift für Musik* (first published 1834).
Turner exhibited his first Venetian paintings: (i) *Bridge of Sighs;* (ii) *Canaletto Painting;* (iii) *Ducal Palace and Custom House, Venice.*
Education Grant Act: first State grant to the two voluntary educational societies.
Chopin: *Piano Concerto in E minor* published.

S. H. Christie invented Wheatstone Bridge (so-called) for measuring unknown electrical resistance.
Gauss: *Intensitas Vis Magneticae Terrestris and Mensuram Absolutam Revocata,* on magnetism and absolute units in physics; defined magnetic field and pole strength; based units on cm., gm., sec.; with Weber, invented declination needle.
Marshall Hall (*1790, †1857) studied reflex action.
Horner: first use of rough principles of cinematography.
Pattison: silver extraction process.
Wheatstone invented the stereoscope.
Invention, at Marseilles, of *machine kryptographique,* fore-runner of typewriter.

1833

Swiss Federal Diet met to amend Federal Pact 1815; rival Diet by League of Sarnen was later dissolved.
†Ferdinand VII of Spain; accession of infant Isabella II: Queen Christina Regent; first Carlist war (to 1838).
Dom Miguel defeated in Portugal; Maria Gloria established as Maria II.
League of Munchengratz: Russia, Austria and Prussia: opposed to Liberalism of England and France; financial support for Don Carlos in Spain.
Otto I, first King of Greece, landed at Naupalis.
Mahmoud II of Turkey sought Russian aid against Mehemet Ali; Treaty of Unkiar Skelessi resulted.

1834

Irish Church question caused resignation of Grey: replaced by Melbourne; Melbourne dismissed; Peel Prime Minister; Tamworth Manifesto.
Grand National Consolidated Trades Union of G.B. and Ireland set up by Robert Owen.
Six Dorchester farm labourers transported for trying to form union: Tolpuddle martyrs.
Central Criminal Court set up.
Abolition of slavery in all British possessions.
St Helena made Crown Colony.
Quadruple Alliance: Britain, France, Spain and Portugal; opposed to Don Carlos.
U.S.A. Indian Territory constituted.
Rising of workmen at Lyons.
Bavaria joined German Zollverein; break up of Southern Customs Union; Saxony joined Zollverein; German Customs Union complete.
Articles of Baden; some Swiss Cantons asserted rights against R.C. Church.
First meeting of Transylvanian Diet since 1811.
Syrian revolt against Ibrahim.
Poor Law Amendment Act.

Balzac: *La Recherche de L'Absolu*, French novel.
Grillparzer: *Der Traum ein Leben*, Austrian play.
Lytton: *The Last Days of Pompeii*, historical novel.
Frederick Marryat (*1792, †1848): *Peter Simple*, a novel.
Musset: (i) *On ne badine pas avec l'Amour*, (ii) *Lorenzaccio*, French dramas of romantic fantasy.
Balzac: *Le Père Goriot*, French novel.

First identification of enzyme (*diastase*).
Vast shower of meteors seen in America.
Anthracite used for iron-smelting.
First full steam crossing of Atlantic; S.S. *Royal William*.
Enterprise steam omnibus in use.
East India Co. deprived of monopoly of China trade; ceased trading and concerned solely with Indian government.

Corot: *View of Santa Maria della Salute*, French painting.
Turner: *Venice, Dogana and San Giorgio Maggiore*, English painting of Italian scene.
Establishment of Institute of British Architects; became Royal in 1837.
Kreutzer: *Das Nachtlager von Granada*, German opera; his most successful.
Delacroix: *Arabic Fantasy*, French painting.
Hokusai: *Hundred Views of Mount Fuji*, prints by great Japanese artist.
Old Houses of Parliament destroyed by fire.
Central Administration of Knights Hospitallers set up in Rome.
Teutonic Order reorganized as religious and military body.

Bessel attributed motion of Sirius to existence of a binary star.
Faraday enunciated laws of electrolysis.
Lenz's Law on induced current in electro-magnetic induction.
Samuel Hall: surface-condenser, producing distilled water for boilers.
Hamilton: *A General Method in Dynamics*, introducing Hamiltonian functions.
Joseph Hansom patented "Hansom cab" (two-wheeler).
F. F. Runge discovered phenol and aniline (see 1826) in coal tar.
Cyrus H. McCormick (*1809, †1884), U.S. inventor, patented harvesting machine.
Julius Plücker (*1801, †1868), German mathematician, defined his six equations on singularities of algebraic curves.
First geological map of the world completed: part of Devonshire.

1835 Resignation of Peel: return of Melbourne as Prime Minister.
Municipal Reform Act for England and Wales.
War in Spain; Louis Pilippe refused to occupy Basque Provinces; Palmerston refused support to Anglo-French intervention; British volunteers, French Foreign Legion supported Queen Christina.
Failure of Fieschi's attempt to assassinate Louis Philippe and sons.
Pope Gregory XVI rejected compromise with Prussia over mixed marriages.

Robert Browning (*1812, †1889): *Paracelsus*, dramatic poem.
Clare: *Rural Muse*, verse.
Théophile Gautier (*1811, †1872): *Mlle de Maupin*, French novel.
Hugo: *Les Chants du Crépuscule*, French poems.
Loennrot, Finnish scholar, published *Kalevala*, national epic.
Musset: (i) *La Nuit de Mai*, (ii) *La Nuit de Décembre*, poems.
Vigny: (i) *Chatterton*, French drama; (ii) *Servitude et Grandeur militaires*, short stories.
Balzac: *Le Lys dans la Vallée*, French novel.

1836 Coal miners strike against yearly employments.
Tithe Commutation Act; tithes made additional rent charge.
Ecclesiastical Commissioners established in Church of England.
London Working Mens' Association formed.
South Australia formed into British Province.
Great Trek of Boers from Cape Colony; Boers founded Republic of Orange Free State.
Arkansas became State in the U.S.A.
Group of Mexicans founded Republic of Texas; Seige of El Alamo; battle of San Jacinto.
Failure of Louis Napoleon to stir up Bonapartist rising in Strasbourg.
Marriage of Maria II of Portugal to Ferdinand of Saxe-Coburg, nephew of Leopold I of Belgium.
Prussian Zollverein became German Customs Union except for Hanse towns, Hanover, Oldenburg and Mecklenburg.

Johann P. Eckermann (*1792, †1854): *Gespräche mit Goethe*, German conversations with Goethe.
Nikolai V. Gogol (*1809, †1852): *The Inspector General*, comedy by the Russian novelist and playwright.
Lamartine: *Jocelyn*, French narrative poem.
Marryat: *Mr Midshipman Easy*, a novel.
Musset: (i) *Il ne faut jurer de rien*, French drama; (ii) *La Nuit d'Août*; (iii) *Lettre à Lamartine*; (iv) *A la Malibran*, poems; (v) *Confession d'un Enfant du Siècle*, tragic love story.

1837 †William IV; accession of Victoria.
Three months' strike of cotton spinners in Glasgow.
Constitutional crisis in Canada; Canada Bill introduced by Lord John Russell (*1792, †1878),

Balzac: *César Birotteau*, French novel.
Browning: *Strafford*, a tragedy.
Carlyle: *The French Revolution*.
Charles Dickens (*1812, †1870): (i) *Pickwick Papers* a novel introducing Mr Pickwick and Sam Weller; (ii) *Oliver Twist*, a story of an

Donizetti: *Lucia di Lammermoor*, Italian opera.
Halévy: *L'Eclair*, French comic opera.
Schumann: *Carnaval*, 20 German piano pieces based on the letters Asch, birthplace of his fiancée.
Corot: *Portrait of the Artist*.
Erection of the Goldsmiths' Company's Hall, London.
Madame Tussaud (*1760, †1850) opened London Waxworks.
Cherubini, Italian composer of church music: *Counterpoint and Fugue*, theory work.
Turner: *Burning of the Houses of Parliament*, painting.

Charles Chubb patented burglar-proof safe (work started by his brother; see 1818).
Samuel Colt (*1814, †1862), U.S. inventor, patented his revolver.
Darwin studied Galapagos Islands; noted effects of their isolation from the world.
Faraday discovered self-induction of a coil of wire.
Gas used for cooking purposes.
Construction of Great Western Railway begun.
Wood-blocks used for some roads in the U.S.A.; three years later in Britain.
Foundation of Melbourne, Australia.
Factory Act passed in Russia; not enforced.

Cherubini: *Requiem in D minor*, Italian composition.
Michael I. Glinka (*1804, †1857): *A Life for the Czar* (now called *Ivan Sussanin),* first Russian opera; composer first worked in Ministry of Communications, but later devoted himself entirely to music.
Philip Hardwicke designed Euston Station, London (reconstruction 1963–7).
Mendelssohn: *St Paul*, an oratorio.
Meyerbeer: *Les Huguenots*, German opera in French style.
Establishment of Huddersfield Choral Society.
London University received its Charter and superseded in its powers the colleges referred to in 1828 and 1829.
Chopin: *Piano Concerto in F minor* published.

John F. Daniell (*1790, †1845) developed his secondary (electric) cell.
E. Davy discovered acetylene (see 1862).
John Ericcson (*1803, †1889), Swedish-U.S. engineer, patented screw-propeller, but was not the earliest to make one (see 1826).
James Marsh (*1794, †1846): test for arsenic: used in criminology.
Pentzoldt developed the centrifuge.
Sorel produced galvanized iron.
Act for registration of births, deaths and marriages.
General Highway Act; General Enclosure Act.
Financial crisis in England and Ireland.
Vauxhall balloon flew 4800 miles: London to Nassau.
Foundation of Adelaide, South Australia.
Stamp Duty on newspapers reduced to 1*d*.

Berlioz: *Requiem* for soldiers killed in Algeria, remarkable for enormous number of performers required.
Constable: *Arundel Mill*, a painting.
Godde and Leseuer built Hôtel de Ville, Paris (to 1849).

Beer and Mädler made first accurate moon-map.
Heinrich W. Dove (*1803, †1879), German meteorologist, found that polar and equatorial air-streams determine European weather.

1837 statesman; rebellion in Canada under Papineau and Mackenzie.
Michigan admitted member state of the U.S.A.
Democratic local-government system introduced into Norway.
Archbishops of Cologne and Posen expelled for opposition to Prussian religious policies.
Seven professors of Göttingen deprived of posts for questioning right of King of Hanover to annul Constitution because it forbade use of state lands for payment of private debts.
Massacres by King Dingaan of Natal.

orphan.
Hugo: *Les Voix intérieures*, French poems.
Musset; *La Nuit d'Octobre*, French poem.
Publication of *Northern Star*.
British introduced *Hindustani* as lingua franca of India.

1838 Lord Durham sent to Canada to report on situation.
Publication of Peoples' Charter at Glasgow; start of Chartism.
Foundation of Anti-Corn Law League in Manchester.
Irish Poor Law Act.
Prison sentences established by Parliament for juvenile offenders.
Aden occupied by Britain.
Austrian troops withdrawn from Bologna; French withdrawn from Ancona.
Greece divided into 24 government districts.
Siege of Herat by Persian army.
Boers defeated Dingaan at Blood River; massacred Dingaan and Zulu followers: "Dingaan's Day", December 16th.
First Afghan War (to 1842).

Grillparzer: *Weh dem, der lügt*, Austrian comedy.
Hugo: *Ruy Blas*, French drama in which a valet loves a queen.
Lamartine: (i) *La Chute d'un Ange*, (ii) *L'Espoir en Dieu*, French poems.
Lady Charlotte Guest translated *Mabinogion* into English.
Eduard Mörike (*1804, †1875): *Gedichte*, German poems by great lyric poet of Swabia.
Vigny: *La Mort du Loup*, French poem advocating resignation to misfortune.

1839 Durham's Report on Canadian government presented to Parliament.
Resignation of Melbourne; Peel sent for: "Bedchamber Question"; Melbourne returned to office.
Chartist Petition presented to Parliament; rejected; Newport Rising.
British force under Keane occupied Kabul.
Treaty of London: Great Powers

Philip Bailey (*1816, †1902): *Festus*, dramatic poem.
Dickens: *Nicholas Nickleby*, a novel.
*Machado de Assis (†1908), Brazilian writer.
Balzac: *Le Curé de Village*, French novel of a priest.
Stendhal: *La Chartreuse de Parme*, French novel.
Vigny: (i) *La Colère de Samson*, (ii) *Le Mont des Oliviers*, French poems.
Opening of University of London Library.

Sir Isaac Pitman (*1813, †1897) introduced his shorthand system, named *Stenographic Soundhand*.
Fitzwilliam Museum, Cambridge, built to house books and engravings bequeathed by Fitzwilliam (see 1816).
Tuned kettledrums introduced into orchestra; untuned-type known some 700 years earlier.
Schumann: *Etudes en forme de Variations*, 12 French studies for pianoforte.

John Gould (*1804, †1881): *Birds of Europe*, ornithological work, completed; excellent drawings.
Paixhan constructed gun to fire shells.
Pouillet: tangent galvanometer, first instrument for measuring current.
Wheatstone and C. F. Cooke (*1806, †1879) constructed *first* railway telegraph.
Samuel B. Morse (*1791, †1872), U.S.A. developed telegraph in the U.S.A.
Last use of pillory in England.
First Canadian Railway.

Berlioz: *Benvenuto Cellini*, French opera.
Corot: (i) *Young Woman*, (ii) *View near Volterra*, French paintings.
Annie Laurie first published; poem by W. Douglas, air by Lady John Douglas Scott.
Queen Victoria's Imperial Crown made.
H. L. Elmes built St. George's Hall, Liverpool; classical Roman architecture.
Sir George Grey (*1812, †1898) discovered aboriginal cave drawings in Western Australia.
Prize Ring rules revised after fatal prize-fight.
Public Record Office, London, founded.
Opening, in Trafalgar Square, of present building of the National Gallery, designed by William Wilkins.

Bessel observed stellar parallax for first time.
Bruce invented type-casting machine.
Daguerre produced photographs using silver salts (*daguerreotype*); had worked with Niepce until †1833 of latter (see 1827, 1829).
Launching of S.S. *Archimedes* (British), first *successful* screw-driven ship.
Regular Atlanticc steamship service: S.S. *Sirius* crossed in 18 days; S.S. *Great Western* in 14½ days.
Royal Agricultural Society founded.
Peking government banned import of opium into China; clash with British (see 1839).
Anglo-Turkish trade treaty: free British trading rights in Turkey and Egypt.

Berlioz: *Roméo et Juliette*, described as a French dramatic symphony.
Turner: *The Fighting Téméraire*, famous sea painting.
First Royal Agricultural Show.
Dispute on religious education in State-aided schools.
Committee of Privy Council to organize administration of public money on education; grant increased; H.M. Inspectors of Schools appointed.
Knights Hospitallers received back Grand

Publication of work of N. H. Abel (*1802, †1829), Swedish, on mathematical analysis.
Davy's collected works published.
Faraday: *Electrostatic Induction and Specific Inductive Capacity*.
William H. Fox Talbot (*1800, †1877): photographic paper; demanded priority over Daguerre (1838); appears to have thought of idea in 1832.
Charles Goodyear (*1800, †1860), U.S.A.: india-rubber vulcanization.
Grove: first cell to produce *steady* current.

	History	Literature
1839	guaranteed perpetual neutrality of Belgium; "Scrap of Paper" of 1914. Armed rising of Parisian artisans against monarchy and middle-class rule. Anglo-Russian accord over Turkey supported by Prussia and Austria. Turkey at war with Mehemet Ali of Egypt; Turks invaded Syria, defeated by Ibrahim; †Mahmoud II; accession of Abdul Mejid, aged 16; Turkish fleet handed to Mehemet Ali. Aden annexed to British India. Outbreak of First Opium War between Britain and China (to 1842.) Republic of Guatemala established.	Austria recognized Magyar as official language in Hungary. *c.* Bradshaw's railway time-table appeared.
1840	Marriage of Queen Victoria and Prince Albert (*1819, †1861) of Saxe-Coburg. Chimney Sweeps Act. Repeal Association founded by O'Connell in Ireland. Transportation of convicts to New South Wales ceased; continued to Tasmania and Western Australia. Canadian Act of Union joined Upper and Lower Canada. Treaty of Waitangi; New Zealand to become British Colony. Foundation of Republic of Natal. Quadruple Convention of London: Britain, Russia, Prussia and Austria; to settle Egyptian question; France declared support for Mehemet Ali; Siege of Acre; Mehemet Ali offered surrender; returned Turkish fleet. Louis Napoleon failed to stir up Bonapartist rising at Boulogne; imprisoned in Ham (to 1846). Abdication of William I of Holland; accession of William II. Resignation of Queen Christina as Regent of Spain.	William H. Ainsworth (*1805, †1882): *The Tower of London*, a novel. R. Browning: *Sordello*, a poem about a poet. Friedrich Hebbel (*1813, †1863): *Judith*, German play. Hugo: *Les Rayons et les Ombres*, French poems. Thomas Babington, Lord Macaulay (*1800, †1859): *Essay on Clive*. Mérimée: *Colomba*, French novel of a vendetta in Corsica. Eugène Scribe (*1791, †1861): *Verre d'eau*, French drama. Thierry: *Récits des Temps Mérovingiens*, early French history brought to vivid life. London Library opened.
1841	Resignation of Melbourne; Peel, Prime Minister. Monster Repeal Meetings in Ireland. Miners' Association of Great Britain formed. "Passionists", Brotherhood of R.C.	Ainsworth: *Old St Paul's*, a novel. Balzac: (i) *Une ténébreuse Affaire*, (ii) *Ursula Mirouët*, French novels. R. Browning: *Pippa passes*, dramatic poem. Carlyle: *On Heroes and Hero-worship*, lectures.

Priories of Lombardy, Venice and Two Sicilies.
Giuseppe Verdi (*1813, †1901), Italian composer: *Oberto, Conte di San Bonifacio,* his first opera, produced at La Scala.
First Henley regatta held.
Grand National steeplechase, first run; Aintree, Liverpool.

James Nasmyth (*1808, †1890) developed steam-hammer.
Theodor Schwann (1810, †1882) showed that ovum is a cell; laid foundations of cell-growth theory.
Electric telegraph on railways: Paddington-West Drayton.
First dental school opened (at Baltimore).
First steel cables introduced: of great value in deep mining.
Wrought iron roof trusses for stations.
Tunnel-kiln developed in Denmark.
Samuel Cunard founded C. Steamship Co.

Alexandre Debain, of Paris, finally evolved the harmonium; his instrument had four stops for one keyboard based on earlier experiments.
Sir James Barry built Westminster Palace, Houses of Parliament (to 1860).
Delacroix: *The Justice of Trajan,* French picture.
Donizetti: (i) *La Favourite,* Italian opera; (ii) *La Fille du Régiment,* comic opera.
Max Schreckenburger (*1819, †1849): *Die Wacht am Rhein,* German national song.
Schumann married Clara Wieck (see 1830); composed 15 sets of songs in same year.
Erection of Nelson's Column; designed by William Railton; statue by E. H. Bailey.
c. Can-can dance in Paris, mainly for visitors.
c. Adolphe Sax (*1814, †1894), Belgian instrument maker, designed the saxophone; originally intended for serious music.

Draper took first photograph of moon.
Elkington's electro-plate process patented (on purchase from John Wright).
Rowland Hill introduced envelopes in England, concurrently with adhesive postage stamps (1*d*. black and 2*d*. blue); envelopes (not stamps) known earlier on Continent.
Liebig: *Chemistry in its Application to Agriculture and Physiology;* dealt with artificial fertilizers.
Kirkpatrick MacMillan made first true bicycle; cranks to drive rear wheels.
Christian F. Schönbein (*1799, †1868), German chemist, identified ozone as a new gas; smelt earlier in electrical experiments.
Erection of first steel cable bridge.
Capt. Wilkes discovered Antarctic coast.
Import of textbooks on anatomy into Russia prohibited on grounds of indecency.
Start of roller-milling in Hungary.
China severed all trade with Britain.
Auckland, largest city of New Zealand, founded.

Corot: (i) *Quai des Pacquis, Geneva,* (ii) *Landscape near Geneva,* French paintings.
Schumann: Symphony No. 1 in B major (*Spring S.*).
Hoffmann von Fallersleben (*1798, †1841): *Deutschland, Deutschland, über Alles,*

Bessel calculated eccentricity of Earth's orbit as 1 : 299.
Braid practised hypnosis.
Faraday experimented on polarization of light by magnetic field.
Rudolph von Kölliker (*1817, †1905), Swiss

1841	Priests founded 1714, settled in London. Proclamation of Union of Upper and Lower Canada. New Zealand became separate British Colony. Sultan of Brunei granted Sarawak to Sir James Brooke. Insurrection at Kabul. Swiss Canton of Aargau suppressed Catholic monasteries; latter protected by Federal Pact 1815. Peace between Sultan and Mehemet Ali; latter made hereditary Pasha of Egypt. Straits Convention; Dardanelles closed to non-Turkish warships.	Dickens: (i) *Barnaby Rudge,* (ii) *The Old Curiosity Shop,* novels. Musset: *Souvenir,* French poem. First issue of *Punch,* humorous and satirical periodical. First publication of *New York (Herald) Tribune.* Louis Kossuth founded *Pesti Hirlap,* Hungarian Liberal reform paper.
1842	Acute industrial crisis in England and Scotland. Second Chartist Petition rejected by Commons; Chartist riots in Staffordshire and Lancashire. Evacuation of Kabul; massacre in Khyber Pass; temporary re-occupation of Kabul by Nott and Pollock. South Australia declared Crown Colony; emigration to Australia encouraged. Maori insurrection due to settlers' infractions of Treaty of Waitangi. Treaty of Nanking: Hong Kong ceded to Britain. Ashburton Treaty; settled boundary dispute over Canadian-U.S. frontier in Maine. French occupied Tahiti. Japan relaxed edict of 1825 against foreign ships visiting ports. Employment of women and children in coal-mines forbidden.	Gogol: *Dead Souls,* Russian novel. Hebbel: *Gedichte,* German poems. Samuel Lover (*1797, †1868): *Handy Andy,* a novel. Macaulay: *Lays of Ancient Rome,* ballads. Sand: *Consuelo,* French novel. Eugène Sue (*1804, †1857): *Les Mystères de Paris,* first French novel to be published as newspaper serial. Tennyson: *Poems.* First publication of *Illustrated London News.* Removal of Press censorship in Denmark.
1843	Irish government prohibited Clontarf Meeting supporting O'Connell's agitation for Repeal of Irish Act of Union. "Rebecca Riots" against Turnpike Toll Bars in South Wales. Establishment of Free Church of Scotland. Natal proclaimed British possession; annexation of Sindh.	Berthold Auerbach (*1812, †1882): *Schwarzwälder Dorfgeschichten,* scenes of Black Forest life. George Borrow (*1803, †1881): *The Bible in Spain,* account of journey by Bible Society agent. Dickens: *A Christmas Carol,* a moral tale. Gautier: *Voyage en Espagne,* French travel sketches. Thomas Hood (*1799, †1845): *Song of the*

German national anthem.
Thomas Cook (*1808, †1892) began his Travel Agency by organizing a temperance meeting excursion to Loughborough.

histologist, first showed function of spermatozoa.
Royal Botanical Gardens, Kew, passed to the nation.
Discovery of Jenolan Caves, N.S.W.
Great Western Railway, London-Bristol, completed.
Royal Mail Steam Packet Co. started service to W. Indies.
Guano, valuable fertilizer, came into use.
British refugees from Canton founded Hong Kong.

Donizetti: *Linda di Chamounix*, Italian opera.
Glinka: *Russlan and Ludmilla*, Russian opera.
Ingres: *Odalisque with Slave*, French painting.
Turner: (i) *Yacht approaching the Coast*, (ii) *Steamer in Snowstorm*, paintings.
Richard Wagner (*1813, †1883), German composer of massive operas, an egotistical man of sybaritic tendency: opera *Rienzi* first performed.
Verdi: *Nabucco*, Italian opera.
Schumann: (i) Three string quartets; (ii) Piano quartet; (iii) Piano quintet.
Establishment of Primary Education in Belgium.
First English skating club, in London; skating, which is much older, probably originated on ice in Scandinavia.

Christian Döppler (*1803, †1853) stated Döppler effect: change of wavelength caused by relative motion of source and observer.
Henson made (abortive) aerial steam-carriage (25–h.p.) engine).
John B. Lawes successfully established use of artificial fertilizers at Rothamsted Experimental Station.
Crawford Long, U.S.A., first used general anaesthetic for an operation.
Carl Gustav Mosander discovered erbium, terbium and yttrium, rare earth metals.
Water-tube boilers first used in steam-ships.
Income Tax reintroduced.
Export of machinery permitted.
Peel reformed Corn Laws; began introduction of Free Trade policies.
Anglo-Russian commercial treaty.
As result of Treaty of Nanking, S. Chinese ports opened to foreign trade.

Race for Royal Hunt Cup first run at Ascot.
Corot: *Tivoli*, French painting.
John Curwen (*1816, †1880), Non-conformist minister, published the *Tonic Solfa*.
Henri Labrouste built Bibliothèque Ste Geneviève, Paris, having an iron frame (to 1850).
Mendelssohn: Music for Shakespeare's play *Midsummer Night's Dream* (see 1819).

James Joule (*1818, †1889) defined mechanical equivalent of heat: 4.18×10^7 ergs per calorie.
F. G. Keller made glass-paper.
Schwabe observed variation of intensity of sun-spots (see 1861).
Sir James R. Ross explored the Antarctic (began 1839).
Thames Tunnel, from Wapping to Rotherhithe, designed by Marc I. Brunel

1843 Isabella II of Spain declared of age to rule.
Formation of Sonderbund in Switzerland.
Nicholas I of Russia formally recognized Leopold I as King of Belgium.

Shirt, poem attacking sweated labour.
Michelet (to 1867): *Histoire de France*.
John S. Mill: (*1806, †1874): *System of Logic* (also 1872).
William H. Prescott (*1796, †1859): *Conquest of Mexico*, account of conflict between native Mexicans and invading Spaniards.
First publication of *News of the World*.
Vicenzo Gioberti (*1801, †1852): *Moral and Political Leadership in Italy*.
Foundation of *The Economist*.

1844 O'Connell tried and sentenced for sedition; verdict reversed by House of Lords, but O'Connell's health and influence were on the wane.
Anglo-French dispute over Tahiti settled.
†Charles XIV of Sweden; accession of Oscar I.
Swiss Sonderbund demanded restoration of monasteries in Aargau; latter demanded expulsion of Jesuits from Switzerland.
Otto I of Greece accepted Liberal Constitution after military revolt.
State visit to Tsar Nicholas I to England.
Peel's Bank Charter Act.
The Rochdale Pioneers founded retail co-operative movement.

Dickens: *Martin Chuzzlewit*, a novel.
Benjamin Disraeli, Earl of Beaconsfield (*1804, †1881)): *Coningsby*, political novel.
Dumas: *Les Trois Mousquetaires*, French novel.
Hebbel: *Maria Magdalena*, German tragedy.
Heine: *Neue Gedichte*, German poems.
Alexander Kinglake (*1809, †1891): *Eothen*, travels in the East.
Sue: *Le Juif Errant*, French novel.
Vigny: *La Maison du Berger*, French poem.

1845 Report of Devon Commission on Irish Land Tenure Systems.
Print Works Act applied Factory Acts to printing works.
Forthcoming potato famine predicted for Ireland.
British Cabinet divided over repeal of Corn Laws; Peel resigned; Russell refused to form ministry; Peel recalled.
Evangelical Alliance: All-Protestant alliance to oppose Roman Catholicism.
F. E. O'Connor's Land Scheme adopted by Chartists.
Captain George Grey appointed first

Friedrich Engels (*1820, †1895), German socialist and life-long friend of Marx, who lived mainly in Manchester: *Condition of the Working Class in England*.
Disraeli: *Sybil*, a novel.
Dumas: (i) *Vingt Ans Après*, (ii) *Le Comte de Monte-Cristo*, French novels.
Edgar Allan Poe (*1809, †1849): *Tales of Mystery and Imagination*, American stories.
Dumas: *La Tulipe noire*, novel of Holland in 17th cent.

Turner: (i) *San Benedetto, looking towards Fusina*, (ii) *Approach to Venice*, paintings.
Donizetti: *Don Pasquale*, Italian comic opera.
Wagner: *The Flying Dutchman*, German opera, first performed.
The tuba introduced into orchestras.
Theatre Act gave greater freedom to musical shows and helped to develop Music Hall.
Foundations: (i) Marlborough College, public school; (ii) Leipzig Conservatory of Music.
John Calcott Horsley (*1817, †1903), artist, designed the first *printed* Christmas card.

(*1769, †1849), opened (begun 1825).
S.S. *Great Britain*, first screw-steamer to cross the Atlantic (3,448 tons).
Half-farthings minted.
Modern sewage system at Hamburg.
Foundation of the Archaeological Association and Institute.
First public telegraph line between Paddington and Slough.
F. H. A. von Humboldt, German explorer: *Asie centrale*, summarizing scientific observations of nine-month journey.

Berlioz: *Traité de l'Instrumentation*, important work on music.
The polka introduced into Britain from Bohemia.
St. Giles's Church, Camberwell, erected by Ruskin.
Turner: *Rain, Steam and Speed*, a painting.
Verdi: *Ernani*, Italian opera, produced at Venice.
Schumann began work on *Scenes from Goethe's Faust*.

Bessel propounded binary motion of stars Sirius and Procyon.
G. Q. Colton (*1814, †1898) and H. Wells (*1815, †1848), U.S.A., used nitrous oxide (laughing gas); not successful at first; reintroduced 1869 for extraction of teeth, using oxygen as well.
H. Grassmann devised four-dimensional geometry.
Kölliker discovered cell-multiplication process (see 1839).
Railway Act: instituted "Parliamentary Train".
Peninsular and Oriental Service extended to Calcutta.
Robert Bunsen (*1811, †1899), German chemist, invented grease-spot photometer.
Larboard (left side of ship) renamed "port" by Admiralty.
Graham's Factory Act.

W. H. Fry (*1813, †1864): *Leonora*, first American opera.
David O. Hill (*1802, †1879) developed artistic photographic portraits.
Ingres: *Contesse d'Haussonville*, French portrait.
A. M. Layard (*1817, †1894) excavated Ninevah.
Mendelssohn: Violin Concerto in E minor.
Wagner: *Tannhäuser*, German opera.
Malicious destruction of the *Portland Vase*, famous Grecian urn; completely restored.
Peel's Maynooth Act: Queen's Colleges founded in Ireland.
Swiss Liberal risings against Jesuit-

John Crouch Adams (*1819, †1892) *calculated* existence of planet Neptune independently done by Leverrier (1846); planet *found* by Galle (1846).
W. G. Armstrong's hydraulic crane.
Erastus B. Bigelow invented Brussels power-loom.
Rudolf E. Clausius (*1822, †1888) discovered ruthenium, rare earth metal.
Faraday's elctromagnetic theory of light.
Fizeau and Foucault photographed the Sun.
James Glaisher (*1809, †1903): tables for finding dew-point from wet and dry thermometers.
General Enclosure Act.

LITERATURE

	HISTORY	LITERATURE
1845	Governor of New Zealand;to 1853. First Sikh War (to 1846); Sikhs defeated by Sir Hugh Gough. War between the U.S.A. and Mexico over boundary disputes to 1848; Florida and Texas admitted to Union. Failure of potato crop in Belgium and Holland; famine. Norwegian religious Dissenters granted freedom of worship. Law limiting hours of child labour in Russia; not enforced.	
1846	Corn Laws repealed by Peel; defeat and resignation of Peel; Russell, Prime Minister of last "Whig" or first "Liberal" Ministry. Secularism founded by G. J. Holyoake (*1817, †1906), pioneer in cooperation. Establishment of responsible government in Canada. Main Maori insurrection suppressed. Gough defeated Sikhs at Aliwal and Sabrao; Treaty of Lahore; Sir Henry Lawrence as British Resident. Labuan ceded to Britain. Oregon Treaty: Canadian-U.S. boundary extended from Great Lakes west along 49th parallel. Iowa entered Union of the U.S.A. Proposed marriages of Isabella II of Spain and her sister, Maria Louisa; created difficulties for Louis Philippe; broke up Anglo-French entente. Election of Pope Pius IX (Pio Nono). Annexation of Cracow by Austria. Japanese repulsed U.S. warships seeking to encourage foreign trade.	*Edmondo de Amicis, Italian novelist (†1908). Balzac: *La Cousine Bette*, French novel. George Grote (*1794, †1871): *History of Greece*, completed 1856. Edward Lear (*1812, †1888): *Book of Nonsense*, verse, including early limericks. Sand: *La Mare au Diable*, French novel. William Makepeace Thackeray (*1811, †1863), novelist, first made his name with *The Book of Snobs*; began *Vanity Fair* (completed 1848) in the same year. Fyodor Mikhailovich Dostoievski (*1821, †1881), Russian novelist: *Poor Folk*, his first novel. John Ruskin (*1819, †1900): *Modern Painters*, on work of J. M. W. Turner.
1847	Poor Law Board replaced Poor Law Commission set up in 1834; Andover Workhouse Scandal. †O'Connell; "Young Ireland" group increased activities. Province of Kaffraria set up in	Jànos Arany (*1817, †1882), Hungarian writer: *Toldi*. Balzac: *Le Cousin Pons*, French novel. Disraeli: *Tancred*, a novel. Charlotte Brontë (*1816, †1855): *Jane Eyre*, a novel.

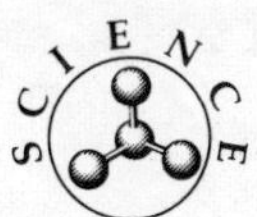

controlled education in Lucerne; suppressed.
Oxford and Cambridge boat race transferred from Henley toPutney.

F. H. A. von Humboldt: *Kosmos* (to 1862); summarized exploration of S. America and Asia; laid foundations of physical geography.
McNaught's compound steam engine.
Ross constructed 22–in. reflector telescope.
Manufacture of breech-loading artillery with rifled barrels at Piedmont.
Foundation of Royal College of Chemistry.
First submarine cable laid across English Channel.
Period of railway speculation (to 1847).
R. W. Thompson patented pneumatic tyre; not adopted until 1888, *q.v.*.
Sturt explored Central Australian desert; copper discovered in Australia.
Naval Academy opened at Annapolis, U.S.A.

J. B. Bunning built Coal Exchange, London, largely of iron and glass.
César Franck (*1822, †1890), Belgian Romantic composer: *Ruth*, oratorio.
Mendelssohn: *Elijah*, German oratorio.
Schumann completed 4th Symphony (so numbered later) in D minor (begun 1841).
W. J. Thomas, antiquary, coined term *folk-lore* to embrace traditions and customs of country people.
Smithsonian Institute founded in Washington.
Fleet Prison pulled down.

Gavin Dalzell made improved bicycle (see 1840).
H. von. Mohl (*1805, †1872) coined name protoplasm and described its behaviour.
Richard March Hoe (*1812, †1886), American inventor, designed rotary printing-press.
Elias Howe (*1819, †1867), U.S.A., invented sewing-machine; put into production by I. M. Singer (1851).
Gooch's "colossal" locomotive: used on G.W.R.
Robinson designed cup anemometer for measuring wind-speed.
Schönbein invented nitro-cellulose and used gun-cotton for firearms.
A. Sobrero, Italian, discovered nitroglycerine.
Warren and Morton, U.S.A., associated in using ether during operation for vascular tumour.
Electric arc-lighting used at Paris Opera House.
Appointment of Railway Commissioners.
Supervision of steamships authorized by Act.
Trade Guilds abolished in Sweden.

Berlioz: *The Damnation of Faust*, French opera.
Delacroix: *St George and the Dragon*, French painting.
Friedrich Flotow (*1812, †1883): *Martha*, German opera, his most successful work.

Gustav Robert Kirchhoff (*1824, †1887), German physicist, enunicated laws of electric currents in network of wires.
Liebig's extract of meat.
James Y. Simpson, surgeon, successfully chloroformed Waldie, chemist; gave rise

	History	Literature
1847	Cape Colony under British supervision. Mormons emigrated to Utah; headquarters at Salt Lake City. Failure of Belgian wheat crop. Famine in Holland led to revolts. United Prussian Diet met at Berlin; Liberals failed to secure constitutional government from Frederick William IV. Federal Diet at Berne declared war on reactionaries; captured Lucerne; dissolved Sonderbund. Liberian Republican Constitution established. Don Pacifico incident in Greece.	Emily Brontë (*1818, †1848), sister of Charlotte: *Wuthering Heights*, her only novel. Heine: *Atta Troll*, German polemic against political poetry; the hero is a dancing bear in the Pyrenees. Marryat: *The Children of the New Forest*, children's novel. Tennyson: *The Princess*, a narrative poem. Mérimée: *Carmen*, French novel with Spain as setting.
1848	Third Chartist Petition; failed. Failure of "Young Ireland" insurrection under Smith O'Brien. General revolt by Sikhs led to Gough's invasion of Punjab. Britain annexed Orange River district in S. Africa. Wisconsin admitted State in the U.S.A. Revolution in Paris; abdication of Louis Philippe; Second Republic; Louis Napoleon elected Prince President. Franco-British grant of independence to Hawaii. Swiss Federal Diet approved new Constitution. Charles Albert granted Liberal Constitution to Sardinia; led revolt against Austria rule; defeated by Radetzky at Custozza. Revolutions in Berlin, Vienna, Venice, Rome, Milan, Naples, Prague and Budapest. German National Parliament summoned to Frankfort; attempted to unify government of German Confederation as hereditary empire. Accession of Francis Joseph as Emperor of Austria. Commission by William II of Holland established new Constitution.	Emile Augier (*1820, †1889): *L'Aventurière*, French play of world of demi-mondaines. Elizabeth Gaskell (*1810, †1865): *Mary Barton*, novel of the weavers of Manchester. Thackeray: *Pendennis* (completed 1850), semi-autobiographical novel. Mill: *Political Economy*.

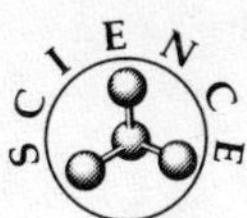

Establishment of Manchester Cathedral, formerly a parish church.
Verdi: (i) *Macbeth*, (ii) *Jérusalem*, Italian operas; the latter was a revised version of an earlier work.

to widespread use of anaesthetics.
Vidi, French, designed aneroid barometer.
Carl Zeiss (*1816, †1888) opened famous optical works at Jena.
15–in. refractor telescope at Cambridge, Mass.
First record of gorilla being known to Western world.
Fielden's Factory Act (Ten Hours Act).
Financial crisis in Britain.
Hamburg-Amerika shipping line founded.
First Swiss railway, Zürich-Baden, opened.

Augustus W. N. Pugin (*1812, †1852), architect, designed Roman Catholic Cathedral of Southwark.
Queen's College London, opened.
Schumann: *Genoveva*, German opera which did not prove to be popular.
c. Honoré Daumier (*1808, †1879): *The Revolt*, French painting.
Pre-Raphaelite Brotherhood (P.R.B.) founded; sought fresh inspiration from Middle Ages and rebelled against Machine Age; included artists Holman Hunt, Burne Jones, Millais, Morris, Rossetti.

R. Böttger first produced safety matches (see 1826).
Charles Ellet built 1,000 ft cable bridge over Ohio River; it collapsed 6 years later.
Strongfellow successfully flew steam-power *model* aircraft.
Wm. Thompson, Lord Kelvin (*1824, †1907), using electric thermometer, determined temperature of absolute zero as –273° C.
Linus Yale, U.S.A., invented cylinder lock.
Proof that Saturn's rings are not solid (Roche's Limit).
Manchester Waterworks began constructing reservoirs.
First commercial milling-machine constructed.
Second cholera epidemic in England; Public Health Act set up Central Board of Health.
Government made loans for land drainage.
Foundation of the Institute of Actuaries.
First discovery of gold in California.
Heyfelder first used ethyl chloride as anaesthetic agent.
First official settlers arrived at Dunedin, New Zealand.
Beginnings of modern psychical research: Fox sisters of New York.
Christian Socialists founded co-operative workshops.

1848

Carlist rising in Catalonia suppressed.

1849

Society for promoting Working-Men's Associations founded.
Irish Encumbered Estates Act.
Riots in Montreal.
Battle of Gujarat; end of Sikh State; Punjab annexed by Britain.
French troops under Oudinot restored Pius IX in Rome.
Frankfort National Parliament offered Imperial Crown to Frederick William IV of Prussia; refused; the Parliament collapsed.
Austro-Sardinian war renewed; Sardinians defeated at Novara; abdication of Charles Albert; accession of Victor Emmanuel II.
Austrians regained Venice; Hungarian revolt crushed with aid from Tsar Nicholas I; Turkey rejected demands for surrender of Hungarian refugees.
†William II of Holland; accession of William III.
Denmark became Constitutional Monarchy.

Matthew Arnold (*1822, †1888): *Poems,* including *The Forsaken Merman.*
C. Brontë: *Shirley,* a novel.
Chateaubriand: *Mémoires d'Outre-Tombe,* French posthumous memoirs.
Dickens: *David Copperfield* (completed 1850), a novel, largely autobiographical.
Sand: *La Petite Fadette,* French novel of rustic manners.
Macaulay: *History of England,* unfinished.
*August Strindberg, Swedish writer (†1912).
Publication of *Who's Who?*

1850

†Sir Robert Peel.
Queen Victoria's Memorandum on Palmerston's methods as Foreign Secretary.
Factory Act defined legal working hours.
Inauguration of Catholic Hierarchy in Britain.
Trade Unionism revived.
Separation of Victoria from New South Wales; General Assembly proposed for all Australia.
British purchased Danish settlements in West Africa.
California admitted to statehood in the U.S.A.
Universal Suffrage abolished in France.
Norwegian National Debt paid off.
Restoration of 1815 German Diet at Frankfort; liquidated final debts arising out of Thirty Years War (1618–48).
Pius IX returned to Rome after end

Elizabeth Barrett Browning (*1806, †1861): *Sonnets from the Portuguese,* expressing her love for her husband.
R. Browning: *Poems.*
*Eminescu (†1889), Roumanian poet.
Nathaniel Hawthorne (*1804, †1864): *The Scarlet Letter,* American tragic story of adulteress.
Hebbel: *Herodes und Mariamne,* German tragedy based on Jewish history.
Charles Kingsley (*1819, †1875): *Alton Locke,* a novel of industrial conditions.
Otto Ludwig (*1813, †1865): *Der Erbförster,* German Romantic tragedy.
Alexander Ostrowski (*1823, †1886): *The Bankrupt,* a comedy.
Dante Gabriel Rossetti (*1828, †1882): *The Blessed Damozel,* a poem.
Tennyson: *In Memoriam,* poem on a friend.
Ivan S. Turgenev (*1818, †1883): *A Month in the Country,* Russian play.
Wordsworth: *The Prelude,* long autobiographical poem.

F. R. Cockerell: *The Professor's Dream*, remarkable painting showing all main architectural monuments of history.
Delacroix: *L'Odalisque*, French painting.
Meyerbeer: *Le Prophète*, German opera in French style.
Franz Liszt (*1811, †1886), Hungarian pianist and composer of ornate and elaborate music: Three Concert Studies for Pianoforte.
Extension of Higher Education in Belgium.
Alfred Rethel (*1816, †1859), German historical painter, subject to insanity: *Dance of Death*, inspired by Belgian unrest of 1848.
c. "Bloomers" introduced by Amelia Jenks Bloomer (*1818, †1894), American reformer.

Gustave Courbet (*1819, †1877), realist working-class painter: *Burial at Ornans*, French painting.
William Holman Hunt (*1827, †1910): *Claudio and Isabella*, a painting.
Sir John Everett Millais (*1829, †1896), a founder of the Pre-Raphaelite movement: *Christ in the House of His Parents*, a painting.
Jean-François Millet (*1814, †1875): *The Sower*, French painting.
Schumann: (i) 3rd Symphony (*The Rhenish*), (ii) Cello Concerto.
Wagner: *Lohengrin*, German opera, first produced at Weimar.
c. Brass bands gained popularity in N. England.
c. Municipal libraries in Britain.
Establishment of the Bach Gesellschaft to publish complete works of J. S. Bach; 46 vols in all; the last appeared in 1900.
Royal Commission on Universities of Oxford and Cambridge.
Falloux's Act strengthened Church control of French education.

Fizeau measured speed of light using terrestrial methods.
William Hunt, of the U.S.A., invented the safety pin.
David Livingstone (*1813, †1873) began exploration of Central and South Africa; crossed Kalahari Desert and reached Lake Ngami.
Joseph Monier, French, produced reinforced concrete; this was to revolutionize building (see 1870).
J. F. Herschel: *Outlines of Astronomy*.
Modern English florin (2s. = £1/10) introduced as step towards decimal coinage – not achieved until 1968.
Final repeal of Navigation Laws.
Steel guns manufactured at Krupps armament works.
Petropavlovsk founded in Siberia.

c. Bunsen attributed with design of his gas burner.
Clausius and Kelvin expounded second law of thermodynamics.
J. B. L. Foucault (*1819, †1868), French, constructed pendulum demonstrating rotation of the Earth.
Glaisher established Meteorological Office.
Mercantile Marine Act.
H. L. F. Helmholtz (*1821, †1894), German scientist, invented ophthalmoscope.
Earl of Rosse discovered spiral nebulae.
James Young, chemist, patented synthetic oil production; preparation of paraffin wax by slow distillation.
Beginnings of petrol refining, without which the internal-combustion engine would be useless.
Mercerized cotton produced by treating cotton with caustic soda.
Invention of steam threshing machine.
Nicholaievst founded in Siberia.

1850 of Roman Republic; partial amnesty; refused to restore Constitution.

1851 Palmerston dismissed for acting without consulting Cabinet or Crown.
Formation of Amalgamated Society of Engineers; New Model Unionism.
Conversion of Henry Edward Manning to Roman Catholicism; later Cardinal Manning.
Victoria became separate colony.
Coup d'état placed Louis Napoleon in control of France; rising in Paris ruthlessly suppressed; policy supported by plebiscite.
Conference of Dresden; restored Old Federal Diet of 1815.
Religious freedom granted to Jews in Norway.
Accession of Danilo as Prince of Montenegro.
Nicholas I failed to gain control of Varanger Fjord from Sweden.

Borrow: *Lavengro*, romance of his wanderings with gypsies.
Theodor Fontane (*1819, †1898): *Gedichte*, German poems.
Kingsley: *Yeast*, novel dealing with contemporary social problems.
Eugène Labiche (*1815, †1888): *Le Chapeau de Paille d'Italie*, French comedy.
Herman Melville (*1819, †1891): *Moby Dick*, American story of a whale relentlessly pursued.
Henri Murger (*1822, †1861): *Scènes de la Vie de Bohème*, Bohemian life in Paris.
Sainte-Beuve (to 1862): *Causeries du Lundi*, literary criticism.
Harriet Beecher Stowe (*1811, †1896): *Uncle Tom's Cabin*, American novel exposing evils of negro slavery.
First issue of *New York Times*.

1852 Palmerston brought about fall of Russell in return for 1851 dismissal; Derby Prime Minister; defeated; Coalition Ministry under Aberdeen.
Bribery Act enabled enquiry into corrupt elections.
Engineering Lock-out: Cotton Spinners Union remodelled on federal basis.
†Duke of Wellington.
Sand River Convention: Transvaal received autonomous government.
New Zealand received responsible self-government.
Second Burmese War; annexation of Pegu.
Louis Napoleon issued new Constitution; plebiscite confirmed restoration of Empire under Napoleon III.
New Bailliwick of Brandenburg set up by King of Prussia for Knights Hospitaller; not recognized by R.C. Order.

Arnold, *Poems*.
Sir Edward S. Creasy (*1812, †1878): *Fifteen Decisive Battles of the World*.
Dickens: *Bleak House*, a novel; miseries of a law suit.
Alexandre Dumas fils (*1824, †1895): *La Dame aux Camélias*, romantic novel, later a play.
Gautier: *Emaux et Camées*, poems.
Leconte de Lisle (*1818, †1894): *Poésies antiques*.
Musset: *Poésies nouvelles*.
Theodor Storm (*1817, †1888): *Immensee*, German sentimental tale.
Tennyson: *Ode on the Death of Wellington*.
Thackeray: *Henry Esmond*, historical novel.
Turgenev: *Sportsman's Sketches*.

Belgian Liberals established undenominational teaching in secondary schools.
Foundation of Sydney University, Australia.

The America's Cup, yachting trophy; won regularly by the U.S.A.
Courbet: *The Village Maidens*, French painting.
Lewis Cubitt designed King's Cross Station.
Charles François Gounod (*1818, †1893): *Sapho*, French opera.
Holman Hunt: *The Hireling Shepherd*, oil painting.
Liszt composed 20 *Hungarian Rhapsodies* (to 1886).
Sir Joseph Paxton built Crystal Palace for Great Exhibition at Hyde Park (see 1852).
Verdi: *Rigoletto*, popular Italian opera.
Thos. W. Walter erected the Capitol, Washington, U.S.A. (to 1863).
Ruskin: *Stones of Venice*, treatise on Gothic art.
Constantinople University founded.
Government made first grant towards Evening Schools.

Prince Albert largely responsible for success of Great Exhibition.
Bogardus developed cast-iron framed buildings.
Kelly developed steel-making converter.
Lister and Donisthorpe developed the machine-comb.
Heinrich Daniel Rühmkorff (*1803, †1877), German, invented high-tension induction coil.
Isaac M. Singer (*1811, †1875), U.S.A., manufactured first *practical* sewing-machine (see 1846).
Submarine cable between Dover and Calais.
First double-decker omnibus.
Start of precision tool-making.
Gold discovered in Victoria, Australia.
Cleveland iron-ore deposits opened up.
Repeal of Window Tax; houses taxed instead.

Holman Hunt: *The Light of the World*, a painting of Christ.
Millais: *Ophelia*, a painting.
Paxton re-erected the Crystal Palace at Sydenham (see 1936).
Opening of Victoria and Albert Museum for art treasures.
Johannes Brahms (*1833, †1897), great German pianist and composer who originally had to earn money playing in low establishments: 3 piano sonatas.

Bunsen isolated magnesium (see 1808).
Samuel Fox made steel frames for umbrellas.
Foucault invented the gyroscope.
Morse developed his telegraph code (alphabet).
Mäthysen, Dutch army surgeon, impregnated bandages with plaster.
Elisha Otis: lift safety device, making machine safe for passengers (see 1854).
Land Survey in Britain completed.
London Water Act, safeguarding purity of supply; not fully implemented for 33 years.
Salt water aquarium in London.
Third cholera epidemic.
Wells Fargo and Co., U.S. Express company, founded.
Haarlem Lake drained for conversion to pasture.
Tasmania ceased to be convict settlement.
Henri Giffard (*1825, †1882), French inventor, built first aero-engine for non-rigid airship.

1852

History:
Mantuan Trials: infamous punishments on Republican plotters.
War between Montenegro and Turkey; Turkey compelled to withdraw forces by Nicholas I.

1853

History:
Gladstone's first budget; duty on 123 articles abolished; death duties introduced.
Preston spinners' strike.
Kaffir war led to British annexation of Kaffraria.
Cape Colony received responsible government.
Van Diemen's Land renamed Tasmania in honour of its discoverer.
Marriage of Napoleon III to Eugenia di Montijo, widow of Spanish General.
Regulation of Antwerp; religious teaching in Belgian secondary schools to be in accordance with religious views of majority of pupils.
Roman Catholic bishops permitted in Holland.
Russo-Turkish war; Russians attacked and occupied Moldavia and Wallachia; Turkish fleet destroyed at Sinop.

Literature:
Arnold: (i) *Sohrab and Rustum*, (ii) *The Scholar-Gipsy*, poems.
C. Brontë, *Villette*, novel set in Brussels.
Gaskell: *Cranford*, a novel.
Hawthorne: *Tanglewood Tales*, U.S. mythology for children.
Heine: *Neueste Gedichte*, German poems.
Gwilym Hiraethog (*1802, †1883): *Aelwyd F'Ewythr Robert*, pioneer Welsh novel.
Hugo: *Les Châtiments*, poems attacking Napoleon III.
Kingsley: *Hypatia*, historical novel of 5th-cent. Alexandria.
Charles Reade (*1814, †1884): *Peg Woffington*, a novel.
Thackeray: (to 1855) *The Newcomes*, a novel.

1854

History:
Offices of Secretary of State for War and Colonies added to existing Secretaryships.
Cardwell's Railway Act.
Outbreak of Crimean War: Battles of Alma, Balaclava, Inkerman; start of siege of Sebastopol; growing discontent with conduct of war.
Usury Laws.
Act providing for committal of juvenile offenders to reformatories.
First meeting of Cape Parliament; Orange Free State returned to Boers.
Annexation of Nagpur.
Successful risings in Madrid and elsewhere against misrule of Isabella II.
Swedish government gained control

Literature:
Augier: *Le Gendre de M. Poirier*, social drama in prose.
Dickens: *Hard Times*, a novel.
Gustav Freytag (*1816, †1895): *Die Journalisten*, German comedy of small town political life.
Gottfried Keller (*1819, †1890): *Der grüne Heinrich*, Swiss autobiography.
Theodor Mommsen (*1817, †1903): *Römische Geschichte*, German history of Rome.
Tennyson: *Charge of the Light Brigade*, poem on the charge at Balaclava.
Henry D. Thoreau (*1817, †1862): *Walden*, American tale of author's life in the woods.
Josef V. von Scheffel (*1826, †1886): *Der Trompeter von Säkkingen*, German verse romance.

Johann C. Dahl (*1788, †1857): *Winter Landscape*, Norwegian painting.
Schumann: Fantasia for Violin and Orchestra.
Henry E. Steinway founded New York firm of piano manufacturers of that name; originally Steinweg of Brunswick.
Verdi: *Il Trovatore*, Italian opera, his second success; *La Traviata*, in same year, did not score corresponding initial popularity.
Foundation of Wellington College, public school, from subscriptions in memory of Duke of Wellington.
Foundation of Melbourne University, Australia.
Balmoral Castle rebuilt (to 1855) by Albert, Prince Consort.

Queen Victoria allowed John Snow to administer chloroform to her during birth of Prince Leopold; ensured place of chloroform as anaesthetic in Britain.
Hamilton's lecture on quaternions published.
Noble's improved wool-combing machine; widely used in Britain.
M. F. Maurey, U.S.A.: *Physical Geography of the Sea*, standard work on winds and currents.
U.S. Commodore Perry proposed trade relations with Japan; rejected.
Alexander Wood: hypodermic syringe for subcutaneous injections.
Vaccination against smallpox compulsory in England.
Reaping-machine came into general use.
Completion of Cherbourg breakwater (2½ miles long).
Opening of railway from Vienna to Trieste, through the Alps.
Abolition of duty on newspaper advertisements.
Opening, at Regent's Park, of the first public aquarium.

Baron Haussmann, Prefect of Seine, began reconstruction of Paris; broad boulevards less easy to barricade by insurgents.
Courbet: *Bonjour, Monsieur Courbet*, French realist painting.
Wm. Frith (*1819, †1909): *Ramsgate Sands*, a painting; artist was very popular with the "man in the street".
Delacroix: *The Tiger Hunt*, French painting.
Millet: *The Reapers*, French painting.
Wagner: *Der Ring des Nibelungen*, cycle of German operas, comprising: (i) *Das Rheingold*; (ii) *Die Walküre*; (iii) *Siegfried*; (iv) *Götterdammerung* (completed 20 years later).
Tragic insanity and attempted suicide of Schumann.
Foundation of London Working Men's College.
University Reform Bill.

Sir George B. Airy (*1801, †1892): mine experiment to determine Earth's density.
Marcellin P. E. Berthelot (*1827, †1907), French chemist: *Sur les combinaisons de la glycérine avec les acides*, his first major work.
M. P. R. Garcia, professor of singing, designed laryngoscope; of value to throat surgeons.
Geissler's electric discharge tube.
Otis, U.S.A., invented hydraulic lift.
Georg F. B. Riemann (*1826, †1866): *Über die Hypothesen welche der Geometrie zu Gründe liegen*; developed non-Euclidean geometry.
Sinsteden made first accumulators (see 1859).
S.S. *Brandon*, first ship with compound expansion engines.
Millwall docks opened.

Year	History	Literature
1854	of brandy manufacture; first stage to control of drunkenness.	
1855	William Howard Russell (*1821, †1907), *The Times* correspondent, revealed mismanagement of British forces in Crimea. Fall of Aberdeen Ministry; Palmerston Prime Minister. Committee of Enquiry into Crimean matters. State visit of Victoria and Albert to France. Fall of Sebastopol. Tasmania granted representative government. British occupied island of Perim on sea route to India. Sardinia under Cavour joined France, Britain and Turkey against Russia in Crimea. Spain given more Liberal Constitution. Sweden made treaty with Britain and France; guaranteed against Russian attack. †Tsar Nicholas I; accession of Alexander II.	Michelet: *Histoire de France, Les Temps Modernes*. John L. Motley (*1814, †1877): *Rise of the Dutch Republic*, history. R. Browning: *Men and Women*, poems. Dickens: *Little Dorrit* (completed 1857), a novel. Freytag: *Soll und Haben*, German novel. Hebbel: *Agnes Bernauer*, German tragedy. Paul Heyse (*1830, †1914): *L'Arrabiata*, German short story. Kingsley: *Westward Ho!*, historical adventure novel. Henry Wadsworth Longfellow (*1807, †1882): *Hiawatha*, U.S. poem. George Meredith (*1828, †1909): *Shaving of Shagpat*, oriental tale. Tennyson: *Maud and Other Poems*. Anthony Trollope (*1815, †1882): *The Warden*, a "Barchester" novel. Walt Whitman (*1819, †1892): *Leaves of Grass*, American poetry. First publication of: (i) *The Daily Chronicle*; (ii) *The Daily Telegraph*.
1856	Treaty of Paris ended Crimean War; privateering abolished; merchantmen henceforth to be unarmed. Outbreak of Second Anglo-Chinese War and war with Persia (to 1857). Natal became separate Colony. Oudh annexed by Lord Dalhousie. Successful counter-revolution in Spain; Liberal measures annulled. Visit of Emperor Francis Joseph to Lombardy and Venice; appointment of Liberal-minded Archduke Maximilian as Governor of provinces.	James A. Froude (*1818, †1894): (to 1870) *History of England*, in 12 vols. Alexis de Tocqueville (*1805, †1859): *L'Ancien Régime*, French study of pre-Revolution period. Edmond About (*1828, †1885): *Le Roi des Montagnes*, French novel. Mrs Craik (*1826, †1887): *John Halifax, Gentleman*, a novel. Ralph Waldo Emerson (*1803, †1882): *English Traits*, by American essayist and poet. Gustave Flaubert (*1821, †1880): *Madame Bovary*, French realistic novel of provincial doctor's wife.

Opening of Cheltenham Ladies' College, girls' public school.
Taylor excavated Ur of the Chaldees, Sumerian settlement.

Russians used land-mines in Crimean War.
New Public Health Board appointed.
English coastal trade opened to ships of all nations.
Trade treaty between Japan and the U.S.A.
Turin-Genoa railway opened.

Ford Maddox Brown (*1821, †1893), last English Historical Painter and follower of Pre-Raphaelite style: *The Last of England*.
Courbet: *The Artist's Studio*, French painting.
Liszt: *Faust* Symphony.
First printing of *Londonderry Air*.
Crystal Palace concerts began; held weekly until 1901.
Civil Service Commission appointed; entry examination (not open) set up.
International Exhibition in Paris.
Federal Polytechnic School opened in Zürich.

Thomas Addison described disease named after him.
Audemars produced nitro-cellulose *thread* (rayon); see 1846.
Sir Joseph Bazalgette modernized London sewers after outbreak of cholera.
David E. Hughes (*1831, †1900) constructed telegraph printer.
Köller, Austrian, developed tungsten steel (see 1857).
Florence Nightingale (*1820, †1910) saved hundreds of lives in Crimea by introducing hygiene into military hospital wards.
Alexander Parkes invented celluloid, so named later by J. W. and I. S. Hyatt, U.S.A. (1873).
Robbins and Lawrence Co., Vermont, U.S.A., introduced turret-lathe.
Sale of methylated spirits authorized for commercial purposes in Britain.
Royal Victoria docks opened.
First iron Cunard steamer crossed Atlantic in 9½ days.
Ferdinand de Lesseps (*1805, †1894) granted concession to construct Suez Canal.
Livingstone discovered Victoria Falls.
Sir Richard Burton (*1821, †1890): *Pilgrimage to Mecca*, travel book.
Abolition of duties on newspapers.

Karl Bechstein (*1826, †1900) founded in Berlin the piano-manufacturing company bearing his name.
Courbet: *Girls on the Banks of the Seine*, French painting.
Alexander Sergeivitch Dargomejsky (*1813, †1869), self-taught Russian composer: *Russalka*, an opera.
Edgar Degas (*1834, †1917); French impressionist best known for ballet scenes: *Self-Portrait*.
Holman Hunt: *The Scapegoat*, a painting.
Millais: *Autumn Leaves*, a painting.
Institution of the Victoria Cross for outstanding gallantry in action; to be won

Sir Henry Bessemer's (*1813, †1898) converter introduced into steel industry.
William H. Perkin discovered first synthetic dye, Perkin's mauve, later called Tyrian purple.
Pringsheim observed fertilization of female plant; 24 years later did similar work with animals.
Ruskin erected Oxford Museum of Science.
Cocaine, in impure form, extracted from coca leaves (see 1859).
Discovery of skull of primitive man, estimated as 100,000 years old, at Neanderthal.
Cheap fine cotton yarns made possible by

1856

History

Hatti-humayum of Treaty of Paris promised reforms in Turkey; not effected by 1867.

Literature

Hugo: *Les Contemplations,* French poems.
Keller: *Die Leute von Seldwyla,* five Swiss tales.
Kingsley: *The Heroes,* Greek mythology for children.
Ludwig: *Zwischen Himmel und Erde,* German novel.
Reade: *It's Never Too Late to Mend,* a novel.

1857

History

Palmerston defeated over Chinese policy; resigned; returned with larger majority.
Chinese fleet destroyed by British; British entered Canton.
Anglo-Persian peace treaty signed in Paris.
Indian, or Sepoy, Mutiny; Siege of Lucknow; Sir H. Lawrence killed; massacres at Cawnpore; Relief of Lucknow; capture of Delhi.
End of transportation.
Anti-Revolutionary National Society founded in Italy to secure unity under Sardinia and House of Savoy.
Copenhagen Act placed Danish local government in hands of well-to-do citizens.

Literature

Charles Baudelaire (*1821, †1867): *Les Fleurs du Mal,* French poems.
Borrow: *Romany Rye,* sequel to *Lavengro.*
C. Brontë: *The Professor,* a novel.
E. B. Browning; *Aurora Leigh,* narrative poem.
George Gee, of Denbigh, started *Y Faner,* national Welsh weekly.
Thos. Hughes (*1822, †1896): *Tom Brown's Schooldays,* novel of public school life.
Scheffel: *Ekkehard,* historical novel.
Herbert Spencer (*1820, †1903): *Essays.*
Thackeray: (to 1859) *The Virginians,* sequel to *Henry Esmond.*
Trollope: *Barchester Towers,* a novel.

1858

History

Defeat of Palmerston on Conspiracy to Murder Bill; resigned; Derby's second ministry.
Abolition of Property Qualification for M.P.s.
National Miners' Association founded.
Jews admitted to Parliament.
Anglo-Chinese Treaty of Tientsin.
Irish Republican Brotherhood (Fenians) founded in the U.S.A. by J. O'Mahony.
Suppression of Indian Mutiny; East India Co. finally abolished; government of India transferred to Crown.
Vancouver Island and British Columbia became Crown Colonies; Ottawa selected as Capital of Canada.
Orsini Plot; unsuccessful attempt to assassinate Napoleon III.
First recorded miracle at Lourdes.
Compact of Plombières: agreement between Napoleon III and Cavour;

Literature

Carlyle: *Frederick the Great,* history.
"George Eliot" (pseudonym of Mary Ann Evans) (*1819, †1880): *Scenes from Clerical Life,* three stories.
Eben Fardd (*1802, †1863), Welsh poet: *Brwydr Maes Bosworth.*
Frederick W. Farrar (*1831, †1903): *Eric, or Little by Little,* a moral tale.
Gautier: *Le Roman de la Momie,* French novel.
Oliver Wendell Holmes (*1809, †1894): *The Autocrat of the Breakfast-Table,* imaginary conversations in a boarding-house.
Longfellow: *Courtship of Miles Standish,* American narrative poem.
William Morris (*1834, †1896): *Defence of Guenevere,* poetry.
Trollope: *Dr Thorne,* novel in "Barsetshire" series.
Henrik Johan Ibsen (*1828, †1906), Norwegian poet and dramatist: *The Vikings in Helgoland,* a play.
Crockford's Clerical Directory first appeared.

by all ranks of the Army and Royal Navy.
Evan and John James: *Hen Wlad fy Nhadau*, Welsh National Anthem.
Rebuilding of Westminster (to 1862).

Heilmann's combing-machine.
Louis Pasteur (*1822, †1895), French chemist, began study leading to understanding of bacteriology.
Construction of railways in Russia commenced.

L. J. Duc built the Palais de Justice, Paris (to 1868).
Liszt: (i) Piano Concerto in E♭;
(ii) Hungarian organ fugue on the name of *BACH*; (iii) *Dante* Symphony first performed.
Millet: *The Gleaners*, French peasant scene.
Sir Charles Hallé (*1819, †1895), pianist and conductor, founded the Hallé Concerts at Manchester.
George Bizet (*1838, †1875): *Chloris et Clotilde*, French cantata, for which he gained Grand Prix de Rome.
Original foundation of Bombay University.

Robert Mushet discovered tungsten-carbon steel (see 1855).
John Scott Russell built first steel steamship.
Excavation of Mont Cenis tunnel, 8 miles long (to 1871).
Queen Victoria opened S. Kensington Museum (later The Science Museum).
Lissajous figures, formed by perpendicular harmonic motions, demonstrated.
Financial panic in Britain caused by over-speculation in U.S. railways; Bank Charter Act suspended.
Free Trade introduced into Sweden.
Livingstone: *Missionary Travels in South Africa*.

Brahms: Piano Concerto in D minor (No. 1).
Gounod: *Le Médécin malgré lui*, French opera.
Ingres completed painting *La Source* (see 1807).
Jacques Offenbach (*1819, †1880): *Orpheus in the Underworld*, gay German-French operetta; the most popular of his 90 operettas.
Battersea Park designed.
Royal Opera House, London, opened at Covent Garden; third on site.
Frith: *Derby Day*, a painting.
New York Symphony Orchestra gave its first public concert.
Foundation of Keble College, Oxford.
Big Ben (so named after Sir Benjamin Hall), great 13½-ton bell of the Houses of Parliament clock tower, cast at Whitechapel Bell Foundry.

Appearance of Donati's comet.
First Atlantic cable laid; largely successful because of work of Kelvin on stranded wire and insulation (see 1866).
Joseph Lister (*1827, †1912) studied coagulation of blood.
A. Nadar, of Paris, took first aerial photographs.
Plücker discovered cathode rays.
Launching of S.S. *Great Eastern*, largest ship of her day; propelled by paddles and screw.
Introduction of ironclads into French navy; two years later into R.N.
Use of steam stone-crusher in the U.S.A.
Pasteur explained that lactic acid fermentation is caused by bacteria.
Banking Companies' Act: extended limited liability to banking companies except in respect of banknotes.
Public Health Board dissolved; new Public Health Act.
First meeting of General Medical Council in London.
John H. Speke (*1827, †1864) and Sir Richard F. Burton (*1821, †1890) discovered

1858 French support for Sardinia in war with Austria.
Prince William of Prussia, brother of Frederick William IV, became Regent when King became insane.
Turks invaded Montenegro; defeated at Grahovo by Prince Danilo.

1859 Reform Bill introduced by Disraeli; defeated; Derby Government fell; Palmerston Prime Minister for second time.
Peaceful picketing during strike legalized.
London building strike.
Fenian movement active in Britain.
Outbreak of third Anglo-Chinese war.
Queensland became separate colony.
Oregon admitted as State in the U.S.A.
Napoleon III issued General Amnesty.
Treaty of Turin between France and Sardinia; confirmed terms of Plombières.
War between Austria and Sardinia; Austrians defeated at Magenta and Solferino; Milan captured from Austria; Armistice of Villafranca; confirmed in Treaty of Zürich; Cavour resigned because terms inadequate.
Sardinia received Lombardo-Venetia, ceded to France by Austria.
Monaco became independent of France (Protectorate since 1644).
War between Spain and Morocco.
Russia conquered Eastern Caucasus.
†Oscar I of Sweden; accession of Charles XV.

Dickens: *Tale of Two Cities*, novel of French revolution.
Edward FitzGerald (*1809, †1883) translated the *Rubáiyát* (see 1050).
Eliot: *Adam Bede*, a novel.
Hugo (to 1883): *La Legende des Siècles*, French epic poems.
Meredith: *Ordeal of Richard Feverel*, a novel.
Mill: *On Liberty*, a treatise.
Frédéric Mistral (*1830, †1914): *Mireille*, French poem.
Sand: *Elle et Lui*, a work on her affair with Musset.
Sophie, Comtesse de Ségur (*1799, †1874): *Les Vacances*, French children's novel.
Samuel Smiles (*1812, †1904): *Self-Help*; how to succeed in life.
Tennyson: *Idylls of the King*, poems on adventures of King Arthur.
Dostoievski: *Village of Stepanchikovo*, Russian humorous novel.

1860 Gladstone introduced Free Trade Budget; completed free-trade system in England.
Cobden Free Trade Treaty with France.
British captured Peking; end of Third Chinese War.
Napoleon III issued decree changing

William Wilkie Collins (*1824, †1889): *Woman in White*, mystery novel.
Dickens: (i) *Great Expectations*, a novel; (ii) *Uncommercial Traveller*, twenty miscellaneous papers.
Eliot: *Mill on the Floss*, a novel.
*Salvatore di Giacoma, Italian poet and novelist (†1834).

Lake Tanganyika.
Speke discovered Lake Victoria, source of River Nile.
Formation of Suez Canal Co.
Oil-well at Wietze, Hanover; first in Europe.

T. B. Bishop, Maine, U.S.A.: *John Brown's Body*, to commemorate the hanging of Brown after the raid at Harper's Ferry.
Wm. Butterfield built All Saints Church, Margaret St, London; Gothic style.
Wm. Dyce: *Pegwell Bay, Kent*, painting.
Emmett, "Negro minstrel": *Dixie*, American song.
Gounod: *Faust*, famous French opera, performed in Paris.
James A. McNeill Whistler (*1834, †1903), American Impressionist painter: *At the Piano*.
Millet: *The Angelus*, French painting.
Opening of Scottish National Gallery.
Vauxhall Pleasure Gardens closed.
Foundation of Corps of Commissionaires.
Adelina J. M. Patti (*1843, †1919), great soprano born in Spain, appeared as *Lucia* in New York.

Bunsen carried out spectrum analysis.
Darwin: *The Origin of Species*, great work on natural history; laid foundations of modern evolutionary theory.
Kirchhoff explained Fraunhöfer lines (see 1814) in spectrum analysis using flame spectrometer.
De Lesseps commenced work on Suez Canal, 92 miles long (see 1869).
Livingstone discovered Lake Nyasa.
Neimann isolated pure cocaine (see 1856).
Planté's lead accumulator; improved form (see 1855).
G. M. Pullman, of New York, invented Pullman luxury railway coaches.
Weston invented the differential pulley.
Coupled driving-wheels introduced on British locomotives.
Opening, at Cranleigh, of first cottage hospital.
Invention of steam-roller in France.
Foundation of Port Said, Egypt.
First American oil-wells drilled; at Titusville, Pennsylvania.
Russia reduced tariffs.

Félix Clément (*1822, †1885): *Histoire Général de la Musique religieuse*, French standard textbook.
Corot: (i) *The Studio*, (ii) *Pensive Girl*, French paintings.
Degas: *Spartan Boys and Girls exercising*, French painting.
Delacroix: *Horses going in the Sea*, French

Lenoir constructed gas-driven internal-combustion engine.
Picinotti, of Italy, invented early form of dynamo.
Frederick Walton produced cork linoleum.
First English tramway (horse-drawn) at Birkenhead (see 1832).
Berthelot: *Chimie organique fondée sur la*

1860 Autocratic Empire into Liberal Empire.
October Charter restored Austrian Imperial Government to state of pre–1848; failed because of Hungarian opposition.
Cavour returned to office in Sardinia; Nice and Savoy ceded to France; Tuscany, Emilia, Bologna, Parma, Modena and Piacenza united with Sardinia; first Italian National Parliament at Turin.
Garibaldi and "Thousand" invaded and captured Sicily and Naples; Naples, Sicily and Umbria united with Sardinia; Sardinians invaded Papal States.
Failure of Carlist Rising in Spain.
Charles XV of Sweden accepted petition for governmental reforms.
Assassination of Danilo, Prince of Montenegro.
Accession of Michael Obrenovich to throne of Serbia.
Turkish massacre of Christians at Damascus.
Knights Hospitallers lost lands of Great Priory of Messina.

Labiche: *Le Voyage de Monsieur Perrichon*, French comedy.
John Motley (*1814, †1877): *History of the United Netherlands*.
Friedrich Spielhagen (*1829, †1911): *Problematische Naturen*, German novel.
Algernon Charles Swinburne (*1837, †1909): *The Queen Mother*, a drama.
Thackeray: *The Four Georges*, on the Hanoverian kings.
First Welsh National Eisteddfod under aegis of the Gorsedd.
Charles Bradlaugh (*1833, †1891), atheist politician (see 1860 *et seq*.) began running the *National Reformer*.

1861 †Albert, Prince Consort; Victoria retired to Windsor.
The "Trent" case.
Lagos ceded by native ruler to Britain.
Boers in Transvaal set up separate state.
Abraham Lincoln (*1809, †1865), President of the U.S.A.; Kansas admitted State of U.S.A.; outbreak of American Civil War; main battles: Bull Run and Lexington.
France, Britain and Spain sent troops into Mexico to enforce payment of financial debts; Britain and Spain later withdrew; France purchased Mentone and Roquebrune from Monaco.
Benito Juarez, Mexican patriot, occupied Mexico City; President 1861–62.
Sardinians captured Gatea; Italy, except Rome and Venice, united

Mrs Beeton (*1836, †1865): *Book of Household Management*.
Eliot: *Silas Marner*, a novel of a lone weaver.
Fontane: *Balladen*, poetry.
Friedrich Max Müller (*1823, †1900): *Science of Languages*, German study by comparative philologist.
Francis T. Palgrave (*1824, †1897): *Golden Treasury*, celebrated anthology.
Reade: *The Cloister and the Hearth*, novel introducing Luther and Erasmus.
Sand: *Le Marquis de Villemer*, a novel.
Turgenev: *Fathers and Sons*, Russian novel, in which Nihilism first appeared.
Italian National Library formed.
Dostoievski: *The House of the Dead*, Russian, book recalling his time in prison.

painting.
Daumier: *The Uprising*, French painting.
Gounod: *Philémon et Baucis*, French opera.
Holman Hunt: *The Finding of Christ in the Temple*, a painting.
Collection of Liszt's 55 songs.
Sir George Gilbert Scott (*1811, †1878), built Foreign Office, London.
Antoine Vallon (*1833, †1900): *Le Moulin de la Galette*, French painting.
Courbet: *La Toilette de la Mariée*, French painting (unfinished).
c. Manet: *Concert at the Tuileries Gardens*,French painting.
Bedford College, London, founded (for women).
Construction of Parliament buildings at Ottowa.

Corot: *Le Lac de Terni*, French painting.
Charles Garnier (*1825, †1898), French architect, won competition for designing new Opera House in Paris; very ornate, it was opened in 1875 and cost 50 million francs (a substantial sum at the time).
Hallé commenced playing Beethoven sonatas from memory, against strong opposition; beginnings of memorized concert performances.
Henri Lambrouste built the great Bibliothèque Nationale, Paris (to 1869).
c. Degas: *The Bellelli Family*, French painting.
c. Millet: *The Wash Tub*, French painting.
Queen Victoria instituted Order of the Star of India.
Newcastle Commission Report on state of Popular Education in England.
Erection of Sandringham House (to 1870), country house of the Queen.

synthèse, French work on synthesis of organic chemicals.
c. C. L. Sholes (*1819, †1890), of the U.S.A., invented a form of typewriter.
c. Whitworth's standard measurements for screws adopted throughout Britain.
Foundation of Bank of Russia.
Construction of the *Warrior*, first British ironclad.
J. M. Sturt, explorer, reached centre of Australia.
Mines Regulation Act introduced checkweighers and better safety precautions.
Copper coins replaced by bronze in England.
National Rifle Association inaugurated at Bisley by Queen Victoria.
Training courses for nurses at St Thomas's Hospital, London.
London Trades Council established.
Johan Philip Reis (*1834, †1874), German, invented magnetic telephone, superior to Bell's of 1876.
Bunsen and Kirchhoff discovered caesium, an alkali metal.
First oil refinery built; at Titusville, Pennsylvania (see 1859).

Bunsen and Kirchhoff discovered rubidium, using electroscope.
Work of Sir William Crookes (*1832, †1919) led to discovery of thallium.
Soda-making process by Solvay, in Belgium.
Thomas Graham (*1805, †1869) recognized colloidal state of liquids.
Spörer's sun-spots law; maximum every 13 years approx.
G. F. Train introduced first horse-drawn trams in London.
Daily weather forecasts in Britain.
Discovery of archaeopteryx, fossil bird.
Use of magazine rifles; in American Civil War.
Krupp's steelworks produced its first gun.
Establishment of Post Office Savings Bank.
Gladstone abolished duty on paper.
Lace Works Act.
Telegraph line across the U.S.A. completed.
Danube Navigation Statute.

1861 under Victor Emmanuel of Savoy.
Regent of Prussia became King William I of Prussia.
Union of Moldavia and Wallachia to form Roumania; Alexander I, Prince of Roumania; Herzegovina revolted against Turks; defeated; Serbs joined revolt.
Serfdom abolished in Russia by Alexander II.

1862 Foundation of Ironworkers' Association.
Industrial Provident Societies Act; encouraged federal co-operative developments.
American Civil War battles: Mill Springs and Williamsburg.
French war in Mexico (continued to 1867).
Reform Union in Germany; advocated Pan-German State with Austria as President.
Otto von Bismarck appointed Prime Minister of Prussia.
Local self-government given to Communes in Sweden.
Garibaldi invaded Papal States; defeated and captured by Italians at Aspromonte; later released.
Russia adopted liberal policies towards Poland.
Military rising in Greece; deposition of Otto I.
Montenegrin revolt against Turks; crushed; Turkish suzerainty recognized.
Obrenovich secured withdrawal of Turks from all but four Serbian towns including Belgrade.

Borrow: *Wild Wales,* Englishman learns Welsh and discovers Wales.
E. B. Browning: *Last Poems.*
Eliot: *Romola,* novel of medieval Florence.
Flaubert: *Salammbô,* French novel of Carthage.
Hebbel: *Die Nibelungen,* a tragedy.
Hugo: *Les Misérables,* epic novel on a convict.
Leconte de Lisle: *Poèmes barbares,* poems.
Christina Rossetti (*1830, †1894): *Goblin Market,* poetry.
Ruskin: *Unto this Last,* advanced essays on employment and wages.
Spencer: *First Principles,* by philosopher and social scientist.
Mrs Henry Wood (*1814, †1887): *The Channings,* a novel.
Ibsen: *Love's Comedy,* Norwegian satire.
Dostoievski: *The Insulted and the Injured,* Russian novel.

1863 Marriage of Edward, Prince of Wales, to Alexandra of Denmark.
Britain returned Ionian Islands to Greece.
Abolition of slavery proclaimed in the U.S.A.
Lincoln: *Gettysburg Address,* famous speech at dedication of Gettysburg cemetery.
American Civil War Battles:

*D'Annunzio (†1938), Italian poet, novelist and dramatist.
Joseph Sheridan le Fanu (*1814, †1873): *The House by the Churchyard,* weird story.
Eugène Fromentin (*1820, †1876): *Dominique,* French novel.
Gautier: *Le Capitaine Fracasse,* French novel and historical fantasy.
Kingsley: *The Water Babies,* humorous fairy tale of little chimney sweep.

U.S.A. introduced passport system.
Establishment of Amalgamated Society of Carpenters and Joiners.
Start of Lancashire cotton famine.
Pneumatic power used in construction of Mont Cenis tunnel.

Berlioz: *Beatrice et Bénédict*, French opera.
Degas: *Gentlemen's Race, before the Start*, French painting.
Franck: Six pieces for the Organ.
Frith: *The Railway Station*, a painting.
*Edward German (†1936), well known for light opera *Merrie England*.
Gounod: *La Reine de Saba*, French opera.
Hughes and Richards: *God bless the Prince of Wales*, patriotic song.
Liszt: *The Legend of St Elizabeth*, Hungarian oratorio.
Millet: *Man with a Hoe*, French painting.
Verdi: *La Forza del Destino*, Italian opera.
Julia Ward Howe (*1819, †1910): *Battle Hymn of the Republic*, sung by Union forces in American Civil War.
Foundation of Clifton College, public school, at Bristol.
Revised Code of Education set up payment by results.

Confederate battleship *Alabama* left builders' yard on Mersey.
Brown, U.S.A., invented universal milling-machine.
Clark identified Sirius B in the heavens, as forecast by Bessel.
Foucault measured speed of light in laboratory, using a mirror.
Richard Gatling (*1818, †1903), of the U.S.A., patented his machine-gun.
Gould: *Birds of Great Britain*, fine ornithological work.
Glaisher and Coxwell ascended 7 miles in balloon.
Nasmyth's slot-drilling machine.
Wöhler produced acetylene from calcium carbide.
Act requiring *two* shafts to be sunk for safety in new coal mines.
Companies Act: flotation simplified; limited liability applied to small concerns.
Highways Act: authorized compulsory combination of parishes to maintain highways.
Lincoln issued first legal U.S. paper money ("Greenbacks").
Speke became first European to visit Uganda.
First all-steel hulled ship (not the *Alabama*) left the builders' yard on the Mersey.

Bizet: *Les Pêcheurs de perles*, French opera, his first major work.
Eugène Boudin (*1824, †1898): *Beach at Trouville*, French painting.
Degas: *Portrait of Duchess Morbilli*, French painting.
Liszt: (i) Symphony in A, (ii) *Psalm XIII*, Hungarian oratorio.
Edouard Manet (*1832, †1883: (i) *Déjeuner sur l'Herbe*, French painting, first rejected

Sir Francis Galton (*1822, †1911): *Meteorographica*, first work to establish theory of anticyclones.
James Clerk Maxwell (*1831, †1879), physicist, propounded mathematically existence of electro-magnetic waves.
Angelo Secchi (*1818, †1878), Italian astronomer, classified stars into types, using method of stellar spectroscopy.
In Central London was begun the first

1863 Nashville, Winchester, Gettysburg, etc.
West Virginia admitted to statehood in the U.S.A.
French troops entered Mexico City: Archduke Maximilian proclaimed Emperor of Mexico.
†Frederick VII of Denmark; raised succession question in duchies of Schleswig and Holstein; William of Denmark elected King of Greece.
Polish rising against Russia; Russo-Prussian convention closed Prussian frontier to refugee Poles.
British bombardment of Kagoshima; reprisal for Japanese murder of Englishman.

Hippolyte Taine (*1828, †1893): *Histoire de la Litérature Anglaise*, by a French scholar.
George Whyte-Melville (*1821, †1878): *The Gladiators*, a novel.

1864 First Trade Union Conference.
International Working Mens' Association met; "First International".
Britain declared neutrality over Schleswig-Holstein question.
Nevada admitted State of the U.S.A.
American Civil War battles; Petersburg, Cedar Creek, Farmville, etc.
Franco-Italian Convention: France to withdraw from Rome 1866; Italy to recognize Temporal authority of Papacy.
Encyclical *Quantum Cura* asserted independence of Church.
War between Denmark and Austro-Prussian alliance, over duchies; Allies occupied Schleswig and Holstein; Treaty of Vienna in favour of Austria and Prussia.
New democratic Constitution in Greece; Greeks occupied Corfu.
Local government reforms in Russia; Polish rising crushed; Nihilism militant in Russia; conquest of West Caucasus.

R. Browning: *Dramatis Personae*, collection of poems.
Dickens: *Our Mutual Friend*, a novel.
Le Fanu: *Uncle Silas*, mystery novel.
John Henry Newman (*1801, †1890): *Apologia pro Vita sua*, on conversion to Roman Catholicism.
Tennyson: *Enoch Arden*, narrative poem.
Vigny: *Les Destinées*, French poetry.
Edmond (*1811, †1896) and Jules (*1830, †1870) de Goncourt: *Renée Mauperin*, French novel of a modern young woman.
de Ségur: *Les Malheurs de Sophie*, French novel for children.
Wilhelm Raabe (*1831, †1910): *Der Hungerpastor*, German novel.
Edmond Erckmann (*1822, †1899) and Alexandre Chatrian (*1826, †1890): *L'Histoire d'un Conscrit de 1813*, French historical novel.
Ibsen: *The Pretenders*, Norwegian play.

1865 †Palmerston; Russell, Prime Minister.
Negro insurrection in Jamaica.
Surrender of Confederate General Lee at Appomattox Court House ended American Civil War; assassination of Abraham Lincoln,

"Lewis Carroll" (Charles Dodgson) (*1832, †1898): *Alice in Wonderland*, children's book.
Meredith: *Rhoda Fleming*, a novel.
Newman: *Dream of Gerontius*, a poem later set to music by Elgar.
"Ouida" (Louise de la Ramée) (*1838,

as indecent; (ii) *Olympia*.
Claude Monet (*1840, †1926): *Salon des Refusés*, Frenching painting.
Scott erected Albert Memorial, London (to 1872).
Johann Barthold Jongkind (*1819, †1891): *Beach at Sainte-Adresse*, water-colour.
Secondary and Technical Education in Holland promoted by law.

Anton Bruckner (*1824, †1896), Austrian composer: Symphony in D minor (*Die Nullte*); revised 1869.
Gounod: *Mireille*, French opera.
Hunt: *The Shadow of Death*, a painting.
Manet; *Races at Longchamp*, French painting.
Monet: *The Breakwater at Honfleur*, French impressionist painting.
Offenbach: *La Belle Hélène*, German-French operetta.
Foundation of Royal Society of Organists.
Peter Ellis built Oriel Chambers, Liverpool, largely of iron (to 1865).
Whistler: *The Green Screen: Caprice in Purple and Gold*, American painting.
Educational reforms in Russia.
National Scandinavian Society founded in Sweden.
Auguste Rodin (*1840, †1917), French sculptor: *L'homme au nez cassé*.
Public Schools Act listed nine great schools.

Queensberry Rules, governing boxing, drawn up.
Paul Cézanne (*1839, †1906), essentially self-taught artist whose overbearing manner hid intense timidity: *Uncle Dominique as a Monk*, French painting.

Underground Railway construction in the world (see 1890).
Wilbrand manufactured trinitrotoluene (T.N.T.)
c. H. Mège-Mouris, French chemist, produced margarine.
Abolition of Dutch tolls on the Scheldt.
Estblishment of Co-operative Wholesale Society.
Reich and Richter discovered indium, rare metal.
Nadar constructed *Le Géant*, largest gas-filled balloon of its day.
Opening at Broadmoor, Berks, of State Institution for the criminally insane.

Sir Samuel White Baker discovered Lake Albert.
William Cotton's power-driven hosiery machine.
Henri Dunant (*1828, †1910), Swiss philanthropist, founded International Red Cross.
Svend Foyn invented harpoon gun.
Sir William Huggins (*1824, †1910) proved irresoluble nebulae to be gaseous; confirmed Herschel's theory.
Peaucellier's cell for mathematical inversion.
Siegfried Markus, Austrian, fitted engine to a hand-cart.
Siemens-Martin open-hearth furnace.
Metric system approved in Britain but restricted to use in scientific work.
Chimney Sweeps Act: forbade employment of children; ineffective.
Liquidation of Turnpike Trusts began.
Collapse of Dale Dyke reservoir, Sheffield; heavy loss of life.
Twelve-hour working day in Sweden.
American import duty 47% (to 1897).

Gregory J. Mendel (*1822, †1884), Austrian, enunciated his law of heredity, based on work of cross-fertilization of peas.
Maxwell's mathematical equations of electro-magnetic induction.
Refining of copper by electrolytic process.
First 4–4–0 locomotive (G.N.S.R.).

1865 President of the U.S.A.
First recorded American train robbery, in Iowa.
Biarritz Meeting: Napoleon III and Bismarck; former to be neutral in event of Austro-Prussian war.
Convention of Gastein; Austria and Prussia agreed to hold Holstein and Schleswig respectively.
Austrian Imperial Constitution cancelled.
Swedish Diet reformed.
Florence succeeded Turin as capital of Italy.
Turkestan conquered by Russia.
Alliance of Argentine, Brazil and Uruguay against Paraguay.

†1908): *Strathmore*, a novel.
Ruskin: *Sesame and Lilies*.
Swinburne: *Atalanta in Calydon*, dramatic poem.
John G. Whittier (*1807, †1892), U.S.A.: poems.
Erckmann-Chatrian: *Waterloo*, French novel.
Goncourt frères: *Germinie Lacerteux*, a novel.
Hugo: *Chansons des Rues et des Bois*, poems.
Wilhelm Busch (*1832, †1908), German: *Max und Moritz*, amusingly illustrated.
Leo Nikolaievich Tolstoy (*1828, †1910): *War and Peace*, great Russian novel.
Censorship of Press in Russia relaxed.

1866 Gladstone's Reform Bill defeated; Government resigned; Derby, Prime Minister; Reform riots in Hyde Park.
Sheffield outrages against non-trade unionists.
Fenian conspiracy in Ireland.
Civil Rights Bill (Negroes) passed by U.S. Chamber and Senate.
Austro-Prussian relations over Schleswig-Holstein led to war; Austria defeated in Seven Weeks War at Sadowa (Königgratz); Treaty of Prague.
Prusso-Italian defensive alliance: Italy declared war on Austria; defeated at Custozza; received Venice but not Tyrol at Treaty of Prague (Italia irredentia).
Two military risings suppressed in Madrid.
Alexander I of Roumania deposed; Charles of Hohenzollern-Sigmaringen elected; new Constitution.
Crete, supported by Greece, gained measure of self-government from Turkey.

Eliot: *Felix Holt*, a novel.
Kingsley: *Hereward the Wake*, historical novel.
Ruskin: *Crown of Wild Olive*, lectures.
Swinburne: *Poems and Ballads*.
Charlotte Mary Yonge (*1823, †1901): *The Dove in the Eagle's Nest*, historical romance.
François Coppée (*1842, †1908): *Le Reliquaire*, collection of French poems.
Emile Gaboriau (*1832, †1873): *L'Affaire Lerouge*, French detective novel.
Sully Prudhomme (*1839, †1907): *Poèmes*, French philosophical verse.
Catulle Mendès (*1841, †1909): *Le Parnasse contemporain*, anthology of poems of the Parnassian school.
Paul Verlaine (*1844, †1896): *Poèmes saturniens*, French poems.
Robert Hamerling (*1830, †1871): *Ahasver in Rom*, German novel of the Wandering Jew.
Dostoievski: *Crime and Punishment*, Russian novel.

Franck: *La Tour de Babel*, French oratorio.
Degas: *Woman with Chrysanthemums*, French painting.
Giuseppe Mengoni constructed Galleria Vittorio Emanuele, Milan, having great iron and glass roof.
Monet: *Le Déjeuner sur l'Herbe*, French painting (not to be confused with that of 1863 by Manet).
Wagner: *Tristan and Isolde*, German opera, first performed; Hans von Bülow (*1830, †1894) conducted it without musical score.
Whistler: (i) *Old Battersea Bridge*, (ii) *Courbet at Trouville*, paintings.
Nicholas A. Rimsky-Korsakov (*1844, †1908), Russian composer, one of the "Five". Symphony in E♭ minor (later, in E minor; revised 1884).
Pierre Auguste Renoir (*1841, †1919): *Le Cabaret de la Mère Anthony*, French painting.
University of Odessa founded.
Overarm bowling first allowed in cricket.

Establishment of Metropolitan Fire Service.
First British concrete roads.
Pierre Lallement, of Paris, designed "boneshaker" bicycle with rotary pedals.
Construction of Amsterdam-North Sea Canal begun.
Union Chargeability Act: modified Poor Law System.
Pasteur cured silk-worm disease (*pébrine*) and saved the French silk industry.
Massachusetts Institute of Technology founded.

Courbet: *Deer at the Brook*, French painting.
Degas: *Steeplechase*, French painting.
Manet: *The Fifer*, French painting.
Monet: (i) *Le Jardin de l'Infante*, (ii) *Camille*, (iii) *Terrace near Le Havre*, French paintings.
Offenbach: *La Vie Parisienne*, German-French operetta.
Renoir and Sisley painted at Marlotte.
Bedřich Smetana (*1824, †1884): *The Brandenburgers in Bohemia*, Czechoslovakian opera.
Suppé: *Light Cavalry*, Austrian operetta.
Liszt: (i) *Deux Légendes*, Hungarian piano music; (ii) *Christus*, an oratorio.
c. Berlioz: *Les Troyens*, French opera.
c. Cézanne: (i) *The Orgy*, (ii) *The Man in a Blue Cap*, French paintings.
Organs permitted to be used in Established Church of Scotland.
Erection of Palais de Justice, Brussels, enormous square building with huge collonaded tower (to 1883).
Restoration (to 1880) of St David's Cathedral, Bangor, Wales.

Weldon process for preparation of cholorine.
Winchester developed his repeating rifle.
Atlantic cable in use (see 1858).
U.S.A. approved metric system but proceeded as did Britain in 1864.
Royal Aeronautical Society founded as Aeronautical Society of Great Britain.
Robert Whitehead developed propelled submarine torpedo from earlier experiments of Fulton and Bashnell.
Financial crisis due to over-speculation in new joint-stock companies.
Mary Baker Eddy (*1821, †1910), after studying mental reactions, made remarkable recovery from an injury after reading Gospels; led to her propounding the concept of Christian Science.
Pasteur: *Études sur le vin*, regarding diseases of the wines, are said to have saved France millions of pounds.

	History	Literature
1866	Attempt to assassinate Tsar Alexander II by Karakosof failed; Tsar returned to reactionary policies.	
1867	*Hornby v. Close* Case; trade unions declared illegal associations. Second Parliamentary Act; vote given to artisans in towns. Royal Commission on Trade Unions. Fenian rising in Ireland; outrages in Clerkenwell Prison. Confederation of Dominion of Canada begun; Quebec and Nova Scotia joined. U.S.A. bought Alaska from Russia: "Alaska Purchase". Conference of London; Luxembourg recognized as independent and neutral. North German Confederation formed: Federal State of 27 members. Imperial Constitution problem in Austria solved by *Ausgleich*; Dual Monarchy, under Francis Joseph. Italian Government confiscated Church property worth £80 millions; Garibaldi invaded Papal States, defeated by French at Mentana; French action alienated Italians. Mexican rebels under Juarez executed Emperor Maximilian. Turks withdrew from Belgrade. Pasha Ismail made Hereditary Khedive of Egypt. †Emperor Komei of Japan; accession of Meiji; resignation of Shogun Keiki; restoration of Imperial control of affairs.	Arnold: *New Poems*. Walter Bagehot (*1826, †1877): *The English Constitution*. Edward Augustus Freeman (*1823, †1892): *History of the Norman Conquest of England*. "Mark Twain" (pseudonym of Samuel Clemens) (*1835, †1910): *The Celebrated Jumping Frog*, first story to bring fame to the American humorist. Meredith: *Vittoria*, a novel. Morris: *Life and Death of Jason*, a poem. "Ouida": *Under Two Flags*, a novel. Swinburne: *Song of Italy*, poetry. Emile Zola (*1840, †1902): *Thérèse Raquin*, naturalistic French novel. Karl Marx (*1818, †1883): *Das Kapital*, German foundation of international socialism. Ibsen: *Peer Gynt*, Norwegian poetic drama. Dostoievski: *The Gambler*, Russian story.
1868	First regular Trades Union Congress held at Manchester. Disraeli's first Ministry February-December; Gladstone's first ministry (to 1874). Gangs Act forbade employment in farming of children under eight; no women and children to be employed in gangs with men. Labrador incorporated into Canada.	Louisa May Alcott (*1832, †1888): *Little Women*, American story; of Jo March and her three sisters. R. Browning: *The Ring and the Book*, a poem; crime from many points of view. Collins: *The Moonstone*, early detective novel. Morris: *Earthly Paradise*, collection of narrative poems. Queen Victoria (*1819, †1901): *Leaves from a*

Bizet: *La Jolie Fille de Perth*, French opera.
Corot: *At Rheims*, French landscape painting.
Francis Fowke built (to 1871) the Albert Hall, London; great concert hall.
Gounod: *Roméo et Juliette*, French opera.
Sir Edwin H. Landseer (*1802, †1873): animal painter, modelled the Lions in Trafalgar Square.
Liszt: *Hungarian Coronation Mass*.
Manet: *View of the Paris World's Fair*, French painting.
Monet: (i) *The Beach at Sainte-Adresse*, (ii) *Women in the Garden*, French paintings.
Renoir: (i) *Lise with a Sunshade*, (ii) *The Boat*, French paintings.
Sterndale Bennett (*1816, †1875): *The Woman of Samaria*, an oratorio.
Johann Strauss (*1825, †1899): *The Blue Danube*, Viennese waltz.
Sir Arthur Sullivan (*1842, †1900), who had great gift of musical parody, set Morton and Burnand's *Cox and Box* to music.
Verdi: *Don Carlos*, Italian opera.
Wagner: *Die Meistersinger von Nürnberg*, his most light-hearted opera.
Albert Institute, Dundee, erected.
Ice hockey first played; in Canada.

Lister used carbolic antiseptic; great milestone in medicine; the basis of aseptic surgery, his work has saved countless lives.
Alfred B. Nobel (*1833, †1896), Swedish engineer and founder of Nobel prizes, produced dynamite.
Pokorny dated trees by their ring-markings.
Sir William Siemens (*1823, †1883) produced his dynamo.
Livingstone explored the Congo (until 1873).
Discovery of South African diamond fields.
Royal Commission on Employment of Children in Farming.
First *modern* type bicycle.
H. C. Parker, U.S.A., designed motor torpedo.
Factory Act: factory hours extended to cover workshops.
Transportation of convicts to Western Australia ceased.
Heinrich Gerber built, over the Main at Hassfurt, Germany, the first modern cantilever bridge.

Camille Pissarro (*1830, †1903), French impressionist: *Street in Pontoise*, a painting.
Frédéric Bazille (*1841, †1870): *Family Gathering*, French painting; his best known work.
Manet: (i) *The Balcony*, (ii) *Portrait of Émile Zola*, French paintings.
Monet: *Argenteuil-sur-Seine*, French painting.
Modest Mussorgsky (*1839, †1881), one of

Deacon process of producing chlorine: atmospheric oxygen plus copper chloride catalyst.
Sir Norman Lockyer (*1836, †1920) discovered helium in sun's spectrum; not discovered on Earth until later (see 1895).
Leclanché's secondary electric cell.
Scottish Co-operative Wholesale Society founded.

1868 Foundation of Ku Klux Klan by Southern States after American Civil War.
Military pact between Hamburg and Prussia; Lübeck joined German Customs Union.
Military rising in Spain; abdication and flight of Isabella II.
Assassination of Michael of Serbia; election of fourteen-year-old Milan Obrenovich.
Khanate of Bokhara surrendered to Russia after capture of Samarkand.
Japanese court moved to Yedo, now renamed Tokyo and proclaimed as capital.

Journal of our Life in the Highlands.
Alphonse Daudet (*1840, †1897): *Le Petit Chose,* French semi-autobiographical novel.
Dostoievski: *The Idiot,* Russian novel with epileptic hero.
*Maxim Gorky (†1936), Russian novelist.

1869 Trade Union (Protection of Funds) Act did not give legal recognition to the unions.
Wage regulation in iron industry; wages tied to selling price.
Abolition of imprisonment for debt.
Establishment of Labour Representation League.
Irish Church Disestablishment Act.
Hudson Bay Territory joined Dominion of Canada.
Napoleon III changed Constitution; proclaimed Parliamentary Empire.
Spanish Cortes elected by universal suffrage; Carlist rising quelled.
Vatican Council summoned at Rome by Pius IX.
Nihilist Congress held at Basle.

Arnold: (i) *Collected Poems,* (ii) *Culture and Anarchy,* essays.
Richard Doddridge Blackmore (*1825, †1900): *Lorna Doone,* historical novel.
Sir William Schwenk Gilbert (*1836, †1911): *Bab Ballads,* humorous poems.
William Edward Lecky (*1838, †1903): *History of European Morals.*
Mill: *Subjection of Women.*
Mark Twain: *Innocents Abroad,* gullible American travellers in Europe.
Tennyson: *Holy Grail and Other Poems.*
Daudet: *Letters de mon Moulin,* tales of life in Provence.
Flaubert: *L'Education sentimentale,* a novel.
Verlaine: *Fêtes Galantes,* poems.
Ibsen: *The League of Youth,* Norwegian political satire.
Foundation of Metaphysical Society.

1870 Irish Land Act.
British Honduras became Crown Colony.
Red River insurrection suppressed;

Dickens: *Mystery of Edwin Drood,* unfinished novel.
Francis Brett Harte ("Bret Harte") (*1836, †1902): *The Luck of Roaring Camp,* short

the "Five": *Boris Godounov*, Russian opera; first produced 1874.
Rimsky-Korsakov: Symphony No. 2 ("Antar", revised 1875 and 1897).
c. Cézanne: (i) *The Negro Scipio*, (ii) *Portrait of the Artist's Father*, French paintings.
c. Corot: *The Bridge at Mantes*, French painting.
Renoir: *Sisley and his Wife*, French painting.
c. Development of Impressionist style (see 1874).

Robert Mushet's tungsten-vanadium steel for drills.
Wiliam Griggs' process of photochromolithography.
Pasteur: *Études sur le vinaígre*, a sequel to earlier work on wines (see 1866).

Alexander Borodin (*1833, †1887), one of the "Five": First symphony (in E♭ major, composed 1862–67) performed.
Brahms: *Ein Deutsches Requiem*, German cantata of remembrance, completed.
Michele Cammarano: *Piazza San Marco*, Neapolitan painting.
Cézanne: (i) *The Railway Cutting*, (ii) *The Black Clock*, French paintings.
Courbet: *Calm Sea*, French impressionist painting.
Manet: *Portrait of Berthe Morisot*, French painting.
Monet: *The Pheasant*, French painting.
Renoir: (i) *In Summer*, (ii) *La Grenouillère*, French paintings.
Alfred Sisley (*1839, †1899), French artist of English descent: *View of Montmartre*, French painting.
Foundation of Girton College (for women) at Hitchin; transferred to Cambridge, 1873.
Establishment of the Headmaster's Conference.
Foundation of National Education League and National Education Union.
Endowed Schools Act; reform of Grammar Schools.
c. Degas: *Head of a Young Woman*, French painting.

Thomas Andrews (*1813, †1885) discovered critical temperature for liquefaction of carbon dioxide.
Galton: *Hereditary Genius*; laid foundations of eugenics.
Dmitri Ivanovich Mendeleyev (*1834, †1907), Russian scientist, arranged chemical elements in order: periodic law.
Gabriel de Mortellet drew up tables of prehistoric culture.
Reverdin introduced free skin graft.
Ammonia-soda process introduced into Britain from Belgium; superseded le Blanc process of alkalis.
Suez Canal opened by Empress Eugénie of France (see 1859).
Union Pacific, first American transcontinental railway, completed.
Royal Commission on Sanitation.
Repeal of tax on hairpowder (introduced 1795).
First publication of *Whitaker's Almanack*.
Construction of Blackfriars Bridge, London.
John W. Hyatt, U.S.A., organized Albany Dental Plate Co. to market cellulose nitrate plastic.
Launching of the *Cutty Sark*, famous sailing-ship.
Vanadium (discovered by Del Rio in 1801) isolated by Roscoe.

Cézanne: *Melting Snow at L'Estaque*, French painting.
Corot: (i) *Mother and Child on the Beach*, (ii) *The High Wind*, French paintings.

Demolition of fortifications of Luxembourg.
Ferro-concrete building developed, using Monier's discovery (see 1849).
T. H. Huxley (*1825, †1895): theory of

1870 Manitoba joined Dominion of Canada.
Outbreak of Franco-Prussian War; French defeated at Sedan; siege of Paris; end of Second Empire; third Republic proclaimed.
Spanish throne offered to Leopold of Hohenzollern; led to Franco-Prussian war, although throne was refused; offered to Duke of Aosta, who accepted.
French troops withdrawn from Rome; Sardinians entered Rome; Romans elected to join Kingdom of Italy.
Vatican Council promulgated doctrine of Papal Infallibility; emergence of group of "Old Catholics" opposed to this dogma.
Brigandage suppressed in Greece.
Revolts in Roumania; mass of people loyal to dynasty and Charles.
Form of local self-government introduced into St Petersburg, Moscow and Odessa.
Russia repudiated Black Sea clauses of Treaty of Paris 1856.

American story.
D. G. Rossetti, *Poems*.
Spencer: *Principles of Psychology*.
William Stubbs (*1825, †1901): *Select Charters*, from earliest times to Edward I.
Edward Whymper (*1840, †1911): *Scrambles amongst the Alps*, by the pioneer alpinist who conquered the Matterhorn.
Ludwig Anzengruber (*1839, †1889): *Der Pfarrer von Kirchfeld*, Austrian play of peasant life.
Dostoievski: *The Eternal Husband*, Russian story.

1871 Trade Union Act; unions given full legal recognition.
Local Government Act; Local Government Board set up.
Dutch possessions in Guinea ceded to Britain.
Vancouver and British Columbia joined Dominion of Canada.
Ku Klux Klan officially dissolved in the U.S.A.; not effective.
Fall of Paris after siege of 4 months; Treaty of Frankfurt ended war.
The Commune in Paris; supressed by Thiers.
Wiliam I of Prussia proclaimed Emperor of Germany at Versailles.
First *Reichstag* met in Berlin; Bismarck Imperial German Chancellor (to 1890).
Accession of Amadeus of Savoy to throne of Spain; ruled to 1873.
Rome became capital of united Italy; Pope refused terms of Law of

Eliot: *Middlemarch*, a novel.
Benjamin Jowett (*1817, †1893): translated *Dialogues of Plato*.
Lear: *Nonsense Songs and Stories*.
Meredith: *Harry Richmond*, a novel.
Swinburne: *Songs before Sunrise*, poetry.
Hugo: *L'Année terrible*, poems.
Zola: *Les Rougon-Macquart*, a series of novels; the history of a family in the Second Empire.
German language only to be used in schools of Alsace-Lorraine.
Old Catholic professors and teachers dismissed and excommunicated by Vatican decrees; German government refused sanction; start of *Kulturkampf*.
Attack on liberal intelligentsia in Russia; admission to universities restricted.

Degas: *Portrait of Madame Camus*, French painting.
Clément P. L. Delibes (*1836, †1891), mainly an opera composer: *Coppélia*, classic French ballet music.
Millais: *Boyhood of Raleigh*, the painting which made his name.
Monet: (i) *Mme Monet in a Red Cape*, (ii) *Hotel des Roches Noires*, French paintings.
Théodore Fantin-Latour: *The Studio at Les Batignolles*, French painting.
Pissarro: (i) *The Road*, (ii) *Snow at Lower Norwood* (during a visit to England), French paintings.
Sisley: *Snow at Louveciennes*, French painting.
Smetana: *The Bartered Bride*, Czech opera, produced.
Oscar Straus (*1870, †1954): *The Chocolate Soldier*.
Foundation, in France, of Société Nationale de Musique.
First Elementary Education Act (Forster's) set up School Boards.

biogenesis; i.e. living matter solely created by earlier living matter; coined the word *agnostic*.
T. G. Thomas, of New York, performed caesarian operation; named after Julius Caesar, who was, according to tradition, removed from the womb of his dead mother.
Moving-coil galvanometer invented.
Diamond-mining in South Africa.
G.P.O. took control of telegraph services in Britain.
Introduction of ½*d*. postage and stamped postcards in Britain.
Weather service introduced in the U.S.A.
Bunsen invented ice-calorimeter.
Civil Service opened to competitive examination.

Rugby Union founded to regulate the game.
Courbet: *Still Life with Apples*, French painting.
Monet: *Houses of Parliament seen from Westminster Bridge*, French painting of London scene.
Pissarro: (i) *Penge Station, Upper Norwood*, (ii) *Dulwich College*, French paintings of England.
Charles C. Saint-Saëns (*1835, †1921): *Omphale's Spinning Wheel*, first French symphonic poem.
Verdi: *Aïda*, Italian opera, performed at the opening of the Opera House, Cairo.
Whistler: *Arrangement in Grey and Black*, American portrait of artist's mother.
Foundation of Newnham College, Cambridge (for women).
c. Cézanne: *The Man with the Straw Hat*, French portrait.
c. Degas: *A Carriage at the Races*, French painting.

Darwin: *Descent of Man*, his second great work on evolution.
Samuel Ingersoll, U.S.A., invented pneumatic rock-drill.
Clerk Maxwell stated light is of electromagnetic form.
Sand-blasting used in glassworks.
Railway Act: Board of Trade empowered to enquire into accidents.
Stanley met Livingstone in East Africa: "Dr Livingstone, I presume."
Maddox: dry photographic plate (silver bromide).
Completion of Mount Cenis Tunnel, Switzerland (begun 1860).
Griqualand West, including Kimberley diamond field, ceded to Britain.
Purchase of commissions in British armed forces abolished.
Great Fire at Chicago.

1871 Guarantees; became "Prisoner in the Vatican"; temporal power abolished.
Introduction of annual *Storthings* in Norway.

1872 Ballot Act: Vote by secret ballot in Britain.
Licensing Act: Bruce's Act: public-houses to close at midnight in London; 10.0 p.m. in country.
Metalliferous Mines Act: employment of women and children prohibited.
Agricultural Workers' Union founded by Joseph Arch (see 1885).
Arbitration Tribunal in Geneva decided Alabama case between the U.S.A. and Britain in favour of former.
Ulysses S. Grant re-elected President of the U.S.A..
General Amnesty Act pardoned most ex-Confederates in the U.S.A.
Jesuits expelled from Germany.
League of Three Emperors (*Dreikaiserbund*) among Germany, Russian and Austria.
Norwegian *Storthing*'s policy negatived by Oscar II of Sweden.
Spanish Cortes hostile to Amadeus declared in favour of Alfonso, son of Isabella II; outbreak of Second Carlist War in Spain (to 1876).

Guildhall Library, London, founded.
Samuel Butler (*1835, †1902), who became a New Zealand sheep farmer: *Erewhon*, satirical novel of an ideal commonwealth.
Coppée: *Les Humbles*, poems.
Daudet: *Tartarin de Tarascon*, French novel with a comic hero.
Thomas Hardy (*1840, †1928): *Under the Greenwood Tree*, novel of country life.
William W. Reade (*1838, †1875): *Martyrdom of Man*, prose.
Tennyson: *Gareth and Lynette*, Arthurian poem.
Dostoievski: *The Possessed* (begun 1871), Russian novel.

1873 Supreme Court of Judicature Act; reformed English judicial system.
Start of industrial and agricultural depression in Britain.
Start of Ashanti War (to 1874).
Final payment of French war indemnity; German evacuation completed.
Monarchist restoration in France frustrated by refusal of Comte de Chambord to accept Tricolor as national flag.
"May Laws" in Germany restricted powers of Church.
Election Law in Austria; election to *Reichsrath* directly rather than through local Diets.
Abdication of Amadeus of Savoy

Robert Bridges (*1844, †1930): *Poems*, by a doctor who turned from medicine to literature.
Butler: *The Fair Haven*, satirical study of Christian miracles.
Daudet: *Contes du Lundi*, French stories.
Hardy: *A Pair of Blue Eyes*, a novel.
Mill: *Autobiography*.
Arthur Rimbaud (*1854, †1891): *Une Saison en Enfer*, French prose and verse, "psychologically autobiographical".
Jules Verne (*1828, †1905): *Le Tour du Monde en 80 jours*, French scientific novel, later filmed.
Editors of Russian newspapers compelled to reveal names of contributors.

Oxford and Cambridge Universities opened to non-Anglicans.
Offical opening of Royal Albert Hall, London.

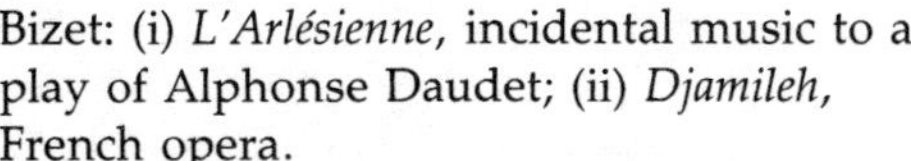

Bizet: (i) *L'Arlésienne*, incidental music to a play of Alphonse Daudet; (ii) *Djamileh*, French opera.
Corot: *The Forest of Coubron*, French painting.
Dargomejsky: *The Stone Guest*, Russian work completed by Cui and Rimsky-Korsakov.
Degas: *The Dance Foyer at the Opera*, French ballet painting.
Antonin Dvořák (*1841, †1904): *Hymnus*, Czech choral work.
Franck: *Rédemption*, French oratorio.
Money: (i) *Windmills in Holland* , (ii) *Sunrise*, French paintings.
Pissarro: *The Wash-house*, French painting.
Sisley: (i) *Place a l'Argenteuil*, (ii) *The Canal*, French paintings.
Aberystwyth University College founded.

Berthelot: *Sur la force de la poudre*, French work on explosives.
Richard Dedekind (*1831, †1916), German mathematician; theory of irrational numbers.
G. A. Hansen discovered the bacillus of leprosy.
Robert Koch (*1843, †1910), German bacteriologist, began his work at Wollstein.
Public Health Act.
Oré of Lyons gave first intravenous anaesthesia; injected chloral hydrate.
Pullman designed his dining-car for trains.
George Westinghouse (*1846, †1914), U.S. engineer, invented the automatic air brake.
Overland telegraph in Australia.
St Gotthard Tunnel commenced (see 1881).
French Assembly authorized 3 milliard franc loan; 21 milliards subscribed.
Penny-farthing bicycle in general use.

Degas: *The Cotton office at New Orleans*, French painting.
Delibes: *Le Roi l'a dit*, French opera.
Manet: *The Croquet Party*, French Impressionist painting.
Monet: (i) *The Corn-Apples*, (ii) *Pleasure Boats*, French paintings.
Pissarro: *The Oise near Pontoise*, French painting.
Rimsky-Korsakov: *Ivan the Terrible* (originally named *Pskovitianka*), Russian opera.
Foundation of the Carl Rosa Opera Company.
c. Cézanne: *Dr Cachet's House at Auvers*, French painting.
c. Whistler: *Miss Cecily Alexander*, American portrait.

Christian Billroth (*1829, †1894), Viennese surgeon known as "Father of Gastric Surgery", removed a cancerous larynx.
Joseph F. Glidden, U.S.A., invented barbed wire.
Peters discovered the asteroid Electra.
Sholes and Glidden, U.S.A., designed the first commercially successful typewriter (marketed 1874 *q.v.*).
Van der Waal's equation for gases.
Commencement of Severn Tunnel; completed 1886.
Co-operative Wholesale Society began manufacture of certain goods.
Railway Commissioners to administer 1854 Railway and Canal Act efficiently.
Prince Edward Island joined Dominion of Canada.

1873 from Spanish throne; Republic proclaimed; Carlist rising in Basque provinces.
Russian students tried to promote cause of social reform among peasants.
Russian occupation of Khiva in Turkestan; gained territory along Oxus.

1874 Resignation of Gladstone's first ministry; Disraeli Prime Minister.
First Trade Union ("Labour") M.P.s, A. Macdonald and T. Burt, elected.
Formation of Women's Trade Union League.
Annexation of Fiji by Britain.
Democrats won control of House of Representatives in the U.S.A.
Bonapartist revival in France forced alliance of Orleanist and Republican forces.
Annam became French Protectorate.
Obligatory civil marriage established in Germany.
French frigate for papal protection left Civita Vecchia.
Storthing's policy again negatived by Oscar II of Sweden.
Spanish Bourbons restored in Alfonso XII.
Revolt of Herzegovinian peasants against Turkish rule; supported by Bosnia.

Flaubert: *La Tentation de S. Antoine,* the life of the saint in the desert.
John Richard Green (*1837, †1883): *Short History of the English People.*
Hardy: *Far from the Madding Crowd,* a novel.
Keller: *KleiderMachen Leute.*
Leopold von Sacher-Masoch (*1835, †1895): *Die Messalinen Wiens*, German novel.
Sir Leslie Stephen (*1832, †1904): *Hours in a Library*, prose.
Swinburne: *Bothwell, a Tragedy.*
Verlaine: *Romance sans Paroles*, poems with musical values.

1875 Carnarvon revived Grey's proposal for South African Federation.
Establishment of Central Parliament in New Zealand.
Third Republic constituted in France.
French law strengthening army caused crisis with Germany.
Dissolution of monasteries in Prussia.
Union of followers of Marx and Lasalle in Germany promoted growth of Socialism.
Russo-British intervention averted danger of Franco-German war.
Representative Committee set up in Alsace-Lorraine to act as Diet.

Mary Baker Eddy: *Science and Health,* teachings of the religion of Christian Science; later the title of the book had *with Key to the Scriptures* added.
Heinrich Schliemann (*1822, †1890), German: *Troy and its Remains,* story of excavation of sites mentioned by Homer.
Tolstoy: *Anna Karenina,* a novel.
c. Afrikaans first became a written language.

Irish University Bill rejected by Commons.
First University Extension Classes set up at Cambridge.
Italian government secularized Roman Catholic convents.

Mark adopted as unit of standard coinage in Germany.
Financial crises in Germany and Austria; industrial unrest.
Sultan of Zanzibar closed slave market on British pressure.
Uniform Imperial Civil Code established in the German Empire.

Cézanne: (i) *Vase of Flowers*, (ii) *View of Auvers*, French paintings.
Manet joined Monet at Argenteuil; they painted in the open air.
Monet: (i) *An Impression*, French painting; "Impressionism" is named after it (see 1868).
Morisot: *At Maurecourt*, French painting.
Renoir: *The Opera Box*, French painting.
Saint-Saëns: *Danse Macabre*, French orchestral work.
Sisley: *Regatta near London*, French painting.
J. Strauss: *Die Fledermaus*, Austrian operetta.
Verdi: *Requiem*, Italian mass.
Hertford College, Oxford, originally Hart Hall, refounded.
c. Degas: *Racehorses at Longchamp*, French painting.
Invention, in England, of the game of lawn tennis.

David Ferrier mapped areas of monkey's brain responsible for different functions.
Andrew T. Still (*1828, †1917), of the U.S.A., laid foundations of osteopathy.
Sliding scale of wages in mining industry, based on selling price of coal.
Factory Act; 10–hour day; minimum age raised to 9 years (10 after 1875).
Italian government extended tobacco monopoly to Sicily.
First zoological gardens in the U.S.A. opened in Philadelphia.
E. Remington and Sons, gunsmiths, manufactured and sold Sholes and Gliddon typewriters (see 1873), which bore name *Remington* from 1876 onwards.

Bizet: *Carmen*, French opera; his most popular work.
Dvořák: Symphony No. 5 in F (originally called the First), Czech composition (revised 1887).
Sir Wm. Gilbert (*1836, †1911) and Sullivan: *Trial by Jury*, light opera produced by d'Oyly Carte.
Manet: *The Grand Canal in Venice*, French Impressionist painting.
Monet: *Sailing Boats at Argenteuil*, French painting.
c. Cézanne: *The Buffet*, French painting showing the artist's interest in geometrical pictures.
c. Holman Hunt: *The Triumph of the Innocents*, a painting.

Disraeli's social reforms included Public Health Act; Artisans' Dwellings Act; Sale of Food and Drugs Act; Climbing Boys Act; Enclosure of Comons Act; Act controlling use of explosives.
Khedive Ismail's shares in Suez Canal bought by Disraeli on behalf of British government.
Completion of drainage system for London.
Percy C. Gilchrist and Sidney G. Thomas began method of extracting phosphorus from iron, made low-grade ores suitable for Bessemer and Siemens steel-production processes.
Ernest Giles crossed Australia from Adelaide to Perth and back.

1875 Carlists driven out of Catalonia and Valencia.
Anglo-Portuguese dispute over Delagoa Bay settled in Portugal's favour.
Union of followers of Deak and Tisza in Hungary to form Liberal Party.
Andrássy Note: attempt by Austria to secure reforms in Turkey; policy resisted by Disraeli.
Japan expelled from Sakhalin.
Japanese legislative body formed by decree, not popular vote.

1876 Legalization of peaceful picketing during strikes.
British missionary work begun in Nyasaland.
Franco-British dual control in Egypt.
Southern Democrats in the U.S.A. regained control of State Governments; systematic disfranchisement of Negroes.
Only disputed election for U.S. Presidency; between Republican Hayes and Democrat Tilden; Hayes adjudged winner.
Battle of Little Big Horn: "Custer's Last Stand".
Colorado admitted member state of the U.S.A.
Liberal Constitutional Monarchy in Spain; Carlists defeated; Royal army to occupy Basque Provinces.
Accession of Abdul Hamid II, the "Damned", as Sultan of Turkey.
Andrássy Note of 1874 accepted by Disraeli and Sultan.
Berlin Memorandum: attempt to check fighting in Balkans.
Bulgaria joined revolt against Turkey; Turkish Bulgarian atrocities.
Russian law courts established in Poland.
Treaty of Jacobabad: Britain to garrison Quetta on Afghan frontier; check on Russian advance.
Russian conquest of Khanate of Khokand.

Daudet: *Jack*, French novel.
Carroll: *Hunting of the Snark*, a fantasy.
Stéphane Mallarmé (*1842, †1898): *L'Après-midi d'un Faune*, French poem which inspired Debussy.
Conrad Ferdinand Meyer (*1825, †1898): *Jürg Jenatsch*, novel with Swiss 17th-cent. background.
Mark Twain: *Tom Sawyer*, adventures of a naughty boy in an American town.
Meredith: *Beauchamp's Career*, political novel.
Jean Richepin (*1849, †1926): *Chanson des Gueux*, poems of beggars, in argot (slang).
Turgenev: *Virgin Soil*, Russian novel.

Smetana: *My Country*, six Czechoslovakian symphonic poems.
Sisley: *La Route de la Princesse à Louveciennes*, French painting.
Church Missionary Society sponsored work in Uganda.

Dutch reclamation in River Y estuary greatly extended.
Foundation of Universal Postal Union at Berne.
c. Roller skating became popular; first rinks constructed.
Japan, while recognizing independence of Korea, retained three trading ports.
Grenville Steam Carriage, oldest mechanical vehicle still in running order, constructed.

Borodin: Symphony No. 2 in B minor completed.
Brahms: Symphony No. 1 in C minor.
*Pablo Casals, great Spanish cellist (†1973).
Cézanne: *The Hermitage, Pontoise*, French painting.
Degas: (i) *The Dancing Class*, (ii) *At the Seaside*, French paintings.
Delibes: *Sylvia*, French ballet.
Edvard Hagerup Grieg (*1843, †1907) *Peer Gynt* suite, Norwegian music based on Ibsen's play, first performed.
Renoir: (i) *Le Moulin de la Galette*, (ii) *Au Théatre; La Première Sortie*, French Impressionist paintings.
Sandon's Act: School attendance 5–10 years compulsory; to 14 without proficiency certificates; parents penalized for withholding children.
Heinrich Schliemann first excavated Mycenae; discovered many gold treasures.
Foundation of Ducie School, Manchester, later to become a pioneer school for science and engineering.

Alexander Graham Bell (*1847, †1922), of Edinburgh, moved to the U.S.A., invented the telephone (see 1860).
Melville R. Bissell invented carpet sweeper.
Arthur Cayley (*1821, †1895), mathematician: *Elliptic Functions*.
Lord Kelvin designed the dry card compass.
Koch discovered the anthrax bacillus.
H. J. Lawson invented the safety rear-driven bicycle.
Linde invented the ammonium refrigerator.
N. A. Otto (*1832, †1891), German, invented four-stroke-cycle horizontal gas engine (hence Otto Cycle).
S. Plimsoll proposed his statutory maximum loading line for ships.
Development of contact process for sulphuric acid.
First compound locomotive constructed.
Grey squirrel introduced into Britain from N. America.
Sanitary Institute, for public health, founded in Britain.
Opening of Royal Albert Docks, London.
†Last pure-blooded Tasmanian.
Quebec and Maritime Provinces of Canada linked by railway.
Geographical Congress at Brussels: International Association founded to suppress slavery and develop Congo basin.
Reichbank in Germany, which became Free Trade country.
Scheme for State purchase of Indian railways.
First Chinese railway constructed.

Year	History	Literature
1876		
1877	Victoria proclaimed Empress of India. Annexation of Transvaal; 9th Kaffir War. National Liberation Association formed; Gladstone's Midlothian Campaign. Irish Nationalist M.P.s began serious obstruction of business in House of Commons. Great American railway strike; first major industrial dispute in the U.S.A. Bismarck tendered resignation; refused by William I. Norwegian *Storthing* and Oscar II continued dispute. Russia intervened in support of Serbia against Turkey. London Protocol: Powers approved Turkish Constitution, but retained right to protect Christian populations; Sultan rejected control. Russia invaded Turkey: Roumania proclaimed independence from Turkey. Turks failed to defend Plevna against Russians. Satsuma rebellion in Japan; Samurai force defeated by conscript army; destroyed feudal concept.	Henry James (*1843, †1916): *The American*, a novel by the U.S. novelist who later became a British citizen. Anna Sewell (*1820, †1878): *Black Beauty*, autobiography of a horse. Daudet: *Le Nabob*, a novel of the world of high finance. Flaubert: *Trois Contes*, three short stories. Hugo: *L'Art d'être Grandpère*, collection of poems. Zola: *L'Assommoir*, a novel of the saloon. Giosuè Carducci (*1835, †1907): *Odi barbare*, volume of Italian poems. Ibsen: *Pillars of Society*, a play. Keller: *Züricher Novellen*, Swiss story cycle.
1878	Second Afghan War (to 1880). Anglo-German approval for France's policies in Algeria and Tunis. Unsuccessful attempt to assassinate Emperor William I of Germany; State of Siege proclaimed; laws against Socialists. †Victor Emmanuel II of Italy; accession of Humbert. †Pope Pius IX; election of moderate Leo XIII. End of series of revolts in Spanish Cuba. Russian occupation of Adrianople; Russo-Turkish armistice; Treaty of San Stefano.	Hardy: *Return of the Native*, novel set in Wessex. Heinrich Leuthold (*1827, †1879): *Gedichte*, poems by Swiss lyric poet. Hector Malot (*1830, †1907): *Sans Famille*, French children's story of a foundling boy. Sir Henry M. Stanley (*1841, †1904): *Through the Dark Continent*, by the explorer of Central Africa. Robert Louis Stevenson (*1850, †1894): *An Inland Voyage*, canal journey in Belgium and France. *c.* Sewing-machines used for book-binding.

Work begun on the Channel Tunnel.
Opening of North Sea canal, in Netherlands (18 miles long).

Brahms: Symphony No. 2 in D major.
Degas: (i) *Café-Concert at the Ambassadeurs,* (ii) *Two Dancers on the Stage,* (iii) *Carlo Pellegrini,* French paintings.
Monet: *Le Pont de L'Europe,* French painting.
Saint-Saëns: *Samson and Delilah,* French opera.
First presentation of *Swan Lake* ballet; music by Peter Ilyich Tschaikowsky (*1840, †1893), Russian composer, who wrote his well-known 4th symphony (in F minor) in the same year.
Renoir: *In a Café,* French Impressionist painting.
c. Cézanne: (i) *Portrait of Victor Chocquet,* (ii) *Madame Cézanne in a Red Easy Chair,* French portraits.
Elementary education between ages of 6 and 9 compulsory in Belgium.
Discovery at Olympus of Praxiteles's statue of Hermes.
Rodin: *L'âge d'airain,* French sculpture which caused a sensation.
Columbus Statue, Mexico City, erected.
International lawn tennis matches held at Wimbledon.

Cailletet (French) and Pictet (Swiss) independently liquefied oxygen.
Thomas Alva Edison (*1847, †1931), U.S. inventor, patented the phonograph; see 1888, 1894; British name "gramophone" later, then "record-player", now "stereo".
De Laval invented the cream-separator.
Pasteur observed action of antibiotics on anthrax bacillus.
Giovanni V. Schiaparelli (*1836, †1910), Italian, observed "canals" of Mars (found *not* to be canals, 1969); A. Hall discovered Phobos and Deimos, the Martian moons.
Elisha Thomson, of the U.S.A., developed electric welding.
Argentine first exported frozen meat to Europe.
Ball-bearings used in bicycles.
Rivers Pollution Act.
Ministry of Commerce and Waterways in Holland.
Portugal began effective development of African colonies.
Between this date and 1907, the 17 rare-earth metals (atomic numbers 21, 39 and 57–71) were identified.

Order of the Indian Empire founded by Queen Victoria.
Cézanne: (i) *The Quayside at Bercy,* (ii) *The Pool at the Jas de Bouffan,* French paintings.
Degas: (i) *The Ballet (Dancer with Bouquet),* (ii) *Café Singer wearing a Glove,* French paintings.
Garnier constructed Monte Carlo Casino.
Manet: *Blonde Half-Nude,* French painting.
Renoir: *Mme Charpentier and her Children,* French painting.
Saint-Saëns: Symphony No. 2 in A minor.
Sisley: *The Banks of the Oise,* Anglo-French painting.
Gilbert and Sullivan: *H.M.S. Pinafore,* light opera.
Belgian School Laws: attempted to

Start of decline of English wheat prices.
Berthelot: *Mécanique chimique,* French work relating chemistry to laws of mechanics.
Mannlicher produced his repeater rifle.
Sédillot gave name microbes to minute organisms.
First use of iodoform as an antiseptic.
Fur farming commenced in Canada, on Prince Edward Island.
Invention of gelignite.
Red Flag Act: mechanical road vehicles to have maximum speed 4 m.p.h. and to be preceded by man with red flag.
Criminal Investigation Department (C.I.D.), New Scotland Yard, established.
An Act of this year defined the Imperial Standard Yard (established 1856) as a

Year	History	Literature
1878	Powers objected to terms of San Stefano; Congress of Berlin summoned to deal with Eastern question; Russian gains in Turkey wiped out; Austria to occupy Bosnia-Herzegovina; Britain to administer Cyprus; some self-government for Crete. Berlin Settlement led to adoption of terrorism by Russian Slavophils.	
1879	Formation of Irish Land League under presidency of Charles Stewart Parnell, leader of Irish Nationalist M.P.s. Zulu War: Zulus defeated at Rorke's Drift and Ulundi; Boers in revolt. Treaty of Gandamak: Khan of Afghanistan to receive British Embassy at Kabul; British Resident murdered; British forces, under Roberts, entered Kabul and, under Stewart, Kandahar. Church of Christ Scientist founded in Boston. Prince Imperial, son of Napoleon III, killed in Zululand. Amnesty granted to Communards of 1871. Bismarck abandoned Free Trade Policies; introduced Protection. Austro-German Dual Alliance (to 1918). Organic Laws: established constitution of Bulgaria; Alexander of Battenburg elected Prince of Bulgaria. Slavophil movement in Russia under control of extremist Mikhailloff; four attempts to murder Tsar Alexander II by 1880.	William Barnes (*1801, †1886): *Poems of Rural Life in the Dorset District.* Bridge: *Poems.* James: *Daisy Miller,* short story of unconventional American girl in Europe. Andrew Lang (*1844, †1912) and Butcher translated the *Odyssey.* Meredith: *The Egoist,* novel with a humourless hero (Sir Willoughby Paterne). Keller: *Der grüne Heinrich* (new ed.), autobiographical tales of young artist. Ibsen: *A Doll's House,* Norwegian drama. Stevenson: *Travels with a Donkey in the Cevennes.* Dostoievski: *The Brothers Karamazov,* Russian novel. Henry George: *Progress and Poverty,* influenced socialist movements.
1880	Disraeli lost Election; Gladstone Prime Minister for second time. Burials Act: burial of Nonconformists permitted in Anglican churchyards. Charles Bradlaugh, atheist, elected M.P. for Northampton; not allowed	Hardy: *Trumpet Major,* a novel. Joel Chandler Harris (*1848, †1908): *Uncle Remus,* American tales of Brer Rabbit and his friends. Pierre Loti (*1850, †1923): *Le Mariage de Loti,* exotic French novel.

complete secular control of education.
Cleopatra's Needle brought to Great Britain; now on Thames Embankment.
Foundation of Lady Margaret Hall, Oxford, for women.
Foundation of Cyclists' Touring Club; incorporated 1887.

certain distance between two marks on a bar of Baily's metal.
Factories and Workshops Act: extended factory laws.
Phylloxera in French vineyards; American vines excluded from France; devastated lands excused from taxes until 1882.
Baron Nordenskjöld (*1832, †1901), Swedish explorer, sailed from Gothenburg to Yokohama along Arctic shore of Asia; North East Passage.
Karl Benz (*1844, †1879) built motorized tricycle which reached 7 m.p.h.

Cézanne: *Aix Paysage Rocheau*, French painting.
Manet: (i) *In a Boat*, (ii) *Portrait of George Moore*, French paintings.
Renoir: (i) *At the Grenouillère*, (ii) *Roses*, French paintings.
Tschaikowsky: *Eugene Onegin*, Russian opera.
Foundation of Somerville College, Oxford, for women.
c. Degas: (i) *Dancers awaiting their Cue*, (ii) *Dancers in Yellow*, French paintings.
Suppé, Vienese light opera composer: *Boccaccio*.

Crookes developed tube to demonstrate existence of cathode rays, later shown by Kelvin to be streams of electrons.
Crompton lit St Enoch's Station, Glasgow, by electricity.
Fahlberg and Remsen discovered saccharine.
Sir W. McEwen diagnosed brain tumour and successfully removed it.
Edison, U.S.A., produced successful carbon-filament incandescent electric light.
James Ritty, of the U.S.A., invented cash register.
Stefan's law on black-body radiation.
First steam-tanker for oil transport; used on Caspian Sea.
Demonstration, at Berlin Trade Exhibition, of first electric tram.
Failure of City of Glasgow Bank; led to Limited Liability Act.
Collapse of Tay Bridge.
Foundation of British United African Company.
Britain and France joint controllers of Suez Canal.
Stanley set out with Belgian expedition to explore Upper Congo.

Brahms: *Hungarian dances*, piano duets.
Degas: (i) *Little fourteen year old Dancer*, (ii) *At the Theatre*, French paintings.
Gilbert and Sullivan: *The Pirates of Penzance*, light opera.
Monet: *Still Life—Apples and Grapes*, French painting.

F. M. Balfour (*1851, †1882): *Comparative Embryology*, basis of modern study of the subject.
Joseph Swann developed incandescent lamp in England, independently of Edison (see 1879).

1880 to affirm; committed to Clock Tower.
10,000 Irish evictions; outbreak of "boycotting".
British forces defeated by Afghans at Maiwand; Roberts' march from Kabul to Kandahar; Khan deposed; pro-British Khan appointed.
French Parliament returned to Paris from Versailles.
Formation of "Socialist Workers" in France.
Jesuits, Benedictines and Carmelites expelled from France.
Pioneer Salvation Army party sent to the U.S.A.
Repeal of "May Laws": relaxation of *Kulturkampf* in Germany; Prussian parliament gave German Government power to set aside laws.
Revolutionary committee in Tiflis; demanded self-government for Armenia.
Norwegian government refused to publish *Storthing* policy; dismissed.

Guy de Maupassant (*1850, †1893): *Contes* (to 1890), French short stories.
"Ouida": *Moths,* a novel.
Lew Wallace (*1827, †1905): *Ben Hur,* historical novel with famous chariot race, by the American.
Zola: *Nana,* novel of the demi-monde.

1881 †Disraeli, Earl of Beaconsfield.
Bradlaugh re-elected; ejected from Commons by ten policemen.
Report on Royal Commission on agricultural depression.
British forces defeated Boers at Laing's Neck and Majuba Hill.
Sudanese revolt under Mahdi.
President Garfield of the U.S.A. shot and wounded; died two months later.
French invaded Tunis; occupied Bizerta; Treaty of Bardo established protectorate over Tunis; Italians hostile.
Franco-British intervention secured most of Thessaly and part of Epirus for Greece.
Prince Alexander of Bulgaria suspended Organic Laws; took absolute power for seven years.
Alexander II of Russia accepted Melikov's proposal for Consultative Committee for reform; assassinated same day.

Revised version of the New Testament.
Flaubert: *Bouvard et Péchet,* French novel, posthumously published.
Anatole France (*1844, †1924): *Le Crime de Sylvestre Bonnard,* French novel.
Ibsen: *Ghosts,* Norwegian drama concerned with venereal disease.
James: *Portrait of a Lady,* Anglo-American novel.
Edouard Pailleron (*1834, †1899): *Le Monde où l'on s'ennuie,* French play satirizing society.
Leopold von Ranke (*1795, †1886): *Weltgeschichte,* German history.
Reed: *The Fifth Form at St Dominic's* novel of schoolboy life.
D. G. Rossetti: *Ballads and Sonnets.*
Stevenson: *Sagesse,* poems.
Oscar Wilde (*1854, †1900): *Poems.*
Liberty of public meeting and Press granted in France.

Pissarro: *The Outer Boulevards*, French painting of Paris.
Renoir: (i) *Little Nude in Blue*, (ii) *Place Clichy*, French paintings.
Tschaikowsky: (i) *1812 Overture*, (ii) *Capriccio Italien*.
Foundation of Guildhall School of Music.
c. Cézanne: (i) *The Village Street*, (ii) *Medea*, French paintings. (iii) *Château de Médan*, water-colour.
Mundella's Education Act: attendance at school compulsory to 13.
Foundation of Regent St. Polytechnic.

James Finlay built iron suspension-bridge, Pennsylvania.
Mikuliez-Radecki first repaired perforated gastric ulcer.
James Wimshurst invented his electrostatic generator.
Introduction of gas-fire.
Discovery that anopheles mosquito carries malaria.
Employers Liability Act.
Forth Bridge opened to traffic.
Use of wood-pulp for production of cheap paper.
First cargo of frozen mutton arrived in London from Australia.
Triple expansion steam engine; 80% more economical than Watt's engine.
Abolition of public dues on French canals.

Gabriel Fauré (*1845, †1924): *Ballade*, for piano and orchestra.
Franck: *Rébecca*, Belgian oratorio.
Gilbert and Sullivan: *Patience*, light opera.
H. L. Higginson founded Boston Symphony Orchestra.
Tales of Hoffmann completed after †Offenbach.
*Anna Pavlova (†1931), Russian prima ballerina.
Renoir: (i) *Les Bataliers*, final painting of his series on Parisian life, (ii) *Gondola in Venice*, (iii) *Venice*.
c. Cézanne: (i) *The Turn in the Road*, French painting, (ii) *Dish and Bowl with Fruit*, still-life.
Tschaikowsky: *Joan of Arc*, Russian opera.
Queen's College, Dundee, founded; became part of St Andrew's University in 1953.

Billroth successfully operated on the abdomen; discovered streptococci in same year.
Sir Alexander Ogston discovered staphylocci.
Koch worked on the destruction effect of certain chemicals (disinfectants) on microbes.
Pasteur developed immunization against anthrax.
Completion of St Gotthard tunnel, linking Göschenen and Airolo, Switzerland (see 1872).
Opening, at Kensington, of the Natural History Museum.
Second Irish Land Act: Land Courts to fix fair rents.
British North Borneo Co. chartered.
Stanley founded Leopoldville in the Congo.
De Lesseps and Gustave Eiffel (*1832, †1923), French engineers, began constructing the Panama Canal.
French Ministry of Agriculture established.
Abolition of flogging in Army and Navy.

1881

Russia captured Denghil-tepe; strengthened influence in Turkestan.
Constitution and national parliament promised to Japanese before 1891.

1882

Epping Forest given to nation by Queen Victoria.
Bradlaugh again expelled from Commons; re-elected; not allowed to sit.
Municipal Corporations Act.
Irish "No rent" Manifesto; Parnell imprisoned; Kilmainham Treaty, Parnell released.
Lord Frederick Cavendish, Chief Secretary of Ireland, and Burke, Under Secretary, assassinated in Phoenix Park, Dublin.
Catholic League formed in Britain.
British fleet bombarded Alexandria; marines occupied Suez; end of Franco-British Dual rule.
Lord Rippon proposed scheme for local Indian self-government.
Mahdi (*1848, †1885) proclaimed himself Messiah in Sudan.
Revolt of Arabi Pasha against Khedive Tewfik defeated at Tel-el-Kebir.
French captured Hanoi; China asserted suzerainty over Annam.
Italy formed Triple Alliance with Austria and Germany (to 1914).
Austrian anarchists adopted policy of terrorism.
"Jewish Pale" in Russia; Jews compelled to live in 15 provinces.

F. Anstey (*1856, †1933): *Vice Versa*, novel with father and son reversed.
Henry Becque (*1837, †1899): *Les Corbeaux*, French play.
Fontane: *L'Adultera*, realistic novel of Berlin life.
Ibsen: *An Enemy of the People*, Norwegian play.
Hardy: *Two on a Tower*, novel of love of young astronomer.
Richard Jefferies (*1848, †1887): *Bevis*, memories of childhood.
George Saintsbury (*1845, †1933): *A Short History of French Literature*.
George Bernard Shaw (*1856, †1950), great playwright: *Cashel Byron's Profession*, novel about a boxer.
Stevenson: (i) *Treasure Island*, tale of pirates; (ii) *New Arabian Nights*, fantastic tales.
Swinburne: *Tristam of Lyonesse*, a poem.
Lord Rippon granted freedom to Press in India.

1883

Ripon attempted to place British and Indian magistrates on equal terms.
Social Democratic Federation founded by H. M. Hyndman; opposed to existing Liberal-Labour alliance.
Dynamite gangs at work in London.
Mahdi's followers in Sudan defeated Hicks Pasha; Gladstone favoured evacuation of Sudan; Gordon sent to effect this policy.
Stephen John Paul Kruger elected

Jefferies: *Story of my Heart*, idealized autobiography.
Lang, Leaf and Myers translated the *Iliad*.
Loti: *Mon frère Yves*, novel of the sea, set in Brittany.
Detlev von Liliencron (*1844, †1909): *Gedichte*, German lyric poems with new realism.
Friedrich Nietzsche (*1844, †1900): *Also sprach Zarathustra* (to 1891), salvation of society is 'will to power".
B. Bjørnson (*1832, †1910) *Beyond our Power*, Norwegian drama.

Foundation of Society for Physical Research.
Gilbert and Sullivan: *Iolanthe*, light opera.
Gounod: *The Redemption*, French oratorio.
Manet: (i) *Peonies in an Ovoid Vase*, (ii) *The Bar at the Folies-Bergère*.
Monet: *The Cliff Walk, Pourville*, French painting.
Renoir: *The Two Sisters*, French painting.
Foundation of Selwyn College, Cambridge.
University College, Liverpool (later Liverpool University—see 1903), founded.
Cézanne: *Self-Portrait*.
c. Degas: (i) *The Millinery Shop*, (ii) *The Laundresses*, French paintings.
Anglo-Australian cricket "Ashes" started.
University of Prague divided into two sections, German and Czech.
Oderbank Clubs formed in Italy.
Berlin Philharmonic Orchestra founded.

Alphonse Bertillon (*1853, †1914), French statistician, developed anthropometric method of identification of criminals.
Koch discovered tuberculosis bacillus; made great advances in microscopy, using stained slides, at about this time.
Kynoch developed brass cartridge-case.
H. W. Seeley, of the U.S.A., invented electric flat iron.
Electric trains at Leytonstone, London, and at Berlin.
Present Eddystone lighthouse erected.
Reinforced concrete bridges built in Europe.
Extension of Allotments Act: trustees of parish lands authorized to let them as allotments.
Cessation of work on Channel Tunnel project.
British Royal Niger Company founded.
Severe commercial crisis in France.
Foundation of German Colonial Society.
Russian Factory Act prohibited child labour.
Joseph Breuer, Viennese physician, used hypnosis to treat hysteria; beginnings of psychoanalysis.
c. The quagga, rare zebra striped on forepart only, became extinct.

Brahms: Symphony No. 3 in F major.
Delibes: *Lakmé*, French comic opera.
Dvořák: *Stabat Mater*.
Renoir: (i) *By the Seashore*, (ii) *The Artist's son, Jean*, French paintings.
Statue of Liberty presented by France to the U.S.A.
Opening of Metropolitan Opera House, New York.
Foundation of Cardiff University.
Central Board of Education set up by co-operative movement in Britain.
Establishment of Boys' Brigade at Glasgow.

Galton: *Human Faculty*, his second major work on eugenics.
Introduction of liquid compass.
First electric tramway (see 1860) at Portrush, Ireland; electric transport popularized by Chicago Exhibition.
Opening of Brooklyn Bridge, New York.
General acceptance of *zone time*, standard times at intervals of whole numbers of hours from Greenwich.
Institution of parcel post in Britain.
Channel Tunnel Development Bill rejected for the first time.

1883 President of Transvaal; re-elected 1888, 1893, 1898.
Britain annexed part of New Guinea.
†Henri, Comte de Chambord, last male Bourbon heir to French throne; united Legitimists and Orleanists.
French captured Majunga and Tamatave in Madagascar.
Re-establishment of French protectorate in Annam; Franco-Chinese war.
German protectorate declared over West African coast from Angra Pequena to Orange River.
Anti-Magyar riots in Bosnia.
Bulgarian Constitution restored by Alexander.

Olive Schreiner (*1855, †1920): *The Story of an African Farm*, novel of a Boer farmer's life.
Emile Verhaeren (*1855, †1916): *Les Flamandes*, Belgian poems.
Zola: *Au bonheur des Dames*, French novel of department store.

1884 Third English Reform Act: extended franchise to agricultural labourers.
William Morris founded Socialist League in England.
General Gordon arrived at Khartoum to withdraw Egyptian garrison; escape route cut.
Convention of London: Gladstone restored autonomy of Transvaal.
French artisans and peasants allowed to form trade unions.
Fournier's Convention: China recognized French protectorate over Annam; withdrawal of French garrisons misunderstood.
Catholic majority returned at Belgian elections.
Berlin Conference: set up independent Congo State under Leopold II of Belgium.
Extreme Liberals, Progressives and Left Wing openly hostile to Bismarck.
Germany secured grant of 60,000 square miles of Zanzibar.
Bismarck's first "Re-insurance" Treaty with Russia.
Agreement of Skierniewice; renewed *Dreikaiserbund*.
Martial Law in Austria to check anarchists.

Revised version of the Old Testament.
Henri F. Amiel (*1821, †1881), Swiss critic: *Fragments d'un Journal intime*.
Daudet: *Sapho*, French novel; the adventures of a model.
Joris Karl Huysmans (*1848, †1907): *A Rebours*, French novel with hero seeking perverse sensations.
Ibsen: *The Wild Duck*, Norwegian play, a satirical tragi-comedy.
Jean Moréas (*1856, †1910): *Les Syrtes*, French poems.
Mark Twain: *The Adventures of Huckleberry Finn*, sequel to *Tom Sawyer*.
First part of the *Oxford English Dictionary* (completed 1928).
Foundation of the Fabian Society, research organization for Socialism.

Belgian government withheld salaries of priests solely engaged in teaching.
Alexander E. Chabrier (*1841, †1894), French composer: *España*, orchestral rhapsody.
Establishment of Royal College of Music (originally set up as National Training School of Music, in 1872).
Women's Co-operative Guild established.

Explosion of Krakatoa, volcanic island near Java; vast tidal wave caused great loss of life.
Bismarck: insurance against illness in Germany.
Royal Red Cross Order founded by Queen Victoria.
Railway Act: block signalling system and interlocking points and signals.
Railway and Canal Traffic Act: permanent commission to deal with appeals against freight rates.
Sir Joseph Swan manufactured first artificial silk.

Degas: (i) *The Ironers*, (ii) *Café Singer*, French pastels.
Sir Edward Burne-Jones (*1833, †1898): *King Cophetua and the Beggar-Maid*, pre-Raphaelite painting.
Peter Carl Fabergé (*1846, †1920), Russian goldsmith, made first of his famous jewelled Easter eggs for the tsar.
Antonio Guardi began Sagrada Familia, Barcelona; strange church with tall thin towers, still incomplete.
Jules Massenet (*1842, †1912): *Manon*, French opera.
Georges Seurat (*1859, †1891), noted for pointillism (pure dots of unmixed colour): *Une Baignade Assière*, French painting.
Tschaikowsky: *Mazeppa*, Russian opera.
c. Cézanne: (i) *Bay of Marseilles seen from l'Estaque*, French painting; (ii) *Pot of Flowers on a Table*, still-life.
Foundation of Bangor (North Wales) University College.
Catholic clergy in Belgium regained control of religious education.
Report of Royal Commission on Technical Instruction.

Carl Köller used cocaine as local anaesthetic.
Sir Charles A. Parsons (*1854, †1931) invented first practical steam-turbine engine; earlier attempts had failed.
Hiram S. Maxim developed recoil-operated machine-gun.
Ilya Mechnikov (*1845, †1916) proposed theory of phagocytes—white blood corpuscles destroying bacteria (accepted by 1892).
Royce began manufacturing motorcars at Manchester (see 1904).
First deep tube underground railway built in London.
Royal Commission on Housing set up.
Discovery of gold in Transvaal; rise of Johannesburg.
British acquired Somaliland.
U.S.A. received Pearl Harbour as Pacific naval base.
French manufacture of sugar and cultivation of beetroot protected.
Insurance against accidents introduced into Germany industry.
German trade treaties with West African chiefs.
Germany annexed Northern New Guinea; Britain took the rest.

	History	Literature
1884	Oscar II of Sweden conceded Law of Norwegian *Storthing*. Electoral system in Portugal improved. Russians seized Merv in Turkestan.	
1885	Redistribution Act: single member constituencies in Britain. Resignation of Gladstone: Salisbury's "Caretaker" government to 1886. Anglo-Russian crisis over Afghan boundary. Joseph Arch, farm labourer, M.P. for Northampton. Agitation for disestablishment of Church of England. Third Burmese War; Burma absorbed into India. Southern Nigeria became British protectorate; Bechuanaland annexed. Fall of Khartoum; †Gordon. Russia offended by release from prison of anarchist, Kropotkin. French protectorate over Annam recognized by China. French influence extended along Senegal River; Germany, France and Great Britain agreed on Pacific spheres of influence. Italy occupied Massowah on Red Sea. †Alfonso XII of Spain; Maria Christina of Austria proclaimed Regent. Bulgaria acquired Eastern Roumelia from Turkey; Serbo-Bulgarian war of 14 days. Russia seized Pendjeh, Afghan territory. China and Japan agreed to allow Korea self-government. First meeting of Indian National Congress.	Burton, traveller (see 1858) and orientalist, said to understand 35 languages, translated *The Arabian Nights* (to 1888), Oriental tales. Sir H. Rider Haggard (*1856, †1925): *King Solomon's Mines*, African adventure novel. William Henry Hudson (*1841, †1922): *The Purple Lane*, S. American story by the naturalist. Meredith: *Diana of the Crossways*, a novel. Tennyson: *Tiresias and Other Poems*. Becque: *La Parisienne*, French naturalistic drama. Daudet: *Tartarin sur les Alpes*, French novel. France: *Le Livre de mon Ami*, French novel. Jules Laforgue (*1860, †1887): *Les Complaintes*, French poems. Maupassant: *Bel-Ami*, French novel with unscrupulous hero. Zola: *Germinal*, French novel about miners. Russian made official language in baltic provinces.
1886	Fall of Salisbury; Gladstone's third administration; Irish Home Rule Bill introduced by Gladstone, defeated; resignation of Gladstone; Salisbury in office (to 1892). Bradlaugh allowed to take seat by Speaker.	Alcott: *Jo's Boys*, popular book for children. Frances Eliza Hodgson Burnett (*1849, †1924): *Little Lord Fauntleroy*, U.S. novel with child hero. Marie Corelli (pseud. of Mary Mackay) (*1854, †1924): *A Romance of Two Worlds*, a novel.

Brahms: Symphony No. 4 in E minor.
Cézanne: (i) *The Judgment of Paris*, (ii) *Flowers and Fruit*, (iii) *Paul Cézanne* (his son), French paintings.
Degas: (i) *Jockeys at Training*, (ii) *After the Bath*, French paintings.
Dvořák: Symphony No. 2 in D minor.
Gilbert and Sullivan: *The Mikado*, probably their finest light opera.
Gounod: *Mors et Vita*, French oratorio.
Ferdinand Hodler (*1853, †1918): *Woodland*, Swiss painting.
Belgian Education Law made religious education compulsory.
J. Strauss: *Die Zigeunerbaron (The Gipsy Baron)*, Viennese operetta.
The buildings of the Sorbonne were again reconstructed.

Karl Auer: incandescent gas mantle; developed by Welsbach (see 1887).
Balmer: hydrogen spectrum lines.
Benz, German engineer, built his first car; 3-wheeler.
William Burroughs, of U.S.A., invented earliest commercial adding machine.
Mannesmann patented seamless metal tubes.
The Rover Co. marketed Lawson's safety bicycle, chain-driven to back wheel.
William Stanley, of the U.S.A., invented transformer.
Use of Stephenson's rail-gauge.
First English electric tram-car at Blackpool.
Impure aluminium extracted by E. H. and A. C. Cowles by electric furnace.
Canadian Pacific Railway, Montreal to British Columbia, completed.
Comte de Charbonnet started artificial silk industry in France.
France imposed duty on imported wheat.
Russia forbade sale of Polish land to foreigners.
Pasteur successfully inoculated a child bitten by a dog infected by rabies.
Norwegian military service restricted to home defence; reduced value of Swedish-Norwegian force.
Gottleib Daimler (*1834, †1900), German engineer, developed his light-weight high-speed petrol engine.

Cézanne: (i) *Landscape with Viaduct, La Montaigne Sainte-Victoire*, (ii) *Gardanne*, French paintings.
Degas: (i) *Ballet Scene*, (ii) *Seated Dancer tying her Slipper*, French paintings.
Hodler: *Meditation*, Swiss painting.
Mastel invented the celesta (musical

E. von Berzmann steam-sterilized surgical instruments.
Daimler produced a motor-cycle.
R. H. Fitz, U.S.A., recognized appendicitis.
Goldstein discovered positive rays.
C. M. Hall, of U.S.A., and P. L. T. Héroult, of France, independently produced

1886

Liberal Party split into Liberals and Unionists over Home Rule.
British protectorate over Zanzibar (to 1890).
American Federation of Labour replaced federation of unions.
All claimants to throne expelled from France.
Boulanger appointed French Minister of War; popular because favoured recovery of Alsace-Lorraine.
Socialist-inspired strikes suppressed by troops in Belgium.
Reichstag refused to renew military grants in Germany.
German-Spanish dispute over Carolines settled by Leo XIII in favour of Spain.
*posthumous Alfonso XIII of Spain.
Treaty of Bucharest ended Serbo-Bulgarian War; Alexander of Bulgaria forced to abdicate.
Greece forced to keep peace with Turkey by allied blockade.
Russia fortified Batoum in defiance of Congress of Berlin (1878).
Annexation of Upper Burma by U.K.

Hardy: *The Mayor of Casterbridge,* novel of a man who sells his wife and child.
Rudyard Kipling (*1865, †1936): *Departmental Ditties,* verse on Anglo-Indian life.
Stevenson: (i) *Dr Jekyll and Mr Hyde,* a "scientific" novel: (ii) *Kidnapped,* a novel of 1751.
Tennyson: *Locksley Hall, sixty years after,* a poem.
Loti: *Pêcheur d'Islande,* French novel of Brittany and Iceland.
Georges Rodenback (*1855, †1898): *La Jeunesse blanche,* Belgian poetry.
Nietzsche: *Jenseits von Gut und Böse,* German philosophy.
Czech language on equal footing with German in Bohemia.

1887

Parnell accused of complicity in Phoenix Park Murders (1882 *q.v.*).
Irish Coercion Act; Irish Lane Act.
Franco-German crisis over actions of Boulanger in Schnaebele case.
German *Reichstag* dissolved; alliance of Imperialists, Conservatives, some National Liberals—the *Kartel*—gave Bismarck majority in new *Reichstag*; military grants renewed.
Renewal of Russo-German "Reinsurance" Treaty; and Triple Alliance.
Expiry of *Dreikaiserbund.*
Bismarck refused permission for Russia to raise loans in Berlin; France advanced Russia 350 million francs.
Italian force annihilated by Ethiopians at Dogali; designs on Tripoli conditionally supported by Britain and Germany.

Sir Hall Caine (*1853, †1931): *The Deemster,* novel of the Isle of Man.
Sir Arthur Conan Doyle (*1859, †1930): *A Study in Scarlet,* first Sherlock Holmes novel.
Rider Haggard: (i) *She,* novel of Ayesha; (ii) *Allan Quartermain,* novel set in Africa.
Hardy: *The Woodlanders,* a novel.
Goncourt frères: *Journal* (concluded 1896).
Mallarmé: *Poésies.*
August Strindberg (*1849, †1912): *The Father,* Swedish play of a man tormented by his wife.
Hermann Sudermann (*1857, †1928): *Frau Sorge,* German novel.
Zola: *La Terre,* French novel of ugly peasant life.
L. L. Zamenhof (*1859, †1917) published first book on Esperanto.

instrument).
Millais: *Bubbles*, sentimental painting.
Seurat: *Sunday Afternoon on the Island of the Grande Jatte*, French painting.
Foundation of St Hugh's College, Oxford, for women.
Olympia, Hammersmith, erected.
c. Beginnings of post-Impressionism; lasted 20 years, until cubism.
Saint-Säens: (i) Symphony in E minor with organ, French composition; (ii) *La Carnaval des Animaux*, published 1922.
Colonial and India Exhibition at S. Kensington.
Ceremony of dedication of Statue of Liberty, New York.
c. Vincent Van Gogh (*1853, †1890), "father of expressionism", who frequently used brilliant yellow: *La Guinguette*, Dutch painting.

aluminium by electrolysis.
Manufacture of optical glass at Zeiss works, Jena.
Hydro-electric scheme at Niagara Falls.
Development of electric ophthalmoscope.
Opening of Severn and Liverpool-Birkenhead railway tunnels.
Tilbury docks opened for Eastern trade and travel.
German East Africa Co. formed to develop Zanzibar colony.
Abolition of slavery in Spanish Cuba.
Law of Settlement in Germany: authorized finance to purchase Polish lands in Posen and W. Prussia for German colonization.
Russian Factory Act strengthened inspection; made strikes illegal.

Cézanne: *The Blue Vase*, French painting.
Claude A. Debussy (*1862, †1918), French composer and founder of the Impressionist school of music: *Le Printemps*, orchestral suite.
Monet: *Fields in Spring*, French painting.
Sir John Stainer (*1840, †1901): *The Crucifixion*, an oratorio.
c. Van Gogh: (i) *Le Moulin de la Galette*, (ii) *Boulevard de Clichy*, Dutch paintings of Montmartre.
Verdi: *Othello*, Italian opera.
Golden Jubilee of Queen Victoria ended Windsor retirement.
Richard Strauss (*1864, †1949): (i) *Macbeth*, (ii) *Aus Italien*, German tone-poems.
Chabrier: *Le Roi malgré lui*, French opera.

Edison and Swan combined to produce "Ediswan" electric lamp for domestic use.
Mach (*1838, †1916), Austrian, defined MACH number, now widely used in high-speed flight.
Michelson and Morley's important experiment on relative velocity of light in perpendicular directions; no difference of speed found; results led later to Einstein's relativity theory.
Goodwin invented celluloid film.
Cyanide process used for extraction of gold and silver proposed; at first ridiculed (see 1890).
Svante A. Arrhenius (*1859, †1927), Swedish physical chemist, proposed ion theory of electrolysis.
C. A. von Welsbach demonstrated practical incandescent gas mantle.
Construction of first British torpedo cruiser.
Allotments Act: local authorities empowered to acquire land compulsorily for allotments.

1887
Macao recognized as Portuguese by China.
Bulgarian parliament elected Ferdinand of Saxe-Coburg as Prince.
Anglo-Russian treaty fixed Russo-Persian frontier along Oxus River.
British Baluchistan, including Quetta, established.

1888
Commission to examine charges against Parnell.
County Councils Act: elected councils to take over administrative duties of J.P.s.
Miners Federation of Great Britain formed; demand for minimum wage.
Foundation of Scottish Labour Party.
Mashonaland and Matabeleland declared British sphere of influence.
Boulanger supported by Monarchists in France; popularity threatened Third Republic.
Main portion of Bremen incorporated into German Customs Union; parts of Weser estuary remained Free Port.
†Emperor William I of Germany; accession of Frederick III March—June; accession of Emperor William II.
Unemployment demonstration in Rome suppressed by military.
More liberal constitution granted to Serbia by Milan.
Convention of Constantinople: Suez Canal declared open to ships of all nations and free from blockade.
Sarawak and Brunei placed under British protection.
General Buller founded R.A.S.C. (Royal Army Service Corps).
Jack the Ripper murdered six women in London.

Charles Doughty (*1843, †1926): *Travels in Arabia Deserta*.
Hardy: *Wessex Tales*.
Kipling: (i) *Soldiers Three*, (ii) *Plain Tales from the Hills*, short stories of India.
George Moore (*1852, †1933): *Confessions of a Young Man*, autobiography.
Morris: *Dream of John Bull*, dream of socialist commonwealth.
Sir Arthur Quiller-Couch (*1863, †1944): *Troy Town*, novel of Cornwall.
Stevenson: *The Black Arrow*, novel of the War of the Roses.
Wilde: *Happy Prince and Other Tales*.
Georges Courteline (*1860, †1929): *Le train de 8h.47*, French barrack life.
Iannis Psichari (*1854, †1929), one of creators of modern Greek literary language, *My Journey*, written in demotic tongue.
Fontane: *Irrungen, Wirrungen*, German novel.
Use of Danish language forbidden in schools in German N. Schleswig.

1889
Great London Dock Strike; the "Dockers' Tanner"; growth of unskilled workers' unions; New Unionism; Gasworkers Union formed.
Act to prevent cruelty to children.
Transvaal claimed to be "encircled"

Sir James Barrie (*1860, †1937): *A Window in Thrums*, sketches of Scottish village life.
R. Browning: *Asolando*, poetry.
Conan Doyle: *The Sign of Four*, a novel.
Jerome K. Jerome (*1859, †1927): (i) *Idle Thoughts of an Idle Fellow*, (ii) *Three Men in a Boat*, amusing stories.

Coal Mines Regulation Act: boys not to work underground until 13 or at surface under 12.
U.S. Interstate Commerce Act: federal control of interstate railways.
Work begun on Kiel Canal.
Daimler 4-wheeled motor car produced.

Cézanne: *Peasant in a Blue Smock*, French painting.
Gilbert and Sullivan: *The Yeoman of the Guard*, light opera.
Van Gogh: (i) *Sunflowers*, (ii) *Portrait of Armand Roulin*, (iii) *La Mousme*, (iv) *Drawbridge at Arles*, Dutch paintings.
Monet: *Cap d'Antibes*, French Impressionist painting.
Rimsky-Korsakov: *Scheherazade*, Russian symphonic suite.
Seurat: *Fishing Fleet at Port-en-Bessin*, French painting.
Tschaikowsky: Fifty Symphony, in E minor.
Henri de Toulouse-Lautrec (*1864, †1901): *Trace Horse of the Bus Line, Place Clichy*, French painting by the cripple who specialized in Paris night life.
Final report on Commission on Elementary Education Acts in England.
English Priory of Knights Hospitallers authorized by Royal Charter.

Heinrich Hertz (*1857, †1894), German physicist, produced electro-magnetic waves; identified wireless waves as belonging to same family as light waves; Sir Oliver Lodge made same discovery (independently) in same year: Hertz used induction coil; Lodge used Leyden jars.
Dunlop's pneumatic tyre, which has yet to be improved on in principle, developed.
Fridtjof Nansen (*1861, †1930), Norwegian explorer, crossed Greenland icefield.
Nickolas Tesla (*1856, †1943) made first alternating-current motor.
Sir J. Dewar and Sir F. Abel invented cordite.
Mercerizing process introduced into cotton manufacture; facilitated later development of artificial silk industry.
Foundation of London General Omnibus Co.
British East Africa Co. founded.
Emile Berliner improved the phonograph (gramophone); see also 1894.
Reconstructed free port of Hamburg opened.
Agricultural depression caused Sweden to abandon Free Trade.
Foundation of Institut Pasteur.
Hudson and Sclater: *Argentine Ornithology*.
George Eastman (*1854, †1932), made photographic paper roll-film.

Dvořák: Symphony No. 4 in G major.
Gilbert and Sullivan: *The Gondoliers*, light opera.
Renoir: *Girls picking Flowers*, French painting.
Seurat: *The Side Show*, French painting.
Van Gogh: (i) *Man with a Pipe*, self-portrait;

Eiffel completed his Tower at Paris, 985 ft high.
Hollerith's punched-card system; now widely used in industry.
Eastman's Kodak camera came into production, using photographic film.
Mering and Minkowski showed that

1889

by Rhodes' concessions in East Africa.
North and South Dakota, Montana and Washington admitted States in Union of the U.S.A.
Flight of Boulanger on threat of treason charge.
Congress of French Revolutionary Labour Party at Bordeaux.
Mayerling tragedy: suicide of Crown Prince Rudolph of Austria and Baroness Maria Vetsera.
Treaty of Acciali: Ethiopia made Italian protectorate.
Portuguese under Pinto tried to extend influence in Zambesi Valley; Anglo-Portuguese dispute.
End of Portuguese Empire in Brazil; Republic proclaimed.
Abdication of King Milan of Serbia; accession of Alexander.
Russian jurors to be nominated by Government.
Aristocratic "Land Captains" replaced elected J.P.s in Russia.
Promulgation of Japanese Constitution.

Mark Twain: *A Connecticut Yankee in King Arthur's Court*, a novel.
Stevenson: *Master of Ballantrae*, novel of time of '45 uprising.
William Butler Yeats (*1865, †1939): *The Wanderings of Oisin*, narrative poem.
Paul Bourget (*1852, †1935): *Le Disciple*, psychological novel.
France: *Thaïs*, a novel.
Gerhart J. Hauptmann (*1862, †1946): *Vor Sonnenaufgang*, German realistic play.
Sudermann: *Die Ehre*, German play.

1890

Parnell vindicated of Phoenix Park murder charges; ruined by O'Shea divorce petition; rejected as leader of Irish Nationalists in Commons.
Omnibus strike in London settled on basis of 12–hour day.
Work of Rhodes Pioneers begun in Southern Rhodesia.
Britain annexed Uganda.
Britain recognized French Protectorate over Madagascar.
Idaho and Wyoming recognized as States of American Union.
Workmen in France allowed compensation for contracts broken by employers.
Treaty of Busah: improved Franco-British relations in West Africa.
†William III of Holland; Luxembourg passed to Duke of Nassau.
Fall of Bismarck; Caprivi, Imperial Chancellor; start of personal rule of William II.

Barrie: *My Lady Nicotine*.
Booth: *In Darkest England*.
Caine: *Bondman*, a novel.
Sir James George Frazer (*1854, †1941): *The Golden Bough* (to 1915), comparative folk-lore.
Morris: *News from Nowhere*, Socialistic prose romance.
Sir William Watson (*1858, †1935): *Wordsworth's Grave*, poetry.
Whistler: *The Gentle Art of Making Enemies*; the painter had a quarrelsome nature.
Paul Claudel (*1868, †1955): *Tête d'Or*, French play.
Stefan George: *Hymnen*, German poetry.
Arno Holz (*1863, †1929): *Die Familie Selicke*, German realistic drama.
Ibsen: *Hedda Gabler*, Norwegian play.
Zola: *La Bête humaine*, French railroad novel.

(ii) *The Olive Grove*, Dutch paintings.
c. Cézanne: *Harlequin*, French painting.
Paris Exhibition: proof of industrial development in France.
Lectures at Dorpat University to be in Russian; German forbidden in schools.
Tschaikowsky: *The Sleeping Princess*, ballet music.
Richard Strauss (*1864, †1949), German prolific composer: *Tod und Verklärung*, tone-poem.

pancreas prevented diabetes.
International metre length of platinum and iridium adopted (see 1799).
Brunner-Mond Salt Union formed; combination of 64 firms.
Establishment of Telephone Co.
First linotype machines in use.
Private tolls abolished on French canals.
Work on Panama Canal stopped; company bankrupt.
Bismarck introduced Old Age Insurance into Germany.
Board of Agriculture became Government Department with Minister.
Panhard and Levassor began using Daimler's engines in French cars; used modern layout.
General Booth: *Survey of London Life and Labour.*
Erection of Tacoma Building, Chicago; 13 storeys high; first sky-scraper.
Technical Education Act: County Councils to levy 1*d*. rate for technical and manual instruction.

†Franck, Belgian organ composer who received acclaim shortly before he died.
Cézanne: *Mme Cézanne in the Conservatory*, French portrait.
Degas: *Dancers in Blue*, French painting.
Pietro Mascagni (*1863, †1945): *Cavalleria Rusticana*, Italian opera—his one success.
Van Gogh: (i) *Portrait of Dr Gachet*, (ii) *Street in Auvers*, Dutch paintings.
Russian opera *Prince Igor*, commenced by Borodin (†1887), completed by Glazunov and Rimsky-Korsakov.
Tschaikowsky: *Queen of Spades*, Russian opera.
Discovery of Cleopatra's tomb.
Olderbank Clubs (see 1882) in Italy suppressed.
Sir B. Baker and Sir J. Fowler completed cantilever Forth Bridge (for railway) at Queensferry, near Edinburgh; length 1⅓ miles; additional (suspension) bridge (for road traffic) alongside in 1964.
Gilbert: *Original Comic Operas.*

Bertillon: *La Photographie judiciare*, in which he explained his anthropometry (see 1882).
Emil von Behring (*1854, †1917), German bacteriologist, discovered immunity to tetanus could be given by use of serum; introduced name "antitoxin".
Halstead, at Johns Hopkins hospital, first used rubber gloves in surgery.
French miners to elect delegates to supervise safety while working.
Opening of first underground railway, City and South London line.
In Chicago, the first entirely steel-framed building was erected.
London-Paris telephone line opened.
Financial panic in London and in Paris.
Moving-picture films, precursor of cinematography (see 1894), shown in New York.
Cyanide process of preparation of gold from crude ore developed in South Africa (see 1887).
Lunacy Act gave management of asylums to visiting committees.

LITERATURE

1890

Zanzibar Settlement: Tanganyika became Imperial German Colony; Germany excluded from Upper Nile; British protectorate over Zanzibar.
Britain ceded Heligoland to Germany.
Zemstva Law in Russia; limited franchise in local government; excluded intellectual professions.
Russia attempted to limit Finnish control over customs and money.
First meeting of Japanese Legislature under new Constitution.

1891

James Keir Hardie elected M.P.; first Independent Labour Party Member.
†Parnell.
Brooklands Agreement: basis for wage negotiations in cotton industry.
Anglo-Portuguese Convention on E. Africa.
Nyasaland became British Protectorate.
Behring Sea Arbitration Treaty signed.
Suicide of Boulanger at Brussels.
French Labour Department formed; Labour Exchanges projected.
French fleet paid official visit to Kronstadt; Franco-Russian entente.
Massacre of Europeans following Arab revolt in Belgian Congo.
Plan to introduce universal military service in Holland failed.
Triple Alliance, Germany, Austria, Italy renewed to 1902.
Law for Protection of Workers: restricted hours for German workers.
Anglo-Italian Agreement: spheres of influence defined in N.E. Africa.
Republican rising in Oporto; failed.
Formation of Young Turk Movement to secure liberal reforms; Committee established at Geneva.
Maxim Gorky began influence towards class war in Russia.

Barrie: *The Little Minister*, novel of love (dramatized 1897).
Conan Doyle: *Adventures of Sherlock Holmes*, detective stories.
Hardy: *Tess of the D'Urbervilles*, a novel.
Henley: *Lyra Heroica*, verse.
Kipling: *The Light that Failed*, novel of a hero who goes blind.
Shaw: *Quintessence of Ibsenism*, tract in praise of Ibsen.
Wilde: (i) *Lord Arthur Savile's Crime*, (ii) *Picture of Dorian Gray*, novels.
Maurice Barrès (*1862, †1923): *Le Jardin de Bérénice*, French novel.
André Gide (*1869, †1951): *Les Cahiers d'André Walter*, French autobiography in fictional form.
Huysmans: *Lá-bas*, French novel of black magic.
Hauptmann: *Einsame Menschen*, German play.
Frank Wedekind (*1864, †1918): *Frühlings Erwachen*, German play.
Selma Lagerlöf (*1858, †1940): *Gösta Berling*, Swedish novel.
Independent Labour Party newspaper, *The Clarion*, published.

Lockyer's theory of stellar evolution.
P. Rudolph's anastigmatic camera lens.
Housing of Working Classes Act.
French explorer Monteil's journey Niger-Kano-Tchad-Tripoli; completed 1892.
First Chinese cotton mill constructed.

Cézanne: (i) *Man with Pipe*, (ii) *Card Players*, French paintings.
Paul Gauguin (*1848, †1903), French artist who contracted venereal disease in later years: (i) *Women on the Beach*, (ii) *Vahini with Gardenia*, French-Tahitian paintings.
All English elementary education to be free.
Tschaikowsky: *Caisse-Noisette* (to 1892), his third and last ballet music; also incidental music for *Snow-Maiden*.
Sir George E. W. Robey (*1869, †1954), comedian, began his professional career.

Dewar liquefied oxygen in quantity.
Beginnings of wireless telegraphy based on work of Clerk Maxwell and Hertz.
René Panhard, French, produced his car chassis.
Tesla further developed high-tension induction coil (1,000,000 volt).
G. E. Hale (*1868, †1938), U.S. astronomer, and Deslandris independently invented the spectro-heliograph.
c. Tuffier, of Paris, performed early lung operation for tuberculosis.
Factory Act: no child under 11 to work in factories.
Small Holdings Act: County Councils empowered to purchase land for letting as smallholdings (under 50 acres).
Eugene Dubois discovered pithecanthropus.
W. L. Judson, of the U.S.A., invented zip fastener, but first *practical* design 1913.
Indian Mint closed to silver.
British South Africa Co. granted use of port of Beira by Portugal.
Bank failures in the U.S.A. and Australia.
Bank of Portugal suspended payment for 60 days.
Widespread famine in Russia.
Building of Trans-Siberian Railway commenced.
Sebastian Z. de Ferranti (*1864, †1930) built Deptford power station for London Electricity Supply Corporation.

LITERATURE

1892

Resignation of Salisbury; Gladstone P.M. for fourth and last time.
Three Independent Labour Party M.P.s elected.
Dr Wilfred Grenfell arrived in Labrador to work for Royal National Mission to Deep Sea Fishermen.
Papal Encyclical *Inter Inumeras* forbade French Catholics to secure political power; urged obedience to civil power.
Failure of Panama Scheme revealed corruption in French Government.
Anarchist outrages in Paris.
French-speaking communes of Alsace-Lorraine ordered to conduct official correspondence in German.
India Councils Act.

Kipling: *Barrack-Room Ballads*, on soldier-life in India.
Yeats: *Countess Kathleen*, poetic play.
Israel Zangwill (*1864, †1926): *Children of the Ghetto*, novel of Jewish life.
Cymru'r Plant, Welsh children's magazine first published.
France: *L'Étui de Nacre*, French short stories.
Maurice Maeterlinck (*1862, †1949): *Pelléas et Mélisande*, Belgian play.
Zola: *Le Débâcle*, French novel.
Hugo von Hofmannsthal (*1874, †1929): *Der Tod des Tizian*, return of Romanticism to German theatre.
Ibsen: *The Master Builder*, Norwegian play.

1893

Gladstone's second Irish Home Rule Bill; rejected by Lords.
National mining strike in Britain.
Durand Agreement: frontier between India and Afghanistan defined.
Matabele War.
U.S. marines overthrew native government in Hawaii.
Bomb thrown at President of France in Chamber.
Ivory Coast became French Colony; French captured Dahomey.
Franco-Russian Alliance with secret military agreements.
Nyssens Electoral Law: universal suffrage in Belgium.
Belgian General Strike: serious riots suppressed by troops.
Proposal for universal suffrage in Holland failed.
Italians defeated Dervishes at Agordat.
First Social Democrats elected to Council of Copenhagen.

Edward F. Benson (*1867, †1940): *Dodo*, a novel.
Conan Doyle: *Memoirs of Sherlock Holmes*, detective stories.
Gerard Manley Hopkins (*1844, †1899): *Poets and Poetry of the Century*, ed. Bridges.
Stevenson: *Catriona*, sequel to *Kidnapped*.
Francis Thompson (*1859, †1907): *Hound of Heaven*, a poem.
Wilde: (i) *Lady Windermere's Fan*, a drama; (ii) *Salome*, a play.
Yeats: *Celtic Twilight*, prose.
Mallarmé: *Vers et Proses*.
Victorien Sardou (*1831, †1908): *Madame Sans-Gêne*, French play.
Ricarda Huch (*1864, †1947): *Ludolf Ursleu*, German novel.
Max Halbe (*1865, †1945): *Jugend*, German drama.

Cézanne: *Still Life with Apples and Primroses.*
Ruggiero Leoncavallo (*1858, †1919): *I Pagliacci*, Italian opera, produced at Milan.
Edvard Munch (*1863, †1944): *Portrait of a Lady in Black*, Norwegian painting.
Gauguin: *Fatata Ti Miti*, French-Tahitian painting.
Renoir: *Noirmoutiers*, French painting.
Toulouse-Lautrec: *A Corner in the Moulin de la Galette*, French painting.
Systematic excavations begun at Delphi by French School at Athens.
Great masonry dam, over 1,000 ft long, in Montgomeryshire, across River Vyrnwy.
Edward German (*1862, †1936): incidental music for *Henry VIII*.

C. F. Cross and E. J. Bevan discovered viscose process for manufacture of rayon.
Salomons and Pyke developed A.C.—D.C. converter.
Sir Frederick Hewitt introduced first practical nitrous oxide apparatus with mixing chamber.
Hudson: *A Naturalist in La Plata*.
Final abandonment of Brunel's wide-gauge on British railways.
Heavyside propounded existence of conducting-layer ionosphere in upper atmosphere.
Construction of Blackwall Tunnel, London, commenced.
British South Africa Co. took over Northern Rhodesia.
Gold discovered in Western Australia.
Bank of Portugal suspended payment of interest on National Debt to some foreign investors.
Russian famine of 1891 continued.
Hendrik A. Lorentz (*1853, †1928), Dutch physicist, who introduced Lorentz transformation, extended Maxwell's electromagnetic theory.

Dvořák: *From the New World*, Czech symphony in E minor.
Engelbert Humperdinck (*1854, †1921): *Hansel and Gretel*, German opera.
Gauguin: *Tahitian Landscape*, French-Tahitian painting.
Arnold Dolmetsch (*1858, †1940): *Interpretation of Music of 17th and 18th Centuries*, standard work.
Munch: *The Cry*, Norwegian expressionist painting.
Gilbert and Sullivan: *Utopia Limited*, light opera.
Tschaikowsky: Symphony No. 6 in B minor (the "Pathetique").
Toulouse-Lautrec: *The Clown Boum-Boum at the Cirque Fernando*, French painting.
Verdi: *Falstaff*, Italian opera based on *Merry Wives of Windsor*.
c. Cézanne: *Boy in a Red Waistcoat*, French painting.
Foundation of Bournemouth Municipal Orchestra.
Foundation, at Oxford, of Home-Students (later becoming St Anne's College) and St

Hermann Dresser introduced acetylsalicylic acid (trade name—aspirin).
Henry Ford (*1863, †1947), American motor manufacturer, designed his first "gasoline buggy".
Otto Lilienthal (*1848, †1896) successfully flew a glider; crashed in 1896 after some 2,000 flights.
Liverpool overhead electric railway built; closed 70 years later.
Opening of Imperial Institute in London.
Erection of 33-in. refractory telescope at Meudon, France.
End of Russian famine (since 1891).
Britain acquired Solomon and Gilbert Islands.
Uganda became British protectorate.
Opening of Corinth Canal (4 miles long).
c. Wilhelm Maybach's float-feed carburettor (original carburettor by Daimler 1876).

1893

Compulsory civil marriage in Hungary.
Alexander Obrenovitch of Serbia declared himself of age.
Formation of Polish Socialist Society.

1894

Retirement of Gladstone; Lord Rosebery P.M.
Harcourt's Budget raised Death Duties.
Parish Councils Act: Parish, Rural and Urban District Councils established.
Alfred Dreyfus (*1859, †1935), French artillery officer, found guilty of treason (see 1906).
President Carnot of France assassinated by Italian anarchist.
French under Joffre captured Timbuktu.
Hawaii became republic.
Sicilian bread riots led to martial law and suppression of Italian socialist societies.
Italians defeated Dervishes at Kassala.
Kurds massacred Armenians at Sassoun.
National Society founded in Greece to extend Greek authority in Balkans.
†Alexander III of Russia; accession of Nicholas II, last Romanov Tsar.
Sergius Witte became Minister of Finance in Russia.
Outbreak of war between Japan and China; Japanese naval victory at Yalu River; capture of Port Arthur.
Alexander Obrenovitch annulled liberal constitution of 1889.

George du Maurier (*1834, †1896): *Trilby*, a novel of Svengali mesmerist.
George (*1847, †1912) and Weedon (*1853, †1919) Grossmith: *Diary of a Nobody*.
Anthony Hope (*1863, †1933): *The Prisoner of Zenda*, novel of "Ruritania".
Kipling: *Jungle Book* animal stories for children.
Moore: *Esther Waters*, a novel.
Stanley Weyman (*1855, †1928): *Under the Red Robe*, historical novel.
Wilde: *A Woman of No Importance*, a play.
Yeats: *Land of Hearts' Desire*, poetic play.
The Yellow Book (to 1897), literary journal, illustrated by Aubrey Beardsley.
France: *Le Lys rouge*, French novel.
Zola: *Lourdes*, French novel.
Shaw: (i) *Arms and the Man*, (ii) *Candida*, plays.

1895

Compulsory retirement of aged Duke of Cambridge as Com. in Chief of British Army.
Liberals defeated at General Election; Salisbury again P.M.
Freetown, Sierra Leone, granted municipal status and privileges.
Anglo-French interests began to conflict in Nile Valley.
U.S. intervened in Anglo-

Grant Allen (*1848, †1899): *The Woman who did*, a novel.
Barrie: *Sentimental Tommy* a novel.
Joseph Conrad (*1857, †1924): *Almayer's Folly*, novel of a Borneo trader.
Corelli: *The Sorrows of Satan*, a novel.
Kenneth Grahame (*1859, †1932): *The Golden Age*, imaginative tales.
Hardy: *Jude the Obscure*, a novel.
Meredith: *The Amazing Marriage*, a novel.

Hilda's College, both for women; Federal University of Wales also founded.

Napoleon Bird, barber of Stockport, played piano marathon of 48 hours non-stop without repetition, from memory.
Debussy: *L'Après-Midi d'un Faune*, French tone-poem by composer who used whole-tone scale and overtones.
Toulouse-Lautrec: *Les Deux Amis*, French painting.
Publication of FitzWilliam Virginals Book (see 1816).
c. Degas: *Femme à sa Toilette*, French painting.
Guaranty Building, Buffalo, early metal-framed building, erected.
R. Strauss: *Guntram*, his first opera, produced at Weimar.
Monet: *Rouen Cathedral*, French painting.
Baron Pierre de Coubertin initiated congress reviving Olympic games.
Beginning of motor-car racing: Paris—Rouen.
Blackpool Tower (518 ft high) opened.

Halstead (U.S.A.) explained his operation for breast-cancer (mastectomy).
Sir William Ramsey (*1852, †1916) and Lord Rayleigh discovered argon; establishment of existence of zero valency.
Flagstaff Observatory, Arizona (Lowell), erected.
Oliver and Schäfer discovered the nature of adrenalin.
Thirlmere dam, for Manchester water supply, completed; aqueduct 96 miles long.
Automatic loom invented in the U.S.A. by J. H. Northrop.
Louis Lumière (*1864, †1948), French, invented the cinematograph.
Berliner modified earlier work on gramophone by using horizontal disc, instead of cylinder, as record; not fully satisfactory until 1897.
Water-tube boilers fitted in H.M. ships *Hornet* and *Sharpshooter*.
Launching of *Turbinia*, first steam-turbine ship.
Merchant Shipping Act; Masters, Mates and Engineers to hold Board of Trade Certificates.
Railway and Canal Traffic Act: fixed existing rates as maxima.
Official opening of Manchester Ship Canal (begun 1887).
Sale of spirits resumed in Russia as State Monopoly.
Formation of French Agricultural Mutual Loan Society.

Cézanne: (i) *Bathers*, French painting, one of several, mainly of nude figures; (ii) *Still Life with Onions*, and other still life studies.
Degas: *Dancers at the Practice Bar*, French painting.
Petipa and Ivanov: *Le Lac des Cygnes*, Russian ballet to music by Tschaikowsky.
Renoir: *Reading*, French painting.
Toulouse-Lautrec: *The Clowness Cha-U-Kao*, French painting.

Wilhelm Konrad Röntgen (*1845, †1923), German physicist, experimented with Crooke's tubes (see 1879) and discovered rays (X-rays) which penetrated glass and other media; terrible injuries suffered by early scientists who did not realize the dangerous nature of these rays.
Ramsey obtained helium, identified by its spectrum with gas observed in sun in 1868, *q.v.*

1895

Venezuelan border dispute; arbitration in Britain's favour.
Dreyfus was refused new trial by French President, Faure.
Nyssens Law extended to Belgian provinces and communes.
Germany, France and Russia united to compel Japan to return Liaotung peninsula to China.
New revolt in Spanish Cuba; brutal suppression led to U.S. protests.
Armenian demonstration in Constantinople led to massacre of 50,000 Armenians.
National League founded in Poland; aimed at autonomy under Russian suzerainty.
Frontiers of Pamirs fixed by Commission of Russians, Afghans and British.
Treaty of Shimonoseki; end of Sino-Japanese war.

Sir Arthur W. Pinero (*1855, †1934): *The Second Mrs Tanqueray*, drama of a woman with a past.
Herbert George Wells (*1866, †1946): *The Time Machine*, science fiction.
Wilde: *The Importance of Being Earnest*, a comedy.
Yeats: *Poems*.
Edmond Rostand (*1868, †1918): *La Princesse Lointaine*, French play.
Verhaeren: *Les Villes Tentaculaires*, poems.
Henry Sienkiewicz (*1846, †1916): *Quo Vadis*, Polish novel of the days of Nero.

1896

Beginning of period of rising prices and falling wages to 1914.
Truck Act: regulated deductions from wages of fines for bad workmanship.
Conciliation Act: boards could settle industrial disputes if both sides willing.
British protectorates established in Sierra Leone and East Africa.
Start of Kitchener's campaign against Khalifa in Sudan.
Jameson Raid in South Africa: British negotiations with Boers (to 1899) failed; Kruger Telegram: Kaiser William II congratulated Kruger of Transvaal on defeat of Jameson Raid.
Utah admitted as State of the Union in the U.S.A.
France annexed Madagascar.
Anglo-French treaty settled boundaries in Siam.
State visit of Tsar Nicholas II to Paris.
Von Houten's Franchise Bill; extended Dutch franchise.
French Tunisian protectorate recognized by Italy.

Sir Max Beerbohm (*1872, †1956), critic, author and caricaturist: *Works of Max Beerbohm*.
Conrad: *An Outcast of the Islands*, novel set in E. Indies.
Corelli: *The Mighty Atom*, a novel.
A. E. Housman (*1859, †1936): *A Shropshire Lad*, lyrics.
William Wymark Jacobs (*1863, †1943): *Many Cargoes*, humorous stories.
Wells: *Island of Dr Moreau*, novel of horror.
Edouard Estaunié (*1862, †1942): *L'Empreinte*, French novel.
Pierre Louÿs (*1870, †1925): *Aphrodite*, French novel.
Hauptmann: *Die Versunkene Glocke*, popular German drama.
Fontane: *Die Poggenpuhls*, German novel.
Anton Pavlovich Chekhov (*1860, †1904): *The Seagull*, Russian play, which was at first a failure.
The Harmsworths began *The Daily Mail*, newspaper.
Russian newspapers granted temporary licences; imported books and newspapers strictly censored.

Sir Henry Wood (*1868, †1944) started Queen's Hall Promenade Concerts.
Marie Wurm gave extemporization concert on themes handed her by an audience in London.
Royal Commission's report on Secondary Education.
Frederick Delius (*1862, †1934): *Over the hills and far away*, orchestral work (performed 1897 at Eberfeld); English composer, first recognized in Germany, later popularized by Beecham in Britain.
R. Strauss: *Till Eulenspiegel's Merry Pranks*, German tone-poem.
National Trust incorporated by Act of Parliament.
On 28th Dec., in the Hotel Scribe, in Paris, was the first public film show in the world.

Thomas Armat of Washington developed modern cinema projection principle.
First motor-car exhibition in London.
Electrification of first *mainline* railway.
Construction of Uganda railway commenced.
Introduction of diphtheria antitoxin.
British East Africa Co. surrendered Kenya as British protectorate.
Completion of Kiel Canal (61 miles long); Germany now a North Sea power.
King C. Gillette, of the U.S.A., invented safety razor.
Hudson: *British Birds*, ornithological work.
Lorentz: *Versuch einer Theorie der electrischen und optischen Erscheinungen in bewegten Körpern*, continuing his electromagnetic studies.

Gauguin: *Why are you angry?*, French-Tahitian painting.
Gilbert and Sullivan: *The Grand Duke*, light opera.
Sir William Nicholson (*1872, †1949), painter and engraver: *The Square Book of Animals*, wood-cuts.
Giacomo Puccini (*1858, †1924): *La Bohème*, Italian opera, produced at Turin; his first major success.
Toulouse-Lautrec: *Maxime Dethomas*, French painting.
Foundation, by 10 members, of the Académie Goncourt.
Royal Victorian Order founded as personal Order of Sovereign.
First public film show in the U.S.A.
F. Strauss: *Also sprach Zarathustra*, German tone-poem.
Edward Macdowell (*1861, †1908), American composer became director of the new Music Department of Columbia University, New York; wrote *Indian Suite* in the same year, using North American Indian airs.
Rimsky-Korsakov: *Sadko*, Russian opera.
First modern Olympic Games; held at Athens (see 1894).

†Nobel and establishment of Nobel Prizes, five annually, for: (i) physics; (ii) physiology or medicine; (iii) chemistry; (iv) literature; (v) furtherance of cause of peace.
Guglielmo Marconi (*1874, †1937), Italian electrical engineer, demonstrated on Salisbury Plain practicability of wireless telegraphy.
Emile Achard first described para-typhoid fever.
Antoine Henri Becquerel (*1852, †1908), French physicist, observed radiation from uranium affected photographic plate; discovery of radio-activity.
Samuel P. Langley (*1834, †1906), U.S. scientist, successfully flew a steam-driven *model* aircraft.
Rehn, of Frankfort, sutured a heart wound; beginnings of heart surgery.
Zeeman observed light emitted by a substance placed in a magnetic field underwent change.
At West Hartlepool was built first all-steel English building.
Locomotives Act: repeal of "Red Flag" restriction; maximum speed raised to 14 m.p.h.
Earliest record of water-chlorination, during typhoid outbreak in Italy.

1896 Italians defeated by Menelek of Abyssinia at Adowa; Treaty of Addis-Ababa; Italian protectorate ended.
Massacre of Armenians by Kurds and Circassians supported by Sultan.
Insurrection in Crete against Turkish rule.

1897 Report of Royal Commission (Eversley) on agricultural depression.
Employers' Liability Act: responsibility for injuries to and compensation of employees injured at work.
Dingley Tariff: high protective duties in the U.S.A. consolidated.
State visit of President Faure of France to St Petersburg cemented Franco-Russian Alliance.
Two German missionaries murdered in Shantung; German interest in China.
Introduction of universal suffrage into Austria.
Austro-Russian treaty on Balkans relaxed tension caused by 30–day war between Greece and Turkey in Macedonia.

Conrad: *The Nigger of the Narcissus*, a tale of the sea.
Henry Havelock Ellis (*1859, †1939): *Studies in Psychology of Sex.*
Wells: *The Invisible Man*, a novel of a scientist who makes himself invisible.
Gide: *Les Nourritures terrestres*, poetic prose.
Loti: *Ramuntcho*, a novel set in the Basque country.
Rostand: *Cyrano de Bergerac*, a drama of a hero sensitive about the size of his nose.
James: *The Spoils of Poynton*, Anglo-American novel.

1898 Britain secured lease of Wei-hai-wei from China.
Battle of Omdurman: British under Kitchener defeated Khalifa and Dervishes.
U.S.A. annexed Hawaii.
End of state of debtor nation, existing from 1783, for the U.S.A.; foreign investments $500 million.
Franco-British tension following "Fashoda Incident".
Personal military service introduced into Holland.
German fleet seized Kiaochow; secured 99–year lease from China.
Foundation of *Flottverein* (Navy League) in Germany; *Reichstag* passed first Navy Act.
U.S. battleship *Maine* blown up in Havana harbour.
Spanish-American War: Spain

Bridges: *Poetical Works.*
Hardy: *Wessex Poems.*
Maurice Hewlett (*1861, †1923): *The Forest Lovers*, romantic novel.
Hope: *Rupert of Hentzau*, another "Ruritanian" novel.
James: *The Turn of the Screw* (contained in *The Two Magics*), on the supernatural.
Shaw: *Plays Pleasant and Unpleasant.*
Wells: *War of the Worlds*, science fiction.
Wilde: *Ballad of Reading Gaol*, a poem; study of a condemned man.
Huysmans: *La Cathédrale*, French novel.
George: *Das Jahr der Seele*, German poems.

Commencement of Klondyke gold rush.
Sudanese railway extended to Wadi Haifa.
Foundation of Russo-Chinese Bank.
Widespread famine in India (to 1897).
Cassini Treaty: China gave Russia right to construct railway through Manchuria to Port Arthur.

Paul Dukas (*1865, †1935), French composer, *The Sorcerer's Apprentice*, symphonic poem.
Gauguin: *Girls bathing in Tahiti*, French-Tahitian painting.
Pissarro: *Night Effect; Boulevard Montmartre*, French painting.
Henri Rousseau (*1844, †1910), untutored artist known as the "Douanier": *The Sleeping Gipsy*.
Sir Henry Tate presented the Tate Gallery to the nation.
Toulouse-Lautrec: *Marcelle*, French painting.
Diamond Jubilee celebrations of Queen Victoria.
R. Strauss: *Don Quixote*, German tone-poem.
First Women's Institute in the world; established at Stoney Creek, Canada.

Sir J. J. Thomson (*1856, †1940) discovered the electron (negatively charged particle).
J. McCreary patented an air-washer intended to purify air in a building; beginnings of air-conditioning.
Foundation of Royal Automobile Club, London.
Trunk telephone wires tranferrred to control of G.P.O.
Sir Ronald Ross (*1857, †1932), bacteriologist, identified cause of malaria and studied the disease.
Berthelot: *Thermochemie*, extending his *Méchanique chimique* (see 1878).
Trained nurses only to be employed in hospitals.
Beginnings of Monotype system of typesetting.
†S. A. Andrée, when attempting to explore Polar regions in free-flying balloon.

H. P. Beridge erected Amsterdam Bourse.
Samuel Coleridge-Taylor (*1875, †1912), coloured composer of Croydon: *Hiawatha's Wedding Feast*.
Cézanne: *The Montaigne Sante-Victoire seen from Bibemus*, French Impressionist painting.
Gauguin: *Whence do we come? Who are we? Where are we going?*, huge painting in Tahiti.
Giordano: *Fedora*, opera noted for introducing bicycles on the stage.
Degas: *Woman drying her neck*, French nude study.
University of London Act reorganized it as teaching university.
Agitation against growth of ritualistic practices in the Church of England.
Rimsky-Korsakov: *Tsar Saltan*, Russian opera.
Sergei Rachmaninoff (*1873, †1943),

Pierre Curie (*1859, †1906) and Marie Curie (*1867, †1934), French, discovered radium and polonium.
Pickering, using photographic plate, found the 9 moons of Saturn.
First record of myxomatosis (rabbit disease).
Ramsay discovered xenon, krypton and neon, inert atmospheric gases.
Electrification of underground railway from Mansion House to Waterloo.
Rudolf Diesel (*1858, †1913), German engineer, demonstrated his diesel engine (requiring no sparking-plug).
French quick-firing "75" gun produced.
M. J. Owens, of the U.S.A., designed automatic machine for making bottles.
Marconi established wireless communication between Bournemouth and Isle of Wight.
K. Shiga, of Japan, discovered the bacillus of dysentery.

1898 defeated at Santiago and Manila; Treaty of Paris ended war; Cuba independent; the U.S.A. acquired Philippines.

Powers appointed Prince George of Greece as High Commissioner in Crete; under Turkish suzerainty.

Workmens' Social Democratic Party formed in Russia.

"Hundred Days of Reform" in China; deposition of Kuang-Hsu and reinstatement of Empress Dowager; suppression of Reform.

1899 London County Council established; lasted to 1965.

General Federation of Trade Unions in England formed.

Anglo-Egyptian condominium over Sudan established.

War between Boers and British in South Africa; Boers invaded Natal; British defeated at Magersfontein, Stormberg, Colenso; Siege of Ladysmith.

Permanent Court of Arbitration set up at the Hague.

Anglo-French Convention settled spheres of influence in West Africa.

Macedonian Committee formed at Sofia.

Nicholas II ended independence of Finland.

Russian persecution of Armenians in Caucasus.

Migration of Russian peasants made easier by State Council.

Ernest W. Hornung (*1866, †1921): *The Amateur Cracksman*, adventures of Raffles.

Kipling: *Stalky and Co.*, schoolboy adventures.

James Moffat (*1870, †1944): colloquial translation of *New Testament*.

Pinero: *Trelawny of the Wells*, comedy of stage life.

Somerville and Ross (pseudonym of Edith Somerville (*1858, †1949) and Violet Martin): *Some Experiences of an Irish R.M.*

Yeats: *The Wind among the Reeds*, poems.

René Bazin (*1853, †1932): *La Terre qui meurt*, French novel.

Moréas: *Les Stances*, poems.

Tolstoy: *Resurrection*, Russian novel.

Ibsen: *When We Dead Awaken*, Norwegian play, his last important work.

1900 Labour Representation Committee set up; commencement of Labour Party.

Tonga placed under British protection.

Commonwealth of Australia Constitution Act; established federalism.

Roberts replaced Buller in South Africa; Relief of Ladysmith, Mafeking, Kimberley; Boer leader Kronje surrendered at Paardeberg; Transvaal and Orange Free State annexed by Britain.

Conrad: *Lord Jim*, a novel.

Theodore Dreiser (*1871, †1945): *Sister Carrie*, U.S. novel of an actress.

Shaw: *Three Plays for Puritans* [(i) *The Devil's Disciple*, (ii) *Caesar and Cleopatra* (ii) *Captain Brassbound's Conversion*].

Wells: *Love and Mr Lewisham*, a novel.

Henri Bergson (*1859, †1941): *Le Rire*, philosophy.

Sidonie G. Colette (*1873, †1954): *Claudine à l'École*, French novel.

Charles Péguy (*1873, †1914) founded *Cahiers de la Quinzaine* (1900–14).

Rainer Maria Rilke (*1875, †1926):

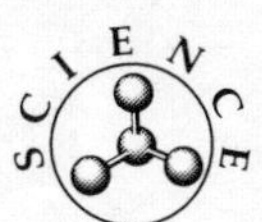

Russian composer, invited to conduct in London as result of composition of C minor prelude.

Konstantin Tsiolkovski stated principles of rocket reaction propulsion.
Introduction of Imperial Penny Postage.
Work begun on Aswan Dam.
British goods given preferential tariff in Canada.
Congo railway completed to Stanley Pools.
Swiss railways nationalized.
Serious food riots in Italy.
Russia secured 25–year lease of Port Arthur from China.

Coleridge-Taylor: *The Death of Minnehaha*, choral work.
Dvořák: *Kate and the Devil*, Czech opera.
Gauguin: *The Tahitian Women with Mangoes*, French-Tahitian painting.
Sir (William) Edward Elgar (*1857, †1934): *Enigma Variations*, music representing his acquaintances.
Jean Sibelius (*1865, †1957): *Finlandia*, Finnish tone-poem.
Toulouse-Lautrec: *At the Circus*, 39 drawings, mainly in crayon.
Foundation of Ruskin College, Oxford (not part of the University), by Walter Vrooman, American, for socialistic education.
Establishment of Board of Education.
Russian universities closed because of student disorders.

A. L. Debierne discovered actinium, heaviest rare-earth metal.
Parsons' turbo-alternator developed.
Lummer and Pringsheim studied black body radiation.
First R.N. turbine ships, destroyers *Cobra* and *Viper*, built.
Wireless telegraphy from England to France.
First garden city; established at Letchworth.
Further famine in India.
Organization of Board of Labour in France.
D. Hilbert (*1862, †1943): *Grundlagen der Geometrie*, German modern axiomatic research based on Greek geometry.
S.S. *Oceanic*, White Star Line, launched; first large luxury liner.

Coleridge-Taylor: *Hiawatha's Departure*, choral work.
Elgar: *The Dream of Gerontius*, an oratorio.
Gustav Holst (*1874, †1934): *Cotswolds Symphony*, his first notable work.
Pablo Picasso (*1881, †1973): *Le Moulin de la Galette*, Spanish painting of Montmartre.
c. Renoir: *Building in progress in the Sacré-Cœur*, French painting.
c. Rousseau: *The Customs House*, French painting.
Puccini: *La Tosca*, Italian opera.
German: music for *Nell Gwynn*.

G. Ricci and T. Levi-Civita developed the absolute differential calculus from earlier concept of tensors.
Max Planck (*1858, †1947) first proposed quantum theory.
Peter N. Lebedev (*1866, †1912), Russian physicist, demonstrated the existence of light-pressure.
J. E. Brandenburger invented cellophane.
Construction of first Zeppelin.
Central London Underground opened; London's tubes electrified.
Escalator, invented in the U.S.A., exhibited in Paris Exhibition.

LITERATURE

	History	Literature
1900	Franco-Italian Treaty concerning North African colonies. Proportionate Representation in Belgium. Tirpitz induced German *Reichstag* to pass Navy Act doubling navy by 1920. Germany received Samoa in Pacific. Assassination of King Humbert of Italy; accession of Victor Emmanuel III. Socialist Revolutionary Party formed in Russia; advocated Terrorism. Russians occupied Manchuria; massacred 45,000 Chinese. Boxer Rebellion in China: national resentment at foreign intervention; suppressed.	*Geschichten vom lieben Gott.* Rostand: *L'Aiglon*, French play with Napoleon II as hero.
1901	†Victoria; accession of Edward VII. Inauguration of Australian Commonwealth. Peace Protocol with China after Boxer Rebellion. Taff Vale Case: Trade Unions in Britain liable for actions of tort. Northern Nigeria became British protectorate. President McKinley, U.S.A., assassinated; succeeded by Theodore Roosevelt. Law of Associations: gave French Roman Catholics right to form Associations, if neither secret nor illegal. Labour Councils in France to settle disputes between masters and men. Franco-Italian agreement defined spheres of interest in Mediterranean. Compulsory military service in Sweden and Norway. New Constitution in Serbia issued by Alexander. Creation of North Western Frontier Province in India.	Barrie: *Quality Street*, a play. Butler: *Erewhon Revisited*, sequal to *Erewhon*. Kipling: *Kim*, novel of Indian life. Sir John Rhys: *Celtic Folklore*. Yeats: *Poems*. Sir Owen M. Edwards (*1858, †1920): *Wales*, the story of a nation. Bazin: *Les Oberlé*, novel about Alsace and Lorraine. Frank Norris (*1870, †1902), American novelist: *The Octopus*, first part of a trilogy on wheat. Strindberg: *The Dance of Death*, a play of the duel to the death between husband and wife. Thomas Mann (*1875, †1955): *Buddenbrooks*, German novel describing the decline of a Lübeck family; this work brought him fame.
1902	Resignation of Salisbury; Arthur Balfour succeeded as P.M. First celebration of Empire Day;	Hilaire Belloc (*1870, †1953): *The Path to Rome*, a travel walk. Enoch Arnold Bennett (*1867, †1931): *The Grand Babylon Hotel*, a novel.

W. Nicholson: *Characters of Romance*, woodcuts.
Sindacalisti, revolutionary society, formed in Italy.
National Brass Band contests instituted (at the Crystal Palace).
School leaving age raised to 14.
Foundation of Birmingham University.
Wallace Collection opened in London.
Davis Cup presented for men's international lawn tennis.

Royal Niger Co.'s territories taken over by British Government.
Working day in France limited to 10 hours.
2,000 km. of new canals completed in France since 1876.
60% of Russian railways brought under State control by Witte.
Yangtze Convention: Britain and Germany, guaranteed freedom of trade, to uphold Chinese integrity.
Hugo de Vries (*1848, †1935), Dutch botanist: *The Mutation Theory*, (to 1903) modern evolution theory.
F. E. Dorn, German, discovered radon, heavy gas.
Benjamin Holt, of the U.S.A. invented caterpillar tractor.
Sigmund Freud (*1856, †1936): *Traumdeutung*, Austrian interpretation of dreams.

Dvořák: *Russalka*, Czech opera.
Elgar: *Cockaigne*, an overture.
Gauguin: *Still Life with Apples*, French painting.
Picasso: *Bal Tabarin*, Spanish painting.
Renoir: *Young Renoir drawing*, French painting.
Walter Sickert (*1860, †1942), noted for atmosphere: *Interior of St Mark's, Venice*, a painting.
Cockerton Judgment: illegal to provide secondary education out of rate levied by Schools Board under 1870 Act.
Boxing recognized as legal sport in England.
German completed Sullivan's light opera *The Emerald Isle*.
Opening of Wigmore Hall, London.

Marconi transmitted morse wireless signals from Poldhu, Cornwall, to St John's, Newfoundland.
First award of Nobel Prizes.
Becquerel discovered dangerous effects of radioactivity on humans.
First isolation of adrenalin, a hormone.
Peter Cooper-Hewitt produced mercury vapour-lamp; invented by Arons in 1892.
First electric tram ran in London.
First British submarine launched at Barrow-in-Furness.
Uganda railway reached Lake Victoria.
U.S. Steel Corporation organized under J.P. Morgan and Co., bankers.
Opening of Trans-Siberian railway.
Hay-Pauncefort Treaty gave U.S. power to build and police Panama Canal if open to shipping in peace or war.
Robert Falcon Scott (*1868, †1912) commanded the *Discovery* on antarctic exploration.

Enrico Caruso (*1873, †1921), Italian tenor, made his first gramophone record; in all, 154 recordings.
Gauguin: *The Call*, French painting.

Establishment of Metropolitan Water Board, supplying London.
Telegraphy applied to ships.
Trans-Pacific Cable laid.

	History	Literature
1902	renamed Commonwealth Day in 1959. Joseph Chamberlain advocated return to Protection and Imperial Preference. Anglo-German fleet seized Venezuelan fleet to recover debts and reparations. Peace of Vereeniging; ended Boer War. Franco-Italian secret treaty: Italy to remain neutral if France were attacked by third power. Failure of second Belgian General Strike. Triple Alliance (Germany, Austria, Italy) renewed to 1914. Italian designs on Tripoli conditionally approved by France and Austria. Russo-Japanese Convention: Russians agreed to evacuate Manchuria in 18 months. Anglo-Japanese Treaty: for mutual defence and to maintain *status quo* in Far East.	Conrad: *Youth*, stories. Conan Doyle: *The Hound of the Baskervilles*, Sherlock Holmes story. James: *Wings of the Dove*, a novel. Kipling: *Just So Stories*, animal stories for children. Arthur Edward Woodley Mason (*1865, †1948): *The Four Feathers*, a novel. Beatrix Potter (*1866, †1943): *Peter Rabbit*, children's story. Walter de la Mare (*1873, †1956): *Songs of Childhood*, poetry for children. Yeats: *Cathleen Ni Houlihan*, a drama. Gide: *L'Immoraliste*, French novel. Charles Maurras (*1868, †1952): *Les Amants de Venise*, on the Sand-Musset love story. Chekhov: *Three Sisters*, Russian play.
1903	Britain and France agreed to settle disputes through International Court at The Hague. Joseph Chamberlain began Tariff Reform campaign. Women's Social and Political Union formed to demand votes for women. Wyndham's Act: Irish landlords to be bought out; peasant ownership; repayments over 68½ years. Alaskan frontier question between Canada and U.S.A. settled by arbitration. British expeditionary force sent to Tibet. Exchange of State visits between London and Paris; Arbitration Treaty established *Entente Cordiale*. Dutch Democratic Labour Party formed: General Strike suppressed by troops. Mursteg Programme: Austro-Russian proposals to solve Macedonian problems; failed.	Barrie: *The Admirable Crichton*, a play. Butler: *The Way of All Flesh*, semi-autobiographical novel of middle-class life published posthumously. Erskine Childers (*1870, †1922): *The Riddle of the Sands*, a novel. Conrad: *Typhoon*, short story. George Gissing (*1857, †1903): *Private Papers of Henry Ryecroft*, a novel, largely autobiographical. James: *The Ambassadors*, a novel. Jack London (*1876, †1916): *The Call of the Wild*, American novel with a dog hero. Shaw: *Man and Superman*, a play. René Boylesve (*1867, †1926): *L'Enfant á la Balustrade*, French novel: study of narrow provincial life. T. Mann: *Tonio Kröger*, a short novel.

Debussy: *Pelléas et Mélisande*, French opera.
Picasso: *Nude, Back View*, Spanish painting.
Sir Giles Gilbert Scott (*1880, †1960) designed Liverpool Cathedral.
Institution of the Order of Merit for distinguished service to the State; limited to 24 holders at one time.
Education Act: abolished School Board system; local control in hands of Town and County Council; Secondary Education authorized out of rates.
British Academy granted Royal Charter.
Esperanto introduced into England.
Elgar: *Coronation Ode*, choral work.
German: *Merrie England*, light opera.

Completion of Aswan Dam in Egypt.
French working day reduced to 9½ hours.
Public Health Act in France improved artisan living conditions.
White settlement of Kenya Highlands began.
St Pierre, Martinique, destroyed by earthquake.
Abdul Hamid gave Germany concessions to build railway to Baghdad; rail system to stretch from Hamburg to Persian Gulf.
Tientsin Sanitary Police established: first Chinese public health measure.
F. A. Krupp (*1854, †1902) took over Germania shipbuilding yard at Kiel; great armaments firm developed.

Coronation Durbar for Edward VII, King-Emperor, at Delhi.
Degas: *Dancers in Yellow Skirts*, French pastel.
Elgar: *The Apostles*, an oratorio.
German: *A Princess of Kensington*, light opera.
Pissarro: *Bridge at Bruges*, French painting.
First *recording* of an opera; Verdi's *Ernani*.
Foundation of Universities at Liverpool and Manchester.
Establishment of Workers' Educational Association.
Building of Letchworth Garden City.
R. Strauss: *Symphonia domestica*, German tone-poem.
Picasso: (i) *Guitarist*, (ii) *La Tragédie*, (iii) *La Famille Soler*, Spanish painting.

First radio press messages published by *The Times*.
Orville (*1871, †1948) and Wilbur (*1867, †1912) Wright, of the U.S.A., who experimented as early as 1900, made first flight in heavier-than-air machine; used 12–h.p. engine.
Tsiolkovski published a paper on astronautics.
Henry Ford, American, founded his famous motor company.
Wilhelm Einthoven invented the electro-cardiograph (for measuring heart contractions).
Phenobarbitone, long-acting sedative, discovered.
Road speed limit in England increased to 20 m.p.h.
Introduction of Belgian Old Age Pension scheme.
Foundation of Bank of Persian Loans with large Russian interests.
J. J. Thomson: *Conduction of Electricity through Gases*.
Bertrand Arthur William Russell (*1872,

LITERATURE

	History	Literature
1903	Alexander Obrenovitch and Queen Draga of Serbia assassinated; Peter Karageorgevitch elected king. Russian massacre of Jews at Kishinyov. Russia refused to evacuate Manchuria under terms of Russo-Japanese Convention.	
1904	*Entente Cordiale* strengthened; helped to settle Anglo-Russian difficulties after Dogger Bank incident. Election of Theodore Roosevelt as President of U.S.A. (to 1909). Franco-British accord over Egypt. Kaiser William II urged Tsar of Russia to form league with France and Germany against Britain. Revolt of Hereros of S.W. Africa; resented German interference with their pastures. Italian General Strike. Cretans demanded union with Greece; Powers refused; Cretans rebelled. Union of Liberators formed in Russia. Outbreak of Russo-Japanese War; Port Arthur besieged by Japanese, by land and sea; Russians defeated at Liaotung and on the Shaho. Zemstvo members at St Petersburg demanded constitutional reform in Russia; promised but not effected.	Barrie: *Peter Pan*, play for children. Belloc: *The Old Road*. Bennett: *Anna of the Five Towns*, novel. Gilbert Keith Chesterton (*1874, †1936): *Napoleon of Notting Hill*, a novel. Conrad: *Nostromo*, novel of South American life. Hardy: *The Dynasts*, poem dealing with the Napoleonic wars. "O. Henry" (*1862, †1910): *Cabbages and Kings*, American short stories. Wells: *The Food of the Gods*, a novel. Romain Rolland (*1866, †1944): *Jean-Christophe* (written 1904–1912) French novel. Hermann Hesse (*1877, †1964): *Peter Camenzind*, German novel of adolescence. Wedekind: *Die Büchse der Pandora*, German play. Chekhov: *The Cherry Orchard*, Russian play.
1905	Resignation of Balfour; Liberals under Campbell-Bannerman in power. Royal Commission (to 1909) on Poor Law. Organization of Sinn Fein Party in Ireland. Saskatchewan and Alberta became separate provinces of Canada. French law separating Church and State passed. French aims in Morocco checked by Germany. Treaty of Björko: Russo-German alliance; Tsar forced to rescind	Bennett: *Sacred and Profane Love*, novel. Ernest Dowson (*1867, †1900): *Poems*. Edward Morgan Forster (*1879, †1970): *Where Angels Fear to Tread*, his first novel. Baroness Emmuska Orczy (*1865, †1947): *The Scarlet Pimpernel*, novel of the French revolution. Shaw: *Major Barbara*, a play; the heroine joins the Salvation Army. J. M. Synge (*1871, †1909): *Riders to the Sea*, tragedy of fisher folk. Wells: *Kipps*, novel of a draper's apprentice. Wilde: *De Profundis*, essay of confession written in prison. Heinrich Mann (*1871, †1950): *Professor*

†1970): *Principles of Mathematics*.
G.W.R. introduced early motor-bus service from Helston to the Lizard; initiation of bus services largely came from railway companies.

Dvořák: *Armida*, Czech opera.
Pierre Bonnard (*1867, †1947): *The Boulevard*, French painting.
Holst: *The Mystic Trumpeter*, for soprano solo and orchestra.
Picasso: *The Two Sisters*, Spanish nude painting.
Puccini: *Madame Butterfly*, Italian opera.
Paul Signac (*1863, †1935): *Venice, The Yellow Sail*, by the French Impressionist painter.
The London Symphony Orchestra gave its first concert.
William Archer and Harvey Granville Barker produced proposals for National Theatre.
Foundation of Leeds University.
Work begun on Liverpool Anglican Cathedral, largest in Britain.
Rimsky-Korsakov: *Kitezh*, Russian opera.
Rodin: (i) *Ugolin*, (ii) *Le Penseur*, French sculptures.
Construction of Apulian aqueduct begun.
Completion of Great Salt Lake Viaduct (11.8 miles of bridging), Utah, U.S.A.
Excavation by Gustavson of fine Oseberg burial ship (*c*. 850).

Sir John A. Fleming (*1849, †1945) used thermionic valve, having filament and anode, for detection of wireless waves; de Forest later added a grid, creating a triode valve.
F. S. Kipping discovered silicones.
C. S. Rolls became interested in the fine cars built by H. Royce (see 1884); led to foundation of Rolls-Royce Ltd. in 1906.
First engine-driven life-boat built.
Licensing Act: compensation to publicans when licence revoked.
Formation of Ladies' Automobile Club.
Anglo-French settlement of Fishing Rights disputes in Newfoundland.
Construction of Panama Canal resumed.
Freud: *Psychopathology of Everyday Life*, major work of Austrian psychiatrist.
Photo-electric cell developed through J. Elster and H. Geitel.
Anschütz-Kaempfe: gyro-compass (see 1911).

Cézanne painted last of some 60 pictures of La Montagne Sainte-Victoire.
Humperdinck: *The Sleeping Beauty*, German opera.
Franz Lehár (*1870, †1948): *The Merry Widow*, Hungarian light opera.
Macdowell, American composer, became insane.
Munch: *The Bridge*, Norwegian painting.
Picasso: (i) *La Belle Hollandaise*, Spanish painting sold to Queensland Art Gallery for £55,000; (ii) *La Boule*, painting of two acrobats.
Rousseau: *Banks of the Oise*, French painting.

Albert Einstein (*1879, †1955) completely explained Brownian molecular movement; began work on relativity at about the same time; also in same year started extending Planck's quantum theory.
Discovery of Cullinan diamond (world's largest) of over 3,000 carats; presented to Edward VII in 1907.
Mount Wilson observatory, California, built.
Herbert Austin (*1866, †1941) began manufacturing his cars.
Motor-driven fire engines brought into commission.
Motor-buses first used in London.

1905 treaty because contrary to Franco-Russian *Dual Entente*.
Italian protectorate established in Somaliland.
Norwegian *Storthing* dissolved Swedish-Norwegian Union; Oscar II accepted this; Prince Charles of Denmark elected King of Norway, as Haakon VII.
Universal suffrage introduced into Hungary.
Russians surrendered Port Arthur; Russian Baltic fleet destroyed by Togo at Tsushima; Treaty of Portsmouth (New Hampshire) ended Russo-Japanese War.
Many unions in Russia; Union of Unions formed by Miliukov.
Revolution in Russia following "Blood Sunday"; St Petersburg Soviet under Leon Trotsky.
October Manifesto: Nicholas II promised a *Duma* with full legislative powers; ended Autocracy in Russia.
Partition of Bengal: unrest in India.

Unrat, German novel, by the brother of Thomas Mann, showing the decline of a schoolmaster.
Rilke: *Das Stundenbuch*, German lyric poetry.
Hesse: *Unterm Rad*, German novel.
Pio Baroja (*1872, †1956), Spanish novelist: *La lucha por la vida* (begun 1904), trilogy of Madrid underworld.

1906 General Election resulted in great Liberal victory; supported by Irish Nationalists and Labour Party in Commons.
Trades Disputes Act: Unions exempted from actions for tort (see 1901).
Workmen's Compensation Act: to include domestic servants.
Responsible government granted to Transvaal.
Government of Papua transferred to Australia.
Court of Appeal declared Dreyfus innocent of treason; restored to Army rank (see 1894).
Conference at Algeciras; French rights in Morocco recognized.
Pope Pius X ordered French Catholics not to join denominational Associations.
Establishment of Colonial Department in German Foreign Office.

Sir Winston Spencer Churchill (*1874, †1965): *Lord Randolph Churchill*, biography of his father.
Conrad: *Mirror of the Sea*, memories and impressions.
De la Mare: *Poems*.
William De Morgan (*1839, †1917): *Joseph Vance*, a novel.
Henry Watson Fowler (*1839, †1934), lexicographer and grammarian: *The King's English*.
John Galsworthy (*1867, †1933): *The Man of Property*, first novel in the *Forsyte Saga*.
London: *White Fang*, novel of a wild dog.
Upton Sinclair (*1878, †1968), *The Jungle*, U.S. novel of life in the raw in Chicago.
Edgar Wallace (*1875, †1932): *The Four Just Men*, crime novel.
Publication of *John Bull* begun by Horatio Bottomley.

R. Strauss: *Salome*, German opera produced at Dresden.
Aldwych and Kingsway theatres opened in London.
Sheffield University founded.
Sir Thomas Beecham (*1879, †1961) first appeared as a conductor in London.
Manuel de Falla (*1876, †1946), Spanish composer, first gained recognition by opera *La Vida Breve*.
Establishment of Kingsmead, Quaker missionary training-college at Selly Oak, as result of Cadbury's gift (1903) of Woodbrooke to the society.
Binet-Simon intelligence tests published (for classification of backward children).
First real cinema opened at Pittsburgh, U.S.A.

Cawdor Memorandum: proposed annual construction of four Dreadnoughts.
First Motor Exhibition opened at Islington.
Regular steam-boat services established on Thames.
Building of first German Dreadnought begun.
State to take over Italian railways; railway workers to be denied the right to strike.
Financial Commission, supported by international fleet, in Macedonia.
Sultan Abdul Hamid gave Germans permission to build branch of Berlin-Baghdad railway towards Mecca.
Commercial manufacture of rayon yard by viscose process, based on work of C. F. Cross and E. J. Bevan and, later, Stearn, Topham and Mueller.

Elgar: *The Kingdom*, an oratorio.
Michel Fokine (*1880, †1942): *Chopiniana*, later became *Les Sylphides*, a ballet to Chopin's music.
Cézanne: (i) *Portrait of Vallier*, (ii) *Still Life with Chair, Bottles and Apples*, French paintings.
Rousseau: *Summer, the Pasture*, French painting.
c. Beginnings of *Fauves* (wild beasts) Movement started by Henri Matisse (*1869, †1954) and André Derain (*1880, †1954); pure violet colour and simplified form used.
Rachmaninoff: *Francesca da Rimini*, Russian opera.
Ralph Vaughan William (*1872, †1958), composer keenly interested in folk-song: Three Norfolk rhapsodies.
Picasso: *Gertrude Stein*, Spanish portrait.
Dame Ethel M. Smyth (*1858, †1944): *The Wreckers*, an opera.
First French Grand Prix (for motor cars).

Launching of H.M.S. *Dreadnought*, first battleship in modern style; turbine driven and heavily armed; speed 21 knots.
Launching of liner *Lusitania*.
Bakerloo and Piccadilly tube lines opened in London.
Tungsten-filament electric lamps in use.
German Navy Act: strengthened navy and made Kiel Canal usable by dreadnoughts.
Agricultural reforms in S. Italy to relieve distress.
Franco-British loans to Russia after war with Japan.
Official opening of Vauxhall Bridge.
Opening of Simplon Tunnel, 12½ miles long; begun 1896.
San Francisco suffered severe earthquake followed by widespread fire.
Clement von Pirquet introduced term *allergy* in medicine.
Roald Amundsen (*1872, †1928), Norwegian explorer, traversed North-West Passage (begun 1903); determined position of magnetic North Pole.

Year	History	Literature
1906	Annual average emigration of Germans dropped from 750,000 (1870–1900) to 20,000. Young Turks Committee transferred from Geneva to Salonika. Meeting of First *Duma* in St Petersburg; failed to establish good relations with Tsar's ministers; dismissed; Viborg Manifesto.	
1907	Women allowed to serve on Local Government Councils. Territorial Army introduced into Britain by Haldane, War Minister. Railway Conciliation Boards established. United Methodist Church established. Responsible government granted to Orange River Colony. New Zealand received Dominion status. Anarchy in Morocco; murder of French workmen at Casablanca. Oklahoma admitted to Statehood in the U.S.A. Revolt of Hereros crushed by German troops. General League of German Trade Unions formed. Germany refused armament limitations proposed by Hague Peace Conference. Guaranteeing Treaty between: (1) Norway, and (2) Britain, Russia, Germany and France. Parliamentary rule suppressed in Portugal by Carlos I. Edward VII visited Nicholas II of Russia; Anglo-Russian differences settled; *Dual Entente* became *Triple Entente* of France, Russia, Britain. Hague Peace Conference to limit armaments: failed; rejected ban on aerial bombing in war. Meeting of Second Russian *Duma*; Stolypin chief minister; *Duma* dissolved; election of Third *Duma*.	Belloc: *Cautionary Tales for Children*, poems. Conrad: *The Secret Agent*, a novel. Forster: *The Longest Journey*, a novel. "George Brown" (*1863, †1927): *Memoirs of a Surrey Labourer*. Sir Edmund William Gosse (*1849, †1928): *Father and Son*, autobiography published anonymously. Synge: *Playboy of the Western World*, a drama, which provoked riots in the Abbey Theatre, Dublin. Yeats: *Deirdre*, a drama. George: *Der Siebente Ring*, German poetry. Strindberg: *The Ghost Sonata*, Swedish drama. Jacinto Benavente (*1866, †1954): *Los Intereses Creados*, Spanish play of two young men who use their wits to succeed. Pope Pius X ordered Benedictine Order to revise *Vulgate*. Italian bishops urged to suppress Modernist teaching in schools and press.
1908	†Campbell-Bannermann; Herbert Asquith Prime Minister to 1916. Children's Act: Separate Juvenile Courts established.	Barrie: *What Every Woman Knows*, a play. Bennett: *The Old Wives' Tale*, a novel of two sisters.

First International Conference for cancer research; at Heidelberg and Frankfurt.
Education Authorities to provide meals for poor children.

Delius: *A Village Romeo and Juliet*, opera.
Sergei Pavlovich Diaghilev (*1872, †1929), Russian impresario called the "Father of Ballet", began popularizing the art and producing operas in the capital cities.
Elgar: *The Wand of Youth*, orchestral work (to 1908).
German: *Tom Jones*, light opera.
Holst: *Somerset Rhapsody*, based on folk-song.
Gustav Mahler (*1860, †1911), Austrian composer: Symphony No. 8 in E♭ major ("The Symphony of a Thousand").
Picasso and Georges Braque (*1882, †1963) evolved the Cubist Movement: "Paint not what you see but what you know is there", often several aspects of a subject in the same picture.
Rousseau: *The Snake Charmer*, French painting.
Formation of Joint Committee of Oxford University and Workers' Educational Association.
Rolland: *Vie de Beethoven*, French biography of the composer.

Henri Farman (*1874, †1958) made a successful biplane.
G. Urbain separated ytterbium and lutecium, rare metals.
Jannsky discovered the four principal blood groups (O, A, B, AB) in man; led to successful blood transfusions.
August von Wassermann (*1866, †1925) discovered his test for syphilis, determining the seriousness of the infection.
William Willett (*1856, †1915) proposed "daylight saving"; adopted 1916, *q.v.*.
Introduction of medical inspection of school-children.
Opening of Northern Line of London Underground Railway.
Brooklands Motor Racing Circuit opened.
Companies Act: limited-liability principle applied to private companies.
Taxi-cabs first legally recognized in Britain.
Channel Tunnel Scheme rejected by Parliament.
Electric washing-machine invented by Hurley Machine Co., of the U.S.A.
First airship flew over London.
c. First attempts at preservation of fruit by freezing.
S.S. *Mauretania*, 30,700 tons, launched; speed 26 knots.
Imperial College of Science and Technology, part of London University, created by amalgamating Royal College of Science, City and Guilds Tech. Coll. and Royal School of Mines.

Elgar: Symphony No. 1 in A♭.
Benno Moiseiwitsch (*1890, †1963), pianist, made his début at Queen's Hall, London.
Monet: (i) *The Island of San Giorgio Maggiore*,

Agricultural Smallholdings Act: tenant farmers free to choose own husbandry methods; National Farmers' Union founded.

1908

Coal Mines Regulation Act: 8–hour-day underground.
First woman Mayor; elected at Aldeburgh, Suffolk.
Foundation of Women's Freedom League.
Abdul Aziz of Morocco deposed by Mulai Hafid; French occupied Casablanca.
Expropriation Law: authorized further German settlement in Poland.
Baltic and North Sea Convention.
Assassination of Carlos I of Portugal and Crown Prince; accession and flight of Manuel II.
Austria annexed Bosnia; protectorate since 1878.
Ferdinand proclaimed himself Tsar of independent Bulgaria.
Cretans again demanded union with Greece.
Revolt in Constantinople against loss of Crete: Sultan Abdul Hamid proclaimed Liberal Constitution.
Russian *Duma* permitted to discuss of Budget.
Russian Government took control of Finnish affairs.
Formation of Muslim League in India.
†Tz'u-hsi, Dowager Empress of China; end of prestige of Manchu rulers.

Chesterton: *The Man Who Was Thursday,* a novel.
William Henry Davies (*1871, †1940): *The Autobiography of a Super-Tramp,* by the Welsh poet.
Forster: *A Room with a View,* a novel.
Grahame: *The Wind in the Willows,* a novel and fantasy of animal life.
Joseph Bédier (*1864, †1938): *Les Légendes épiques,* a study of old French epic poetry.
Jules Romains (*1885, †1972): *La Vie unanime,* French poems.

1909

People's Budget introduced by Lloyd George.
Introduction of Labour Exchanges in Britain.
Osborne Judgment: subscriptions to political levy by trade unionists illegal.
Women's Suffrage movement became militant.
Report on Poor Law and Unemployment (1905); no government action.
South Africa Act: Union of Cape Colony, Transvaal and Orange Free State.
Postal workers struck in France to demand right to form Trade Union.

John Buchan (*1875, †1940): *Prester John,* a novel.
Evans: *Scripta Minoa,* on pre-Phoenician Minoan script.
Galsworthy: (i) *The Silver Box,* (ii) *Strife,* plays on social problems.
Ezra Pound (*1885, †1973) *Personae and Exultations,* U.S. poetry.
George Macaulay Trevelyan (*1876, †1962): *Garibaldi and the Thousand,* history.
Wells: (i) *Ann Veronica,* (ii) *Tono Bungay,* novels.
Barrès: *Colette Baudoche,* French novel of a young girl of Metz.
Gide: *La Porte Étroite,* French novel.
Maeterlinck: *L'Oisèau bleu,* Belgian-French play.

(ii) *The Ducal Palace*, French Impressionist paintings.
Mary Pickford (*1839, †1979), appeared in film, *The Little Teacher*.
Rimsky-Korsakov: *Le Coq d'Or*, Russian opera, his last work, performed; prohibited 1910 because of satire on government.
Rousseau: *Père Juniet's Cart*, French painting.
First Boy Scout Troop set up in England by Baden-Powell.
Erich W. Korngold (*1897, †1957), German composer: *Der Schneemann, (The Snowman)*, pantomine music.
Maurice Ravel (*1875, †1937), French composer: *Ma Mère l'Oye*, piano duet.
Granville Bantock (*1868, †1946), composer and conductor, became professor of music at Birmingham University (until 1934).

Contributory Old Age Pension Scheme in Britain.
Galton, anthropologist: *Memories of my Life*.
Landsteiner and Popper first isolated virus of poliomyelitis (infantile paralysis).
H. K. Onnes (*1853, †1926), Dutch physicist, liquefied helium.
First production of model T Ford motor car, of which 15,000,000 were to be sold.
Opening of Rotherhithe Tunnel.
Establishment of Port of London Authority.
Hudson River tunnel completed.
Adoption of Weston Cell (1.0183 V) as standard.
60–in. reflecting telescope erected at Mount Wilson.
Great meteorite fell in Siberia.
Intense earthquake destroyed much of Sicily and Calabria; loss of life estimated at over 150,000.
Gas used for refrigeration.
Sir Ernest H. Shackleton (*1874, †1922) took expedition to within 100 miles of South Pole; knighted on return in 1909.
Discovery, in Montana, of remains of *tyrannosaurus rex*, huge, carnivorous, prehistoric reptile.
Anglo-Russian Chamber of Commerce set up at St Petersburg.
Wilbur Wright flew aeroplane for 30 miles in 40 minutes.

Diaghilev successfully launched his Ballet Company in Paris.
Lehár: *The Count of Luxembourg*, Hungarian opera.
R. Strauss: *Elektra*, German opera, first performed at Dresden.
Rousseau: *Equatorial Jungle*, French painting.
Maurice Utrillo (*1883, †1955): (i) *Place du Tértre*, (ii) *Rue Muller*, (iii) *Renoir's Garden*, French paintings.
Official opening of existing Victoria and Albert Museum buildings.
Foundation of Universities of Bristol and Belfast (Queen's University); also of University College, Dublin (R.C.)
First Boy Scout Rally, at Crystal Palace.

Robert E. Peary (*1856, †1920), U.S. explorer, claimed to be first to have reached the North Pole.
Louis Blériot, French airman, made first cross-Channel flight from Calais to Dover, in 37 minutes.
Farman made first 100–mile flight.
Oil refinery established at Abadan.
Sir A. V. Roe (*1887, †1958) began manufacturing aeroplanes in Britain.
Housing and Town Planning Act.
Selfridge's London store opened.
High protective tariffs continued in the U.S.A. by Payne-Aldrich Tarriff.
American Col. S. F. Cody established the (then) British air record of one hour's flight.

LITERATURE

	History	Literature
1909	Leopold II handed Congo State to Belgium as colony. Universal suffrage in Sweden. Insurrection at Barcelona. Sultan Abdul Hamid II deposed by Young Turks. Powers left Macedonian problem in hands of "liberal" Young Turks. Russo-Bulgarian secret treaty against Germany and Austria. *Duma* investigated Russian police actions: fewer executions. Morley-Minto reforms in India.	First appearance of *La Nouvelle Revue française*. Ferenc Molnar (*1878, †1952): *Liliom*, Hungarian play.
1910	†Edward VII: accession of George V. Constitutional Crisis over Parliament Bill, which was aimed at reducing powers of House of Lords. January election reduced Liberal majority to 124. Round Table Conference over Parliament Bill; failed to reach agreement. December election; government majority 126; 84 Irish Nationalists, 42 Labour Members; Conservatives and Liberals tied. Cape Colony, Natal, Orange Free State, Transvaal united into Dominion of South Africa. Revolution in Portugal: abandonment of throne by Manuel II; Portugal declared a Republic. Prince Nicholas of Montenegro assumed title of king. Formal annexation of Korea by Japan.	Sir Norman Angell (*1874, †1967): *The Great Illusion*, written to show futility of war, even for victors. Belloc: *Verses*. Bennett: *Clayhanger*, a novel. Forster: *Howard's End*, a novel. Galsworthy: *Justice*, a play. Charles E. Montague (*1867, †1928): *A Hind Let Loose*, a novel. Wells: *The History of Mr Polly*, a novel. Claudel: *Cinq grandes Odes*, French poems. Péguy: *Le Mystère de la Charité de Jeanne d'Arc*, French drama, in prose and verse. Hauptmann: *Der Narr in Christo, Emanuel Quint*, German religious novel. Hermann Löns (*1866, †1914): *Der Wehrwolf*, German novel of peasant life in 30 Years' War.
1911	Parliament Act: reduced powers of Lords and life of parliament. Payment of M.P.s introduced; £400 per annum. Strikes and industrial unrest in Britain: dockers, railwaymen, weavers. Conciliation Act: board of workers and employers under permanent	Beerbohm: *Zuleika Dobson*, a novel. Bennett: (i) *Hilda Lessways*, (ii) *The Card*, novels. Chesterton: *The Innocence of Father Brown*, detective stories. Fowler: *Concise Oxford Dictionary*. David Herbert Lawrence (*1885, †1930): *The White Peacock*, a novel. Katherine Mansfield (*1888, †1923): *In a*

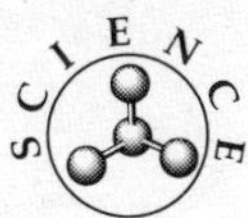

First Rugby football match to be played at Twickenham.

Leo H. Baekeland, U.S.A., discovered "bakelite".
Trade Boards established in "sweated" industries.
Russian Land Law: conditions of peasants improved.
Development and Road Improvements Fund Act.

Ernest Bloch (*1880, †1959), American composer: *Macbeth*, lyrical drama.
Braque: *The Sacré-Cœur*, French Cubist painting.
Wassily Kandinsky (*1866, †1944): *First Abstract Work*, by Russian post-Impressionist painter.
Oskar Kokoschka (*1886, †1980): *Frau Loos*, Austrian portrait.
Picasso: *Ambroise Vollard*, Cubist drawing.
Rousseau: *The Waterfall*, French painting.
Igor Stravinsky (*1882, †1971), Russian-born composer: *The Fire Bird*, ballet music.
The tango, which originated in S. America a few years earlier, gained popularity in the U.S.A. and Europe.
Negro dance-band at Memphis, Tennessee, said to have introduced the "blues", frequently using minor 3rd and 7th.
Consecration of Westminster Roman Catholic Cathedral (begun 1895).
Girl Guides Association founded in England by Lady Baden-Powell.
Ferruccio B. Busoni (*1886, †1924): *Fantasia contrapuntistica*, Italian orchestral work.
Mexico University re-established.

Mme Curie isolated radium from its chloride.
Bertrand Russell and A. N. Whitehead: *Principia Mathematica* (vol. 1, 1910; vol. 2, 1912; vol. 3, 1913; later revised).
Crippen, murderer, arrested on board ship; 'SS Montrose'; first capture of a criminal by use of radio.
Last appearance of Halley's comet, due to reappear in 1987.
First air-mail service organized in England.
Louis Paulhan won *Daily Mail* prize for powered flight from London to Manchester.
First German Zeppelin *Deutschland* crashed.
200,000 km. of new roads completed in France since 1871.
J. J. Thomson began work on deflection of rays in magnetic field; this was to lead to discovery of numerous isotopes.
Paul Ehrlich (*1854, †1915), German bacteriologist, developed salvarsan (arsenical compound) as cure for syphilis; one of the great discoveries in history, this was the 606th chemical he had endeavoured to use for the purpose.
Discovery of 520,000–carat aquamarine at Marambaia, Brazil; world's largest gem-stone.

Irving Berlin (*1888, †1989): *Alexander's Rag-Time Band*, early U.S. jazz tune.
Coleridge-Taylor: *A Tale of Old Japan*, light opera.
Elgar: *Symphony No. 2 in E♭*.
Piet Mondrian (*1872, †1944), Dutch painter: *Horizontal Tree*, rectangular-based abstraction.
Renoir: (i) *Young Shepherd resting*, (ii)

Lord Rutherford (*1871, †1937) enunciated theory of atomic structure: positively charged nucleus round which electrons (negative) move in orbits.
Charles F. Kettering, of the U.S.A., invented self-starter (for cars).
Amundsen became first man to reach the South Pole.
Claude developed tubular neon light.

LITERATURE

1911

History

official to settle disputes.
Men's co-operative Guild established.
Riots in Morocco over rival French and German interests; French entered Morocco to aid Sultan; Spain occupied north coast of Morocco.
German gunboat *Panther* set to Agadir; Agadir Crisis.
Convention of Berlin: France to establish protectorate in Morocco.
Italo-Turkish war: Turkey opposed to Italian policy in Tripoli.
Young Turks refused to open Dardanelles to Russian warships.
Assassination of Stolypin, Chief Minister of Russia, at Kiev.
Imperial Durbar at Delhi presided over by George V, King Emperor; Bengal Partition repealed.
Revolution in China; Manchu dynasty overthrown by middle class.

Literature

German Pension, N.Z. short stories.
John Masefield (*1878, †1967): *The Everlasting Mercy*, narrative poem.
"O. Henry": *The Gift of the Wise Men*, short story.
Pound: *Canzoni*, poetry.
Shaw: *Fanny's First Play*, play.
Wallace: *Sanders of the River*, a novel.
Hugh Walpole (*1884, †1941): *Mr Perrin and Mr Traill*, a novel on school life.
Wells: *The New Machiavelli*, a novel in autobiographical form.
Hauptmann: *Die Ratten*, German play.

1912

History

Shops Act: half-holiday for assistants.
Coal Miners' Strike: led to Coal Mines (Minimum Wages) Act.
Disestablishment of Welsh Church effected.
New Mexico admitted to statehood in the U.S.A.
Franco-British Naval Agreement: French fleet transferred to Mediterranean; Britian to defend N. and W. coasts of France.
German Socialists declared themselves anti-war; asserted international proletarian solidarity.
Italy bombarded entrance to Dardanelles; seized Rhodes; Turks defeated at Derna.
Treaty of Ouchy; ended Italo-Turkish war; Turkey ceded Tripoli and Cyrenaica to Italy.
Formation of Balkan League: Serbia, Bulgaria, Greece, Montenegro; Turks massacred Bulgarians at Kotchana and Berana; First Balkan War.

Literature

Edmund C. Bentley (*1875, †1956); *Trent's Last Case*, mystery novel.
William S. Houghton (*1881, †1913): *Hindle Wakes*, play dealing with Lancashire cotton towns.
Shaw; (i) *Androcles and the Lion*, (ii) *Pygmalion*, plays.
James Stephens (*1882, †1950): *The Crock of Gold*, prose fantasy fairy stories.
Ernst Barlach (*1870, †1938): *Der tote Tag*, German drama of a son wishing to break away from his mother.
Waldemar Bonsels (*1881, †1952): *Die Biene Maja*, German nature story.
"Alain Fournier" (*1886, †1914): *Le Grand Meaulnes*, French novel of adolescent love.
France: *Les Dieux ont soif*, French historical novel.
Huch: *Der grosse Krieg in Deutschland*, German novel of Thirty Years War.
Daily Herald published (to 1964).
Establishment of modern Copyright Law.

Gabrielle with a Rose, French paintings.
The *Mona Lisa* stolen from the Louvre; recovered 1913.
Utrillo: *Les Moulins de la Galette*.
Stravinsky: *Petroushka*, Russian ballet.
R. Strauss: *Der Rosenkavalier*, German opera.
Sir Robert Lorimer erected Chapel of the Order of the Thistle, St Giles's Cathedral, Edinburgh.
Assemblies of students at Russian universities forbidden.
Amadeo Modigliani (*1884, †1920), tragic Italian artist: *Paul Alexandre*, portrait (one of three of the subject).
Cecil Sharp (*1859, †1924) founded English Folk-Dance Society.
Arnold Schönberg (*1874, †1951): *Harmonielehre*, treatise on harmony by the Viennese self-taught composer.
Hong Kong University set up.

Elmer A. Sperry (*1860, †1930), of the U.S.A., invented *successful* gyro-compass.
First use of aircraft for offensive measures; by Italians in Libya.
Escalators installed in Britain (see 1900).
On 9th August temperature at Greenwich reached 100°F.
British Government bought control of National Telephone Co.
National Insurance Act.
First woman admitted to membership of Royal College of Surgeons, London.
Germans permitted to extend Baghdad railway to Alexandretta.
Coal Mines Act; new safety regulations; no boy younger than 14 years of age to work below ground or younger than 12 at the surface.
S.S. *Olympic*, 46,400 tons, launched; speed 23 knots.
Charles T. R. Wilson (*1869, †1959), physicist, invented the cloud chamber for detection of the path of an atom.

Bonnard: *Place Clichy*, French painting.
Bramwell Booth (*1856, †1929) succeeded his father, William Booth, as General of Salvation Army.
Busoni: *Die Brautwahl*, German opera.
Marc Chagall (*1887, †1985): *The Cattle Dealer*, Russian Expressionist painting.
Debussy: *Jeux*, ballet music.
Delius: *Song of the High Hills*, choral work.
Jascha Heifetz (*1901, †1987), violinist from Vilna, began touring as a soloist.
Mrs J. Gordon Lowe established Girl Guides in the U.S.A.
Kandinsky: *Improvisation*, Russian painting.
Picasso: *L'Aficionado*, Spanish cubist painting.
Ravel: *Daphnis and Chlöe*, French ballet music.
Signac: *The Seine near St Cloud*, French pointillist painting.
R. Strauss: *Ariadne auf Naxos*, German opera.
Utrillo: *Terrace in the Rue Muller*, French painting.
Erection of County Hall, London; designed by Ralph Knott.

Berry made first parachute descent *from an aircraft*.
Laurence Oates (*1880) vainly sacrified himself (March 17th) in Antarctica to save Scott and the rest of the party (who perished March 29th) after they had reached the South Pole.
Wilson published cloud-chamber photographs; later used to detect protons and electrons.
P. Debya: theory of specific heat of solids.
Victor F. Hess (*1883, †1964) discovered cosmic radiation by studying ionization of air in closed vessel in a balloon.
Ehrlich introduced acriflavine as an antiseptic.
Discovery of skull of Piltdown man, believed to be 50,000 years old; hoax exposed 1953.
Formation of Royal Flying Corps.
S.S. *Titanic* sank after collision with iceberg near Cape Race; led to International Convention of Safety of Life at Sea.
Selandia, first ocean-going motor-vessel built at Copenhagen; *Jutlandia* completed on Clyde 5 months later.

	History	Literature
1912	Albania declared an independent state. Yuan Shih-k'ai, first Chinese war-lord, emerged as ruler in new republic. †Emperor Meiji Tenno, who established Japan as modern world power.	
1913	Trade Union Act: Trade Unionists allowed to contract out of Political Levy (Osborne Judgment, 1909). Marconi Scandal: Lloyd George, Rufus and Isaacs Master of Elibank, accused of corrupt practices; acquitted. First woman magistrate in Britain. Woodrow Wilson elected President of the U.S.A. Underwood Act: small reduction in U.S. tariffs. *Reichstag* coalition passed first recorded censure on Imperial German Government Settlement and Expropriation Laws. Assassination of King George of Greece at Salonika. Treaty of London: ended First Balkan War; Turkey renounced claim to Crete. Second Balkan War, June to August: Montenegro, Serbia, Greece, Roumania allied against Bulgaria and Turkey. Treaty of Bucharest: Balkan States, for first time, settled their own quarrels; partitioned Balkans. Treaty of Constantinople: Bulgaria and Turkey settled differences. Convention of Athens: Turkey and Greece settled ownership of Aegean Islands. Appointment of a German as Inspector-General of Turkish Army. Fourth *Duma*: last elected parliament of Imperial Russia.	James Elroy Flecker (*1884, †1915): *The Golden Journey to Samarkand*, collection of poems. Robert Frost (*1875, †1963): *A Boy's Will*, American poetry. D. H. Lawrence: *Sons and Lovers*, a novel. Sir Compton Mackenzie (*1883, †1972): *Sinister Street*, a novel in a series. Masefield: *Dauber*, narrative poem of an artist-sailor. "Guillaume Apollinaire" (*1880, †1918): *Alcools*, poems with "cubist" characteristics. Barrès: *La Colline inspirée*, symbolic novel. Roger Martin de Gard (*1881, †1958): *Jean Barois*, novel in dialogue form. Marcel Proust (*1871, †1922): *A la Recherche du Temps Perdu*, very long novel in seven sections (to 1922). T. Mann: *Der Tod in Venedig*, short story. Rilke: *Das Marienleben*, poetry. Franz Werfel (*1890, †1945): *Wir sind*, Austrian lyrics. Miguel de Unamuno (*1864, †1936): *Del Sentimiento Trágico de la Vida*, Spanish philosophy.
1914	Irish Home Rule Act restored Irish Parliament; 42 M.P.s to sit at Westminster. Ulster volunteers formed by Carson to oppose integration with	Johannes Robert Becher (*1891, †1958): *Verfall und Triumph*, German prose and verse collection. Bourget: *Le Démon de Midi*, a novel. Edgar Rice Burroughs (*1875, †1950),

First Alexandra Rose Day held.

German Navy Law introduced by Tirpitz: to give Germany 41 battleships and 20 cruisers by 1920.

Elgar: *Falstaff*, orchestral work.
H. W. Williams: *Tipperary*, to become song of World War I.
Jacob Epstein (*1880, †1959), American sculptor: *Two Doves*, marble group.
Holst: *St Paul Suite* for Strings.
Kandinsky: *Black Lines*, Russian expressionist painting.
Kokoschka: *Self-portrait*.
Lilli Lehmann (*1848, †1929): *Mein Weg*, autobiography of the soporano.
Max Liebermann (*1847, † 1935): *Shooting in the Dunes*, German Impressionist painting.
Cecil B. de Milne (*1881, †1959): *The Squaw Man*, U.S. film, one of his first.
Schönberg: *The Lucky Hand*, drama with music.
Alexander Scriabin (*1872, †1915): *The Poem of Fire (Prometheus)*, Russian orchestral work in which instructions were given for light to be projected on a screen.
Sibelius: *The Bard*, Finnish symphonic poem.
Stravinsky: *The Rite of Spring (Le Sacré du Printemps)*, ballet which created a great sensation.
Woolworth Building, New York City, completed; 792 ft high.
Establishment of a film censor.
First Charles Chaplin (*1889, †1977) film.

Sir W. H. and W. L. Bragg, father and son, understood crystalline structures using X-ray spectrometer.
H. N. Russell's theory of stellar evolution.
Friedrich Bergius (*1884, †1949), German chemist, using high-pressure hydrogen on coal dust converted it directly into oil.
Max Bodenstein developed concept of chemical chain-reactions.
Niels Bohr (*1885, †1962), Danish physicist, applied quantum theory to the structure of the atom; also explained the line spectrum of ionized helium.
H. Geiger invented his counter to measure radioactivity.
René Lorin expounded the basic ideas of jet propulsion.
British Medical Research Council founded.
Coiled tungsten-filament lamp, filled with inert gas, developed.
Existence of Vitamin A first recognized by McCollum and Davis.
Nationalization of British telephone system; transferred, except Hull, to G.P.O.
Seaplanes first carried on board ship (in H.M.S. *Hermes*).
First Federal Income Tax introduced into the U.S.A.
French military service extended from two to three years.
Harry Brearly produced stainless steel.

Vaughan Williams: (i) *Hugh the Drover*, an opera; (ii) *London Symphony*, by the founder of the English Symphony School.
Percy Wyndham Lewis (*1884, †1957), author and artist, founded Vorticism,

Robert H. Goddard, American, undertook practical experiments with rockets..
E. C. Kendall, U.S.A., prepared pure thyroxin for treatment of endocrine deficiencies, particularly thyroid.

1914 Southern Ireland; Curragh Incident; all-party conference at Buckingham Palace on Ulster failed.
Confucianism to be State religion of Republican China.
Northern and Southern Nigeria united as one colony.
Egypt and Cyprus declared British protectorates.
World War I: Assassination of Archduke Franz-Ferdinand at Sarajevo; Austrian attack on Serbia; Austria and Germany at war with Russia; Germany declared war on France, invaded Belgium; British declared war on Germany and Austria; Japan declared war on Germany; Battle of Mons began; Russians defeated at Tannenberg; Anglo-German engagement in Heligoland Bight; Battle of Marne began; Craddock defeated by Graf Spee at Coronel; H.M.A.S. *Sydney* destroyed German raider *Emden*; Graf Spee's squadron destroyed at Falklands; British forces captured German Togoland; ANZAC troops occupied Samoa and German New Guinea; Japanese captured Kiaochow and German North Pacific isles.

American novelist: *Tarzan of the Apes*, first of the Tarzan books.
Chesterton: *The Wisdom of Father Brown*, further adventures of the R.C. priest.
Frost: *North of Boston*, poetry.
Constance Holme (*1880, †1955): *The Lonely Plough*, a novel.
James Joyce (*1882, †1941): *Dubliners*, short stories and sketches.
D. H. Lawrence: *The Prussian Officer*, short story.
Bertrand Russell: *Our Knowledge of the External World*, philosophy.
Shaw: *Misalliance*, a play.
Gide: *Les Caves du Vatican*, French novel.

1915 *World War I: Western Front*: Battles of Ypres, Neuve Chapelle, Aisne, Loos; Nurse Edith Cavell executed by Germans; Italy joined war on Allied side;
Eastern Front: Russians retreated from East Prussia and Galicia, defeated Turks at Kars; Austro-German invasion of Poland;
Southern Front: Bulgarians invaded Serbia; Britain declared war on Bulgaria; Central Powers overran Serbia; Allied landings at Gallipoli and Salonika; siege of Kut;
Naval War: Battle of the Dogger Bank; Germany declared blockade of British Isles; S.S. *Lusitania* sunk by German submarine;
Colonial War: Botha completed conquest of German West Africa.

Rupert Brooke (*1887, †1915): *1914 and Other Poems*.
Buchan: *The Thirty-Nine Steps*, a novel.
Conrad: *Victory*, a novel.
D. H. Lawrence: *The Rainbow*, a novel.
William Somerset Maugham (*1874, †1965): *Of Human Bondage*, a novel, semi-autobiographical in content.
Virginia Woolf (*1882, †1941): *The Voyage Out*, a novel.
Jakob Wassermann (*1873, †1934): *Das Gänsemännchen*, a novel

partly a derivation of Futurism and Cubism.
Busoni: (i) *Indian Fantasy*, (ii) *Nocturne Symphonique*, Italo-German orchestral works.
Chagall: *The Rabbi of Vitebsk*, a painting.
Delius: *North Country Sketches*, orchestral music.
Diaghilev presented *Le Coq d'Or* as a ballet.
Beniamino Gigli (*1890, †1957), Italian tenor, made début (in *La Gioconda*).
John Marin (*1870, †1953): *Sunset*, American water-colour.
Massine came into prominence in ballet.
Picasso: *The Small Table*, Spanish cubist painting.
Sibelius: *The Oceanides*, composed for his visit to America.
Stravinsky: *Rossignol*, a ballet.

Marconi transmitted wireless telephone messages between Italian ships 50 miles apart.
H. Shapley studied period luminosity of certain stars (Cepheid pulsation).
Bank of England authorized to issue paper money in excess of statutory limit.
Britain conditionally agreed to extension of Baghdad railway to Basra.
First single-seater fighter planes made in Britain.
First Zeppelin raid took place.
Completion of the Panama Canal.
Grand Trunk Pacific Railway completed in the U.S.A.

Chagall: *Poète Allongé*; one of the original Surrealists, the artist painted pictures as seen in dreams.
Debussy: *Études* for piano.
Raoul Dufy (*1877, †1953), member of the Fauve group: *Homage to Mozart*, French painting.
Douglas Fairbanks Senior (*1883, †1939) began starring as silent-film hero.
Juan Gris (*1887, †1927): *Still Life and Landscape*, Surrealist painting.
Hubert Parry: modern setting of hymn *Jerusalem* to words of William Blake.
R. Strauss: *Eine Alpensinfonie*, German tone-poem.
First Women's Institute introduced into Britain by Mrs Alfred Watt; first British one set up in Anglesey.
University Library, Mexico City, erected;

Georg Cantor (*1845, †1918): *Contributions to the Founding of a Theory of Transfinite Numbers*.
Einstein: General Theory of Relativity (see 1905).
Sir Chas. R. Fairey (*1887, †1956) founded his aviation company.
British troop train disaster near Gretna Green; 200 killed.
Discovery of dwarf stars, through W. S. Adams, resulted from study of Sirius B spectrum.
Establishment of Ministry of Munitions under Lloyd George.
First automatic telephone exchange in Britain.
Formation of National Register in Britain.
Munitions of War Act.
National War Workshops established.
Rent Restriction Act: prohibited increases

1915 Asquith's Coalition government formed.
Haig succeeded French as Com. in Chief.
British Army in France; Robertson appointed British C.I.G.S.
Secret Pact of London: between Allies and Italy; led to Italian alliance against Central Powers.
Islands by Britain.
Treaty between Britain and Ibn Saud.
Fall of Viviani ministry in France; Briand, Prime Minister.
Gregory Rasputin effective ruler of Russia.
Yuan Shih-K'ai (†1916) attempted to restore Chinese monarchy under himself.
Japan's Twenty-one Demands on China: would have robbed China of remaining freedom; demands modified.

1916 *World War I: Western Front*: Battles of Verdun, Somme and Ancre; Italy declared war on Germany; forced to retreat on Trentino front; Portugal declared war on Germany;
Eastern Front: Brussilov's offensive south of Pripet; Roumania declared war on Germany and Austria;
Southern Front: Allies evacuated Gallipoli; British surrendered Kut to Turks; Turkish attack on Egypt repulsed; Bulgarians invaded Greece;
Naval War: Battle of Jutland; Kitchener drowned.
Colonial War: General Smuts to command German East Africa; British conquest of Cameroons completed.
Asquith's Coalition government resigned; Lloyd George Prime Minister.
Imperial War Conference met in London.
Germans tried to land arms in Ireland; Easter rebellion in Dublin; suppressed; Sir Roger Casement executed.

Barrie: *A Kiss for Cinderella*, a play.
Bridges: *The Spirit of Man*, prose and verse.
Buchan: *Greenmantle*, war story.
Flecker: *Collected Poems*.
Joyce: *A Portrait of the Artist as a Young Man*, autobiographical novel.
Sheila Kaye-Smith (*1887, †1956): *Sussex Gorse*, novel of country life.
Moore: *The Brook Kerith*, novel of life of Jesus.
Edith Sitwell (*1887, †1969) and Osbert Sitwell (*1892, †1964): *Twentieth Century Harlequinade*, poetry.
Henri Barbusse (*1873, †1935): *Le Feu*, realistic war novel.
Franz Kafka (*1883, †1924): *Die Verwandlung*, a story.
Georg Kaiser (*1878, †1945): *Von Morgens bis Mitternachts*, German play.

remarkable building having flat decoration in colour on the outside.
Panama-Pacific International Exhibition at San Francisco.
Keep the Home Fires Burning, wartime song, published.

in rent or mortgage rates in cases of small properties.
Second Budget: Excess Profits Duty 50%; McKenna Duties on imported goods.
S.S. *Campania* converted into first large aircraft carrier.
Zeppelin raid on Tyneside.
Germans used poison gas at Ypres.
German *flammerwerfer* (flame-thrower) used in war.
Completion of Canadian Northern Railway.
Panama Canal opened to commerce.
Ford farm tractor developed.

Delius: (i) *Requiem*, choral work, (ii) violin concerto, (iii) concerto for violin and cello.
Elgar: *The Spirit of England*, orchestral work.
de Falla: *Noches en los jardines de España*, for piano and orchestra.
Enrique Granados (*1867, †1916): *Goyescas*, Spanish opera performed in New York; composer perished on way back to Europe.
Holst: *The Planets*, musical suite, of which the ominous *Mars* is probably the best known, completed.
Arthur Honegger (*1892, †1955): *Le Chant de Nigamon*, Swiss orchestral work; the composer helped to form the *Nouveaux Jeunes* group in the same year.
Korngold: *Violanta*, one-act opera performed at Munich.
Modigliani: *Portrait of Lapoutre*.
George Robey appeared in *The Bing Boys are Here*, began career in revue (to 1932).
Stanford and Forsyth: *A History of Music*.
Chu Chin Chow, musical comedy, began its run of 2,238 shows.
D. W. Griffith: *Intolerance*, great epic film introducing modern techniques.

Sir Arthur Eddington (*1882, †1944) began investigating internal constitution of the stars.
Jonnesco successfully performed sympathectomy for relief of angina pectoris.
H. de Roche-Lima isolated typhus (see 1576).
Allied Economic Conference in Paris; pooling of resources agreed.
Compulsory Military Service in Britain.
First tank, *Little Willie*, used by Heavy Machine Gun Corps (later Royal Tank Corps).
Invention of amatol (an explosive).
Foundation of Federation of British Industries.
Introduction of British Summer Time (B.S.T.).
Refrigeration of blood for transfusion.
Unemployment insurance extended to cover munition trades.
Wheat Commission and Food Control established.
First successful British airship (dirigible), R9, built.
Great Zeppelin raids on Britain; first Zeppelin destroyed over the country.

	History	Literature
1916	German Peace Note; rejected by Allies. Sykes-Picot (Anglo-French secret) Agreement on Partition of Turkish Empire. Joffre named Marshal of France. Resignation of Tirpitz, founder of German Navy; von Falkenhayn dismissed. †Francis Joseph of Austria; accession of Karl I. Assassination of Rasputin.	
1917	*World War I: Western Front*: Battles of Messines, Passchendaele, Cambrai; British captured Nesle, Chaulnes, Peronne, Canadians captured Vimy Ridge, French victory on Aisne; *Eastern Front*: Russian collapse on Revolution; Armistice with Germany; *Italian Front*: Italians defeated by Austrians at Caporetto. *Southern Front*: Siege of Kut: Turks defeated at Gaza; Allenby captured Jerusalem; Constantine I, pro-German Greek king, abdicated. U-boat war intensified; Haig made Field-Marshal. Whitley Committee proposed joint industrial councils; failed through Trade Union influences. Balfour Declaration: Jewish National Home in Palestine. Establishment of Ministry of Labour. U.S.A. declared war on Germany; sent expeditionary force to Europe. Cuba entered war on side of Allies. Prohibition proposed in the U.S.A. by Congress (see 1920). Fall of Briand government in France; Ribot, Prime Minister. Foch and Pétain replaced Nivelle after failure of latter's Western Front offensive. Mutinies in French army. Ribot replaced by Painlevé; in turn replaced by Clemenceau. Russian Revolution: Liberal Revolution in March; Nicholas II	Barrie: (i) *Dear Brutus*, (ii) *The Old Lady shows her Medals*, plays. Norman Douglas (*1868, †1952): *South Wind*, a novel. John Drinkwater (*1882, †1937): *Poems*. Thomas Stearns Eliot (*1888, †1965) who became British in 1927: *Prufrock*, American poems. Siegfried Sassoon (*1886, †1967): *The Old Huntsman*, poetry. Alec Waugh (*1898, †1981): *The Loom of Youth*, novel of public school life. Yeats: *The Wild Swans at Coole*, poetry. Paul Valéry (*1871, †1945): *La Jeune Parque*, long French poem. Reinhard Goering (*1887, †1936): *Seeschlacht*, German drama. Luigi Pirandello (*1867, †1936): *Cosi è se vi pare*, Italian play; three facets of truth, presented in turn. *Bonnet Rouge* Affair: attack in Press on war and Anglo-French alliance.

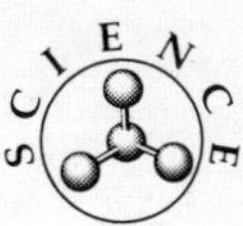

Krupp's works at Essen bombed by the French.
First celebration of ANZAC day in London.
Mrs. Margaret Sanger opened *birth-control* clinic in U.S.A.

Bonnard: *Rue Tholozé*, French painting.
Delius: *Eventyr*, orchestral work.
Holst: *The Hymn of Jesus*, choral work.
Ravel: *Le Tombeau de Couperin*, French piano music.
Reinhardt, Hofmannsthal and R. Strauss founded the Salzburg Festival.
John Singer Sargent (*1856, †1925): *Boats at Anchor*, water-colour.
Bells of St Mary's, war-time song, published.
British Royal Family assumed name of Windsor.
Order of British Empire founded to recognize war services of men and women.
Completion of Quebec (railway) Bridge (1,800 ft long).
c. John Nash: *Oppy Wood*; like his brother, he painted the effects of war upon Nature.
Foundation of Imperial War Museum a memorial to World War I: present museum in Lambeth opened 1936.

British shipping, wool, cotton and food under state control; British government took over all dollar securities; Excess Profits Duty increased to 80%; Corn Production Act: minimum prices guaranteed to farmers; Agricultural Wages Board; minimum wages for farm workers; New War Loan.
Formation of British Tank Corps.
Proposal for British decimal coinage; supported by Chamber of Commerce; quashed by Royal Commission (1920); resuscitated in the 1960s for introduction in 1971.
Gold sovereigns withdrawn from circulation; manufacture in small numbers continued.
100-in. reflecting telescope at Mount Wilson, California.
Germans used liquid fire at Cambrai; also used mustard gas, causing heavy Allied casualties.
Gotha, German twin-engined biplane; first aircraft especially designed for bombing.
Completion of railway line linking Eastern and Western Australia.
U.S.A. purchased Dutch West Indies.

LITERATURE

1917 abdicated; October Revolution: Bolsheviks seized control.
Finland declared independence from Russia.

1918 *World War I: Western Front*: Ludendorff offensive against Allies failed; Foch forced German retreat; Allied-German Armistice;
Eastern Front: Russo-German Treaty of Brest-Litovsk; Germans occupied Esthonia; Roumanian peace with Germany; Bulgaria retired from War; unconditional surrender of Austria-Hungary;
Naval Front: German Navy mutinied at Kiel; German fleet surrendered at Rosyth.
"Coupon Election" in Britain renewed Government's mandate.
Franchise Act: women over 30 given vote.
Conscription applied to Ireland; Irish M.P.s proclaimed Irish Republic; civil war in Ireland.
President Wilson, U.S.A., announced his "Fourteen Points" as basis for settlement of World War I.
Foch Com. in Chief. Allied forces.
Abdication of Kaiser William II; Germany proclaimed a Republic.
Emperor Karl I abdicated; Austria became a Republic.
Hungary declared independent Republic.
Poland proclaimed a Republic.
Tsar Ferdinand of Bulgaria abdicated; accession of Boris.
Tsar Nicholas II of Russia and family murdered at Ekaterinburg.
Latvia proclaimed independence from Russia.

Drinkwater: *Abraham Lincoln*, a play.
Hopkins: *Poems*, posthumously published.
Joyce: *Exiles*, a play.
D. H. Lawrence: *New Poems*.
Sassoon: *Counter Attack*, poetry.
Giles Lytton Strachey (*1880, †1932): *Eminent Victorians*, irreverent biographies.
Edward Thomas (*1878, †1917): *Last Poems*.
Wells: *Joan and Peter*, a novel.
Apollinaire: *Calligrammes*, poems.
Pierre Benoit (*1886, †1962): *Koenigsmark*, French novel on Germany.
Georges Duhamel (*1884, †1966): *Civilisation*, French war sketches.
André Maurois (*1885, †1967): *Les Silences du Colonel Bramble*, French description of English soldiers.
Oswald Spengler (*1880, †1936): *Der Untergang des Abendlandes*, German philosophy.

1919 Treaty of Versailles between Allies and Germany.
Treaty of Saint-Germain between Allies and Austria.
Treaty of Neuilly between Allies and Bulgaria.
First woman M.P., Lady Astor, took her seat in the Commons.

"W. N. P. Barbellion" (*1889, †1919): *The Journal of a Disappointed Man*, autobiography.
Beerbohm: *Seven Men*, stories.
Buchan: *Mr Standfast*, a novel.
James Branch Cabell (*1879, †1958): *Jurgen*, American novel purporting to be retold from old chronicles.

Sir Adrian Boult (*1889, †1983) first gained prominence as a conductor.
Chagall: *The Green Violinist*, French painting.
Alfred Denis Cortot (*1877, †1962), French pianist and conductor founded École Normale de Musique at Paris.
Egan and Whiting: *Till We Meet Again*, popular song.
Matisse: *By the Window*, French painting.
Modigliani: *Portrait of Madame Anna Zborowska*, Italian painting.
Paul Nash (*1889, †1946) exhibited paintings of Western Front Battlefields, which brought him recognition.
Picasso: (i) *Madame Olga Picasso*: (ii) *Seated Pierrot*, Spanish paintings; (iii) *Harlequin with Guitar*, cubist painting.
Francis Poulenc (*1899, †1963): *Mouvements Perpetuels*, French pianoforte compositions.
Renoir: *Woman tying up her Shoe*, French painting.
Stravinsky: *Histoire du Soldat*, ballet with voice.
Fisher Education Act: raised school-leaving age to 14; Act never fully implemented.

Shapley made a reasonable estimate of the shape of the Galaxy.
The Department of Scientific and Industrial Research (D.S.I.R.), appointed 1915, took control of the National Physical Laboratories (N.P.L.), founded 1899.
Cunliffe Committee recommended end of government borrowing; produced deflationary monetary policy.
Trade Boards Act: extended system to wide range of new trades.
Russia adopted the metric system.
Russia abandoned Julian Calendar and adopted Gregorian (Julian 13 days behind Gregorian).
Large-scale industrial enterprises in Russia nationalized by Bolshevik government.
Opening of Quebec Bridge of the St Lawrence (begun 1904).
U.S.A. inaugurated first regular airmail service.
World-wide influenza epidemic began; in the period (to its termination in 1918) it is estimated that 20,000,000 people died.
Royal Flying Corps (R.F.C.) became Royal Air Force (R.A.F.).
First increase in letter postage rate since the 1d charge of 1840; new rate 1½d; many increases since 1918.

Jack Dempsey (*1895, †1983) became world heavyweight boxing champion.
Elgar (i) cello concerto; (ii) piano quintet; (iii) string quartet.
de Falla: *El sombrero de tres picos (The three-cornered Hat)*, Spanish ballet.
Holst: music for Walt Whitman's *Ode to Death*.

John Maynard Keynes (*1883, †1946): *The Economic Consequences of the Peace*, economics.
Russell: *Introduction to Mathematical Philosophy*, written in prison.
Great year for flying records: (i) Hawker and Grieve flew from Newfoundland across Atlantic; (ii) Sir Ross Smith flew from

1919 Railway strike in Britain.
Working week of 48 hours became general.
Britain appointed to mandate over Palestine.
Rebel Irish M.P.s met as parliament of Ireland, *Dail Eirann*.
Treaty of Rawalpindi: end of 3rd Afghan War.
Revolt against British rule in Egypt.
Punjab riots; Amritsar Massacre.
Danzig restored as Free City.
Royalist rising in Portugal suppressed.
Adolf Hitler (*1889, †1945) founded National Socialist German Workers' Party.
Communist (Spartacist) rising in Berlin crushed.
Civil War in Bavaria: right-wing government established.
German Republic adopted Weimar Constitution.
Benito Mussolini formed *Fascia di combattimento*.
Gabriel d'Annunzio seized Trieste; later forced to withdraw.
Soviet Republic established in Russia; Comintern formed (see 1943); Civil War (to 1921) in Russia; "White" forces led by Koltchak and Denikin; Allied intervention against Bolsheviks failed.
Seventy-one warships of the German fleet were scuttled at Scapa Flow.

Conrad: *The Arrow of Gold*, a novel.
Masefield: *Reynard the Fox*, narrative poem.
Maugham: *The Moon and Sixpence*, novel of stockbroker turned artist.
Shaw: *Heartbreak House*, a play.
Walpole: *Jeremy*, a novel.
Benoit: *L'Atlantide* adventure novel.
"Roland Dorgelès" (*1886, †1973): *Les Croix de Bois*, French war novel.
Gide: *La Symphonie pastorale*, a tale.
Vicente Blasco Ibañez (*1867, †1928): *The Four Horsemen of the Apocalypse*, Spanish novel of World War I.

1920 Treaty of Trianon between Allies and Hungary.
Treaty of Sèvres between Allies and Turkey (later modified).
Spa Conference: Allies agreed on German war-reparation payments.
Emergency Powers Act: British government could declare state of emergency if need arose.
First Archbishop in disestablished Church of Wales enthroned.
British civil administration of Palestine under League of Nations mandate.

Barrie: *Mary Rose*, a play.
Agatha Christie (*1891, †1976): *The Mysterious Affair at Styles*, her first mystery novel.
Galsworthy: (i) *In Chancery*, a novel in the *Forsyte Saga*; (ii) *The Skin Game*, a play.
D. H. Lawrence: *Women in Love*, a novel.
Sinclair Lewis (*1885, †1951): *Main Street*, American novel of small town life.
Mansfield: *Bliss and Other Stories*.
Wilfred Owen (*1893, †1918): *Poems*, by a brave soldier who hated war.
Pound: *Umbra*, poetry.
Wells: *Outline of History* (of the world).

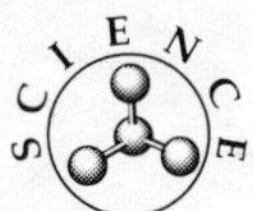

Modigliani: *Gypsy Woman with Baby*, Italian painting.
Picasso: (i) *The Balcony, Saint Raphael*, (ii) *Pierrot and Harlequin*, Spanish gouaches.
R. Strauss: *Die Frau ohne Schatten*, German opera.
Harold Bauer, pianist, founded Beethoven Association of New York.
Sigfrid Karg-Elert (*1877, †1933), German organ composer, began instructing at Leipzig Conservatory.
Ignacy Jan Paderewski (*1860, †1941), famous pianist, became first Prime Minister of free Poland.
Geoffrey Whitworth founded British Drama League.
Foundation of League of Nations Union.
Formation of American Legion of Ex-Servicemen.

England to Australia; (iii) Alcock and Brown made first non-stop transatlantic flight (Newfoundland to Ireland); (iv) British airship R34 crossed Atlantic.
Daily London-Paris air service began.
Fokker invented radio-controlled aircraft.
Local Government Board replaced by Ministry of Health.
Preventative serum produced to combat yellow fever.
Discovery of the proton, sub-nuclear particle.
Rent Act: rateable values increased; 10% rent increase allowed.
Addison's Housing and Town Planning Act.
Housing (Additional Powers) Act: subsidies for working-class houses.
Electricity (Supply) Act: Central Electricity Commission set up to supply cheap electricity.
Ministry of Transport established.
Sankey Commission on coal industry: recommended nationalization.
Land Settlement Facilities Act: to settle ex-service men on smallholdings.
Holland inaugurated Zuider Zee reclamation project.

Alessandrescu (*1893, †1959): *Acteon*, Roumanian symphonic poem.
Louis Kentner (*1905) pianist, first began recitals.
Paul von Klenau (*1883, †1946), Danish composer and conductor, founded Copenhagen philharmonic concerts.
W. Nicholson: *Sunflowers*, a painting.
Picasso: (i) *The Wounded Bird*, (ii) *Women Bathing*, Spanish pastels.
Roger Quilter (*1877, †1953), light composer: *Children's Overture*.
Ravel: *La Valse*, French orchestral music.
Stravinsky: *Symphonies of Wind Instruments*.

J. de la Cierva invented the autogyro, precursor of the helicopter.
Sir Geoffrey de Havilland (*1882, †1965) founded his aircraft company.
Michelson measured the diameter of Betelgeuse; first accurate measurement of a star.
Slipher noted shift of spectra of galaxies towards the red (Döppler effect).
Marconi Company opened first British public broadcasting station (near Chelmsford); later in same year first American station transmitted at East Pittsburgh.

1920 Fourth Irish Home Rule Bill: two Irish parliaments, Belfast and Dublin, offered; rejected by Sinn Fein; civil war; "Black and Tans" introduced by British government; †T. J. MacSwiney, Irish patriot, on hunger strike in British prison.
Sacco and Vanzetti murder case in the U.S.A.
American women given vote.
U.S.A. refused to ratify Treaty of Versailles; France ratified the Treaty.
French Presidential Election: Deschanel preferred to Clemenceau; Millerand Prime Minister.
Franco-Polish attack on Ukraine; Curzon Line rejected as Polish-Russian frontier; Poles driven back to Warsaw; Weygand reorganized Polish army; Russians driven out of Warsaw.
"Little Entente" of Czechoslovakia, Roumania and Yugoslavia.
Kapp *putsch* in Germany to effect Nationalist counter-revolution; defeated by Berlin workers.
Fall of Orlando government in Italy; Giolotti returned to office.
Unrest in Italy; Workers' Societies in many factories.
Russia recognized Esthonian independence.
Britain annexed Kenya colony.
Canonization of Joan of Arc (†1431).

"Alain" (*1868, †1951): *Les Propos d'Alain*, chats on philosophy.
Duhamel: *La Confession de Minuit*, French novel.
Proust: *Le Côte de Guermantes*, French novel.
Valéry: *Le Cimetière marin*, French poetry.
Pirandello: *Six Characters in Search of an Author*, a play.
Ernst Toller (*1893, †1939): *Masse Mensch*, German play.
Werfel: *Spiegelmensch*, German play.
Time and Tide magazine began publication.
F. Scott Fitzgerald (*1896, †1940), American novelist: *This Side of Paradise*, experiences at Princeton.

1921 First British woman barrister.
Irish Treaty: ended rebellion; Southern Ireland given Dominion Status.
Establishment of Chamber of Princes in India.
Franco-Polish mutual security Pact.
Resignation of Italian Prime Minister Giolotti; succeeded by Facta.
First Fascist parliamentary representation in Italy.
Greece defied League of Nations and declared war on Turkey; defeated at Sakarya.

Galsworthy: *To Let*, a novel in the *Forsyte Saga*.
Aldous Huxley (*1894, †1963): *Crome Yellow*, his first novel.
Kaye-Smith: *Joanna Godden*, a novel.
Percy Lubbock (*1879, †1965): *The Craft of Fiction*.
Eugene O'Neill (*1888, †1953): *The Emperor Jones*, U.S. play of an American Negro.
Shaw: *Back to Methuselah*, mammoth play cycle in five parts.
Strachey: *Queen Victoria*, a biography.
Francis Carco (*1886, †1958): *L'Homme traqué*, French novel of life in Montmartre.
Estaunié: *L'Appel de la Route*, a novel.

Roger Fry (*1866, †1934): *Vision and Design*, by the art critic and painter.
King George V unveiled the Cenotaph in Whitehall; Unknown Soldier buried in Westminster Abbey.
First meeting of the League of Nations.
Conditions of award of the Victoria Cross extended to R.A.F. women of military nursing service and civilians acting under Service authority.
Oxford University admitted women to degrees.
First World Jamboree of Boy Scouts held in London.
Introduction in the U.S.A. of Dalton Plan, educational system produced by Helen Parkhurst.

Gramophone discs first electrically recorded.
Silver coins in Britain, hitherto 92.5% silver, reduced to 50% purity.
Dye Stuffs (Regulation) Act: controlled import of dyestuffs.
Rent Restriction Act still further modified.
Unemployment Insurance extended to wider groups of workers.
Court of Enquiry on Dock Labour: national minimum wage and decasualization of labour recommended.
Cranwell Royal Air Force College founded.
First automatic telephone introduced into England.
Foundation of Calcutta School of Medicine.
U.S. seaplane piloted by A. C. Read from Newfoundland to England via Azores.
All factories in Russia employing more than 10 workers nationalized.
Prohibition introduced into the U.S.A.
North West Mounted Police, founded 1873, took name of Royal Canadian Mounted Police.
Worst outbreak of foot-and-mouth disease, mainly in Germany and France.

Publication of Burt's standardized tests for educational attainment at school.
Paul Hindemith: (i) *Sancta Susanna*, one-act Swiss opera; (ii) *Mörder, Hoffnung der Frauen*.
Fritz Höger erected Chilehaus, Hamburg, fine modern building (to 1923).
Honegger: *King David*, oratorio with spoken dialogue, performed at Lausanne; play by Morax.
Picasso: *The Three Musicians*, Spanish cubist painting.
Sergei Prokofiev (*1891, †1953); Russian modernistic composer: *The Love for Three Oranges*, an opera.
Frank Buchman (*1878, †1961) founded

Howard-Burg discovered footprints of the *yeti* (abominable snowman) in the Himalayas; further discoveries made from time to time (e.g. Shipton, 1951); theory now largely discredited.
Thompson sub-machine gun invented in the U.S.A.
Jewish people began to utilize chemicals from the Dead Sea.
Opening of King George V Dock, London.
Airship R34 exploded over the Humber.
Railway Act: amalgamation of British railway companies into four main companies: L.M.S., L.N.E.R., S.R., G.W.R.
Safeguarding of Industries Act: second step

1921 Turkist Nationalist government set up at Ankara; adopted popular sovereignty law and ministerial responsibility.

Italians agreed to evacuate Anatolia.

Franco-Turkish Treaty; French withdrew from Cilicia.

Formal Treaty between Turkish Nationalists and Soviet Russia.

End of British mandate in Iraq; Hashemite kingdom established (to 1958).

Treaty of Riga: ended Russo-Polish war.

Anti-Bolshevik mutiny by sailors at Kronstadt naval base; ruthlessly crushed.

Establishment of Soviet Commissariat of Internal Affairs (and Secret Police) N.K.V.D.

Mongolian independence declared.

Paul Morand (*1888, †1976): *Ouvert la nuit*, French novel of the "Jazz Age".

Grazia Deledda (*1872, †1936): *La Madre*, Italian novel.

Karel Čapek (*1890, †1938): *The Insect Play*, Czech allegorical drama prophesying totalitarianism.

1922 Carlton Club Meeting: subordinate Conservative ministers led by Baldwin revolted against Coalition government; defeated leaders.

Resignation of Lloyd George; end of Coalition government; return to party politics; Bonar Law Prime Minister.

Irish election endorsed Dominion Status; rejected by Sinn Fein; civil war.

Assassination of Michael Collins (*1890), Irish leader.

Treaty of Rapallo: Russo-German treaty.

Mussolini: (i) declared in favour of Constitutional Monarchy; (ii) led Fascist march on Rome; (iii) was made Italian Prime Minister.

†Pope Benedict XV; accession of Pope Pius XI.

Republic proclaimed in Greece.

Turks, led by Mustapha Kemal, rejected Treaty of Sèvres.

Greeks routed by Turks; fall of Smyrna.

Deposition of Sultan of Turkey.

Egypt declared an independent state; end of British protectorate.

Eliot: *The Waste Land*, a poem.

Flecker: *Hassan*, a play in verse.

Galsworthy: (i) *The Forsyte Saga* (in one volume); (ii) *Loyalties*, a play.

Joyce: *Ulysses*, a novel of characters in Dublin.

Sinclair Lewis: *Babbitt*, novel of the Middle West in the '20s.

Mansfield: *The Garden Party*, short stories.

John Middleton Murry (*1889, †1957): *The Problem of Style*, literary criticism.

O'Neill: *Anna Christie*, American play.

Edith Sitwell: *Façade*, poetry.

Walpole: *The Cathedral*, a novel.

Yeats: *Later Poems*.

François Mauriac (*1885, †1970): *Le Baiser au Lépreux*, French novel.

Valéry: *Charmes*, poems.

Berthold Brecht (*1898, †1956): *Baal*, early play of German dramatist.

Hans Carossa (*1878, †1956): *Eine Kindheit*, German autobiography.

Moral Rearmament Movement, in the U.S.A.
Education Act: regulated age and conditions of work for children under 14.
Foundation of British Legion by Earl Haig.

towards abolition of Free Trade.
Excess Profits Duty repealed.
Decontrol of coal industry; followed by coal lock-out.
First Birth Control Clinic in England, opened in London.
Anglo-Russian Trade treaty.
German reparations fixed at £6,000,000,000.
Period of great famine in Russia.
International Conference at Washington to secure armaments limitation.
Austin first produced his "Austin 7s".
Act requiring all new dentists to be fully qualified.

Sir Arthur Bliss (*1891, †1975), composer: *Colour Symphony*, experimental work on tone and vision.
Epstein: *Nan*, American sculpture.
Paul Klee (*1879, †1940): *A Girl's Adventure*, Swiss Surrealist painting.
Marin: *Deer Isle Islets, Maine*, American painting.
c. Matisse: *Still Life: Apples on a Pink Tablecloth*, French painting.
Picasso: *Two Women running on the Beach*, Spanish gouache.
Prokofiev began writing ballets for Diaghilev's company.
Ravel: Cello Sonata.
Vaughan Williams: *A Pastoral Symphony*.
Charlie Chaplin appeared in the film *The Kid*.
Northern Union Rugby Football adopted name of Rugby League.
Tomb of Tut-ankh-Amen discovered at Luxor by Howard Carter and Lord Carnarvon.
Chagall settled in France.

Sir F. G. Banting and C. H. Best, of Toronto, isolated insulin from pancreas; widely used in the treatment of diabetes; synthesized 1964.
Barnard won the King's Cup Air Race.
A temperature of 136° F. was recorded at Azizia, N.W. Libya.
British Broadcasting Co., a private monopoly under charter, made first regular broadcasts for entertainment in the world (see 1927); Broadcasting Licenses (10s.) instituted in Britain.
Balfour Note: proposed cancellation of War Debts; rejected by France and the U.S.A.
Washington Naval Treaty: naval strength stabilized among the U.S.A., Britain and Japan.
Last recorded case of rabies (hydrophobia) in Britain (until 1969).
Vilhelm Friman Koren Bjerknes (*1862, †1951), Norwegian meteorologist, explained the polar-front theory of air circulation and its effect on the weather.

1922 End of civil war in Russia (from 1917).
Union of Soviet Socialist Republics established in Russia (U.S.S.R.).
Stalin became General Secretary of Communist Party.
O.G.P.U. Secret Police established in Russia; dissolved 1934.

1923 Resignation of Bonar Law through ill-health; Baldwin Prime Minister.
Parliament dissolved; Government in minority after General Election December.
Foundation of Canberra as Federal Capital of Australia.
Internal self-government granted to Southern Rhodesia.
Calvin Coolidge elected President of the U.S.A. (to 1929).
French occupation of Rühr on German default in reparations; breach with Britain; "rupture cordiale".
Failure of Hitler's Nazi *putsch* at Munich; Hitler imprisoned.
Corfu incident: Italian bombardment of Greek-held Corfu after murder of Italian general on Greco-Albanian frontier.
General Primo de Rivera became dictator in Spain.
Tangier international zone established; ended 1956.
Proclamation of Turkish Republic; end of Ottoman Empire (founded 1298); Mustapha Kemal first President; Ankara new capital of Turkey.
Treaty of Lausanne: undid injustices of Treaty of Sèvres; restored old Anglo-Turkish friendship.
Transjordan declared independence.
Egypt declared herself a hereditary constitutional monarchy.
Chinese Nationalist government established by Sun Yat Sen (†1925) at Canton; Kuomintang reorganized by Sun, assisted by Russian, Borodin.

Bennett: *Riceyman Steps*, novel of miserly bookseller.
Bourn: *The Wheelwright's Shop*, account of village craft.
Conrad: *The Rover*, a novel.
Davies: *Collected Poems*.
Frost: *New Hampshire*, poetry.
A. Huxley: *Antic Hay*, a novel.
D. H. Lawrence: *Birds, Beasts and Flowers*, poetry.
Pelham Grenville Wodehouse (*1881, †1975): *Leave it to Psmith*, novel with comic upper-class characters.
Colette: *La Maison de Claudine*, French novel.
Jacques Maritain(*1882, †1973): *Eléments de Philosophie* (1923–9).
Maurois: *Ariel ou la Vie de Shelley*, French biography of the poet.
Hitler: *Mein Kampf* (completed 1927), the blueprint of Nazism.
Boris Pasternak (*1890, †1960), Russian poet: *Themes and Variations*.
First publication of *The Radio Times*.
Wallace Stevens (*1879, †1955), American poet: *Harmonium*, his first volume of poems.

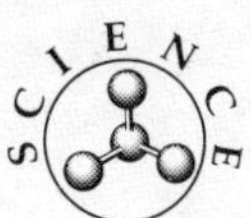

Ronald Coleman made film début in *The White Sister*.
de Falla: *El retablo de Maese Pedro*, Spanish opera.
Holst's *The Perfect Fool*, opera-ballet performed.
Honegger: *Pacific 231*, tone-poem about a locomotive.
Klee: *Landscape with Yellow Birds*, Swiss painting.
Zoltán Kodaly (*1882, †1967): *Psalmus Hungaricus*, for voice, orchestra and organ.
Kokoschka: *View of Dresden*, Austrian painting.
King Oliver (Creole Jazz Band): *Dippermouth Blues*, early jazz form for various formal occasions.
Picasso: *The Woman in White*, Spanish painting.
P. A. Scholes: *Listener's History of Music* (to 1929), 3 vols.
Stanley Spencer (*1892, †1959): commenced painting *The Resurrection, Cookham*.
William Walton (*1902, †1983): *Façade*, burlesque ballet, originally to accompany Edith Sitwell's poems; choreography by Ashton.
Poulenc: *Les Biches*, ballet music for Diaghilev.
Crossword puzzles appeared in U.S. newspapers.
Wightman Cup presented for U.K. and U.S.A. women's team lawn tennis championship.

A. H. Compton studied scattering of X-rays by matter; illustrated particle structure of electromagnetic radiation.
E. P. Hubble demonstrated that the galaxies lie beyond the Milky Way.
Julian Sorell Huxley (*1887, †1975): *Essays of a Biologist*.
Hale constructed spectroheliograph.
de Pescara's helicopter made successful flight.
First American broadcasts heard in Great Britain.
Demonstration, in New York, of sound films (talkies); see 1928.
Terrible earthquakes in Tokyo and Yokohama; estimated 140,000 lives lost.
Word *robot* appeared in Capek's play, *R.U.R.* (Rossum's Universal Robots).
Anglo-U.S. War Debt agreement; ill-feeling between the two countries.
Housing Act: Government subsidy over 20 years to assist local authorities to build houses.
Rent restrictions modified.
Chimes of Big Ben first broadcast.
At Bradford, Yorks, first Local Records Office established in Britain.
Commercial treaty between Canada and the U.S.A.
German inflation; currency stabilized; one new gold mark for one billion old marks.
Establishment of Interpol (International Criminal Police Control) in Vienna.
Military academy established in China, under Chiang Kai-chek, (*1887, †1975).
Twenty-four hour annual race for G.T. and sports cars instituted at Le Mans.

1924 Defeat of Baldwin Government, January; succeeded by first British Labour Govt under Ramsay Macdonald (*1866, †1937).
Dawes' Plan: attempt to make reparations practicable; failed.
Protocol of League of Nations Union enforced compulsory arbitration on member state of League in event of dispute.
Ramsay MacDonald first British Prime Minister to attend Assembly of League of Nations.
"Zinoviev Letter" Affair; fall of Labour government; Baldwin's second ministry.
Formation of short-lived Rural Party in Britain.
U.S. limited immigration under national quota scheme.
Italy gained control of Fiume; surrendered to Yugoslavia 1947; now called Rijeka.
Murder of Mateotti, Italian politician, openly opposed to Mussolini.
Turkish Caliphate abolished; Royal House exiled.
†Lenin (Vladimir Ilyich Ulianov, *1870), creator of modern Russia.
Petrograd renamed Leningrad in honour of Lenin.
Republic of Outer Mongolia joined the U.S.S.R.
Unsuccessful Communist-inspired revolution in Esthonia.
Chinese National government accorded diplomatic recognition to Soviet Russia.

Noel Coward (*1899, †1973): *The Vortex*, a play.
Forster: *A Passage to India*, a novel, his best known work.
Dame Rose Macaulay (*1881, †1958): *Orphan Island*, a novel.
Mansfield: *Something Childish*, short stories.
Alan Alexander Milne (*1882, †1956): *When we were Very Young*, poems for Christopher Robin, his young son.
Moffat: colloquial translation of *Old Testament*.
Shaw: *St Joan*, a play.
Mary Webb (*1881, †1927): *Precious Bane*, a novel of Shropshire.
Wodehouse: *The Inimitable Jeeves*, novel of a perfect butler.
James Woodforde (*1740, †1803): *Diary of a Country Parson*.
Mauriac: *Génitrix*, French novel.
T. Mann: *Der Zauberberg*, German novel.
Werfel: *Verdi*, German novel.
André Breton (*1896, †1966): *Manifeste du Surréalisme*, by the founder of the movement.

1925 League of Nations Protocol on Arbitration rejected by Britain.
Locarno Treaties: Great powers undertook to submit disputes to arbitration.
Pensions Act: provided Old Age Pensions, Widows' Pensions and Orphans' Pensions.
Samuel Commission set up to examine coal industry.
Coal subsidy of £223 million paid by government.

Coward: *Fallen Angels*, a play.
Warwick Deeping (*1877, †1950): *Sorrell and Son*, a novel.
Dreiser: *An American Tragedy*, a novel.
Eliot: *The Hollow Men*, poetry.
Ronald Firbank (*1886, †1926): *Prancing Nigger*, a novel.
Fitzgerald: *The Great Gatsby*, American novel.
A. Huxley: *Those Barren Leaves*, a novel.
Anita Loos (*1893, †1981): *Gentlemen Prefer*

George Gershwin (*1898, †1937), American composer: *Rhapsody in Blue*, for piano and jazz orchestra.
Holst: *At the Boar's Head*, an opera.
Vladimir Horowitz (*1904, †1989), Russian pianist, began to gain fame in Berlin.
Kandinsky: *Composition with Red Background*, Russian abstract water-colour.
Yehudi Menuhin (*1916), American violinist, made his debut at the age of 7.
Picasso: *Still Life with Biscuits and Green Tablecloth*, Spanish cubist painting.
Puccini: *Turandot*, Italian opera unfinished at his death (see 1926).
R. Strauss: *Intermezzo*, German opera.
Dame Ninette de Valois (Edris Stannus) joined the Diaghilev ballet company; later became one of the great figures in the art.
George V opened British Empire Exhibition at Wembley.
Inauguration of the Winter Olympics.
Consecration of Liverpool Anglican Cathedral.
Kemal Pasha began Westernization of Turkish life.
Nina Bang, first woman to obtain cabinet rank, became Danish Minister of Education 1924–26.
University of Florence refounded (see 1272).

L. de Broglie modified quantum theory.
Walter Chrysler (*1875, †1940), American, produced his first car; founded Chrysler Corporation in the following year.
Flettner, German, invented rotor ships.
Rice-Kellogg (U.S.A.) invented loudspeaker.
Formation of Imperial Airways, taken over by British Overseas Airways Corporation (B.O.A.C.) in 1940.
Photographs first transmitted across the Atlantic by wireless telegraphy from Britain to the U.S.A.
Agricultural Wages (Regulation) Act.
Housing (Financial Provisions) Act: increased amount of subsidy.
Channel Tunnel Scheme abandoned by British government.
End of British South Africa Co.'s control in Northern Rhodesia, which became Crown Colony.
Australopithecus africanus, primitive man-like creature, of 1,000,000 years ago, discovered in the region of the Vaal River, Union of South Africa.
Japan adopted the metric system.
Col. E. F. Norton's attempt to conquer Everest; Mallory and Irvine last seen at 28,239 ft.

Braque: *Still Life*, French cubist painting.
Chaplin appeared in the film *The Gold Rush*.
Derain: *Landscape*, French painting.
S. M. Eisenstein: *The Battleship Potemkin*, Russian film.
Epstein: *Rima*, Hudson Memorial in Kensington Gardens.
c. Klee: *Fish Magic*, Swiss painting.
Matisse: *Still Life with Pineapple*, French painting.
Picasso: (i) *Still Life with an Antique Bust*, (ii)

Sir E. V. Appleton and M. A. F. Barnett determined the position of the ionosphere (Heaviside Layer) which reflects radio waves.
R. A. Millikan, U.S. scientist, discovered cosmic rays.
Permanent institution of British Summer Time (B.S.T.) during lighter months of each year.
Echo-sounding gear used for measuring depth of ocean.
Irving Langmuir (*1881, †1957), American

	History	Literature
1925	Dominions Office set up by British government. Cyprus made British Crown Colony; Republic 1960. French troops began evacuation of Ruhr. Revolt against French rule in Syria. Hindenburg became President of Germany (to 1934). Nazi Party in Germany reconstituted. Mussolini embarked on creation of Fascist State. Albania, a principality, became Republic (until 1928). Kurd rebellion against Kemal Pasha; suppressed. Reza Khan Pahlevi, prime minister of Persia, elected Shah. †Sun Yat Sen, founder of Chinese Republic.	*Blondes*, American novel of the "gold-diggers" of the '20s. Séan O'Casey (*1884, †1964): *Juno and the Paycock*, play of Dublin slum family. T. F. Powys (*1875, †1953): *Mr Tasker's Gods*, a novel. Woolf: *The Common Reader*, essays on literary criticism. "Alain": *Propos sur le Bonheur*, French philosophic chats. Proust: *Albertine disparue*, a novel. Lion Feuchtwanger (*1884, †1958): *Jud Süss*, German novel with Jewish hero. Kafka: *Der Prozess*, novel known in Britain as *The Trial*. Sigrid Undset (*1882, †1949): *Olav Audunsson*, Norwegian novel. *Daily Graphic* absorbed by *Daily Sketch*.
1926	General Strike in Britain, May 1st to 12th. Coal Mines Act: legalized 8–hour day. Marriage of parents legitimized children born out of wedlock in England. Adoption of children legalized in England. Germany admitted to membership of League of Nations. Republican government in Portugal overthrown by Army coup led by General Gomez da Costa. Commencement of Italian policy of infiltration into Albania (see 1939). New Penal Code replaced Moslem religious law in Turkey. Plot to assassinate Kemal Pasha made the excuse for removal of last leaders of Young Turk Movement. Anglo-Egyptian Treaty: British forces withdrawn from Egypt to Suez Canal Zone. Proclamation of Ibn Saud as King of the Hedjaz. Chiang Kai-chek set out to unify China; provisional government set up at Hankow.	Christie: *The Murder of Roger Ackroyd*, detective novel, sensational because the murderer is the narrator. Edna Ferber (*1887, †1968): *Show Boat*, American novel, later to become musical show. Thomas Edward Lawrence (*1888, †1935), explorer: *Seven Pillars of Wisdom*, desert adventures in World War I. Milne: *Winnie-the-Pooh*, children's book. Colette: *La Fin de Chéri*, novel of a woman and a young lover. Gide: (i) *Les Faux-Monnayeurs*, French novel; (ii) *Si le Grain ne meurt*, autobiography. Henry de Montherlant (*1896, †1971): *Les Bestiaires*, French novel. Kafka: *Das Schloss*, incomplete novel. Hans Grimm (*1875, †1959): *Volk ohne Raum*, German novel. Georges Bernanos (*1888, †1948): *Sous le Soleil de Satan*, French novel. C. K. Ogden (*1889, †1957) began work on BASIC (British-American-Scientific-International-Commercial) English, using only 850 words.

Still Life with Fishing Net, Spanish paintings.
Ravel: *L'Enfant et les sortilèges*, French opera.
Sibelius: *Tapiola*, Finnish symphonic poem.
Vaughan Williams: *Concerto accademico* for violin.
Madame Tussaud's Waxworks burned down.
Idea of Signature Tunes, now widely used for broadcast programmes, originated with various dance bands.
Foundation of Miami University, Florida.
Wearing of the fez in Turkey forbidden.
Alban Berg (*1885, †1935): première of *Wozzeck*, opera (completed 1921).

chemist, invented atomic hydrogen welding process.
Pneumatic tyres first used on London buses.
An aircraft at Farnborough made a vertical ascent.
Britain returned to the Gold Standard.
Work begun on Mersey Tunnel, Liverpool-Birkenhead (see 1934).
First regular weekly British Broadcasting Company's broadcast to the Continent.
First transatlantic broadcast.
Empire Marketing Board established.
Further protective measures to safeguard British trade against foreign competition.
Agreement on fishing between Canada and the U.S.A.
Development of paratroops in Russia.

Braque: *Aria of Bach*, French painting.
Epstein: *The Visitation*, figure sculpture.
Hindemith: *Cardillac*, Swiss opera.
Klee: *Around the Fish*, Swiss painting.
Constant Lambert (*1905, †1951), later conductor (1937 *et seq.*) of Sadler's Wells ballet: music for ballet *Romeo and Juliet*.
Nellie Melba (Helen Mitchell) (*1859, †1931), Australian operatic soprano: *Melodies and Memories*.
Jely Roll Morton (Red Hot Peppers Band): *The Chant*, jazz.
Picasso: *Still Life with Foliage*, Spanish painting.
Dmitri Shostakovich (*1906, †1975), Russian composer: First Symphony (in F major) performed at Leningrad.
Vaughan Williams: *Sancta Civitas*, choral work.
Opera *Turandot*, begun by Puccini (see 1924), completed by Alfano.
Sir William Hadow's first Report on Education.
University Extension College at Reading became Reading University.
Huge organ installed at Liverpool Cathedral.
Film *Metropolis*, science fiction of futuristic city.

Amundsen and Ellsworth flew, in the dirigible *Norge*, Spitzbergen-North Pole-Alaska.
John Logie Baird (*1888, †1946), inventor, first demonstrated television; he used a mechanical scanning disc.
Richard Evelyn Byrd (*1888, †1957), American naval officer, made first aeroplane flight to the North Pole.
Busch demonstrated lens property of magnetic coils; foundation of electron microscope (see 1932).
Goddard, of the U.S.A., who had earlier experimented with solid fuels, produced first liquid-fuel rocket.
Schneider Trophy (air race) won by Italy at speed of 256 m.p.h.
The Electricity (Supply) Act established the Central Electricity Board, which, within seven years, created the Grid system.

1927 Trades Disputes and Trade Union Act: General Strikes made illegal; repression of trade-union activity; repealed 1945.
Release of Oscar Slater, wrongfully imprisoned in England for 19 years.
Simon Commission investigated Moslem problems in India.
Fianna Fail, political party, founded in Ireland by Eamon de Valera.
Mob attack on Vienna law courts led to formation of *Heimatschutz*, an armed conservative force.
Trotsky, co-founder with Lenin of modern Russia expelled from Russian Communist Party; Stalin's struggle for power in Russia.

Mazo de la Roche (*1885, †1961): *Jalna*, Canadian novel.
Harley Granville-Barker (*1877, †1946): *Prefaces to Shakespeare*.
Ernest Hemingway (*1898, †1961): *Men without Women*, American short stories.
Mansfield: *Journal*.
Sir Harold Nicolson (*1886, †1968): *Some People*, stories introducing real people.
Upton Sinclair: *Oil!*, a novel.
Walpole: *Jeremy at Crale*, a novel.
Thornton Niven Wilder (*1897, †1975): *Bridge of San Luis Rey*, American novel.
Henry Williamson (*1895, †1977): *Tarka the Otter*, moving novel of a wild animal.
Woolf: *To the Lighthouse*, a novel.
Julien Benda (*1867, †1956): *La Trahison des Clercs*, French attack on intellectuals who become party men.
Mauriac: *Thérèse Desqueyroux*, French novel.
Arnold Zweig (*1887, †1968): *Der Streit um dem Sergeanten Grischa*, German war novel.
Sir John Morris-Jones (*1864, †1929): *Caniadau*, Welsh poems.

1928 Fifth English Reform Act: votes given to women on same terms as men.
Shop (Hours of closing) Act.
†Mary Nutter (*1856), last so-called "Lancashire Witch".
South Africa granted Germany preferential duties.
French military service reduced to one year.
Kellog-Briand Pact denouncing War signed in Paris.
Salazar assumed direction of Portuguese government.
Italian Fascist trade unions

Edmund Blunden (*1896, †1974): *Undertones of War*.
Leslie Charteris (*1907): *The Saint meets the Tiger*, first of his "Saint" books.
A. Huxley: *Point Counter Point*, a novel.
Joyce: *Anna Livia Plurabelle*, fragment of a novel.
D. H. Lawrence: *Lady Chatterley's Lover*, a novel.
Wyndham Lewis (*1894, †1969): *The Childermass*, a novel.
T. F. Powys: *Mr Weston's Good Wine*, a novel.
Sassoon: *Memoirs of a Fox-hunting Man*, autobiography.

Lambert: *Pomona*, a ballet.
Vaughan Williams: *Riders to the Sea*, an opera.
Braque: *Still Life with Grapes*, French painting.
Dufy: *Casino de Nice*, French painting.
Epstein: *Madonna and Child*, figure sculpture.
Holst: *Egdon Heath*, orchestral work.
Klee: *Air-Tsu-Drie*, abstract ink drawing.
Kodaly: *Hary Janos* suite, Hungarian orchestral work.
Kokoschka: *Lyons*, Austrian painting.
Ernst Krének (*1900): *Jonny spielt auf*, Czech opera utilizing jazz idiom.
Picasso: *The Painter and his Model*, Spanish cubist painting.
Diego Rivera (*1886, †1957): *Delfina Flores*, Mexican painting of a child.
Jaromir Weinberger (*1896, †1967): *Schwanda the Bagpiper*, Czech opera.
Prokofiev: *The Gambler*, orchestral work.
Shostakovich: Symphony No. 2 (October Symphony).
B.B.C. took over control of Promenade Concerts.
First film with dialogue included: *The Jazz Singer*.
Discovery of tomb of Prince Mes-Kalam-Dug (–3500) at Ur of the Chaldees.
International Peace Bridge, linking Canada and U.S.A., opened.
Menin Gate Memorial unveiled in Belgium.

Baird, at Glasgow, demonstrated colour television.
c. Davisson and L. Germer, and independently G. P. Thomson and A. Reid, confirmed experimentally L. de Broglie's theory (1924) that every moving particle possesses an associated wave.
B. C. P. Jansen and W. F. Donath isolated vitamin B (thiamine).
Charles Augustus Lindbergh (*1902, †1974), U.S.A., first solo flight over Atlantic.
J. H. Oert demonstrated that the centre of the Galaxy lies in Sagittarius.
Seagrave drove racing car at a speed exceeding 200 m.p.h.
R. Wideröe constructed first resonnance accelerator: foundation of linear accelarator and cyclotron.
Communication established across the Atlantic by radio-telephone.
Australian broadcast first heard in Britain.
Establishment, by Royal Charter, of British Broadcasting Corporation (B.B.C.), which superseded the privately run British Broadcasting Company (see 1922).
Automatic 'phone service in London.
George V opened Gladstone Dock.
Reginald Joseph Mitchell (*1895, †1937), aircraft designer, became recognized for Schneider Trophy seaplanes (see also 1937).
Britain won Schneider Trophy at speed of 281 m.p.h.
c. Introduction, into Britain, of the coypu (or nutria), a huge rat, from Argentina.
British army abandoned lance as weapon except for ceremonial purposes.

Louis Armstrong (Savoy Ballroom Five): *West End Blues*.
Braque: *Still Life, the Table*, French painting.
Walt Disney (*1901, †1968), American film-maker: first Mickey Mouse cartoon: *Plane Crazy*.
Eisenstein: *October*, Russian revolutionary film.
Gershwin: *An American in Paris*, American tone-poem in jazz style.
Honegger: *Rugby*, Swiss tone-poem.
Krének: (i) *Der Diktator*, (ii) *Schwergewicht oder die Ehre der Nation*, Czech operas.
Ravel: *Bolero*, French orchestral work.
Shostakovich: *The Nose*, Russian satirical

Byrd's first Antarctic expedition (see 1933, 1939).
Paul A. M. Dirac (*1902) predicted existence of the positron (see 1932).
Eddington, astronomer: *The Nature of the Physical World*.
Sir Alexander Fleming (*1881, †1955), discovered *penicillium notatum*, a green mould, caused destruction of nearby bacteria on a culture plate by producing a substance, which he called penicillin (the first antibiotic): see 1940.
Sir Charles Edward Kingsford-Smith (*1897, †1935), Australian airman, flew across the Pacific Ocean.

1928 empowered to submit names for Fascist Grand Council.
Republic of Albania became monarchy under Zogu Ahmed Bey (King Zog) (*1895, †1961).
Italo-Turkish non-aggression pact.
Start of first Five Year Plan in Russia; declared achieved 1932, nine months ahead of schedule.
*Dalai Lama.
Chiang Kai-chek captured Peking; unification of Republican China.
Kuomintang/Communist split: Chiang Kai-chek established rival Nationalist government to Communists at Nanking; Nanking new capital of China.
Assassination of Marshal Chang Tso-Lin, warlord of Manchuria.

Evelyn Waugh (*1903, †1966): *Decline and Fall*, a novel.
Woolf: *Orlando*, a novel.
Jean Giraudoux (*1882, †1944): *Siegfried*, French play.
André Malraux (*1901, †1976): *Les Conquérants*, French novel.
Marcel Pagnol (*1895, †1974): *Topaze*, French play.
Brecht: *Dreigroschenoper*, German play adapted from *The Beggar's Opera*.
"Ludwig Renn" (*1889): *Krieg*, German war book.
Opening of first Malvern Drama Festival.
European alphabet adopted in Turkey.

1929 Young Plan for final settlement of reparations proposed.
Hunger March of unemployed Glasgow workers from Blytheswoode Square, Glasgow, to Trafalgar Square.
Local Government Act (Neville Chamberlain); abolished Poor Law and Boards of Guardians in England.
Hatry case in England: £14,000,000 frauds revealed in court action.
Resignation of Baldwin government; Second Labour government under Ramsay Macdonald.
First English woman Cabinet Minister, Miss Margaret Bondfield, Minister of Labour (to 1931).
Agricultural De-rating Act.
Term *apartheid* first used at Kroonstad to describe separate development of black and white cultures.
India granted Dominion status.
Agricultural Marketing Board in U.S.A. established federal loan board to encourage orderly

Richard Aldington (*1892, †1972): *Death of a Hero*, war novel.
Elizabeth Bowen (*1899, †1973): *The Last September*, a novel.
Bridges: *The Testament of Beauty*, a poem.
Lord David Cecil (*1902, †1986): *The Stricken Deer*, biography of W. Cowper.
William Faulkner (*1897, †1962): *The Sound and the Fury*, American novel.
Robert Graves (*1895, †1985): *Goodbye to All That*, autobiography.
Hemingway: *A Farewell to Arms*, a novel.
Richard Hughes (*1900, †1976): *A High Wind in Jamaica*, a novel.
Sinclair Lewis: *Dodsworth*, a novel.
Eric Linklater (*1899, †1974): *Poet's Pub*, a novel.
J. B. Priestley (*1894, †1984): *The Good Companions*, a novel.
Elmer Rice (*1892, †1967): *Street Scene*, American play.
Robert Cedric Sherriff (*1896, †1975): *Journey's End*, play of World War I.
Woolf: *A Room of One's Own*, essays.
Claudel: *Le Soulier de Satin*, French play.
Cocteau: *Les Enfants terribles*, French novel of bourgeois life.

opera, based on Gogol's story.
Stravinsky: (i) *Apollon Musagète*, (ii) *Le Baiser de la Fée*, ballets.
Utrillo: *Square St Pierre and Sacrécœur, Montmartre*, French painting.
First full-length talkie film: *The Lights of New York*, directed by Bryan Foy.

Amelia Earhart (*1898, †1937), U.S., became first woman to fly the Atlantic.
Hans Fischer (*1881, †1945), German scientist, discovered *hematin*, artificial blood pigment.
Discovery of the Appleton Layer, from which short-wave radio waves are reflected.
B.B.C. transmitted still pictures by television.
First sound films (talkies) shown at cinemas.
Opening of Piccadilly Underground Station, London.
Currency and Bank Notes Act.
Dunlop Rubber Co. developed latex foam rubber.
Companies Act: all companies, public and private, to keep proper accounts.
Work begun on Boulder Dam on the Colorado River.
Huge hailstones fell at Potter, Nebraska (July 6th) weighing up to 1½ lb.

Braque: *The Round Table*, French painting.
Coleman Hawkins (Mound City Blue Blowers): *One Hour*, romantic jazz.
Augustus John (*1878, †1961): *Mimosa*, a painting.
Lambert: setting of S. Sitwell's *Rio Grande*, for chorus, piano and other instruments.
Paul Nash (*1889, †1946): *Wood on the Downs*, a painting.
Picasso: (i) *Figure by the Sea*, (ii) *Woman in a Red Armchair*, Spanish cubist paintings.
Ottorino Respighi (*1879, †1936): *Roman Feast*, Italian composition.
Grant Wood (*1881, †1945): *Woman with Plants*, American painting.
Demolition of old Lambeth Bridge built 1862.
Boxing in Britain placed under control of Amateur Boxing Association and British Boxing Board of Control.
Foundation of Museum of Modern Art in New York.
Teutonic Order transformed from religious into Mendicant Order.
Foundation of St Peter's Hall, Oxford, in memory of F. J. Chavasse.

Berger described electrical changes in the human brain; beginnings of electro-encephalography.
Admiral Byrd, U.S.N., flew over the South Pole; discovered Marie Byrd Land, Antarctica.
Van der Graaf constructed his insulated rotating-belt accelerator for high-voltage generation.
Seagrave drove the *Golden Arrow* (racing car) at 231 m.p.h.
Isolation of first steroid sex hormone.
First regional broadcasting station in Britain.
B.B.C. began experimental television programmes.
New Tilbury Dock opened.
Airship *Graf Zeppelin* flew from New York to Freidrichshaven in 55½ hours; completely circumnavigated the Earth in 21 days 7 hours.
Commencement of Maginot Line, fortifications in France, which proved to be abortive, as they did not extend entirely around the frontiers.
New volcanic island, Anak Krakatoa (Child of Krakatoa) emerged in the Pacific (see 1883).

1929 marketing and to stabilize prices.
Lateran Treaty between Italy and Vatican established latter as independent sovereign state.
Election of all-Fascist parliament in Italy.
Savage anti-British riots in Palestine: repressed; concessions granted.
Leon Trotsky banished from Russia by Stalin.
Strict rationing system introduced into Russia to stimulate productivity.

Giraudoux: *Amphitryon 38,* French play retelling an old legend.
Pagnol: *Marius,* play.
Erich Kästner (*1899, †1974): *Emil und die Detektive,* novel of a schoolboy.
Axel Munthe (*1857, †1949): *The Story of San Michele,* memories of a Swedish doctor (translated into 41 languages).
First edition of *The Listener* published.
Daily Herald placed under control of Odhams Press and T.U.C.

1930 Ratification of London Naval Treaty.
Coal Mines Act: legalized 7½-hour working day.
Housing Act (Greenwood's); tackled problem of slum clearance.
French evacuation of Rhineland.
End of occupation of Germany by Allied troops.
End of dictatorship of Primo de Rivera in Spain.
Election of 107 Nazis to Reichstag.
Return of Carol of Roumania (*1893, †1953) to throne he renounced as Crown Prince; succeeded his son Michael.
Formation of parliamentary opposition permitted in Turkey; Liberal Republican Party.
Proclamation of Kingdom of Ethiopia as Empire under rule of Haile Selassie (Ras Tafari).
Destruction of Russian Kulaks; property and equipment presented to collective farms.
London Naval Treaty led to resignation of chief of Japanese Naval Staff and assassination of Prime Minister Hamaguchi.

"James Bridie" (*1888, †1951): *The Anatomist,* a play.
Eliot: *Ash-Wednesday,* poetry.
Maugham: *Cakes and Ale,* a novel.
Victoria Sackville-West (*1892, †1962): *The Edwardians,* a novel.
Shaw: *The Apple Cart,* a play.
E. Waugh: *Vile Bodies,* a novel.
Walpole: *Herries Chronicle* (to 1933) historical novels set in the Lake District.
Francis Charles Yeats-Brown (*1886, †1944): *Bengal Lancer,* autobiography.
Stève Passeur (*1899, †1966): *L'Acheteuse,* French play.
Jules Supervielle (*1884, †1960): *Le Forçat innocent,* French poetry.
Josef Ponten (*1883, †1940): *Volk auf dem Wege* (1930–41), novels depicting German emigration.
Ina Seidel (*1885): *Das Wunschkind,* German novel.
José Ortega y Gasset (*1883, †1955): *La Rebelión de las masas,* Spanish philosophy applied to the mass mind.
Daily News and *Daily Chronicle* amalgamated to form *News Chronicle.*

Collapse of New York Stock Exchange; Wall Street financial disaster; world financial depression began.
Metric system adopted in China.
Opening of Welland Canal, in Canada (25 miles long).

Bela Bartók (*1881, †1945): *Cantata Profana*, choral music.
Dufy: (i) *Regatta at Henley*, (ii) *Château and Horses*, French paintings.
Hindemith: *Concert Music* for brass and strings.
Holst: *Choral Fantasia*.
Klee: *Floating city*, abstract painting.
Kodály: *Marosszék Dances*, Hungarian orchestral music.
Matisse: *The Odalisque*, French painting.
Picasso: *The Acrobat*, Spanish cubist painting.
c. Georges Rouault (*1871, †1958): *Afterglow, Galilee*, French painting.
Shostakovich: (i) *May the First*, Russian symphony (his third), (ii) *The Golden Age*, ballet.
Gilbert Spencer: *Cotswold Farm*, a painting.
William Grant Still (*1895, †1978): *Afro-American Symphony*.
Stravinsky: *Symphony of Psalms*, choral work.
Hadow's second report on Education of the Adolescent.
Youth Hostels Association (Y.H.A.) founded.
Courtauld Institute of Fine Art founded in London.
Chrysler Building, New York City, completed; 1046 ft high.
B.B.C. Symphony Orchestra founded.
Film, *The Blue Angel*, with Marlene Dietrich (*1901).
E. S. Harkness (*1874, †1940), U.S. philanthropist, founded Pilgrim Trust.

D'Ascanio, of Italy, designed helicopter (see 1923, 1939).
E. D. Lawrence and M. S. Livingstone, U.S.A., invented the cyclotron, particle accelerator used in atomic physics.
Seagrave killed in speedboat travelling at 100 m.p.h. on Lake Windermere.
Max Theier (*1899) successfully used serum for immunization against yellow fever.
c. Tombaugh discovered planet Pluto, calculated to exist by Lowell.
Sir Frank Whittle commenced experiments with gas turbines for jet propulsion.
First use of telephone for messages from ship to shore.
B.B.C. first attempted television broadcasts.
Channel Tunnel scheme rejected by government.
Road Traffic Act.
Airship R101 destroyed during flight to India; Britain abandoned manufacture of airships.
First non-stop transatlantic flight Paris to New York.
First polders, large areas of reclaimed arable land, in Zuider Zee.
Albert Canal, Belgium, constructed (to 1939).
Creation of Ural-Kuznetsk scheme of mining and metallurgical development in Russia (became main supply base 1942–45).
Worst flood in history laid waste Yangtze Valley in China.
German liner *Europa* gained Blue Riband.

1931 Statute of Westminster: British Dominions became sovereign states under British Crown.
May Committee: set up by Parliament to enquire into financial state of Britain; Report led to heavy foreign withdrawals from Bank of England.
Financial crisis in Britain: Cabinet split over economies.
Resignation of Labour government; formation of National government with Macdonald as Prime Minister; confirmed by General Election.
National Economy Act: salaries cut by 10%.
Sir Oswald Mosley left Labour Party; founded New Party.
London Round Table Conference on India: Mahatma Gandhi insisted on all-India government; opposed by Moslems of Pakistan; failed.
Hoover Moratorium; proposed final settlement of German war debts.
Revolution in Spain: departure of Alfonso XIII; proclamation of Republic.
Proposed Austro-German Customs Union abandoned through French pressure.
Sudeten Party withdrew from Czechoslovakian Coalition government.
Peasant unrest in Russia led to serious grain shortages (and again in 1932).
Japanese invasion of Manchuria: Chinese total boycott of Japanese trade.

Pearl S. Buck (*1892, †1973): *The Good Earth*, American novel.
Ivy Compton-Burnett (*1892, †1969): *Men and Wives*, a novel.
Coward: *Cavalcade*, patriotic play, the history of a family.
Philip Guedalla (*1889, †1944): *The Duke*, biography of Wellington.
O'Neill: *Mourning becomes Electra*, plays.
Anthony Powell (*1905): *Afternoon Men*, a novel.
Robert Sherwood (*1896, †1955): *Reunion in Vienna*, a comedy.
Dodie Smith: *Autumn Crocus*, a play.
Jean Giono (*1895, †1970): *Le Grand Troupeau*, French novel.
Giraudoux: *Judith*, French play.
André Obey (*1892, †1975): *Noé*, French play.
Antoine de Saint-Exupéry (*1900, †1944): *Vol de Nuit*, French novel about flying.
Hermann Broch (*1886, †1951): *Die Schlafwandler*, Austrian prose trilogy of novels.
Georges Simenon (*1903, †1989) published first Maigret novel.

1932 Ottawa Conference: attempt to establish Imperial trading policies.
Import Duties Act: (Neville Chamberlain) full-scale protection reintroduced into Britain; Free Trade abandoned.
Resignation of Snowden and Samuelite Liberals from National

Erskine Preston Caldwell (*1903, †1987): *Tobacco Road*, American novel.
Eliot: *Sweeney Agonistes*, fragment of a verse play.
Stella Gibbons (*1902, †1989): *Cold Comfort Farm*, a novel.
Louis Golding (*1895, †1958): *Magnolia Street*, novel of Jewish life.

Chagall: *Synagogues in Jerusalem*, French painting.
Chaplin appeared in the film *City Lights*.
Salvador Dali (*1904, †1989): *Persistence in Memory*, Spanish surrealist painting by a leader of the movement.
Epstein: *Genesis*, a sculpture.
Keynes: *Job, a Masque for Dancing*, to the music of Vaughan Williams (Camargo Society).
Lambert: *Music for Orchestra*.
Filippo de Pisis: *Portico of the Church of San Moisé*.
Ravel: Concerto for piano (left-hand only) and orchestra.
Utrillo: *Montmartre*, French painting.
Walton: *Balshazzar's Feast*, oratorio in the modern style.
Rachmaninoff's music banned in Russia as "bourgeois".
Foundation of National Trust for Scotland.
Films: (i) *Frankenstein*, with Boris Karloff; (ii) *Emil and the Detectives* (see 1929, Literature).
Empire State Building, New York, erected; 1250 ft high containing 102 storeys (see 1950, Science).
Formal opening of New Delhi, new capital of India.
Mikhail Botvinnik (*1911), Russian grandmaster, first won Soviet chess championship.

L. Beardmore crossed the English Channel in a glider.
Karl Jansky (*1905, †1949) discovered radio waves emanating from the Milky Way.
Kuhn, Lederer and Winterstein successfully developed chromatography for chemical analysis; orginally discovered by M. S. Tsvett, Russian.
Auguste Piccard (*1884, †1962), Swiss physicist, constructed stratosphere balloon; ascended to height of 53,000 ft (1931–2).
Jacob Schick, of the U.S.A., invented electric razor.
Vickers-Armstrong designed amphibious tank.
Records: (i) Schneider Trophy (379 m.p.h.); (ii) G.W.R. express (78 m.p.h.); (iii) Airspeed (407 m.p.h.) by Stainforth.
First outside television broadcast; finish of Derby Race.
Opening of King George V Dock, Glasgow.
First London trolley-bus ran.
New Zoological Gardens opened at Whipsnade.
Protective duties of 50% levied on certain foreign manufactures.
Horticultural tax on imported fresh fruits, vegetables and flowers.
Agricultural Marketing Act: marketing boards set up.
Severe earthquake tremor recorded in London.
Destructive earthquake at Hawkes Bay, New Zealand.
Neon tubes used for advertising.
First pocket battleship, *Deutschland*, launched in Germany.
International Leprosy Association formed to combat the disease.
Failure of Austrian Credit Anstalt and important German banks.

Children and Young Persons Act: reformed juvenile court procedure; emergence of Approved Schools.
Sir Thomas Beecham founded the London Philharmonic Orchestra.
Benjamin Britten (*1913, †1976): *A Boy Was Born*, choral work.
Edward Burra (*1905, †1976): *The Café*,

Anderson discovered the positron, positively charged particle of same mass as electron, in cosmic rays.
J. Chadwick discovered the neutron, uncharged sub-nuclear particle.
J. D. Cockcroft and E. T. S. Walton first observed artifically accelerated particles disintegrating a nucleus.

1932 government following Protectionist policies.
Outbreak of economic war with Irish Free State.
Reorganization of British Post Office: close Treasury control relaxed; enterprise encouraged.
Great Hunger March of unemployed to London.
Wesleyan Methodist groups united as Methodist Church of Great Britain and Ireland.
British Union of Fascists founded by Mosley.
De Valera came to power in Irish Free State; land-purchase repayments to British government stopped.
Lausanne Conference settled reparations and war debts.
Election of Franklin Delano Roosevelt (*1882, †1945) as President of the U.S.A.
Family Allowance system introduced into France.
Assassination of President Doumer of France; succeeded by Lebrun (to 1940).
Nazis held 230 seats, largest single party, in German Reichstag.
Dollfuss became Chancellor of Austria.
Japanese punitive expedition against China using neutral international settlement at Shanghai; Chinese defeated.
Japanese established puppet state of Manchukuo.
Nationalists assassinated Japanese Prime Minister, Tsuyoshi Inukai, in Tokyo.

Hemingway: *Death in the Afternoon*, essays on bullfighting.
A. Huxley: *Brave New World*, novel of world without dignity or passion.
Charles Morgan (1884, †1958): *The Fountain*, a novel.
Damon Runyon (*1884, †1946): *Guys and Dolls*, American short stories.
Bergson: *Les deux Sources de la Morale et de la Religion*, French philosophy.
Mauriac: *Le Noeud de Vipères*, French novel.
Romains: *Les Hommes de bonne Volonté* (1932–46), cyclic novel in 27 vols.
Benedetto Croce (*1866, †1952): *Storia d'Europa nel secolo decimono*, Italian work.
Oxford English Dictionary (formerly *Murray's English Dictionary*) published.
First publication of literary quarterly *Scrutiny* edited by F. R. Leavis.

1933 Lytton Report to League of Nations Union on Manchukuo settlement: rejected by Japanese, who withdrew from League.
Fulham East By-Election: seat went to a Pacifist.
Opening of World Economic Conference in London by King George V; total failure.
Housing (Financial Provisions Act)

Churchill: *Marlborough, his Life and Times*, biography of an ancestor.
James Hilton (*1900, †1954): *Lost Horizon*, a novel.
John Cowper Powys (*1872, †1963): *A Glastonbury Romance*, a novel.
Stephen Spender (*1909): *Poems*.
James Thurber (*1894, †1961): *My Life and Hard Times*, humour of American life.
Marcel Aymé (*1902, †1967): *La Jument*

expressionist painting.
Derain: *Flowers in a Vase*, French painting.
Grant Still: *Spring Landscape*, American painting.
Munch: *Mrs. Thomas Olsen*, Norwegian expressionist painting.
Schönberg: *Moses and Aaron*, Austrian opera (twelve-tone composition).
Films: (i) *Farewell to Arms*; (ii) *Shanghai Express*; (iii) *Morning Glory*.
First of Disney's *Silly Symphonies (Trees and Flowers*, in colour).
F. Lang's war strategy film, *M*.
The Green Table, ballet of the Ballet Joos de Monte Carlo.
Shakespeare Memorial Theatre opened at Stratford-on-Avon.
Opening of new Lambeth Bridge, over the Thames, replacing that demolished in 1929.
Opening of Sydney Harbour Bridge.
Turkey admitted to League of Nations.
George Washington Bridge, over the Hudson, opened.
Autobahn built from Cologne to Bonn.

Dunham identified carbon dioxide in atmosphere of Venus.
J. B. S. Haldane: *The Causes of Evolution*.
C. G. King and W. A. Waugh isolated vitamin C (ascorbic acid).
Knoll and Ruska's two-stage projection microscope.
H. Urey first isolated deuterium, heavy hydrogen isotope.
Records: (i) Campbell drove *Bluebird* (racing car) at 253 m.p.h.; (ii) Garwood's speedboat record (111 m.p.h.); (iii) Amy Mollison (née Johnson) flew Lympne-South Africa in 4 days 6 hr. 54 min.; (iv) J. A. Mollison flew Atlantic (Dublin-New Brunswick) in 30¼ hr.; (v) Scott flew England-Australia in 8 days 20 hr. 44 min.
Salter Report followed conference on British Road and Rail Transport.
Town and Country Planning Act.
Wheat Act: System of quotas and deficiency payments to provide British producers with secure market and enhance price for home-grown wheat.
Short-acting barbiturates introduced for use in intravenous anaesthesia.
Imperial Economic Conference at Ottawa.
Completion of Zuider Zee drainage scheme (begun 1919).

Ashton: *Les Rendezvous*, ballet to the music of Auber.
George Balanchine and Lincoln Kirstein founded a school of American ballet.
Disney: *The Three Little Pigs*, Silly Symphony.
Epstein: *Ecce Homo*, a sculpture.
Kodály: *Dances of Galanta*, Hungarian orchestral music.
Charles Laughton acted in Korda's film, *The*

Andrews, Laidlaw and Wilson Smith first isolated influenza virus.
Byrd's second Antarctic expedition (to 1935); on this journey he undertook solitary meteorological duties in a small hut for the six-month winter of 1934.
Campbell: new car speed record of 272 m.p.h.
Irène Curie and Frédéric Joliot produced radio-active isotopes of certain elements.

1933 subsidies abolished except for purposes of slum clearance.
Anglo-Russian trade dispute following trial of Metropolitan Vickers engineers for espionage.
President Roosevelt announced new legislative policy in U.S. "New Deal".
Prohibition repealed in the U.S.A.
Conservative Right Wing gained control of Spanish government.
Foundation of Falange in Spain; Spanish Fascist Party.
Hitler appointed Chancellor of Germany.
German Catholic and Social Democratic Parties suppressed.
Local Government constitutions of Hamburg and Bremen set aside.
Reichstag fire in Berlin; Communists accused.
Concentration Camps started in Germany.
Austrian prohibition of tourist traffic from Germany; anti-Nazi move.
Permanent Council of Little Entente (1920) established.
Graeco-Turkish non-aggression pact signed.
Russia established diplomatic relations with the U.S.A. for first time since Revolution in 1917.
Second Russian Five-Year Plan; dissolution of Third International.

Verte, French novel.
Duhamel: *Chronique des Pasquier,* French saga of bourgeois family.
Malraux: *La Condition humaine,* French novel.
Ignazio Silone (*1900, †1978): *Fontamara,* Italian novel of peasants.
Sholem Asch (*1880, †1957): *Three Cities,* Russian trilogy.
Federico Garcia Lorca (*1899, †1936): *Boda de Sangre (Blood Wedding),* Spanish rural tragedy.
British Museum purchased *Codex Sinaiticus,* 4th- and 5th-cent. manuscripts for £100,000, from Russia.

1934 Incitement to Disaffection Act: reversed decision in Wilkes Case (1766) that general powers of search were illegal.
Stavisky affair: suicide of shady financier involved French politicians.
Status Act: South Africa declared a sovereign independent state.
Anti-republican riots in France.
Assassination of King Alexander of Yugoslavia and French Foreign Minister at Marseilles.
France, supported by Britain and Italy, opposed German terms for rearmament.
Balkan Entente signed at Athens.

Graves: *I, Claudius,* historical novel.
A. Huxley: *Beyond the Mexique Bay,* travel book.
John O'Hara (*1905, †1970): *Appointment in Samarra,* American novel.
Priestley: *English Journey.*
Alphonse James Albert Symons (*1901, †1941): *The Quest for Corvo,* biography.
Arnold Toynbee (*1899, †1975): *A Study in History* (1934–54) of the principal civilizations.
Cocteau: *La Machine infernale,* French play on Oedipus theme.
Montherlant: *Les Célibataires,* French novel.
Armand Salacrou (*1899): *Les Frénétiques,* French play, satire on movie world.

Private Life of Henry VIII.
Matisse: *The Dance*, French expressionist painting.
P. Nash took part in "Unit One" group movement towards surrealism.
R. Strauss: *Arabella*, German opera.
Stravinsky: *Persephone*, Russian opera.
National Playing Fields Association received Royal Charter from George V.
Foundation of British Film Institute.
Discovery of Tassili rock paintings in Sahara by Lt. Brenans of Camel Corps.
Germany left the League of Nations.
Foundation of British Interplanetary Society.
Opening of White Sea Canal (141 miles long) linking Baltic and White Sea.

Eddington, astronomer: *Expanding Universe*.
P. Karrer established chemical nature of vitamin A.
R. Kuhn, P. György and T. Wagner von Jauregg recognized riboflavin as a vitamin (B_2).
L. M. Milne-Thomson: *The Calculus of Finite Differences*, systematic treatment of an important part of actuarial mathematics.
Erwin Schrödinger (*1887, †1961), Austrian physicist, received Nobel Prize for his work in advancing the knowledge of wave mechanics.
Pauli proposed the existence of the neutrino (identified 1956).
Discovery of polythene by I.C.I. scientists.
Discovery II sailed from Britain on voyage of exploration of the Antarctic.
London omnibus companies, tramways and underground railways amalgamated into London Passenger Transport Board.
Road and Rail Traffic Act: established carriers' licences subject to condition of vehicles and non-excessive hours for drivers.
Taxation of heavy motor vehicles greatly increased.
Second Agriculture Marketing Act: prices of home-produced foods raised by limiting imports; controlled home production.

Dali: *William Tell*, surrealist painting.
Hindemith: *Mathis the Painter*, German opera.
Kandinsky: *Composition*, Russian abstract painting.
Klee: *Temptation*, Swiss abstract painting.
Kokoschka: *Venice*, expressionist painting.
Nash: *Genesis*, twelve wood-engravings.
Picasso: *Bull-fight*, Spanish cubist painting.
John Piper (*1903): *Rye Harbour*, a painting.
Respighi: *La Fiamma*, Italian opera.
Shostakovich: *Lady Macbeth of Mzensk*, Russian opera, which caused him to fall into disfavour with Soviet authority in 1936.
Rev. Dick Sheppard founded Peace Pledge Union.
Opening at Glynde, of the Glyndebourne

Jean Batten flew England-Australia in 14 days 23 hr. 25 min, fastest time for woman pilot.
W. Beebe (*1877, †1962), U.S.A., descended more than ½ mile into the ocean in his bathysphere.
*Dionne quintuplets, all girls, in Canada.
T. Hay observed white spot on Saturn.
W. R. Park, U.S. bacteriologist, discovered his vaccine for poliomyelitis.
J. Prentice observed bright nova in Hercules.
Scott and Black won London-Melbourne air race in 2 days 23 hr. in de Havilland Comet.
Mumps first isolated.

	History	Literature
1934	†Albert I of Belgium in Ardennes climbing accident; accession of Leopold II (to 1951). †President Hindenburg of Germany; Hitler became Reichsführer. Munich Putsch: Hitler's purge of followers including Rohm and Schleicher; "Night of the Long Knives". Rhineland finally evacuated by Allied forces. Polish-German ten year non-aggression pact. Socialist strikes in Austria vigorously suppressed by Chancellor Dollfuss. Dollfuss murdered by Nazi supporters; succeeded by Kurt Schuschnigg (to 1938). Assassination of S. M. Kirov, head of Leningrad Bolsheviks, led to Stalin's "Treason trials" and Communist purges. N.K.V.D., became M.V.D.; O.G.P.U. dissolved. Parliamentarian system in Esthonia replaced by dictatorship. Henry Pu-Yi, last Emperor of China (1912), made Japanese puppet Emperor of Manchukuo; deposed 1945.	Friedrich Wolf (*1888): *Professor Mamlock*, German play. Opening of Manchester Central Library, containing more than 500,000 books.
1935	Resignation of Ramsay Macdonald as Prime Minister; succeeded by Baldwin, P.M. for third time. Sir Samuel Hoare dismissed as Foreign Secretary following Hoare-Laval Pact, in which Anglo-French foreign ministers made deal with Italy over her invasion of Abyssinia; succeeded by Anthony Eden. Railway Staff National Tribunal: to deal with work, wages and conditions; National Wages Board abolished. Stresa Conference: Foreign Ministers of Britain, Italy, France denounced unilateral repudiation of treaties as danger to European peace. British Council established.	Archibald J. Cronin (*1896, †1981), medical practitioner: *The Stars Look Down*, a novel. Eliot: *Murder in the Cathedral*, poetic drama. Graham Green (*1904): *England Made Me*, a novel. Christopher Isherwood (*1904, †1986): *Mr. Norris changes Trains*, a novel. Clifford Odets (*1906, †1963): *Waiting for Lefty*, American play. John Steinbeck (*1906, †1968): *Tortilla Flat*, American novel. Giraudoux: *La Guerre de Troie n'aura pas lieu*, French play. Montherlant: *Les jeunes filles* (1935–40) 4–vol. novel. Lorca: *Llanto por Ignacio Sanchez Mejias*, lament for dead bull-fighter and other Spanish poems. †Aircraftsman "Shaw" (Lawrence of

Festival Theatre, by John Christie (*1882, †1962).
House of Commons refused to accept a fixed date for Easter.
Excavation of Maiden Castle, Dorset.
Russia admitted to membership of League of Nations.

British iron and steel industry reorganized; quota system of production; wasteful competition eliminated.
Colwyn Committee recommended reorganization of cotton industry.
Cunard and White Star shipping lines merged.
First vertical lift-bridge built at Middlesbrough.
Government subsidy £9½ million for construction of *Queen Mary* and sister ship.
Mersey Tunnel at Liverpool opened by George V (see 1925).
Unemployment Act: children admitted to Insurance Fund on leaving school; Unemployment Assistance Board set up Means Test for relief.
Workmen's Compensation Act: licensed greyhound racing tracks; totalisator betting permitted.
Appointment of special Commissioners for Depressed Areas.

Max Beckmann (*1884, †1950): *Tulips*, German expressionist painting.
Chagall: *The Red Horse*, Russian surrealist painting.
Dali: *Nostalgic Echo*, a painting.
Dufy: *Deauville*, French painting.
Films: (i) *Anna Karenina*, with Greta Garbo; (ii) *David Copperfield*; (iii) *Mutiny on the Bounty*.
Gershwin: *Porgy and Bess*, American opera.
Benny Goodman: *After You've Gone*, jazz trio music; began developing swing music from jazz.
Nash: *Megalithic Landscape*, influenced by surrealism.
Ben Nicholson (*1894, †1982): *White Relief*, abstract painting.
Picasso: (i) *Woman's Head*, (ii) *The Muse*, Spanish cubist paintings.

Campbell: new land speed record 301.7 m.p.h.
Amelia Earhart flew Honolulu-California in 18¼ hr.
C. C. Magee, of the U.S.A., invented parking-meter.
A. Stevens and O. Anderson, U.S.A., ascended 74,000 ft into the stratosphere in a helium balloon.
Sir Robert Watson-Watt (*1892, †1973) originated plan for radio pulse-echo aircraft detection, leading to the establishment of radar stations; five were erected as early as 1936.
Yukawa predicted the existence of the meson (see 1937).
Hore-Belisha introduced pedestrian crossings and 30 m.p.h. speed limit in built-up areas of Great Britain.

1935 Lusaka established as capital of Northern Rhodesia.
U.S. Labour Relations Act: part of Roosevelt New Deal; labour given right to organize freely; to bargain without coercion from employers.
Franco-Soviet peace pact signed.
Croix de Feu: quasi-Fascist organization founded in France.
Rexists: Belgian Fascist Party founded by Degrelle.
League of Nations imposed economic sanctions against Italy; rejected Abyssinian appeals for help against Italy.
Nuremberg Laws: deprived Jews of citizen rights; persecution of Jews.
Saar plebiscite returned district to German rule.
Anglo-German naval agreement.
Full conscription restored in Germany contrary to Treaty of Versailles.
Promulgation of new Austrian Constitution.
Restoration of monarchy in Greece.
Russian rationing system replaced by incentives policy; wage differences varied in accordance with social value of work done.
Defence alliance among Russia, France, Czechoslovakia.

Arabia) following motor-cycle accident.
Cyril Connolly (*1903, †1974): *The Rock Pool*, a novel about artists on the Riviera.

1936 January: † George V; accession of Edward VIII.
December: Constitutional crisis: abdication of Edward VIII; accession of Albert, Duke of York, as George VI.
Churchill demanded re-armament; Defence White Paper; Naval Programme; Air force improved; Hore-Belisha's Army reforms.
Naval Pact among Britain, France and the U.S.A.
Front Populaire: French Left parties' union; government under M. Blum.
Croix de Feu dissolved by Socialist government in France.
Popular Front Coalition in Spain defeated Conservatives.
Falange led by General Franco and

W. H. Auden (*1907, †1973) and Isherwood: *The Ascent of F.6*, a play.
Alfred Jules Ayer (*1910, †1989): *Language, Truth and Logic*, doctrines of positivist "Vienna" philosophers.
Eliot: *Collected Poems*.
Winifred Holtby (*1898, †1935): *South Riding*, a novel.
George S. Kaufmann (*1889, †1961) and Moss Hart (*1904, †1961): *You Can't Take it With You*, American comedy.
F. R. Leavis: *Revaluation*, Literary criticism.
Margaret Mitchell (*1900, †1949): *Gone with the Wind*, American novel, later filmed.
Morgan: *Sparkenbroke*, a novel.
Terence Rattigan (*1911, †1977): *French Without Tears*, a play.
Dylan Thomas (*1914, †1953), Welsh poet and playwright: *Twenty-Five Poems*.

Spencer: *The Bridle Path, Cookham*, a painting.
R. Strauss: *Die schweigsame Frau*, German opera.
Anthony Tudor: *The Descent into Hell*, ballet to the music of Ernest Bloch (Ballet Rambert).
Ninette de Valois: *The Rake's Progress*, Vic-Wells ballet to music of Gavin Gordon.
Vaughan Williams: 4th Symphony, in F minor.
Appearance of the rumba.
Silver Jubilee of George V celebrated.
First British National Park set up in Snowdonia.
Production of the Hammond organ in the U.S.A.

Hayden Planetarium opened in New York City.
Mussolini completed second reclamation of Pontine Marshes.
First Battersea power station (105 megawatts) built.
London Green Belt Scheme brought into operation.
Ribbon Development Act.
Great Western Railway centenary.
First chimpanzee born at London Zoo.
Silver Jubilee train travelled at 112 m.p.h.
Institution of British Sugar Corporation.
Radio-telephone service established to Japan.
Iraq oil pipe-line from Kirkuk to Haifa opened.
Completion of Appenine Tunnel (11½ miles long), Italy.
Great Beujon Hospital, Paris, opened.
Formation of German air force.
Disastrous earthquake at Quetta, India.
Sale of Chinese Eastern Railway by Russia to Manchukuo government.
U.S. Social Security Act: introduced unemployment systems and old-age pensions.
Opening of Princess Juliana Canal, in the Netherlands (20 miles long).

XIth modern Olympiad at Berlin under Hitler's leadership.
Ashton: *Apparitions*, ballet to the music of Liszt.
Hindemith: *Funeral Music*.
Kodály: *Te Deum*, Hungarian choral work.
Albert Marquet (*1885, †1947): *The Island of San Giorgio Maggiore*, French painting.
Picasso: *Still-Life with Lemons and Oranges*, Spanish cubist painting.
Prokofiev:*Peter and the Wolf*, fairytale for children; spoken dialogue with orchestra.
Rachmaninoff: Symphony No. 3 in A minor.
Schönberg: *Violin Concerto*.
Shostakovich: 4th Symphony, Russian composition, withdrawn during rehearsal.
Stravinsky: *Chronicles of my Life*, autobiography by the composer.

J. M. Keynes: *General Theory of Employment, Interest and Money*.
Turing, of Manchester, published theory of electronic computing machines.
Flying records: (i) Amy Mollison flew England-Cape Town in 3 days 6 hr.; (ii) J. A. Mollison flew Newfoundland-Croydon in 13 hr. 17 min.; (iii) Jean Batten flew solo to New Zealand in 11 days 56 min.
Opening, at Alexandra Palace, of first high-definition television broadcasts using electronic scanning (developed since 1934) in place of mechanical scanning; station closed on outbreak of World War II; reopened 1946.
S.S. *Queen Mary*'s maiden voyage, gained Blue Riband.
Public Health Act consolidated all earlier Acts.

1936 supported by Germany and Italy revolted; Spanish Civil War (to 1939); Republican government moved from Madrid to Valencia.
Italians captured Addis Ababa; Victor Emmanuel III of Italy proclaimed Emperor of Abyssinia.
Anti-Italian sanctions lifted by League of Nations.
Belgium requested release from Locarno Agreement.
Germany re-occupied Rhineland without Allied protest.
Germany abrogated Locarno Pact.
Anti-Comintern Pact signed by Germany and Japan.
Convention of Montreux.
†Faud I of Egypt; accession of Farouk (to 1952).
New Russian Constitution: universal franchise with equal, direct and secret voting.
Execution of former Bolshevik leaders, including Kamenev and Zinoviev, following Kirov murder (1934).
Azerbaijan established as Republic of U.S.S.R.
Esthonian referendum abolished dictatorship; authoritarian constitution introduced; political parties forbidden.
Chiang Kai-chek kidnapped by Communists; forced to co-operate against Japanese aggression.

George Malcom Young(*1882, †1959): *Victorian England*, portrait of an age.
Jean Anouilh (*1910, †1987): *Le voyageur sans Bagages*, French play.
Louis Aragon (*1897, †1982): *Les Beaux Quartiers*, French novel.
Bernanos: *Le Journal d'un Curé de Campagne*, French novel.

1937 Marriage of Duke of Windsor (ex Edward VIII) to Mrs Simpson, American divorcée.
British government announced rearmament policy.
Resignation of Baldwin; Neville Chamberlain Prime Minister.
Nyon Conference for suppression of submarine piracy in Mediterranean arising from Spanish Civil War.
Divorce legalized in Britain for grounds other than adultery.
Punjab became autonomous province of India.
Aden became British Crown Colony.

Phyllis Bottome (*1884, †1963): *The Mortal Storm*, a novel.
Cronin: *The Citadel*, novel of doctor's career from mining town to London society.
Mackenzie: *The Four Winds of Love*, a novel.
Priestley: *Time and the Conways*, a play.
Victoria Sackville-West: *Pepita*, a romantic biography.
Dorothy L. Sayers (*1893, †1957), best-known for her Lord Peter Wimsey stories: *The Zeal of thy House*, a play.
Steinbeck: *Of Mice and Men*, a novel.
Giraudoux: *Électre*, French play; individual version of the Greek story.
Emil Ludwig (*1881, †1948): *Franklin*

Utrillo: (i) *Christmas in Montmartre*, (ii) *Maison Mimi*, French paintings.
Work commenced on Guildford Cathedral.
Werner March: Olympic Stadium, Berlin (begun 1934).
Destruction of Crystal Palace by fire (see 1852).
Broadway Melody, American revue film.
Sir Donald George Bradman (*1908) became captain of the Australian cricket XI (until 1948).

Construction of Germany's West Wall, Siegfried Line, begun.
Devaluation of French franc.

Bliss: *Checkmate*, ballet music.
Britten: Variation (for strings) on a theme of Frank Bridge.
Disney: *Snow White and the Seven Dwarfs*, his first full-length cartoon.
Honegger: *L'Aiglon*, Swiss opera.
Klee: *Travelling Circus*, Swiss painting.
Picasso: (i) *Seated Woman*, (ii) *Guernica*, Spanish cubist works.
Shostakovich: 5th Symphony (in D minor), Russian composition.
Joe Louis (*1914, †1981) won World Heavyweight Boxing Championship; retained title until 1948.
Lord Nuffield founded Nuffield College, Oxford.

Aiken, U.S.A., at work on electronic computing.
Anderson discovered existence of mesons, small charged particles, in solar radiation (see 1935).
Amelia Earhart lost on Pacific flight.
C. A. Elvehjem, R. J. Madden, F. M. Strong and D. W. Woolley isolated niacin (anti-pellagra vitamin).
Campbell's land-speed record broken by George E. T. Eyston (*1897, †1979) at a speed of 311 m.p.h.
Air Raid Precautions (A.R.P.) introduced.
B.B.C. first broadcast British Quiz programme.
By this date motor-taxation receipts were

	History	Literature
1937	Cagoulard Plot to overthrow Third Republic in France; failed. Fall of Blum government in France: collapse of Front Populaire. Internal civil war among Spanish Republicans, who moved capital from Valencia to Barcelona. Guernica, Spain, bombed by German planes. Religious persecution in Germany:Protestant and R.C. priests arrested. Rome-Berlin Axis formed. Lübeck lost last political independence; incorporated in Schleswig-Holstein. Hansestadt Hamburg created by inclusion of Altona, Harburg and surrounding area. Pact of Saadabad: frontiers of Turkey, Iraq, Afghanistan and Persia stabilized by non-aggression pact. First elections under new Russian Constitution: only one list of candidates. Executions for Kirov murder continued. Resumption of Sino-Japanese war (to 1945): Japanese seized Shanghai and Peking; Chinese government forced to leave Nanking for Hankow; Chiang Kai-chek united with Communists led by Mao Tse-tung and Chou-en-Lai to resist Japanese.	*D. Roosevelt*, German biography of the U.S. President. Nikolai Ostrovsky (*1904, †1937): *The Making of a Hero*, Russian novel of the young Communists of the early Revolution. Stevens: *The Man with the Blue Guitar*, American poems. *The Morning Post* (newspaper) absorbed by *The Daily Telegraph*.
1938	Resignation of Anthony Eden, Foreign Secretary, over Chamberlain's policy towards Mussolini; Eden succeeded by Halifax. Act of Parliament established holidays with pay. Estimated that ⅓ British families lived below poverty line; ⅓ just above it. De Valera's new constitution for Ireland; Eire to be independent but retain Commonwealth membership. Fair Labour Standards Act in the U.S.A.: Roosevelt New Deal;	Bowen: *The Death of the Heart*, a novel. Greene: *Brighton Rock* a novel; adolescent criminal at Brighton race-course. Francis Kilvert (*1840, †1879): *Diaries* published; life of 19th-cent. vicar. Cecil Day Lewis (*1904, †1972): *Overtures to Death*, poems. Daphne du Maurier (*1907, †1989): *Rebecca*, novel. Dorothy Richardson (*1873, †1957): *Pilgrimage*, novels. Rex Warner (*1905, †1986): *The Professor*, a novel. Emlyn Williams (*1905, †1987): *The Corn is Green*, play based on author's youth in

Zoltan Korda and Flaherty's film *Elephant Boy*.
Coronation of George VI; last parade of British Empire.
Sir Billy Butlin (*1899, †1980) opened his first holiday camp (at Skegness).
Education Act: School-leaving age raised to 15 (to be implemented in 1939); abandoned because of war.
The Golden Gate Bridge, San Francisco, completed; single span, 4200 ft long.

applied entirely for general purposes; insidious practice begun in 1926.
Government subsidy for oats and barley.
Mitchell posthumously was to earn gratitude of Britain for Spitfire fighter (designed 1936–37).
National Maritime Museum opened at Greenwich.
Power Jets Ltd established; first successful jet engine tested.
S.S. *Normandie* gained the Blue Riband for France; crossed Atlantic in 3 days 23 hr. 2 min.
Sodium-vapour lamps in use.
Zeppelin *Hindenburg* destroyed by fire when landing at Lakehurst, U.S.A.
Storstrom Bridge, Denmark, opened.

Bartók: *Violin Concerto*, Hungarian composition.
Burra: *Mexican Church*, a painting.
Chaplin appeared in the film *Modern Times*.
Dufy: (i) *Regatta*, (ii) *Joinville*, (iii) *Santa Maria Della Salute*, (iv) *Scuola di San Marco*, French paintings.
Werner Egk (*1901, †1983): *Peer Gynt*, German opera.
Hindemith: (i) *Mathis der Maler*, Swiss opera (completed 1935) performed; (ii) *Nobilissima Visione*, ballet music.
Honegger: *Jeanne d'Arc au Bûcher*, Swiss-French narrative oratorio (words by Claudel) performed.

Grote Reber, U.S.A. (*1911), using dish-type radio telescope, received short waves from the Milky Way; beginnings of radio-astronomy.
P. Karrer, H. Salomon and H. Fritzsche synthesized vitamin E (the α-, β- and γ-tocopherols) first recognized in 1922.
Isolation of pyridoxine (vitamin B_6).
Sulphanilomide drugs developed (May and Baker 693) from sulpha prototype of G. Domagk (1935).
New theory of stellar energy propounded by Bethe and von Weizsäcker independently.
Discovery of nylon, strong synthetic fibre, in the U.S.A.; commercial production 1939.

1938 minimum and maximum wages fixed; abolition of child labour.
Franco-German declaration of Friendship.
Italian Manifesto: defined principles of Fascist racialism.
First anti-Jewish measures in Italy.
Failure of Schuschnigg to unite non-Nazi Austrians against Germany; led to German *Anschluss,* in which Hitler annexed Austria.
Hitler assumed command of German army.
Munich Pact: European powers agreed to German seizure of Sudetenland.
Mainly Turkish area around Alexandretta became autonomous republic of Hatay.
Third Russian Five Year Plan: interrupted 1941 by German invasion.
Japanese captured Hankow; Chiang Kai-chek retreated to Chungking.
Friction between Chinese Nationalists and Chinese Communists.
Signatories of Washington Treaty (1921) met at Brussels; failed to bring Japan to conference.
Spanish Republican victory at River Ebro; Nationalist forces reached Mediterranean near Castellon dividing Republican Spain; final Nationalist offensive against Catalonia.

Wales.
Bernanos: *Les Grands Cimetières sous la Lune,* polemic against Franco.
Mauriac: *Asmodée,* a play.
Jean-Paul Sartre (*1905, †1980): *La Nausée,* a novel.
Picture Post, British illustrated weekly, first published.

1939 British government's guarantee against foreign aggression to Poland: extended to Greece and Roumania.
Salaries of M.P.s in Britain raised to £600 per annum.
Ministry of Information: war-time ministry in Britain (to 1946).
Lebrun re-elected President of France (to 1940).
Failure of Anglo-French mission to Moscow.
French Communist Party dissolved for supporting Russo-German Pact.
Barcelona captured by Nationalists under Franco; surrender of Madrid

Joyce Cary (*1888, †1957): *Mister Johnson,* a novel.
Eliot: *The Family Reunion,* a play.
Eric Ambler (*1909): *The Mask of Dimitrios,* a thriller set in the Balkans.
C. S. Forester (*1899, †1966): *Captain Hornblower,* a novel; one of a series of tales of a naval officer of bygone days.
Isherwood: *Goodbye to Berlin,* stories of life in the city.
Joyce: *Finnegan's Wake,* a novel written in a language unintelligible without concentrated study.
Steinbeck: *The Grapes of Wrath,* American novel.

Leslie Howard appeared in film *Pygmalion*.
Lambert: *Horoscope*, a ballet.
Carl Orff (*1895, †1982): *Carmina Burana*, choral work.
Picasso: (i) *Still Life and Guitar*, (ii) *Still Life with Red Bull's Head*, (iii) *Woman in an Armchair*, Spanish cubist works.
R. Strauss: *Daphne*, German opera.
Report of Spens Committee on secondary education in Britain.
Rheims Cathedral, destroyed in World War I, restored and reopened.
James Monroe High School, New York City, had 10,000 pupils.
Opening of Marine Studios, Florida, world's first oceanarium.
C. F. Carlson (*1906, †1968) made first xerographic print.

Discovery of coelacanth skin, primitive fish, off East London, South Africa (live specimen found 1952).
Georg Biro, of Hungary made first *practical* ball-point pen, originally invented in 1888.
Brilliant display of *aurora borealis* seen in many parts of Britain.
H.M.S. *Rodney* became first ship to be equipped with radar.
Graf Zeppelin, virtually the last rigid airship, went out of commission; later airships were *blimp* type used in World War II, inflated like toy balloons.
Food and Drugs Act consolidated and improved earlier Acts.
Issue of civilian gas masks in Britain during Munich crisis.
British first-line aircraft increased by 124; Germany's by 742.
Low-voltage fluorescent lighting introduced commercially into Britain.
Discovery of new nickel-chrome alloy for use in jet engines.
Anglo-U.S. trade treaty marked retreat from Ottawa tariff agreement.
Lady Reading founded W.V.S. (Women's Voluntary Service).
Anglo-Irish Agreement; end of trade war.
Bartlett Dam, Arizona, completed; multiple-arch erection 286 ft high.

Bartók: *6th String Quartet*, Hungarian work.
Lennox R. F. Berkeley (*1903, †1989): *Serenade for Strings*.
Epstein: *Adam*, a sculpture.
Fokine: *Paganini*, ballet for Colonel de Basil.
Hindemith: (i) Violin Concerto; (ii) Violin Sonata in C major.
Honegger: *La Danse des Morts*, Swiss musical composition.
Marin: *Fisherman and Boats*, American painting.
Henry Moore (*1898, †1986): (i) *Reclining Figure*, a sculpture; (ii) *Landscape with Figures*, expressionist painting.
Ivor Novello (*1893, †1951): *The Dancing*

Byrd's third expedition to Antarctica (to 1941).
Hans von Chain, of Heinkel's, flew world's first jet aircraft in Germany.
Otto Hahn (*1879, †1968) and Fritz Strassman discovered nuclear fission in uranium (U^{235}).
Paul Müller (*1899, †1965) synthesized DDT (powerful insecticide commercially produced in 1942).
Igor Sikorsky, of the U.S.A., made first serviceable helicopter.
Balloons used as barrage to protect Britain against aircraft attack.
Radar stations in operation around coast of

1939 to Nationalists; end of Spanish Civil War.
Mussolini's invasion and conquest of Albania.
†Pope Pius XI; accession of Pius XII.
German unilateral denunciation of Anglo-German naval pact and Polish non-aggression pact.
Salzburg Conference of Rome-Berlin Axis powers.
Czechoslovakia invaded and occupied by Germany (to 1945); Slovakia declared independent state.
Germany annexed Memel.
World War II
Europe: German invasion of Poland, occupation of Danzig: started World War II; Britain and France declared war on Germany; Warsaw surrendered.
Russian Front: Russian invasion of Poland; Fourth Partition of Poland between Germany and Russia; Russian attack on Finland.
Naval: (i)Anglo-German action of River Plate; *Graf Spee* scuttled; (ii) *Rawalpindi*, armed merchant cruiser, sunk by German battleships after gallant action.
Hatay (see 1938) incorporated into Turkey.
Britain and France to assist Turkey in case of aggression.
Esthonia forced into alliance with Russia.
Japanese adopted seceded Chinese leader Wang Ching-wei as puppet ruler in Nanking.

Flora Thompson (*1877, †1947): *Lark Rise*, a novel.
Gide: *Journal*, diary 1885–1939.
Saint-Exupéry: *Terre des Hommes*, tales of an airman.
T. Mann: *Lotte in Weimar*, a novel.

1940 *World War II.*
European Front: Altmark incident in Norwegian waters; German invasion of Denmark, Norway, Low Countries; fall of Holland, Belgium; evacuation of Dunkirk by British; fall of France; Battle of Britain.
Russian Front: Russo-Finnish war ended.
Mediterranean Front: Italy declared war on Britain and France, invaded France; British fleet incapacitated

Ambler: *Journey into Fear*, a thriller.
Sir Arthur Bryant (*1899, †1985): *English Saga*, panorama of our national life.
Raymond Chandler (*1888, †1959): *Farewell my Lovely*, a novel.
Greene: *The Power and the Glory*, novel of dissolute Catholic priest in Mexico.
Hemingway: *For Whom the Bell Tolls*, a novel.
Arthur Koestler (*1905, †1983), Anglo-Hungarian author: *Darkness at Noon*, a novel.

Years, musical play.
Picasso: *The Poet Jaime Sabartés*, Spanish cubist work.
Piper: *Hamsey Church*, a painting.
Shostakovich: 6th Symphony, Russian composition.
Graham Sutherland (*1903, †1980): *Entrance to a Lane*, a painting.
Utrillo: *La Tour Saint Jacques*, French painting.
Films: (i) *Gone with the Wind*, with Vivien Leigh and Clark Gable; (ii) *Ninotschka*, with Greta Garbo.
Excavation of Sutton Hoo burial ship (Anglo-Saxon) in Suffolk.
National Identity Cards introduced into Britain; abolished 1952.
Opening of Opera House, Blackpool; largest in Britain.
Song *We'll Hang out the Washing on the Siegfried Line*. It became well known over 2nd World War years.

Britain; proved of great value in giving early warning of aircraft approach (see 1935).
I.F.F. radar (identification, friend or foe) developed.
Morden-East Finchley underground railway, having 17–mile-long tunnel, constructed.
Gloster Aircraft Co. of Britain to build plane suitable for jet engines.
First British transatlantic Air Mail Service opened.
Ministry of Supply established to deal with war-time production; dissolved 1959.
Excess profits tax in Britain on outbreak of war.
National Service (Conscription) introduced into Britain; to 1960.
White Paper on Civil Defence.
German battleship *Bismarck* launched.
Severe earthquakes in Chile (January) and Anatolia (December); tens of thousands died.
Extermination of anopheles mosquito in Brazil begun (later: Egypt 1944, Cyprus 1946).

Disney's *Fantasia*; probably his greatest achievement; coloured cartoons set to classical music.
Chaplin appeared in the film *The Dictator*, lampooning Hitler.
Duke Ellington: *Jack the Bear*, orchestral jazz.
Hindemith: Violin Concerto.
Hitchcock, (*1899, †1980) film: *Rebecca*.
Kodály: Concerto for orchestra, Hungarian work.
Lambert: *The Prospect Before Us*, a ballet.

Formation of Home Guard in Britain (first known as Local Defence Volunteers, L.D.V.).
Fire Watching, against enemy air attacks, compulsory in Britain.
Introduction (to 1953) of food rationing in Britain.
British Council incorporated by Royal Charter.
Purchase Tax introduced.
Britain leased naval and military bases to the U.S.A.

1940

French fleet at Oran; Italian invasion of Greece; British naval attack on Italian fleet at Taranto; British offensive against Italians in Western Desert.
Naval: naval battle of Narvik; S.S. *Jervis Bay*, armed merchant cruiser, sunk by *Admiral Scheer*, German pocket battleship, after gallant action.
Far Eastern Front: Japan joined Rome-Berlin Axis.
Resignation of Chamberlain ministry; Coalition ministry under Winston Churchill (to 1945).
German forces occupied Channel Islands (to 1944).
President Roosevelt elected in the U.S.A. for third term.
French government left Paris for Touraine; Paris occupied by Germans; government moved to Bordeaux.
Marshal Pétain became Prime Minister of France; Franco-German armistice signed at Compiègne in Foch's railway coach, which was afterwards burned.
Government of unoccupied France moved to Vichy.
French Indo-China invaded by Japanese.
Abdication of Carol II of Roumania; accession of son, Michael (to 1947).
Russia re-occupied Latvia, Lithuania, Esthonia, lost after World War I; all admitted to Soviet Union.
Leon Trotsky (co-founder with Lenin of modern Russia) in exile in Mexico, assassinated by Stalin's orders.
Installation of Dalai Lama in Tibet.
Assistance to Chinese Nationalists via French Indo-China ended by Japanese; Burma Road only route open.

Clive Staples Lewis (*1898, †1963): *The Problem of Pain*, on Christian behaviour.
Morgan: *The Voyage*, a novel.
Michael Sadleir (*1888, †1957): *Fanny by Gaslight*, a novel.
Dylan Thomas: *Portrait of the Artist as a Young Dog*, short stories.
Aragon: *Le Crève-cœur*, anti-Vichy poetry.
Mikhail Sholokhov (*1905, †1984): *Tikhi Don (The Silent Don)*, Russian novel in 4 vols.

1941

World War II
European Front: Roumania and Bulgaria joined Axis partners.
Mediterranean Front: Italian air

Cary: *A House of Children*, a novel.
Cronin: *The Keys of the Kingdom*, a novel.
John Phillips Marquand (*1893, †1960): *H. M. Pulham, Esq.*, American novel.

Sir David Low (*1891, †1963): anti-Nazi cartoons.
Matisse: *Still Life with Oysters*, French painting.
Moore: (i) *The Bride*, wire sculpture; (ii) *The Two Seated Women*, expressionist painting.
Picasso: *Café at Royan*, Spanish painting.
Shostakovich: Piano Quintet, Russian composition.
Stravinsky: Symphony in C major.
R. Strauss: *Love of the Danae*, German opera.
George VI instituted George Cross and George Medal.
German destruction of Coventry Cathedral in "Baedeker Raid"; new design by Sir Basil Spence approved 1951.
Tragic loss of ballets *Checkmate* and *Horoscope* in Holland during the German invasion.
Discovery, in France, of Lascaux caves; famous for prehistoric wall paintings (−25,000 to −14,000).

Shell Oil Co. provided design for new combustion chamber for jet engines.
Blood plasma used instead of red blood in transfusions.
Invention of cavity magnetron; development of centimetric radar for ships and land-mass detection.
S.S. *Queen Elizabeth* (83,673 tons) launched.
Germans used paratroops.
Completion of Baghdad Railway (commenced 1888).
Sir Howard Florey and Dr. E. Chain experimented successfully with penicillin as an antibiotic; obtained concentrated extracts; published results in *Lancet* 1940, 1941, 1943; one of the milestones of medicine, the discovery of penicillin (see 1928) has saved countless lives, e.g. in cases of infection by staphylococcus, streptococcus, pneumococcus, gonococcus, syphilis, anthrax and diphtheria.
G. T. Seaborg (*1912) and his team in California obtained plutonium by bombarding uranium with deuterons.

Berlin: *White Christmas*, popular song.
Egk: *Columbus*, German oratorio.
Hindemith: Symphony in E flat.
Marin: *Circus Elephants*, American painting.

Donald Bailey invented the military bridge named after him (first used 1942, North African campaign).
Hans Haas, later widely known for

1941 attacks on Malta; British occupation of Italian Somaliland; Addis Ababa recaptured from Italians by British; Germans invaded Greece (occupied to 1944) and Yugoslavia; battle for Crete; Free French and British entered Syria; British offensive in Western Desert.
Russian Front: Germany invaded Russia; German forces entered Persia; Germans captured Kiev, Kharkov, Rostov; attack on Moscow and siege of Leningrad commenced; Russian counter-offensive in Ukraine.
Far Eastern Front: Russo-Japanese neutrality pact; Japanese mobilization; Japanese air-attack on U.S. Pacific fleet at Pearl Harbor; Japanese captured Hong Kong.
Naval actions: British defeat of Italians at Cape Matapan.
Conscription applied to women in Britain.
Rudolph Hess, Nazi leader, landed in Britain on "peace" mission.
Meeting of Churchill and Roosevelt: Atlantic Charter signed.
U.S.A. declared war on Axis powers.
French government under control of Admiral Darlan.
Resistance to German occupation begun by French.
Dismissal of Weygand as G.O.C. French army.
Italian occupation of Dalmatian provinces of Yugoslavia.
Turkey forced into non-aggression pact with Germany.
Abdication of Reza Khan Pahlevi, Shah of Persia.
Lebanon proclaimed its independence of French Mandatory rule (1920).

Warner: *The Aerodrome*, novel of clash of militarism and rural life.
Vernon Watkins (*1906, †1967): *The Ballad of the Mari Lywd*, poetry.
Brecht: *Mutter Courage und ihre Kinder*, German play.
Fitzgerald: *The Last Tycoon*, American novel.
Werfel: *Das Lied von Bernadette*, German novel of healing at Lourdes.

1942 *World War II*
European Front: R.A.F. increased bombing attacks on Germany.
Mediterranean Front: Second German counter-offensive in Western Desert: Rommel captured British-held Tobruk; Axis forces reached El

Eliot completed *The Four Quartets*, a religious sequence consisting of (i) *Burnt Norton* (1935), (ii) *East Coker* (1940), (iii) *The Dry Salvages* (1941), (iv) *Little Gidding* (1942).
C. S. Lewis: *The Screwtape Letters*, book about Christian behaviour.

Matisse: *The Two Girl Friends*, French painting.
Moore: *People Sleeping in the Underground during an Air Raid*.
Nash: *Bomber over Berlin*, painting by the official war artist.
Picasso: *Seated Woman with a Cat*, Spanish cubist painting.
Piper: *View of Windsor Castle*, watercolour, pen and ink.
Shostakovich: 7th Symphony (written during the siege of Leningrad), in C major.
Orson Welles's film *Citizen Kane*, which made his reputation.
Norwood Report on curricula and examinations in English secondary schools.
Early appearance of bebop dance.
Outward Bound Sea School created for young people.

television underwater film series, began subaquatic photography.
First flight by P. E. G. Sayer, of Gloster jet fighter, Britain's first jet aircraft; based on work of Whittle (see 1930).
J. R. Whinfield and J. T. Dickson produced terylene; not available until 1950.
Air Training Corps (A.T.C.) established in Britain.
Royal Navy first used frigates, small escort vessels (entirely unlike 17th-cent. three-masted wooden frigates).
National Fire Service (N.F.S.) established in Britain to deal with war emergencies; dissolved 1948.
Income Tax reached 10*s*. in the £.
System of points rationing in Britain as war-time measure.
Mosquito fighter aircraft in use.
Identification of landmarks and urban areas possible from aircraft, at night and in poor visibility, through use of H2S radar set.
U.S.A. introduced "lease-lend" system of aid to Britain.

Braque: (i) *The Kitchen Table*, (ii) *The Fish Bowl*, French paintings.
Britten: 1st String Quartet.
Burra: *Soldiers*, surrealist painting.
Matisse: *The Idol*, French painting.
Picasso: (i) *Woman with an Artichoke*, (ii) *Still Life with Pigeon*, Spanish cubist paintings.

A. C. Harley (*1889, †1960), engineer, invented device for clearing fog from airfields; code name F.I.D.O.
J. S. Huxley: *Evolution, the Modern Synthesis*.
Max Mueller, of Junkers, developed successful turbo-prop engine.
K. A. Strand discovered planet of extreme

1942 Alamein; Rommel defeated by Montgomery at El Alamein; retreat of Axis forces westwards from Egypt; Allied landings in French North Africa.
Russian Front: Germans captured Sebastopol, Voroshilovsk, Krasnodar; battle of Stalingrad begun.
Far Eastern Front: Japanese captured Manila; invaded Dutch East Indies; Japanese captured Singapore, Rangoon, Mandalay, Philippines; defeat of Japanese at Milne Bay; Allied counter-offensive in New Guinea.
Naval actions: American-Japanese air-sea battles of Coral Sea and Midway.
Germans entered unoccupied France.
Riom Trials: former French leaders Blum, Daladier, etc., accused; failed.
French fleet sunk at Toulon; sabotage.
Darlan assassinated at Algiers.
Iberian Bloc: formed by Spain and Portugal.
Hitler declared himself Germany's supreme "Law Lord".
Strong American air force built up in Free China; saved Chungking from destruction.

Elliot Paul (*1891, †1958): *A Narrow Street*, American reminiscences of life in Paris.
Anouilh: *Eurydice*, French play.
Paul Eluard (*1895, †1952): *Poésie et Vérité*, French poetry.
Sartre: *Les Mouches*, French play.
Ilya Ehrenburg (*1891, †1967): *The Fall of Paris*, Russian novel.
Albert Camus (*1913, †1960), French writer and journalist: (i) *L'Étranger*, a novel, (ii) *Le Mythe de Sisyphe*, philosophical essay.

1943 *World War II*
European Front: Allied "round the clock" bombing of Germany began.
Mediterranean Front: British captured Tripoli; Allied offensive in Tunisia, Axis forces surrendered; Allied invasion of Sicily and landings on Italian mainland; Italian government surrendered to Allies; German resistance in Italy continued; Allied Volturno offensive; Italy joined Allies in war against Germany; Allied crossing of River Sangro.
Russian Front: Surrender of German army under Paulus at Stalingrad; Russians captured Rostov, Kharkov;

Nigel Balchin (*1908, †1970): *The Small Back Room*, a novel about scientists.
Denis Brogan (*1900, †1974): *The English People*.
Davies: *Collected Poems*.
Thomas: *New Poems*.
T. Rowland Hughes: (*1903, †1949): *O Law i Law (From Hand to Hand)*, a poignant story of the slate quarries of North Wales.
Germans burned Neapolitan archives before retreating.

Shostakovich: Symphony No. 8 in C major.
R. Strauss: *Capriccio*, German opera.
Sutherland: *Red Landscape*, expressionist painting.
Greer Garson appeared in the film *Mrs. Miniver*.
Disney cartoon film *Bambi*.
George Cross awarded to Island of Malta by George VI.
Discovery of Mildenhall Treasure: hoard of Roman silver-ware in Suffolk.
Destruction of Assembly Rooms, Bath, during air raid; reconstructed and reopened 1963.

density, affecting motion of 61 Cygni β.
Beveridge Plan: *Report on Social Security and National Insurance* published in England.
Report of Scott Committee on Land Utilization in Rural Areas.
Royal Electrical and Mechanical Engineers (R.E.M.E.) established separately from R.A.S.C.
War-time "National Loaf" introduced into Britain.
Terms of U.S. "Lease-lend" scheme to Britain made reciprocal.
Construction, at Chicago University, of world's first nuclear reactor.
Enrico Fermi (*1901, †1954), Italian physicist, awarded Hughes Medal for work on artificial radio-active sources; valuable contribution to atomic energy research.

Ashton: *The Quest*, ballet, to music by Walton.
Hindemith: (i) *Ludus Tonalis*, twelve fugues for piano; (ii) Overture, *Cupid and Psyche*.
Picasso: (i) *The Square of the Vert-Galant*, Spanish painting; (ii) *Woman in a Wicker Chair*, cubist painting.
Poulenc: *La Figure Humaine*, French cantata, one of his finest works.
Schönberg: Variations in G minor.
Vaughan Williams: 5th Symphony, in D minor, based on folk-lore.
Establishment of Ministry of Town and Country Planning in Britain.
Foundation of Nuffield Trust.
Opening of Howrah Bridge at Calcutta.

Selman A. Waksman (*1888, †1973), Russian-born scientist, first isolated streptomycin (antibiotic).
Chubb Crater, largest known meteorite crater, discovered at Northern Ungava, Canada, from the air.
Rolls-Royce "Welland" jet engine developed.
Anglo-American agreement with Chinese Nationalists to withdraw their special trading concessions and "treaty ports" in China.
Between 1943 and 1944 it is estimated that 4,000,000 people were murdered at Auschwitz (concentration camp).
J. S. Huxley: *Evolutionary Ethics*.

LITERATURE

1943 crossed Dnieper, regained Kiev and continued offensive west.
Japanese Front: Australians landed in Salamanua and Lae; took Buna; Guadalcanal evacuated by Japanese; Americans landed in Aleutians; captured Munda in Solomon Islands; landed on Treasury Island; invaded Gilbert Island.
Naval actions: American air-sea victory over Japanese in Bismarck Sea.
Casablanca Conference: Churchill-Roosevelt meeting; agreed "unconditional surrender" terms for Germany.
National Liberation Front founded in Algiers by de Gaulle and Giraud.
Corsica liberated from Vichy France.
Worker-Priest movement started in France: banned by Vatican 1959; restored 1965.
Victor Emmanuel III of Italy dismissed Mussolini, who was imprisoned; Italian Fascist Party dissolved; Mussolini rescued from prison by German raiding party.
Moscow Patriarchate of Orthodox Church (destroyed by Peter the Great) restored.
Dissolution of Comintern (see 1919).

1944 *World War II*
European Front: Allied bombing intensified; Allied landings in Normandy: Second Front (see D Day, opposite); German retreat from Normandy commenced; Allied landings in South of France; Liberation of Paris and Brussels; Battle of Arnhem: Allied air-borne landings failed; Germans cleared from Belgium; German counter-attack in Ardennes.
Mediterranean Front: Allied landings at Anzio; bombardment of Monte Cassino; Rome surrendered to Allies; Axis *Gothic Line* broken; Allied landings in Greece.
Russian Front: Russian offensive in Ukraine; Russians entered Roumania: captured Bucharest;

Cary: *The Horse's Mouth,* a novel of an artist.
Leslie Poles Hartley (*1895, †1972): *The Shrimp and the Anemone,* a novel.
Rosamund Lehmann (*1903), *The Ballad and the Source,* a novel.
Maugham: *The Razor's Edge,* a novel.
Trevelyan: *English Social History.*
Anouilh: *Antigone,* a play in modern costume of the old Greek legend.
Camus: *Caligula,* French play.
Sartre: *Huis Clos,* a play.

Francis Bacon (*1910): *Crucifixion*.
Bliss: *Miracle of the Gorbals*, tragic ballet.
Braque: *The Slice of Pumpkin*, French painting.
Matisse: *The White Dress*, French painting.
Picasso: (i) *Seated Woman in Blue*, (ii) *The Tomato Plant*, Spanish cubist paintings.
Prokofiev: Symphony No. 5 in B♭.
Rivera: *The Rug Weaver*, Mexican painting.
Rouault: *Homo Homini Lupus*, grim French painting denouncing violence.
R. Strauss: *Danae*, German opera.
Sutherland: *Sunset*, a painting.
Report of Fleming Committee on Public Schools in England.
Butler Education Act: secondary education for all children established: Ministry of Education superseded Board of Education.

Allied invasion of German-held Western Europe. D Day (June 6th), the greatest invasion of all time; highly scientific in concept; over 700 ships and 4,000 landing craft involved; remarkable oil pipe-line (PLUTO) laid across bed of English Channel to provide fuel for mechanised troops; Mulberry Harbour assembled off Normandy coast to aid Allied landings.
R.A.F. dropped *Grand Slam* bombs (22,000 lb.) on concrete U-boat pens.
V1 and V2 rockets used by Germans to bombard Britain; reached height in excess of 70 miles in flight.
Medical Council created to investigate hearing aids.
Bretton Woods Conference on international monetary policy.
Proposed British National Health Service (N.H.S.) published as White Paper.

1944 Crimea cleared of Germans; Bulgaria invaded by Russians: Belgrade captured; Russian offensives on Karelian and Central fronts.

Far Eastern Front: American invasion of Marshall and Admiralty Islands; Madang captured by Australians; Americans relanded in Philippines; Kalewa (Burma) captured by British.

Pétain imprisoned in Belfort.

Women's suffrage introduced into France.

France regained Lorraine (seized by Germany 1940).

Vietnam declared itself independent of France under Ho Chi Minh.

Abdication of Victor Emmanuel III of Italy; accession of Umberto II.

Execution of Count Ciano, Italian Fascist Foreign Secretary.

Iceland declared herself independent of Denmark.

Bunker bomb plot against Hitler failed.

Agreement on Allied zones of occupation of Germany and Berlin.

Moscow Conference: Allies declared intention to restore Austrian independence.

Russians invaded Hungary; captured Budapest; Horthy's dictatorship (begun 1920) ended.

Roosevelt elected for fourth term as President of the U.S.A.

Dumbarton Oaks Conference at Washington: led to establishment of United Nations Organization (U.N.O).

1945 *World War II*

European Front: German counter-offensive in Ardennes broken; Allied forces crossed Rhine; Germany overrun from West; American and Russian forces joined at River Elbe; suicide of Hitler; unconditional surrender of Germany (May 8th).

Mediterranean Front: Allies reached River Po; Italian partisans liberated Milan; Turkey declared war on

John Betjeman (*1906, †1984): *New Bats in Old Belfries*, verse.

Connolly: *The Unquiet Grave*, essays written under the pseudonym "Palinurus".

Nancy Mitford (*1904, †1973): *The Pursuit of Love*, a novel.

Percy Howard Newby (*1918): *A Journey to the Interior*, novel of the Orient.

"George Orwell" real name Eric Blair (*1903, †1950): *Animal Farm*, a novel; satire on the progress of a revolution: animals revolt against a farmer.

Ministry of National Insurance set up in Britain.
H.M.S. *Vanguard*, Britain's largest battleship, launched; displacement 42,000 tons; cost £11m; commissioned 1946.

Britten: *Peter Grimes*, an opera.
Epstein: *Lucifer*, a sculpture.
Honegger: *Sinfonie Liturgique*, his third symphony.
Kodály: *Missa Brevis*, Hungarian choral work.
Charlie Parker sextet: *Groovin' High*, transitional jazz.
Picasso: *The Charnel House*, Spanish cubist painting.
Prokofiev: *Cinderella*, Russian ballet.
Rouault: *Head of a Clown*, French painting.

First atomic explosion (experimental) at Alamogordo New Mexico (July 16th); atomic bombs dropped on Hiroshima (August 6th) and Nagasaki (August 9th); tremendous loss of life (estimated at 91,000 in Hiroshima alone) resulted; in consequence, war with Japan was greatly shortened.
By this time aero-engines developing 2,500 h.p. were in use.
Establishment of Harwell Atomic Research Centre in England.

1945 Germany; unconditional surrender of German army in Italy (April 29th).
Russian Front: Hungary, Poland and Austria overrun by Russians; fall of Warsaw and Vienna; Germany overrun from East: Russians captured Berlin (May 2nd).
Far Eastern Front: Australian landings in Japanese-held Borneo; U.S. Marines captured Bataan in Philippines; Russia declared war on Japan and invaded Manchuria; unconditional surrender of Japan (August 14th).
Yalta Conference: Last meeting of Roosevelt-Churchill-Stalin.
Potsdam Conference: Allies met to settle problems of reconquered Europe: serious differences.
Fall of war-time Coalition government in Britain; Churchill headed "Caretaker government".
General Election in Britain: Labour government headed by Clement Attlee (to 1951).
†Roosevelt, U.S. President since 1933; succeeded by Truman.
Revival of Ku Klux Klan in America by Samuel Green.
Former Japanese-held Korea occupied by U.S. and U.S.S.R. troops.
Third Republic (begun 1871) in France ended by referendum.
Execution of Pierre Laval, French collaborator with Germans (1940–45) and Vidkun Quisling (*1887), puppet P.M. of Norway.
Saar administered by France (to 1956).
Danzig (renamed Gdansk) assigned to Poland; German population (95%) expelled.
Opening of Nuremberg War Crimes Tribunal; ended 1946.
Division of Austria into four zones of military occupation.
Mussolini executed by partisans.
Galicia, formerly Polish territory, annexed by Russia.
Formation of Arab League in Cairo.

O. Sitwell: *Left Hand, Right Hand*, autobiography (to 1950).
Thurber: *The Thurber Carnival*, humour.
Romain Gary (*1915, †1980): *Education européenne*, French novel.
Sartre: *Les Chemins de la Liberté*, French novel in 4 vols.
Carlo Levi (*1902, †1975): *Christ stopped at Eboli*, Italian novel.

Shostakovich: Symphony No. 9 in E♭ major.
R. Strauss: complex variations for 23 instruments, based on *Eroica* funeral march.
Stravinsky: *Symphony in Three Movements*.
B.B.C. introduced Light Programme.
Opening of new Waterloo Bridge over the Thames.
San Francisco Conference: formation of United Nations; Charter signed at San Francisco; Security Council of U.N.O. established power of veto; Falangist Spain refused admission to U.N.O. (declared unfit by Potsdam Conference); Turkey represented as an ally.
Women's suffrage adopted in Italy.

SCIENCE

Family allowance system introduced into Britain.
Purified curare used to produce relaxation in patients under light general narcosis (see 1595).
Completion of Sturrock Dock, Cape Town; graving dock 1212 ft long.

1945 Communist government of Vietnam established.
Chinese Nationalists under Chiang Kai-chek took Formosa from Japan.
Russo-Chinese Agreement: Russia to support Nationalist China in return for concessions in Manchuria.
Japan under Allied occupation (to 1952).

1946 Churchill's "Iron Curtain" speech at Fulton, U.S.A.
Trades Disputes and Trade Union Act: repealed 1927 Act.
Execution of William Joyce ("Lord Haw-Haw") for anti-British broadcast propaganda (1939–45).
Mutiny in Indian navy at Bombay.
Sarawak ceded to British Crown by Rajah Sir Charles Brooke.
Independence of Transjordan recognized by Britain: State became Kingdom of Jordan.
French Fourth Republic accepted by referendum (to 1958).
Italian plebiscite ended monarchy and set up Republic.
Republic of Hungary proclaimed.
King Zog of Albania deposed in his absence; Republic proclaimed.
Bulgaria established Communist People's Republic.
Turkish Electoral Law reformed: new political parties permitted.
French completed evacuation of Lebanon.
Fourth Five Year Plan announced in Russia (completed 1950).
Philippines established as independent republic.
Nanking restored as capital of China; U.S. failed to bridge gap between Nationalists and Communists; Chiang Kai-chek promulgated new Constitution for China; Communists refused to take part in discussions.
First African nominated for Kenya Legislative Council.
Civil War in Indo-China (ended 1954).

Henry Green (*1905, †1973): *Back,* a novel.
John Hersey (*1914): *Hiroshima,* American account of atomic bomb explosion.
Hartley: *The Sixth Heaven,* a novel.
Rattigan: *The Winslow Boy,* play of a cadet falsely accused of theft.
Denton Welch (*1895, †1948): *In Youth is Pleasure,* a novel.
Edmund Wilson (*1895, †1972): *Memoirs of Hecate Country,* American collection of sketches.
Cocteau: *L'Aigle a deux Têtes,* French play.
Montherlant: *Le Maître de Santiago,* French play.
Jacques Prévert (*1900, †1979): *Paroles,* French collection of poems.
Salacrou: *Les Nuits de la Colère,* play on the French Resistance.
Sartre: (i) *La Putain respectueuse,* French play; (ii) *L'Existentialisme est un Humanisme,* philosophical treatise setting forth author's ideas.
Opening of New Bodleian Library, Oxford.
B. A. W. Russell: *History of Western Philosophy.*

Bliss: *Adam Zero*, ballet music.
Britten: *The Rape of Lucrece*, an opera.
Carlo Carrà: *Seascape in Venice*.
Honegger: *Deliciae Basilienses*, his fourth symphony.
Fernand Léger (*1881, †1955): *Composition with Branch*, French abstract painting.
Matisse: (i) *Lady with a White Dress*, French painting; (ii) *1001 Nights*, collage.
Moore: (i) *Family*, a bronze; (ii) *Family Group*, pen, chalk and watercolour.
Picasso: *Sea Urchins*, Spanish cubist work.
Piper: *Landscape with Rocks*, pen and gouache.
Shostakovich: 9th Symphony.
New Towns Act in Britain.
B.B.C.: (i) television service resumed from Alexandra Palace; (ii) Third Programme begun on radio.
League of Nations Union superseded by United Nations Organization (U.N.O.); first General Assembly of U.N.O. held in London.
U.N.E.S.C.O. (United Nations Educational, Scientific and Cultural Organization) established (4th Nov.).

Z.Bay received radar echoes from moon.
D. W. Fry built the first linear accelerator for electrons.
Nationalization in Britain of: (i) Bank of England; (ii) civil aviation; (iii) coal industry.
Opening of London Airport (now Heathrow); extended, and new terminal built, 1955.
Coinage Act: "silver" coins in Britain (50% pure silver since 1920) replaced by cupro-nickel.
Regular attenders at House of Lords received travelling expenses.
Proposed experimental rocket range at Woomera, Australia.
First U.S. Navy atomic bomb tests at Bikini and Eniwetok Atolls, in Marshall Islands; U.S. battleship *Arkansas* sunk by the blast.
Invention, in the U.S.A., of electric blanket (with thermostatic switch).
International Bank for Reconstruction and Development established.
Woolwich and Sandhurst combined to form Royal Military Academy, Sandhurst.
Benjamin Spock (*1903): *The Common Sense Book of Baby and Child Care*, advocated relaxation of controls over children.

1947

Crown Proceedings Act: Crown liable to legal proceedings.
India Independence Act: India partitioned into two Dominions; India (Hindu) and Pakistan (Moslem); Punjab partitioned between the two.
Kashmir disputed between India and Pakistan; state conceded to India.
Burma Independence Act: Union of Burma outside British Commonwealth.
Ceylon Independence Act: Ceylon became self-governing Dominion.
Legislative Council established at Aden.
U.S.A. voted funds to protect Greece and Turkey from Russian pressures.
Vincent Auriol elected President of France.
Revolt against French rule in Madagascar.
Industrial unrest in France inspired by Communists.
Breakdown of London Four Power Conference of Foreign Ministers on Germany.
Bi-zonal agencies set up by British and American authorities in Germany.
Bremen created a "Land" within American zone of occupation.
Prussia liquidated as separate German state.
Allied peace treaty with Italy; British and American troops left.
Communist government set up in Poland.
Roumania abolished monarchy; abdication of King Michael.
Russo-Finnish peace treaty.
Nationalist troops in China captured Communist capital of Yenan.
New, and more democratic, constitution in Japan.
Failure of attempted Communist revolt in Burma.

Herbert Ernest Bates (*1905, †1974): *The Purple Plain*, a novel.
Forster: *Collected Short Stories*.
Hartley: *Eustace and Hilda*, a novel.
Mackenzie: *Whisky Galore*, a novel.
Newby: *Agents and Witnesses*, a novel.
Tennessee Williams (*1914, †1983): *A Streetcar Named Desire*, U.S. play of the Deep South.
Camus: *La Peste*, French novel of pestilence in Oran.
Julien Green (*1900): *Si j'étais vous*, French novel.
Diary of Anne Frank published: by a Jewess who died in Belsen Concentration Camp, Germany (1945).
Discovery of the Dead Sea Scrolls, in Wadi Qumran, Palestine; the scrolls appear to date from –22 to 100; five scrolls are in Jerusalem and five in Syria; the reconstruction was carried out by Prof. Wright Baker, of Manchester University.

1948

Representation of the People Act: abolition of plural voting in Britain.

Churchill: *The Second World War*, history, by one who made it.

Britten: *Albert Herring*, an opera.
Dufy: *Music*, French water-colour.
Hindemith: *Day of Judgment*, work for choir and orchestra with 7th cent. wording.
Kokoschka: (i) *The Matterhorn*, (ii) *Whirlwind of Sion*, Russian expressionist paintings.
Matisse: *The Young English Girl*, French painting.
Prokofiev: (i) *War and Peace*, Russian opera; (ii) Symphony No. 6 in E♭ minor.
Schönberg: *A Survivor from Warsaw*, Austrian cantata.
Foundation of St. Benet's Hall, Oxford University.
No further appointment to be made to British Indian Orders of Chivalry.
School-leaving age raised to 15 in Britain (see 1937).
Town and Country Planning Act in Britain.
Dominions Office became Commonwealth Relations Office.
Free passages to Australia for emigrant British ex-servicemen.
Christian Dior (*1905, †1957) opened his salon in Paris; immediately revolutionized ladies' fashion with his "New Look".
Richard Attenborough (*1923) appeared in the film *Brighton Rock*.

K. Arnold first reported "flying saucers" in the U.S.A.
John Cobb drove Railton Special car at 394 m.p.h.
British Leprosy Relief Association Research Unit at Uzuakoli, Nigeria, found oral treatment of leprosy, using dapsone, effective.
Experimental gas-turbine ship developed.
First British nuclear reactor built (at Harwell).
Formation of General Agreement on Tariffs and Trade (G.A.T.T.).
Greenwich Observatory removed from Greenwich to Herstmonceux, Sussex, because London lights interfered with astronomical observation.
Government-supported ground-nuts scheme in Tanganyika; failed; cost the nation between £10m and £40m.
Nationalization of British electric power supply.
Transport Act: railways, canals and road transport nationalized in Britain (last-named de-nationalized 1953).
Most severe winter in Britain for 53 years.
Marshall Plan instituted: U.S. aid for European post-war recovery.
Pilotless U.S. aircraft flew the Atlantic.
Harvard Observatory discovered new comet.
Great meteorite fell in Siberia.

Braque: *The Bird*, French painting.
Britten rewrote music for Gay and

Bardeen, Brattain and Shockley, U.S.A., invented the transistor, a solid-state

1948 Conscientious Objectors Tribunals (National Service Act).
Formation of World Council of Churches.
Criminal Justice Act: abolition of trial of Peers by Peers.
Commencement of withdrawal of British troops from Egypt.
Mosley revived Fascist party in Britain.
Assassination of Gandhi, leader of Indian independence movement.
†Mohammed Ali Jinnah, founder of Pakistan.
Burma became independent republic outside British Commonwealth (1947).
Beginning of terrorism in Malaya.
Ceylon became self-governing Dominion within British Commonwealth (1947).
South African government adopted *apartheid* as official policy.
Formation of Organization of American States (O.A.S.).
Political *Third Force* formed in France; between Gaullists and Communists.
Abdication of Queen Wilhelmina of Holland; accession of Juliana.
Soviet Union withdrew from Allied Control Council in Berlin.
Para-military "police" in Soviet occupation zone of Germany.
Russian blockade of West Berlin began: Allied "air lift".
Communist coup in Czechoslovakia; People's Republic established.
Communist People's Republic established in Roumania.
Bulk of Palestine taken over by Zionist Jews who declared new, independent state of Israel.
Communist forces invaded China from Manchuria; captured Honan; set up North China People's Republic; advanced towards Chinkiang, North Korea became Communist republic; South Korea republic under U.S. influence.

C. D. Lewis: *Collected Poems.*
Greene: *The Heart of the Matter,* a novel.
Leavis: *The Great Tradition,* literary criticism.
Norman Mailer (*1923): *The Naked and the Dead,* American novel.
Alan Paton (*1903, †1988): *Cry the Beloved Country,* South African novel.
Irwin Shaw (*1913, †1984): *The Young Lions,* American novel.
E. Waugh: *The Loved One,* novel of Californian burial customs.
Eluard: *Poèmes politiques.*
Prévert: *Histoires,* collection of French satirical poems.
Sartre: *Les Mains sales,* French play.

Pepusch's *Beggar's Opera* (see 1728).
Chagall: *Evening Enchantment*, Russian surrealist painting.
Dufy: *The Band*, French lithograph.
Kokoschka: *Boats near the Dogana*, Russian expressionist painting.
Picasso: (i) *The Kitchen*, (ii) *Lobster and Bottle*, Spanish cubist paintings.
Sutherland: *The Large Vine Pergola*, a painting.
Vaughan Williams: 6th Symphony.
United Nations adopted Declaration of Human Rights.
Aldeburgh Festival established.
Institute of Contemporary Arts founded in London.
University College of Nottingham became Nottingham University.
Children Act: Local Authorities responsible for children without proper homes.
Foundation of New South Wales University of Technology, Australia, and of University of Bergen, Norway.
Malraux: *Psychologie de l'Art*, French study of art in 4 volumes.
XIV Olympic Games: in London.

amplifying electronic device largely to supersede the thermionic valve.
J. Derry, in de Havilland aircraft, reached supersonic speed.
Kinsey: *Sexual Behaviour in the Human Male*.
Completion of 200–in. Hale reflecting telescope at Mount Palomar, California.
World Health Organization (W.H.O.) set up as part of United Nations; began large-scale D.D.T. spraying against malaria.
Organization of European Economic Co-operation (O.E.E.C.) established.
Nationalization of British Health Services.
London Passenger Transport Board replaced by London Transport Executive.
Steady state theory of the universe evolved by Hermann Bondi and Thomas Gold.
Revised Uganda development plan involved construction of Owen Falls Dam.
Copenhagen Conference: international broadcasting wavelengths settled (British wavelengths altered 1950).
National Assistance Act passed.
Italy joined European Recovery Programme.
Local Government Act: Block Grant replaced by Exchequer Equalization Grant.

1949 Legal Aid and Advice Act.

Parliament Act: Reduced Lords' delaying powers.

North Atlantic Treaty signed at Washington.

British North America Act: Newfoundland, formerly Dominion, became Canadian province.

Ireland Act: Republic of Ireland recognized as outside the Commonwealth.

Indo-Pakistan cease-fire in Kashmir; Indian- and Pakistani-controlled governments set up in Hindu and Moslem areas of state.

Laos became independent state within French Union.

Indonesia declared herself a republic independent of Holland.

Cambodia and Vietnam granted independence as Associate States of French Union (Cambodia fully independent 1955, Vietnam 1954).

Federal Republic in West Germany; Konrad Adenauer first Chancellor; Bonn established as capital.

Russian blockade of Berlin lifted; end of Allied air-lift.

German Democratic Republic established in Soviet Zone of Germany.

Communist régime established in Hungary.

Arab-Israeli Armistice: Partition of Jerusalem between Israel and Jordan.

Chiang Kai-chek withdrew from presidency of China; Nanking evacuated; Communists invaded remaining Chinese provinces; Communist People's Republic of China under Mao Tse-tung.

Bates: *The Jacaranda Tree*, a novel.

Simone de Beauvoir (*1908, †1986): *The Second Sex*, feminist essay.

Faulkner: *Knight's Gambit*, a novel.

Christopher Fry (*1907): *The Lady's Not for Burning*, a verse drama.

Jean Genet (*1910, †1986): *Our Lady of the Flowers* (French publication 1946).

Greene: *The Third Man*, a long short story.

Orwell: *Nineteen Eighty Four*, a novel, terrifying in its implications of the future.

Louis MacNeice (*1907, †1963): *Collected Poems*.

Arthur Miller (*1915): *Death of a Salesman*, American play of a pathetic salesman at the end of his career.

Elizabeth Taylor (*1912, †1976): *A Wreath of Roses*, a novel.

Angus Wilson (*1913): *The Wrong Set*, short stories.

1950 Outbreak of war between United Nations and North Korea; latter supported by Chinese; ended 1951.

General Election in Britain: Labour government returned without overall majority.

India declared herself an independent republic within the British Commonwealth.

William Cooper (*1910): *Scenes from Provincial Life*, a novel.

Lawrence Durrell (*1912): *Sappho*, a verse play.

Eliot: *The Cocktail Party*, a play.

Fry: *Venus Observed*, a play.

Hartley: *The Boat*, a novel.

E. Waugh: *Helena*, a novel.

Hemingway: *Across the River and Into the Trees*, American war novel.

Bliss: *The Olympians*, ballet music.
Chagall: *Red Sun*, Russian surrealist painting.
Sir Kenneth Clark (later Lord Clark) (*1903, †1983): *Landscape into Art*, by the Slade Professor of Fine Art.
Miles Davis orchestra: *Godchild* (composed by Gerry Mulligan), modern jazz.
Moore: *Sculptured Objects*, lithograph.
Picasso: *Woman with a Fish Hat*, Spanish cubist painting.
University College of North Staffordshire founded at Keele.
Formation of a Council of Europe; Italy became a member.
Hindemith: (i) Horn Concerto, (ii) Concerto for Trumpet, Bassoon and Orchestra, German compositions.
The Third Man, film starring Orson Welles, and famous for *Harry Lime Theme*, played on the zither.
Natal University, S. Africa, founded.
Work begun on huge Lomonosov University of Moscow, containing 40,000 rooms (completed 1953).
University of Malaya established.

Nationalization of British gas industry.
Publication of Report by Royal Commission on Population.
Devaluation of the pound sterling.
100,000 gold sovereigns minted.
Helicopter freight service in Britain.
Mount Palomar Observatory, U.S.A., opened; first test photographs made.
Firing of first stage rocket at White Sands, New Mexico.
First Russian atomic explosions recorded.
Charlemagne Prize established in Aachen for service to European co-operation and understanding.

Berlin: *Call Me Madam*, musical comedy.
Braque: (i) *Bowl of Fruit* (ii) *The Terrace*, French paintings.
Hindemith: *A Requiem for those we love*, setting to music of Whitman's poems.
Honegger: 5th Symphony, Swiss composition.
Krének: *Tarquin*, Austrian opera, first performed.

Anglo-Persian dispute over Persian nationalization of oilfields: settled in 1954.
H.M.S. *Ark Royal* launched; designed to carry 110 aircraft.
S.S. *Galathea*, Danish research vessel, found living organisms at depth exceeding 34,000 ft in Pacific Ocean.
End of polygamy in China.
Severe earthquake in Assam.

1950 Anglo-Egyptian dispute over future of Sudan and Suez Canal Zone began (Suez Crisis 1956).
Nairobi (Kenya) received Royal Charter of Incorporation.
McCarthy Committee of Enquiry into Un-American activities began work.
Pleven Plan for European Army.
Polish-German frontier fixed permanently on Oder-Neisse Line by agreement between Poland and German (East) Democratic Republic.
Dalai Lama assumed ruling power in Tibet.
Italian Somaliland, under control by Britain 1941–1949, came under U.N. trusteeship (to 1960); became independent 1960

1951 General Election in Britain: Conservatives returned under Churchill with overall majority of 17 (to 1955).
Durham County Council applied "Closed Shop" principle for its employees.
Fraudulent Mediums Act: repealed Witchcraft Act of 1735.
Operation performed on King George VI for lung resection.
Guy Burgess and Donald Maclean, British diplomats, defected to Russia.
Dock strike in Britain.
Egypt abrogated Treaty of 1936 and Condominium Agreement of 1899 with Britain; British troops occupied Canal Zone.
Leopold III of Belgium abdicated in favour of his son, Prince Baudouin.
French government under Pleven resigned on issue of electoral reform.
†Pétain, French C.-in-C. in 1917, who collaborated with Germans in 1940.
First General Election in Gold Coast Colony.

F. S. Chapman: *Memoirs of a Mountaineer*.
Richard Church (*1893, †1972): *The Growth of the English Novel*.
Frost: *Complete Poems*.
Fry: *A Sleep of Prisoners*, verse drama.
Nevill Coghill (*1899, †1980): *The Canterbury Tales*, Chaucer's tales in modern English.
Sir Victor Gollancz (*1893, †1967): *A Year of Grace*, anthology by the founder of the Left Book Club.
Jacquetta Hawkes (*1905): *A Land*.
Edward Hyams (*1910): *Sylvester*, satirical novel.
James Jones (*1921): *From Here to Eternity*, American novel.
Nicholas Monsarrat (*1910, †1979): *The Cruel Sea*, novel on the Battle of the Atlantic.
Sir Steven Runciman (*1903): *A History of the Crusades* (completed 1954).
Jerome David Salinger (*1919): *The Catcher in the Rye*, American novel.
Angus Wilson: *Hemlock and After*, a novel.
Sartre: *The Psychology of Imagination*.
Hermon Wouk (*1915): *The Caine Mutiny*, American novel.
Arden Edition of Shakespeare begun.
History Today, monthly periodical first

Picasso: *Winter Landscape*, Spanish cubist painting.
Rouault: *Winter*, French painting.
Utrillo: *Suburban Street*, French painting.
Scottish Nationalists stole Coronation Stone (Stone of Scone) from Westminster Abbey; stone recovered in 1952.
Foundation of St. Antony's College, Oxford University.
College of Europe opened at Bruges.
Samba, modern dance, gained popularity.
State Secret, film on dictatorship theme.
c. Cool Jazz developed from bebop.
At St. Chad's, Winsford, Cheshire, campanologists working continuously rang 21,600 changes in 12 hr. 56 min.

European Payments Union agreement reached.
Colombo Plan (South and South East Asia).
Nationalization of British steel industry: denationalized 1952.
Rover Motor Co. in Britain produced world's first gas-turbine powered car.
Myxomatosis first used to destroy rabbits in Australia; used in Britain in 1952.
International airport opened at Livingstone, Northern Rhodesia.
Burmese government reopened Rangoon-Mandalay road.
Schumann Plan for European Coal and Iron Community.
Formation of European Broadcasting Union.
First Sociology World Congress at Zürich.
Television tower added to Empire State Building, New York; overall height raised to 1474 ft.
Arrest of Klaus Fuchs for sale of atomic secrets to enemy agents.

Britten: *Billy Budd*, an opera.
Peter Racine Fricker (*1920): Concerto for Violin and Small Orchestra.
Emilio Greco (*1913): *Seated Figure*, Italian sculpture.
Picasso: (i) *Baboon and Young*, (ii) *Head of a Woman*, Spanish bronzes.
Rodgers and Hammerstein: *South Pacific*, American musical play.
Stravinsky: *The Rake's Progress*, an opera.
Vaughan Williams: *The Pilgrim's Progress*, an opera.
Abbey Theatre, Dublin, destroyed by fire.
Competition for design of new Coventry Cathedral won by Basil Spence.
Festival of Britain opened by King George VI.
Manchester Free Trade Hall rebuilt after destruction in 1941; Hallé Orchestra returned.
Foundation stone for National Theatre laid.
Royal Festival Hall, designed by R. Matthew and J. L. Martin, opened.
Walker Art Gallery, Liverpool, reopened after 12 years.
"X Certificate" introduced by British film censors for films unsuitable for persons under 16.

De Havilland *Comet*, first turbo-jet airliner.
First peaceful uses of atomic energy: (i) heating of Harwell Atomic Reasearch Establishment, (ii) production of electric power at Arco, Idaho.
New calibre for small arms adopted by Britain.
Census in Britain (first since 1931).
Census in India: population 356,891,624.
Dangerous Drugs Act.
Dartmoor National Park of 365 square miles created.
European Coal and Steel Community Treaty signed in Paris.
Foreign Exchange Market reopened in London for first time since 1939.
Forestry Act.
Introduction of Health Service charges split Labour Party; Bevan and Wilson resigned.
Margam Steelworks at Port Talbot completed.
Largest oil refinery in Europe opened at Fawley, Hampshire.
Persian government under Dr Musadiq nationalized oil industry.
Rain-making experiments in U.S.A.
Submarine *Affray* disaster off Isle of Wight; 75 lives lost.

1951 Greece elected to Security Council of United Nations.
Treaty of Peace with Japan signed by 49 nations.
Assassination of King Abdullah of Jordan.
India and Pakistan in dispute over future of Kashmir.
Libya bacame independent state.
Assassination of Ali Khan, Premier of Pakistan.
General Ali Razmara, Prime Minister of Persia, assassinated.
Colombo Plan, for development of S. and S.E. Asia, came into operation.
Chinese Communist forces occupied Tibet.
U.S. President Truman dismissed General MacArthur as Supreme Commander Allied Powers.
Pacific Security Treaty signed by United States, Australia and New Zealand.

issued.
Oxford Companion to the Theatre.

1952 †King George VI; accession of Elizabeth II.
Defamation Act revised law of libel and slander.
Identity Cards (see 1939) abolished.
New Towns Act.
Craig and Bentley murder case.
Straffen murder case: problem of relationship of crime and mental illness.
European Defence Community Treaty.
European Coal and Steel Community's common market in these products in the six participating countries.
Arab League security pact.
†D.S. Senanayaka, Prime Minister of Ceylon; succeeded by Dudley Senanayaka.
China accused U.S. of waging germ warfare in Korea.
Batista Y Zaldivar, a former president, overthrew Cuban government.
Egypt:General Mohammed Neguib (*1900, †1984) seized power; King Farouk abdicated.

Jean Anouilh: *Waltz of the Toreadors*, French play.
Bates: *Love for Lydia*, a novel.
Agatha Christie: *The Mousetrap*, longest running play in the history of the theatre (still running 1991).
Peter Fleming (*1907): *A Forgotten Journey*, on a journey through Russia.
Fry: *The First-Born*, a play.
Sir Arthur Grimble (*1888, †1956): *A Pattern of Islands*, reminiscences.
Hemingway: *The Old Man and the Sea*, short novel.
Frederick Knott: *Dial M for Murder*, a play.
Doris Lessing (*1919): *Martha Quest*, a novel.
Somerset Maugham: *The Vagrant Mood*, essays.
Gavin Maxwell (*1914, †1969): *Harpoon at a Venture*.
C. Morgan: *The River Line*, a play.
H. Nicholson: *King George the Fifth, His Life and Reign*.
Laurens van der Post (*1906): *Venture to the Interior*, travel.
Hilda F. M. Prescott (*1896, †1972): *The Man on a Donkey*, historical novel.

Three-dimensional films shown in *Telecinema* built on South Bank festival site.
The African Queen, film with Katharine Hepburn and Humphrey Bogart.
An American in Paris, film with Gene Kelly.
The Browning Version, film version of Terence Rattigan's play, with Michael Redgrave.
The Lavender Hill Mob, comedy film with Alec Guinness.
Oliver Twist, film with Alec Guinness, Robert Newton and John Howard Davies.
A Streetcar Named Desire (see 1947), film with Vivien Leigh and Marlon Brando.
The Archers, a radio series.
The Final Test, television play by Terence Rattigan.
Balance of Payments crisis in Britain.

International Conference on Tariff and Trade.
42,000 people in Britain owned television sets.
Compulsory Purchase Order for 80 acres in City of London for redevelopment.

Bliss: *Solo Cantata*, composed for Kathleen Ferrier.
Pierre Boulez (*1925): *Structures*, French composition for two pianos.
Dali: *St. John of the Cross*, purchased by Glasgow Art Gallery.
Iain Hamilton (*1922): Clarinet Concerto.
Moore: *Time-Life Screen*, sculptures for Time-Life Building, London.
Antoine Pevsner (*1886, †1962): *Column*, bronze and brass.
Franz Reizenstein (*1911, †1968): *Voices in the Night*, a cantata of poems selected by Christopher Hassall.
Germaine Richier (*1904, †1959): *The Bat*, plaster.
John Veale (*1922): *Symphony*, in one movement.
Vaughan Williams: (i) 7th Symphony, *Antarctica*, (ii) *The Scholar Gypsy*, setting of passages from Matthew Arnold, (iii) *Romance for Harmonica*, composed for Larry Adler.
"Action Painting", a form of abstract expressionism, in vogue.
Society for the Promotion of New Music formed.

First British atomic bomb exploded at Monte Bello Islands, Australia.
Anglo-U.S. Metals Agreement.
Worst railway accident in Britain: 112 killed at Harrow.
British North Greenland expedition.
Largest dam in Britain (at Claerwen) completed.
Dispute with Iceland over extension of fishing limits.
Government plan to denationalize iron and steel industry.
John Cobb killed on Loch Ness.
Coelacanth, thought extinct for 50 million years, caught alive near Madagascar.
Contraceptive pill first made.
Douglas civil airliner flew polar route from Vancouver to Copenhagen.
Cosmic rays produced at Brookhaven Laboratory, New York.
De Havilland 100 jet fighter flew faster than the speed of sound.
30 people killed during annual Farnborough Air Display.
First gas turbine generator installed by British Electricity Authority at Manchester.
Giant hydro-electric power station built at

1952

Federation of Eritrea with Abyssinia.
Successive French governments under Pleven, Favre and Pinay.
Bonn Conventions granted sovereignty and ended occupation by Western Powers of German Federal Republic (W. Germany).
Heligoland restored to German Federal Republic.
Dr Kwame Nkrumah (*1909, †1972), first Prime Minister of Gold Coast.
Greece and Turkey joined N.A.T.O.
Greek constitution revised.
General Election in India: Pandit Nehru (*1889, †1964) formed government.
Hussein (*1935) succeeded Talal as King of Jordan.
Mau Mau activities in Kenya.
First General Election in Libya.
Revolt in Nepal suppressed by army.
Inaugural session of first parliament of Nigeria.
Apartheid policy of segregation of black and white races in S. Africa.
Self-government in Sudan.
General Dwight D. Eisenhower (*1890, †1969) elected U.S. President.

Priestley and Jacquetta Hawkes: *Dragon's Mouth*.
Rattigan: *The Deep Blue Sea*, a play.
D. Talbot Rice (*1903): *English Art (871–1100)*.
Sir John Rothenstein (*1901): *Modern English Painters: Vol. 1: Sickert to Smith* (1956: *Vol. 2: Lewis to Moore)*.
D. Thomas: *Collected Poems*.
E. Waugh: *Men at Arms*, a novel.
English Historical Documents, General Editor: David C. Douglas (12 vols.).

1953

†Queen Mary, aged 85.
Anglo-Egyptian agreement on self-government for the Sudan.
Treaty of Alliance between Britain and Libya.
British forces sent to Guiana to suppress Cheddi Jagan's Communist-inspired independence movement.
Bermuda Conference of Western Powers attended by Eisenhower, Churchill and Laniel.
Dag Hammarskjöld (*1905, †1961) elected as Secretary-General of U.N.
Treaty of Economic Unity between Argentina and Chile.
Census in Australia: pop. 8,795,778.
Revolution in Bolivia suppressed.

Anouilh: *The Lark*, French play.
James Baldwin (*1924): *Go Tell It on the Mountain*, novel.
Churchill awarded Nobel Prize for Literature.
A. Duff Cooper (*1890, †1954): *Old Men Forget*, political autobiography.
The Faber Book of Children's Verse, edited by Janet Adam Smith.
Brian Fawcett: *Exploration Fawcett*, a record of his lost father's expedition.
Faulkner: *Requiem for a Nun*, American novel.
Patrick Leigh Fermor (*1915): *A Time to Keep Silence*, on monastic life.
Ian Fleming (*1908, †1964): *Casino Royale*, first James Bond adventure.
Norman Gash (*1912): *Politics in the Age of Peel*.

Hatfield New Town, designed by Lionel Brett.
University of Southampton founded.
Wellington Museum opened at Apsley House.
High Noon, film with Gary Cooper.
Limelight, film with Charles Chaplin and Claire Bloom.
The Outcast of the Islands, film of Conrad's novel, with Ralph Richardson, Trevor Howard and Robert Morley.
The Sound Barrier, film with original script by Terence Rattigan.
Crown Film Unit disbanded by British government.
XV Olympic Games: in Helsinki.
Kathleen Kenyon (*1906, †1978) excavated site of ancient Jericho.
Abolition in Britain of W.W.2 "Utility" goods system.

Donzère-Mondaragon, in Rhône Valley.
First hydrogen bomb exploded by U.S. at Eniwetok Atoll, Pacific.
First commercial jet airline service (London to Johannesburg).
Immunization by injection against poliomyelitis.
Construction began on first atomic-powered submarine, U.S.S. *Nautilus*.
Radio-active carbon used for dating prehistoric objects.
Remains of *telanthropus man*, 1 million years old, found at Swartzkraus, near Krugersdorp, S.A.
World's largest radio telescope under construction at Jodrell Bank.
120–inch telescope for Lick Observatory, Mount Hamilton, California.
Television in Scotland, from transmitter at Kirk O'Shotts.
Farewell journey of last London tram.
S.S. *United States* won Blue Riband; 3 day 10 hr.40 min. Atlantic crossing.

Beecham produced opera, *Irmelin*, by Delius (composed 1892).
Bliss appointed Master of the Queen's Music.
Britten: (i) *Spring Symphony*, (ii) *Gloriana*, an opera.
Reg Butler (*1913): *The Unknown Political Prisoner*, abstract sculpture.
Eliott: *The Confidential Clerk*, verse-drama.
Fricker: Viola Concerto.
Hamilton: *Cyrano de Bergerac*, his first symphony.
Frederick Loewe (*1901): *Paint Your Wagon*, American musical.
Matisse: *L'Escargot*, French gouache on cut and pasted paper.
Moore: *King and Queen*, bronze.
Ben Nicholson: *Vertical Seconds*, abstract painting.

British atomic weapon exploded on Woomera Rocket Range in Australia.
First atomic shell tested successfully in Nevada.
Study of cosmic rays.
Sir John Hunt's expedition conquered Mt. Everest; Edmund Hillary and Sherpa Tensing reached summit.
Kuhrang Dam constructed in Persia with technical aid of British company.
H.M. submarine *Andrew* crossed Atlantic without surfacing.
Ministry of Agriculture inquiry into the disposal of Crichel Down.
Exploration by Gas Council of underground natural gas.
Isle of Grain oil refinery.
Myxomatosis epidemic.
"Smog" in Britain.

	HISTORY	LITERATURE
1953	Political crisis in Buganda: Britain forced the Kabaka to leave. General Elections in: (i) Canada, (ii) Hungary, (iii) Japan. *Coup d'État* in Colombia by Pinilia. New constitution in Denmark abolished Upper House and increased membership of Lower House of Parliament. Egypt became a republic under Neguib; Nasser, Deputy Premier. French political crisis: M. Reynaud named France "The Sick Man of Europe". Treaty of Friendship among Greece, Turkey and Yugoslavia. Fighting in Indo-China: French troops occupied Dien Bien Phu. Laos invaded by Viet Minh forces. Japan set up National Defence Force. Jomo Kenyatta sentenced on charges of managing Mau Mau in Kenya. Armistice in Korea. Rioting in Pakistan. *Coup d'État* by Royalists in Persia; Dr Mussadiq arrested. Cardinal Wyszynsky, Primate of Poland, arrested. Federation of Northern and Southern Rhodesia and Nyasaland. Russia renounced claims to Turkish territory. †Stalin; succeeded by Malenkov. Crisis over the Saar administration. Nationalist Party under Dr Malan elected in S. Africa. New constitution in Yugoslavia: Marshal Tito President.	Rupert Gunnis: *Dictionary of British Sculptors, 1660–1851.* Graves: *Poems.* Gerald Hanley (*1916): *The Year of the Lion,* a novel. Sir John Hunt (*1910): *The Ascent of Everest.* Hyams: *Gentian Violet,* a novel. Lehmann: *The Echoing Grove,* a novel. C. D. Lewis: *An Italian Visit,* poems. Maurois: *Cecil Rhodes,* a biography. C. Morgan: *The Burning Glass,* a play. Sean O'Faolain (*1900): *South to Sicily,* sketches of Calabria. Tennessee Williams: *Camingo Real,* American play. Cecil Woodham-Smith (*1896, †1977): *The Reason Why,* on the Charge of the Light Brigade.
1954	Colonial Service replaced by Her Majesty's Overseas Service. Landlord and Tenant Act: security of tenure to occupying tenants. Increase in number of West Indian immigrants to Britain. I.R.A. attacked military barracks in Omagh, N. Ireland. Anglo-Egyptian agreement on the Suez Canal base. Berlin Conference of Britain, France,	Kingsley Amis (*1922): *Lucky Jim,* satirical novel. Bates: *The Feast of July,* a novel. Betjeman: *A Few Late Chrysanthemums,* poems. H.M. Colvin (*1919): *Biographical Dictionary of English Architects, 1660–1840.* John van Druten: *I Am a Camera,* drama. Fry: *The Dark is Light Enough,* a play. Sir Keith Feiling (*1884, †1977): *Warren Hastings.*

Picasso: *Bouquet*, Spanish bronze.
Edmund Rubbra (*1901): Viola Concerto.
Shostakovich: Symphony No. 10.
Walton: (i) *Orb and Sceptre*, Coronation March, (ii) *Te Deum*.
Guys and Dolls, American musical based on Runyon's stories.
Historic Buildings and Ancient Monuments Act.
Institute of Classical Studies founded by University of London Senate.
New terminal buildings, London Airport (architect: Frederick Gibberd).
Coronation of Elizabeth II televised.
The Cruel Sea (see 1951), film with Jack Hawkins and Donald Sinden.
From Here to Eternity (see 1951), film with Frank Sinatra.
Genevieve, film comedy, with Dinah Sheridan, John Gregson and Kay Kendall.
The Robe, first Cinemascope film, with Richard Burton and Jean Simmons.
Roman Holiday, film with Gregory Peck and Audrey Hepburn.
Moulin Rouge, film of Toulouse-Lautrec, with José Ferrer.

Disastrous North Sea floods on coasts of Britain and Holland: 307 and 1800 deaths respectively.
Piltdown Man exposed as a fraud by chemical tests.
Bone of *Folsom Man* (10,000 B.C) discovered in New Mexico.
Pyramid discovered at Sakkara by Dr Zakaria Goneim.
Research on (i) air pollution, (ii) oil pollution of the sea.
Structure of D.N.A. molecule elucidated by Watson and Crick.
Discovery of new scale of space outside the Solar System.
International Laboratory for Nuclear Research at Meyrin, near Geneva.
Piccard descended 2 miles under the ocean in Bathyscaphe *Trieste*.
Russia exploded hydrogen bomb.
Experiments in colour television in the U.S.

Roger Bannister (*1929) first man to run a mile in under 4 minutes.
Berkeley: *Nelson*, an opera.
Britten: *The Turn of the Screw*, an opera.
Aaron Copland (*1900): *The Tender Land*, American opera.
Fricker: *Rhapsodia Concertante* for violin and orchestra.
Carlo Menotti (*1911): *The Saint of Bleeker Street*, American opera.

Atomic Energy Authority Act in Britain.
B.B.C. received permission to build V.H.F. broadcasting stations.
British Medical Council approved use of pain-relieving vapour of *trilene* by midwives.
Civil Service introduced Equal Pay for women.
End of food rationing in Britain.
New solar telescope, second largest in world, opened at Oxford.

1954

History

U.S. and Russia: Russia rejected proposals to reunify Germany.
Friction between Aden Protectorate and State of Yemen.
New constitution in British Honduras.
Upsurge of Algerian nationalism: 20,000 French troops despatched to suppress terrorism.
State of Emergency in Buganda.
Communist China *Chargé d'Affaires* opened in London.
Fulgencio Batista elected President of Cuba.
Disturbances in Cyprus and Greece over question of *Enosis* (unity with Greece).
Nasser assumed power in Egypt.
Communist China threat to "liberate" Formosa: U.S. Mutual Defence Treaty with Nationalist China.
Revolution in Guatemala.
French settlements in India became part of that country.
Indo-China armistice; declaration of Geneva Conference.
Trieste Territory divided into Italian and Yugoslav zones.
S.E. Asia Defence Treaty to prevent spread of Communism in that area.
Treaty of Friendship between Turkey and Pakistan.
Ho Chi Minh headed government in North Vietnam.
Communist Vietnamese captured Dien Bien Phu.
Members of Organization of American States pledged action against Communist infiltration.
U.S. Senate's vote of censure on Senator McCarthy's methods.
Communist Party outlawed in U.S.
Mutual Defence Agreement between U.S. and Japan.

Literature

Robert Gittings (*1911):*John Keats: The Living Year*.
William Golding (*1911): *Lord of the Flies*, a fantasy.
Derek Hudson (*1911): *Lewis Carroll*, a biography.
A. Huxley: *The Doors of Perception*.
C. D. Lewis: *Collected Poems*.
Wyndham Lewis: *Self Condemned*, a novel.
John Masters (*1914, †1983): *Bhowani Junction*, a novel.
Edwin Muir (*1887, †1959): *Autobiography*.
Iris Murdoch (*1919): *Under the Net*, a novel.
Rattigan: *Separate Tables*, a play.
Francoise Sagan (*1935): *Bonjour Tristesse*, novel.
C. P. Snow (*1905, †1980): *The New Men*, a novel.
D. Thomas: *Under Milk Wood*, radio play.
John R. R. Tolkien (*1892, †1973): *Fellowship of the Ring* (Part 1 of Trilogy, *Lord of the Rings*).
Sir Mortimer Wheeler (*1890, †1976), archaeologist: *Rome Beyond the Imperial Frontiers*.
John O'London's Weekly ceased publication.
The European Inheritance, edited by Sir E. Barker, Sir G. Clark and P. Vaucher.

1955

History

Churchill resigned; Eden Prime Minister; subsequent General Election: Conservatives returned with overall majority of 60.
Britain's dispute with Argentina and Chile over Falkland Islands

Literature

Amis: *That Uncertain Feeling*, a novel.
Samuel Beckett (*1906): *Waiting for Godot*, a play.
Charles Carrington (*1897): *Rudyard Kipling*, a biography.
Cary: *Not Honour More*, a novel.

Moore: *Internal and External Forms*, elmwood sculpture.
Sutherland: *Portrait of Sir Winston Churchill*
Julian Slade (*1930): *Salad Days*, a musical.
Walton: *Troilus and Cressida*, an opera.
Concert organ installed in Royal Festival Hall.
2nd-cent. Temple of Mithras unearthed in City of London.
Musique Concrète, electronically produced music played at Aldeburgh Festival.
The Caine Mutiny (see 1951), film with Humphrey Bogart.
Alfred Hitchock's film *Dial M for Murder* (see 1952).
Doctor in the House, film with Dirk Bogarde and Kenneth More.
Walt Disney's film: *The Living Desert.*
The Purple Plain, film with Gregory Peck.
Renato Castellani's film version of *Romeo and Juliet*.
On the Waterfront, film with Marlon Brando.
First L.C.C. comprehensive school at Kidbrooke.
Historic Buildings Councils for England and Wales set up.
Barbican scheme for redevlopment of site N.E. of St. Paul's
Growth of new towns in Britain.
University of Hull founded.
Chinese University founded at Singapore.
Steps to integrate racially segregated schools in U.S.
Designs for U.N.E.S.C.O. headquarters in Paris approved.

Television Act set up Independent Television Authority.
Decision to develop Gatwick as alternative airport to London Heathrow.
European Atomic Energy Society to promote industrial uses of atomic energy.
World-wide concern about fall-out from atomic explosions and disposal of radio-active waste.
First regular trans-Arctic air service (Copenhagen to Los Angeles) inaugurated by Scandinavian Airlines.
"Flying Bedstead", vertical take-off aircraft, made first controlled flight.
New element No. 99, *Eka-holmium*, produced at University of California.
Italian expedition climbed K2 (Mount Godwin Austen), second highest peak in the world (28,250 ft).
Investigation into pollution of air and sea.
Use of radio-isotopes in medicine, scientific research and industry.
Saint Lawrence Seaway commenced.
Relationship established between smoking and cancer of the lung.
Bell Telephone Co. developed a solar battery converting the sun's radiation into electricity.
Total eclipse of the sun (next eclipse, A.D. 2115).
Eurovision TV network established.
U.S.S. *Forrestal* launched, 59,650–ton aircraft carrier, largest warship in the world.
Half a million children vaccinated against poliomyelitis in U.S.A.

Pietro Annigoni (*1910): *Portrait of H.M. the Queen*.
Bloch: Symphony.
Bliss: (i) Violin Concerto, (ii) *Meditations on a Theme by John Blow*.
John Bratby (1928): *Still Life with Chip-Fryer*.

Commencement in Britain of (i) V.H.F. broadcasting, (ii) Commercial TV.
Britain announced decision to produce the hydrogen bomb.
Plans for construction of 12 nuclear power stations in Britain.

1955 submitted to International Court.
British government's major road construction scheme to cost £147 million.
Attlee retired; Gaitskell Leader of Labour Party.
Oil in Navigable Waters Act for prevention of pollution.
Western European Union inaugurated.
Baghdad Pact of mutual co-operation between Iraq and Turkey; joined later by Persia.
Britain signed treaty with Iraq and acceded to Baghdad Pact.
Armed rebellion and general strike in Argentina; Perón resigned and went into exile.
Austria re-established as sovereign state; military occupation ended.
Kabaka returned to Buganda.
Hostilities between Nationalist and Communist China in the area of Matsu and Quemoy Islands.
Internal unrest in China: purge of Communist Party.
Outbreak of violence in Cyprus; State of Emergency ordered.
Defence Alliance between Egypt and Syria signed.
Russia formally ended state of war with Germany.
Occupation of West Germany ended.
West German Federal Republic joined N.A.T.O.
Russia signed Warsaw Treaty setting up unified East European command and annulling Anglo-Soviet and Franco-Soviet Treaties.
Soviet Chairman Malenkov resigned; collective leadership of Khrushchev and Bulganin ensued.
Malta requested political union with United Kingdom.
State of Emergency in Pakistan.
South Vietnam became republic under Ngo Dinh Diem.
Tanganyika new constitution in force.

Richard Church: *Over the Bridge,* autobiography.
William Empson (*1906, †1984): *Collected Poems.*
Greene: (ii) *Loser Takes All,* (ii) *The Quiet American,* novels.
John Gunther (*1901, †1970), American journalist: *Inside Africa.*
The Manuscript Poems of A. E. Housman, edited by T. B. Haber.
John Harvey (*1911): *English Mediavel Architects.*
T. E. Lawrence: *The Mint,* posthumous work describing his life as "Aircraftman Shaw".
Miller: *A View from the Bridge,* American play.
Alfred Leslie Rowse (*1903): *The Expansion of Elizabethan England.*
Sherriff: *The Long Sunset,* a play.
History of Technology, edited by Charles Singer, E. J. Holmyard and A. R. Hall.
Stephen Spender (*1909): *Collected Poems, 1928–53.*
E. Waugh: *Officers and Gentlemen,* a novel.
Cecily Veronica Wedgwood (*1910): *The King's Peace, 1637–1641,* history.
Tennessee Williams: *Cat on a Hot Tin Roof,* a play.
A. Wilson: *The Mulberry Bush,* a play.
Bill for the suppression of "Horror Comics" in Britain.

Le Corbusier (C. E. Jeanneret) (*1887, †1965): *Le Modulor 2 (Le Modulor— 19548)*, work on architecture.
Rolf Liebermann (*1910): *School for Wives*, an opera.
Michael Tippet (*1905): *Midsummer Marriage*, an opera.
Inaugural debate of Cambridge University Women's Union held.
University of Exeter founded.
University College of Rhodesia and Nyasaland founded.
Commercial TV commenced in Britain from Croydon.
London Airport new terminal buildings opened (Heathrow).
The Dam-Busters, war film with Richard Todd.
Walt Disney's *Lady and the Tramp*, first all-cartoon feature in Cinemascope.
Marty, short film with Ernest Borgnine and Betsy Blair.
The Prisoner, film with Alec Guinness.
Richard III, film of Shakespeare's play, with Laurence Olivier; music by Walton.
Summer Madness, film with Katherine Hepburn.
Lightning injured 44 people and killed one at Ascot Races.

Rapidly increasing use of automation in industry.
Cambridge University teams, led by Dr. F. Sanger, identified structure of insulin molecule.
Atomic Energy: Britain and U.S. signed agreement.
Geneva Congress on Peaceful Uses of Atomic Energy; 72 countries represented.
Mount Kangchenjunga climbed by British expedition led by Charles Evans.
Comet III airliner completed 30,000-mile trip round the world in 66 hr. 43 min. of flying time.
Audouin Dollfus and his son made photo-electric observations of the Earth from an altitude of 4½ miles.
Dorothy Hodgkin elucidated structure of vitamin B_{12}, liver extract used for treatment of pernicious anaemia.
Techniques at M.I.T. for sending V.H.F. radio waves over distance of 380 miles, obviating the need for many TV relay stations.
"Credit Squeeze" introduced in Britain to control inflation.
Development of electronic computers for use in weather forecasting.
B. F. Burk, at the Carnegie Institute, discovered the emission of radio waves from planet Jupiter.
First section of *Photographic Atlas of the Universe* published by Mount Palomar Observatory.
Element No. 101, *Mendelivium*, discovered.
Deaths from tuberculosis in Britain fell by 64% in 6 years.
Egypt planned dam at Aswan creating lake 100 miles long and submerging dwellings of 50,000 Sudanese.
Scientists at University of California discovered the negative proton.
New anti-poliomyelitis vaccine developed by J. E. Salk at Pittsburgh University.

1956 Restrictive Trade Practices Act.
Small Lotteries and Gaming Act; bingo and small gaming legalized.
I.R.A border raids in Ulster; N. Ireland outlawed *Sinn Fein* and *Fianno Uladh* political parties.
Mysterious disappearance of frogman Commander Crabb, R.N., at Portsmouth during Russian naval visit.
Russian leaders Bulganin and Khrushchev visited Britain.
Suez crisis; Nasser seized Canal; Israel attacked Egypt; Britain and France sent ships and troops; Russia threatened to intervene; U.N. called for cease-fire, accepted by participants.
Terrorism continued in Cyprus; Makarios deported to Seychelles.
Pakistan an Islamic republic; remained in British Commonwealth.
Welensky Federal Prime Minister of Rhodesia and Nyasaland Federation.
Khrushchev denounced Stalin; "de-Stalinization" of policies by E. Europe Communist states.
Hungary: de-Stalinization policy; people demanded greater democratic freedom; Warsaw Treaty renounced; invasion by Russia crushed revolt; János Kádár President; many refugees fled; U.N. ignored; martial law proclaimed.
General Glubb dismissed from command of Arab Legion.
400,000 French troops in Algeria failed to crush revolt.
France recognized Tunisian independance.
National People's Army formed in East Germany.
West Germany introduced conscription.
Rainier III of Monaco married actress Grace Kelly.
Mass arrests in Johannesburg.
Morocco became independent state.
Sudan proclaimed an independent republic; admitted to Arab League.

Copyright Act.
Bates: *The Sleepless Moon*, a novel.
Churchill: *A History of the English-Speaking Peoples* (completed 1958).
James Gould Cozzens (*1903, †1978): *By Love Possessed*, a novel.
A. Huxley: *Adonis and the Alphabet*, essays.
Hammond Innes (*1913): *The Mary Deare*, sea story.
Pamela Hansford Johnson (*1912, †1981): *The Last Resort*, a novel.
R. Macaulay: *The Towers of Trebizond*, a novel.
Monsarrat: *The Tribe that Lost its Head*, a novel.
John Osborne (*1929): *Look Back in Anger*, a play.
Rowse: *The Early Churchills (The Later Churchills*, 1958).
Wilson: *Anglo-Saxon Attitudes*, a novel.
Colin Wilson (*1931): *The Outsider*.
Anouilh: *Poor Bitos*, French play.
Brendan Behan (*1923, †1964): *The Quare Fellow*, Irish play.
H. Werner Keller: *The Bible as History*.
30–letter Latin alphabet to replace 30,000 ideographic characters in Chinese writing.

Bush: *Men of Blackmoor*, an opera.
Alan Davie (*1920): *Sacrifice*, abstract painting.
Fricker: Sonata for Violincello and Pianoforte.
Moore: *Three Upright Figures*, a sculpture.
Tippett: Pianoforte Concerto.
Vaughan Williams: Symphony No. 8 in D Minor.
Walton: *Johannesburg Festival Overture*,
"Rock and Roll" music popular.
David Copperfield, 13–part TV play, adapted by Vincent Tilsley.
B.B.C. began using new TV transmitter at Crystal Palace.
Decline of cinema attendances.
Stained glass windows for Coventry Cathedral designed by Geoffrey Clarke, Lawrence Lee and Kenneth New.
Design Centre opened in The Haymarket, London.
Sir William Holford, published plan for new setting for St Paul's Cathedral.
XVI Olympic Games: in Melbourne.
Discovery in Egypt of (i) Temple of The Pharaoh Amenophis III, (ii) 5,000–year-old tomb of Queen Her Nit.
First boarding schools in Russia.
A Town Like Alice, film of novel by Nevil Shute, with Virginia McKenna and Peter Finch.
Reach for the Sky, film of Douglas Bader's life, with Kenneth More.
The King and I, film with Yul Brynner and Deborah Kerr.
Mike Todd's *Around the World in Eighty Days*, film with David Niven and Cantinflas (see 1873).

World's first large-scale nuclear power station inaugurated at Calder Hall, Cumberland.
Dido, heavy-water reactor, completed at Harwell.
A.E.I. constructed, at Aldermaston, first privately owned atomic reactor.
Campaign for Nuclear Disarmament (C.N.D.); protest march from Aldermaston.
Clean Air Act.
Petrol rationing reintroduced in Britain.
Macmillan introduced Premium Savings Bonds.
Road Traffic Act: vehicle testing and parking meters.
Milford Haven to be oil port able to handle the largest oil tankers.
Air speed record, 1,132 m.p.h., set up by Peter Twiss flying a Fairey *Delta*.
Transatlantic telephone service linking Britain with N. America inaugurated.
F. W. Müller, U.S.A., developed an ion microscope giving a magnification of 2¾ million times; individual atoms seen.
Discovery of (i) *neutrino* (see 1933) atomic particle, at Los Alamos Laboratory, U.S.A., (ii) *anti-neutron* at the University of California.
Discovery in Siberia of extensive deposits of diamonds, coal, iron ore, gold, silver and other minerals.
Pei Wen-Chung discovered in China fossil remains of *Gigantopithecus*, apeman possibly 500,000 years old.
Arend-Roland Comet discovered.

LITERATURE

1956 Eisenhower again President of U.S.A.

1957 Eden resigned; succeeded as Prime Minister by Harold Macmillan.
Homicide Act abolished Death Penalty except for certain kinds of murder (e.g. of a police officer).
Rent Act.
Wolfenden Report on Homosexuality and Prostitution.
Committee of Privy Councillors investigated telephone tapping by British police.
Home Guard, re-formed during Korean War, disbanded.
British armed forces reduced; amalgamation of many regiments.
British and French companies in Egypt "Egyptianized".
W. Europe relaxed trade restrictions with Communist China.
Suez Canal reopened.
Treaty of Rome set up European Economic Community (the Common Market) among six nations: France, Italy, West Germany, Belgium, Holland and Luxembourg.
†Haakon VII of Norway.
The Saar politically united with West Germany.
Rebellion in Oman led by the Imam quelled by Sultan with British help.
Women given the vote in Persia and Egypt.
Crisis in Jordan: political parties dissolved; martial law proclaimed.
Tunisia abolished monarchy; republic, headed by Habib Bourguiba, proclaimed.
Polygamy abolished in Tunisia.
Guerrilla activity in Cuba under Fidel Castro against dictator Batista.
Ghana, formerly the Gold Coast, became independent state.
Political crisis in Indonesia: Dutch industries seized.
Independence granted to the Federation of Malaya.
Civil Rights Act in U.S.A.
Race riots in Southern U.S.A.;

Beckett: *End-Game*, a play.
Sir Maurice Bowra (*1908, †1971): *The Greek Experience*, Ancient Greece.
John Braine (*1922, †1986): *Room at the Top*, a novel.
Vera Brittain (*1896, †1970): *Testament of Experience*, autobiography.
Bryant: *The Turn of the Tide*, World War II, 1939 to 1943.
Sir Kenneth Clark (*1903): *The Nude*, on art.
Lawrence Durrell (*1912, †1990): (i) *Bitter Lemons*, about Cyprus, (ii) *Justine*, a novel.
Grimble: *Return to the Islands*.
Ted Hughes (*1930): *The Hawk in the Rain*, first poems.
D. Lessing: *The Habit of Loving*, a novel.
C. D. Lewis: *Pegasus*, miscellaneous poems.
MacNiece: *Visitations*, short poems.
G. Maxwell: *A Reed Shaken by the Wind*, life in the marshes of Iraq.
H. V. Morton (*1892, †1979): *A Traveller in Rome*.
Murdoch: *The Sandcastle*, a novel.
J. Osborne: *The Entertainer*, a play.
Cyril Northcote Parkinson (*1909): *Parkinson's Law*, a satire on office organization, ominously true to life.
Edith Sitwell: *Collected Poems*.
Patrick White (*1912): *Voss*, a novel.
C. Wilson: *Religion and the Rebel*.
New Cambridge Modern History.
The Oxford Dictionary of the Christian Church.

M. Arnold: Symphony No.3.
Britten: *Prince of the Pagodas*, a ballet.
Copland: *Piano Fantasy*, American music.
Davie: *The Farmer's Wife, No. 2*, abstract expressionist painting.
Epstein: *Christ in Majesty*, a sculpture for Llandaff Cathedral.
Hindemith: *Harmonie der Welt*, Swiss opera.
Moore: *Seated Woman*, a sculpture.
Poulenc: *Dialogues des Carmélites*.
Rubbra: Symphony No. 7 in C Major.
Stravinsky: *Agon*, abstract ballet.
Victor Vasarely (*1908): *Cassiopée*, "optical" painting.
Walton: Concerto for Violoncello and Orchestra.
Loewe: *My Fair Lady*, musical, based on Shaw's *Pygmalion*.
University of Leicester founded.
Society for Mediaeval Archaeology founded.
Compulsory registration of independent schools in Britain.
School Broadcasting on TV started in Britain.
TV news series *Tonight*, featuring Cliff Michelmore.
Formation of the Civic Trust in Britain.
Paintings by apes exhibited at the Institute of Contemporary Arts, London.
Work commenced on new capital city of Brazil, called Brasilia, designed by Lucio Costa.
Across the Bridge, film with Rod Steiger.
The Prince and the Showgirl, film with Laurence Olivier and Marilyn Monroe.

First British hydrogen bomb exploded at Christmas Island (in Pacific).
Electricity Act.
Epidemic of Asian Influenza in Britain.
U.K. Atomic Energy Authority's experimental apparatus *Zeta* came into operation at Harwell.
Institute of Computer Science (reconstituted 1964) founded as University of London Computer Unit.
Radio telescopes at Jodrell Bank and Cambridge completed.
Radar used in Britain to check on speeding motorists.
Laying of cross-Channel cable to connect power supply systems of Britain and France.
International Atomic Energy Agency inaugurated.
Euratom Treaty signed by the six Common Market countries to collaborate on the peaceful uses of atomic energy.
New element No. 102, *Nobelium*, discovered.
International Geophysical Year: large-scale exploration of Antarctic, including British expedition led by Fuchs and Hillary; new low temperature record of $-100.4°$ F recorded at South Pole.
Project to build huge system of dams and hydro-electric power stations at Peace River Valley in the Canadian Rocky Mountains.
Russia launched (i) *Sputnik I*, first artificial Earth satellite, (ii) *Sputnik II*, carrying Eskimo dog, (iii) Inter-Continental Ballistic Missile.
Nuclear-powered Russian ice-breaker *Lenin* (16,000 tons) launched.

1957 violence at Little Rock, Arkansas, over integration of Negroes in senior high school.

1958 Charles became Prince of Wales.
Empire Day renamed Commonwealth Day.
Race riots in Nottingham and Notting Hill.
Matrimonial Causes (Property and Maintenance) Act.
Life Peerages Act.
Litter Act.
Talks between British government and Mintoff failed; State of Emergency in Malta.
Crisis in Pakistan: martial law; constitution abrogated; Ayub Khan President.
Singapore gained independence.
West Indies Federation inaugurated.
Fourth French Republic ended; de Gaulle (*1890, †1970) President; referendum successful; Fifth Republic began; French troops left Tunisia and Morocco.
Iceland extended territorial fishing waters to 12 miles.
†Pope Pius XII; succeeded by John XXIII.
Russian demand to establish Berlin as "Free City" resisted by N.A.T.O. powers; emergence of popular leader, Willy Brandt.
Bulganin dismissed; Khrushchev became Soviet Premier.
Imre Nagy, Minister-President during Hungarian uprising, executed.
Egypt and Syria formed United Arab Republic: Nasser President; joined by Yemen to form United Arab States.
Military coup in Iraq; republic proclaimed; Feisal II and family murdered; El Kassem Prime Minister.
Arab Federation of Iraq and Jordan; dissolved after Iraqi revolution.
Yemeni attacks on Aden border.
Army assumed power in the Sudan.

Amis: *I Like It Here*, a novel.
Betjeman: *Collected Poems*.
Truman Capote (*1924, †1984): *Breakfast at Tiffany's*, American work.
Eliot: *The Elder Statesman*, a play.
Fermor: *Mani*, travel book about Southern Greece.
Gunther: *Inside Russia Today*.
Jack Kerouac (*1922, †1969): *On the Road*, American novel of "Beatnik" life.
Norah Lofts (*1904, †1983): *Scent of Cloves*, historical novel.
Alberto Moravia (Alberto Pincherle) (*1907): *Two Women*, Italian novel.
Murdoch: *The Bell*, a novel.
Pasternak: *Dr Zhivago*, Russian novel.
Runciman: *The Sicilian Vespers*, history of the rebellion in 1282.
Peter Shaffer (*1926): *Five Finger Exercise*, a play.
Snow: *The Conscience of the Rich*, a novel.
Ludwig Wittgenstein (*1889, †1951): *The Blue Book and The Brown Book*, his philosophical ideas.

Boulez: *Le Soleil des Eaux*, French music.
Britten: *Noye's Fludde*, miracle play set to music.
Max Ernst (*1891, †1976): *Après Moi le Sommeil*, French painting.
Moore: *Reclining Figure*, 20–ton marble for U.N.E.S.C.O. Building, Paris.
Shostakovich: Symphony No. 11.
Tippett: (i) *Crown of the Year*, cantata with text by Christopher Fry; (ii) Symphony No. 2.
Walton: *Partita* for orchestra.
Vaughan Williams: Symphony No. 9 in E Minor.
Leonard Bernstein's *West Side Story*, American musical.
Ondine, a ballet; choreography by Ashton, music by Hans Werner Henze (*1926).
Gatwick Airport, designed by Yorke, Rosenberg and Mardall, completed.
Brussels Exhibition showed international architectural achievements.
U.N.E.S.C.O. Building in Paris, designed by Breuer, Nervi and Zehrfuss.
Seagram Building, New York, designed by Van der Rohe.
R.B. Fuller: geodesic dome for Union Tank Car Co., Louisiana; 384–ft span.
Design for Cumbernauld New Town, near Glasgow, by L. Hugh Wilson.
Stereophonic gramophone records introduced.
Stereophonic broadcasting developed by the B.B.C.
TV news series *Panorama*, featuring Richard Dimbleby.
Your Life in their Hands, TV series on hospital treatment.
Carve Her Name with Pride, war film with Virginia McKenna.
The Inn of the Sixth Happiness, film with Ingrid Bergman.
Mon Oncle, French comedy film with Jacques Tati.
The Wind Cannot Read, film with Dirk Bogarde and Yoko Tani.

Electronic computers introduced in research, industry and commerce.
Britain's experimental rocket *Black Knight*.
Last steam locomotive manufactured at Crewe.
Herstmonceux Observatory completed.
Work begun on Forth Road Bridge.
Restoration work at Stonehenge.
Vision Electronic Recording Apparatus (V.E.R.A.) developed by B.B.C.
U.S. submarine *Nautilus* travelled 1,830 miles under Arctic ice-cap.
U.S.A. successfully fired *Atlas* I.C.B.M.
Space exploration: (i) U.S.A. *Explorer I* (its first earth satellite), *Vanguard I, Explorer III* and *IV*, and *Atlas* (relay station); *Pioneers I, II* and *III* aimed at Moon; (ii) Russia launched *Sputnik III*.
Van Allen radiation belt around the Earth discovered.
Discovery of huge submarine current, 250 miles wide, flowing 3,500 miles across Pacific.
Radio-active Carbon–14 technique used to date Jericho as world's oldest city.
Reports of *Yeti* (Abominable Snowman) in Central Asia.
Chinese marine engineers built 22,000–ton ship, *Leap Forward*, in 58 days.
Industrial and agricultural production stepped up in China.
New French franc created.
Air crash at Munich cost lives of 7 of Manchester United football team.

1958 Civil strife in Lebanon.
†Strijdom, South African Premier; Verwoerd succeeded.
Military coup in Siam.
Communist Chinese bombarded Quemoy Islands.
Alaska became 49th state of U.S.A.
French Guinea became independent.
Women first voted in Mexico.

1959 General Election: Conservatives under Macmillan returned to power.
Street Offences Act removed prostitutes from the streets.
Mental Health Act.
Obscene Publications Act.
European Free Trade Association (E.F.T.A.) established by "Outer Seven": Austria, Britain, Denmark, Norway, Portugal, Sweden and Switzerland.
Cyprus became a republic; Makarios President; Britain retained military bases on the island.
European Monetary Agreement.
World Refugee Year.
Pope John XXIII called first Vatican Council since 1870 in search for Church unity.
United Nations condemned *Apartheid*.
Census in Russia: population 208,826,650.
Army revolt in Iraq suppressed.
Dispute between India and China over Ladakh; border clash.
First elected government in Nepal.
Uprising in Tibet against Chinese rule: Dalai Lama escaped to India; revolt suppressed.
Riots in Leopoldville: beginning of Civil War in Belgian Congo.
End of State of Emergency in Kenya (from 1952).
Mali, former French colony, became independent.
State of Emergency in Nyasaland: Hastings Banda, leader of African National Congress, arrested.
Cuba: Batista fled; revolutionary

Behan: *The Hostage*, Irish play.
Braine: *The Vodi*, a novel.
William Burroughs (*1914): *The Naked Lunch*.
Cary: *The Captive and the Free*, his last novel.
Compton-Burnett: *Heritage and its History*, a novel.
Shelagh Delaney (*1939): *A Taste of Honey*, a play.
William Golding: *Free Fall*.
Graves: *Collected Poems*, 1959.
Greene: *The Complaisant Lover*, a play.
A. Huxley: *Brave New World Revisited*.
Laurie Lee (*1914): *Cider with Rosie*, Cotswold village life.
Colin MacInnes (*1914, †1976): *Absolute Beginners*, novel on teenage problems.
Garrett Mattingly (*1900, †1962): *Defeat of the Spanish Armada*, history.
Iona and Peter Opie: *The Lore and Language of Schoolchildren*.
James Pope-Hennessy (*1916, †1974): *Queen Mary*, a biography.
Thurber: *The Years with Ross*, American humour.
Van de Post: *The Lost World of the Kalahari*.
Arnold Wesker (*1932): *Roots*, a play.
Anouilh: *Becket*, French play.
Eugène Ionesco (*1912): *Le Rhinocéros*, French play.
15 to 18: Report of the Central Advisory Council for Education (England) (Crowther Report).
Paperbacks became increasingly popular.
Manchester Guardian renamed *The Guardian*.

Bratby: *Coach House Door*, a painting.
Benjamin Frankel (*1906, †1973): Symphony No. 1.
Seymour Lipton (*1903): *Mandrake*, bronze.
Moore: *Two-Piece Reclining Figure*, bronze.
Poulenc: *La Voix Humaine*, French opera.
Jerome Robbins (*1918): *L'Après-Midi d'un Faune*, American ballet.
Shostakovich: Violoncello Concerto.
Design for Churchill College, Cambridge, won by Sheppard, Robson & Partners.
Bernard Miles' Mermaid Theatre opened in London.
Sheffield University Library completed.
Frank Lloyd Wright (*1869, †1959): Guggenheim Museum, New York.
Pirelli Building in Milan: skyscraper designed by Gio Ponti.
University of Malaya established.
First section of Britain's motorway (M1), London-Birmingham, opened.
Caravanning increasingly popular in Britain.
Look Back in Anger (see 1956), film with Richard Burton.
The Horse's Mouth (see 1944), film with Alec Guinness.
Room at the Top (see 1957), film with Laurence Harvey.
I.T.V.'s three new stations: Anglia, Tyne-Tees and Ulster.
Face to Face, TV series with John Freeman.
South African government refused to introduce television.
Le Corbusier designed monastery at La Tourette.

Hovercraft invented by Christopher Cockerell and built by Saunders-Roe Ltd.; 2–hr Channel crossing, Calais to Dover.
British Gas Council experimented with *natural* gas.
First British experimental surgery unit opened at Hammersmith: research on organ transplantation.
First British drive-in bank opened in Liverpool.
Work begun on 98–inch telescope, largest in Britain, for Royal Observatory.
Shell tanker *Avris* propelled by gas turbine.
H.M. dockyard at Malta transferred to Bailey (Malta) Ltd.
Charles Ford of Harwell made human chromosomes visible.
Driest British summer for 200 years.
Graduated Contributions and Superannuation Benefits related to incomes.
National Coal Board to close up to 240 mines by 1965.
Vienna Cancer Institute started first bone-marrow bank.
General Electric Research Laboratory, U.S.A., made synthetic diamonds.
Luis Alvarez at Berkeley, California, discovered neutral *xi* particle.
U.S. launched: (i) atomic submarine, *George Washington*, armed with Polaris missiles; (ii) atomic-powered cargo ship *Savannah*.
U.S. and Russia began training astronauts; two monkeys recovered unharmed from space by U.S.
Moon probes: (i) Russia launched *Lunik I, II* and *III*; back of the Moon photographed; (ii) U.S. launched *Pioneer IV*.
Soviet expedition reached South Pole.
Arctic submarine plateau discovered.
Louis Leakey discovered "Nut-cracker"

1959 forces under Fidel Castro seized power; agrarian reforms introduced.
Self-government by Jamaica within West Indies Federation.
Hawaii became 50th state of the U.S.A.

1960 Marriage of Princess Margaret and Antony Armstrong-Jones.
Betting and Gaming Act.
Noise Abatement Act.
Road Traffic Act.
Charities Act.
First joint Anglican-Methodist church dedicated at Hernes Bay, Kent.
Payment of Wages Act: repealed sections of Truck Acts; permitted payment of wages by cheque on request.
Abortive Four-Power (U.S., Russia, Britain and France) Conference in Paris.
Women priests ordained in Lutheran Church of Sweden.
Brezhnev became President of U.S.S.R.
Communist ideological dispute between Russia and China.
Military coup in Turkey, Menderes overthrown; General Gürsel became Head of State.
U.A.R. National Assembly inaugurated.
Belgian Congo became Congo Republic; Lumumba Prime Minister; mutiny and disorder; Katanga Province under Tshombe seceded; civil war followed.
Sharpeville shooting: 67 Africans killed in Pan-African demonstration.
African states of Cameroons, Dahomey, Ghana, Ivory Coast, Mali, Niger, Nigeria, Senegal, Somali, Togo and Upper Volta became independent republics.
Abortive *Coup d'État* in Ethiopia.
Attempted assassination of Verwoerd.
Military *Coup d'État* in Laos.
Brasilia became capital of Brazil.

Ayer: *Logical Positivism*, philosophy.
Stan Barstow (*1928): *A Kind of Loving*, novel.
Betjeman: *Summoned by Bells*, autobiography in verse.
Robert Bolt (*1925): *A Man for All Seasons*, play on Sir Thomas More.
Durrell: *Clea*, a novel.
Lillian Hellman (*1906, †1984): *Toys in the Attic*, a play.
C. D. Lewis: *The Buried Day*, autobiography.
Maxwell: *Ring of Bright Water*, otter story.
Harold Pinter (*1930): *The Caretaker*, a play.
Rattigan: *Ross*, play on Lawrence of Arabia.
Sherriff: *A Shred of Evidence*, a play.
Snow: *The Affair*, a novel.
Wesker: *I'm Talking about Jerusalem*, a play.
Wilson: *Ritual in the Dark*, a novel.
The *Daily Herald* severed ties with Labour Party; became independent newspaper.
News Chronicle and *The Star* ceased independent publication.
Public Lending Right campaign by Sir A. Herbert; proposed that libraries pay fees for books borrowed from them.
Penguin Books published "unexpurgated edition" of *Lady Chatterley's Lover* (see 1928); found "Not Guilty" of issuing obscene work.
Teilhard de Chardin (*1881, †1955): *Le Milieu Divin*, a philosophical work.

man, 600,000 years old, in Olduvai Gorge, Tanganyika (now Tanzania, see 1964).

Michael Ayrton (*1921, †1975): *Icarus III*, bronze.
Britten: *Midsummer Night's Dream*, an opera.
Lynn Chadwick (*1914): *The Watchers*, bronze.
Fricker: Symphony No. 3.
Rubbra: Violin Concerto.
Walton: Symphony No. 2.
National Gallery for Modern Art for Scotland at Inverleith House, Edinburgh, opened.
Herbert Art Gallery opened in Coventry.
B.B.C. White City Television Centre, designed by Norman and Dawbarn, opened.
U.S. Embassy building Grosvenor Square opened; architect: Eero Saarinen.
Stiletto-heeled shoes fashionable.
Sculptural construction made from materials found.
Barbara Moore, aged 56, walked from John O'Groats to Land's End.
22 new galleries opened at the Louvre, Paris.
XVII Olympic Games: in Rome.
Butterfield 8, film of O'Hara's novel, with Elizabeth Taylor.
The Entertainer (see 1957), film with Laurence Olivier.
The Millionairess, film with Peter Sellers and Sophia Loren.
The Alamo, film with John Wayne.
Tunes of Glory, film with Alec Guinness and John Mills.
Alfred Hitchcock's film *Psycho*.
Saturday Night and Sunday Morning, film with Albert Finney.
Hiroshima, mon Amour, French film.
Fings Ain't Wot They Used To Be, film version of Lionel Bart's musical.

Farthing ceased to be legal tender.
New £1 banknote issued.
Last British tram ran at Sheffield.
U.S. and Britain agreed to build missile Early Warning Station at Fylingdales, Yorkshire.
Polaris missiles fired from underwater by U.S. submarine *George Washington*.
Britain agreed to provide facilities for Polaris submarines in Holy Loch.
U.S.S. *Enterprise*, atomic-powered carrier, launched.
U.S. submarine *Triton* made first undersea round-the-world voyage, in 84 days.
U.S. Navy bathyscaphe *Trieste* dived 35,000 ft to bottom of Challenger Deep in Western Pacific.
U.S. X15 research aircraft: air speed record of 2,196 m.p.h.
U.S. launched communications satellites *Echo I* and *Courier IB*, and meteorological satellites *Tiros I* and *II*.
Development of optical maser (laser) in U.S. laboratories.
R. L. Mossbauer's work with gamma rays (*Mossbauer Effect*).
Galaxy 6,000 million light years distant photographed by R. Minicowski at Mount Palomar Observatory, U.S.A.
International Development Association established.
France exploded her first nuclear bomb in Sahara.
Kariba Dam opened and work commenced on Aswan High Dam.
Russian satellite *Sputnik V*, with two live dogs, orbited Earth 17 times; successfully recovered.
Everest climbed by Chinese using Northern Route.
Annapurna II climbed by British-Indian-Nepalese expedition.
Earthquakes destroyed Agadir in Morocco and Lar in Persia.

1960 U.S. reconnaissance aircraft shot down by Russians in the Urals; pilot Gary Powers imprisoned.
John Kennedy (*1917, †1963) first R.C. President of U.S.A.
U.S. property on Cuba seized; Cuba aligned herself with Communist bloc; U.S. ended aid.
Eichmann, former Gestapo Chief, captured by Israeli Security Service in Argentina.

1961 Census in Britain: population 51,295,000.
Dr Fisher, Archbishop of Canterbury, resigned; Dr Ramsey succeeded.
Betting Levy Act; Consumer Protection Act; Factory Act; Rating and Valuation Act.
Britain applied to join the Common Market.
West Indian and Asian immigrants poured into Britain.
Lonsdale, Blake and the Krogers spy trials in U.K.
†Dag Hammarskjöld (*1905), Secretary-General of the U.N., in air crash, succeeded by U Thant.
East Germany sealed border between E. and W. Berlin: Berlin Wall built.
Referendum on Algeria endorsed de Gaulle's policy: terrorism by Organisation de L'Armée Secrete (O.A.S.); State of Emergency in France.
Albania expelled from Soviet bloc.
Census in India: population 438,000,000.
India seized Portuguese possessions of Goa, Damao and Diu.
Dispute over official language (Sinhala) in Ceylon; State of Emergency.
Coup d'État in Syria; secession from U.A.R.; independence restored.
Iraq claimed Kuwait: British troops despatched; later replaced by Arab League forces.
Pahlavi Foundation acquired Shah of Persia's £47,500,000 property.

New English Bible: New Testament (Old Testament, 1970; Apocrypha 1970).
Beckett: *Comment C'Est*, a novel.
Asa Briggs (*1921): *Birth of Broadcasting*, History of the B.B.C., Vol. I.
Compton-Burnett: *The Mighty and Their Fall*, a novel.
Graves: *More Poems 1961*.
Greene: *A Burnt-Out Case*, a novel.
Joseph Heller (*1923): *Catch 22*, satire on war.
Hughes: *The Fox in the Attic*, a novel.
Letters of Sigmund Freud, 1873–1939.
C. S. Lewis: *An Experiment in Criticism*.
R. Macaulay: *Letters to a Friend*.
Masefield: *Bluebells and Other Verse*.
Murdoch: *A Severed Head*, a novel.
Ogden Nash (*1902, †1971), American: *Collected Verses*.
Obsorne: *Luther*, a play.
Pasternak: *Poetical Works*, posthumous Soviet edition.
Sartre: *Critique de la Raison Dialectique*, French philosophy.
Muriel Spark (*1918): *The Prime of Miss Jean Brodie*, a novel.
Gwyn Thomas (*1913): *The Keep*, a play.
E. Waugh: *Unconditional Surrender*, a novel.
Patrick White: *Riders in the Chariot*, Australian novel.
Tennessee Williams: *Night of the Iguana*, American play.
John Whiting (*1917, †1963): *The Devils*, a play.
Sunday Dispatch merged with *Sunday Express*.

Severe earthquakes in Chile.
Hong Kong struck by typhoon.

Arnold: Symphony No. 5.
Frederick Ashton's ballet to Stravinsky's *Persephone*.
Lionel Bart (*1930): *Oliver*, a musical.
Britten: Sonata for Violoncello and Pianoforte.
Fricker: Twelve Studies for Pianoforte.
Goya's *Duke of Wellington* stolen from N.G.; recovered 1965
Kodaly: Symphony.
Moore: *Standing Figure (Knife-edge)*, bronze.
Hardwick's Doric portico of Euston Station demolished despite protests.
Walton: *Gloria*.
University of Sussex founded at Brighton.
University of Essex founded at Colchester.
University of Ghana founded.
The Royal Ballet visited Leningrad and Moscow.
End of *Children's Hour* on B.B.C.
New Towns Commission set up in Britain.
Sixty-storey Chase Manhattan Bank H.Q. in Manhattan completed.
Guildford Cathedral consecrated.
B.B.C. TV series: *The Age of Kings*, Shakespeare's historical plays.
Walt Disney's *One Hundred and One Dalmations*, film cartoon.
Exodus, Otto Preminger's film adapted from novel by Leon Uris.
El Cid, film with Charlton Heston and Sophia Loren.
Whistle Down the Wind, film with Hayley Mills.
Breakfast at Tiffany's (see 1958), film with Audrey Hepburn.
La Dolce Vita, Italian film.
Mirror Group H.Q. building in London, designed by Sir Owen Williams & Partners, completed.

Yuri Gagarin, first man in space in 5-ton Soviet spaceship *Vostok*, orbited the Earth in 1 hr 48 min.
Second man in space, Alan B. Shepard, U.S.A., made successful suborbital flight to 115-mile height.
Barnett Ventilator, electronic lung pump, developed.
Robert Beeching appointed Chairman of British Transport Commission.
Bradshaw's Railway Time-table ceased publication (see 1839).
U.S. scientists Claus and Nagy discovered extra-terrestrial life on meteorites.
Crick and Brenner's work with D.N.A.
Denny 70-seater Hoverbus for inland waterways.
Jodrell Bank team transmitted radio waves which reflected back from Venus.
Ryle's theory that the Universe changed with time conflicted with "Steady State" view of Hoyle.
Atlas computer, world's largest and fastest, at Harwell for use in atomic research and meteorology.
British and French electric power grids linked by Channel cables.
Central Electricity Board built £2 million laboratory at Berkeley for nuclear power research.
Mini-cabs operating in London.
South Africa introduced decimal currency: the Rand.
Tanganyika conference on Preservation of African Wild Life.
Eclipse of the Sun televised.
New vaccine *Covexin* to treat 7 different sheep diseases.
U.S. Saturn rocket made successful test flight.

1961 South Africa became republic; withdrew from Commonwealth.
Southern Rhodesia: new constitution.
Tanganyika, Sierra Leone, Ruanda became independent African states.
Congo Republic: Lumumba murdered; fighting between U.N. troops and Katanga; secession of Katanga ended.
Casablanca Conference: independent African states drew up African Charter.
Nationalist uprising in Angola.
Abortive invasion of Cuba by U.S.
Tristan da Cunha's 262 people evacuated to England following volcanic eruption; returned 1964.
Eichmann (see 1960) condemned to death.

1962 Joint Committee on Reform of the House of Lords recommended that successor to a peerage could renounce it for life.
Commonwealth Immigrants Act.
Road Traffic Act.
Transport Act.
Archbishop of Canterbury, Dr Ramsey, visited U.S.S.R.
British businessman, Greville Wynne, arrested in Hungary and taken to Russia on charges of spying.
William Vassall, Admiralty clerk, sentenced to 18 months imprisonment for spying for Russia.
European Economic Community: second stage of integration.
Geneva Disarmament Conference on nuclear weapons.
Second Vatican Council (first 1870, *q.v.*) opened in Rome.
Attempted assassination of de Gaulle, at Le Petit-Clamart, near Paris.
Declaration guaranteeing Laotian neutrality signed by 13 states of Geneva Conference.
U.S. established a military command in S. Vietnam.

Edward Albee (*1928): *Who's Afraid of Virginia Woolf?*, American play.
Anthony Burgess (*1917): *A Clockwork Orange*, novel.
Faulkner: *The Reivers*, American novel.
Roy Fuller (*1912): *Collected Poems 1936–61*.
Isherwood: *Down There on a Visit*, a novel.
Jean Kerr (*1923): *Mary, Mary*, a play.
C. D. Lewis: *The Gate*, poems.
Murdoch: *An Unofficial Rose*, novel.
Vladimir Nabokov (*1899, †1977): *Pale Fire*, Russian-U.S. novel.
Pasternak: *In the Interlude*, Russian poems.
Pinter: *The Collection*, a play.
Powell: *The Kindly Ones*, a novel.
Rothenstein: *Augustus John*, a biography.
Rowse: *Ralegh and the Throckmortons*, history.
Anthony Sampson (*1926): *Anatomy of Britain*.
Alexander I. Solzhenitsyn (*1918): *One Day in the Life of Ivan Denisovich*, Russian novel.
Wesker: *Chips with Everything*, a play.
Restrictive Practices Court upheld Net Book Agreement.

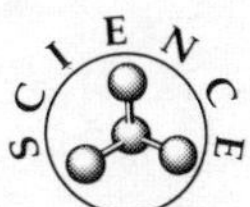

Palazzo del Lavoro, Turin, Exhibition Hall designed by Luigi Nervi.

U.S. Bell X15 rocket-powered aircraft flew at 3,545 m.p.h.
Pompeii excavations: 8 calcified bodies found (see A.D.79).
Orient Express: last journey from Paris to Budapest (after 78 years).
Hurricane in British Honduras: †190 people; 65,000 homeless.

Bliss: *The Beatitudes*, a cantata.
Britten: *War Requiem*.
Frankel: Symphony No. 2.
Gilbert and Sullivan operettas out of copyright: D'Oyly Carte Company monopoly ceased.
Alexander Goehr (*1932): Violin Concerto.
Barbara Hepworth (*1903, †1975): *Single Form (Memorial)*, a bronze.
Leonardo da Vinci's cartoon *Virgin and Child* purchased for National Gallery from Royal Academy for £800,000.
Stravinsky: *The Flood*, Russian-American opera.
Tippett: *King Priam*, an opera.
University of Singapore founded.
Chichester Theatre, first public theatre in Britain with arena stage, opened.
Commonwealth Institute opened.
Coventry Cathedral consecrated; tapestry by Graham Sutherland; windows by John Hutton, John Piper and Lawrence Lee; sculpture by Epstein.
32-storey Hilton Hotel built in Park Lane, London.
Philharmonic Hall, of Lincoln Center, New York (designed by Max Abramovitz), opened.
Trans-World Airlines building at Idlewild, New York, opened.

Royal College of Physicians published report on Smoking and Health.
To reduce tooth decay, Minister of Health backed schemes to include fluorine in water.
Thalidomide drug given as sedative to pregnant women caused deformities in babies and was withdrawn.
Alex Moulton's new bicycle design.
Speculative Gains Tax introduced in Britain.
Knightsbridge-Piccadilly underpass opened.
Meteorological office began using Centigrade scale in weather reports.
Maiden flights of British airlines Vickers V.C.10 and de Havilland *Trident*.
Britain and France signed agreement for joint construction of *Concorde*, world's first supersonic airliner.
U.S. launched communications satellite *Telstar*; live TV and radio signals relayed from America to Europe.
Three U.S. spaceflights by astronauts John Glenn, Malcolm Scott Carpenter and Walter Schirra.
U.S. launched rocket *Mariner* to study Venus and British satellite *Ariel* to study cosmic radiation.
U.S. *Ranger* spacecraft hit the Moon.

1962 New constitution in Pakistan: system of government with Ayub Khan as President.
Chinese offensive on Indian border at N.E. Frontier and Ladakh area.
Algeria became independent.
South Africa introduced "Self-Rule" for the Transkei.
Tanganyika became a republic.
Uganda became independent.
Western Samoa became independent.
Federation of the West Indies dissolved: (i) Jamaica, (ii) Trinidad and Tobago became independent states.
Cuban crisis: confrontation of U.S. and Russia over establishment of Russian missile base in Cuba; Russia finally dismantled the base.
Coup d'État by armed forces in Peru: new government headed by General Godoy.

1963 Macmillan resigned; succeeded as Prime Minister by Sir Alec Douglas-Home (*1903).
†Gaitskell; Harold Wilson elected Leader of Labour Party.
John D. Profumo, Secretary for War, involved in scandal, resigned; enquiry, under Lord Denning, held no breach of security.
Contracts of Employment Act.
Matrimonial Causes Act.
Offices, Shops and Railway Premises Act.
Great Train Robbery of £2½ million from Glasgow-London mail train at Cheddington, Bucks.
Philby discovered to be "Third Man" in the Burgess-Maclean affair (see 1951).
Conversations between Anglicans and Methodists proposed eventual union.
Brussels negotiations for British entry into Common Market failed.
Nuclear Test Ban Treaty signed by U.S., Russia and Britain.
†Pope John XXIII; succeeded by Paul VI.

Amis: *One Fat Englishman,* a novel.
Alvar Ellegard, using electronic computer to record frequency of stylistic traits, claimed that Sir Philip Francis was "Junius".
Günter Grass (*1927): *Hundejahre,* German novel.
Rolf Hochhuth (*1931): *The Representative,* German play.
Ionesco: *Exit the King,* French play.
MacNeice: *The Burning Perch,* poems.
Mary McCarthy (*1912, †1989): *The Group,* a novel.
Murdoch: *The Unicorn,* a novel.
V. S. Naipaul (*1932): *Mr Stone and the Knights Companion,* a novel.
Pinter: (i) *The Dwarfs,* (ii) *The Lover,* plays.
John A. T. Robinson, Bishop of Woolwich (*1919): *Honest to God,* controversial statement on outdated concepts of Christianity.
John Updike (*1932): *The Centaur,* American novel.
Rowse: *William Shakespeare: a biography,* claimed to solve a number of outstanding problems.
John Cleland's novel *Fanny Hill* published in U.S. but banned in Britain.

Dr No, "James Bond" film, with Sean Connery.
How the West was Won, Cinerama film with Karl Malden.
Lawrence of Arabia, film with Peter O'Toole.
To Kill a Mockingbird, film with Gregory Peck.
U.S. Air Force Academy Chapel near Colorado Springs, containing places of worship for three denominations, dedicated.

Chudinov, Russian scientist, claimed to have revived fossil algae over 250 million years old.
Great St Bernard Tunnel between Italy and Switzerland completed.
Coalmine disaster at Völklingen in the Saar: 298 miners killed.
Severe earthquake in Persia destroyed 300 villages and killed 12,000 people.
Avalanche in North Peru, down Mt Huascarán, buried village and killed over 3,000.

Goehr: *Little Symphony*.
Menotti: *The Last Savage*, American opera.
Victor Pasmore (*1908): *Abstract in White, Ochre and Black*; transparent projective relief, painted wood and plastic.
Tippett: Concerto for Orchestra.
Walton: *Variations on a Theme by Hindemith*.
Newsom Report on Secondary Education in Britain: *Half Our Future*.
Robbins Report on Higher Education in Britain.
London Opera Centre opened.
Old Vic Company gave last performance; Old Vic became home of National Theatre.
University of Newcastle-upon-Tyne reconstituted.
University of York founded.
University of Guyana founded.
Gallery of Modern Art, New York, designed by Edward Durrell Stone.
Metered television licensed in Britain.
No. 10 Downing Street restored by Raymond Erith.
Le Corbusier's Carpenter Center for the Visual Arts completed.
Beatles "Pop" Group achieved international fame.
"Pop Art" and "Hard Edge Art" in vogue.

Beeching Report on British Railways recommended closing half the stations and one-third of track.
Development of British T.S.R.-2 supersonic bomber.
Buchanan Report, *Traffic in Towns*, published.
Rachel Carson (*1907, †1964): *The Silent Spring*, drew attention to dangerous long-term effects of the use of chemical pesticides.
Consumers' Association published critical report on contraception.
Development Council in Britain.
Perec Rachmann, landlord, evicted tenants from rent-controlled properties.
Construction of the Victoria Underground Line commenced.
Teaching machines used in education.
Report of British and French Working Group recommended construction of Channel Tunnel.
Anti-matter atomic particle *anti-xi-zero* discovered.
Friction welding invented.
Vaccine for measles developed.
U.S. nuclear submarine *Thresher* lost with crew of 129 in Atlantic.

LITERATURE

1963

Former British colony of Aden joined Federation of South Arabia.
Army overthrew Kassem's government in Iraq; Kassem killed.
Kenya became independent state.
Nigeria became a republic.
Zanzibar became independent state.
Central African Federation dissolved.
Independent African states agreed to Charter of Organization of African Unity.
First of the Bantustans in the Transkei, South Africa.
Federation of Malaysia created.
S. Vietnam government of Ngo Dinh Diem overthrown by Army coup; Diem shot.
Direct "Hot Line" established between U.S. and Russia.
President Kennedy assassinated at Dallas, Texas; succeeded by Lyndon Johnson; Lee Oswald, accused of murder, shot dead by Jack Ruby.
Martin Luther King led Campaign for negro Civil Rights in Birmingham, Alabama; rioting; Kennedy presented Civil Rights Bill to U.S. Congress.

114–day strike of newspaper printers in New York; *New York Mirror*, ceased publication.

1964

*Prince Edward.
General Election: Labour majority of four; Wilson Prime Minister.
Hire Purchase Act.
Libraries and Museums Act.
Resale Prices Act.
"Mods" and "Rockers" rioting at seaside resorts.
Use of contraceptive pills banned to British Roman Catholics.
Fighting between Greek and Turkish communities in Cyprus; U.N. peace-keeping force sent.
Malta became independent.
Khrushchev resigned; replaced as First Secretary by Leonid Brezhnev (*1906, †1982) and as Prime Minister by Aleksei Kosygin (*1904, †1980).
Pope Paul VI went on pilgrimage to Holy Land.
Saud of Saudi Arabia deposed; Prince Feisal crowned King.

Saul Bellow (*1915): *Herzog*, American novel.
Coghill: *Shakespeare's Professional Skills*, literary criticism.
William Golding: *The Spire*.
Graves: *Man Does, Woman Is*, poems.
Christopher Hassall (*1912, †1963): *Rupert Brooke*, a biography.
Hemingway: *A Movable Feast*, posthumous American autobiography.
Philip Larkin (*1922, †1985): *The Whitsun Weddings*, poetry.
Philip Magnus (*1906): *King Edward VII*, a biography.
Mauriac: *De Gaulle*, French biography.
Miller: *After the Fall*, American play.
Osborne: *Inadmissible Evidence*, a play.
Pinter: *The Homecoming*, a play.
Sartre: *Les Mots*, French autobiography.
Snow: *Corridors of Power*, a novel.
Gore Vidal (*1925): *Julian*, American novel.

Cleopatra, film with Elizabeth Taylor.
The L-Shaped Room, film with Tom Bell and Leslie Caron.
Billy Liar, film with Tom Courtenay.
This Sporting Life, film of David Storey's novel, with Richard Harris and Rachel Roberts.
Tom Jones, film of Fielding's novel, with Albert Finney.

U.S. placed belt of copper needles in orbit 2,000 miles up for military world radio communication.
U.S. astronaut Major Gordon Cooper orbited earth 22 times in *Mercury* capsule.
Russian astronaut Valentina Tereshkova, first woman in space, in three-day orbital flight.
Flood disaster in N. Italy killed over 2,000.
Cyclone in E. Pakistan killed over 10,000.
Hurricane *Flora* killed 6,000 in Caribbean.

Britten: Symphony with Solo Violoncello.
Alan Rawsthorne (*1905, †1971); Symphony No. 3.
University of East Anglia founded.
University of Kent at Canterbury founded.
University of Lancaster founded.
University of Stirling founded.
University of Strathclyde founded.
B.B.C. opened second television channel: B.B.C. 2.
B.B.C. television series *The Great War*.
Windmill Theatre in London closed.
University of Malawi founded.
Huntingdon Hartford Gallery of Modern Art opened in New York.
XVIII Olympic Games: in Tokyo.
Becket, film with Richard Burton and Peter O'Toole.
Dr Strangelove, film with Peter Sellers.
My Fair Lady (see 1957), film with Audrey Hepburn and Rex Harrison.

Ministry of Technology formed.
15% Import Surcharge to aid Balance of Payments.
Forth Road Bridge opened.
Blue Streak rocket successfully launched by Britain.
Typhoid outbreak in Aberdeen; 400 cases confirmed.
British Government's plan *The South-East Study, 1961–1981* published.
European Launcher Development Association (E.L.D.O.) formed.
British Satellite *Ariel II* launched in Virginia.
Royal Air Force bomber T.S.R.2 made maiden flight.
U.S. *Ranger 7* spacecraft successfully launched to Moon; 4,000 photographs sent back; *Ranger 9* televised moon 1965.
U.S. spacecraft *Mariner IV* launched to explore planet Mars; transmitted photographs of Mars 1965.

1964 Indonesia invaded Malaysia; protest to U.N.; confrontation ended 1966.
War in South Vietnam between Government troops and Vietcong; U.S. increasingly involved.
Kenya became a republic.
Former British colony of Nyasaland became independent state of Malawi.
Bantu Laws Amendment Bill: *Apartheid* in South Africa.
Referendum in S. Rhodesia favoured independence.
Tanganyika and Zanzibar united to form new Republic of Tanzania.
Zambia, formerly N. Rhodesia, became a republic.
Canada's new national flag omitted Union Jack.
U.S. Presidential Election: Johnson returned.
Warren Report on the assassination of President Kennedy published.
U.S. Negro leader Luther King awarded Nobel Peace Prize.
Riots in Panama over U.S. administration of Canal Zone.

The Oxford Book of Nineteenth Century Verse, edited by John Hayward.
The Sun, new British daily newspaper, first published.

1965 †Sir Winston Churchill (*1874).
Edward Heath (*1916) became Leader of Conservative Party.
Government decided to cut Territorial Army by 70,000 men.
Mrs Elizabeth Lane became first Woman High Court judge in England.
Prices and Incomes Board set up: Aubrey Jones, M.P., Chairman.
Murder (Abolition of Death Penalty) Act.
Race Relations Act.
Gerald Brooke, British lecturer, imprisoned for subversive activities in Moscow; released in exchange for the Krogers, 1969.
U.N. Security Council enlarged from 11 to 15.
Spain renewed claim on Gibraltar; restricted movement of Colony's inhabitants.
Terrorism in Aden by National

John Arden (*1930): *Armstrong's Last Goodnight*, a play.
Baldwin: *The Amen Corner*, a play.
John Le Carré (*1931): *The Looking-Glass War*, spy thriller.
Graves: (i) *Collected Poems*, (ii) *Collected Short Stories*.
Robert Lowell (*1917, †1977): *For the Union Dead*, American poems.
Mailer: *An American Dream*, American novel.
Frank Marcus (*1928): *The Killing of Sister George*, a play.
Murdoch: *The Red and the Green*, a novel.
Bill Naughton (*1910): *Spring and Port Wine*, a play.
Osborne: *A Patriot For Me*, a play.
Sylvia Plath (*1932, †1963): *Ariel*, poems.
Spark: *The Mandelbaum Gate*, a novel.
Wesker: *The Four Seasons*, a play.
Boots' Circulating Libraries closed in Britain.
India adopted Hindi as official language.

Walt Disney's *Mary Poppins*, film with Julie Andrews.
Zorba the Greek, film with Lila Kedrova and Anthony Quinn.
Cassius Clay became World Heavy-weight Boxing Champion.
"Pirate" ship *Radio Caroline* operating outside British territorial waters attracted large audience.
Topless dresses worn in London.

Russian three-man spaceship *Voskhod* orbited Earth.
Discovery of *quasars*, quasi-stellar objects.
China exploded her first nuclear bomb.

Henze: *Der Junge Lord*, German opera.
Moore: *Lincoln Center Reclining Figure*, his largest bronze, 28 ft by 17 ft.
Malcolm Williamson (*1931): (i) *Symphonic Variations*, (ii) *Violin Concerto*.
Local Authorities asked to submit plans for comprehensive schools in Britain.
New University of Ulster founded at Coleraine, Co. Londonderry.
University of Warwick founded at Coventry.
First Commonwealth Festival of the Arts held in Britain.
Northern Aviary at Regent's Park Zoo, designed by Lord Snowdon and Cedric Price, opened.
Post Office tower, London's tallest building, opened.
A Policy for the Arts, White Paper published in Britain.
Institute of United States Studies founded in London.
Institute of Latin-American Studies founded in London.

Natural gas discovered in North Sea by British Petroleum Company.
Capital Gains Tax in Britain.
White Paper *Steel Nationalization* published.
Cigarette advertising banned on Commercial TV in Britain.
First commercial communications satellite, *Early Bird*, launched.
Fertility drugs caused multiple pregnancies in women.
France converted dollar assets into gold to curb U.S. investment; pressure on pound sterling resulted.
France boycotted all meetings of E.E.C. after disagreement over common farm policy; boycott ended 1966.
France launched her first satellite, A–1, from Sahara.
Russian cosmonaut Alexei Leonov left spacecraft *Voskhod II* and floated in space for 20 minutes.
U.S. two-man spacecraft *Gemini 5* orbited for eight days; *Gemini 6* and 7 made successful rendezvous in orbit.

1965	Liberation Front; Britain assumed direct rule. Singapore seceded from Malaysia and became independent state. Gambia, former British colony, became independent. Unilateral Declaration of Independence (U.D.I.) by Rhodesia; Premier Ian Smith. De Gaulle re-elected President of France. Pope created 27 new cardinals. Communist-led "coup" in Indonesia failed; led to repressive measures against Chinese population. U.S. bombed N. Vietnam and increased military forces in S. Vietnam to 125,000. Negro riots in Watts district of Los Angeles; 35 dead 800 seriously injured; $100 million damage. Ku Klux Klan members shot dead Mrs Viola Liuzzo, U.S. Civil Rights worker. Revolt in Dominican Republic: government overthrown; U.S. sent troops to restore order.	*The Penkovsky Papers*, supposedly based on notes of the Russian, Oleg Penkovsky, an American agent; Russia declared the book a forgery.
1966	Sir Edward Compton (*1906) first Parliamentary Commissioner (Ombudsman). General Election: Labour Party returned to power under Wilson; majority of 97. Prices and Incomes Act. British Colonial Office, created in 1854, dissolved; colonial responsibility assumed by new Commonwealth Office. Wilson, on board H.M.S. *Tiger*, met Ian Smith, Rhodesian Prime Minister, for talks; British proposals rejected; U.N. resolution for sanctions against Rhodesia. Bechuanaland and Basutoland, former British territories in Africa, became independent states of Botswana and Lesotho respectively. Former British colony of Barbados became independent state. Former colony of British Guiana	Anouilh: *The Fighting Cock*, French play. Auden: *Collected Shorter Poems, 1927–1957*. Capote: *In Cold Blood*, American study of two men convicted of murder. Charles Dyer (*1928): *Staircase*, a play. Greene: *The Comedians*, a novel. David Mercer (*1928, †1980): *Belcher's Luck*, a play. Murdoch: *The Time of the Angels*, a novel. H. Nicolson: *Diaries and Letters*, edited by Nigel Nicolson (3 vols. completed 1968). Jean Rhys (*?1890, †1979): *Wide Sargasso Sea*, novel. Paul Scott (*1920, †1978): *The Jewel in the Crown*, first volume of "Raj Quartet". Updike: *Of the Farm*, American novel. Rebecca West (*1892, †1983): *The Birds Fall Down*, a novel. Patrick White: *The Solid Mandala*, a novel. Yevgeny Yevtushenko (*1933): *Poetry*, translated from the Russian by George Reavey.

B.B.C. Third Programme used ex-exclusively for serious music.
Twenty-Four Hours, B.B.C. television news programme.
University of Zambia founded.
Gateway Arch, sheathed in stainless steel, at St. Louis, U.S.A., designed by Saarinen, completed.
The Sound of Music, film musical with Julie Andrews.
The Spy who came in from the Cold, film of Le Carré's novel, with Richard Burton.
Doctor Zhivago (see 1958), film with Omar Sharif and Julie Christie.
Growing craze for Bingo in Britain; run-down cinemas used as bingo-halls.

SCIENCE

Massive power failure paralysed New York City and surrounding district for 12 hours.
Avalanche at Mattmark Dam, Switzerland, killed 100.
Severe earthquake in Chile caused 400 deaths.

Britten: (i) *The Poet's Echo*, a song-cycle, (ii) *The Burning Fiery Furnace*, an opera.
Henze: Symphony No. 4.
Alun Hoddinott (*1929): *Variants*.
Rawsthorne: 'Cello Concerto.
Tippett: *The Vision of St Augustine*, choral work.
Williamson: *The Violins of St Jacques*, an opera.
Harrogate Festival of Arts and Sciences began.
University of Bradford founded.
Brunel University founded at Uxbridge, Middlesex.
City University, London, founded.
Heriot-Watt University founded at Edinburgh.
Loughborough University of Technology founded.
University of Surrey incorporated by Royal Charter.
Centre Point, 33–storey London office block, completed; still empty 1974.

Drastic economy measures in Britain.
Announcement that Britain would have decimal currency, based on £ sterling, in 1971.
Ministry of Social Security to replace Ministry of Pensions and National Insurance.
Selective Employment Tax (S.E.T.) and Corporation Tax in Britain.
Britain's atom-smashing particle accelerator *Nina* built at Daresbury in Cheshire.
Work begun on fast breeder reactor at Dounreay in Scotland: prototype for new nuclear power stations.
Britain's first Polaris submarine H.M.S. *Resolution* launched at Barrow.
Aberfan mining village disaster: torrential rain caused landslide of tip; school engulfed; 116 children and 28 adults killed.
Tay Road Bridge, longest in Britain, opened.
Severn Bridge completed.

1966 became independent state of Guyana.
Verwoerd, South African Prime Minister, assassinated by Demitrio Tsafendas; succeeded by B. J. Vorster (*1915).
Nkrumah, President of Ghana, deposed by military coup of General Ankrah.
†Lal Bahadur Shastri, Indian Prime Minister; succeeded by Mrs Indira Gandhi (*1917).
Tashkent Declaration between India and Pakistan to restore mutual friendship.
Sir Robert Menzies (*1894), Prime Minister of Australia since 1949, resigned; succeeded by Harold Holt.
France withdrew from N.A.T.O.
"Cultural Revolution" in China; purge of "Revisionists" by organized bodies of youths known as "Red Guards".
Serious Negro race riots in Chicago, Cleveland and Brooklyn.
International Treaty on peaceful uses of outer space.

Billy Graham (*1918), American evangelist, opened Greater London crusade.
The Times newspaper taken over by Lord Thomson; news on front page for first time.
New York Herald Tribune ceased publication.

1967 Abortion Act: permitted termination of pregnancy on recommendation of two doctors.
Criminal Justice Act: introduced majority verdicts in criminal trials.
Decimal Currency Act: decimal currency to be introduced in Britain in 1971.
Road Safety Act: police authorized to give breath tests to drivers.
Sexual Offences Act: homosexual acts between consenting adults ceased to be an offence.
Defence White Paper: drastic cuts in armed forces; run down of Far Eastern commitments.
Jo Grimond (*1913), Liberal Party Leader, resigned; Jeremy Thorpe (*1929) succeeded.
France blocked Britain's entry into Common Market.
Australian Prime Minister Holt drowned; succeeded by Deputy, John McEwen (*1900).

Aleksei Arbuzov (*1908): *The Promise*, Russian play.
John Barth (*1930): *Giles Goat-Boy*, a novel.
Jules Feiffer (*1929): *Little Murders*, a play.
Golding: *The Pyramid*, a novel.
Isherwood: *A Meeting by the River*, a novel.
Lowell: (i) *Benito Cereno*, a play, (ii) *Near the Ocean*, poetry.
Edward Lucie-Smith (*1933): *The Liverpool Scene*, poems.
Desmond Morris (*1928): *The Naked Ape*, describing man's habits as a mammal.
Naipaul: *The Mimic Men*, a novel.
The Rubáiyát of Omar Khayyám, translated by Robert Graves and Omar Ali-Shah (see 1050, 1859).
Spark: *Collected Poems, Vol 1.*
Tom Stoppard (*1937): *Rosencrantz and Guildenstern are Dead*, a play.
Wilson: *No Laughing Matter*, a novel.
Publishers' Association introduced Standard Book Numbering.
New *Catholic Encyclopaedia* published.

Opening of Parliament televised for first time.
Pay-TV, coin-box operated television, in London.
Football: England won the World Cup, defeating W. Germany 4–2 in Final.
New York Metropolitan Opera House completed.
Whitney Museum, New York, designed by Marcel Breuer, completed.
University of Chittagong founded.
Khartoum, film with Laurence Olivier and Charlton Heston.
A Man for all Seasons (see 1960), film with Paul Scofield.
Modesty Blaise, film with Monica Vitti and Dirk Bogarde.
Who's Afraid of Virginia Woolf? (see 1962), film with Elizabeth Taylor and Richard Burton.
Serious flooding in N. Italy damaged art treasures in Florence.
South Hampshire Study, planning report by Colin Buchanan & Partners.

Extensive mergers and "take-over" bids in British companies.
Six Common Market countries adopted Common Farm Policy.
Volta River hydro-electric scheme inaugurated.
Earthquake at Varto, in Turkey: over 2,000 killed.
Australian decimal currency: new dollar worth 10 old Aus. shillings.
Fossil bacteria found in rocks estimated to be 3,000 million years old by Harvard scientist.
Plastic heart used by U.S. surgeons kept patient alive for several days.
U.S. *Gemini 10* spacecraft located and locked onto *Agena* vehicle in space; astronaut "Buzz" Aldrin made spacewalk of 5 hr 35 min. from *Gemini 12*.
U.S. *Surveyor 1*, unmanned spacecraft, made soft landing on Moon, transmitted photographs of lunar surface; *Lunar Orbiter 1* photographed possible landing sites.

Richard Rodney Bennett (*1936): Symphony No. 2.
Francis Chichester sailed alone around the world in *Gipsy Moth IV*; knighted by the Queen at Greenwich.
Goehr: Quartet.
Henze: Double Concerto for Oboe, Harp and Strings.
René Magritte (*1898, †1967): *La Folie des Grandeurs*, Belgian surrealist bronze sculpture.
Liverpool Roman Catholic Cathedral consecrated: designed by Gibberd; stained glass by Traherne, Piper and Reyntiens; sculpture by Elisabeth Frink.
Plowden Report: *Children and Their Primary Schools*, published.
Queen Elizabeth Hall, London's new concert hall on South Bank, opened; architect: Hubert Bennett.
Royal College of Art granted Royal Charter.
University of Dundee founded.
University of Salford founded.

First British colour TV broadcast; 625–line definition used.
Donald Campbell killed on Coniston Water attempting to break his own water speed record in *Bluebird*.
Decasualization of dock labour in Britain.
Devaluation of pound sterling by 14.3 per cent.
Foot and mouth disease in Britain: 422,000 animals slaughtered.
Cunard liner *Queen Elizabeth II* launched by Queen.
Last voyage of Cunard liner *Queen Mary*.
98–inch reflecting Newton telescope, largest in Europe, at Royal Observatory at Herstmonceux.
Liberian tanker *Torrey Canyon* aground off Land's End; bombed in attempt to prevent large-scale pollution of beaches.
First heart transplant operation by Dr Christian Barnard at Cape Town; patient died after 18 days; 1968: Dr Philip Blaiberg survived a transplant for 19 months.
Hydrogen bomb exploded by China.

LITERATURE

1967 Referendum held in Gibraltar: overwhelming decision to remain with Britain.
R. Hubbard, "Scientology" leader, refused re-entry to Britain.
Communist-inspired riots in Hong Kong.
South Arabian Federal Government dissolved; Aden became People's Republic of South Yemen.
Greece: Bloodless *Coup d'État* by army; Constantine II fled to Rome; military government led by George Papadopoulos; press censorship.
Six-day war between Israel and Arab States of Egypt, Jordan and Syria; Arab forces defeated; Israel occupied Gaza Strip, Sinai and West bank of Jordan River.
Civil war in Nigeria: breakaway region of "Biafra" led by Ojukwu; Biafra defeated 1970.
President Sukarno of Indonesia deposed; succeeded by T. N. J. Suharto (*1921).
"Che" Guevara (*1928), Latin-American revolutionary, killed during guerrilla warfare in Bolivia.

1968 Clean Air Act.
Commonwealth Immigration Act: to restrict immigration of Kenyan Asians.
Theft Act.
Race Relations Act.
Trade Descriptions Act.
British Foreign and Commonwealth Offices merged.
Labour government introduced bill to reform House of Lords; bill abandoned 1969.
Civil Rights disturbances in Londonderry, Northern Ireland.
Wales: bomb outrages by Welsh Home Rule group; Welsh Language Society campaign.
Argentina claimed Falkland Islands: Britain refused to cede colony against wishes of Islands' population.
Former British colonies, Mauritius

Amis: *I Want it Now*, a novel.
Auden: *Collected Longer Poems*.
Michael Frayn (*1933): *A Very Private Life*, a novel.
Fuller: *New Poems*.
Graves: *Poems 1965–1968*.
Christopher Hampton (*1946): *Total Eclipse*, a play.
Hochhuth: *Soldiers: An Obituary for Geneva*, German play.
C. D. Lewis appointed Poet Laureate.
Peter Luke (*1919): *Hadrian the Seventh*, a play.
Miller: *The Price*, American play.
Murdoch: *The Nice and the Good*, a novel.
Percy Howard Newby (*1918): *Something to Answer For*, a novel.
George Orwell: *Collected Essays, Journalism and Letters*, edited posthumously by Ian Angus and Sonia Orwell.
Osborne: *The Hotel in Amsterdam*, a play.
Powell: *The Military Philosophers*, a novel.

Court Lees Approved School closed by Home Secretary.
B.B.C. radio programmes reorganized, becoming Radio 1, 2, 3 and 4; new Radio 1 exclusively "pop" music; local radio stations started.
B.B.C. television serial, *The Forsyte Saga*, in 26 episodes.
Canada staged *Expo 67* exhibition at Montreal to celebrate centenary.
Centre Le Corbusier Heidi-Weber completed at Zurich.
Bonnie and Clyde, film with Faye Dunaway and Warren Beatty.
Camelot, film with Vanessa Redgrave and Richard Harris.
Walt Disney's cartoon film: *The Jungle Book* (based on Kipling's stories).
Thoroughly Modern Millie, film with Julie Andrews.

Leakey discovered fossil remains of man-like creature *kenyapithecus africanus*, claimed to be 20 million years old.
Mangla Dam, large-scale irrigation and hydro-electric project, completed in Pakistan.
Russian spacecraft *Venus IV* made soft landing on planet Venus.
Unmanned Russian satellites linked up in space: possible basis for future space-station building.
Sweden adopted right-hand side driving for road traffic system.
First laser surgery operating theatre; in Cincinnati, U.S.A.
Scientists at Stanford University, California, manufactured primitive form of life in a test tube.
Discovery of virus causing chicken disease (Marek's Disease).

Britten: *The Prodigal Son*, church parable.
Henze: (i) Piano Concerto No. 2, (ii) *Medusa*, German oratorio.
Menotti: *Help, Help, the Glotolinks*, American space opera for children.
Rawsthorne: Concerto for two pianos and orchestra.
Alec Rose sailed alone around the world in yacht *Lively Lady*; knighted.
Vasarely: *Arny*, optical painting.
Williamson: Symphony No. 2.
Howard Winstone, Welshman, won World Featherweight Boxing Championship.
London Bridge sold for £2.4 million to U.S. Oil company; re-erected over Colorado River.
London Opera Society launched.
New Euston Station opened.
First report of Public Schools Commission (Newsom Report) recommended gradual integration with State Schools.
South Africa refused to accept M.C.C.

British Standard Time, one hour in advance of Greenwich Mean Time, adopted; ended 1971.
Fulton Report on future of the British Civil Service published.
Post Office two-tier system: First and Second Class letter mail.
End of steam locomotion on British Railways.
Fertility drug administered to a Birmingham woman resulted in her giving birth to six babies.
Structure of haemoglobin molecule determined by Dr Max Perutz, of Cambridge.
Britain's first heart transplant patient, Frederick West, survived operation for 46 days.
Cambridge radio astronomers, leader Sir Martin Ryle, discovered *pulsars*, radio stars emitting regular pulses of energy.
Biochemists of Imperial College, London,

1968 and Swaziland, became independent.
Treaty on non-proliferation of nuclear weapons signed by U.S.A., Russia, Britain and 58 other states.
Rioting in Belgium over Flemish language question; General Election.
Liberal reform measures by Czech government led by Alexander Dubček; Russian invasion; Czech leaders arrested but later released.
Students of Sorbonne University in anti-government riots; joined by trade unions; French General Election; majority of Gaullist Party increased.
Spanish government took drastic measures to curb Basque Nationalists.
Rann of Kutch dispute between India and Pakistan resolved by international tribunal.
Martin Luther King assassinated at Memphis, Tennessee.
Senator Richard Nixon (*1913), Republican, elected President of U.S.A.
Senator Robert Kennedy shot at Los Angeles; Sirhan Bishara Sirhan, Jordanian Arab, charged with murder.
U.S.S. *Pueblo* captured by North Korean forces; crew accused of spying but later released; ship not returned.

Snow: *The Sleep of Reason*, a novel.
William Styron (*1925): *The Confessions of Nat Turner*, a novel.
Updike: *Couples*, American novel.
Vidal: *Myra Breckinridge*, American novel.
Solzhenitsyn: (i) *Cancer Ward* (Part II, 1969), (ii) *The First Circle*, Russian novels.
End of censorship by the Lord Chamberlain in the English Theatre.

1969 Representation of the People Act lowered voting age from 21 to 18; Family Law Reform Act lowered age of majority to 18.
Divorce Reform Act: breakdown of marriage sole ground for divorce in Britain.
Parliament voted for permanent abolition of Death Penalty.
Redcliff-Maud Report on reform of local government in England.
Investiture of Prince Charles as Prince of Wales by the Queen at Caernarvon Castle.
White Paper *In Place of Strife* on

Amis: *The Green Man*, a novel.
Anouilh: *Cher Antoine*, French play.
Auden: *City Without Walls*, poetry.
Brigid Brophy (*1929): *In Transit*, a novel.
Cozzens: *Morning, Noon and Night*, a novel.
Murdoch: *Bruno's Dream*, a novel.
Nabokov: *Ada*, Russian-American novel.
Peter Nichols (*1927): *The National Health*, a play.
Philip Roth (*1933): *Portnoy's Complaint*, American novel.
David Storey (*1933): *The Contractor*, a play.
Charles Wood (*1932): *"H"*, a play.

cricket team which included Basil D'Oliveira.
XIX Olympic Games: in Mexico City.
B.B.C. stereo broadcasting on V.H.F. Radio 3 programme.
Canterbury Tales, musical based on Chaucer's stories.
The Charge of the Light Brigade, a film.
Chitty Chitty Bang Bang, film with Dick Van Dyke.
Oliver!, film version of Lionel Bart's musical.
Star, film of life of Gertrude Lawrence, with Julie Andrews.

led by Professor E. B. Chain, developed *statalon*, highly resistant anti-virus compound.
Central Banks' two-tier marketing system for gold permitted commercial dealings at a free price.
International Research and Development Corporation produced revolutionary type of superconducting electric motor.
France exploded a hydrogen bomb.
Major earthquake in North-east Persia killed over 12,000 people.
U.S. spacecraft *Apollo 8*, with three astronauts aboard, journeyed 240,000 miles to the Moon and returned safely after completing ten lunar orbits.
U.S. launched unmanned satellite: orbiting astronomical observatory to study X-ray sources.
Physicists of Maryland University claimed to have detected gravitational waves.

Bennett: *Victory*, an opera.
William Mathias: Symphony No. 1.
Olivier Messiaen (*1908): *The Transfiguration*, an oratorio.
Thea Musgrave (*1928): Clarinet Concerto.
John Tavener (*1944): *Celtic Requiem*.
Tippett: *The Knot Garden*, an opera.
Walton: *Battle of Britain*, film music.
The Queen ended her traditional 'live' Christmas broadcast.
Open University founded on a new concept of teaching through television and radio.
Consultant architects' reports on conservation of Bath, Chichester, Chester and York.

British Petroleum discovered large oil deposit in Alaska.
Concorde supersonic airliner made successful maiden flight from Toulouse.
British Trans-Arctic Expedition successfully crossed Arctic ice-cap.
Human egg fertilized in a test tube ("Test-tube Baby") at Cambridge.
British Post Office became a public corporation.
Cunard liner *Queen Elizabeth II* made her maiden voyage.
Outbreak of Asian 'flu in Britain.
Structure of insulin determined by Dr Dorothy Hodgkin at Oxford.

LITERATURE

1969 reform of trade unions published.
Catherine McConnachie first woman minister in Church of Scotland.
Bomb outrages in Wales by Welsh National extremists.
Civil disturbances in N. Ireland: increased activity of I.R.A.; resignation of Prime Minister O'Neill; succeeded by James Chichester-Clark; Eire demanded end of partition; British troops sent to restore order.
Anguilla incident: independence demanded by self-appointed president Webster; troops and police sent by British government; later withdrawn.
De Gaulle resigned after defeat in referendum; succeeded by Georges Pompidou (*1911, †1974).
Willy Brandt (*1913) elected Chancellor of West Germany.
Greece left Council of Europe.
Franco named Prince Juan Carlos as his eventual successor in Spain.
R.C. Church removed 46 saints from its calendar.
Mrs Golda Meir (*1898, †1978) succeeded Eshkol as Prime Minister of Israel.
Border clashes between Chinese and Russian troops in Sinkiang area.
Tom Mboya (*1926), leading Kenyan politician, assassinated.
Hi-jacking of airliners: new international problem.
Lieut. William Calley charged with responsibility for shooting by U.S. soldiers of Vietnamese civilians in My Lai.

1970 Equal Pay Act.
Administration of Justice Act.
General Election in Britain: Conservatives elected; Edward Heath Prime Minister.
Industrial Relations Bill.
Britain reopened negotiations to enter Common Market.
Two C.S. gas bombs thrown in

Albee: *Tiny Alice*, American play.
Bellow: *Mr Sammler's Planet*, American novel.
Bolt: *Vivat! Vivat Regina!*, a play.
Fry: *A Yard of Sun*, a play.
Germaine Greer (*1959): *The Female Eunuch*, study of female stereotyping.
Hampton: *The Philanthropist*, a play.
P. H. Johnson: *The Honours Board*, a novel.

£22 million scheme for St Katherine's Dock, London, published.
52–storey headquarters of the Bank of America in San Francisco, tallest building in the world, opened.
Boris Spassky, Russian, became World Chess Champion, defeating Tigran Petrosian.
Broadcasting in the Seventies, B.B.C. publication outlining its future policy.
Civilization, B.B.C. television series presented by Sir Kenneth Clark.
Battle of Britain, film with Laurence Olivier.
Funny Girl, film musical with Barbra Streisand.
Midnight Cowboy, film with Dustin Hoffman and John Voight.
Oh! What a Lovely War, film with Richard Attenborough and star cast.
Women in Love, film of D. H. Lawrence's novel.
First new British decimal coin, seven-sided 50–pence piece, circulated; halfpenny withdrawn.

First fully automatic navigational buoy, designed eventually to replace the lightship, launched in London.
Victoria Line opened: first underground railway built in London for 60 years.
Longhope (Orkney) Lifeboat lost with entire crew in Pentland Firth.
Quarantine increased to 8 months in Britain.
Russian Venus probes discovered surface conditions on planet too hot to support life.
Russian cosmonauts' welding experiments in spacecraft *Soyuz 6* while orbiting Earth.
Neil Armstrong, commander of U.S. spacecraft *Apollo 11,* became first man to set foot on the Moon; televised pictures of landing transmitted to Earth; rock samples brought back in the spacecraft.
Hurricane *Camillo* struck southern U.S.A.; 400 killed.
U.S. scientists "seeded" hurricane *Debbie* with silver iodide crystals dropped from aircraft; intensity reduction claimed.
Problems of the Human Environment, U.N. scientific report, stressed urgent need for conservation.
Discovery of fossil skull of prehistoric reptile *lystrosaurus* in Antarctica supported theory of continental drift.

Bliss: Concertino for 'Cello and Orchestra.
Elliott Carter (*1908): Piano Concerto.
Frankel: Symphony No. 7.
Goehr: *Symphony in One Movement.*
Nicholas Maw (*1935): *The Rising of the Moon,* an opera.
Robbins: *Dances at a Gathering,* a ballet.
Shostakovich: Symphony No. 14.
Record price of £2,310,000 paid at Christie's

British Rail developed a passenger train capable of a speed of 150 m.p.h.
Industrial dispute led to electricity power cuts in Britain; emergency powers declared.
Oil discovered in North Sea by British Petroleum Co.
Financial crisis of Rolls Royce Company: saved by government aid.

1970 House of Commons by a demonstrator.
Shooting and bomb outrages in N. Ireland; public processions banned.
Rhodesia became a republic.
Pacific islands of Fiji, Tonga and Western Samoa became independent states.
Czech Liberal reformers, including Dubček, gradually stripped of office and expelled from Communist Party.
Rioting in Gdansk and other Polish Baltic towns against widespread price increases; Gomulka resigned.
West German treaties with Poland and Russia recognizing national boundaries.
Divorce permitted in Italy.
Civil War in Jordan between Palestinian guerrillas and government forces; order restored.
Hi-jacking of three airliners to Jordan by Palestinian guerrillas: aircraft blown up; passengers and crews held hostage, later released.
Attempt to assassinate Pope Paul VI at Manila Airport during Far Eastern tour.
†Nasser; succeeded as President of Egypt by Anwar Sadat (*1918, †1981).
Outbreak of kidnapping of diplomats by political extremists in Canada and Latin America.
Attempted invasion of Guyana by troops from Portuguese Guinea.
U.S. forces attacked Communist bases in Cambodia.
National Guard fired on rioting students at Kent State University, Ohio, killing five.

1971 Terms agreed for U.K. entry into E.E.C.
First postal strike in U.K.; strikes against Industrial Relations Bill; unemployment highest since 1940.
Immigration Bill to end right of Commonwealth citizens to settle in U.K.

1970
Lowell: *Notebook*, American poems.
Murdoch: *A Fairly Honourable Defeat*, a novel.
Proust: *Time Regained*, translated from the French by Andreas Mayor.
Nabokov: *Poems and Problems*, Russian-American work.
New transcription of Pepys's *Diary* by Robert Latham and William Matthews.
Snow: *Last Things*, novel.
Spark: *The Driver's Seat*, a novel.
Shaffer: *The Battle of Shrivings*, a play.
Mary Stewart (*1916): *The Crystal Cave*, historical novel.
Storey: *Home*, a play.
Updike: *Bech: A Book*, American novel.
Vidal: *Two Sisters*, American novel.
Solzhenitsyn: *In the Interests of the Cause*, Russian novel.
Henri Charrière: *Papillon*, adventures in a French penal colony.

1971
Amis: *Girl, 20*, novel.
Alan Ayckbourn (*1939): *Time and Time Again*, play.
Alan Bennett (*1934): *Getting On*, play.
Burgess: *MF*, novel.
le Carré: *The Naive and Sentimental Lover*, novel.

for Velasquez portrait *Juan de Pareja*.
The Great Waltz, musical comedy on life of Johann Strauss.
New theatre company, The Young Vic, formed.
New barracks for Household Cavalry, incorporating 300–ft tower block, designed by Spence.
Government decision to charge for admission to national galleries and museums.
Expo 70 held in Japan: 76 nations took part.
World-wide anti-*Apartheid* feeling in sport: South Africa expelled by International Olympics Committee and banned from Davis Cup; English cricket tour cancelled.
New censorship gradings by British Board of Film Censors: (a) U and A. (all ages), (b) AA (14+), (c) X (18+).
Anne of the Thousand Days, film with Richard Burton and Geneviève Bujold.
Butch Cassidy and the Sundance Kid, film with Paul Newman and Robert Redford.
Cromwell, film with Richard Harris and Alec Guinness.
Ned Kelly, film with Mick Jagger.
Paint Your Wagon (see 1953), film musical with Lee Marvin.
Waterloo, film with Rod Steiger and Christopher Plummer.

First commercial radio stations planned in U.K.
Closure of *Daily Sketch*, oldest tabloid newspaper in Britain.
Opening of Kennedy Arts Centre, Washington.
Demolition of Les Halles market, Paris.

Roskill Commission chose Cublington as site for London's third airport; after public protest Foulness, Essex, chosen in 1971.
Hovertrain passenger service inaugurated in France.
European Conservation Year: world-wide attention on need to conserve the Earth's natural resources.
First use of nuclear-powered heart "pace-makers".
China launched her first satellite.
Russian two-man spacecraft *Soyuz 9* made record 18 days' orbit of Earth.
Russia landed eight-wheeled robot vehicle *Lunokhod 1* to explore moon's surface from unmanned spacecraft *Luna 17*.
Boeing 747 "Jumbo Jet" airliner.
Explosion on U.S. spacecraft *Apollo 13* half-way to the moon; crew used Lunar module *Aquarius* as "space lifeboat"; emergency rescue measures resulted in safe return of astronauts.
Cyclone and tidal wave struck East Pakistan: enormous damage; half a million deaths estimated.
Earthquake disaster in N. Peru destroyed towns of Yungay and Ranrahirca: 50,000 killed.
Worst flood disaster in Roumania in living memory: crops destroyed and communication disrupted; 161 people died.

Decimal currency introduced in U.K.
Aswan high dam opened.
Apollo 14 made moon landing; *Apollo 15* astronauts first to drive vehicle on moon; *Mariner 9* in orbit of Mars; first orbit of another planet.
Russian spacecraft *Soyuz 10* docked with space station *Salyut*.

1971 U.K. expelled 90 Russian diplomats and officials for alleged spying.
End of Royal Navy's Far East Command.
Almost 50% increase in petitions for divorce since Divorce Reform Act (1969).
N. Ireland: internment without trial; serious disturbances in Belfast; 100th death since troubles began.
Admission of communist China to U.N.; expulsion of Formosa; Kurt Waldheim appointed U.N. Secretary General.
Treaty banning nuclear weapons from seabed.
U.S. Supreme Court allowed newspaper publication of Pentagon Papers, secrets of Vietnam war.
U.S.A.: anti-war demonstrations; trade embargo on China lifted; 26th amendment to Constitution extended voting rights to 18–year-olds; Lt. William Calley found guilty of My Lai massacre of S. Vietnamese civilians, 1968 (see 1969).
Strategic Arms Limitation Talks agreed to limit anti-ballistic missiles.
Uganda: army coup put Idi Amin in power.
Switzerland: women given the vote.
Pakistan-India war; declaration of E. Pakistan as independent state of Bangladesh; Ali Bhutto became President of Pakistan.
Haiti: †Francois Duvalier, President, succeeded by son Jean-Claude (ousted 1986).
Laos: incursion by S. Vietnamese troops, supported by U.S. forces; U.S. losses in Vietnam passed 45,000.
Syria broke off relations with Jordan; Syria, Libya and Egypt formed Federation of Arab Republics; Libya nationalized BP's assets.
Iraq: expulsion of many Iranians.
Emirate of Bahrain became independent of Britain; Sierra

David Caute (*1936): *The Confrontation*, a trilogy.
Compton-Burnett: *The Last and the First*, posthumous novel.
Forster: *Maurice*, posthumous novel.
Golding: *The Scorpion God*, novel.
Simon Gray (*1936): *Butley*, play.
Greene: *A Sort of Life*, autobiography.
Hartley: *The Harness Room*, novel.
Geoffrey Hill (*1932): *Mercian Hymns*, prose poems.
Isherwood: *Kathleen and Frank*, biography.
Lessing: *Briefing for a Descent into Hell*, novel.
McCarthy: *Birds of America*, novel.
Adrian Mitchell (*1932) *Ride the Nightmare*, poetry; *Tyger*, play.
Murdoch: *An Accidental Man*, novel.
Naipaul: *In A Free State*, fiction (Booker Prize).
Nichols: *Forget-me-not Lane*, play.
Osborne: *West of Suez*, play.
Pinter: *Old Times*, play.
Powell: *Books Do Furnish a Room*, novel.
Vernon Scannell (*1922): *The Tiger and the Rose*, autobiography.
Tom Sharpe (*1928): *Riotous Assembly*, comic novel.
Solzhenitsyn: *August 1914*, Russian novel (Paris publication).
Storey: *The Changing Room*, play.
William Trevor (*1928): *Miss Gomes and the Brethren*, novel.
Wouk: *The Winds of War*, novel.

Work began on preservation of temples of Philae, Egypt.
Parthenon reported to be imperilled by atmospheric corrosion.
Opening of London Bridge, reconstructed in Arizona desert.
Opening of Disney World leisure complex, Florida.
Bernstein: *Mass for the Late President Kennedy*.
John Joubert (*1927): Symphony No. 2.
Rubbra: Symphony No. 8.
Britten: *Canticle IV*, vocal work.
John McCabe (*1939): Symphony No. 2.
Tate Gallery: major exhibition of work of Andy Warhol (*1931, †1987), exponent of Pop Art.
Anastasia, ballet by Kenneth MacMillan.
†Louis Armstrong, jazz trumpeter.
Official dissolution of Beatles pop group.
The French Connection, film.
Death in Venice, film by Visconti with Dirk Bogarde.
Love Story, film directed by Arthur Hiller.
The Go-between, film by Joseph Losey from novel by Hartley.
Sunday, Bloody Sunday, film by John Schlesinger.
A Clockwork Orange, film by Stanley Kubrick.
Macbeth, film version by Polanski.
Follies, musical by Stephen Sondheim.
Godspell, American musical, opened in London.
The Search for the Nile, B.B.C. television dramatised documentary.
Edna, The Inebriate Woman, television play by Jeremy Sandford.
Collapse of crush barriers at Ibrox football stadium, Glasgow: 66 spectators killed.
Joe Frazier beat Muhammed Ali for world heavyweight boxing championship.

Three *Soyuz 11* cosmonauts died during longest ever flight.
U.S. and U.S.S.R. launched space probes towards Mars.
Plans to develop high-speed Advanced Passenger Train in U.K.
End of free school milk in Britain.
Crash helmets compulsory for motorcyclists in U.K.
Japan: world's first major plane crash; 162 killed.
Chay Blyth made first solo yacht voyage round world in westerly direction.
Hormone responsible for human growth reported to have been synthesized.
Rolls-Royce declared bankrupt.
Experimental air-cushion vehicle had first trials at Cambridge, U.K.
First use of computers in air-traffic control.
International concern over pollution of environment; I.C.I. developed catalysts to reduce pollution levels from car exhausts.
Auction of areas for exploitation of N. Sea oil fields.
Important investment in cancer research in U.S.
Royal College of Physicians re-affirmed link between smoking and lung cancer; government agreed to warning notices on cigarette packets.
W. Germany: first experiments in genetic engineering to reduce levels of amino-acids in children.
Self-administered pregnancy tests advertised in U.K.
First major national commitment to prevention and treatment of alcholism in U.S.
India: cyclone killed 5,000 and destroyed about 1,000,000 homes.
54 countries signed International Telecommunications Satellite Consortium agreement.

1971 Leone became republic within Commonwealth; Congo renamed Zaire.

1972 Miners' strike in U.K.: extensive power cuts nationally; industry restricted to 3–day week; State of Emergency.
Pound floated and sank to record low; 90–day freeze on increases in pay, prices, dividends and rents to curb inflation; Bank of England's minimum lending rate highest since 1914.
Unemployment over 1 million; nearly 24 million days lost through strikes, highest figures since 1926.
Local Government Act established new counties and districts.
Reginald Maudling, Home Secretary, resigned because of involvement with bankrupt.
U.K. dispute with Iceland over fishing limits ("Cod War"); ended 1973.
President Nixon re-elected: ordered resumption of bombing in Vietnam; visited China and Moscow.
Arrests at Watergate building, Washington, H.Q. of Democratic Party, during attempted bugging; former White House aides indicted.
U.S. Senate passed Equal Rights amendment.
Continuation of troubles in N. Ireland: IRA bomb in Belfast store injured 55; British Embassy burned down in Dublin; 13 killed in Londonderry "Bloody Sunday"; direct rule from London imposed; 100th British soldier killed; total deaths now over 500.
Strategic Arms Limitation Treaty (S.A.L.T.) signed by U.S. and U.S.S.R.
First British ambassador to communist China appointed.
Pakistan left Commonwealth; Bangladesh joined.
26 killed by terrorists in Tel Aviv airport; military incidents between

Richard Adams (*1920): *Watership Down*, novel.
Ayckbourn: *Absurd Person Singular*, comedy.
Beckett: *The Lost Ones*, fiction; *Not I*, play.
Quentin Bell (*1910): *Virginia Woolf*, biography.
John Berger (*1926): *G*, fiction (Booker Prize).
Donald Davie (*1922): *Poems 1950–70*.
Margaret Drabble (*1939): *The Needle's Eye*, novel.
Frederick Forsyth (*1938): *The Odessa File*, novel.
Graves: *Poems 1970–2*.
James Herriot (*1916): *It Shouldn't Happen to a Vet* and *All Creatures Great and Small*, novels.
P. J. Kavanagh (*1931): *A Happy Man*, novel.
Miller: *The Creation of the World and Other Business*, play.
Osborne: *A Sense of Detachment*, play.
van der Post: *A Story Like the Wind*, account of African life.
Kathleen Raine (*1908): *The Lost Country*, poetry.
Roth: *The Breast*, novel.
Snow: *The Malcontents*, novel.
Stoppard: *Jumpers*, play.
Storey: *Pasmore*, novel.
Alexander Theroux (*1939): *Three Wogs*, short stories.
Eudora Welty (*1909): *The Optimist's Daughter*, novel.
Wesker: *The Old Ones*, play.
E. A. Whitehead (*1933): *Alpha Beta*, play.
Wood: *Veterans*, play.
Betjeman appointed Poet Laureate.
Russia refused to allow Nobel Prize to be presented to Solzhenitsyn.

Official opening of new Stock Exchange building.
Five Oxford men's colleges announced plans to admit women.
Karlheinz Stockhausen (*1928): *Momente*, spatial music.
Henze: *Das Floss der Medusa*, dramatic oratorio.
Shostakovich: Symphony No. 15.
Tippett: Symphony No. 3.
Harrison Birtwistle (*1934): *The Triumph of Time*, music.
Treasures of Tutankhamun, exhibition at British Museum.
Jesus Christ Superstar, musical by Andrew Lloyd Webber and Tim Rice.
Tommy, rock-theatre by The Who (rock group).
A Little Night Music, musical by Stephen Sondheim.
The Godfather, film by Francis Ford Coppola with Al Pacino and Marlon Brando.
Avanti, film by Billy Wilder.
Roma, film by Fellini.
Young Winston, film by Richard Attenborough.
Discreet Charm of the Bourgeoisie, film by Bunuel.
Sleuth, film with Olivier and Michael Caine.
Last Tango in Paris, film by Bertolucci with Marlon Brando.
School-leaving age in Britain raised from 15 to 16.
Longford Committee proposed penalties for pornographers in U.K.
Pope abolished tonsure.
Rhodesia expelled from Olympic movement. Olympic games at Munich: Arab guerrillas kidnapped nine Israeli athletes, killing two more; athletes and kidnappers killed in rescue attempt; first major incident of international terrorism.
U.S. swimmer Mark Spitz won record seven Olympic gold medals.
Bobby Fischer beat title-holder Boris Spassky in world chess championship, Reykjavik.

U.N. Conference on the Human Environment, Stockholm.
International convention to prevent dumping at sea.
International conference of Broadasting Unions adapted uniform rules for intercontinental television transmissions by satellite.
B.B.C. announced development of Ceefax information system.
U.S. and Russia agreed to co-operate in matters of science and technology.
U.S. approved expenditure for manned space-shuttle research.
Crews of U.S. *Apollo 16* and *17* spacecraft continued exploration of moon; nuclear-powered laboratory placed on moon; *Pioneer 10* unmanned spacecraft launched, first to observe Jupiter.
World's most powerful radio telescope, Mullard Observatory, Cambridge, U.K.
World's most powerful atom-smashing machine, Batavia, U.S.A.
First kidney and pancreatic tissue transplant. U.K. government announced kidney-donor card scheme.
Evidence of link between eating of blight-infected potatoes and birth of children with spina bifida.
London *Sunday Times* prevented by High Court from publishing articles about thalidomide (1962); government offered £3 million to help child victims.
Discovery in Kenya of skull said to be 2.6 million years old, possibly earliest known "missing link.".
Important exploration of Mediterranean and Red Sea seabeds by *Glomar Challenger*, drilling and sampling ship.
First pocket calculators using microchip technology.
Introduction of computerized fault-location system for car repairs.
First electronic cash registers linked to stock distribution systems.
Britain's first hypermarket opened.
Worst crash in history of U.K. aviation: 118 killed at Heathrow; another air crash,

1972 Israel and Egypt, Lebanon and Syria.
Iraq nationalized Iraq Petroleum Co. based in London.
West Berliners permitted to enter E. Berlin.
Leaders of Baader-Meinhof, German terrorist group, arrested.
Uganda: Amin announced expulsion of all Asians: U.K. agreed to admit 25,000 with British passports.
Vietnam: withdrawal of last U.S. ground forces. Peace talks.

1973 Britian, Ireland and Denmark became members of E.E.C.; reduction of tariffs between E.E.C. countries; agreement on common agricultural policy.
U.K.: pay and prices freeze continued, followed by strict counter-inflation controls; State of Emergency following widespread strikes.
Value Added Tax (10%) replaced Purchase Tax and Selective Employment Tax.
New Northern Ireland Bill with anti-terrorist measures including trial without jury.
N. Ireland: plebiscite showed large majority in favour of continued membership of U.K.; capital punishment abolished; new Ulster Assembly, by proportional representation, in Stormont; terrorist bomb campaign, including car and letter bombs, in London and elsewhere.

U.S. military operations in Indochina officially ended; ceasefire in Vietnam; U.S. troops departed.
Yom Kippur War: Israel, invaded by Egypt and Syria (later supported by Iraq), counter-attacked; ceasefire after three weeks; U.N. peace-keeping force established in Middle East. Oil states increased oil prices by 70–100% and cut production. Beginning of major energy crisis.
Watergate affair: four senior aides of President Nixon resigned following

Ayckbourn: *The Norman Conquests*, play trilogy.
Beryl Bainbridge (*1934): *The Dressmaker*, novel.
Bennett: *Habeas Corpus*, play.
Edward Bond (*1934): *Bingo*, play.
Burroughs: *Exterminator!* science fiction.
J. G. Farrell (*1935, †1979): *The Siege of Krishnapur*, novel (Booker Prize).
Greene: *The Honorary Consul*, novel.
Hampton: *Savages*, play.
R. Hughes: *The Wooden Shepherdess*, novel.
Lessing: *The Summer before the Dark*, novel.
Lowell: *The Dolphin*, poems.
Mailer: *Marilyn*, biography of Monroe.
Murdoch: *The Black Prince*, novel.
Powell: *Temporary Kings*, novel.
Thomas Pynchon (*1937): *Gravity's Rainbow*, novel.
Peter Redgrove (*1932): *In the Country of the Skin*, novel.
Shaffer: *Equus*, play.
Sharpe: *Indecent Exposure*, novel.
Solzhenitsyn: *The Gulag Archipelago* (published Paris), novel.
Spark: *The Hothouse by the East River*, novel.
Storey: *A Temporary Life*, novel.
R. S. Thomas (*1913): *Selected Poems 1946–68*.
Kurt Vonnegut (*1922): *Breakfast of Champions*, novel.
White: *The Eye of the Storm*, novel.
Tennessee Williams: *Out Cry*, play.
Wilson: *As If By Magic*, novel.

at Moscow, killed 176.
Nicaragua: earthquake killed about 10,000 people; 200,000 homeless.

Opening of new London Bridge (1968) and New London Theatre, Drury Lane.
Opening of J. Paul Getty Museum, Malibu, California; Sydney Opera House, Australia, designed by Utzon; World Trade Centre, New York; Bosphorus suspension bridge, Turkey, longest outside U.S.A, linking Europe and Asia.
Opening of London Broadcasting Company (L.B.C.) and Capital Radio, first legal U.K. commercial radio stations.
Treasures of Chinese Art exhibition, London and Paris.
Arts sales: Japanese became dominant buyers.
Krzysztof Penderecki (*1933): Symphony No. 1.
Havergal Brian (*1876, †1972); Symphony No. 2.
Britten: *Death in Venice*, opera.
The Rocky Horror Show, musical.
Everything You Wanted To Know About Sex . . . , film by Woody Allen.
O Lucky Man!, film by Lindsay Anderson.
Live and Let Die, film based on novel by Fleming.
The Day of the Jackal, film by Fred Zimmerman of novel by Forsyth (1971).
Serpico, film by Sidney Lumet.
Parade, film by Jacques Tati.
The Sting, film with Paul Newman and Robert Redford.
Badlands, film by Terence Malick.
Sleeper, film by Woody Allen.
The Way We Were, film with Barbra Streisand and Robert Redford.
Some Mothers Do 'Ave 'Em, B.B.C. television comedy series.

U.N. adopted Declaration on the Human Environment.
Skylab, unmanned space station, launched into orbit; three manned missions launched to conduct experiments from it; colour pictures of Jupiter received from *Pioneer 10* (see 1972).
European Space Agency formed in Brussels: Europe to pool resources in joint space projects.
U.S.-U.S.S.R. exchange of data about Mars.
Compensation for thalidomide victims agreed after 11–year court proceedings.
International protests at French resumption of nuclear tests in Pacific.
Famine in Ethiopia: 100,000 feared dead.
7–year drought continued in W. Africa.
Heart disease caused ½ million deaths in U.S. ¾ million new cases of gonorrhea per year reported in U.S.
Widespread development of microprocessor designs and markets.
First computer-controlled petrol station.
Wedding of Princess Anne seen by 500 million television viewers worldwide.
First intercontinental stereophonic television transmission.
Foreign cars took record share of British market. Japanese cars becoming common in U.K. for first time.
E. F. Schumacher: *Small is Beautiful – A Study of Economics as if People Mattered*, treatise on "alternative" technology.
Worst flooding on record in Pakistan, Bangladesh and India.
Worst flooding in 200 years in Mississippi River valley.
C.E.R.N. (European atom-smashing

LITERATURE

1973 allegations of political espionage on Democratic party at Watergate (1972). Senate Select Committee began investigation; subpoenas served on Nixon following his refusal to release secret tape recordings of conversations with people allegedly involved.
Asian traders expelled from Kenya.
Afghanistan proclaimed republic after army-backed coup.
Greece: army takeover.
Argentina: General Juan Peron, former dictator, elected president.
Australia: aborigines granted vote.
Bahamas became independent of U.K.

1974 World shortage of oil; exporting countries increased prices and embargoed certain countries in wake of Israeli-Arab war; I.M.F. announced help to nations hit by quadrupled oil prices.
U.K. train drivers' and miners' strike.
General Election: Labour government without overall majority; Harold Wilson Prime Minister.
End of State of Emergency and 3–day week.
"Social Contract" between government and T.U.C. to restrain pay increases.
Autumn election: Labour returned with small overall majority.
Serious inflation: 20% increase in cost of living; wage increases of 26%; petrol prices up 75%.
Health and Safety at Work Act.
Prevention of Terrorism Act.
N. Ireland: 1,000 death since beginning of troubles; spate of I.R.A. bombs in Buckinghamshire, Yorkshire, Westminster Hall, Guildford; Birmingham pub bombings killed 26.
Watergate: Grand Jury claimed President involved in conspiracy to cover up political espionage; Supreme Court demanded White

Adams: *Shardik*, allegory.
Amis: *Ending Up*, novel.
Ayckbourn: *Absent Friends* and *Confusions*, plays.
Baldwin: *If Beale Street Could Talk*, novel.
J. G. Ballard (*1930): *Concrete Island*, novel.
Carl Bernstein and Robert Woodward: *All the President's Men*, journalists' account of Watergate.
Peter Brook's production of *The Ik* at Paris Festival.
Burgess: *The Clockwork Testament*, novel.
Durrell: *Monsieur*, novel.
Athol Fugard (*1932): *Statements: Three Plays*.
David Hare (*1947): *Knuckle*, play.
Heller: *Something Happened*, novel.
Thomas Keneally (*1935): *Blood Red, Sister Rose*, historical novel.
Larkin: *High Windows*, poetry.
Mike Leigh (*1943): *Babies Grow Old* and *The Silent Majority*, plays.
Murdoch: *The Sacred and Profane Love Machine*, novel (Whitbread Award).
Nikolaus Pevsner (*1902): final volume of series *The Buildings of England*.
Roth: *My Life as a Man*, first of novel sequence.
Cornelius Ryan (*1920, †1974): *A Bridge Too Far*, war history.
Sharpe: *Porterhouse Blue*, novel.
Stoppard: *Travesties*, play.
Storey: *Life Class*, play.
Solzhenitsyn expelled from Russia; collected Nobel Prize.

The Ascent of Man, B.B.C. television documentary series.
The World at War, television documentary series.
Italian government announced plans to prevent Venice from sinking into sea.
U.S.S.R. signed Geneva Universal Copyright Convention.
Pulitzer Prize awarded to *Washington Post* for public service during Watergate affair.

research organisation): unification of electromagnetic and weak forces, important step towards formulating single set of laws to describe structure and behaviour of universe.

English National Opera (formerly Sadlers Wells Opera) established at London Coliseum, performing in English.
Charges for admission to national art galleries and museums in U.K.
Major exhibition of works by Turner, Royal Academy.
Nine Elms replaced Covent Garden Market.
First major building (shopping centre) in Milton Keynes new town.
Halifax Building Society's new head office (Building Design Partnership), Halifax, Yorkshire.
First professional Sunday soccer.
Pop festival at Windsor: battles between hippies and police.
Opening of Gladstone pottery museum, Stoke-on-Trent.
Russian ballet dancer Mikhail Baryshnikov defected to U.S.
†Duke Ellington (*1899), jazz musician.
Bennett: *Concerto for Orchestra*.
Henze: *Voices* (songs) and *Tristan*.
Birtwistle: *Imaginary Landscape*.
Musgrave: *The Voice of Ariadne*, opera.
Hoddinott: *The Beach at Falesá*, opera.
Williamson: *Elevamini*, first symphony (first performance; composed 1957).
Murder on the Orient Express, film by Sidney Lumet.
The Conversation, film by Francis Ford Coppola.
The Towering Inferno, disaster film.

U.N.I.C.E.F. stated that 400 million children in underdeveloped countries faced malnutrition.
World's first "test-tube" babies officially announced to have been born.
Commercial exploitation of microcomputers.
Oil companies announced discovery of major oil fields in North Sea.
Beginning of trans-Alaska oil pipeline.
Anxiety over damage to ozone layer by chemical propellants in aerosol cans, leading to higher levels of ultra-violet radiation on Earth and increased risk of cancer.
Development of genetic engineering, using D.N.A.
Spock's child-rearing theories blamed for development of "permissive society".
U.S. astronauts returned from *Skylab* after longest space flight (84 days). First close-up pictures of Venus and Mercury from *Mariner 10*. *Pioneer 11* passed Jupiter on way to Saturn.
First heart transplant without removal of existing heart.
Free family planning available on National Health Service.
Paris: opening of Charles de Gaulle airport.
Police national computer opened in U.K.
First broadcast of Ceefax Teletext information service by B.B.C. television.
Explosion at Flixborough chemical plant destroyed village and killed 29.

1974 House tapes; Nixon resigned under threat of impeachment; replaced by Gerald Ford, Vice-President.
Israeli forces withdrew from Suez Canal; hostilities between Israel and Syria eased; Israeli air attacks on Palestinian refugee camps in Lebanon; Palestinian guerrillas claimed responsibility for 88 deaths in Greek plane crash; U.N. recognized Palestinian Liberation Organisation (P.L.O.) as representing Palestinian people; border clashes between Iran and Iraq.
Cambodia: fighting between government and communist rebels (Khmer Rouge).
Uganda: 250,000 alleged deaths since Amin took power.
Argentina: †Juan Peron, succeeded by wife Isabel.
Greece: civilian government replaced military rule; free elections held; monarchy deposed.
Ethiopia: Emperor Haile Selassie deposed; left-wing regime took power.
Portugal: military coup ousted right-wing regime.

1975 U.K. wage inflation passed 28%; electricity prices up 33%; over 1¼ million unemployed; wage increases limited; price controls extended; record level of bankruptcies; government requested £1 billion loan from I.M.F.
Sex Discrimination Act; Equal Pay Act.
Margaret Thatcher elected leader of Conservative party.
Direct Grant grammar schools to be phased out.
British Leyland car firm taken over by government.
National referendum: 67% in favour of continued membership of Common Market.
First meeting of N. Ireland Convention.
"Balcombe Street Siege": I.R.A.

Ayckbourn: *Bedroom Farce*, play.
Bainbridge: *Sweet William*, novel.
Bellow: *Humboldt's Gift*, novel.
Malcolm Bradbury (*1932): *The History Man*, satirical novel.
Maureen Duffy (*1933): *Capital*, fiction.
Constantine FitzGibbon (*1919): *The Golden Age*, fiction.
Gray: *Otherwise Engaged*, play.
Trevor Griffiths (*1935): *Comedians*, play.
Seamus Heaney (*1939): *North*, poetry.
Lessing: *The Memoirs of a Survivor*, fiction.
David Lodge (*1935): *Changing Places*, satirical novel.
Murdoch: *A Word Child*, novel.
Naipaul: *Guerrillas*, novel.
Pinter: *No Man's Land*, play.
Powell: *Hearing Sweet Harmonies*, final volume of series "A Dance to the Music of Time."
Willy Russell (*1947): *Breezeblock Park*, play.

Blazing Saddles, film by Mel Brooks.
The Great Gatsby, film by Jack Clayton.
The Odessa File, film by Ronald Neame.
The Godfather Part II, film by Francis Ford Coppola.
Alice Doesn't Live Here Anymore, film by Martin Scorsese.
Tommy, film by Ken Russell.
Soccer: W. Germany won 10th World Cup, Munich.

Major air disaster: 346 killed in crash near Paris.
Bangladesh: monsoon floods submerged more than half the country; 10 million homeless; 1,500 dead; international aid.
Opening of first McDonald's hamburger and fast-food restaurant in London.

European Architectural Heritage Year focussed attention on protection of important buildings.
First live radio broadcast of proceedings of House of Commons (see 1978): one-month trial period.
China: discovery of "terra cotta army" of 6,000 life-sized warriors (*c.* -206) at tomb near Xian.
Water Tower Place, Chicago, opened: world's tallest reinforced concrete building.
Canadian National communications tower, Toronto: world's tallest free-standing structure.
McCabe: *The Chagall Windows*, orchestral music.
Peter Maxwell Davies (*1934): *Ave Maris Stella*, chamber music.
Malcolm Williamson appointed Master of the Queen's Music.

World population reached 4 billion (see 1987).
First North Sea oil delivered to U.K. mainland. First underwater pipeline opened. Collapse of Burmah Oil, U.K.'s second largest oil company.
Deaths at Windscale atomic energy plant, apparently of leukaemia.
European Space Agency formed to develop European launch vehicle.
Joint Russian and American space flight: U.S.A. *Apollo* and U.S.S.R. *Soyuz* docked and carried out joint experiments.
End of current U.S. manned space programme. U.S.S.R. *Soyuz 17* and *18* docked with *Salyut* space station to conduct research; U.S.S.R. space probes landed on Venus; first pictures of planet's surface.
Spread of Dutch Elm Disease killed 6.5 million trees in U.K.

1975 terrorists held London couple hostage for 6 days.
End of Vietnam war: communist troops captured capital, Saigon.
Khmer Rouge took control in Cambodia; fall of capital, Phnom Pen; end of 5-year war.
Watergate: jail sentences on ex-President Nixon's former aides, including former Attorney-General.
U.S.A.: schools disrupted by objections to "bussing" to end racial segregation.
Lebanon: civil war in Beirut between Christians and Muslims.
Portugal: first free elections for 50 years; socialists in majority; independence granted to Angola (civil war began) and Mozambique.
Helsinki Agreement: 37 countries signed pact on security, co-operation and human rights.
Vienna: 70 hostages taken at O.P.E.C. meeting by pro-Palestinian terrorists.
Suez Canal re-opened to international shipping after 8 years.
Spain: †Franco; restoration of monarchy.
Andrei Sakharov, Soviet human rights campaigner, awarded Nobel Peace Prize.
First visit to Germany by Israeli Prime Minister.
†Chiang Kai-chek, president of nationalist China (Taiwan).

Scott: *A Division of the Spoils*, final volume of series "Raj Quartet".
Mike Stott (*1944): *Funny Peculiar*, play.
Paul Theroux (*1941): *The Great Railway Bazaar*, travel.
E. P. Thompson (*1924): *Whigs and Hunters*, history.
Ben Travers (*1886, †1980): *The Bed Before Yesterday*, farce.
William Trevor (*1928): *Angels at the Ritz*, short stories.
Updike: *A Month of Sundays*, novel.
Last World Theatre Season in London.

1976 Resignation of Prime Minister, Harold Wilson, succeeded by James Callaghan.
U.K. government applied to I.M.F. for £2.3 billion loan to support sterling; £ fell below $2 for first time; strikes in protest at cuts in public sector spending.
Bill to make comprehensive education compulsory.
Bill to nationalize shipbuilding and aircraft industries.
Criminal Law Bill ended trial by jury for minor crimes.
Race Relations Bill published.

Albee: *Counting the Ways*, play.
Amis: *The Alteration*, novel.
Ayckbourn: *Just Between Ourselves*, play.
Bainbridge: *A Quiet Life*, novel.
Howard Brenton (*1942): *Weapons of Happiness*, play.
Frayn: *Donkey's Years*, play.
Judith Guest (*1936): *Ordinary People*, novel.
Thom Gunn (*1929): *Jack Straw's Castle*, poetry.
Alex Haley (*1921): *Roots*, historical reconstruction.
Hampton: *Treats*, play.
Hughes: *Season Songs*, poetry.
Keneally: *Season in Purgatory*, novel.

Jaws, film by Steven Spielberg.
The Romantic Englishwoman, film with Glenda Jackson.
Rollerball, film.
The Passenger, film by Antonioni.
The Rocky Horror Picture Show, film by Jim Sharman.
The Day of the Locust, film by John Schlesinger.
Barry Lyndon, film by Stanley Kubrick.
One Flew Over the Cuckoo's Nest, film by Milos Forman.
Picnic at Hanging Rock, film by Peter Weir.
Monty Python and the Holy Grail, film.
Fawlty Towers, television comedy series with John Cleese.
The Naked Civil Servant, television play (Prix Italia).
Days of Hope, television films by Ken Loach and Tony Garnett.
The Evacuees, television play by Jack Rosenthal.
A Chorus Line, musical play.
Jeeves, musical play by Lloyd Webber, libretto by Ayckbourn.
First ascent of Everest by S.W. face.
John Walker (N.Z.) ran mile in 3 mins. 49.4 secs.
First cricket World Cup, won by West Indies.

Opening of National Theatre building, South Bank, London, designed by Denis Lasdun.
Opening of Museum of London, the National Exhibition Centre, Birmingham, The Royal Exchange Theatre, Manchester, and the National Air and Space Museum, Washington, U.S.A.
Tate Gallery exhibited *Low Sculpture* by Carl Andre, consisting of 120 firebricks in two oblong layers.
Retrospective exhibition of works of L. S. Lowry (*1887, †1976), British painter, at Royal Academy.
Britten: *String Quartet No. 3*.

Uterine cancer linked to taking of oestrogen.
First successful treatment in womb to prevent mental handicap by correcting chemical deficiency.
Clinical inauguration of whole-body X-ray scanner.
Identification of enkephalin (brain chemical).
Development of floppy discs and portable computers.
Microprocessors used in automatic cash dispensers at banks.
First domestic videocassette recorders introduced.
Dutch radio-astronomers (Leiden University) mapped radio galaxy 3C236, largest object in universe, spanning 18 million light years.
41 killed in worst-ever crash of London tube train, Moorgate.
Draught continued in Ethiopia and Somalia: estimated 40,000 dead.
Severe earthquake in E. Turkey destroyed town of Lice.
Hurricane Eloise caused damage from Puerto Rico to Florida and N.E. America.
Discovery of fossil remains of pterosaur with 50–foot wingspan, twice the size of any previous discovery.

General acceptance of safety guidelines for work on D.N.A. opened way for genetic engineering to become major interest of science.
Successful synthesis of wholly man-made gene by Har Gobind Khorana.
First successful decoding of complete genetic code of a whole living organism, Cambridge, U.K.
First use of solid-state integrated circuits in telephones.
Field trials of optical fibre cables for telecommunications, permitting carriage of much more information than copper cable.
Digital watches available very cheaply.

1976

Bill to create separate assemblies for Scotland and Wales.
Ulster Convention dissolved.
N. Ireland: British Ambassador killed by landmine; launch of women's peace movement.
Third fishing dispute between U.K. and Iceland ended.
U.K. broke off diplomatic relations with Uganda.
Palestinian terrorists hijacked plane with 250 passengers; 91 Jewish hostages rescued at Entebbe airport, Uganda, by Israeli commandos.
Egypt banned Soviet warships from Egyptian ports.
Lebanon: civil war continued, with Syrian intervention; evacuation of British and Americans.
Warsaw Pact countries invited West to join pact barring first use of nuclear weapons.
S.E. Asia: Vietnam reunified (see 1954); Hanoi became capital; last U.S. troops left Thailand.
†Mao Tse-Tung, chairman of Chinese Communist party, succeeded by Hua Kuo-Feng.
Angola: success of communist forces, supported by U.S.S.R. and Cuba, over U.N.I.T.A. nationalist movement.
Rhodesia announced transition to black majority rule; border incidents with Mozambique.
S. Africa: rioting in Soweto over government education policy.
Transkei became first independent black homeland.
Portugal: first free presidential election for 50 years.

Lowell: *Selected Poems*.
Brian Moore (*1921): *The Doctor's Wife*, novel.
Murdoch: *Henry and Cato*, novel.
Robert Nye (*1939): *Falstaff*, fictional biography.
Osborne: *Watch It Come Down*, play.
Simon Raven (*1927): *The Survivors*, novel.
Rhys: *Sleep It Off, Lady*, short stories.
Sharpe: *Wilt*, comic novel.
Spark: *The Takeover*, novel.
Storey: *Saville*, novel (Booker Prize)
P. Theroux: *The Family Arsenal*, novel.
Trevor: *The Children of Dynmouth*, novel (Whitbread Award).
Vonnegut: *Slapstick: Or Lonesome No More*, fiction.
White: *A Fringe of Leaves*, novel.
Collected Poems of W. H. Auden.

1977

Lib-Lab pact kept government in office; collapse of Social Contract; return to free collective bargaining over wages.
Prices Commission given power to freeze prices (up 69.5% since 1974).
British Leyland car company threatened to shut factories because of strikes; government threatened to withhold public money.

Ayckbourn: *Ten Times Table*, play.
Bainbridge: *Injury Time*, novel (Whitbread Award).
Bennett: *The Old Country*, play.
Bolt: *State of Revolution*, play.
Bruce Chatwin (*1940, †1989): *In Patagonia*, fiction.
John Cheever (*1912, †1982): *Falconer*, novel.
John Fowles (*1926): *Daniel Martin*, novel.

Malcolm Arnold (*1921): *Philharmonic Concerto.*
Maxwell Davies: *Symphony No. 1* (first performance 1978).
Ruskin College, Oxford: James Callaghan launched "Great Debate" on education in U.K.: need for core curriculum and greater relevance to modern industrial society asserted.
Vogue of punk rock.
Side by Side by Sondheim, review.
Pacific Overtures, musical by Sondheim.
Popularity of films with Kung-fu interest.
Marathon Man, film by Schlesinger.
Rocky, film with Sylvester Stallone.
The Omen, film by Richard Donner.
Family Plot, film by Hitchcock.
Bugsy Malone, film by Alan Parker.
Face to Face, film by Bergman.
Bill Brand, television series by Trevor Griffiths.
Wesker: *Love Letters on Blue Paper,* television drama.
I, Claudius, B.B.C. television serial epic.
When The Boat Comes In, television series.
The Glittering Prizes, six television plays by Frederic Raphael.
Dixon of Dock Green, popular television series, ended after 21 years.
Montreal Olympics boycotted by African countries because of N. Zealand's sporting links with S. Africa; Lasse Viren (Finland) first to win both 5,000m. and 10,000m. races in successive Olympics; Nadia Comaneci (Roumania), aged 14, first to achieve perfect score in gymnastics.

Development of computerized cash-registers and check-out devices in retail industry, industrial robots with computer memories, word processors, and networked data-processing services.
Successful end of W.H.O.'s 2–year campaign to eradicate smallpox.
First outbreak of Legionnaires disease.
First commerical flights of Anglo-French supersonic airliner *Concorde.*
Worst mid-air crash killed 176, Zagreb, Yugoslavia.
Seat-belts in cars compulsory in U.K.
Dangerous release of dioxin after accident at chemical plant, Seveso, Italy.
Spacecraft landed on Mars after 11–month voyages; discovered ingredients for life, but no life; first-ever photographs from Mars.
Completion of U.S. space shuttle, first re-usable spacecraft.
Violent earthquakes at Tangshan, China (about 900,000 killed), in Guatemala (23,000 killed, ½ million homeless) and in Turkey (6,000 killed).
Greater London Council abandoned high-rise housing.
India: Government initiative to slow population growth.
U.K. had worse drought for 250 years.
Report of Royal Commission on pollution.

Pompidou Centre for the arts, designed by Renzo Piano and Richard Rogers, opened in Paris.
Founding of Robinson College, Cambridge.
Fund launched to save Acropolis from decay by atmospheric pollution.
Annan Report on future of British broadcasting recommended fourth television channel to encourage independent programme makers.

U.S. company Apple produced first boom in sale of home computers.
2-in. television screen produced commercially in U.K.
U.K. government announced plans to develop solar power.
International protest marchers clashed with 5,000 riot police at construction site of fast breeder nuclear reactor, Creys-Malville, France.

1977

Conservatives won control of Greater London Council.
Violence on picket-lines at Grunwick film-processing laboratories following refusal to unionize involved thousands of police and demonstrators.
Riots at demonstrations for and against National Front in London and Birmingham.
N. Ireland: fire-bombs caused £1 million damage; founders of Women's Peace Movement awarded Nobel Peace Prize.
Jimmy Carter inaugurated as U.S. President; cut aid to Argentina, Uruguay and Ethiopia because of their civil rights records.
S. Africa: U.N. banned arms sales to country; Commonwealth leaders demanded policy changes; †Steve Biko (*1946), black civil rights leader, in detention.
Uganda: Amnesty International claimed thousands killed under Amin regime; Archbishop of Uganda murdered.
Central African Republic: President Bokassa crowned himself Emperor at $30 million ceremony.
Djibouti, France's last African colony, became independent.
Israel established settlements on West Bank, captured from Jordan in Six Day War (1967); Egyptian President Sadat visited Israel and addressed Knesset.
5–day hijack of plane by Palestinian terrorists ended at Mogadishu, Somalia, by German and British commandos; 86 hostages freed unharmed.
Border conflict between Cambodia and Vietnam; Vietnamese "boat-people" began to flee communist regime.
Pakistan: military coup ousted Bhutto; replaced by General Zia.
Czechoslovac intellectuals issued Charter 77 demanding civil rights.
S.E.A.T.O. (1954) dissolved as outdated.

J. K. Galbraith (*1908): *The Age of Uncertainty*, history and sociology.
Grass: *Der Butt*, novel.
Isherwood: *Christopher and his Kind*, memoirs.
Dan Jacobson (*1929): *The Confessions of Josef Baisz*, novel.
Erica Jong (*1942): *How to Save your own Life*, novel.
Barrie Keefe (*1945): *A Mad World, My Masters*, play.
Jerzy Kosinski (*1933): *Blind Date*, novel.
Lowell: *Day by Day*, poetry.
David Mamet (*1947): *American Buffalo*, play.
Gabriel García Márquez (*1928): *The Autumn of the Patriarch*, novel.
Nichols: *Privates on Parade*, play.
Priestley: *Instead of the Trees*, autobiography.
Rattigan: *Cause Célèbre*, play.
Roth: *The Professor of Desire*, novel.
James Saunders (*1925): *Bodies*, play.
Scott: *Staying On*, novel (Booker Prize).
P. Theroux: *The Consul's File*, stories.
Tolkien: *The Silmarillion*, posthumous novel.

U.K. newspaper *Gay News* fined £1,000 for blasphemy.
Tippett: *The Ice Break*, opera; fourth symphony.
Carter: *Symphony for Three Orchestras*.
Every Good Boy Deserves Favour, words by Stoppard, music by André Previn.
George Balanchine: *Viennese Waltzes*, ballet.
A Bridge Too Far, film by Richard Attenborough.
Saturday Night Fever, film with John Travolta, created fashion for disco-dancing.
Annie Hall, film by Woody Allen.
Valentino, film by Ken Russell with Rudolf Nureyev.
Star Wars, film, biggest-ever box-office success.
Close Encounters of the Third Kind, film by Steven Spielberg.
Our Day Out, television play by Willy Russell.
Jesus of Nazareth, television production by Franco Zeffirelli.
Age of Uncertainty, television series on economics by Galbraith.
Marie Curie, television biography by Peter Goodchild.
Annie, musical play.
Red Rum first horse to win Grand National three times.
Nigel Short, aged 11, youngest-ever qualifier for national chess championship.
†Elvis Presley (*1935), popular singer; Maria Callas (*1923), opera singer; Groucho Marx (*1895), film comedian; Bing Crosby (*1904), singer and film actor.

Millions of gallons of oil polluted N. Sea after accident on oil rig in Ekofisk field.
First oil flow in trans-Alaska pipeline.
U.S. space shuttle *Enterprise* had first tests; *Voyager 2* probe launched towards Jupiter and Saturn, possibly Uranus and Neptune.
Presence of rings round Uranus detected.
German radio-astronomers reported water molecules in nebula 2.2 million light-years away, indicating possibility of other solar systems with our physical conditions.
U.K. scientists reported discovery of complete genetic structure of a virus, disproving belief that each gene carries code for reproduction of only one type of protein molecule.
British Aerospace formed to run nationalized aviation industry.
U.S.S.R. supersonic airliner *TU–144* made first scheduled flight.
First cut-price shuttle flights London-New York.
Two jumbo jets collided on ground at Tenerife; 582 killed; world's worst aviation disaster.
More U.K. purchases of foreign than British cars for first time.
First European weather satellite launched.
Last run of Paris-Istanbul Orient Express after 94 years.
Roumania: earthquake destroyed large part of Bucharest, killing 1,500.
Lightning caused massive power failure in New York; 3,200 looters arrested.

1977 S.E.A.T.O. (1954) dissolved as outdated.

1978 Britain refused to join European Monetary System.
Government announced new 5% pay-increase guidelines; rejected by unions and by Labour Party Conference.
Ford car workers given 17% wage rise after 9-week strike.
Inflation held at 8.4%.
U.K. expected to be self-sufficient in N. Sea oil within 2 years.
Bingham Report revealed breaches of oil sanctions against Rhodesia by U.K. oil-companies.
P.L.O. London representative shot by Arab gunmen in London.
N. Ireland: I.R.A. bomb killed 14 at restaurant near Belfast.
Rhodesia: agreement to end white rule by end of year.
U.S.A.: Camp David peace agreement between Egypt and Israel.
Israel: Arab terrorists killed 37 in attack on bus; Israeli reprisals against P.L.O. camps in S. Lebanon.
Lebanon: U.N. troops installed.
Iran: 430 killed in cinema fire begun by Shi-ite Muslim extremists; violent demonstrations against Shah's rule; martial law declared; strike of oil workers cut off oil exports.
Somalia failed in war against Ethiopia.
S. Africa: Vorster resigned, succeeded by P. W. Botha.
Moscow: civil rights dissidents Orlov, Shcharansky and Ginsburg jailed.
Italy: Aldo Moro, former premier, abducted and murdered by Red Brigade terrorists.
†Pope Paul VI; †Pope John Paul I after 33 days; election of John Paul II, first non-Italian Pope since 1542.
Nicaragua: serious disturbances; Sandinista National Liberation Front opposed President Somoza.

Amis: *Jake's Thing*, novel.
Martin Amis (*1949): *Success*, novel.
Ayckbourn: *Joking Apart*, play.
Bainbridge: *Young Adolf*, novel.
Bond: *The Woman*, play.
Brophy: *Palace Without Chairs*, novel.
Burgess: *1985*, novel.
Brian Clark (*1932): *Whose Life Is It, Anyway?*, play.
Len Deighton (*1929): *SS-GB*, novel.
Farrell: *The Singapore Grip*, novel.
Greene: *The Human Factor*, novel.
Hare: *Plenty*, play.
John Irving (*1942): *The World According to Garp*, novel.
M. M. Kaye (*1911): *The Far Pavilions*, novel.
Hugh MacDairmid (*1892, †1978): *Collected Poems*.
Mamet: *The Water Engine*, play.
Julia Markus (*1939): *Uncle*, novel.
Mercer: *Cousin Vladimir*, play.
John Mortimer (*1923): *Rumpole of the Bailey*, novel.
Murdoch: *The Sea, The Sea*, novel (Booker Prize).
Pinter: *Betrayal*, play.
Mario Puzo (*1920): *Fools Die*, novel.
Martin Sherman (*1938): *Bent*, play.
Isaac Singer (*1904): *Shosha*, fiction.
Julian Symons (*1912): *The Blackheath Poisonings*, detective fiction.
P. Theroux: *Picture Palace*, novel.
Updike: *The Coup*, novel.
Jeffrey Wainwright (*1944): *Heart's Desire*, poetry.
Wouk: *War and Remembrance*, historical novel.

Live sound broadcasting from House of Commons began (see 1975).
Opening of East Building of National Gallery of Art, Washington, U.S.A., designed by I. M. Pei.
Britain's first atrium building: Coutts Bank, London.
Sainsbury Centre, University of E. Anglia, designed by Foster.
Completion of Anglican cathedral, Liverpool.
Warwick Castle sold to Madame Tussauds.
Penderecki: *Paradise Lost*, opera (composed 1976–78).
Coming Home, film with John Voigt.
Revenge of the Pink Panther, film by Blake Edwards with Peter Sellers.
Pretty Baby, film by Louis Malle.
Grease, film with John Travolta.
The Last Waltz, film by Martin Scorsese.
The Deer Hunter, film with Robert de Niro.
Superman, film by Richard Donner.
Renaldo and Clara, film by Bob Dylan.
National Lampoon's Animal House, comedy film by John Landis.
Evita, musical play by Tim Rice and Andrew Lloyd Webber.
Pennies from Heaven, television drama serial by Dennis Potter.
The Body in Question, television documentary series by Jonathan Miller.
The Voyage of Charles Darwin, television documentary series.
Edward and Mrs Simpson, television series.
Holocaust, television series.
Thames T.V. *This Week* programme on alleged police brutality in N. Ireland banned by Independent Broadcasting Authority.
Publication of *The Times* and *The Sunday Times* suspended indefinitely because of strikes.
Skateboard craze among children cost N.H.S. £6 million.
Britain's first statutory May Day holiday.
Naomi James became first woman to sail single-handed round world.
Bjorn Borg became first hat-trick winner of

Development of computerized information systems raised international anxiety about invasions of privacy.
Production of high-density microcircuit by electron-beam technology.
Sweden became first country to ban aerosol sprays damaging to ozone layer.
U.S. Department of Health warned of dangers from asbestos.
Russian ocean-surveillance satellite with nuclear power-supply re-entered atmosphere accidentally, scattering radioactive debris in Canada.
U.K. government approved plans for nuclear reprocessing plant at Windscale, Cumbria.
Greenpeace environmentalist group prevented culling of grey seals.
Oil tanker *Amoco Cadiz* sank in Channel, spilling 220,000 tons of crude oil; extensive coastal pollution in Brittany.
Tanker-lorry carrying propylene crashed and exploded near camp site in Spain, killing 200.
U.S. astonomers announced discovery of black hole in constellation of Scorpio.
U.S.S.R. cosmonauts spent 139 days in space using *Salyut 6* orbiting station; new record.
Vladimir Remek (Czechoslovakia) first non-Russian/American in space.
U.S. and U.S.S.R. postponed manufacture of neutron bomb.
France: opening of Perpignan-Narbonne autoroute created continuous Amsterdam-Valencia motorway (1,250 miles); first model of high-speed train T.G.V. (Train de Grande Vitesse) (see 1981).
Earthquake in Iran killed 25,000.
Birth of baby following "in vitro" fertilization, Manchester, supervized by Patrick Steptoe.
First crossing of Atlantic by balloon (U.S.A.-France, 137 hours).
Bombay: Boeing 747 exploded in mid-air, killing 213.

1978 Guyana: mass suicide of 913 members of People's Temple, U.S. religious cult.
U.S. granted Panama control of Panama Canal from 1999.
Solomon Islands became independent of Britain.

1979 "Winter of discontent" in U.K.: industrial action against pay restraint by 1 million public sector workers, notably in transport, cleansing and hospital services; disruption of food and fuel supplies.
General Election: Conservatives in power: Margaret Thatcher, first British woman Prime Minister, committed to cutting taxes and public spending, curbing union power, and privatizing nationalized industries; sale of council houses planned.
First direct elections to European Parliament; European Monetary System officially inaugurated; Greece admitted to Common Market; Thatcher demanded £1 billion rebate from E.E.C.
N. Ireland: over 300 army deaths since 1969; I.R.A murdered Lord Mountbatten, close relative of royal family; seizure of £½ million worth of I.R.A. weapons from U.S. supporters.
Airey Neave, Tory M.P., killed by I.R.A. car bomb at House of Commons.
Carter and Brezhnev signed SALT–2 arms limitation treaty.
Mother Teresa, campaigner for the poor, won Nobel Peace Prize.
First visit of a Pope to communist country: Pope John Paul visited Poland, also Latin America, Ireland, U.S.A.
Iranian revolution: exile of Shah; installation of Ayatollah Khomeini as absolute ruler; Islamic republic established; U.S. Embassy occupied.
Saudi Arabia: Muslim extremists

Ayckbourn: *Sisterly Feelings*, and *Taking Steps*, plays.
Baldwin: *Just Above My Head*, autobiographical novel.
Andrew Birkin (*1945): *J. M. Barrie and the Lost Boys*, biography.
Leslie Epstein (*1938): *King of the Jews*, novel.
Penelope Fitzgerald (*1916): *Offshore*, novel (Booker Prize).
Forsyth: *The Devil's Alternative*, novel.
Golding: *Darkness Visible*, novel.
Gray: *Close of Play*, play.
Roger Hall (*1937): *Prisoners of Mother England*, play.
Heller: *Good as Gold*, novel.
Jennifer Johnston (*1920): *The Old Jest*, novel (Whitbread Award).
Keneally: *The Confederates*, historical novel.
Mailer: *The Executioner's Song*, "non-fiction novel".
Mark Medoff (*1940): *Children of the Lesser God*, play.
Mercer: *Then and Now*, play.
Miller: *The American Clock*, play.
Naipaul: *A Bend in the River*, novel.
Roth: *The Ghost Writer*, novel.
Saunders: *Birdsong* and *The Mountain*, plays.
Shaffer: *Amadeus*, play.
Sharpe: *The Wilt Alternative*, novel.
Spark: *Territorial Rights*, novel.
Styron: *Sophie's Choice*, novel.
Vonnegut: *Jailbird*, novel.
White: *The Twyborn Affair*, novel.

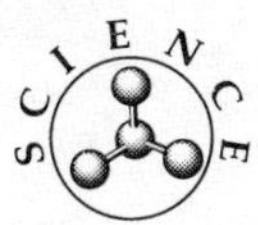

Wimbledon's men's singles for over 40 years.
Muhammed Ali won world heavyweight boxing championship for record third time.

Opening of Tate Gallery Extension, London, and J. F. Kennedy Library, Boston, U.S.A.
All Souls College, Oxford, agreed to admit women (first woman fellow elected 1981).
Plans announced for rebuilding of London docklands.
Royal Academy exhibition: *The Horses of San Marco*.
First complete performance of Berg's opera *Lulu*, completed by Cerha.
Discovery of first Viking fortress in England, at Repton, Derbyshire.
Establishment of National Heritage Fund.
The Times resumed publication after suspension of nearly a year.
Anthony Blunt, art adviser to the Queen, named as former Russian spy.
Apocalypse Now, film by Francis Ford Coppola.
Star Trek, film.
Kramer vs Kramer, film with Dustin Hoffman.
Wise Blood, film by John Huston.
Manhattan, film by Woody Allen.
The Amityville Horror, film.
Tess, film based on Hardy's novel by Roman Polanski.
Monty Python's Life of Brian, film.
Moonraker, film by Lewis Gilbert.
Sweeney Todd, musical by Stephen Sondheim.
Tinker, Tailor, Soldier, Spy, television series with Alec Guinness, from novel by le Carré.
Testament of Youth, television version of memoirs of Vera Brittain.
Not The Nine O'Clock News, television comedy series.
Rumpole of the Bailey, television series by John Mortimer.
Blue Remembered Hills, television play by Dennis Potter.
Sebastian Coe (U.K.) became first world record holder at 800m (1.42.2), one mile

First mass-marketing of computer-based games and toys.
Introduction of Sony Walkman, portable cassette-player with earphones.
Application of fibre-optic cable technology to public telephone and television-based information systems.
Newspapers introduced laser plate making and electronic picture transmission.
Discovery of Jupiter's ring from photographs taken by U.S. spacecraft *Voyager I*; first picture of volcanic eruption in space, on Io, satellite of Jupiter; two U.S.S.R. cosmonauts completed record 175 days in space; U.S. spacecraft *Pioneer 11* first to reach Saturn; *Skylab* disintegrated on re-entry into Earth's atmosphere after 35,000 orbits.
Organic molecules extracted from rocks in Greenland dated at 3.830 million years.
First successful transplant of fallopian tube.
Major accident at Three Mile Island nuclear power station, U.S.A. intensified debate about public safety.
Prediction of 50% increase in number of over–60's by end of century (150% increase in Third World).
International Whaling Commission banned whaling by factory ships, and all whaling in Indian Ocean, to conserve species.
Revolution in Iran led to increased cost of oil internationally.
Major oil spillage: 2.4 million barrels from well in Gulf of Mexico.
Last link in French motorway system from Channel coast to Italian frontier; Beaune-Mulhouse autoroute linked French and W. German motorways.
10,000 homeless in Portugal after worst flooding for a century.
Cyclone in India killed 600; 1 million homeless.
Three quarters of population of Dominica made homeless by hurricane.

1979 seized control of Grand Mosque, Mecca.
Afghanistan invaded by Russia following civil war between Muslim rebels and pro-Marxist government troops.
Rhodesia: Bishop Muzorewa first black Prime Minister of Zimbabwe-Rhodesia; illegal independence ended; U.N. sanctions lifted.
Uganda: Amin ousted.
Cambodia occupied by Vietnam; overthrow of Khmer Rouge; allegations that Pol Pot regime murdered 3 million Cambodians.
Nicaragua: exile of Somoza, replaced by junta of businessmen and Sandinista rebels.
Pakistan: execution of Bhutto; introduction of Islamic laws.

1980 Employment Act.
Housing Act: allowed council house tenants to buy their homes.
Government pursued monetarist policies; 100,000 jobs cut in civil service; state strike-benefit halved; plans to sell off nationalized ferries and railway hotels.
Budget lowered personal taxes and nearly doubled V.A.T.
First national strike in steel industry since 1926 lasted 3 months.
Inflation dropped from 22% to 15%.
Two million unemployed, highest figure since 1935.
E.E.C. agreed 75% reduction in U.K. budget contribution.
N.A.T.O. announced U.S. Cruise missiles to be based in U.K.
London: terrorists occupied Iranian embassy and took hostages; S.A.S. (Special Air Service, counter-revolutionary commando) stormed embassy and ended seige.
U.N. called on Israel to dismantle settlements on West Bank and Gaza strip (see 1977).
Israel declared whole of Jerusalem to be its capital.
Poland: strikes at Lenin shipyards, Gdansk, led by Lech Walesa, ended

Albee: *The Lady from Dubuque*, play.
Amis: *Russian Hide-and-Seek*, novel.
Ayckbourn: *Season's Greetings*, play.
Barstow: *A Brother's Tale*, novel.
Brenton: *The Romans in Britain*, play at the National Theatre (see 1982).
Burgess: *Earthly Powers*, novel.
J. L. Carr (*1912): *A Month in the Country*, novel.
Drabble: *The Middle Ground*, novel.
Frayn: *Make and Break*, play.
Greene: *Dr Fischer of Geneva*, novel, and *Ways of Escape*, autobiography.
Golding: *Rites of Passage*, novel (Booker Prize).
Ronald Harwood (*1934): *The Dresser*, play.
Heaney: *Selected Poems 1965–75*.
Christopher Hope (*1944): *A Separate Development*, first novel.
Lessing: *The Marriages between Zones Three, Four and Five*, science fiction.
Lodge: *How Far Can You Go?*, novel.
Murdoch: *Nuns and Soldiers*, novel.
Pinter: *The Hothouse*, play.
Stanley Price (*1931): *Moving*, play.
Raven: *An Inch of Fortune*, novel.
Russell: *Educating Rita*, play.
Storey: *Early Days*, play.
Wilson: *Setting the World on Fire*, novel.
Nicholas Nickleby, noted production by the Royal Shakespeare Company.

(3.49), and 1500m (3.32.8) simultaneously within 41 days.
Bjorn Borg won Wimbledon men's singles for fourth consecutive year.
Fastnet yacht race hit by Atlantic storms: 17 killed.

Chicago: 274 killed in U.S.A.'s worst air crash.

Humber Bridge completed (opened 1981) with longest main span in world (1,410 metres).
Covent Garden: central market re-opened as shopping centre; London Transport Museum opened.
Alexandra Palace, London, damaged by fire.
Modernization of National Maritime Museum, Greenwich, completed.
Opening of Robinson College, Cambridge.
The Vikings, exhibition, British Museum.
Closure of London Evening News.
Church of England introduced Alternative Service Book.
Simon Rattle appointed principal conductor of the City of Birmingham Symphony Orchestra.
B.B.C. musicians on two-month strike over plans to close 5 orchestras.
Tippett: *Concerto for violin, viola and cello.*
Rubbra: Symphony No. 11.
Penderecki: Symphony No. 2.
Davies: Symphony No. 2.
Breakfast television franchise created in U.K.; plans for cable television announced.
Shogun, television series.
Death of a Princess, controversial television documentary.
Dallas, American television series, first broadcast in U.K.

Growth of "green" and "ecology" parties in Europe.
U.S.A. restricted production of chlorofluorocarbons (CFCs) aerosol propellants.
Nations bordering Mediterranean signed anti-pollution pact.
Seven major industrial nations agreed 50% cut in oil consumption by 1990.
World's largest oil refinery, Abadan, on fire during Iran-Iraq war.
E.C. called for phasing out of all uses of asbestos.
U.K.: 60,000 in biggest anti-nuclear demonstration for nearly 20 years.
Rapid growth of computer technology in banks, libraries, travel agencies and offices.
Development of videodisk to store computerized data.
Inauguration of world's first purpose-built Synchrotron Radiation Source, Daresbury, Cheshire.
W.H.O. announced elimination of smallpox.
Successful synthesis of interferon by genetic engineering.
Frederick Sangster, U.K. scientist, won second Nobel Prize, for work on D.N.A.
World's worst-ever recorded famine: 10 million threatened, including 2 million refugees, in E. Africa.

1980 by government promise of independent trade unions; formation of Solidarity, union federation, supported by R.C. Church, first E. European independent trade union.
Iraq invaded Iran.
Failure of secret mission by U.S. commandos to rescue 53 hostages held in U.S. Embassy, Tehran.
Iran: British Embassy closed; U.S. severed diplomatic relations.
Afghanistan: fighting between Soviet/Afghanistan troops and mujahideen rebel forces.
Islamic Conference demanded Russian withdrawal from Afghanistan.
Zimbabwe-Rhodesia: general election; Robert Mugabe Prime Minister; country became Zimbabwe and joined U.N.
Italy: right-wing terrorists exploded bomb at Bologna station, killing 84.
Somalia: estimated 1.3 million refugees from fighting in Ethiopia.

The State of the Language, essays edited by Leonard Michaels and Christopher Ricks.

1981 Wildlife and Countryside Bill.
British Nationality Act.
Social Democratic Party (S.D.P.) launched by Labour party defectors (Limehouse Declaration).
Plans to privatize British Aerospace (see 1977).
Budget reinforced monetarist policy. Cuts announced in defence spending, grants to universities and number of student places.
5–month strike of civil servants.
2.5 million unemployed; Liverpool-London "People's March for Jobs".
Race riots in Brixton; Asians and skinheads clashed in Southall; riots in Peckham, Toxteth area of Liverpool, and elsewhere; worst civil unrest this century.
N. Ireland: †Bobby Sands, I.R.A. hunger-striker in prison, shortly after election as M.P.; riots in Belfast; 9 other hunger-strikers died.

M. Amis: *Other People*, novel.
Ayckbourn: *Way Upstream*, play.
Bond: *Restoration*, play.
William Boyd (*1952): *A Good Man in Africa*, novel.
James Clavell (*1924): *Noble House*, novel.
Nell Dunn (*1936): *Steaming*, play.
D. J. Enright (*1920): *Collected Poems*.
Frayn: *Noises Off*, comedy.
Brian Friel (*1929): *Translation*, play.
Martin Gilbert (*1936): *Churchill: The Wilderness Years*, biography.
Gray: *Quartermaine's Terms*, play.
Leigh: *Goose-pimples*, play.
Mitchell: *Collected Poems and Songs*.
Julian Mitchell (*1935): *Another Country*, play.
Naipaul: *Among the Believers*, study of Islam.
Nichols: *Passion Play*.
Osborne: *A Better Class of Person*, autobiography.
Jonathan Raban (*1942): *Old Glory*, travel.
Roth: *Zuckerman Unbound*, novel.
Salman Rushdie (*1947): *Midnight's Children*, novel (Booker Prize).

The Shining, film by Stanley Kubrick.
The Empire Strikes Back, film.
The Elephant Man and *The Blues Brothers*, popular films.
U.N.E.S.C.O. report stated that a third of the world's population could not read or write.
†John Lennon, former Beatle, murdered in New York.
Severiano Ballesteros became youngest player to win U.S. Masters golf tournament.
Moscow Olympics boycotted by W. Germany, U.S.A., China and Japan: Daley Thompson first U.K. athlete to win decathlon.
Bjorn Borg won Wimbledon for fifth consecutive year.

First reliable report of variability of sun's luminosity.
U.S.S.R. cosmonauts on *Salyut 6* spent 185 days in space, new record; U.S. *Voyager 1* space probe discovered Saturn's 15th moon.
Alexander Kieland, floating hotel for N. Sea oil-rig workers, collapsed in storm; 123 killed.
Eruptions of Mount St. Helen's, U.S.A. previously dormant volcano.
Summer heatwave killed 1,265 in U.S.A.
Earthquake destroyed most of El Asnan, Algeria; another devastated southern Italy; 3,000 dead, 600,000 homeless altogether.
World's longest road tunnel (10 miles), St Gotthard, Switzerland.
Sixpenny pieces no longer legal tender.
Kielder reservoir opened.

Completion of Barbican Centre for Arts and Conferences, London (opened 1982); designed by Chamberlin, Powell and Bon.
Opening of National Westminster Tower, London, Europe's tallest building.
Re-development of South Dock, Liverpool, announced.
Sale of popular newspapers in U.K. rose by ½ million copies following introduction of bingo competitions.
Church of England voted to ordain women as deacons.
Citizens' Band radio legalized.
Picasso's *Guernica* returned to Spain after 40 years in U.S. following restoration of democracy; self-portrait of Picasso sold for $5.3 million, world record for 20th century painting.
Rodin Rediscovered, major exhibition at National Gallery, Washington.
Taverner: *Akhmatova Requiem*.
Davies: Symphony No. 2 (composed 1980).
The Wild Boy and *Isadora*, ballets by Kenneth MacMillan.
First cable television in U.K.

First reports of A.I.D.S. (acquired immune deficiency syndrome).
Discovery of T.P.A. (converts cancer cells into macrophages).
Successful treatment of children's disease by bone-marrow grafts.
Identification of "passive smoking" link between lung cancer and involuntary inhaling of tobacco smoke by non-smokers; led to widespread demands for smoking bans or restrictions in public places.
U.K. government announced plans to reduce lead content in petrol.
Russian oil-drill reached 10,636 m, world record.
Severn barrage proposed, to provide electricity from tidal flow.
Appearance of first electrically-powered commercial lorry.
Fifty pits, employing 30,000 miners, to close in Britain.
One in eight children in U.K. belonged to one-parent families.
Closure of Royal Docks, London.

1981

150,000 demonstrated in London against siting of Cruise missiles; ¼ million Germans demonstrated against N.A.T.O. deployment of nuclear missiles in Europe; demonstrations in U.S.A., France and Germany against nuclear power stations.
Inauguration of Ronald Reagan as U.S. President; simultaneous release of 52 U.S. Embassy hostages in Teheran after 444 days.
U.S.A. stopped arms sales to Iran.
Geneva: N.A.T.O. and Warsaw Pact countries began arms-limitation talks.
Poland: General Jaruzelski became Prime Minister; national strikes by members of Solidarity, condemned by U.S.S.R.: martial law imposed; U.S. economic sanctions against Poland and Russia.
Greece admitted to European Community.
France: election of socialist president François Mitterand ended 23 years of right-wing power; policy of decentralization introduced.
Egypt: President Sadat assassinated.
Israel attacked Iraq's nuclear reactor in Baghdad, bombed Beirut and annexed Golan Heights.
Lebanon: intense fighting in Beirut; attacks on P.L.O.
"Yorkshire Ripper" sentenced for murder of 13 women, attempted murder of 7 others.

Robert Stone (*1937): *A Flag for Sunrise,* novel.
Stoppard: *On the Razzle,* play.
D. M. Thomas (*1935): *The White Hotel,* novel.
Updike: *Rabbit is Rich,* novel.
Vidal: *Creation,* novel.
John Wells (*1936): *Anyone for Denis?,* play.
The Oresteia, production by Peter Hall at the National Theatre.
Collected Poems by Sylvia Plath, edited by Ted Hughes.

1982

Falklands War: Argentina invaded Falkland Islands; U.N. demanded withdrawal; U.K. Foreign Secretary resigned; U.K. task force dispatched; U.K. imposed 200-mile "exclusion zone" around Falklands; sinking of H.M.S. *Sheffield* by Exocet missile; sinking of Argentine battleship *General Belgrano;* landing of British troops at San Carlos; surrender of Argentine forces at Port Stanley ended fighting; †255 British troops, 652 Argentinians.
Fall of Argentine President Galtieri.
Unemployment passed 3¼ million.

Arden: *Silence among the Weapons,* novel.
Ayckbourn: *Intimate Exchanges,* play.
Bellow: *The Dean's December,* novel.
Bond: *Summer,* play.
Boyd: *An Ice Cream War,* novel.
Burgess: *On Going to Bed,* novel.
Chatwin: *On the Black Hill,* fiction.
Caryl Churchill (*1938): *Top Girls,* play.
Cooper: *Scenes from Metropolitan Life,* novel.
Durrell: *Constance,* novel.
James Fenton (*1949): *The Memory of War,* poetry.
Greene: *Monsignor Quixote,* novel.
Hampton: *Tales from Hollywood,* play.
Hare: *A Map of the World,* play.

Marriage of Prince of Wales and Lady Diana Spencer seen by 750 million television viewers worldwide.
Brideshead Revisited, television version of Waugh's novel by Mortimer.
Smiley's People, television spy series with Alec Guinness.
Hill Street Blues, The Borgias and *Tenko,* popular television series.
Cats, musical by Lloyd Webber based on T. S. Eliot poems; became U.K. longest-running musical, 1989.
Chariots of Fire, film.
The French Lieutenant's Woman, film from novel of John Fowles (1969).
Gregory's Girl, film by Bill Forsyth.
Raiders of the Lost Ark, film by Steven Spielberg.
First woman cox in history of Oxford-Cambridge Boat Race.
Geoffrey Boycott became scorer of most runs in history of test cricket.
New Zealand: protests at visit of South African national rugby team.
Diego Maradona, Argentinian soccer player, transferred for $8 million, record transfer fee.
First London Marathon.

Litre measure introduced at U.K. petrol stations.
Home computers cheaply available; introduction of I.B.M. personal computer.
Launch of first satellites to provide business-data channels to commercial users.
Maiden flight of U.S. space shuttle *Columbia,* first re-usable spacecraft; *Voyager 2* space probe produced new information about Saturn.
Initiation of high-speed train service (T.G.V.) from Paris to S. E. France; new railway speed record of 235 m.p.h.
First cross-channel flight by solar-powered aircraft.
First balloon flight across Pacific, Japan to the U.S.A. (5,300 miles).
Maximum weight of heavy goods vehicles raised from 32.5 to 40 tonnes.
Longest and fastest crossing of Antarctica: team lead by Ranulph Fiennes travelled 2,500 miles in 75 days.
Crew of Penlee lifeboat, Cornwall, drowned during rescue attempt.
St Valentine's Day disco fire in Dublin killed 49, mainly teenagers.

Government approved new British Library building, Euston Road (designed by Colin St. John Wilson).
Raising of *Mary Rose,* flagship of Henry VIII, in Solent (sank 1545).
Inauguration of Channel 4, U.K.'s fourth television service; three new regional commercial television services (Central, T.V. South, T.V. South West).
Completion of Theatre Royal, Plymouth (designer Peter Moro).
Opening of Sutton Place, arts and music centre.
Demise of D'Oyly Carte Opera Company.
U.S.A.: Reagan administration proposed 40

U.N. Environment Programme reported annual loss of 6 million hectares of productive land to desert, and annual clearance of 8 million hectares of rain forest.
Growing anxiety about effect of acid rain on lakes and forests.
Draft international treaty to control release of CFCs from aerosol sprays and refrigerators.
International Whaling Commission voted to ban commercial whaling in 3 years.
Genetic engineering produced abnormal growth in mice: possibility of fast-growing farm animals, and animals producing

1982

8–month pay dispute in Health Service.
Privatization of Britoil.
Collapse of Laker Airways and De Lorean car company.
Serious civil disturbances in St Paul's area of Bristol.
I.R.A. car-bomb in Hyde Park killed 2 horse-guards and 7 horses.
Bomb under bandstand, Regent's Park, killed 6 bandsmen of Royal Green Jackets.
Bomb at Ballykelly pub disco killed 11 British soldiers and 5 civilians.
European Court outlawed corporal punishment in schools.
Establishment of women's peace camp at Greenham Common, U.S. airbase in U.K.
Church of England report advocated unilateral nuclear disarmament.
First visit of a Pope to Britain since 1531.
Spain opened border with Gibraltar to pedestrians (closed 1969, fully opened 1985): joined N.A.T.O.
Poland: food riots following price increases of up to 400%; Solidarity banned; Walesa released from detention after nearly a year.
Israel invaded Lebanon; Beirut beseiged; P.L.O. expelled; Palestinians massacred by Lebanese Christian militia in refugee camps.
Israel handed back Sinai, occupied since 1967 war, to Egypt.
U.S.S.R.: †Brezhnev, succeeded by Andropov.
Nicaragua: Sandinista government suspended civil rights.
Canada: new constitution, severing last colonial link with U.K.
France: nationalization of banks.
Germany: Helmut Kohl Chancellor.

Hughes: *Selected Poems*.
Kazuo Ishiguro (*1954): *A Pale View of the Hills*, novel.
Keneally: *Schindler's Ark* (Booker Prize).
Marquez: *Chronicle of a Death Foretold*, novel.
Timothy Mo (*1953): *Sour Sweet*, novel.
Pinter: *Other Places*, short plays.
Powell: *The Strangers All Are Gone*, memoirs.
Martin Seymour-Smith (*1928): *Robert Graves, His Life and Work*.
Sharpe: *Vintage Stuff*, novel.
Stoppard: *The Real Thing*, play.
John Wain: (*1925): *Young Shoulders*, novel (Whitbread Award).
Edmund White (*1940): *A Boy's Own Story*, novel.
Director of *The Romans in Britain* (1980) on trial for indecency; case abandoned.

1983

General election; Conservatives re-elected; Liberals and S.D.P. gained 25% of votes; Labour manifesto advocated nuclear disarmament and withdrawal from E.E.C.
Neil Kinnock became leader of

Peter Ackroyd (*1949): *The Last Testament of Oscar Wilde*, novel.
Howard Barker: (*1946): *Victory*, play.
Bradbury: *Rates of Exchange*, novel.
Brenton: *The Genius*, play.
le Carré: *The Little Drummer Girl*, novel.

flats in Washington Memorial and a bank in Lincoln Memorial.
Birtwistle: *The Masque of Orpheus* (composed 1974–82).
Penderecki: *Cello Concerto No. 2.*
William Mathias (*1934): *Lux Aeterna,* requiem.
Royal Shakespeare Company transferred to Barbican Theatre; *Poppy,* musical by Nichol, for first season.
Gandhi, film by Richard Attenborough with Ben Kingsley.
E.T., film by Steven Spielberg.
Shoot the Moon, film by Alan Parker.
Annie, film by John Huston.
A Midsummer's Nights Sex Comedy, film by Woody Allen.
Fanny and Alexander, film by Ingmar Bergman.
Tootsie, film with Dustin Hoffman.
Police, television "fly on the wall" documentary.
Boys from the Blackstuff, five television plays by Alan Bleasdale.
Objects of Affection, 5 television plays by Bennett.
Barchester Chronicles, television serial based on Trollope novels.
Daley Thompson (U.K.) became only man to hold Olympic, European and Commonwealth titles and world record simultaneously, in the decathlon.
English cricketers on "rebel" tour of S. Africa were banned from test cricket for 3 years.
Neoli Fairhall became first paraplegic to win gold medal at Commonwealth Games, Brisbane.

pharmaceutically valuable materials.
Successful replacement of diseased human heart by artificial one.
Identification of some genes involved in cancer.
Important advances in treatment of thalassaemia.
First colour television pictures of Venus from U.S.S.R. spaceprobe *Venera 13.*
Rapid commercial exploitation of video-games using microprocessors.
Launch of Sinclair Spectrum computer, U.K. market-leader in home micros.
Japanese government introduced project to develop "intelligent" computer, capable of reasoning and processing knowledge rather than numbers.
First compact discs on sale.
Introduction of disc pocket-camera.
Blas Cabrera reported detection of a magnetic monopole.
Generation of shortest-ever flash of laser light (30 femtoseconds).
Successful testing of nuclear fusion reactor, Princeton University.
Completion of Thames Barrier, Woolwich.
Itaipu Dam (Bolivia/Peru), world's largest hydroelectric scheme.
Discovery of earliest fossil remains linked to *homo sapiens* (4 million years old).
U.K.: inland telegrams and British Telecom telephone monopoly discontinued.
Passenger jet crashed into Potomac River, Washington, killing 78.
Coach crash near Beaune, France, killed 44 children, 9 adults.

Opening of Burrell Collection, Pollock Park, Glasgow.
Opening of National Museum of Photography, Film and Television, Bradford.
Gulbenkian Centre for Modern Art, Lisbon

World's population estimated as 4,721,887,000.
Confirmation of global warming, and forecast of further 5% temperature rises, caused by greenhouse effect.
Acid rain recognized to be man-made,

1983 Labour Party, David Owen of S.D.P.
Taxes and public spending reduced.
White paper on abolition of G.L.C.
Strike ballots to be compulsory by law. N.H.S. required to put support services to private tender.
C.N.D. demonstrations: 14-mile human chain linked research and military establishments; ¼ million in Hyde Park rally; 1 million W. Germans demonstrated.
Franks Report absolved British government from blame for Falklands invasion.
Ireland: 1981 Derby winner Shergar kidnapped; ransom demand for £2 million; 134 I.R.A. prisoners broke out of Maze prison; I.R.A. car-bomb exploded outside Harrods.
U.S.A.: Reagan called U.S.S.R. an "evil empire"; proposed "Star Wars", missile shield in space; supported Contra rebels opposed to Marxist Sandinista government in Nicaragua; invaded Grenada.
Siberia: Korean Airlines passenger jet shot down by Soviet fighter plane, killing 269.
Poland: martial law lifted after 19 months; Pope visited, and supported right to join free trade unions.
Lebanon: army took over control of E. Beirut from Christian militia; suicide attacks by lorries carrying explosives devastated U.S. marine base (†241) and French barracks (†58) of U.N. forces, and U.S. Embassy; P.L.O. left for Tunisia.
Iran: major offensive across border with Iraq.
India: 600 Muslim refugees massacred in Assam, worst sectarian violence since partition.
Sri Lanka: racial violence between Sinhalese and Tamils.
Philippines: murder of Benigno Aquino, opposition leader, on return from exile.
U.K.'s biggest robbery: £25 million gold bars from Brinks-Mat.

J. M. Coetzee (*1940): *Life and Times of Michael K*, novel (Booker Prize).
Nick Dark (*1948): *The Body*, play.
Deighton: *Berlin Game*, novel.
Charles Dyer (*1928): *Lovers Dancing*, play.
John Fuller (*1937): *Flying to Nowhere*, first novel.
Hughes: *The River*, poetry.
Neil Jordan (*1950): *The Dream of a Beast*, novel.
William Kennedy (*1928): *Ironweed*, novel.
Mamet: *Glengarry Glen Ross*, play.
Masters: *Man of War*, novel.
Peter Porter (*1929): *Collected Poems*.
Roth: *The Anatomy Lesson*, novel.
Rushdie: *Shame*, novel.
Neil Simon (*1927): *Brighton Beach Memoirs*, play.
Graham Swift (*1949): *Waterland*, novel.
R. S. Thomas: *Later Poems*.
Trevor: *Fools of Fortune*, novel (Whitbread Award).
Updike: *Bech is Back*, short stories.
Nicholas Wright (*1940): *The Custom of the Country*, play.
"Hitler Diaries" published, then declared to be forgeries.
Diaries of Peter Hall when Director of National Theatre.

(designed by Leslie Martin).
The Genius of Venice exhibition, Royal Academy.
†Joan Miro (*1893), Spanish artist.
Witold Lutoslawski (*1913): Symphony No. 3.
Paul Patterson (*1947): *Mass of the Sea*.
Messiaen: *Saint François d'Assise*, opera.
First early morning television in U.K.: B.B.C.'s *Breakfast Time*.
First prosecution of "video nasty" under Obscene Publications Bill.
The Winds of War, television historical drama.
Kennedy, television series.
An Englishman Abroad, television play by Bennett.
The Old Men at the Zoo, television series by Wilson.
Never Say Never Again, film with Sean Connery.
Zelig, film by Woody Allen.
Local Hero, film.
Yentl, fim with Barbra Streisand.
Amadeus, film by Milos Forman.
Monty Python's The Meaning of Life, film.
Octopussy, film.
Return of the Jedi, film.
Blondel, musical by Tim Rice and Stephen Oliver.
La Cage Aux Folles, musical by Jerry Herman.
Television companies allowed football teams to carry shirt advertising.
English Football League accepted sponsorship and changed name.
First World Athletics Championships, Helsinki.
Christopher Dean and Jayne Torville (U.K.) won third successive world title for ice-skating.
U.S.A. lost Americas Cup (yacht race) to Australia after 132 years.
Martin Luther King's birthday became national holiday in U.S.A. (first observed 1986).

largely by sulphur emissions, especially from power stations.
Forecast that large-scale nuclear war would create global "nuclear winter".
All new cars in U.K. to run on lead-free petrol by 1990.
First election victories of Green Party candidates, W. Germany.
U.K. government ordered enquiry into allegations of high levels of cancer near Sellafield nuclear power station (formerly Windscale).
Public enquiry into plan for power station with pressurized water reactor, Sizewell, U.K.
Joint European experimental fusion reactor, Torus, started up.
Discovery of W and Z bosons, fundamental particles, at European Nuclear Physics Centre (C.E.R.N.).
A.I.D.S. affected 2,000 in U.S.A. and reached Europe.
Development of test to identify people who will suffer from Huntington's Chorea.
World's first man-made chromosome assembled.
Britain's first heart and lung transplant.
U.K. High Court upheld doctor's right to supply contraceptive pills to under-16s without parents' consent.
Computer purchases in U.K. doubled.
U.S. space-shuttle *Challenger* made maiden flight.
First sophisticated scientific laboratory (spacelab) in space.
Queen presented Order of Merit to Mother Teresa of Calcutta.
Egypt: Nile steamer sank, killing 500.
Australia's worst bush-fire killed 69.
New world land-speed record (633.6 m.p.h.) by jet-powered car.
Wheel-clamping of illegally parked cars introduced in London.
Wearing of car seat belts compulsory in U.K.
£1 coin introduced.

1984 Disastrous famine in Ethiopia following drought; massive international relief operation and fund raising.
U.K.: national strike by miners over pay offer and pit closures; violence at Nottinghamshire and Derbyshire pits; battles between riot police and miners at Orgreave coking plant, Yorkshire; High Court ruled strike illegal, fined National Union of Mineworkers and sequestered union funds.
Disruptive action by teachers in support of pay claim (see 1987).
Ban on Union membership at Government Communications Headquarters (G.C.H.Q.), Cheltenham.
Flotation of British Telecom shares, biggest share issue ever.
Matrimonial and Family Proceedings Bill allowed divorce after one year.
I.R.A. bomb exploded at Grand Hotel, Brighton, occupied by Prime Minister, Cabinet and M.P.s during party conference; 5 killed.
W.P.C. Yvonne Fletcher shot dead from Libyan embassy, London, during anti-Gaddafi demonstration.
Women's peace camp, Greenham Common, cleared by bailiffs and police.
Stockholm disarmament conference attended by N.A.T.O. and Warsaw Pact countries.
E.E.C. summit collapsed because of disagreement over U.K. budget contributions.
U.K. and China agreed reversion of Hong Kong to China, 1997.
India: serious riots between Hindus and Muslims; Golden Temple of Amritsar, occupied by Sikh militants, stormed by troops; 802 dead; Sikh bodyguards assassinated Prime Minister, Indira Gandhi.
Beirut: civil war; evacuation of foreign nationals, including U.N. peace-keeping force.

Ackroyd: *T. S. Eliot*, biography.
K. Amis: *Stanley and his Women*, novel.
M. Amis: *Money*, novel.
Ayckbourn: *A Chorus of Disapproval*, play.
Ballard: *Empire of the Sun*, novel.
Barker: *Scenes from an Execution*, play.
Julian Barnes (*1946): *Flaubert's Parrot*, literary commentary.
Brenton: *Bloody Poetry*, play.
Anita Brookner (*1928): *Hotel du Lac*, novel.
Anita Desai (*1937): *In Custody*, novel.
Frayn: *Benefactors; Number One; Platonov*, plays.
Pam Gems (*1925): *Camille*, play.
Gray: *The Common Pursuit*, play.
Heaney: *Sweeney Astray* and *Station Island*, poetry.
Heller: *God Knows*, novel.
Ted Hughes appointed Poet Laureate.
Howard Jacobson (*1942): *Peeping Tom*, novel.
Penelope Lively (*1933): *According to Mark*, novel.
Lodge: *Small World*, novel.
Pinter: *One for the Road*, play.
Stephen Poliakoff (*1952): *Breaking the Silence*, play.
Sue Townsend (*1946): *The Secret Diary of Adrian Mole, Aged 13¾*, fiction.
Updike: *The Witches of Eastwick*, novel.
Vidal: *Lincoln*, novel.
Keith Waterhouse (*1929): *Thinks*, monologue.
Wood: *Red Star*, play.
First distribution of royalties to authors from Public Lending Right.

York Minster's south transept roof destroyed by fire; damage estimated at £1 million.
Prince Charles criticized modern architecture at Royal Institute of British Architects; public enquiry into proposed glass tower (Mies van der Rohe) on Mansion House site.
Washington: Vietnam war memorial, privately funded.
Neue Staatsgallerie extension, Stuttgart, designed by James Stirling.
Turners' *Seascape: Folkestone* sold for £7.37 million; first Turner Prize awarded to Malcolm Morley (*1931).
Cable television introduced in U.K.
Trocadero, Piccadilly Circus, London's first major leisure centre.
Titbits magazine closed after 104 years.
First performance of Symphony in A minor (K.16a) by Mozart (?), written at age 9, discovered in Denmark.
Tippett: *The Mask of Time*, music.
Stockhausen: *Samstag aus Licht*, opera.
Philip Glass (*1937): *Akhnaten*, opera.
Luciano Berio (*1925): *Un Re In Ascolto*, opera.
Starlight Express, roller-skating musical by Lloyd Webber.
Sunday in the Park with George, musical by Sondheim.
Under the Volcano and *The Dresser*, films with Albert Finney.
A Passage to India, film by David Lean from Forster novel.
Beverley Hills Cop, comedy film.
Greystoke, film by Hugh Hudson.
The Killing Fields, film by Roland Joffe.
The Jewel in the Crown, television series.
Do They Know It's Christmas?, record by pop singers (Band Aid) for famine relief.
Thriller, record by Michael Jackson, popular singer, sold 40 million copies, world best-seller.
Los Angeles Olympics, boycotted by U.S.S.R.
Viv Richards, West Indies cricketer, scored 189 not out against England, highest-ever one-day innings.
Oxford won Boat Race in record time (16 min 45 secs).

European Space Agency rocket *Ariane* put world's largest telecommunications satellite into orbit.
First untethered spacewalk, from U.S. space shuttle *Challenger*; first repair of satellite in orbit; maiden flight of space shuttle *Discovery*; Russian cosmonauts spent 238 days in orbit, new record.
Mexico: U.N. conference recommended slowing growth of world population.
Ottowa: ten nations (excluding U.K. and U.S.A.) pledged to reduce sulphur dioxide emissions by 30% to reduce acid rain.
Greenhouse effect blamed for weather of 1981 and 1983, warmest on record.
Monsoon floods in Bangladesh destroyed ½ million homes and stranded 30 million inhabitants; deforestation in India and Nepal blamed.
U.K. government report stated that childhood leukaemia was 10 times the national average near Sellafield nuclear processing plant.
Explosion at chemical factory, Bhopal, India, killed up to 10,000 and injured many more.
10–day-old baby became youngest-ever heart transplant patient.
Newborn baby given baboon's heart.
U.K.'s first test-tube triplets.
A.I.D.S. virus identified by Robert Gallo and Luc Montagnier.
Discovery of top quark at C.E.R.N.
First production of x-rays from lasers.
3.6 million computers in U.K. at beginning of year; first portable computer with full-sized screen; marketing of Apple Macintosh computer, first to use mouse, creating new market of desktop publishing.
Launch by some retail outlets of payment by electronic transfer from customers' bank accounts.
Police video cameras linked to computers to match number plates with those of stolen cars.
U.K.'s first cellular radio network, Vodafone.
Japanese car firm Nissan announced plans for factory in N. E. England.
£1 note and ½p coin phased out.

1984 Poland: 652 political prisoners granted amnesty.
S. Africa: new constitution caused rioting in black townships; peace with Mozambique.
Europe's biggest cannabis seizure: £7 million in U.K.
†Andropov, succeeded by Chernenko as General Secretary.

1985 Miners' strike ended in failure.
Teachers' pay dispute: disruptive action in schools.
Prescription charges increased to £2.
Opinion polls put S.D.P./Liberal Alliance in lead.
£ valued at $1.07, record low; effective 27% devaluation in one year.
Local Government Bill abolished G.L.C. and metropolitan counties.
Liverpool and Lambeth local councillors surcharged £¼ million for failing to set rate.
Anglo-Irish Agreement gave Irish Republic consultative role in N. Ireland affairs.
Ireland: Dublin government bill to seize £5 million worth of I.R.A. assets.
Eviction of 200 protesters from Cruise missile base, Molesworth, Cheshire.
Race riots at Broadwater Farm estate, London; policeman murdered.
First black bishop and council leader in U.K.
Commonwealth Prime Ministers' conference: U.K. refused to impose full-scale economic sanctions against S. Africa.
S. Africa: riots over attempts to move 100,000 black squatters to new townships; end of ban on mixed marriages; state of emergency in 30 black districts.
U.S.S.R.: †Chernenko, replaced by Mikhail Gorbachev as General Secretary, who announced moratorium on missile deployment.
Geneva: Reagan-Gorbachev talks

Ackroyd: *Hawksmoor*, novel.
Ayckbourn: *Women in Mind*, play.
Peter Barnes (*1931): *Red Noses*, play.
Ray Bradbury (*1920): *Death is a Lonely Business*, novel.
Peter Carey (*1943): *Illywacker*, novel.
Don DeLillo (*1936): *White Noise*, fiction.
Douglas Dunn (*1942): *Elegies*, poetry.
Greene: *The Tenth Man*, novel.
Hare and Brenton: *Pravda*, play.
Tony Harrison (*1937): *The Mysteries*, medieval plays versified, and *Collected Dramatic Verse*.
Garrison Keillor (*1942): *Lake Wobegon Days*, novel.
Lessing: *The Good Terrorist*, novel.
Maynard Mack (*1909): *Alexander Pope, A Life*.
Moore: *Black Robe*, historical novel.
Mortimer: *Paradise Postponed*, novel.
Randolf Quirk (*1920) and others: *A Comprehensive Grammar of the English Language*.
Raban: *Foreign Country*, novel.
Shaffer: *Yonadab*, play.
Simon: *Biloxi Blues*, play.
Barry Unsworth (*1930): *Stone Virgin*, novel.
Vonnegut: *Galapagos*, novel.
A. N. Wilson (*1950): *Gentlemen in England*, novel.
Jeanette Winterson (*1959): *Oranges Are Not The Only Fruit*, novel.
Les Liaisons Dangereuses, adapted as a play by Hampton.
The Mahabharata, dramatization by Peter Brook.

U.K. and U.S.A. withdrew from U.N.E.S.C.O.
Oxford University refused to grant honorary degree to Mrs Thatcher because of education cuts.
Treasure Houses of Britain exhibition, National Gallery, Washington.
Opening of Picasso Museum, Paris.
Mantegna's *Adoration of the Magi* became world's most expensive painting (£8.1 million).
Renoir exhibition, Hayward Gallery, London.
Victoria and Albert Museum introduced voluntary charge for admission.
Robert Venturi selected to design National Gallery extension, following Prince Charles's criticism (1984).
First live television from House of Lords.
John Eaton (*1935): *The Tempest*, opera.
Musgrave: *Harriet: The Woman Called Moses*, opera.
Andrew Lloyd Webber (*1948): *Requiem Mass*.
Les Miserables, musical.
Heimat, film by Edgar Reitz.
A Chorus Line, film by Attenborough.
The Colour Purple, film by Spielberg.
Out of Africa, film by Sidney Pollack.
Witness, film by Peter Weir.
Prizzi's Honour, film by Huston.
My Beautiful Laundrette, film by Stephen Frears.
Edge of Darkness, television drama by Tony Martin.
B.B.C. television documentary on N. Ireland in *Real Lives* series dropped after government pressure; journalists went on strike; programme later shown.
Live Aid, appeal by Bob Geldorf and rock musicians for Ethiopian famine relief, raised £60 million; simultaneous 10 hour

U.N. Office of Emergency Operations stated 19 million Africans still faced famine.
U.S.-Canadian study of acid rain agreed.
U.N. estimated 6.9 million square kilometres of Africa under threat of desertification.
World Wildlife Fund began campaign to conserve wetlands.
European Community environment ministers agreed emission standards for vehicle exhausts.
Evidence of black hole at centre of our galaxy.
A.I.D.S.: first British baby to die; screening of all blood-donors; W.H.O. proclaimed epidemic.
Fewer than one in three now smoking in U.K.
Clive Sinclair launched C5, cheap battery-powered single-seater three-wheeled vehicle; failed to catch on.
Amstrad launched P.C.W. 8256, popular domestic word-processor.
Use of robots in microelectronic engineering.
Genetic fingerprinting used for first time to establish paternity.
Development of techniques to identify defective D.N.A. in foetuses.
Application of biotechnology to agriculture: genetically engineered bacteria giving plants built-in insect and frost repellant.
Japanese Boeing 747 crashed near Tokyo: 520 killed; world's worst single crash.
Air India jet blew up over Atlantic, killing 329; terrorist bomb suspected.
Train crash in Ethiopia killed 390.
Bradford City football club grandstand destroyed by fire during match; 52 spectators killed.

LITERATURE

1985 agreed 50% cut in nuclear weapons; improvement in east-west relations.
Lebanon: Shi'ites, backed by Syria, assaulted Palestinian strongholds in Beirut; Isreal released 700 Lebanese Shi'ites in exchange for 39 U.S. hostages from airliner hijacked by Shi'ite Muslims.
Arab terrorism: attacks at Rome and Vienna airports; hijacking of Italian cruise ship *Achille Lauro*, later surrendered.
Nicaragua: U.S.A. banned aid to Contra rebels; trade embargo against Sandinista government.
N. Zealand: alleged sabotage of Greenpeace protest ship *Rainbow Warrior* by French secret service.

1986 Government announced replacement of rates by Community Charge (poll tax) in 1990.
Water industry to be sold off.
Westland affair: two cabinet ministers resigned during controversy over future ownership of helicopter firm.
Education Act abolished corporal punishment in schools.
Violence between striking print workers and police at Wapping printing plant.
London Stock Exchange deregulated: "Big Bang" introduced computerized trading, admitted foreign companies, and ended fixed commission rates and other controls.
Privatization of Trustee Savings Bank and British Gas attracted 4 million applications for shares in both cases.
Gorbachev-Reagan summit, Reykjavik.
U.S.S.R.: Gorbachev proposed elimination of all nuclear arms by 2000; attacked policies of Brezhnev; advocated perestroika (reconstruction) and glasnost (openness) to democratise U.S.S.R.; freeing of Shcharansky and

K. Amis, *The Old Devils*, novel (Booker Prize).
Margaret Atwood (*1939): *The Handmaid's Tale*, novel.
Paul Bailey (*1937): *Gabriel's Lament*, novel.
Barnes: *Staring at the Sun*, novel.
Bennett: *Kafka's Dick*, play.
Brookner: *A Misalliance*, novel.
Burgess: *The Pianoplayers*, novel.
le Carré: *A Perfect Spy*, novel.
Caute: *News From Nowhere*.
Coetzee: *Foe*, novel.
Gems: *The Danton Affair*, play.
Hare: *The Bay at Nice*, play.
Hemingway: *The Garden of Eden*, posthumous novel.
Hughes: *Flowers and Insects*, poetry.
Dusty Hughes (*1947): *Futurists*, play.
Ishiguro: *An Artist of the Floating World*, novel (Whitbread Awards).
P. D. James (*1920): *A Taste for Death*, novel.
Mo: *An Insular Possession*, novel.
Newby: *Leaning in the Wind*, novel.
Powell: *Fisher King*, novel.
Piers Paul Read (*1941): *The Free Frenchman*, novel.
P. Theroux: *O-Zone*, fiction.
Updike: *Roger's Version*, novel.
Hugh Whitemore (*1936): *Breaking the Code*, play.
Completion of *Oxford English Dictionary*.
Spycatcher affair: government attempted to

concerts in London and Philadelphia; television showing reached 1½ billion viewers.
Boris Becker (17) became youngest-ever Wimbledon men's singles champion.
English football clubs banned from European competitions because of spectators' behaviour:
British football hooliganism at Heysel stadium, Belgium, led to death of 41 spectators, mainly Italian.

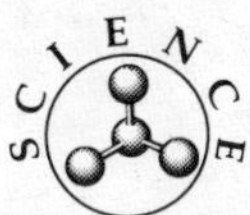

Bangladesh: cyclone and tidal wave killed 10,000.
Mexico City: most devastating earthquake this century killed 7,000.
Colombia: volcano obliterated four towns, killing 25,000.
Italian Dolomites: reservoir burst, flooding villages and killing 210.

Opening of Swan Theatre, Stratford-upon-Avon.
Opening of Musée d'Orsay and Parc La Villette (Museum of Science, Technology and Industry), Paris.
Opening of Museum of Contemporary Art, Los Angeles, designed by Arata Isozaki.
Lloyd's building, London, designed by Richard Rogers.
Headquarters of Hong Kong and Shanghai Bank, designed by Norman Foster.
B.B.C. launched full day-time television service.
Peacock Committee on future of broadcasting proposed replacement of B.B.C./I.T.V. duopoly by multiplicity of channels; B.S.B. (British Satellite Broadcasting) awarded first franchise for direct broadcasting by satellite.
French government announced privatization of T.F.–1, first sale of public service television channel to private owners.
Launch of *The Independent* and *Today*, new newspapers.
Control of South Bank arts and complex passed from G.L.C. to South Bank Board.
30 million people worldwide took part in "The Race Against Time" to raise money for refugees in Africa (Sportaid).
Menotti: *Goya*, opera.
Davies: *Violin Concerto*.

U.S. space shuttle *Challenger* exploded soon after lift-off, killing all 7 crew, including schoolteacher Christa McAuliffe.
Voyager 2 photographed Uranus.
Agreement on construction of Channel tunnel, initially to be rail only.
Explosion at Chernobyl nuclear reactor, U.S.S.R., caused escape of tonnes of radioactive material; world's worst nuclear accident.
Escape of carbon dioxide and hydrogen gas from volcanic lake in Cameroons killed 1,700.
Rhine extensively polluted by 30 tons of liquid pesticides and mercury following fire in chemical warehouse in Basle, Switzerland.
Forecasts that greenhouse effect would produce desert conditions in mid-Asia and N. America by 2050 unless controlled.
Hole detected in ozone layer in atmosphere above Spitzbergen for first time.
U.K. government launched biggest-ever health campaign (cost £20 million) to combat A.I.D.S; 278 deaths reported so far.
First triple (heart, lung and liver) transplant, Cambridge, U.K.
First use of lasers to dispel blockage in coronary artery; tests on use of lasers to remove tissue from cornea.
Anti-malaria protection by vaccine made by genetic engineering.

1986

Sakharov, leading dissidents.
Polish government released 225 political prisoners.
U.S.A.: Irangate scandal; arms supplied to Iran in exchange for hostages, with profits diverted to Nicaraguan Contra rebels after Congress refused funding.
U.S. and Libyan forces clashed in Gulf of Sirte; U.S. aircraft, some British-based, bombed Libya.
Arab terrorist bombing campaign in Paris.
China: student demonstrations demanded democratic reforms.
S. Africa: 8,500 detained under State of Emergency following continued anti-apartheid unrest; riots in Soweto.
Civil wars in Aden and Uganda.
Philippines: ousting of President Marcos, replaced by Mrs Corazon Aquino (see 1983).
Sweden: assassination of Olaf Palme, Prime Minister.
Spain and Portugal joined E.C.
Mario Soares became first civilian president of Portugal since 1926.
Trial of 474 alleged Mafia gangsters began in Italy.

stop publication of memoirs of Peter Wright, former secret service officer.

1987

General Election: Conservatives elected for third term with large overall majority.
S.D.P. voted to merge with Liberals; breakaway S.D.P. formed.
Settlement imposed in teachers' pay dispute; Teachers' Pay and Conditions Act abolished Burnham Committee, negotiating body.
Privatization of British Airways, Rolls Royce, British Airports Authority and B.P.; flotation of Eurotunnel.
Child Benefit frozen.
House prices in S. England, up 25% this year, now double prices elsewhere.
Stock exchange collapse: 20% drop in share prices in London (Black

Ackroyd: *Chatterton*, novel.
Ayckbourn: *A Small Family Business*, play.
A. L. Barker (*1918): *The Gooseboy*, novel.
Nina Bawden (*1925): *Circles of Deceit*, novel.
Bellow: *More Die of Heartbreak*, novel.
Boyd: *The New Confessions*, novel.
Chatwin: *Songlines*, fiction/anthropology.
Churchill: *Serious Money*, play.
Edgar: *That Summer*, play.
Richard Ellman (*1918, †1987): *Oscar Wilde*, biography.
Heaney: *The Haw Lantern*, poetry.
Keneally: *The Playmaker*, novel.
Lively: *Moon Tiger*, novel (Booker Prize).
Mamet: *Speed-the-Plow*, play.
Tony Marchant (*1959): *Speculators*, play.
Ian McEwan (*1948): *The Child in Time*, novel.

Lloyd Webber: *Phantom of the Opera*, musical.
The Monocled Mutineer, television play by Alan Bleasdale.
The Singing Detective, television series by Dennis Potter.
Hannah and her Sisters, film by Woody Allen.
Crocodile Dundee, film with Paul Hogan.
The Sacrifice, film by Andrei Tarkovsky.
Sid and Nancy, film by Alex Cox.
Mona Lisa, film with Bob Hoskins.
The Mission, film by Roland Joffe.
Platoon, film by Oliver Stone.
A Room with a View, film.
Mike Tyson became youngest ever world heavyweight boxing champion at 20.
Virgin Atlantic Challenger II, speed-boat, crossed Atlantic in record time.
Argentina won World Cup, Mexico.

World's first test-tube quins born in London.
20% of children now born outside marriage in U.K.
Halley's Comet visible from Earth; photographed by European space probe *Giotto*.
Discovery of high-temperature superconductors (Alex Muller, Zurich).
Experimental aircraft *Voyager* flew round world non-stop on one tank of fuel in 9 days.
First permanently armed police patrolling Heathrow airport.
Japanese Nissan car company opened new plant at Sunderland, U.K.
Introduction of smart cards by Honeywell and Bull.
First pocket telephones.

Opening of Theatre Museum, Covent Garden.
Clore Gallery (extension of Tate), designed by James Stirling.
Buildings in U.K. eligible for listed status after 30 years instead of 50.
Wortham Centre (opera house) and museum for Menil collection, designed by Renzo Piano, in Houston, Texas.
British Art of the 20th Century exhibition, London and Stuttgart.
Major retrospective exhibitions of work of Le Corbusier, London and Paris.
Exhibition of works of Lucien Freud (*1922), Washington and Paris.
Age of Chivalry exhibition, Royal Academy.
Sale of Van Gogh's *Irises* (£30 million in New York, world record) and *Sunflowers* (£24.7 million in London).

World population passed 5 billion (see 1975).
U.N. World Food Programme warned of famine in Ethiopia (facing 3 million people), Mozambique and Angola.
Drought in India: a third of population short of water.
Montreal: 70 nations agreed to maintain use of CFCs at 1986 level, to be reduced by half by 1999; 90% thinning of ozone layer over Antarctica observed and attributed to release of CFCs by industrial nations.
Predictions that greenhouse effect would cause 13 cm rises in sea levels by 2025, and make hurricanes more destructive.
U.K.: one person a day now dying of A.I.D.S.
First radiation detected from exploded Milky Way supernova, nearest observed

1987 Monday), 23% in New York.
Charges of illegal share-dealing against Guinness brewing firm.
End of year-long picketing at Wapping (see 1986) over manning levels for new newspaper-printing technology.
I.R.A. bomb at Remembrance Day parade, Enniskillen, N. Ireland, killed 11, injured 63; bomb at British military base in W. Germany injured 31.
U.S.S.R.: Gorbachev demanded democratization of communist party and state bodies; offered to remove all Russian short-range missiles from E. Europe; pardoned 140 dissidents.
Hungary: demonstrations in support of liberal reform.
Washington summit: Reagan and Gorbachev agreed dismantling of all land-based, intermediate-range weapons.
U.S.A.: Tower Commission criticized President's role in Irangate (1986).
Saudi Arabia: rioting by Iranian zealots during Muslim pilgrimage, Mecca; 400 dead.
Persian Gulf: U.S. minesweepers recovered mines laid in shipping lanes by Iran.
Lebanon: Terry Waite, representative of Archbishop of Canterbury, presumed kidnapped on hostage-release mission.
Sri Lanka: government planes attacked Tamil separatists.
Trials began of alleged war criminals in Israel and France; †Hess, Hitler's deputy, last prisoner in Spandau jail, Berlin.

Miller: *Timebends*, autobiography, and *Danger, Memory!*, one act plays.
Moore: *The Colour of Blood*, novel.
Murdoch: *The Book and the Brotherhood*, novel.
Naipaul: *The Enigma of Arrival*, fiction.
Poliakoff: *Coming in to Land*, play.
Roth: *Counterlife*, novel.
Shaffer: *Lettice and Lovage*, play.
Tom Wolfe (*1930): *The Bonfire of Vanities*, novel.

1988 Government announced plans to privatize electricity industry.
Budget reduced top rate of income tax to 40p and standard rate to 25p.
Public spending lowest for 20 years.
Education Reform Act introduced

Ayckbourn: *Henceforward*, play.
Barker: *The Bite of the Night*, play.
Bennett: *Single Spies*, play.
Carey: *Oscar and Lucinda*, novel (Booker Prize).
Chatwin: *Utz*, novel.

24–hours-a-day television launched in Britain.
B.B.C. offices raided by Special Branch to remove television material on Zircon spy satellite project.
Nigel Osborne (*1948): *The Electrification of the Soviet Union*, opera.
Amadeus Quartet disbanded.
†Jacqueline du Pre (*1945), British cellist.
Prick Up Your Ears, and *Sammy and Rosie Get Laid*, films by Stephen Frears.
Beverley Hills Cop II, comedy film.
Cry Freedom, film by Richard Attenborough.
Fatal Attraction, film.
Comrades, film by Bill Douglas.
Little Dorrit, film by Christine Edzard.
Hope and Glory, film by John Boorman.
Jean de Florette and *Manon des Sources*, French films by Claude Berri from novels by Pagnol.
My Life as a Dog, Swedish film by Lasse Hallstrom.
The Last Emperor, film by Bernardo Bertolucci.
World Athletics Championships, Rome.

since 1604.
Paul Chu showed superconductivity possible at above 90 degrees Kelvin: possibility of production of cheap magnetic fields for power transmission, magnetically-levitated transport, cheaper hospital scanners, etc.
World's most powerful wind-powered generator, Burgar Hill, Orkneys.
I.B.M. computer company introduced OS/2, with capacity to "multitask" (show several programmes simultaneously on screen "windows").
Compact cassette replaced vinyl gramophone record as main medium for sale of recorded music; introduction of digital audio tape cassettes, providing opportunity for home recordings with quality similar to compact discs.
Devastating hurricane (110 m.p.h.) over S. E. England; 15 million trees uprooted; insurance claims reached £1.3 billion; worst storm in U.K. for 300 years.
Flooding in Bangladesh: 24 million homeless, 670 dead.
Herald of Free Enterprise, cross-channel car-ferry, sank at Zebrugge, Belgium, with 192 deaths.
Fire at King's Cross underground station killed 30.
Hungerford massacre: gunman killed 16, wounded 14, then shot himself in U.K.'s worst shooting incident.

M.P.s voted for televising of House of Commons proceedings.
Opening of Museum of the Moving Image, South Bank.
Tate Gallery Liverpool opened at Albert Dock.

Between 5 and 10 million people infected by A.I.D.S. virus HIV.
First heart and lung transplant patient to give birth.
Marilyn Monk suggested genetic abnormalities could be detected early

1988 national curriculum and testing, devolution of responsibilities from local authorities to schools, and freedom to opt out of local control; first G.C.S.E. examinations, replacing O level and C.S.E.
Abolition of right to silence in N. Ireland courts.
"Clause 28" forbidding promotion of homosexuality as a "pretended family relationship", became law.
G.C.H.Q. workers dismissed, first civil servants sacked for union membership.
Liberalization of public house licensing hours.
Charges for eye tests and dental treatment.
Liberals and official S.D.P. merged into S.L.D.P.
Gibraltar: British soldiers killed 3 I.R.A. members; at their Belfast funeral, loyalist killed 3 mourners; at funeral of one of these, 2 British soldiers murdered.
U.S.S.R. began military withdrawal from Afghanistan.
U.S.S.R.: Gorbachev made president; unrest in Armenia, Azerbaijan, Latvia and Lithuania; supreme Soviet approved contested elections.
U.N.: Gorbachev announced big unilateral troops reductions in E. Europe, suggesting end of Cold War; Yasser Arafat, P.L.O. leader, condemned terrorism and recognized Israel's right to exist.
Iraqi forces killed 5,000 in gas attack on Iranian-occupied territory; Iran-Iraq cease-fire agreed.
U.S. warship mistakenly shot down Iranian airbus over Gulf, killing 290.
11-day hijack of Kuwaiti jumbo jet in attempt to secure release of 17 Arabs from Kuwaiti jails.
Manuel Noriega, Panamanian dictator, indicted for drug smuggling.
†President Zia of Pakistan in midair explosion; election of Benazir Bhutto.

Fitzgerald: *The Beginning of Spring*, novel.
Friel: *Making History*, play.
Gilbert: *Never Despair*, final volume of Churchill biography.
Hare: *The Secret Rapture*, play.
Stephen Hawking (*1942): *A Brief History of Time*, scientific best seller.
Alan Hollinghurst (*1954): *The Swimming Pool Library*, first novel.
Larkin: *Collected Poems*.
Lodge: *Nice Work*, novel.
Márquez: *Love in the time of Cholera*, novel.
O'Brien: *The High Road*, novel.
Pinter: *Mountain Language*, play.
Rushdie: *The Satanic Verses*, novel.
Stoppard: *Hapgood*, play.
Vonnegut: *Bluebeard*, novel.
Fay Weldon (*1933): *Leader of the Band*, novel.
Wright: *Mrs Klein*, play.
Law Lords allowed newspapers to publish allegations made in *Spycatcher*.
Sale of original manuscript of Kafka's *The Trial* for £1.1 million, highest price for 20th century work.
Manchester University sold off 94 books from John Rylands Collection for £1.8 million.
The Plantaganets, notable production of Shakespearean history plays by Royal Shakespeare Company.

Hereford Cathedral decided to sell *Mappa Mundi* to restore and endow cathedral.
Opening of riverside development, Richmond, designed by Quinlan Terry.
Prince Charles's B.B.C. television documentary *Visions of Britain* attacked modern architecture in favour of vernacular and classical and of community-based projects.
Creation of Broadcasting Standards Council to create code curbing violence and explicit sex.
White Paper on future of broadcasting promised hundreds of television and radio channels.
Government ban on radio and television interviews with members of I.R.A. and other N. Ireland organizations.
Major international exhibitions of works of Degas and Gauguin.
Retrospective exhibition of paintings of David Hockney (*1937), British painter, Tate Gallery.
Stockhausen: *Montag aus Licht*, opera.
Distant Voices, Still Lives, film by Terence Davies.
A Fish Called Wanda, film with John Cleese directed by Charles Crichton.
Who Framed Roger Rabbit?, film by Robert Zemeckis.
Babette's Feast, film by Gabriel Axel.
Rain Man, film by Levinson.
Mississippi Burning, film by Alan Parker.
Last Temptation of Christ, film by Martin Scorsese.
A Very British Coup, television drama.
Talking Heads, television monologues by Bennett.
Tumbledown, television play about Falklands, by Richard Eyre.
Death on the Rock, Thames T.V. investigation of Gibraltar killings (see History) shown despite government protests.
Olympic Games in Seoul: winner of 100 metres stripped of gold medal after failing drug test.

enough to destroy embryo and avoid abortion.
Anxieties about salmonella in eggs.
Claims that consumption of convenience foods caused decline in intelligence, reversible by vitamin tablets.
N. European viral epidemic killed hundreds of seals.
Record flood levels in Bangladesh and China; 1½ million homeless in Nile floods.
Most violent hurricane on record devastated Jamaica and Caribbean region.
Worst drought in U.S. midwest since 1930s dust bowl.
Severe earthquakes in Armenia (26,000 dead, ½ million homeless) and India.
Personal computers using optical rather than magnetic storage discs (256 megabytes of capacity).
Development of compact discs capable of recording.
First pocket-sized video recorder and television set (Video Walkman by Sony).
Incidents of large-scale international "hacking" (unauthorized computer tapping).
Tests revealed Turin Shroud dated from 1260–1390 A.D.
U.S. space craft *Discovery* launched.
First absolute proof of existence of planets other than those of solar system.
Inauguration of Australia Telescope, most powerful in southern hemisphere.
First trans-Atlantic optical fibre telephone cable linked U.K. and U.S.A.
Lockerbie, Scotland: London-New York jumbo crashed after bomb exploded on board; 270 dead, including all passengers and crew, and 11 townspeople; Palestinian terrorism suspected.
N. Sea oil platform Piper Alpha exploded, killing 166.
Clapham Junction train crash killed 35, worst U.K. rail accident for 20 years.

1988 †Chico Mendes, leader of rubber tappers in Amazonian rainforest, assassinated; international outcry focusses world attention on politics of rainforest destruction.

ARTS

SCIENCE

Index

A

B

C

D

F

G

H

I

K

L

M

N

O

Q

S

T

U

V

W